Lecture Notes in Computer Scien

Commenced Publication in 1973
Founding and Former Series Editors:
Gerhard Goos, Juris Hartmanis, and Jan van Leeuwen

Kaushal Solanki   Kenneth Sullivan
Upamanyu Madhow (Eds.)

Information Hiding

10th International Workshop, IH 2008
Santa Barbara, CA, USA, May 19-21, 2008
Revised Selected Papers

 Springer

Volume Editors

Kaushal Solanki
Kenneth Sullivan
Mayachitra Inc.
5266 Hollister Avenue, Suite 229
Santa Barbara, CA 93111, USA
E-mail: {solanki, sullivan}@mayachitra.com

Upamanyu Madhow
University of California
Department of Electrical and Computer Engineering
Santa Barbara 93106, USA
E-mail: madhow@ece.ucsb.edu

Library of Congress Control Number: 2008938111

CR Subject Classification (1998): E.3, K.6.5, K.4.1, K.5.1, D.4.6, E.4, C.2

LNCS Sublibrary: SL 4 – Security and Cryptology

ISSN   0302-9743
ISBN-10   3-540-88960-4 Springer Berlin Heidelberg New York
ISBN-13   978-3-540-88960-1 Springer Berlin Heidelberg New York

Springer is a part of Springer Science+Business Media

springer.com

© Springer-Verlag Berlin Heidelberg 2008

Typesetting: Camera-ready by author, data conversion by Scientific Publishing Services, Chennai, India
Printed on acid-free paper   SPIN: 12550937   06/3180   5 4 3 2 1 0

Preface

It is our great pleasure to present this volume of the proceedings of the 10th edition of Information Hiding (IH 2008). The conference was held in Santa Barbara - the American Riviera, California, USA, during May 19–21, 2008. It was organized by three Santa Barbarans on fire, from both industry (Mayachitra) and academia (UCSB).

Over the years, Information Hiding (IH) has established itself as a premier forum for presenting research covering various aspects of information hiding. Continuing the tradition, this year, we provide a balanced program including topics such as anonymity and privacy, forensics, steganography, watermarking, fingerprinting, other hiding domains, and novel applications. We received a total of 64 papers from all over the globe, and would like to take this opportunity to thank all the authors who submitted their paper to IH 2008 and thus contributed to the consolidation of the reputation of the conference. The papers were refereed by at least three reviewers who provided detailed comments, which was followed by discussion amongst the Program Committee members. Only 25 papers were selected for presentation. This rigorous review process will certainly strengthen Information Hiding's position as the top forum of our community.

We would like to thank all the members of the Program Committee and all the external reviewers for the enormous amount of effort that they put into the review process. We thank Mary Jo Comer from Santa Barbara Travel for her help in all the arrangements throughout the process. We are thankful to the volunteers from UCSB whose tireless efforts were crucial in making this event successful. Finally, we are extremely grateful to our sponsors, MovieLabs, Thomson, and VRL-UCSB, for their valuable support to the conference, and to INRIA for passing on the leftover funds from IH 2007.

We hope that you will enjoy reading these proceedings and find inspiration for your future research.

May 2008

Kaushal Solanki
Kenneth Sullivan
Upamanyu Madhow

Organization

Organizing Committee

General Chair

Kaushal Solanki   Mayachitra Inc., USA

Program Chairs

Kenneth Sullivan   Mayachitra Inc., USA
Upamanyu Madhow   University of California, Santa Barbara, USA

Program Committee

Ross Anderson   University of Cambridge, UK
Mauro Barni   Università di Siena, Italy
Patrick Bas   Gipsa-lab, France
Jack Brassil   HP Labs, USA
Jan Camenisch   IBM Zurich Research Laboratory, Switzerland
François Cayre   Gipsa-lab, France
Ee-Chien Chang   National University of Singapore, Singapore
Christian Collberg   University of Arizona, USA
Ingemar J. Cox   University College London, UK
Gwenaël Doërr   University College London, UK
Jessica Fridrich   SUNY Binghamton, USA
Teddy Furon   INRIA Rennes, France
Neil F. Johnson   Booz Allen Hamilton, USA
Stefan Katzenbeisser   Philips Research, The Netherlands
Darko Kirovski   Microsoft Research, USA
Upamanyu Madhow   University of California, Santa Barbara, USA
John McHugh   Dalhousie University, Canada
Ira S. Moskowitz   Naval Research Laboratory, USA
Andreas Pfitzmann   Dresden University of Technology, Germany
Phil Sallee   Booz Allen Hamilton, USA
Kaushal Solanki   Mayachitra Inc., USA
Kenneth Sullivan   Mayachitra Inc., USA

Local Coordinator

Anindya Sarkar   University of California, Santa Barbara, USA

Volunteers

Lakshmanan Nataraj	Malavika Bhaskaranand	R. Pravin Kumar
Sandeep Bhat	Vivekanandan N.	Vivek Kankanhalli

External Reviewers

Giacomo Cancelli	Qiming Li	Ryutarou Ohbuchi
Alessandro Piva	Ben Zhao	Victor Raskin
Wei-Jen Li	Andrew Ker	Roberto Caldelli

Sponsoring Institutions

Motion Pictures Laboratories, Inc., USA
Thomson, USA
Lecture Notes in Computer Science (LNCS)
Vision Research Lab, UCSB, USA
INRIA , France

Table of Contents

Anonymity and Privacy

A Display Technique for Preventing Electromagnetic Eavesdropping
Using Color Mixture Characteristic of Human Eyes 1
  Takashi Watanabe, Hiroto Nagayoshi, and Hiroshi Sako

Hiding a Needle in a Haystack Using Negative Databases 15
  Fernando Esponda

Information Leakage in Optimal Anonymized and Diversified Data 30
  Chengfang Fang and Ee-Chien Chang

Steganography I

Perturbation Hiding and the Batch Steganography Problem 45
  Andrew D. Ker

Maximizing Steganographic Embedding Efficiency by Combining
Hamming Codes and Wet Paper Codes 60
  Weiming Zhang, Xinpeng Zhang, and Shuozhong Wang

Forensics

Detecting Re-projected Video 72
  Weihong Wang and Hany Farid

Residual Information of Redacted Images Hidden in the Compression
Artifacts 87
  Nicholas Zhong-Yang Ho and Ee-Chien Chang

Novel Technologies/Applications

Trusted Integrated Circuits: A Nondestructive Hidden Characteristics
Extraction Approach 102
  *Yousra Alkabani, Farinaz Koushanfar, Negar Kiyavash, and
  Miodrag Potkonjak*

Reversible Watermarking with Subliminal Channel 118
  Xianfeng Zhao and Ning Li

Watermarking I

Watermarking Security Incorporating Natural Scene Statistics 132
  *Jiangqun Ni, Rongyue Zhang, Chen Fang, Jiwu Huang,
  Chuntao Wang, and Hyoung-Joong Kim*

Block-Chain Based Fragile Watermarking Scheme with Superior
Localization   147
   Hong-Jie He, Jia-Shu Zhang, and Heng-Ming Tai

Steganalysis

Generic Adoption of Spatial Steganalysis to Transformed Domain   161
   Andreas Westfeld

Weighted Stego-Image Steganalysis for JPEG Covers   178
   Rainer Böhme

Practical Insecurity for Effective Steganalysis   195
   Johann Barbier and Stéphanie Alt

Other hiding Domains I

Authorship Proof for Textual Document   209
   J. Wu and D.R. Stinson

Linguistic Steganography Detection Using Statistical Characteristics of
Correlations between Words   224
   Zhili Chen, Liusheng Huang, Zhenshan Yu, Wei Yang, Lingjun Li,
   Xueling Zheng, and Xinxin Zhao

Steganography II

A Data Mapping Method for Steganography and Its Application to
Images   236
   Hao-tian Wu, Jean-Luc Dugelay, and Yiu-ming Cheung

Benchmarking for Steganography   251
   Tomáš Pevný and Jessica Fridrich

Other Hiding Domains II and Network Security

Other Hiding Domains

Information Hiding through Variance of the Parametric Orientation
Underlying a B-rep Face   268
   Csaba Salamon, Jonathan Corney, and James Ritchie

A Supraliminal Channel in a Videoconferencing Application   283
   Scott Craver, Enping Li, Jun Yu, and Idris Atakli

Network Security

C-Mix: A Lightweight Anonymous Routing Approach   294
   Vinayak Kandiah, Dijiang Huang, and Harsh Kapoor

Watermarking II

Strengthening QIM-Based Watermarking by Non-uniform Discrete
Cosine Transform 309
    Xianfeng Zhao, Bingbing Xia, and Yi Deng

Distortion Optimization of Model-Based Secure Embedding Schemes
for Data-Hiding 325
    *Benjamin Mathon, Patrick Bas, François Cayre, and
    Fernando Pérez-González*

Fingerprinting

On the Design and Optimization of Tardos Probabilistic Fingerprinting
Codes 341
    Teddy Furon, Arnaud Guyader, and Frédéric Cérou

Iterative Detection Method for CDMA-Based Fingerprinting Scheme ... 357
    Minoru Kuribayashi and Masakatu Morii

Author Index 373

A Display Technique for Preventing Electromagnetic Eavesdropping Using Color Mixture Characteristic of Human Eyes

Takashi Watanabe, Hiroto Nagayoshi, and Hiroshi Sako

Hitachi, Ltd., Central Research Laboratory
1-280 Higashi-koigakubo Kokubunji-shi, Tokyo, Japan
{takashi.watanabe.dh,hiroto.nagayoshi.wy,hiroshi.sako.ug}@hitachi.com

Abstract. The security problem of screen image leakage on a cathode-ray tube (CRT) through electromagnetic radiation from several meters away, "transient electro-magnetic pulse emission surveillance technology" (TEMPEST), has attracted wide interest by security researchers since Van Eck wrote about this problem. On the industry side, the problem is considered a serious risk, especially for computers used in operations related to such areas as critical business and information management at banks. To solve the problem, techniques for reducing the S/N ratio of emanating information by signal reduction and noise generation have been investigated as countermeasures. We have developed a technique that introduces noise to displayed images. With this technique there is less of a quality penalty on the visible images. This is a result of using a human visual characteristic known as additive color mixing, which occurs when an eye is continuously exposed to quickly changing colors. Although we used hardware to implement this technique, using software for low-cost systems is possible. We tested and confirmed the effectiveness of the technique using both analog and digital systems: a computer connected with a CRT or LCD by an analog RGB cable.

Keywords: TEMPEST, Compromising Emanation, Side Channel Analysis, Electromagnetic Radiation.

1 Introduction

After Van Eck published his paper [1] in 1985, the risk of information leakage through electromagnetic radiation from a display unit, not only cathode-ray tube (CRT) but also liquid-crystal display (LCD) [2], has been widely known. The technique to capture information through electromagnetic (EM) radiation is now referred to as "TEMPEST" (transient electro-magnetic pulse emission surveillance technology) or "compromising emanations". However, little information on guidelines or requirements for preventing TEMPEST has been unveiled, though some companies have been selling TEMPEST testing devices.

The most significant literature on TEMPEST that is publicly available is a thesis by Markus Kuhn [3]. He states that million-dollar devices were required

K. Solanki, K. Sullivan, and U. Madhow (Eds.): IH 2008, LNCS 5284, pp. 1–14, 2008.

to eavesdrop EM information from ordinary display units a few decades ago. Although such high-end products cost the same today, lower-range products, those costing as little as thousands of dollars, are nearly capable of capturing partial information from a few meters away, which is due to improvements in radio management technologies. Furthermore, with rapid advances in software definition radio (SDR) and field programmable gate array (FPGA), the cost of information retrieval is expected to decrease to less than a thousand dollars in the near future. Because of these changes, development of low-cost countermeasures applicable to ordinary computers is required.

Countermeasures are woven to reduce the S/N ratio of leakage information and are categorized as signal reduction and noise generation. For signal reduction, smoothing devices such as a low-pass filter or Gaussian filter are applied to screen fonts [4,5] and entire images. For noise generation, an additional noise source is placed near the sources of signal emission, and in addition they are synchronized with a pixel clock to effectively cover the frequency range of information leakage.

Our technique increases noise by spreading information in a time domain and then introduces noise on the displayed images. The visible images, however, maintain their quality by reducing the noise on the human eye. In our technique, we use the human visual characteristic known as the additive mixing of colors, which occurs when quickly changing colors are seen. From a technical standpoint, sub-images are generated from an original image and a noise pattern and then sub-images are displayed in a quick flipping manner. The images seen by the user on the display and those seen by the attacker who is monitoring EM radiation are different, even when he is an averaging attacker [6], because the information that travels through EM radiation is effectively modulated by our technique. Furthermore, since the information is randomized by noise, the attacker cannot retrieve any information on what the user sees.

With the same objective, Kuhn [3] suggests a technique that randomizes the lower significant bits of pixels, which are those that do not significantly affect image quality. Our technique introduces a large amount of noise with less of an image quality penalty.

This paper is organized as follows. In the following chapter, we describe a leakage model, a test setup for eavesdropping, and the preliminary results of our test. In the third chapter, we describe our technique for preventing information leakage and show test results.

2   Leakage Model and Test Setup

2.1   Leakage Source

A target (or victim) system is illustrated in Fig. 1. It consists of a personal computer (PC) connected to a CRT or an LCD by an analog RGB cable. In the system, the picture to be displayed on the CRT screen is generated in a CPU or a GPU and then stored in the RAM of the PC or the GRAM of a graphic board. The graphic board is equipped with a digital-to-analog converter that accesses the RAM or the GRAM to retrieve the picture and convert it in digital form to analog form in order to transmit the analog value to the CRT through the analog RGB cable. The CRT receives the analog value and activates a regulator to modulate the strength of an electron beam to an adequate level. The electron beam then activates the phosphorogen coated layer on the screen so that the luminance at the position reaches the expected value corresponding to the picture. In some CRTs, the regulator is directly controlled by the input analog signal. On the other hand, various CRTs buffer incoming analog values in digital form by an analog-to-digital converter. Then, after digital filters are applied, a digital-to-analog converter is used to activate the electron beam. In either case, analog voltages corresponding to the luminance of the pixels in the picture are transmitted in the system.

A conventional desktop PC and a CRT are connected by an analog RGB cable, which transmits luminance information pixel-by-pixel. Each pixel is made up of three colors: red, blue, and green of the RGB color system. Color information is represented by a 0.7-Vpp analog signal and is divided into 256 levels so that each level has a 30-mV margin. Pixels are transmitted in order from the top left to the bottom right by raster scanning, which is illustrated in Fig. 1, where the addresses (0,0) and $(w-1, h-1)$ are respectively located at the top left and bottom right parts of the screen. Here, w and h are the width and height of the screen. In raster scanning, the pixel at (0,0) is transmitted first, followed by (1,0), (2,0), etc. Once the scan reaches the rightmost address $(w-1, 0)$, the scan goes to the next line (0,1), (1,1), (2,1), etc. After $(w-1, h-1)$, the scan goes back to the top left, (0,0). This scanning sequence of one screen is called

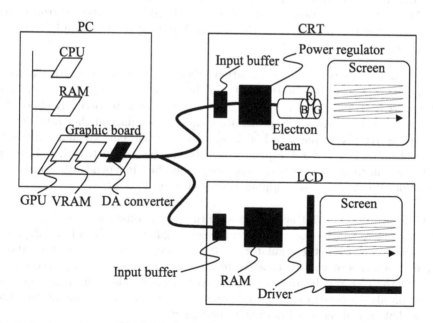

Fig. 1. Leakage sources (thick black lines) in system of computer and CRT or LCD connected by analog RGB cable

a "frame". In ordinary PCs and CRTs, the frame rate is set to between 60 and 85 Hz. The human visual system cannot follow such high-frequency images and thus identifies them as smooth motion pictures.

As illustrated in Fig. 1, sources of information leakage, represented by thick black lines, are spreading nearly throughout the system. The leakage spreads from the output of the graphic board's VRAM to the CRT's regulator of the electron beam and the LCD drivers. If an attacker can couple an antenna to the leakage source, they can retrieve information from a distance without having to be near the target device. Even worse, EM analysis is passive and so evidence of information leakage is not detectable.

2.2   Leakage Model

As Maxwell's theorem states, current fluctuation in a circuitry board generates electromagnetic radiation using wires as antennas. The point where there is the most leakage in the system is the ground line, where a large current modulated by signal activity is present in the circuit.

If a PC and a CRT are connected by an analog RGB cable, the system operates as described below.

1. Through an input port, analog RGB, horizontal sync, and vertical sync signals are received.
2. The pixel clock, the horizontal sync, and the vertical sync signals locate the angle of the electron beam at the target position.
3. At the target position, depending on the RGB signal, the electron beam stimulates phosphorogen on the screen, resulting in the material glowing with corresponding luminance.

In 1 and 3, electromagnetic radiation related to current fluctuation occurs, caused by a pixel value (RGB signal). In the analog system, which consists of an analog RGB cable and a CRT, since a pixel value is numerically expressed by voltage level, current vibrations are caused depending on the transition of two successive pixel values. In Fig. 2, an EM radiation pattern that represents successive $t - 1$, t and $t + 1$ pixel values is shown. As illustrated, red, green and blue information is treated separately and thus independently cause EM radiation. What we see is a combination of these radiations.

CRT System. In a CRT system, most of the power consumption is used by the electron beam, which is controlled by a power regulator of which input depends on a pixel value. For the regulator, a 100-V power source is boosted to about a few thousands of voltage to activate the electron beam. Because the power level of the electron beam corresponds to the pixel value, the resultant EM radiation also depends on the pixel value and thus an attacker monitoring the EM radiation can retrieve information on this value.

If a screen size becomes larger, decreasing the transition speed of the electron beam is necessary. When an interval between spotting times of adjacent pixels is

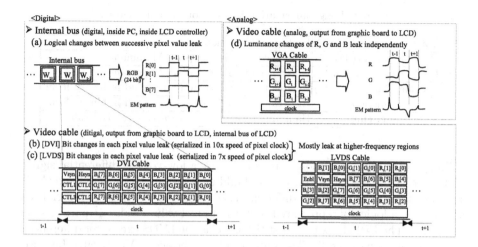

Fig. 2. Encoding of digital (a) 24-bit parallel bus, (b) digital DVI, (c) 24-bit LVDS and analog, (d) RGB

long, the beam is controlled by the ZR (zero return) method, which zeroizes the voltage of the beam before the next pixel value is charged. In this case, the pixel value itself leaks. On the other hand, if the interval is short, zeroizing the beam is difficult, thus the beam keeps the voltage and starting from it, changes to the next voltage level. In this case, the differences of two successive pixel values leak. The latter case is common today, and in a system with an analog RGB cable and a CRT, the difference of pixel values in the raster scanning order is the basic leakage information.

LCD System. If the CRT is replaced by an LCD, we need to consider a more complex leakage model because LCDs are digitally different from CRTs. In the LCD system, the RGB cable leaks pixel values in a numerical manner, as described above, whereas the LCD leaks pixel values in a logical manner.

At an input port of an LCD, an analog pixel value from the RGB cable is sampled at a high frequency and then converted to a digital form by an analog-to-digital converter. The output digital data are stored in an internal RAM. Then, when one frame, or one line, of data is filled, the data are transmitted to a digital-to-analog converter to generate a charge current for the capacitors on each TFT. The digital data are transmitted through buses, which are pre-charge and static buses. In the pre-charge bus, the bus is charged to 0 or 1 before a datum is transmitted. On the other hand, the static bus keeps the previous datum and then it directly changes to the next datum state. Apparently, leakage information is different in either bus. For high-speed systems, the static bus is preferred.

The following is the leakage information in the digital system.

1. Hamming distance of two successive pixel values. (static bus)
2. Hamming weight of a pixel value. (pre-charge bus)

Table 1. Image information leakage source and its forms

Leakage source	Leakage information
RGB cable (analog DVI-Ij	Difference of adjacent pixels' luminance.
CRT electron beam part	Difference of adjacent pixels' luminance.
DVI cable (digital DVI-D)	Relates to a pixel value represented in binary form.
LVDS transmission	Relates to a pixel value represented in binary form.
LCD logical circuit	Hamming distance of two successive pixel values.

Today, most high-resolution display units use a low-voltage differential signal (LVDS) or FPD-Link for the purpose of building a system with a high bandwidth and fewer wires. The LVDS is a differential signaling bus, and because it serializes pixel values, a logically represented pattern of pixel values leaks: 4^7 patterns for 8-bit value. The FPD-Link is almost the same as the LVDS except for differences related to encoding (Fig. 2). The digital video interface (DVI) is same because the DVI uses the TMDS (transaction minimized differential signaling) format, also shown in Fig. 2.

Note that in the digital system, there is more information leakage than in the analog system, as summarized in Table 1.

2.3   Test Setup

Figure 3 illustrates connections between evaluation devices. This setup consists of two systems: a target system and an eavesdropping system, which are connected only by electromagnetic waves. The wide-band receiver captures electromagnetic radiation by searching a full range of frequencies between 10 MHz and 1 GHz. The power sources of the two systems are also separated because electronic information travels through these sources.

2.4   Preliminary Test Result

The center and right-side pictures in Fig. 4 show the results of a test using the previously described system (Fig. 3), targeting a PC and an LCD connected by an analog RGB cable. In our experiment, one CRT and two LCDs were tested. The values of the horizontal sync and vertical sync signals used are shown in Table 2.

As shown in Table 1, and described in the previous section, we can extract various types of images showing leakage, which are distributed over frequencies of at least between 10 MHz and 1 GHz, as illustrated in Fig. 5. We thus need to suppress not only the "edge" leakage but also the "bit pattern" leakage, especially when we connect a computer and an LCD using an analog RGB cable.

When hsync or vsync signals are generated on an attacker's system and are inconsistent with those of the target device, displayed eavesdropping images scroll vertically or horizontally or both. To stabilize the images, we need to match the value at the 6th to 7th precision.

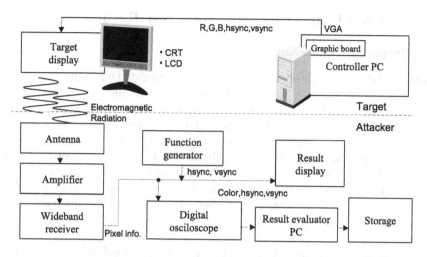

Fig. 3. Structure of electromagnetic leakage evaluation system

Fig. 4. Displayed image (left) and eavesdropped images (center and right)

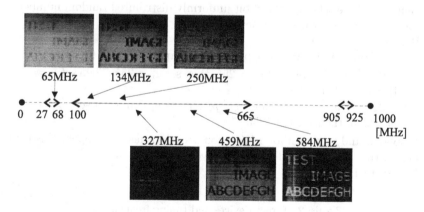

Fig. 5. Frequencies of image leakage (represented by lines and arrows) and eavesdropped images

3   Proposed Countermeasure and Test Results

3.1   Proposed Countermeasure

Our countermeasure adds or subtracts randomly generated n sets of values to the original pixels, so that $n + 1$ sub-images are generated, and then it quickly displays these images in turn. Since the sub-images change over a short period, their average luminance can be seen by people. Thus, if we add a value to the original image in one sub-image and subtract the value from the original image in the other sub-image, a person can see the original image in his/her brain even though the randomized sub-images are displayed on the display unit. This human characteristic is also used for blur reduction of movies on an LCD by inserting a black or lower luminance image between actual images by doubling the frame rate.

Because it does not compromise generality, we restrict the number of sub-images to two.

The proposed technique first generates a noise pattern randomly and then adds and subtracts values to and from the original pixel value to make two sub-images. In other words, a random value is added to the original pixel value to generate the pixel value of the first sub-image, and the random value is subtracted from the original pixel value to generate the pixel value of the second sub-image. Consequently, the average pixel value of the first and second sub-images becomes the same as that of the original image. This averaging function is achieved by quickly changing the screen between the first and second sub-images.

Here we describe our algorithm. The pixel values p_i are numbered in the order of raster scanning from the origin (0,0). The u_i and v_i are the pixel values of the first and second sub-images, respectively, which are numbered in the same way as previously described.

1. Generate three sets of $w \times h$ 8-bit uniformly distributed random numbers r_i. (or only one set for a grayscale image.)
2. Read the input value p_i.
3. For each pixel and each color plane, RGB, apply (a) and (b) in turn.
   (a) Calculate $u_i = p_i + r_i$. If $u_i > 255$, then set $u_i = 255$. Then set $v_i = p_i - r_i$. If $v_i < 0$, then set $v_i = 0$.
   (b) Calculate $u_i = p_i - r_i$ and $v_i = p_i + r_i$. If $u_i < 0$, then set $u_i = 0$, and if $v_i > 255$, then set $v_i = 255$
4. Display u and v in turn for 1/60 seconds each or faster. (Repeat this for the period that p is expected to be displayed, as shown in Fig. 6)
5. Return to 1.

Table 2. Target devices and tuning frequencies

Target device	Hsync(kHz)	Vsync(Hz)
A (CRT)	48.47327212	75.0962
B (LCD)	48.38397523	60.0987
C (LCD)	48.53026104	60.0248

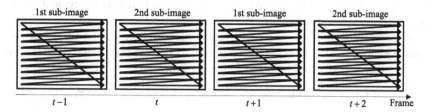

Fig. 6. Display technique with two sub-images

As previously mentioned, the electromagnetic radiation depends on the difference of two successive pixel values, and the displayed pixel values are randomized, thus the leaking information is randomized. We can improve the randomness of the sub-images by increasing the number of these images. However, changing the screen in such a short period to activate human color-mixture characteristics becomes more difficult because display units may not be able to process such quick changes.

Here we explain how our system works. Consider the screen resolution $w \times h$ and the pixel value at location (x,y) as $p_{x,y}$. If we describe the power of electromagnetic radiation at time t by $w(t)$, it is:

$$w(f) = a \cdot |p_{X_i,Y_i} - p_{X_{i-1},Y_{i-1}}|$$

where:

$$X_t = f_p \cdot t \bmod w \,, \; Y_t = (f_p \cdot t - X_t)/w \bmod h$$
$$X_{t-1} = f_p \cdot (t-1) \bmod w \,, \; Y_{t-1} = (f_p \cdot (t-1) - X_{t-1})/w \bmod h$$

Here, a is a coefficient that depends on leakage sources.

Our technique generates a noise value $\alpha_{x,y}$ and then $p'_{x,y} = p_{x,y} - \alpha_{x,y}$, $p''_{x,y} = p_{x,y} + \alpha_{x,y}$ from the original pixel value $p_{x,y}$. Although the noise value $\alpha_{x,y}$ is independent of the location (x,y), the value is constant at each location.

When we quickly change the sub-images over a short period, the human eye can see the average value:

$$\frac{(p'_{x,y} + p''_{x,y})}{2} = \frac{(p_{x,y} - \alpha_{x,y} + p_{x,y} + \alpha_{x,y})}{2} = p_{x,y}.$$

This value is equal to the original pixel value.

The above equation is also valid for X_t, Y_t rather than x, y. Therefore leakage from the first sub-image $w'(t)$ and second sub-image $w''(t)$ are:

$$w'(f) = a \cdot |p'_{X_t,Y_t} - p'_{X_{t-1},Y_{t-1}}| = a \cdot |c_{X_t,Y_t} - \alpha_{X_t,Y_t} + \alpha_{X_{t-1},Y_{t-1}}|$$
$$w''(f) = a \cdot |p''_{X_t,Y_t} - p''_{X_{t-1},Y_{t-1}}| = a \cdot |c_{X_t,Y_t} + \alpha_{X_t,Y_t} - \alpha_{X_{t-1},Y_{t-1}}|$$

Here, c_{X_t,Y_t} is set to $c_{X_t,Y_t} = p_{X_t,Y_t} - p_{X_{t-1},Y_{t-1}}$, which is equivalent to the leakage without a countermeasure.

If the horizontal and vertical sync signals match those of the target device, the image visible to the attacker corresponds to the average value of $w'(t)$ and $w''(t)$. The result is divided into the following four cases.

i) $c_{X_t,Y_t} - \alpha_{X_{t-1},Y_{t-1}} + \alpha_{X_{t-1},Y_{t-1}} \geq 0$, $c_{X_t,Y_t} + \alpha_{X_{t-1},Y_{t-1}} - \alpha_{X_{t-1},Y_{t-1}} \geq 0$

$$\frac{w'(f) + w''(f)}{2}$$
$$= \frac{a \cdot (c_{X_t,Y_t} - \alpha_{X_t,Y_t} + \alpha_{X_{t-1},Y_{t-1}}) + a \cdot (c_{X_t,Y_t} + \alpha_{X_t,Y_t} - \alpha_{X_{t-1},Y_{t-1}})}{2}$$
$$= a \cdot c_{X_t,Y_t}$$

ii) $c_{X_t,Y_t} - \alpha_{X_{t-1},Y_{t-1}} + \alpha_{X_{t-1},Y_{t-1}} \geq 0$, $c_{X_t,Y_t} + \alpha_{X_{t-1},Y_{t-1}} - \alpha_{X_{t-1},Y_{t-1}} < 0$

$$\frac{w'(f) + w''(f)}{2}$$
$$= \frac{a \cdot (c_{X_t,Y_t} - \alpha_{X_t,Y_t} + \alpha_{X_{t-1},Y_{t-1}}) - a \cdot (c_{X_t,Y_t} + \alpha_{X_t,Y_t} - \alpha_{X_{t-1},Y_{t-1}})}{2}$$
$$= a \cdot (\alpha_{X_{t-1},Y_{t-1}} - \alpha_{X_t,Y_t})$$

iii) $c_{X_t,Y_t} - \alpha_{X_{t-1},Y_{t-1}} + \alpha_{X_{t-1},Y_{t-1}} < 0$, $c_{X_t,Y_t} + \alpha_{X_{t-1},Y_{t-1}} - \alpha_{X_{t-1},Y_{t-1}} \leq 0$

$$\frac{w'(f) + w''(f)}{2}$$
$$= \frac{-a \cdot (c_{X_t,Y_t} - \alpha_{X_t,Y_t} + \alpha_{X_{t-1},Y_{t-1}}) + a \cdot (c_{X_t,Y_t} + \alpha_{X_t,Y_t} - \alpha_{X_{t-1},Y_{t-1}})}{2}$$
$$= a \cdot (\alpha_{X_t,Y_t} - \alpha_{X_{t-1},Y_{t-1}})$$

iv) $c_{X_t,Y_t} - \alpha_{X_{t-1},Y_{t-1}} + \alpha_{X_{t-1},Y_{t-1}} < 0$, $c_{X_t,Y_t} + \alpha_{X_{t-1},Y_{t-1}} - \alpha_{X_{t-1},Y_{t-1}} < 0$

$$\frac{w'(f) + w''(f)}{2}$$
$$= \frac{-a \cdot (c_{X_t,Y_t} - \alpha_{X_t,Y_t} + \alpha_{X_{t-1},Y_{t-1}}) - a \cdot (c_{X_t,Y_t} + \alpha_{X_t,Y_t} - \alpha_{X_{t-1},Y_{t-1}})}{2}$$
$$= -a \cdot c_{X_t,Y_t}$$

In ii) and iii), the results only depend on the random value, and there is no image leakage, whereas in i) and iv), the result is equivalent to the original leakage without a countermeasure, so the attacker sees the information related to the original picture on his/her screen.

The above equations imply that ii) or iii) tends to be satisfied if a smaller c_{X_t,Y_t} is achieved. If we are not informed in advance about the original picture, one strategy is to accomplish such a situation by generating α_{X_t,Y_t}, $\alpha_{X_{t-1},Y_{t-1}}$ to let $|\alpha_{X_t,Y_t} - \alpha_{X_{t-1},Y_{t-1}}|$ be a larger value. As illustrated geometrically in Fig. 7, the right strategy is better than the one on the left.

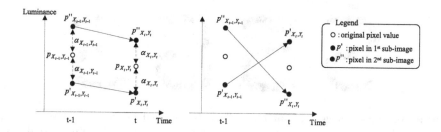

Fig. 7. Example of picture value allocation to first and second sub-images (right case is preferable)

3.2 Test Results

We implemented our technique on an FPGA with RGB input and output ports. The unit was directly connected to the video output port of the computer, and its output port was connected to the CRT or the LCD. This system is able to process pictures in real time with up to XGA resolution.

Figure 8 is the sub-images generated from the original picture in Fig. 4 using our method. Magnified images of character "S" are shown in Fig. 9. If these sub-images are displayed by quickly flipping them on the screen, what we see is virtually depicted in Fig. 8. Notably, the resulting image has less contrast compared with the original picture because we cannot express a pure black or white value using two different values.

CRT System. Results of EM eavesdropping on a CRT system are summarized in Table 3. Without a countermeasure, as shown in the left columns of Table 3, the edges of characters clearly leak at three intervals of frequencies 40 to 80 MHz, 120 to 180 MHz, and 210 to 270 MHz, although only the strongest leak images in each range are shown. These frequencies are recognized as harmonics of the base pixel clock frequency 65 MHz for an XGA screen.

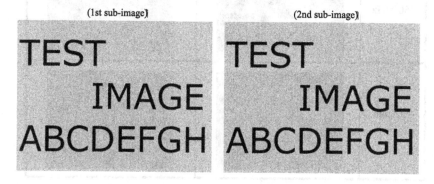

Fig. 8. Generated sub-images using method (corresponds to u and v in section 3.1)

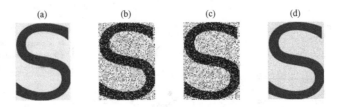

Fig. 9. Magnified images of character "S" in (a) original image, (b) 1st sub-image, (c) 2nd sub-image and (d) visible image on human eyes. (d) is calculated virtually by averaging (b) and (c).

Table 3. Comparison of eavesdropped images from the target system with or without countermeasure in analog system

Tuning frequency	Without countermeasure	Proposed method
65 MHz		
134 MHz		
250 MHz		
Leakage model		

Table 4. Comparison of eavesdropped images in the digital system

Tuning frequency	Without countermeasure	Proposed method
327 MHz		
459 MHz		
584 MHz		
Leakage model		

The right columns in Table 3 show the results of applying our method. The edges of characters found in the left columns are dismissed, implying that retrieving any information about the original image is not possible.

The last row in Table 3 contains estimated leak images made by the leakage model described in the second section. The left picture shows information on the edges of the characters, whereas the right picture shows only noise. Both seem to well explain the test results.

LCD System. The same test was conducted for a system in which a CRT was replaced by an LCD. Table 4 shows the results of this test. Although, as we pointed out for Fig. 5, leakage is seen at lower frequencies, the results for these regions are the same as those in Table 3.

4   Conclusion

We developed a signal reduction and noise generation technique that uses human visual characteristic related to an additive mixture of colors, which is what occurs during continuous exposure to quickly changing colors. We tested the technique using a system of a computer and CRT or LCD connected by an analog RGB cable with an image conversion hardware that is realized by a FPGA board.

With the same goal, Kuhn [3] suggested a technique that randomizes lower significant bits of pixel value that do not significantly affect the quality of an image. Our method introduces a significantly larger amount of noise with less of an image quality penalty.

Although our technique has the drawback of contrast reduction on a displayed image, this can be done at a low cost using software. Furthermore, our method is independent from previously proposed methods, and thus, our method combined with others will effectively improve security against electromagnetic eavesdropping.

References

1. van Eck, W.: Electromagnetic Radiation from Video Display Units: An Eavesdropping Risk? Computer & Security 4, 269–286 (1985)
2. Kuhn, M.: Electromagnetic Eavesdropping Risks of Flat-Panel Displays. In: 4th Workshop on Privacy Enhancing Technologies, pp. 1–20 (2004)
3. Kuhn, M.: Compromising emanations: eavesdropping risks of computer displays. University of Cambridge Technical Report Number 577 (December 2003)
4. Kuhn, M., Anderson, R.: Soft Tempest: Hidden Data Transmission Using Electromagnetic Emanations. In: Aucsmith, D. (ed.) IH 1998. LNCS, vol. 1525, pp. 124–142. Springer, Heidelberg (1998)
5. Tanaka, H., Takizawa, O., Yamamura, A.: Evaluation and Improvement of TEMPEST fonts. In: Lim, C.H., Yung, M. (eds.) WISA 2004. LNCS, vol. 3325, pp. 457–469. Springer, Heidelberg (2005)
6. Shiwei, D., Jiadong, X., Chenjiang, G.: Bit error rate of a digital radio eavesdropper on computer CRT monitors. In: IEEE International Symposium on Communications and Information Technology (ISCIT), vol. 2, pp. 1093–1099 (2004)

Hiding a Needle in a Haystack Using Negative Databases

Fernando Esponda

Department of Computer Science
Instituto Tecnológico Autónomo de México
Mexico City, Mexico
fernando.esponda@itam.mx

Abstract. In this paper we present a method for hiding a list of data by mixing it with a large amount of superfluous items. The technique uses a device known as a negative database which stores the complement of a set rather that the set itself to include an arbitrary number of garbage entries efficiently. The resulting structure effectively hides the data, without encrypting it, and obfuscates the number of data items hidden; it prevents arbitrary data lookups, while supporting simple membership queries; and can be manipulated to reflect relational algebra operations on the original data.

1 Introduction

Data confidentiality has always been a primary concern of individuals and organizations. Before the computer era, important documents were hidden or kept under lock and key. Getting access to them implied a guardian "server", a key, or knowing the document's whereabouts. Many of the same techniques apply today to information kept in a digital form; however, the variety and volume of today's data, together with the number of users and applications it must service, require greater robustness and flexibility in how data may be manipulated.

Consider, for instance, a list of credit-card numbers that is made available to several independent entities; for example, the list records numbers presumably involved in "suspicious" activities or, alternatively, the list of winners of some draw. The numbers in the list should remain confidential, but the presence or absence of a given number must be readily verified (in order to call the authorities, deny service, or present a prize).

Cryptographic hash functions are effective for creating a list of data items whose true identity cannot be easily determined but whose presence can be verified by anyone. Suppose, however, that learning the number of entries in the list is useful for an adversary, or that the data needs to be augmented with the card holders name, or the list restricted to only those cards issued by a specific financial institution (the first digits of the card indicate its issuer). A hashed list fails to conceal the number of items it contains and makes meaningful manipulations difficult, e.g., selecting a subset of the contents according to some criterion. Alternatively, consider hiding the data by mixing it in with items that

K. Solanki, K. Sullivan, and U. Madhow (Eds.): IH 2008, LNCS 5284, pp. 15–29, 2008.

are structurally similar but meaningless—hiding a needle in a haystack. Finding a datum requires sifting through a large amount of chaff; the size of the data set is concealed; and the resulting set can be handled to reflect some manipulations on the hidden data. Verifying the presence of an item, however, requires special, secret knowledge of where to look. The quality of the concealment strongly depends on the nature and size of the set in which the items are hidden.

In this paper we propose a scheme that resembles a combination of both methods discussed above. It efficiently supports membership queries while making arbitrary fishing expeditions hard, it obfuscates the cardinality of the hidden set by including "garbage" entries, and the hidden data can be manipulated using some relational operations. The main difference is that the data is not hashed and can still be manipulated meaningfully, and that the amount of chaff that can be efficiently included with the data is very large. The data-structure we employ is known a negative database—a compressed version of the list containing all of the elements *not* in the original, positive database or list. Storing the complement of the list of interest allows us to include a large amount of superfluous data within it; intuitively, the more chaff the smaller the negative database.

Previous work on negative databases relied on the theoretical difficulty of "reversing" a negative database (deciding whether a negative database is empty or not is NP-complete) and on finding suitably hard instances for its security [10]. Our current proposal does not lean on this property, as it may very well be easy to find entries not included in the negative database; its security relies on the number of superfluous entries included alongside the data and on the infeasibility of retrieving only the valid items. Furthermore, the size of the representations presented here are dramatically smaller that those used in the cited work.

Sections 2 and 3 describe our proposal in detail and give it a theoretical treatment. In section 4 we outline a possible implementation and present the output of several experiments. We discuss our results and give some concluding remarks is Sect.6.

2   Description

The original data is a subset of the set of all binary strings of length t, U_d. Strings belonging to U_d are referred to as *text* strings throughout the document. Our strategy is to embed U_d within a larger universe U, such that U can be partitioned into a set of valid strings and a set of invalid strings denoted U_V and U_I respectively. The universe U is the set $U_d \times \{0,1\}^c$ of strings of length $l = t + c$; the additional c bits are referred to as the *code* and are used to distinguish valid from invalid strings. Accordingly, U_V contains only those text-code combinations that are deemed to be valid in a particular context (and U_I contains the rest of U).

The data to be concealed, the positive database DB, is a subset of U_V. The negative database, NDB, is a compact representation of $U - (DB \cup G)$, where G (the chaff) is a subset of $U - DB$ and includes strings that are not in DB but that are nevertheless included in the positive image of NDB. The positive image of NDB, i.e., the binary strings not represented in DB, is denoted as DB'.

Negative databases should meet the following desiderata:

- NDB must exclude all of DB
- NDB must be created efficiently
- The membership of any specific string in the set characterized by NDB should be easily determined
- G must contain an intractable number of different text strings and an intractable number of different code strings
- The number of strings in G from U_V must be marginal
- The number of strings in DB' within a Hamming Distance S_H from U_V must be insignificant. S_H is a security parameter that discourages using strings that are farther than S_H as starting points for exhaustive searches
- There must be no easy way to enumerate the valid strings NDB negatively represents without also enumerating an intractable number of invalid strings
- All strings in the universe U should be readily classifiable as valid or invalid

In the next section we describe an algorithm for creating negative databases and investigate the properties of the resulting $NDBs$. We then layout the characteristics the code should have to complete our scheme.

3   Generating a Negative Database

In this section we present an algorithm that outputs a negative database, NDB, when given as input the set of strings DB. First, a few definitions:

Positive Database: A positive database is a set of binary strings of length $l = t + c$—the original data, the data to be concealed, has length t and a code of length c is used to augment it

Negative record: Let $\mathbb{Z}_n$ be the set of non-negative integers less than n, e.g., $\mathbb{Z}_2 = \{0,1\}$. A negative record is a k-tuple of pairs, (position,value), defined over $\mathbb{Z}_l \times \mathbb{Z}_2$. For $l{=}10$ and $k{=}2$ the 2-tuple $< (5,0),(7,1) >$ is a negative record with a 0 at position 5 and a 1 at position 7

Negative database: A negative database, denoted NDB, is a set of negative records

Matching: A negative record N_r is said to match a binary string x if and only if for every pair p in the k-tuple, $x[p.position] = p.value$, where $x[i]$ denotes the value of string x projected onto position i. We write $N_r M x$ for a match and N_r DNM x for a mismatch

Membership: A string x is in NDB if and only if it is matched by at least one negative record

A negative database for positive database DB is such that no negative record in NDB matches a string in DB. There might be, however, some binary strings not in DB that are not matched by NDB; we denote the set of all strings not matched by any NDB entry as DB'.

There are a several algorithms in the literature for creating negative databases [7,10,8]. Moreover, since it was shown in [8] that negative databases are linked by a simple transformation to boolean satisfiability formulas, algorithms for generating formulas can be adapted to generate $NDBs$.

The algorithm presented in Fig. 1 was chosen for its simplicity and ease of analysis. One of our priorities is to have an algorithm with as few biases as possible that could potentially be used by an adversary. The current version is straight forward enough to avoid most of these concerns. The algorithm is similar to methods for generating SAT formulae, to techniques for intrusion detection systems [13], and to algorithms for creating digital credentials [7].

Input: *Size, k, l, DB*
Output: *NDB*
$NDB \leftarrow \emptyset$
while($|NDB| < Size$)
      Create a negative record N_r by selecting k distinct
      pairs from $\mathbb{Z}_b \times \mathbb{Z}_2$ uniformly at random, where $b = \lceil \log_2(l) \rceil$
      if $((N_r \notin NDB) \wedge (\forall x \in DB, N_r \; DNM \; x))$
          $NDB \leftarrow NDB \cup N_r$
Sort *NDB*

Fig. 1. Negative Database Generation Algorithm

The algorithm creates a negative database by selecting negative records uniformly at random from the space of possible records, keeping only those that do not match any DB entry. Each record, in turn, has the same number of position-value pairs (k, sometimes referred to as specified positions). The desired size of NDB is given as a parameter and plays an important role for our scheme. The last line of the algorithm requires sorting NDB; the details are purposely left unspecified as any deterministic ordering will suffice. It is important, however, that both the record order within NDB and the tuple order within each record be specified in order to erase the relative order in which they where created. We assume the use of a suitable pseudo random number generator with a large seed space and cycle.

We wish to create just enough negative records so as to match all valid strings not in DB ($U_V - DB$) and at the same time leave a large subset of U_I unmatched. If too many negative records are created DB' will be very close to DB and the task of retrieving an original data record simplified; on the other hand, if NDB is too small, DB' will include a large number of valid strings and the demarcation of DB will be lost—we aim for the inclusion of strings from $U_V - DB$ to be marginal. This requires not only having an NDB of the proper size but for valid strings to be well distributed throughout the space. The code attached to each string, discussed in Sect. 3.2, accomplishes this.

The number of iterations of the algorithm's main loop is roughly $|NDB|e^{|DB|2^{-k}}$ (see Sect. 3.1, eq. 3). A more mindful version of the algorithm postpones eliminating repeated NDB entries until after the main loop (creating a repeated entry is unlikely) and completes NDB as needed. Taking this into account, the main effort in each iteration is searching through DB. The algorithm's asymptotic time complexity is $O(|NDB| \cdot e^{|DB|2^{-k}} \cdot SearchCost(DB))$, where $SearchCost(DB)$ is the cost of determining whether a potential NDB entry matches DB.

3.1 Properties

Assume that U_V is a set of strings selected independently and uniformly at random from U, that the strings in DB are selected independently and uniformly at random from U_V, and that NDB records are independent of each other. We analyze the properties of our scheme under this circumstances and in Sect. 3.2 discuss the properties the code should have to approximate them in a real scenario. In Sect. 4 we test a particular implementation and examine its results.

The probability of a set of independent detectors, NDB, not matching a particular string in $U - DB$, i.e., the coverage of NDB, is approximated by:

$$P_e = (1 - 2^{-k})^{|NDB|} \simeq e^{-|NDB|2^{-k}} \tag{1}$$

The number of entries in a negative database so as to achieve P_e is:

$$|NDB| \simeq -\ln(P_e)2^k \tag{2}$$

Notice how the number of entries in NDB does not depend on the length of DB strings. The number of bits per entry, however, does. Each NDB record requires $k\lceil \log_2(l) \rceil + k$ bits and the total number of bits in a NDB is $|NDB|(k\lceil \log_2(l) \rceil + k)$.

The size of NDB grows exponentially with the number of specified bits, k, per entry (see eq. 2); k, in turn, determines how easy it will be to generate a record that does not match any DB string. We define P_k as the probability that a randomly chosen negative record is a valid NDB entry:

$$P_k = (1 - 2^{-k})^{|DB|} \simeq e^{-|DB|2^{-k}} \tag{3}$$

the value of k is given by:

$$k \simeq \frac{1}{\ln(2)}(\ln(|DB|) - \ln^2(P_k^{-1})) \tag{4}$$

Along with P_e, k determines what size NDB will have and sets an upper bound on how big a DB can be depicted by as many NDB entries. DBs of any size up to this one, can be represented by NDBs with the same number of records and the same number of specified bits per record. The size of NDB leaks only an upper bound on the size of DB.

For fixed values of P_e and P_k the number of NDB entries grows linearly with the size of the positive database (see Fig. 2(a)):

$$|NDB| = \frac{\ln(P_e)}{\ln(P_k)}|DB| \tag{5}$$

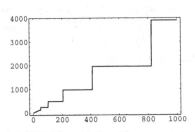

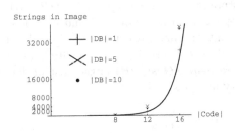

(a) $|NDB|$ growth with respect to $|DB|$. The x axis represents $|DB|$ and the y axis $|NDB|$. The plot was made for a $P_e=2^{-10}$ and a $P_k=0.04$. The resulting k value is rounded up yielding a stepwise growth in NDB

(b) The number of strings in DB' for a text of length 4, code lengths of 8, 12 and 16, and DBs of size 1, 5, and 10. The corresponding NDBs are of size 28, 28 and 56 ($P_m = 0.5$, k=3,3,4). The theoretical results are plotted as a solid line

Fig. 2. Growth behavior of DB, NDB, and DB'

The expected number of strings in NDB's positive image (denoted DB') is $|DB|$ plus the additional strings in $U - DB$ that are not matched by any NDB record:

$$|DB'| = |DB| + P_e|U - DB|$$
$$= |DB| + P_e|U_V - DB| + P_e|U_I| \qquad (6)$$

The expected number of superfluous valid strings included in the positive image is estimated as being $P_e(|U_V - DB|)$ and the expected number of invalid strings as $P_e(|U - U_V|)$ (see Fig.2(b) for an example). Notice that the former does not depend on the size of U while the latter increases as U grows for a given U_V. In what follows we describe a scheme that allows us to control the expected number of false positives by setting P_e, and the expected number of invalid strings by choosing the relative size between U and U_V.

3.2   The Code

Before creating a negative database, the original data must be augmented with a code so as to create a distinction between valid and invalid strings, and to disperse valid strings throughout the space from which DB' is drawn. Consider attaching a unique, uniformly distributed random string to every string in U_d— the set from which the original data is drawn—and creating a NDB with the data to be hidden augmented with its corresponding code (DB). The resulting construction satisfies the first three points laid out in Sect. 2: NDB excludes all of DB; it is created efficiently; and verifying if a data point is in NDB is done by looking up its code and determining if the augmented string is matched by any of NDB's records.

Each negative record matches a subset of U—a hyper-sphere in hamming space—containing all binary strings with the given k positions set to the specified

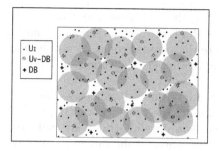

Fig. 3. Graphical depiction of our scheme. The gray circles symbolize the area covered (strings matched) by each NDB entry. The small dark dots are invalid strings, all the rest are valid. DB entries are shown as big dark diamonds. NDB matches most strings in the universe, leaving only DB and an intractable amount of invalid strings unmatched.

values (a total of 2^{l-k} strings). The task of the NDB generation algorithm is to randomly generates those spheres discarding the ones which include any string from DB. If the attached code is sufficiently long, the strings in U_V will be well distributed throughout U making it unlikely that a discarded ball includes a DB entry as well as a $U_V - DB$ string (see Fig. 3). If the algorithm generates an appropriate amount of records (Sect. 3.1 examines this issue), the total number of strings in G will be large with a small number of strings from U_V satisfying the next three properties from Sect. 2 (Sect. 3.2 considers this points). Finally, since the code bears no straightforward relation to the text, there is no efficient way of restricting the retrieval of strings from DB'—the reverse of NDB—to only strings in U_V.

The obvious drawback of this design is the intractable amount of bookkeeping required to distinguish valid from invalid strings (a independent randomly generated code must kept for each DB string). This idealized code, however, brings out the characteristics we want from our code and code generating function g:

- g is computed efficiently. g may be easily invertible
- A small change in the text leads to an arbitrarily large change in the code. For any two distinct strings x and y that are arbitrarily close (in Hamming distance) $g(x)$ and $g(y)$ are arbitrarily far apart
- There is a low probability of code collisions
- It is infeasible to distinguish a valid code from an invalid one without having its corresponding text. It is hard to determine the code having only a small subset of the bits in the text
- The probability of randomly generating a NDB entry for any string in $U_V - DB$ increases with the length of the code
- The resulting code is sufficiently large as to make it hard to recover valid strings from NDB.

An important point is that g may be easy to invert, as the security of the scheme relies on the challenge of finding a valid text-code combination, rather than on the difficulty of recovering the text given the code or vice versa. Finally, note that if a NDB of only codes is created, forgetting about the text altogether, we must additionally ensure that several codes do not decode to the same text, in order to avoid including unwanted valid strings in DB'.

Code Length. The length of the code influences the security of the scheme in two ways: First it determines the proportion of valid to invalid strings in DB'; the longer the code the more invalid strings are included and the more likely to retrieve an invalid string than a valid one in a single try. Second, the length of the code prescribes how many distinct text strings (and code strings) will be included in DB'. This speaks to how easy it is to obtain a valid string given a retrieved entry from DB'. An intractable amount of strings in DB' is not enough to guarantee security unless the number of distinct texts (and codes) is also intractable (it is easy to guide the search away from a few selected strings by including them in NDB (see[9])). The security of the present scheme relies on including an intractable number of strings with distinct texts and codes.

The amount of distinct texts is computed by first estimating the probability of including in DB' a particular string x that is a Hamming distance of h away from the closest string in DB. Let $HD(x, DB)$ be the smallest Hamming distance between a string x and the set of strings DB, and D_h be the number of strings in DB at a distance of h from x.

$$P(x \in DB' | HD(x, DB) = h) = (1 - 2^{-k}(1 - \frac{\binom{l-h}{k}}{\binom{l}{k}})^{D_h})^{|NDB|} \qquad (7)$$

The probability that a DB' includes a given string that is a distance of h away from DB increases as the length of the code increases (see Fig. 4(a)). The expected number of distinct texts in DB' is given by:

$$\sum_{h=0}^{t} \binom{t}{h} P(x \in DB' | HD(x, DB) = h) \qquad (8)$$

As can be seen from this analysis the number of texts in DB' that are close to DB are few in comparison to the total number of distinct texts included in DB' (see Fig. 4(b)). This makes finding a string close to DB increasingly unlikely as the code grows and prevents exhaustive searches from using retrieved strings as a starting point. Section 4 shows how close eq. 4(b) resembles the experimental results for DBs of size one and one hundred.

4   Implementation

This section presents a possible implementation of our scheme and explores its characteristics experimentally. The first step is to choose a code generating function that satisfies the requirements laid out in the previous sections. A straight forward option is to use a hash function and apply it repeatedly to achieve the desired code length. We chose MD5 [21] since it satisfies all of our desiderata,

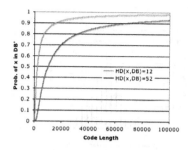

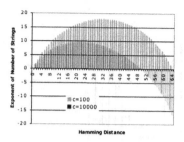

(a) Probability that text x is included in DB' as its attached code increases in length. $|DB| = 1$, x is 64 bits long, $k=3$, and $|NDB| = 366$.

(b) The logarithm (base 10) of the expected number of distinct texts in DB' for codes of length 100 and 10000. $|DB| = 1$, x is 64 bits long, $k=3$, and $|NDB| = 366$.

even though we do not require that it be difficult to recover the text using only the code. In particular, we use MD5 to ensure that a few bits of the code cannot be used to determine the text and vice versa.

In order the generate codes of the desired size MD5 is applied repeatedly to a string $x \in U_d$ as described in Fig. 4.

We conducted experiments for positive databases with one and one hundred elements each, with text strings of 64 bits, and codes of size 128 and 1024. Longer strings and larger databases are possible, but it becomes increasingly harder to handle for the retrieval algorithm (we currently use ZChaff, see below), hindering the ability to collect statistics. The parameter P_e (see Sect. 3.1) was chosen to marginalize the probability of including unwanted valid strings, and k was set to make the creation of NDB agile; however, it could just as easily taken a number of other values yielding different NDB sizes—with $k = 4$ a NDB of size 716 can be readily created for databases of up to 100 elements.

The details of each experiment are shown in the corresponding captions. Each run (an experiment has 10 runs) consists of generating a negative database for the input DB using algorithm 1 and recovering 100,000 strings from the resulting NDB using zChaff [19]—a complete solver for satisfiability formulas.

```
Input: x, c
Output: A code of length c for string x
o ← MD5(x)
while(length(o) < ⌈c/128⌉) //the length of the MD5 code is 128 bits
    o ← o · MD5(x · o)
return the c most significant bits of o
```

Fig. 4. Code Generation Algorithm

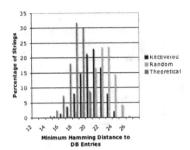

(a) Minimum distance of the recovered texts to the texts in DB (t=64,c=128)

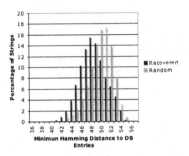

(b) Minimum distance of the recovered codes to the codes in DB (t=64,c=128)

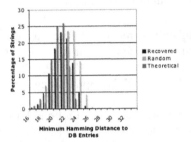

(c) Minimum distance of the recovered texts to the texts in DB (t=64,c=1024)

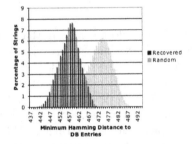

(d) Minimum distance of the recovered codes to the codes in DB (t=64,c=1024)

Fig. 5. Each figure displays the results of an experiment involving ten distinct DBs of size 100 with t=64 and k=7; the DBs of figures (a) and (b) have a code size of 128 and those of (c) and (d) a size of 1024. A NDB of size 5768 was created for each DB and 100,000 "positive" strings recovered from the corresponding $DB's$. The percentage of distinct entries recovered from each DB' for each Hamming Distance was computed and averaged over the ten experiments. Each figure also shows the minimum distance to DB of 50,000 randomly generated strings averaged over the ten DBs. Figures (a) and (c) additionally show the value predicted by using eq. 7 (the recovered and predicted values are very close together, the distance of the random strings are the rightmost values in each figure). Algorithm 1 iterated 12800 times in the worst case.

Using zChaff entails transforming NDB into its equivalent boolean formula (for more on the transformations see [8]) as an intermediate step and converting the solution back to a string in our representation. Each run invokes zChaff 10^5 times with different random seeds to obtain a variety of DB' entries. zChaff uses several advanced heuristics and it's therefore not expected to select solutions uniformly at random; nevertheless, the experimental results (see Fig's. 5 and 6) do not diverge significantly from the theoretical analysis. Indeed, part of our security relies on the infeasibility of leveraging the search towards valid solutions.

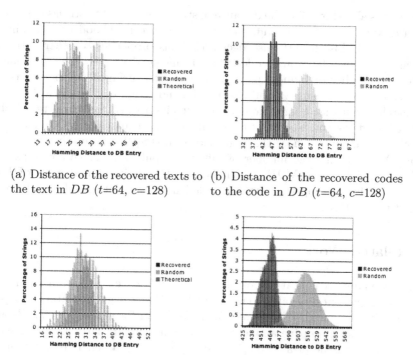

(a) Distance of the recovered texts to the text in DB (t=64, c=128)

(b) Distance of the recovered codes to the code in DB (t=64, c=128)

(c) Distance of the recovered texts to the text in DB (t=64, c=1024)

(d) Distance of the recovered codes to the code in DB (t=64, c=1024)

Fig. 6. Each figure displays the results of an experiment involving ten distinct DBs of size one with t=64 and k=3; the DBs of figures (a) and (b) have a code size of 128 and those of (c) and (d) a size of 1024. A NDB of size 366 was created for each DB and 10^5 "positive" strings recovered from the corresponding $DB's$. The percentage of distinct entries recovered from each DB' for each Hamming Distance was computed and averaged over the ten experiments. Each figure also shows the distance of 50,000 randomly generated strings to DB averaged over the ten DBs and figures (a) and (c) show the value predicted using eq. 7. Algorithm 1 iterated 420 times in the worst case.

The experiments report the percentage of recovered strings (divided into text and code) at a given Hamming Distance from DB (when DB has more than one element we report the distance of the recovered string to the closest DB entry) and show that, for proper parameter settings, it is unlikely to recover a string in DB' that is close enough to DB to use as a starting point for an exhaustive search. No experiment yielded any strings in DB and no valid strings where discovered (recall that there is a slight probability of including valid strings in DB' that are not in DB).

The experiments show that the distance distribution of recovered texts to texts in DB is increasingly similar to the distance distribution of texts guessed at random, and suggest that the likelihood of retrieving a text within a certain distance of the hidden data diminishes as the code grows. Likewise, the experiments also show that the distance of strings recovered to strings concealed increases with their length and, therefore, that the likelihood of retrieving a code (or text) close to DB also decreases. This properties together with the amount of distinct texts and codes that are included in DB' computationally bound the number of strings that can be recovered using NDB before a DB entry can be found using zChaff. Notice that no string can be discarded from the search, given that a large number of text bits are required for a reasonable guess of what its corresponding code will be (the composite MD5 of Fig. 4) and vice versa. Finally, note that our algorithm (Fig. 1) can produce the same output NDB for a large number of different input DBs, since any subset of DB' can possibly cause NDB. This handicaps the ability of analyzing NDB to deduce DB. For appropriate text and code lengths the data is safely hidden by a negative database.

5   Related Work

There are many areas that are of interest and influence to this work. First, is the previous work on negative databases: In [11] the negative database representation is introduced; [7] uses a similar algorithm for generating NDBs and introduces some interesting applications, but relies on NP-hardness for its security. In [10] the issue of attaching a code is proposed, albeit it is used with a different purpose, and [6] is concerned with generating NDBs efficiently. Both consider ways of creating secure NDBs. In contrast to [6], our proposal does not rely on cryptographic primitives for the security of the system, and its construction allows for the stored data to be manipulated via a special algebra (see [12]). Reference [9] discusses several algorithms for updating a negative database once it has been created.

The technique of winnowing and chaffing presented in [20] and further studied in [15] has many similarities with our proposal as does the method presented in [4] (Danezis et.al [6] provide another related example); primarily the notion of hiding valid strings amid invalid ones. The main distinctions are that our technique does not require the use of any shared secrets, anybody with a text can verify if it is in DB, and that the amount of chaff that can be efficiently included alongside DB is far greater (this is one of the main advantages of negative databases). Neither method requires encryption.

The work in [17] has similar goals as our own. Here, queries to an encrypted database are restricted by type and "mass harvesting" queries are computationally inefficient. Our technique impedes mass harvesting without the use of encryption by virtue of the representation, but only processes simple membership queries efficiently. It allows, however, the use of many relational algebra operations on the data without the need for keys or secrets. Other techniques using different principles for restricting the types of information that can be learned from a database include [1,16].

On the topic of representation there are several techniques for creating compact depictions of binary sets, of special interest are Bloom Filters [3] and

Ordered Binary Decision Diagrams [5]. The primary differences between these and our scheme is the need of negative databases to always obtain a compact depiction of the complement of a set without explicitly calculating it, and the difficulty with which the data can be retrieved.

Information Hiding techniques [2,18] like water-marking and steganography [14] focus on concealing data items within some stream of information (while, in a matter of speaking, ours hides information in the garbage). Our approach is similar to these techniques in that, given a negative database, it is infeasible to determine whether it represents any valid string (message) at all, i.e., if the corresponding positive database is non-empty; and in that knowledge of the existence of a message does not facilitate its retrieval. However, the referred techniques allow retrieving the message with special knowledge of its whereabouts, while our present proposal does not.

6 Discussion

In this paper we presented a method for hiding data by placing it amidst garbage. The novelty of our scheme is that instead of storing data plus garbage, we store the complement of this set—the negative database. This enables us to compactly keep an arbitrary amount of invalid strings alongside the data. Other work on negative databases rely on NP-hardness principles or on cryptographic primitives to safeguard the confidentiality of the original data. Our scheme relies on neither, but rather on the amount of garbage and the difficulty of systematically telling it apart from the valuable data. Further, the present scheme surpasses some of its predecessors in keeping the size of the data structure manageable; for instance, a negative database for 100 strings can be maintained with roughly four times as many bits as the positive version ($k = 4$, $P_e = 2^{-(t+1)}$ eq. 2).

Our scheme allows any entity to efficiently verify the presence of a given data item in the structure, while preventing massive data harvesting. The most important differences with methods that offer this same functionality are that negative databases don't use encryption; that they obfuscate the size of the hidden set; that a single dataset has a very large amount of different negative database representations and no easy way to test their equivalence; and that they can be manipulated to express transformations on the hidden set. As an example of the latter consider a list of credit-card numbers (CCN) and balances, and its corresponding NDB; suppose the CCN occupies the 54 most significant bits of each record and the balance the following 20. Appending entry $<(0,55)(0,56)(0,57)>$ to NDB will restrict the list's contents to only those with balance less than 131072 dlls. Further, using the operations described in [12] the NDB can be joined with a negative database of names and CCNs to produce one of names, CCNs, and balances. All without knowledge of the actual contents of the actual lists or their sizes.

In this paper we focused on creating $NDBs$ for text and codes because of the functionality added by the relational algebra operations mentioned above. Possible variations of our work include keeping only the code (loosing said functionality) or having secret codes or code generations mechanisms that allow privileged parties to efficiently limit the search and recover the original data.

The results and analysis presented in this paper strongly suggest that negative database can be used to safely keep data hidden; there is, however, more work to be done. Along with more extensive experimentation, better data structures for representing DB and NDB need be explored (to enable more efficient searches) and the statistical properties of NDBs studied in more detail.

Acknowledgments

The author wishes to thank Elena S. Ackley, Stephanie Forrest, and Joan Feigenbaum for their help and insights; and gratefully acknowledge the support of the PORTIA project (NSF grant 0331548) for partially funding this research.

References

1. Agarwal, R., Srikant, R.: Privacy-preserving data minig. In: Proc. of the ACM SIGMOD Conference on Management of Data, pp. 439–450. ACM Press, New York (2000)
2. Bender, W., Gruhl, D., Morimoto, N., Lu, A.: Techniques for data hiding. IBM Systems Journal (September-December 1996)
3. Bloom, B.H.: Space/time trade-offs in hash coding with allowable errors. Communications of the ACM 13(7), 422–426 (1970)
4. Brinkman, R., Maubach, S., Jonker, W.: A lucky dip as a secure data store. In: Proceedings of Workshop on Information and System Security (2006)
5. Bryant, R.E.: Graph-based algorithms for Boolean function manipulation. IEEE Transactions on Computers C-35, 677–691 (1986)
6. Danezis, G., Diaz, G., Faust, S., Käsper, E., Troncoso, C., Preneel, B.: Efficient negative databases from cryptographic hash functions. In: Garay, J.A., Lenstra, A.K., Mambo, M., Peralta, R. (eds.) ISC 2007. LNCS, vol. 4779, pp. 423–436. Springer, Heidelberg (2007)
7. de Mare, M., Wright Secure, R.: Set membership using 3sat. In: Ning, P., Qing, S., Li, N. (eds.) ICICS 2006. LNCS, vol. 4307. Springer, Heidelberg (2006)
8. Esponda, F.: Negative Representations of Information. PhD thesis, University of New Mexico (2005)
9. Esponda, F., Ackley, E.S., Forrest, S., Helman, P.: On-line negative databases. In: Nicosia, G., Cutello, V., Bentley, P.J., Timmis, J. (eds.) ICARIS 2004. LNCS, vol. 3239, pp. 175–188. Springer, Heidelberg (2004)
10. Esponda, F., Forrest, S., Helman, P.: Protecting data privacy through hard-to-reverse negative databases. International Journal of Information Security 6(6), 403–415 (2007)
11. Esponda, F., Forrest, S., Helman, P.: Enhancing privacy through negative representations of data. Technical report, University of New Mexico (2004)
12. Esponda, F., Trias, E., Ackley, E.S., Forrest, S.: A relational algebra for negative databases. Technical Report TR-CS-2007-18, University of New Mexico (2007)
13. Hofmeyr, S., Forrest, S.: Architecture for an artificial immune system. Evolutionary Computation Journal 8(4), 443–473 (2000)

14. Katzenbeisser, S., Petitcolas, F.A.P. (eds.): Information hiding techniques for steganography and digital watermarking. Artech House computer security series. Artech House Inc., Norwood (2000)
15. McHugh, J.: Chaffing at the bit: Thoughts on a note by ronald rivest. In: Pfitzmann, A. (ed.) IH 1999. LNCS, vol. 1768, pp. 395–404. Springer, Heidelberg (2000)
16. Micali, S., Rabin, M., Kilian, J.: Zero-knowledge sets. In: Proc. FOCS 2003, p. 80 (2003)
17. Narayanan, A., Shmatikov, V.: Obfuscated databases and group privacy. In: CCS 2005: Proceedings of the 12th ACM conference on Computer and communications security, pp. 102–111. ACM, New York (2005)
18. Petitcolas, F.A.P., Anderson, R.J., Kuhn, M.G.: Information hiding-a survey. Proceedings of the IEEE special issue on protection of multimedia content 87(7), 1062–1078 (1999)
19. Princeton. zChaff (2004), http://ee.princeton.edu/~chaff/zchaff.php
20. Rivest, R.L.: Chaffing and winnowing: Confidentiality without encryption. MIT Lab for Computer Science (March 1998), http://theory.lcs.mit.edu/~rivest/chaffing.txt
21. Rivest, R.L.: The md5 message-digest algorithm (1992)

Information Leakage in Optimal Anonymized and Diversified Data

Chengfang Fang and Ee-Chien Chang

School of Computing
National University of Singapore
fangchengfang@nus.edu.sg, changec@comp.nus.edu.sg

Abstract. To reconcile the demand of information dissemination and preservation of privacy, a popular approach generalizes the attribute values in the dataset, for example by dropping the last digit of the postal code, so that the published dataset meets certain privacy requirements, like the notions of k-anonymity and ℓ-diversity. On the other hand, the published dataset should remain useful and not over generalized. Hence it is desire to disseminate a database with high "usefulness", measured by a *utility function*. This leads to a generic framework whereby the optimal dataset (w.r.t. the utility function) among all the generalized datasets that meet certain privacy requirements, is chosen to be disseminated. In this paper,we observe that, the fact that a generalized dataset is optimal may leak information about the original. Thus, an adversary who is aware of how the dataset is generalized may able to derive more information than what the privacy requirements constrained. This observation challenges the widely adopted approach that treats the generalization process as an optimization problem. We illustrate the observation by giving counter-examples in the context of k-anonymity and ℓ-diversity.

Keywords: Data dissemination, Privacy-preserving, k-anonymity and ℓ-diversity.

1 Introduction

Data dissemination and information sharing is required in statistical analysis of a population spreading across different organizations, and is also essential in providing transparency. However, the ease of obtaining and linking different published dataset lead to the concern on the leakage of personal information. To protect privacy we may generalize the attribute values, for example by dropping the last digit of the postal code, before the datasets are released. On the other hand, it is meaningless to disseminate datasets that are over generalized. To achieve the right tradeoff, a widely adopted framework treats the problem of finding the generalized dataset as an optimization problem. The framework takes a requirement of privacy as the constraint, and a *utility function*, which measures the usefulness of a generalized dataset, as the objective function in the optimization problem. In other words, given a dataset, among all the generalized

K. Solanki, K. Sullivan, and U. Madhow (Eds.): IH 2008, LNCS 5284, pp. 30–44, 2008.

datasets that meet the privacy requirements, the one that is optimal with respect to the *utility function* is chosen to be disseminated. The framework provides the assurance that the disseminated dataset meets the privacy requirement, and at the same time is useful. The well-known notions on k-anonymity [18] and ℓ-diversity [13] provide notions and requirements of privacy, and both notions are proposed to be employed in the above-mentioned framework. In this paper, we observe that the optimal generalized dataset might no longer satisfy the privacy requirement. Although the disseminated table is chosen from a collection that meets the privacy requirement, the fact that the disseminated dataset is optimal is an additional piece of information. Taking this piece of information into consideration, an adversary may able to derive more information than what the privacy requirement ensured. We will illustrate our observation by investigating the requirements of k-anonymity and ℓ-diversity.

The notion of k-anonymity requires that every record is indistinguishable from at least $(k-1)$ other records for all possible set of attributes. This ensures that at least k tuples share the same generalized identity and thus individual cannot be identified. To illustrate, consider a scenario where a hospital published information of patients in a particular month as shown in Table 1. To protect privacy, values under the attribute "Name" are removed. Elsewhere, an association released information of dentists with information shown in Table 2. It happens that the combination of age, gender and company postal code is unique for Peter in Table 2. Thus, by linking both tables, one may derive Peter's home postal code and he was hospitalized in that month. Table 3 shows a generalization that is 2-anonymized. From Table 3, it is not easy to identify Peter since there are two tuples matching his identity.

The notion of ℓ-diversity is introduced to prevent data inference that is not addressed in k-anonymity. The attributes are classified as *sensitive* and *non-sensitive*, and it is assumed that the publisher knows which attributes are sensitive. Consider the previous scenario where Table 3 is published, and the attribute "Illness" is sensitive. Suppose Alice knows that Peter is hospitalized and she has access to Table 2. Although there are two tuples in Table 3 matching Peter's identity, both of them share the same sensitive value. Thus, Alice can infer that Peter is having fever. To counter this inference, the ℓ-diversity requirement ensures that, among the records with the same identifiers, the sensitive attribute values consist of at least ℓ well-represented values. There are many ways to

Table 1. Released table

Name	Age	Gender	Home postal	Occupation	Company postal	Illness
	30	F	48546	Crane operator	54832	Anxiety
	41	F	13208	Teacher	11824	Sleeplessness
	43	F	15201	Dentist	11857	Sleeplessness
	32	F	48356	Driver	54832	Anxiety
	26	M	61306	Manager	29054	fever
	22	M	61306	Dentist	29089	fever

Table 2. Public table

Name	Age	Gender	Company postal
...	...	...	...
Peter	22	M	29089
...	...	...	...

Table 3. 2-anonymized table

Name	Age	Gender	Home postal	Occupation	Company postal	Illness
	3*	F	48***	Outdoor	54832	Anxiety
	3*	F	48***	Outdoor	54832	Anxiety
	4*	F	1****	Indoor	118**	Sleeplessness
	4*	F	1****	Indoor	118**	Sleeplessness
	2*	M	61306	Indoor	290**	fever
	2*	M	61306	Indoor	290**	fever

defined the meaning of what being "well-represented" values, and a natural choice is by requiring the entropy of the attribute values is above certain threshold, say $\log_2 \ell$. If the sensitive values are well represented, then we can have an upper bound on the chances that the adversary can successfully guess the correct value.

As mentioned in the first paragraph, it is meaningless to publish a table that is over generalized. Hence, it is desire to find a generalized table that meets certain requirements on privacy, and optimal with respect to a utility function. There are many choices of utility functions, and typically, they measure the distance of the generalized dataset from the original dataset. An example of utility function counts the number *'s in the generalized table. In general, given a dataset, it is not easy to find the optimal. In many interesting settings, the problems are NP-hard [14]. Fortunately, there are extensive works in finding the optimal and many approximation algorithms and effective heuristic are known [12,6,15,17].

The rest of this paper is organized as follows. We discuss the related work in section 2, and give the related background and notations in section 3. In section 4.1 and 4.2 we introduce the formulation and show examples on information leakage of k-anonymized table, then we move on to information leakage of ℓ-diverse table in section 4.3 and give a general theorem in section 4.4. Section 5 gives a conclusion.

2   Related Work

There are extensive works on k-anonymity since Sweeney[18] proposed the notion. The notion of k-anonymity is widely involved in the context of protecting location privacy[7,10], preserving privacy in communication protocol[19,20] data mining techniques[2,9] and many others. There are different way of anonymizing and diversifying a table: achieving via generalization[3,12], via generalization with suppression[16,11] and via data swapping and randomization techniques [1,8]. Meyerson et al. have shown that achieving the optimal generalization is NP-hard for many different settings[14,4,5]. Fortunately, there are many practical approximation and heuristic. Sweeney has proposed an heuristic-based approach[17] in 2002. Samarati has also proposed an algorithm of searching a "k-minimal" group that contains the optimal k-anonymizations based on certain preference[15]. Bayardo et al. have proposed a lattice top-down search strategy[6] for optimal k-anonymized tables while LeFevre et al. have proposed a bottom-up searching algorithm[12]. Machanavajjhala et al. have proposed the idea of ℓ-diversity [13] and we follow most of the term and definitions they used.

3 Background and Notations

In this section, we describe k-anonymity and ℓ-diversity, based on definitions in [13] with slight modifications. The definition given in [13] requires the classification of attributes into sensitive and non-sensitive. However, this requirement is not enforced in some known works and the classification may not be trivial in some real life datasets. Hence, for definition of k-anonymity, we do not classify the attribute.

Each dataset $T = \{t_1, t_2, \ldots, t_n\}$ is a set of tuples, and can be viewed as a table as shown in Table 1, where a row corresponds to a tuple, and a column corresponds to an attribute. For a $t \in T$ and an attribute A, let us denote $t[A]$ the value of attribute A of the tuple t.

3.1 Generalization

Let D to be the domain of an attribute value, for example, D can be $\{0, 1\}$, set of integers or set of strings. We say that D^* is a generalization of D if D^* is a partition of D. That is, D^* is a collection of non-intersecting subsets of D, whose union is D. We say that a $c^* \in D^*$ is the *generalized value* of $c \in D$ if $c \in c^*$. If every value in a table T is replaced by its generalized value for some D^*, then we say that the new table T^* is a generalized table of T. For two generalized domain D_0^* and D_1^*, we say that D_1^* is a generalization of D_0^* if, for any $c_0^* \in D_0^*$, there exists a $c_1^* \in D_1^*$ such that $c_0^* \subseteq c_1^*$. Similarly, if D_0^* and D_1^* is the domain of T_0^* and T_1^* respectively, then we say that T_1^* is a generalization of T_0^*.

For example, the domain of "Home postal" in Table 3 is the set of 5-digits strings. Replacing the string 13205 to 1320* is a generalization. The generalized D_0^* domain contains the set { 13200, 13201, ..., 13209 }.

If the string is further replaced by 132**, the new generalized domain D_1^* contains a set {13200, 13201, ..., 13299 }. Furthermore, D_1^* is a generalization of D_0^*. Since a generalized domain is a partition of the original domain, it is not possible to have both 13*** and 132** appeared in a column of the table.

3.2 k-Anonymity

A set of attributes $\{A_1, A_2, \ldots, A_w\}$ of a table is called a *quasi-identifier*. Let $\mathcal{QI}$ be a collection of quasi-identifiers[1]. We say that a tuple t_1 is k-anonymized, if for any quasi-identifier $C \in \mathcal{QI}$, there exist $k - 1$ other tuples $t_2, \ldots, t_k$ such that $t_1[C] = t_2[C] = \ldots = t_k[C]$. A table T is k-anonymized if every tuple is k-anonymized.

If a table T is k-anonymized, given any quasi-identifier in $\mathcal{QI}$, each tuple cannot be distinguished from at least $k-1$ tuples. For example, in a 2-anonymized table shown in Table 3, even if an adversary knows Table 2, he is unable to identify Peter's tuple in Table 3, since the third and fourth tuple has the same generalized value.

3.3 ℓ-Diversity

Under the notion of ℓ-diversity, each attribute is classified as either *sensitive* or *non-sensitive* but not both. Furthermore, a quasi-identifier contains only non-sensitive attributes. Hence, only the non-sensitive attributes can be linked with other public tables. The publisher is assumed to know which attributes are sensitive before the table is generalized. Note that such classification of attributes is not enforced in k-anonymity.

Given q^*, a value of a quasi-identifier, let us define the q^*-*block* to be the set of tuples with value q^*. Let $n(q^*, s, T)$ denote the number of tuples that has value q^* and value s for a sensitive attribute. For example, in Table 7, the block of tuples with values (130**, M, A-) has two sensitive value, "Anxiety" and "Cancer".

In general, a table is said to be ℓ-diverse if, for every q^*-block, the values of any sensitive attribute is "well-represented" by ℓ values. There are a number of ways to quantify how "well-representative" a block is. A simple requirement is to have at least ℓ sensitive values in every q^*-block. In this paper, we adopt the notion of *entropy ℓ-diverse* as defined in [13].

Entropy ℓ-diverse. A table T is said to be entropy ℓ-diverse if, for every q^*-block, and any sensitive attribute with domain S,

$$-\sum_{s \in S} P(q^*, s, T) \log(P(q^*, s, T)) \geq \log(\ell), \tag{1}$$

$$\text{where } P(q^*, s, T) = n(q^*, s, T) \,/\, \sum_{s' \in S} n(q^*, s', T) .$$

$P(q^*, s, T)$ is the ratio of tuples that has the sensitive value s among the tuples in the q^*-block.

Suppose an adversary has the value q of a quasi-identifier, and the generalized table T^*. Let q^* be the corresponding generalized value of q in the table T^*. Let

---

[1] It is not necessary that $\mathcal{QI}$ contains all possible quasi-identifiers. Some previous works restrict $\mathcal{QI}$ to quasi-identifiers that can be linked with other tables.

us assume that, in the original table T, q is unique, and each tuple in the q^*-block (in the table T^*) is equally likely to be the actual tuple with quasi-identifier q. Hence, if he predicts that the tuple has sensitive value s, his chance of success is the ratio $P(q^*, s, T)$. This can be viewed as the *posterior belief* of the tuple having sensitive value s. Let us write it as,

$$\beta_{q,s} .$$

Hence, the left hand side in inequality (1) is the entropy of the posterior belief.

3.4   Utility Function

Ideally, a utility function measures the amount of information retained in a generalized table T^*. Generally, its value increase as the "distance" between T^* and the original T decreases. Here is an example of a simple utility function which counts the number of $*$'s in the generalized table T^*.

$$U(T^*) = - \sum_{t \in T^*} \sum_{q \in \mathcal{QI}_{T^*}} f(t, q) , \qquad (2)$$

where $f(t, q) = k$ is the number of $*$'s contained in $t[q]$.

There are many choices of utility function, we uses the above function (2), which is widely adopted, in our discussions.

3.5   Optimal Generalized Table

Given a table T, let $\mathcal{C}(T)$ be the collection of all possible generalizations of T. Given a privacy requirement, which can be k-anonymity, and/or ℓ-diversity, let $\mathcal{P}$ to be the set of all tables that satisfy the requirement[2]. Let $\mathcal{G}(T)$ be the table in $(\mathcal{C}(T) \cap \mathcal{P})$ that is optimal with respect to a given utility function. Conversely, given a generalized table T^*, we write $\mathcal{G}^{-1}(T)$ to be:

$$\mathcal{G}^{-1}(T) = \{T \mid T^* = \mathcal{G}(T)\} . \qquad (3)$$

That is, it is the inverse of the function $\mathcal{G}$.

Remarks. Note that the definition of $\mathcal{G}(\cdot)$ relies on the definition of the privacy requirement, and the utility function. Also, note that the set $\mathcal{G}^{-1}(T)$ does not contain generalized tables.

We assume that the optimal is unique, and the generalization process is deterministic. Our main observation can be extended to generalization algorithms that are probabilistic. However, for clarity, we choose to handle deterministic algorithms in this paper.

---

[2] To simplify notations, we do not parameterized $\mathcal{P}$ with the requirements. In the paper, it is always clear from the context which privacy requirement is referred to.

4   Information Leakage

This section gives the formulation of information leakage (Section 4.1 and 4.3). Examples of information leakage in k-anonymized and ℓ-diversified table will be given in Section 4.2 and 4.4 respectively.

4.1   Formulation of Leakage in k-Anonymized Tables

Given a T^*, we say that it can be *inverted* if

1. $|\mathcal{G}^{-1}(T^*)| = 1$, and
2. the table in $\mathcal{G}^{-1}(T^*)$ is not k-anonymized.

That is, from T^*, there is only one table T whose optimal generalized data is T^*. Note that it is more interesting to include the second condition since a table that is already k-anonymized will be published as it is.

In cases where the inverse is not unique, all tables in $\mathcal{G}^{-1}(T^*)$ may still able to be generalized to a single table that is not k-anonymized. Given a generalized T^*, we say that it can be *partially inverted* if there is a T_0^* such that

1. For all $T \in \mathcal{G}^{-1}(T^*)$, T can be generalized to T_0^*, and
2. T_0^* is not k-anonymized.

Hence, if a table can be partially inverted, by linking with certain tables, there exists a tuple t_0 and quasi-identifier Q, such that t_0 shares the same identity (with respect to Q) with at most $(k-2)$ tuples. Thus, the original assurance of k-anonymity is compromised.

4.2   Examples for k-Anonymized Table

Example 1: Inverting a table.   This section gives an optimal generalized table T^* that can be inverted. This simple example provides a simple form that can be extended to larger examples. The original table T contains one attribute Att_1 whose domain is binary strings of length 2. The 2-anonymized table is shown in Table 4 (a).

The original value for 0* can be either 00 or 01. Due to symmetry, there are only 5 possible tables that can be generalized to T^*: either it contains four 00's, three 00's, two 00's, one 00, or none. Let us examine these cases.

1. Four 00's, two 00's and none: In each case, the table already satisfies 2-anonymity, and thus its optimal generalized table is itself. Hence, they are not in $\mathcal{G}^{-1}(T^*)$.
2. Three 00's: In this case, there is only one 01. Hence, it does not satisfy 2-anonymity. However, its optimal anonymized table is not T^*. Instead, the table with three 00's and three *1's attains optimal.
3. One 00: Table 4 (b) shows this case. This table does not satisfy 2-anonymity, and it is easy to verify that T^* is its optimal 2-anonymized table.

Therefore, $\mathcal{G}^{-1}(T^*)$ contains only one table and it does not satisfy 2-anonymity.

Table 4. (a) An optimal 2-anonymized table   (b) The only possible original

(a)
Att_1
11
11
0*
0*
0*
0*

(b)
Att_1
11
11
01
01
01
00

Table 5. An optimal 2-anonymized table

Att_1
0011
0011
000*
000*
000*
000*
**10
**10

Example 2: Partially inverting a table. We now give an optimal 2-anonymized table T^* that can be partially inverted. The original table T contains one attribute $Attr_1$ whose domain is binary strings of length 4. The anonymized table T^* is shown in Table 5.

There are two generalized values, 000* and **01. The original value for 000* can be either 0000 or 0001. Similar to the previous example, by examine each case, we can deduce that the original table has two 0011's, three 0001's, one 0000, for the four 000*'s.

Now, let us consider the two tuples with **01. The *'s appear in the first and second position. If, the values are the same at either the first or the second position, then we can have a generalized table with lower utility. For example, {0001, 0101} can be generalized to 0*01, which requires only two *'s. Thus, their optimal is not T^* and the choices for $\mathcal{G}^{-1}(T^*)$ are narrowed to {0010, 1110} and {1010, 0110}. It is easy to check that both cases have Table 5 as its optimal generalization. Therefore, $\mathcal{G}^{-1}(T^*)$ contains two tables as shown in Table 6 (a) & (b), which can be generalized to the table T_0^* as shown in Table 6 (c). Hence, T^* can be partially inverted.

Table 6. (a) & (b) The two possible original of Table 5. (c) A generalized table T_0^* that does not satisfy 2-anonymity.

(a)	(b)	(c)
Att_1	Att_1	Att_1
0011	0011	0011
0011	0011	0011
0001	0001	0001
0001	0001	0001
0001	0001	0001
0000	0000	0000
0010	0110	**10
1110	1010	**10

4.3 Formulation of Leakage in ℓ-Diversified Tables

Recall the definition of posterior belief $\beta_{q,s}$ in Section 3.3. If the fact that the table T^* is optimal is taken into consideration, the probability that a tuple in the q^*-block having the sensitive value s may change and is not longer $P(q^*, s, T)$. Let us call this probability the *enhanced belief* and write it as:

$$\gamma_{q,s} \ .$$

Consider a table T, and its optimal ℓ-diversified table T^*, in addition, let S be a sensitive attribute, Q a quasi-identifier. We say that T^* suffers *partial disclosure* if there exist some $q \in Q$ and $s \in S$ such that:

$$\beta_{q,s} < \gamma_{q,s} \ .$$

Furthermore, we say that T^* suffers *total disclosure* if

$$\beta_{q,s} < \gamma_{q,s} = 1 \ .$$

4.4 Results for ℓ-Diversified Tables

Example.   We now give an optimal diversified table T^* that suffers total disclosure in this section, and we will extend this example to a more general form later in this section.

The table T^* is shown in Table 7. The attribute "Condition" is the only sensitive attribute and the others are non-sensitive. Similar to previous examples, the utility function is based on the number of *'s. The $\mathcal{QI}$ contains the set of all non-sensitive attributes. The leftmost column indicates different blocks and is not part of the table. This table is an optimal 2-anonymized and entropy 2-diversified table.

Table 7. An optimal 2-anonymized and 2-diversified table

	Postal code	Gender	Blood group	Condition
1	130**	M	A+	Heart Disease
	130**	M	A+	Viral Infection
2	130**	M	A−	Anxiety
	130**	M	A−	Cancer
3	130**	M	B*	Cancer
	130**	M	B*	Fever
	130**	M	B*	Cough
	130**	M	B*	Diabetes

It is entropy 2-diversified because for block 1 and block 2 we have the following for the inequality (1),

$$-2 \cdot \left(\frac{1}{2}\right) \log_2 \left(\frac{1}{2}\right) = \log_2 (2) \ .$$

and for block 3, we have

$$-4 \cdot \left(\frac{1}{4}\right) \log_2 \left(\frac{1}{4}\right) > \log_2 (2) \ .$$

Consider an adversary who has a quasi-identifier value (13021, M, A+), which can be identified with block 3. This block has 4 different sensitive values. Thus, the posterior belief for this identity having "cancer" is $\frac{1}{4}$.

Now, using the fact that the table is optimal, the probability changes. The original value for the attribute "Blood group" for each tuple in block 3 can be either B+ or B−. There are 8 different cases for block 3.

1. The non-sensitive value of the first tuple in block 3 is (130**, M, B+) and the number of the other three tuples in block 3 having original value (130**, M, B+) is:
   - 1 or 3: In these two cases, block 3 is already 2-anonymized and 2-diversified. This is against the assumption that T^* is optimal.
   - 2:   In this case, block 3 contains only 1 tuple having the non-sensitive value (130**, M, B−). This tuple can be generalized with tuples in block 2 as "*−" to achieve one less *. Thus, this case can be eliminated.
   - 0:   Only the first tuple in block 3 has the non-sensitive value (130**, M, B+) with can be generalized with tuples in block 1 to achieve one less *. Thus, this case can also be eliminated.
2. The non-sensitive value of the first tuple in block 3 is (130**, M, B−) and the number of the other three tuples in q^*-block 3 having original value (130**, M, B−) is:

  – 1 or 3: In both cases, the original table is already 2-diversify.
  – 2:   In this case, the optimal generalized table is not T^*
  – 0:   It is easy to verify that its optimal generalized table is T^*.

A generalization of the original table is as shown in Table 8. In addition, for the identity (13021, M, B-) having "cancer", the enhanced belief is 1 which is higher than the posterior belief of $\frac{1}{4}$. Thus, this table suffers total disclosure for tuple (13021, M, B-). Furthermore, this table also suffers partial disclosure for (13021, M, B+) (details omitted).

Table 8. Generalization of the original table for Table 7

	Postal code	Gender	Blood group	Condition
1	130**	M	A+	Heart Disease
	130**	M	A+	Viral Infection
2	130**	M	A-	Anxiety
	130**	M	A-	Cancer
3	130**	M	B-	Cancer
4	130**	M	B+	Fever
	130**	M	B+	cough
	130**	M	B+	diabetes

General Result. The previous example is for $k, \ell = 2$. We now show that total disclosure can occurred for any k, ℓ where $k \geq \ell \geq 2$.

Theorem 1. *For any k, ℓ such that $k \geq \ell \geq 2$, there exists an optimal k-anonymized and ℓ-diversified table T^* that suffers total disclosure.*

Proof:
Let $m = \lceil \frac{k}{\ell} \rceil$ and let n be a large number greater than $3k$. Consider a table containing a non-sensitive attribute $Attr_1$ whose domain is bit string of length 2, and a sensitive attribute $Attr_2$ whose domain is the set $\{A_1, A_2, ..., A_n\}$ and its k-anonymized, ℓ-diversified table T^* as shown in Table 9. For abbreviation, the right-most column indicates the number of tuples with the same values. For example, in the first row, the "m" indicates that T^* contains m tuples with value $(11, A_1)$.

This table T^* is entropy ℓ-diverse because for block 1 and 2 we have $-\ell \cdot (\frac{1}{\ell}) \log_2(\frac{1}{\ell}) = \log_2(\ell) = \log_2(\ell)$ and for block 3 we have $-(n - \ell) \cdot (\frac{1}{n-\ell})$ $\log_2(\frac{1}{n-\ell}) = \log_2(n - \ell) > \log_2(\ell)$.

Suppose an adversary wants to guess the sensitive value of non-sensitive value 00, which is generalized to block 3. His posterior belief for this tuple has sensitive value $A_{\ell+1}$ is $\beta_{0*, A_{\ell+1}} = \frac{1}{n-\ell}$.

Now, let us consider the scenario where the adversary knows the fact that T^* is optimal.

Let us introduce the following lemma.

Table 9. Released table in k-anonymity and ℓ-diversity

	$Attr_1$	$Attr_2$	number of tuples
1	11	A_1	m
	11	A_2	m
	11	A_3	m
	...	...	...
	11	A_ℓ	m
2	10	A_2	m
	10	A_3	m
	10	A_4	m
	...	...	...
	10	$A_{\ell+1}$	m
3	0*	$A_{\ell+1}$	1
	0*	$A_{\ell+2}$	1
	...	...	...
	0*	A_{n-1}	1
	0*	A_n	1

Lemma 2. *Given a q^*-block Q of exactly ℓ different sensitive values, it is entropy ℓ-diverse only if all these ℓ different sensitive values have the same number of tuples in this q^* block.*

This lemma holds because only when all sensitive values are of same number, the entropy $-(\ell) \cdot \frac{1}{\ell} \log_2(\frac{1}{\ell})$ is equal to $\log_2(\ell)$.

In this scenario, we should consider the enhanced belief with the above lemma. Note that the original value for 0* can only be either 00 or 01. We divide the possible original tables to the following cases:

1. The first tuple of block 3 is 01 and the number of other tuples having 01 as their non-sensitive attribute is:
   (a) More than $k - 2$ but less than $n - k$. tuples with 01 and 00 are more than k and they all have different sensitive value. Therefore, the original table is already k-anonymized and ℓ-diversify without generalizing the $Attr_1$. This is against the assumption that T^* is optimal.
   (b) More than $n - k - 1$. The number of tuples having non-sensitive value 00 is less than k and hence the original table is not k-anonymized. However, we can generalize those tuples having 00 with block 1 and reduce the number of *'s. Therefore, this case can be eliminated.
   (c) Less than $k - 1$. We can generalize these tuples with block 2 to reduce the number of *'s. Thus, T^* is not optimal.

2. The first tuple of block 3 is 00 and the number of other tuples having 00 as their non-sensitive attribute is:
   (a) More than $k - 2$ but less than $n - k$. This case can be eliminated as the original table is already k-anonymized and ℓ-diversified.
   (b) More than $n - k - 1$. T^* is not optimal in this case.
   (c) Less than $k - 1$ but more than 0. This case can still be eliminated. As long as there are more than one tuple having the non-sensitive value 00, we can still combine these tuples with block 2 (Lemma 2).
   (d) Zero. T^* is optimal as we cannot add the first tuple of block 3 alone to block 2 (Lemma 2).

Table 10. Original table of Table 9

	$Attr_1$	$Attr_2$	number of tuples
1	11	A_1	m
	11	A_2	m
	11	A_3	m
	...	...	...
	11	A_ℓ	m
2	10	A_2	m
	10	A_3	m
	10	A_4	m
	...	...	...
	10	$A_{\ell+1}$	m
3	00	$A_{\ell+1}$	1
4	01	$A_{\ell+2}$	1
	...	...	...
	01	A_{n-1}	1
	01	A_n	1

Thus, $\mathcal{G}^{-1}(T^*)$ contains only a unique table to as shown in Table 10, and $\gamma_{00,A_{\ell+1}}$ is 1.   □

5   Conclusion

In this paper, we have showed that the framework of choosing an optimal (w.r.t an objective function) table from a collection of candidates that satisfies certain privacy requirements, does not provide the assurance that the chosen table will retain the privacy requirements. This is because the fact that the table is optimal is a piece of additional information, which can be exploited by the adversaries. This observation is demonstrated by counter-examples of optimal anonymized and diversified tables. It is interesting to find out whether such framework has been followed in other formulation of privacy, or other security requirements. On the other hand, it is also interesting to find out whether there is a choice of utility function and privacy requirement that can be securely applied in this framework. Randomization seems to be a natural way to provide privacy protection. However, if it is not applied properly, there are still cases where the information leakage is sufficient for the adversary. For example, if the generalization is done by randomly picking a table among all the optimal solutions, an optimal anonymized table may still be inverted or partially inverted even if the solutions are not unique. Hence, it is also interesting to find out how randomization can be applied to provide assurance on privacy protection.

References

1. Adam, N.R., Wortmann, J.C.: Security-control methods for statistical databases: A comparative study. ACM Computing Surveys, 515–556 (1989)
2. Aggarwal, C.C.: On k-anonymity and the curse of dimensionality. In: 31st International Conference on Very Large Data Bases, pp. 901–909 (2005)
3. Aggarwal, G., Feder, T., Kenthapadi, K., Motwani, R., Panigrahy, R., Thomas, D., Zhu, A.: k-anonymity: Algorithms and hardness. Technical report, Stanford University (2004)
4. Aggarwal, G., Feder, T., Kenthapadi, K., Motwani, R., Panigrahy, R., Thomas, D., Zhu, A.: Anonymizing tables. In: 10th International Conference on Database Theory, pp. 246–258 (2005)
5. Aggarwal, G., Feder, T., Kenthapadi, K., Motwani, R., Panigrahy, R., Thomas, D., Zhu, A.: Approximation algorithms for k-anonymity. Journal of Privacy Technology (2005)
6. Bayardo, R.J., Agrawal, R.: Data privacy through optimal k-anonymization. In: International Conference on Data Engineering, pp. 217–228 (2005)
7. Bettini, C., Wang, X.S., Jajodia, S.: Protecting privacy against location-based personal identification. Secure Data Management, 185–199 (2005)
8. Duncan, G.T., Feinberg, S.E.: Obtaining information while preserving privacy: A markov perturbation method for tabular data. In: Joint Statistical Meetings, pp. 351–362 (1997)
9. Fung, B., Wang, K., Yu, P.: Top-down specialization for information and privacy preservation. In: International Conference on Data Engineering, pp. 205–216 (2005)
10. Gedik, B., Liu, L.: A customizable k-anonymity model for protecting location privacy. In: 25th International Conference on Distributed Computing Systems (2005)
11. LeFevre, K., DeWitt, D.J., Ramakrishnan, R.: Mondrian multidimensional k-anonymity. In: International Conference on Data Engineering (2006)
12. LeFevrea, K., DeWitt, D.J., Ramakrishnan, R.: Incognito: Efficient fulldomain k-anonymity. In: SIGMOD (2005)
13. Machanavajjhala, A., Gehrke, J., Kifer, D., Venkitasubramaniam, M.: ℓ-diversity: Privacy beyond k-anonymity. In: International Conference on Data Engineering, p. 24 (2006)
14. Meyerson, A., Williams, R.: On the complexity of optimal k-anonymity. In: 23rd ACM Symposium on the principles of Database Systems, pp. 223–228 (2004)
15. Samarati, P.: Protecting respondents' identities in microdata release. In: IEEE Transactions on Knowledge and Data Engineering, pp. 1010–1027 (2001)

16. Samarati, P., Sweeney, L.: Protecting privacy when disclosing information: k-anonymity and its enforcement through generalization and suppression. Technical report, CMU, SRI (1998)
17. Sweeney, L.: Achieving k-anonymity privacy protection using generalization and suppression. International Journal of Uncertainty, Fuzziness and Knowledge-Based System, 571–588 (2002)
18. Sweeney, L.: k-anonymity: a model for protecting privacy. International Journal of Uncertainty, Fuzziness and Knowledge-Based System, 557–570 (2002)
19. Xu, S., Yung, M.: k-anonymous secret handshakes with reusable credentials. In: 11th ACM Conference on Computer and Communications Security, pp. 158–167 (2004)
20. Yao, G., Feng, D.: A new k-anonymous message transmission protocol. In: 5th International Workshop on Information Security Applications, pp. 388–399 (2004)

Perturbation Hiding and the
Batch Steganography Problem

Andrew D. Ker

Oxford University Computing Laboratory, Parks Road, Oxford OX1 3QD, England
adk@comlab.ox.ac.uk

Abstract. The batch steganography problem is how best to split a steganographic payload between multiple covers. This paper makes some progress towards an information-theoretic analysis of batch steganography by describing a novel mathematical abstraction we call *perturbation hiding*. As well as providing a new challenge for information hiding research, it brings into focus the information asymmetry in steganalysis of multiple objects: Kerckhoffs' Principle must be interpreted carefully.

Our main result is the solution of the perturbation hiding problem for a certain class of distributions, and the implication for batch steganographic embedding. However, numerical computations show that the result does not hold for all distributions, and we provide some additional asymptotic results to help explore the problem more widely.

1 Introduction

The batch steganography problem was first posed in [1]. It supposes that a steganographer possesses a set of cover objects which, between them, are to conceal a covert payload. The aim is to split the payload into a number of parts and embed the parts, using standard steganographic methods, into some or all of the individual objects. The key question is whether the payload should be spread thinly amongst all the covers, whether a small number of covers should be filled to maximum capacity, or some intermediate choice.

This question is relevant to any scenario in which multiple covers are available, including covert communication and steganographic file systems. In fact, it is hard to imagine many scenarios in which only one cover is made available to the steganographer: if they have a plausible reason to send one cover communication, they almost certainly have a plausible reason to send more than one. Then it becomes important to know how to split the payload between the covers, to evade detection.

The initial analysis of the batch steganography problem in [1] includes only a few special cases, making very strong assumptions about the detector's behaviour, and subsequently there have been some results attacking other limited cases: [2] for a detector which counts observations exceeding a threshold, and [3] under the assumption that steganographic distortion is square in the number of embedding changes. An asymptotic capacity result is found in [4] but does not determine the best method of spreading the payload amongst multiple covers.

K. Solanki, K. Sullivan, and U. Madhow (Eds.): IH 2008, LNCS 5284, pp. 45–59, 2008.

Here we attack the general problem, not constraining the detector, and to do this we propose a mathematical abstraction which we call *perturbation hiding*. It is approached using tools of information theory, but the level of abstraction is different from the usual information-theoretic analysis of steganography [5, 6].

We will now summarise the batch steganography problem and point out some ambiguities in its statement; there follows a brief discussion of the appropriate interpretation of Kerckhoffs' Principle in steganography. In Sect. 2 we pose the perturbation hiding problem, discuss its connection with batch steganography, and solve the problem for a class of cover families: it is best to spread payload equally between the cover objects, even though this denies the opportunity to keep the enemy guessing as to payload distribution. However, this is not a general solution, as some numerical explorations show. Motivated by the numerical results, Sect. 3 suggests some asymptotic results (proved with rather less rigor than the solution of Sect. 2) which point towards more general conclusions. Finally, we will discuss the next steps in Sect. 4.

1.1   The Batch Steganography Problem

We take the role of a steganographer who, for reasons legitimate or not, wishes to conceal a payload in a number of cover objects. If the payload is spread thinly amongst all covers then there is little in each object; on the other hand, if a smaller number of objects are filled to capacity then the complete set of objects (all of which are transmitted) contains many genuinely innocent covers, which could confound the detector. The batch steganography problem is how best to balance those factors, but it is difficult to formalize. The security of an embedding process should be measured by the (un)reliability of detectors, but of course this depends on the choice of detector. The results in [1, 2] fix on a few particular cases of detector, and measure security by the number of false positive detections when the false negative rate is 50%. Such results are of limited applicability.

A detector-independent measure of security was suggested by Cachin in [5] and is now widely used in literature on the theory of steganographic security. Cachin postulated a distribution of covers, a corresponding distribution of stego objects, and considered the *Kullback-Leibler (KL) divergence* [7] between those distributions. KL divergence is nonnegative and zero only for equal distributions. Most importantly, there is a well-known connection with hypothesis testing: error rates for determining whether an observation is from distribution X or distribution Y are bounded below by a function of $\mathrm{D_{KL}}(X \parallel Y)$[1].

Incidentally, the detector's task is not as simple as it may seem: they cannot simply test all the objects, knowing that they need only prove a single example of steganography, because this would compound their false positive errors. By measuring KL divergence we avoid discussion of the detector itself, bounding the

---

[1] Any detector must mistake an observation of X for Y with probability α, and vice versa with probability β, satisfying $\alpha \log \frac{\alpha}{1-\beta} + (1 - \alpha) \log \frac{1-\alpha}{\beta} \leq \mathrm{D_{KL}}(X \parallel Y)$.

performance of any detector (including detectors which choose to ignore some of the available evidence).

KL divergence is used to measure security of batch steganography in [3], but we now demonstrate a weakness in the formulation. For now, we will adopt the same notation as that paper, writing $X_i^{p_i}$ for the random variable corresponding to the i-th object, in which a payload has been embedded causing p_i embedding changes. If we may assume that the objects are independent random variables (for example, the covers should not be successive frames from a video, and the payloads should not be identical) then the additivity property means that the total KL divergence satisfies

$$D_{KL}\big((X_1^0,\ldots,X_n^0)\,\|\,(X_1^{p_1},\ldots,X_n^{p_n})\big) = \sum_{i=1}^{n} D_{KL}(X_i^0\,\|\,X_i^{p_i}) \qquad (1)$$

and it is now, in principle, possible to select the number of changes $p_1,\ldots,p_n$ to minimize (1), thus minimizing the detector's reliability.

There are two problems. First, it is cumbersome to account for the relationship between the *size* of embedded payload and the *number of embedding changes* induced. Apart from the added layer of complexity, evident in [3], there are also implicit assumptions that all embedding changes are equally detectable, and that the number of changes depends deterministically on the payload size but not the cover object. Neither is correct: in digital media it is highly likely that some embedding changes are more obvious than others, and the number of changes varies with random correlations between cover and payload.

Second, and more seriously, there is a paradox in this analysis. Suppose that the steganographer has n (independent) covers drawn from the same distribution, and in just one object makes p embedding changes. The KL divergence between the random vector emitted and a vector of n unaltered objects is

$$D_{KL}(\boldsymbol{X}^0\,\|\,\boldsymbol{X}^p) = D_{KL}(X_1^0\,\|\,X_1^p) + \sum_{i=2}^{n} D_{KL}(X_i^0\,\|\,X_i^0) = D_{KL}(X_1^0\,\|\,X_1^p)$$

(regardless of which object is altered) and this is independent of n. This cannot be right: surely it is harder to detect one stego object in amongst many covers, than to tell a single stego object from a single cover? The explanation is that KL divergence is only appropriate for bounding the performance of a hypothesis test where both null and alternative are *simple*, involving no unknown parameters. When we use KL divergence as a metric we are assuming that the opponent knows everything except whether there is any payload or not, including the object which would be selected to carry the payload. This is surely unrealistic.

We do not use this example to claim that KL divergence is the wrong measure for security. It was an incorrect formulation of the (implicit) hypotheses which caused the paradox, and to avoid such problems we must take care about the information asymmetry in steganalysis scenarios.

1.2   Kerckhoffs' Principle in Steganography

So let us reconsider the security model for steganography. It is traditional, in analysis of cryptographic security, to assume the worst case: the opponent is granted almost omniscience regarding the cryptosystem, and (in the case of protocols) almost omnipotence as respects sabotage of transmitted messages. Such conservatism is justified by the possibility of traitors in the communications system.

This is known as *Kerckhoffs' Principle*, one of six desiderata for cryptosystems suggested by the Dutch cryptographer Auguste Kerckhoffs in 1883:

> Il faut qu'il n'exige pas le secret, et qu'il puisse sans inconvénient tomber entre les mains de l'ennemi [8]

or (approximately) that it must not be necessary to keep the system secret: it should not cause trouble were it to fall into enemy hands. Additionally to Kerckhoff's Principle, cryptographers consider the *chosen-plaintext attack*, when the opponent is given the ability to generate their own cyphertexts.

How should we interpret Kerckhoffs' Principle, and the chosen-plaintext attack, in the context of steganography? This issue is discussed in [9], whose authors point out that the principle is rarely mentioned in steganography literature. First, we can dispose of the full chosen- (or known-) plaintext model, which is not appropriate for covert communication if we assume that the steganographer uses an encryption scheme, secure against chosen-plaintexts, prior to embedding. This is analogous to the usual assumption of perfect cryptography added to the Dolev-Yao threat model for protocol security [10]. But even if the payload bits embedded in the cover are obscured by encryption, the same is probably not true of the number of such bits, i.e. the payload *size*.

So consider what we should grant the opponent. As well as knowledge of the steganographic embedding process for placing payload in individual objects, there seem to be four possibilities involving payload size in the batch situation:

(a) the steganalyst knows nothing about the payload being transmitted;
(b) the steganalyst knows the total payload size, but nothing of the steganographer's strategy for breaking it into components;
(c) the steganalyst knows the sizes of the individual payloads to be embedded in the covers, but does not know which object receives which payload size;
(d) the steganalyst knows the amount of payload in each object, they only lack knowledge of whether any embedding happens at all.

Option (a) is dangerously weak, clearly contradicting the spirit of Kerckhoffs' Principle. We should consider the possibility that the steganalyst might use a confederate to insert a payload of known size into the covert communication channel, or could compromise a recipient after the fact. Option (d) is probably too strong, for it is hard to see how the steganalyst could know so much information without also knowing for certain that the covert channel is being used[2]. The

---

[2] Note that estimating the payload in each object is not the same as knowing it.

correspondence between cover object and payload segment should be considered part of the steganographer's secret key shared with their intended recipient. We believe that reliance on option (d) is a significant weakness of [3].

This leaves (b) and (c), both sensible attack models for covert communication. (c) is the more conservative, but not unreasonably so: if the steganalyst were to obtain the steganographer's embedding software, they might learn the strategy for splitting payload between covers. More practically, option (b) seems difficult to analyse because it cannot be cast as hypothesis test without a compound alternative or an (unjustifiable) prior, and so KL divergence is not a good model for detection accuracy. In this paper, therefore, we focus on option (c).

1.3   Notation

In order to reduce complexity of presentation, we will use the following notational conventions throughout the paper. Random variables will always be given upper case letters, observations lower case, and distribution parameters will be Greek lower case. Vectors (of variables, random or otherwise, or parameters) will be boldface, $x = (x_1, \ldots, x_n)$, and $\bar{x}$ will denote $\frac{1}{n} \sum_{i=1}^{n} x_i$. The set of permutations on n elements is S_n; its members will be denoted π and $\pi(x)$ means $(x_{\pi(1)}, \ldots, x_{\pi(n)})$. If D is a one-parameter family of distributions, with parameter λ, then $X \sim D(\lambda)$ indicates that the random variable X has this distribution with the given parameter. The expectation is denoted $E[X]$ and, where the distribution of X needs clarification, it indicated by a subscript: $E[X]_{X \sim D(\lambda)}$. With random vectors, $X \sim (D(\lambda_1), \ldots, D(\lambda_n))$ means that $X_i \sim D(\lambda_i)$ for each i, and also that the X_i are independent. Finally, $X \sim D(\lambda)^n$ is used when the independent components of X are identically distributed.

2   The Perturbation Hiding Problem

We now present the perturbation hiding problem, draw the connection with batch steganography, and solve for a class of distribution families.

Suppose a fixed one-parameter family of probability distributions $D(\lambda)$[3] defined for $\lambda \geq 0$, an integer $n \geq 2$, and a positive constant l. We must choose a nonnegative vector of parameters $\lambda = (\lambda_1, \ldots, \lambda_n)$ subject to the constraint $\bar{\lambda} = l$, with the aim of making the random vectors X and Y, defined by

$$X \sim D(0)^n$$
$$Y \sim (D(\lambda_1), \ldots, D(\lambda_n)),$$

as close to indistinguishable as possible: it should be difficult for an opponent to classify a realization as either X or Y accurately.

This is called *perturbation hiding* because we are required to choose the perturbation from zero in the n parameters defining the random vector. One could

---

[3] There is nothing in this paper which requires them to be one-dimensional random variables, and the same results will apply to random vectors.

imagine many variations of the problem, when the opponent has more or less knowledge about the choice of $\boldsymbol{\lambda}$, but we will fix on the version best aligned with batch steganography: we grant the opponent knowledge of the components of $\boldsymbol{\lambda}$ *but not their order*. Since the opponent has no information on the order of $\boldsymbol{\lambda}$, their observation is equivalent to one of $\boldsymbol{X}$ or $\boldsymbol{Y}$ with

$$X \sim D(0)^n$$
$$Y \sim \Pi\big(D(\lambda_1), \ldots, D(\lambda_n)\big), \quad \text{where } \Pi \text{ is chosen uniformly from } S_n$$
$$\text{independently of all other random variables.}$$

The perturbation hiding problem is:

$$\text{Choose } \boldsymbol{\lambda}, \text{ subject to } \bar{\lambda} = l \text{ and all } \lambda_i \geq 0, \text{ to minimize } \mathrm{D_{KL}}(\boldsymbol{X} \parallel \boldsymbol{Y}). \qquad (2)$$

2.1   Connection with Batch Steganography

If we suppose that the steganographer has selected an embedding method, and uses a source of covers which are uniform (possessing the same characteristics as regards their potential for information hiding), then we can define $D(\lambda)$ as the distribution of objects with payload of size λ (bits). If the total payload is of size nl, there are n covers, the opponent knows everything about their strategy except which cover receives which payload size, and they know nothing more about the opponent so that KL divergence is the appropriate metric, then we have a direct correspondence with the perturbation hiding problem.

It is worthwhile to contrast this with other information theoretic analyses of steganography. Papers following Cachin [5] focus on optimizing the embedding method for individual objects to minimize $\mathrm{D_{KL}}\big(D(0) \parallel D(\lambda)\big)$. An analysis of *perfectly secure* steganography, in which the KL divergence is zero, is described thoroughly in [6]. Such work considers a cover object to be a sequence of samples emitted by a source with known characteristics. Here, we are taking a different level of abstraction where the source emits entire cover objects, and furthermore our assumption is that a perfectly secure embedding is *not* used. This is reasonable because there are no known perfect schemes which work in genuine digital media, and mathematical models of such media do not accord closely with reality. In our setting, detection is possible; the question is how to minimize the reliability of detection, by allocating payload amongst multiple covers.

The perturbation hiding problem is attractive for a number of reasons. First, it seems to be an interesting mathematical challenge in its own right. Second, it allows use of KL divergence even in a situation when the opponent does not know which cover receives which payload, expressing the problem as a test between two simple hypotheses. This is at the cost of algebraic complexity. Third, it avoids the complications of [3] by folding the relationship between cover changes and transmitted payload into the parameterization of the distribution family $D(\lambda)$. Parameterization is important to this problem: as a simple example, the families $D(\lambda) \sim \mathrm{N}(\lambda, 1)$ and $D'(\lambda) \sim \mathrm{N}(e^\lambda - 1, 1)$ describe the same set of distributions as $\lambda \geq 0$ varies, but they correspond to different batch steganography problems, the latter much less favourable for the steganographer because the distribution $D'(\lambda)$ moves away from $D'(0)$ much faster than $D(\lambda)$ from $D(0)$. (However, Theorem 2 demonstrates that the two problems have the same solution).

In the formulation of [3] the optimal solution – spread the payload equally between all covers – makes sense intuitively. But in the perturbation hiding problem the same solution is not so clearly optimal. For when the payload is spread equally between all covers, the opponent *does* know everything about the allocation of payload. Unevenly-spread payload has an apparent advantage of keeping the opponent guessing about its location.

2.2 Solution for Suitably Convex Exponential Families

Let us write $f(x; \lambda)$ for the density function of the distribution $D(\lambda)$. The solution of (2) can depend on f, but we will demonstrate that the symmetrical vector $\boldsymbol{\lambda} = (l, l, \ldots, l)$ is the solution for a certain class of functions f. Thus, for these distribution families, the disadvantage in allowing the opponent to know everything about the allocation of payload is outweighed by the advantage in having no object containing more payload than the necessary minimum.

Theorem 1. *A sufficient condition for $(l, l, \ldots, l)$ to be the solution to (2) is*

$$\sum_{i=1}^{n} \log \mathrm{E}\left[\frac{f(X; \lambda_i)}{f(X; \bar{\lambda})}\right]_{X \sim D(0)} \leq 0 \tag{3}$$

for all choices of $\boldsymbol{\lambda}$.

Proof. Let us identify the distribution of observations at $\boldsymbol{\lambda} = (\bar{\lambda}, \ldots, \bar{\lambda})$: $\boldsymbol{Z} \sim D(\bar{\lambda})^n$. Assuming (3), we must show that $\mathrm{D_{KL}}(\boldsymbol{X} \| \boldsymbol{Y}) \geq \mathrm{D_{KL}}(\boldsymbol{X} \| \boldsymbol{Z})$ for all choices of $\boldsymbol{\lambda}$. Considering the difference,

$$
\begin{aligned}
&\mathrm{D_{KL}}(\boldsymbol{X} \| \boldsymbol{Y}) - \mathrm{D_{KL}}(\boldsymbol{X} \| \boldsymbol{Z}) \\
&= \mathrm{E}\left[-\log\left(\frac{1}{n!}\sum_{\pi \in S_n}\prod_{i=1}^{n}\frac{f(X_i; \lambda_{\pi(i)})}{f(X_i; 0)}\right) + \log\left(\prod_{i=1}^{n}\frac{f(X_i; \bar{\lambda})}{f(X_i; 0)}\right)\right]_{\boldsymbol{X} \sim D(0)^n} \\
&= \mathrm{E}\left[-\log\frac{1}{n!}\sum_{\pi \in S_n}\prod_{i=1}^{n}\frac{f(X_i; \lambda_{\pi(i)})}{f(X_i; \bar{\lambda})}\right]_{\boldsymbol{X} \sim D(0)^n} \\
&\overset{(1)}{\geq} -\log\left(\frac{1}{n!}\sum_{\pi \in S_n}\mathrm{E}\left[\prod_{i=1}^{n}\frac{f(X_i; \lambda_{\pi(i)})}{f(X_i; \bar{\lambda})}\right]_{\boldsymbol{X} \sim D(0)^n}\right) \\
&\overset{(2)}{=} -\log \mathrm{E}\left[\prod_{i=1}^{n}\frac{f(X_i; \lambda_i)}{f(X_i; \bar{\lambda})}\right]_{\boldsymbol{X} \sim D(0)^n} \\
&\overset{(3)}{=} -\log \prod_{i=1}^{n}\mathrm{E}\left[\frac{f(X; \lambda_i)}{f(X; \bar{\lambda})}\right]_{X \sim D(0)} \\
&= -\sum_{i=1}^{n}\log \mathrm{E}\left[\frac{f(X; \lambda_i)}{f(X; \bar{\lambda})}\right]_{X \sim D(0)} \quad \geq 0.
\end{aligned}
$$

(1) is by Jensen's inequality[4] and linearity of expectation, (2) by identical distribution of the X_i, and (3) by their independence. ∎

Now we demonstrate families of distributions for which the condition in Theorem 1 holds. Recall that a one-parameter family in λ is an *exponential family* [11] if the density function can be written in the form

$$f(x; \lambda) = h(x) \exp\{\eta(\lambda)T(x) - A(\lambda)\}$$

for functions h, η, T and A. Then $T(x)$ is a sufficient statistic, and $A(\lambda)$ is the normalizing constant determined by $\exp(A(\lambda)) = \int h(x) \exp\{\eta(\lambda)T(x)\}\, dx$. When η is invertible the family can be re-parameterized to fit the form $f(x; \mu) = h(x) \exp\{\mu T(x) - \bar{A}(\mu)\}$ and in such cases μ is called the *natural parameter*. Even when the parameterization cannot be chosen (as in the perturbation hiding problem: we must solve the problem for the parameterization we are given) it is often cleaner to phrase results in terms of a natural parameter, as is the case here.

Theorem 2. *A sufficient condition for (3) is that f is a one-parameter exponential family for which a natural parameter exists, such that (a) η is convex nondecreasing, and (b) A'' is nondecreasing in the natural parameter.*

One such case is $D(\lambda_i) \sim N(\phi(\lambda_i), \sigma^2)$, when ϕ is continuous and convex increasing, and σ^2 any positive constant.

Proof. We compute

$$\mathrm{E}\left[\frac{f(X;\lambda_i)}{f(X;\bar{\lambda})}\right] = \int h(x) e^{T(x)\left(\eta(\lambda_i) - \eta(\bar{\lambda}) + \eta(0)\right) - A(\lambda_i) + A(\bar{\lambda}) - A(0)}\, dx$$

$$= \exp\left\{A \circ \eta^{-1}\left(\eta(\lambda_i) - \eta(\bar{\lambda}) + \eta(0)\right) - A(\lambda_i) + A(\bar{\lambda}) - A(0)\right\}$$

because of the relationship $\exp(A(\lambda)) = \int h(x) \exp\{\eta(\lambda)T(x)\}\, dx$. If we write $\bar{A} = A \circ \eta^{-1}$, expressing A in terms of the natural parameter, the log of the expectation is equal to $g(\lambda_i)$ where

$$g(\theta) = \bar{A}\left(\eta(\theta) - \eta(\bar{\lambda}) + \eta(0)\right) - \bar{A}\left(\eta(\theta)\right) + \bar{A}\left(\eta(\bar{\lambda})\right) - \bar{A}\left(\eta(0)\right).$$

Note that $g(\bar{\lambda}) = 0$ and

$$g''(\theta) = \eta'(\theta)\left[\bar{A}''\left(\eta(\theta) - c\right) - A''\left(\eta(\theta)\right)\right] + \eta''(\theta)\left[\bar{A}'\left(\eta(\theta) - c\right) - A'\left(\eta(\theta)\right)\right]$$

where c is the constant $\eta(\bar{\lambda}) - \eta(0)$. Then use our assumptions: η' is nonnegative because η is nondecreasing; for the same reason $c \geq 0$ and so $\bar{A}''\left(\eta(\theta) - c\right) - A''\left(\eta(\theta)\right) \leq 0$ because $\bar{A}''$ is nondecreasing; η'' is nonnegative because η is convex; $\bar{A}'\left(\eta(\theta) - c\right) - A'\left(\eta(\theta)\right) \leq 0$ because $\bar{A}$ must be convex (this is always true for an exponential family). We deduce that $g'' \leq 0$.

---

[4] $\mathrm{E}[\phi(X)] \geq \phi(\mathrm{E}[X])$ for convex ϕ; note that $\phi(x) = -\log x$ is a convex function.

Therefore g is concave, hence

$$\sum \log \mathrm{E}\left[\frac{f(X;\lambda_i)}{f(X;\bar{\lambda})}\right]_{X \sim D(0)} = \sum g(\lambda_i) \le g(\bar{\lambda}) + g'(\bar{\lambda}) \sum (\lambda_i - \bar{\lambda}) = 0.$$

For the Gaussian case mentioned, write the pdf of $N(\phi(\lambda), \sigma^2)$ in the exponential family form: $f(x; \lambda) = \frac{e^{-x^2/2\sigma^2}}{\sqrt{2\pi\sigma^2}} \exp\{\frac{\phi(\lambda)}{\sigma^2} x - \frac{1}{2\sigma^2}\phi(\lambda)^2\}$. ϕ must be invertible, so $\mu = \phi(\lambda)/\sigma^2$ is the natural parameter. By assumption, ϕ is convex increasing, and $A(\mu) = \mu^2\sigma^2/2$ satisfies A'' nondecreasing.   ∎

The given example is relevant because of adaptive source coding. Suppose, as a simple example, that the covers are Gaussian $N(c, 1)$ where c is the number of embedding changes in a cover of size N. It is well-known [12] that the size of transmitted payload p satisfies $c \ge NH^{-1}(\frac{p}{N})$ (H is the binary entropy function), a convex function of p. The relationship between bits transmitted and locations changed should always be convex in efficient codes, so this nonlinear relationship does not affect the conclusion that payload should be equally spread.

The conditions in Th. 2 seem natural. Monotonicity of η precludes the possibility that increasing payload is less detectable (in single objects). Some sort of convexity condition could be expected. And recall that, when A is expressed in terms of a natural parameter, A'' is the variance of the random variable: the condition that A'' is nondecreasing ensures that we do not have more certainty about larger payloads. But we should note that the conditions in Theorems 1 and 2 are stronger than necessary. It is possible to construct exponential families which do not satisfy the conditions of the latter, but do satisfy the former, and we will see next that there are distributions which do not form an exponential family at all, yet the solution to (2) is still (for some choices of n and l) the constant vector $(l, l, \ldots, l)$. We hope to widen the results in future work.

2.3 Explorations with Student t-Families

We now ask whether the preceding results apply more widely, when $D(\lambda)$ is not an exponential family. We might expect that the same conclusions should hold for random variables with exponentially-decaying tails, but for long-tailed distributions it might be optimal to concentrate the payload in a few cover objects. This would be plausible because, in the case of long tails, a small number of extreme observations would be expected even when no payload is present, so mimicking this could be a sensible embedding choice.

To explore this question, we performed some numerical computations. However, accurate estimation of the KL divergence

$$\mathrm{D_{KL}}(\boldsymbol{X} \| \boldsymbol{Y}) = \mathrm{E}\left[-\log\left(\frac{1}{n!} \sum_{\pi \in S_n} \prod_{i=1}^n \frac{f(X_i; \lambda_{\pi(i)})}{f(X_i; 0)}\right)\right]_{\boldsymbol{X} \sim D(0)^n} \qquad (4)$$

– an integral over $\mathbb{R}^n$ of a function with $n!$ terms – represents a huge challenge unless n is very small. But even the cases $n = 2$ and $n = 3$ are suggestive.

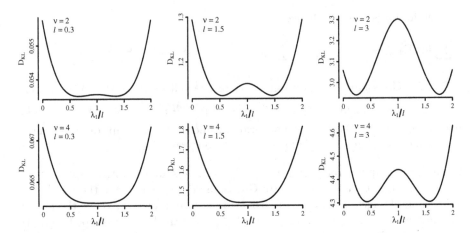

Fig. 1. The case $n = 2$. Numerically-computed $\mathrm{D_{KL}}(\boldsymbol{X} \parallel \boldsymbol{Y})$ as a function of λ_1, when the parent distribution family is Student t with 2 d.f. (above) and 4 d.f. (below). Three different values of l are displayed.

We will concentrate on families of the Student t-distribution, determined by the *degrees of freedom* $\nu > 0$, and parameterized by location:

$$f(x; \lambda) = \frac{\Gamma\left(\frac{\nu+1}{2}\right)}{\sqrt{\nu\pi}\,\Gamma\left(\frac{\nu}{2}\right)} \left(1 + \frac{(x-\lambda)^2}{\nu}\right)^{-\frac{(\nu+1)}{2}}. \tag{5}$$

They were chosen because they never form an exponential family, and describe a continuum of distributions with varying tail weights: as $\nu \to \infty$ the distribution tends to Gaussian, and for $\nu = 1$ it is Cauchy, so heavily-tailed that even the expectation is not defined. Between these extremes, the density function $f(x; \lambda)$ tail decays as $|x|^{-(\nu+1)}$. We are interested in solutions to the perturbation hiding problem, with distribution family determined by ν and total payload by l.

First, we take the case $n = 2$, corresponding to splitting a steganographic payload between just two objects, with λ_1 in one object and λ_2 the other (the opponent does not know which is which), subject to $\lambda_1 + \lambda_2 = 2l$. For a number of different Student t-families $D(\lambda)$, determined by ν, and various values of l, we estimated the KL divergence, using quadrature, as λ_1 varies between 0 to $2l$. A selection of results are shown in Fig. 1, corresponding to the families $\nu = 2$ or $\nu = 4$ and $l = 0.3, 1.5, 3$. The figures are, of course, symmetrical because of symmetry between λ_1 and λ_2.

Regardless of ν, we observed that, as l grows large, the case of equally-spread payload $\lambda_1 = \lambda_2 = l$ eventually becomes the *worst* choice: the optimal choice of λ_1 is somewhere between 0 (concentrate payload) or l (spread equally), decreasing as l increases. Hence the conclusion of Theorem 1 cannot hold universally.

More interestingly, we observed distinct behaviour as $l \to 0$, depending on ν. As appears in Fig. 1, even for very small values of l the choice $\lambda_1 = \lambda_2 = l$ is not optimal for $\nu = 2$, but for l smaller than approximately 1.06 it *is* optimal for $\nu = 4$: although the curve for $\nu = 4$ and small l is very flat near the centre,

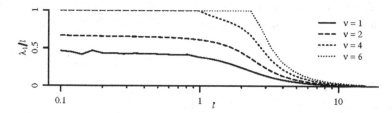

Fig. 2. Below, the numerically-determined optimal values of λ_1 as l varies, when the parent family is from the Student t-family. Four different d.f.s are displayed.

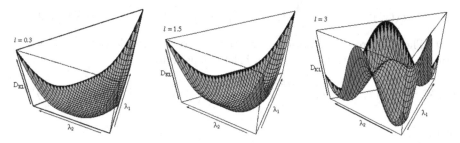

Fig. 3. The case $n = 3$. Numerically-computed $\mathrm{D}_{\mathrm{KL}}(X \parallel Y)$, as a function of λ_1 and λ_2, when the parent family is Student t with 4 d.f.

we do observe a genuine minimum at the central point. Figure 2 examines this further, showing how the optimal value of λ_1 (to minimize (4), assuming $\lambda_1 \leq \lambda_2$) depends on l and ν. For t-families with sufficiently light tails (apparently ν at least approximately 4), we can say that small enough total payloads are best spread equally between the covers, but we cannot say the same of heavily-tailed t-families (this is seen at least for $\nu \leq 3$). These results are only illustrative, but they motivate study of (4) as $l \to 0$; this will be performed in Sect. 3, where the critical change of behaviour near $\nu = 4$ will be explained.

We performed similar experiments for the case $n = 3$; charts for $\nu = 4$ and $l = 0.3, 1.5, 3$ are shown in Fig. 3, but others will not be included for reasons of space. The same features are apparent as for $n = 2$: when $\nu = 4$, for sufficiently small l (less than approximately 1.04), equally-spread payload $\lambda_1 = \lambda_2 = \lambda_3 = l$ gives the lowest KL divergence, but not when $\nu \leq 3$. Additional numerical explorations (of necessity not very thorough) show similar behaviour for $n = 4$ and, pushing our ability to compute (4) numerically to the limit, $n = 5$. The critical values of l do not seem to vary much with n, remaining a little over 1 in all observed cases, suggesting that the limiting result comes into play for larger payloads when there are more objects in which to hide.

3   Asymptotic Results

Motivated by the numerical results, we consider the asymptotics of the perturbation hiding problem. The results are presented briefly and some details are omitted. We will assume considerable regularity without justifying it here. We will consider small payloads, and as $l \to 0$, $\boldsymbol{\lambda} \to \mathbf{0}$. Using the notation

$$\ell(x; \lambda) = \log f(x; \lambda), \quad \ell_\lambda(x) = \frac{\partial}{\partial \lambda} l(x; \lambda)|_{\lambda=0}, \quad \ell_{\lambda\lambda}(x) = \frac{\partial^2}{\partial \lambda^2} l(x; \lambda)|_{\lambda=0},$$

we can show:

Theorem 3. *Assuming sufficient regularity, as $\boldsymbol{\lambda} \to \mathbf{0}$ we have*

$$\mathrm{D}_{\mathrm{KL}}(\boldsymbol{X}, \boldsymbol{Y}) \sim c_1 \left(\sum \lambda_i\right)^2 + c_2 \left(\sum \lambda_i\right)^3 + c_3 \left(\sum \lambda_i^2\right)\left(\sum \lambda_i\right) + O(|\boldsymbol{\lambda}|^4) \quad (6)$$

where

$$c_1 = \frac{1}{2n} \mathrm{E}\left[\ell_\lambda(X)^2\right], \quad c_2 = -\frac{1}{3n^2} \mathrm{E}\left[\ell_\lambda(X)^3\right], \quad c_3 = \frac{1}{2n} \mathrm{E}\left[\ell_\lambda(X)^3 + \ell_\lambda(X)\ell_{\lambda\lambda}(X)\right].$$

Proof. The full proof is laborious but routine, so we include only illustrative sections. In an effort to keep notation brief, let us write

$$F(\boldsymbol{x}; \boldsymbol{\lambda}) = \prod_{i=1}^{n} f(x_i; \lambda_i), \quad F_i = \frac{\partial F}{\partial \lambda_i}, \quad F_{ij} = \frac{\partial^2 F}{\partial \lambda_i \partial \lambda_j}, \quad L = \log\left(\frac{1}{n!}\sum_{\pi \in S_n} F(\boldsymbol{x}; \pi(\boldsymbol{\lambda}))\right).$$

Then

$$\mathrm{D}_{\mathrm{KL}}(\boldsymbol{X} \parallel \boldsymbol{Y}) = \mathrm{E}\left[-\log\left(\frac{\frac{1}{n!}\sum_{\pi \in S_n} F(\boldsymbol{X}; \pi(\boldsymbol{\lambda}))}{F(\boldsymbol{X}; \mathbf{0})}\right)\right]_{\boldsymbol{X} \sim D(0)^n}$$

$$= \mathrm{E}\left[-L(\boldsymbol{X}; \boldsymbol{\lambda}) + L(\boldsymbol{X}; \mathbf{0})\right]$$

$$= -\frac{1}{1!}\sum_{i=1}^{n} \lambda_i \mathrm{E}\left[\frac{\partial L}{\partial \lambda_i}\Big|_{\lambda=0}\right] - \frac{1}{2!}\sum_{i,j=1}^{n} \lambda_i \lambda_j \mathrm{E}\left[\frac{\partial^2 L}{\partial \lambda_i \partial \lambda_j}\Big|_{\lambda=0}\right]$$

$$- \frac{1}{3!}\sum_{i,j,k=1}^{n} \lambda_i \lambda_j \lambda_k \mathrm{E}\left[\frac{\partial^3 L}{\partial \lambda_i \partial \lambda_j \partial \lambda_k}\Big|_{\lambda=0}\right] + O(|\boldsymbol{\lambda}|^4) \quad (7)$$

where, at the last stage, we have assumed sufficient regularity to allow a Taylor expansion of L under the integral, in the second vector parameter, about $\boldsymbol{\lambda} = \mathbf{0}$. The expression will simplify because of the symmetry in L, and

$$\mathrm{E}\left[\frac{F_s(\boldsymbol{X}; \mathbf{0})}{F(\boldsymbol{X}; \mathbf{0})}\right] = \mathrm{E}\left[\frac{F_{st}(\boldsymbol{X}; \mathbf{0})}{F(\boldsymbol{X}; \mathbf{0})}\right] = 0 \quad (8)$$

(in evaluating the expectation, the denominator cancels with the density function, and given sufficient regularity we can take the derivative of the numerator outside the integral; differentiating a constant gives zero).

Therefore for the first- and second-order terms in the Taylor expansion of L,

$$\mathrm{E}\left[\frac{\partial}{\partial \lambda_i} L(\boldsymbol{X}; \boldsymbol{\lambda})\Big|_{\lambda=0}\right] = \mathrm{E}\left[\frac{\sum_\pi F_{\pi^{-1}(i)}(\boldsymbol{X}; \pi(\boldsymbol{\lambda}))}{\sum_\pi F(\boldsymbol{X}; \pi(\boldsymbol{\lambda}))}\Big|_{\lambda=0}\right] = \frac{1}{n}\sum_{s=1}^{n} \mathrm{E}\left[\frac{F_s(\boldsymbol{X}; \mathbf{0})}{F(\boldsymbol{X}; \mathbf{0})}\right] = 0,$$

$$\mathrm{E}\left[\frac{\partial^2}{\partial \lambda_i \partial \lambda_j} L(\boldsymbol{X}; \boldsymbol{\lambda})\Big|_{\lambda=0}\right]$$

$$= \mathrm{E}\left[\frac{\sum_\pi F_{\pi^{-1}(i)\pi^{-1}(j)}(\boldsymbol{X}; \pi(\boldsymbol{\lambda}))}{\sum_\pi F(\boldsymbol{X}; \pi(\boldsymbol{\lambda}))}\Big|_{\lambda=0}\right] - \mathrm{E}\left[\frac{\sum_\pi F_{\pi^{-1}(i)}(\boldsymbol{X}; \pi(\boldsymbol{\lambda}))}{\sum_\pi F(\boldsymbol{X}; \pi(\boldsymbol{\lambda}))}\frac{\sum_\pi F_{\pi^{-1}(j)}(\boldsymbol{X}; \pi(\boldsymbol{\lambda}))}{\sum_\pi F(\boldsymbol{X}; \pi(\boldsymbol{\lambda}))}\Big|_{\lambda=0}\right]$$

$$= \begin{cases} \frac{1}{n(n-1)} \sum_{s \neq t} \sum \mathrm{E}\left[\frac{F_{st}(\boldsymbol{X};\boldsymbol{0})}{F(\boldsymbol{X};\boldsymbol{0})}\right], & \text{if } i \neq j \\ \frac{1}{n} \sum_s \mathrm{E}\left[\frac{F_{ss}(\boldsymbol{X};\boldsymbol{0})}{F(\boldsymbol{X};\boldsymbol{0})}\right], & \text{if } i = j \end{cases} - \frac{1}{n^2} \mathrm{E}\left[\sum_{s=1}^n \frac{F_s(\boldsymbol{X};\boldsymbol{0})}{F(\boldsymbol{X};\boldsymbol{0})}\right]^2$$

$$= 0 - \tfrac{1}{n}\mathrm{E}[\ell_\lambda(X)^2]_{X \sim D(0)} = -2c_1$$

(At the final stage, we used (8) along with independence of $\frac{F_s(\boldsymbol{X};\boldsymbol{0})}{F(\boldsymbol{X};\boldsymbol{0})}$ and $\frac{F_t(\boldsymbol{X};\boldsymbol{0})}{F(\boldsymbol{X};\boldsymbol{0})}$ for $s \neq t$.) We observe that the first two terms of (7) together match the first term of (6). The third term of (7) reduces to the second and third terms of (6) for similar reasons, but the calculations are longer (because there are more types of mixed partial derivative at third order) and we omit them here. ∎

We can draw some useful conclusions from Theorem 3, because the first two terms of (6) cannot be varied by choice of $\boldsymbol{\lambda}$, if $\bar{\lambda} = \frac{1}{n}\sum \lambda_i$ is constrained to equal l. Therefore, a) the steganographer's choice of $\boldsymbol{\lambda}$ can only affect the second-most significant term as $l \to 0$, and b) they should minimize $c_3\left(\sum \lambda_i^2\right)$. If c_3 is positive, the minimum is again at $\lambda_i = l$ (for all i), but if c_3 is negative then the minimum is found on the edge of the feasible region, where some λ_i are zero (we will not proceed to find the location of the minimum, in this paper). We have shown that the sign of $\mathrm{E}\left[\ell_\lambda(X)^3 + \ell_\lambda(X)\ell_{\lambda\lambda}(X)\right]_{X \sim D(0)}$, a constant depending on the distribution family and related to its skewness, determines the optimal strategy for sufficiently small l.

Does this explain the phenomena in Subsect. 2.3, where the degree of freedom parameter appeared critical to whether equal payload was optimal as $l \to 0$? Sadly not, because in a symmetrical distribution, parameterized by location, we always have $c_3 = 0$! We have proved that the effect of payload allocation is (at most) of order l^2 smaller than the leading term in (6) (hence the very flat-looking curves in Subsect. 2.3), but must continue the asymptotic analysis of Th. 3 to the fourth order to understand the asymptotically optimal strategy.

The calculations are of a similar type to those in the proof of Th. 3, but much more complex. We spare the reader the details, and simply state that the fourth-order terms in (6) are

$$c_4\left(\sum \lambda_i\right)^4 + c_5\left(\sum \lambda_i^3\right)\left(\sum \lambda_i\right) + c_6\left(\sum \lambda_i^2\right)^2 + c_7\left(\sum \lambda_i^2\right)\left(\sum \lambda_i\right)^2$$

where

$$c_5 = \tfrac{1}{18n}d_2 - \tfrac{1}{6n}d_3, \quad c_6 = \tfrac{1}{4n(n-1)}d_1 + \tfrac{1}{24n}d_2 + \tfrac{1}{8n}d_3, \quad c_7 = \tfrac{(n-2)}{2n^2(n-1)}d_1 - \tfrac{1}{3n^2}d_2,$$
$$d_1 = \mathrm{E}\left[\ell_\lambda(X)^2\right]^2, \quad d_2 = \mathrm{E}\left[\ell_\lambda(X)^4\right], \qquad\qquad d_3 = \mathrm{E}\left[\ell_{\lambda\lambda}(X)^2\right].$$

(c_4 is not relevant to the location of the minimum). Considering the Hessian at the central point, it can be shown that $\lambda_i = l$ is a (local) minimum if and only if

$$-6d_1 + d_2 + 3d_3 < 0 \qquad\qquad (9)$$

(independently of l and n).

Finally, for the Student t-family (5) one can compute d_1, d_2 and d_3 in terms of the d.f. parameter ν: (9) turns out equivalent to

$$\nu^3 + 2\nu^2 - 15\nu - 20 > 0$$

which is true for $\nu > 3.6367 \cdots$. This explains the behaviour seen in Subsect. 2.3.

4   Conclusions

The batch steganography problem is of importance to covert communication and storage, posing a fundamental question about the allocation of payload between multiple objects. Some other work has addressed special cases, but in this paper we have attacked the general problem. Perturbation hiding is a mathematical abstraction of the batch steganography problem – at a different level of abstraction to most of the literature on information-theoretic analyses of covert communication – and we have given some results about its solutions. It is likely that the results in Subsect. 2.2 can be extended to wider families of distributions, and the asymptotic results of Sect. 3 deserve a more rigorous analytical treatment. An asymptotic result as $n \to \infty$ would also be useful: perhaps Laplace's method can be applied.

We chose the problem formulation after a careful consideration of how much information should be granted to the steganalyst. The model should be seen as conservative: we do not necessarily believe that the steganalyst always knows the size of the individual payloads (without knowing their order), we merely *fear* that they might find out, perhaps by later compromising a recipient: such paranoia is in keeping with the spirit of Kerckhoffs' Principle. It may seem natural for the detector to try to gain information about payload allocation using a *quantitative* steganalysis (such payload size estimators are common) but the use of KL divergence as an insecurity measure limits the ability of *any* detector, including those who first apply estimators.

We would like to conclude that the steganographer's best choice is to spread payload equally between covers (as long as the covers are uniform), and thus the benefits of well-spread payload outweigh the drawbacks of the opponent having no uncertainty about the amount in each object. We have proved that this is so for suitably convex exponential distribution families, and for sufficiently small payloads if the critical value c_3, a constant depending on the distribution family, is positive. However it is not so for when c_3 is negative, or for large payloads. In order to inform the practice of covert communication, and its counterpart in steganalysis, it will be necessary to clarify circumstances under which these dichotomous situations occur. A first stage would be to relate c_3 to the tail behaviour of the family. It would be attractive if a simple test can be developed for genuine cover media, to determine the best embedding strategy.

For tractability and compactness, our analysis in this work has been limited to uniform covers. We note that uniformity does not necessary mean that the covers are truly uniform, merely that the parties do not know how, or do not choose, to take advantage of nonuniformity. Although it is folklore that more data can securely be hidden in "noisier" covers there is not much literature quantifying this, so state-of-the-art steganography is not in a good position to make use of nonuniformity. More work on the perturbation hiding problem may be valuable here, perhaps producing a rule for allocating payload in nonuniform covers.

We have already performed a simple small-payload analysis of the perturbation hiding problem in nonuniform covers, but postpone it to a sequel. The results are quite interesting: it is in the steganographer's interest to distribute payload unevenly between the covers, but also to randomise the distribution: unlike in the uniform case, it does pay to keep the opponent guessing as to the distribution of payload.

Acknowledgements

The author is a Royal Society University Research Fellow.

References

1. Ker, A.: Batch steganography and pooled steganalysis. In: Camenisch, J.L., Collberg, C.S., Johnson, N.F., Sallee, P. (eds.) IH 2006. LNCS, vol. 4437, pp. 265–281. Springer, Heidelberg (2007)
2. Ker, A.: Batch steganography and the threshold game. In: Security, Steganography and Watermarking of Multimedia Contents IX. In: Proc. SPIE, vol. 6505, pp. 0401–0413 (2007)
3. Ker, A.: Steganographic strategies for a square distortion function. In: Security, Forensics, Steganography and Watermarking of Multimedia Contents X. In: Proc. SPIE, vol. 6819 (2008)
4. Ker, A.: A capacity result for batch steganography. IEEE Signal Processing Letters 14(8), 525–528 (2007)
5. Cachin, C.: An information-theoretic model for steganography. Information and Computation 192(1), 41–56 (2004)
6. Wang, Y., Moulin, P.: Perfectly secure steganography: Capacity, error exponents, and code constructions. IEEE Trans. Information Theory (to appear, 2008)
7. Kullback, S., Leibler, R.: On information and sufficiency. Annals of Mathematical Statistics 22, 79–86 (1951)
8. Kerckhoffs, A.: La cryptographie militaire. Journal des sciences militaires IX, 5–38, 161–191 (1883)
9. Cayre, F., Bas, P.: Kerckhoffs-based embedding security classes for WOA datahiding. IEEE Trans. Information Forensics and Security (to appear, 2008)
10. Dolev, D., Yao, A.: On the security of public key protocols. IEEE Trans. Information Theory 29(2), 198–208 (1983)
11. Darmois, G.: Sur les lois de probabilité à estimation exhaustive. Comptes Rendus de l'Académie des Sciences 200, 1265–1266 (1935)
12. Fridrich, J., Soukal, D.: Matrix embedding for large payloads. IEEE Trans. Information Forensics and Security 1(3), 390–394 (2006)

Maximizing Steganographic Embedding Efficiency by Combining Hamming Codes and Wet Paper Codes

Weiming Zhang[1,2], Xinpeng Zhang[1], and Shuozhong Wang[1]

[1] School of Communication and Information Engineering, Shanghai University,
Shanghai 200072, China
[2] Department of Information Research, Information Engineering University,
Zhengzhou 450002, China
zwmshu@gmai.com

Abstract. For good security and large payload in steganography, it is desired to embed as many messages as possible per change of the cover-object, i.e., to have high embedding efficiency. Steganographic codes derived from covering codes can improve embedding efficiency. In this paper, we propose a new method to construct stego-codes, showing that not just one but a family of stego-codes can be generated from one covering code by combining Hamming codes and wet paper codes. This method can enormously expand the set of embedding schemes as applied in steganography. Performances of stego-code families of structured codes and random codes are analyzed. By using the stego-code families of LDGM codes, we obtain a family of near optimal embedding schemes for binary steganography and ± 1 steganography, respectively, which can approach the upper bound of embedding efficiency for various chosen embedding rate.

Keywords: steganography, stego-codes, covering codes, wet paper codes, Hamming codes, embedding efficiency, embedding rate.

1 Introduction

Steganography, the art of conveying information confidentially, is realized by embedding secret messages into innocuous cover-objects such as digital images, audios and videos. The very existence of the communication itself is hidden since the stego-object appears the same as the cover. However, as the cover-object is inevitably changed, the covert communication can still be detected by some statistical means. Given a payload, the steganographer should embed as many messages as possible per change of the cover-object, in other words, seek high embedding efficiency so that possibility of being detected is reduced. Crandall first pointed out that embedding efficiency could be improved by coding methods, and proposed the matrix coding [1]. The relation between steganographic codes (stego-codes for short) and covering codes was studied in [2,3]. It turned out that the stego-code could be defined by the covering

K. Solanki, K. Sullivan, and U. Madhow (Eds.): IH 2008, LNCS 5284, pp. 60–71, 2008.

code [3]. For instance, using an $[N, N - n]$ code with the covering radius R, one gets an (R, N, n) stego-code which can embed n bits of messages into a length-N binary cover block by changing at most R bits. Many binary stego-codes have been constructed using structured codes [3,4,5,6] or random codes [7,8].

Binary stego-codes can be used in binary steganography such as binary value image steganography and least significant bit (LSB) steganography. In LSB embedding, the stego-coding methods may be used in the LSB plane of an image, and adding 1 to a pixel is equivalent to subtracting 1 from the pixel for carrying one secret bit. In fact, the choice of addition or subtraction can also be used to carry information. Therefore each pixel can carry $\log_2 3$ bits of data, that is, a ternary digit, with the pixel gray value modulo 3, which is called "± 1 steganography" and provides higher embedding efficiency than binary steganography. The ± 1 steganography essentially involves a ternary coding problem which can be treated by ternary covering codes. Willems et al. [9] proposed ternary Hamming and Golay codes to improve embedding efficiency of ± 1 steganography. A more efficient method appeared independently in [10] and [11], which introduce a family of stego-codes including the ternary Hamming as a subset. In a revisit of the LSB matching method, Mielikainen [12] proposed to choose addition and subtraction depending both on the original gray values and on a pair of consecutive secret bits. Generalization of the revisited LSB matching method is reported in [13].

The upper bounds of the embedding efficiency, with respect to the embedding rate, for binary and ± 1 steganography have been obtained in [7] and [9], respectively. A main purpose of stego-coding is to design stego-codes in order to approach these upper bounds. Zhang et al. [14] recently presented a double layered embedding method which can employ any binary stego-codes to ± 1 steganography to embed one more bit per change. Moreover it has been shown that, if a binary stego-code can reach the upper bound of embedding efficiency for binary steganography, the corresponding double layered embedding based on this binary stego-code can reach the upper bound of ± 1 steganography [14]. Therefore, constructing good binary stego-codes can solve the problems for both binary steganography and ± 1 steganography.

In this paper we propose a novel method to design stego-codes by exploiting Hamming codes and wet paper codes [15], which can introduce a family of stego-codes from any given binary stego-code. We call it a stego-code (SC) family of the given stego-code. With the proposed method, we can construct stego-codes approaching the upper bound of embedding efficiency for binary steganography and ± 1 steganography at various embedding rates.

The organization of the paper is as follows. Section 2 introduces some notational conventions. Section 3 describes the construction and performance of stego-code families. In Section 4, the stego-code families are modified for applications in ± 1 steganography. The paper is concluded following a discussion in Section 5.

2   Notation

We take images as covers to describe the proposed method. To embed data, the cover image is divided into disjoint segments of N pixels, denoted by $\mathbf{g} = (g_1, \ldots, g_N)$, and let $\mathbf{x} = (x_1, \ldots, x_N)$ be their LSBs which is used as carriers. Because the message is usually encrypted before embedding, it can be considered a binary random sequence, and the message block $\mathbf{m} = (m_1, \ldots, m_n) \in \mathbb{F}_2^n$. A stego-code $SC(R, N, n)$ can embed n bits of messages into N pixels with at most R modifications. The equivalence between stego-codes and covering codes is shown in [3]. Let $\mathcal{C}$ be an $[N, N - n]$ binary code with a covering radius R, then we can construct a stego-code $SC(R, N, n)$ by syndrome coding of $\mathcal{C}$ [5,7]. An example of stego-code based on the Hamming codes will be given in Subsection 3.1.

Note that the covering radius R is the largest number of possible changes while the purpose of stego-coding is to minimize the average number of embedding changes R_a [5,7]. Therefore in the following we will replace R with R_a to denote the stego-code, i.e., when we use the notation $SC(R_a, N, n)$, the first parameter means the average number of changes which is equal to the average distance to the code $\mathcal{C}$ [7]. For perfect codes such as Hamming and Golay codes, the average number of changes can be calculated by $R_a = \frac{1}{2^n} \sum_{i=0}^{R} i \binom{N}{i}$.

For a stego-code $SC(R_a, N, n)$, we define the embedding rate $\alpha = n/N$, which is the number of bits carried by each pixel; define the average distortion $D = R_a/N$, which is the average changing rate of the cover image; and define the embedding efficiency $e = n/R_a = \alpha/D$, which is the average number of embedded bits per change. We use embedding rate α and embedding efficiency e to evaluate the performance of stego-codes.

3   Stego-Code Families

3.1   Basic Hamming Wet Paper Channel

The covering radius of $[2^k - 1, 2^k - k - 1]$ Hamming codes is one for all integers $k \geq 1$, which can be used to construct a stego-code and embed k bits of messages into $2^k - 1$ pixels by changing at most one of them. Taking $[7, 4]$ Hamming code as an example, we explain how to embed and extract 3 bits of messages into 7 pixels. Let $\mathbf{H}$ be the parity check matrix of the $[7, 4]$ Hamming code

$$\mathbf{H} = \begin{pmatrix} 0\,0\,0\,1\,1\,1\,1 \\ 0\,1\,1\,0\,0\,1\,1 \\ 1\,0\,1\,0\,1\,0\,1 \end{pmatrix} . \tag{1}$$

Here we make the columns in the natural order of increasing binary numbers. Given a length-7 block of cover $\mathbf{x}$ and a 3 bits message block $\mathbf{m}$, for instance $\mathbf{x} = (1\,0\,0\,1\,0\,0\,0)$ and $\mathbf{m} = (1\,1\,0)$, compute

$$\mathbf{H} \cdot \mathbf{x}^T = \begin{pmatrix} 1 \\ 0 \\ 1 \end{pmatrix}, \quad \begin{pmatrix} 1 \\ 0 \\ 1 \end{pmatrix} \oplus \begin{pmatrix} 1 \\ 1 \\ 0 \end{pmatrix} = \begin{pmatrix} 0 \\ 1 \\ 1 \end{pmatrix} . \tag{2}$$

Note that the obtained result $(0\,1\,1)$ is the binary representation of three, that is, the third column of $\mathbf{H}$. By changing the third bit of $\mathbf{x}$ and to get $\mathbf{x}' = (1\,0\,1\,1\,0\,0\,0)$, the embedding process is completed. To extract the messages, we only need to compute

$$\mathbf{H} \cdot \mathbf{x}'^T = \begin{pmatrix} 1 \\ 1 \\ 0 \end{pmatrix} = \mathbf{m}^T . \tag{3}$$

In the above embedding process, no change is needed if $\mathbf{H} \cdot \mathbf{x}^T = \mathbf{m}^T$. This occurs with probability $1/2^3$ because the message is a random sequence of cipher text; otherwise we make $\mathbf{H} \cdot \mathbf{x}^T = \mathbf{m}^T$ by changing only one bit of $\mathbf{x}$, with probability $7/2^3$. Therefore the average number of changes made is $7/2^3$, meaning that we have constructed a stego-code $SC(7/2^3, 7, 3)$. In general, with the same method we can get stego-code $SC\left((2^k - 1)/2^k, 2^k - 1, k\right)$ using $[2^k - 1, 2^k - k - 1]$ Hamming code for any integer $k \geq 1$. When $k = 1$ the Hamming stego-code $SC(1/2, 1, 1)$ is just the simple LSB steganography which can embed one bit of message into each pixel and modifies its LSB with probability $1/2$.

We now improve the embedding efficiency of Hamming stego-codes by splitting the LSB embedding channel into two different channels. Without loss of generality, assume that the length of the cover is $L2^k$, and divide it into L disjoint blocks. The corresponding LSB blocks are denoted by

$$(x_1, \cdots, x_{2^k}), \quad \cdots, \quad \left(x_{(L-1)2^k+1}, \cdots, x_{L2^k}\right) . \tag{4}$$

First, compress each block into one bit with an exclusive-or operation:

$$y_i = \bigoplus_{j=1}^{2^k} x_{i2^k+j}, \quad i = 0, 1, \cdots, L-1 . \tag{5}$$

We take $(y_0, \cdots, y_{L-1})$ as the first embedding channel, and apply the simple LSB steganography, i.e., $SC(1/2, 1, 1)$, to it. Therefore each y_i can carry one bit of message and needs to be changed with probability $1/2$.

Second, take the first $2^k - 1$ elements from every cover block, and write

$$\mathbf{x}_1 = (x_1, \cdots, x_{2^k-1}), \quad \cdots, \quad \mathbf{x}_L = \left(x_{(L-1)2^k+1}, \cdots, x_{L2^k-1}\right) . \tag{6}$$

Let $\mathbf{H}$ be the parity check matrix of the $[2^k - 1, 2^k - k - 1]$ Hamming code having a form like (1). In the embedding process of the first channel, if some y_i, for example y_1, needs to be modified, we can flip any one of the 2^k bits in the first block to change y_1, and therefore we can map the first block into any k bits that we need by $\mathbf{Hx}_1^T$. In fact, if $\mathbf{Hx}_1^T$ is just the k bits we want, we can flip x_{2^k} to change y_1, otherwise we make $\mathbf{Hx}_1^T$ equal to any other vector of k bits by changing one of the first $2^k - 1$ bits in this block. With this in mind, we construct the second embedding channel as follows:

$$\mathbf{Hx}_1^T, \quad \mathbf{Hx}_2^T, \quad \cdots, \quad \mathbf{Hx}_L^T . \tag{7}$$

This channel consists of Lk bits. Because in the embedding process of the first channel there are on average $L/2$ y_i's to be changed, with these changes the corresponding $Lk/2$ bits in the second embedding channel (7) can be modified freely as analyzed in the above. Forbidding any change to the rest $Lk/2$ bits, we get a typical wet paper channel with $Lk/2$ dry positions and $Lk/2$ wet positions [15]. With the binary wet paper coding method in [15] we can embed about $Lk/2$ bits of messages on average, and the receiver can extract these messages without any knowledge about the dry positions. For this reason, we call the second embedding channel as the basic Hamming wet paper channel. A detailed method of binary wet paper coding can be found in [15].

In fact, we embed messages using the above channels in two steps. In the first step, we embed L bits into the channel (5), and label the indices of y_i's which need to be changed, but no change is actually made in this step. In the second step, construct Hamming wet paper channel (7) and embed messages with an embedding rate $1/2$ using wet paper coding. In the process of wet paper coding, one bit is flipped in every block with the labelled index i, $1 \leq i \leq L$, which also completes the changes needed by the first step. Combining the two steps, we on average embed $1 + k/2$ bits of messages into a length-2^k block of covers by $1/2$ changes, meaning that we obtain the stego-code $SC(1/2, 2^k, 1 + k/2), k \geq 1$.

3.2   General Framework

To generalize the method described in Subsection 3.1 to any stego-code SC (R_a, N, n), we divide the cover image into disjoint blocks of $N2^k$ pixels and, without loss of generality, assume the cover image consists of $LN2^k$ pixels. Write the LSBs of each block as a matrix as follows:

$$
\begin{matrix}
x_{1,1}, \cdots, & x_{1,N} \\
x_{2,1}, \cdots, & x_{2,N} \\
\cdots & \\
x_{2^k,1}, \cdots, & x_{2^k,N}
\end{matrix}
\qquad (8)
$$

In the first step, compress each column into one bit as

$$
y_i = \bigoplus_{j=1}^{2^k} x_{j,i} \quad i = 1, 2, \cdots, N \; . \qquad (9)
$$

Applying $SC(R_a, N, n)$ to $(y_1, \cdots, y_N)$, we can embed n bits of messages with R_a changes on average. In the second step, let

$$
\mathbf{x}_1 = \left(x_{1,1}, \cdots, x_{2^k-1,1} \right), \quad \cdots, \quad \mathbf{x}_N = \left(x_{1,N}, \cdots, x_{2^k-1,N} \right) \; . \qquad (10)
$$

Construct a Hamming wet paper channel using the same method as in Subsection 3.1

$$
\mathbf{H}\mathbf{x}_1^T, \quad \mathbf{H}\mathbf{x}_2^T, \quad \cdots, \quad \mathbf{H}\mathbf{x}_N^T \; . \qquad (11)
$$

The length of this embedding channel is Nk, including $R_a k$ dry positions and $(N - R_a)k$ wet positions on average. Because there are L blocks in total, each of which can introduce such a Hamming wet paper channel. We can cascade them to employ wet paper coding, and finally embed on average $n + R_a k$ bits of messages into every length-$N2^k$ block with R_a changes. Thus we get a stego-code $SC(R_a, N2^k, n + R_a k)$, $k \geq 0$. In the second step we use only the R_a columns corresponding to the modified positions in the first step to carry extra messages with no additional modification. If any other column is also used to carry k bits of messages, two additional changes are needed with probability $(2^k - 1)/2^k$, which will lead to low embedding efficiency.

The above construction implies that, for any stego-code $SC(R_a, N, n)$, there are a family of stego-codes $SC(R_a, N2^k, n + R_a k)$, $k \geq 0$, associated with it. We denote $SC(R_a, N2^k, n + R_a k)$ with $S(k)$, $k \geq 0$, and $S(0)$ is just $SC(R_a, N, n)$.

Definition 1. *Call $S(k)$, $k \geq 0$, the stego-code family (SCF) associated with SC (R_a, N, n). Because stego-codes and covering codes are equivalent, if $SC(R_a, N, n)$ can be obtained from the covering code C, we also call $S(k)$, $k \geq 0$, as the SCF of C.*

For a stego-code $SC(R_a, N, n)$, its embedding rate $\alpha = n/N$, embedding efficiency $e = n/R_a$ and average distortion $D = R_a/N$. Then the SCF of SC (R_a, N, n), $S(k)$, $k \geq 0$, has embedding rate $\alpha(k)$, embedding efficiency $e(k)$ and average distortion $D(k)$ as follows:

$$\alpha(k) = \frac{n + R_a k}{N2^k} = \frac{\alpha + Dk}{2^k}, \; e(k) = \frac{n + R_a k}{R_a} = e + k, \; D(k) = \frac{R_a}{N2^k} = \frac{D}{2^k} \quad (12)$$

For example, the $[23, 12]$ Golay code, whose covering radius is 3, has the average number of embedding changes

$$R_a = \frac{\binom{23}{1}}{2^{11}} + \frac{\binom{23}{2}}{2^{11}} \times 2 + \frac{\binom{23}{3}}{2^{11}} \times 3 = 2.853 \quad (13)$$

Golay code implies the stego-code $SC(2.853, 23, 11)$, and therefore the stego-code family $SC(2.853, 23 \times 2^k, 11 + 2.85k)$, $k \geq 0$. As shown in Fig.1, the SCF of binary Golay provides a family of stego-coding schemes with embedding efficiency better than the binary Hamming.

The stego-code family $SC(1/2, 2^k, 1 + k/2)$, $k \geq 0$, obtained in Subsection 3.1 is the SCF of $SC(1/2, 1, 1)$, i.e., Hamming code with $k = 1$. Furthermore, every stego-code in [3-6] leads to a family of stego-codes which enormously enlarges the set of coding methods for applications in steganography. However, we found that almost all stego-codes in [3,4,5,6] are below the embedding efficiency curve of SCF of binary Hamming ($k = 1$), except for a few with large embedding rate such as the $[35, 11]$ non-primitive BCH code proposed in the literature [5]. In Fig.1, it is shown that we can get points exceeding the curve of SCF of binary Hamming ($k = 1$) with the SCF of $[35, 11]$ BCH code. Note that the codes used in [3,4,5,6] are structured codes, and we can employ random codes to construct stego-code families even closer to the upper bound of embedding efficiency.

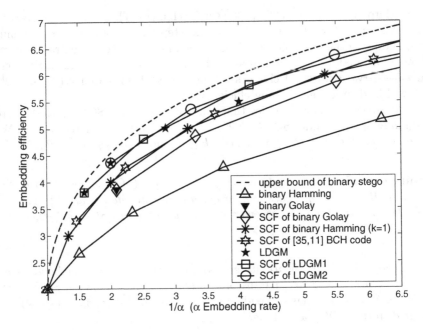

Fig. 1. Performance of stego-code families. The abscissa represents $1/\alpha$ where α is embedding rate.

3.3   SCFs of Random Codes

Binary steganography has the following upper bound [7] of embedding efficiency e with respect to a given embedding rate α.

$$e(\alpha) \le \frac{\alpha}{H^{-1}(\alpha)}, \quad 0 \le \alpha \le 1 , \tag{14}$$

where $H(y) = -y \log_2 y - (1-y) \log_2(1-y)$ is the binary-entropy function, and H^{-1} is the inverse function of H.

It has been shown [2,7] that binary random linear codes can achieve the bound (14) asymptotically with the code length $N \to \infty$. The drawback of random codes is high computational complexity for encoding. However, Fridrich et al. presented an embedding scheme with random linear codes in [7] and they also proposed a more efficient method using LDGM codes in [8] recently, which can achieve embedding efficiency very close to the bound (14) with reasonable complexity when the embedding rate α is relatively large.

For instance, by taking LDGM code with length $N = 10000$, Fridrich et al. reported four stego-codes in [8] with embedding rate and embedding efficiency (α, e) as follows:

$$(0.63, 3.808), (0.50, 4.360), (0.35, 5.010), (0.25, 5.495) . \tag{15}$$

The four stego-codes are labelled as LDGM in Fig.1, indicating that when the embedding rate is larger than or equal to 0.5, embedding efficiency of LDGM can almost achieve the upper bound. Therefore we use the first two codes in (15) to generate two SCFs. Calculating average distortions by $D = \alpha/e$ and applying (12), we can obtain the following performance of the two SCFs:

$$\alpha_1(k) = \frac{0.63 + 0.165k}{2^k}, \quad e_1(k) = 3.808 + k, \quad k \geq 0 ; \tag{16}$$

$$\alpha_2(k) = \frac{0.50 + 0.115k}{2^k}, \quad e_2(k) = 4.360 + k, \quad k \geq 0 . \tag{17}$$

These two SCFs are labelled "SCF of LDGM1" and "SCF of LDGM2" in Fig.1, respectively. It is observed that the SCFs of LDGM codes are closer to the upper bound than SCFs of structured codes.

We find that SCFs is still close to the upper bound (14) even when the embedding rate drops, i.e., the k value increases. As an example, the distance between "SCF of LDGM2" (17), for $0 \leq k \leq 10$, and the upper bound (14) is listed in Table 1. All new generated codes, i.e., codes for $1 \leq k \leq 10$, keep small distances from the upper bound, i.e., less than 0.25, only with slight fluctuation. This implies that SCF can provide embedding efficiency close to the upper bound for even very small embedding rate α. One merit of random codes in [7,8] is that they can provide a continuous family of stego-codes dependent on the embedding rate α. Thus, if we generate stego-codes using random codes for all large embedding rates, e.g., $\alpha \geq 0.5$, and collect all their SCFs, then we can get a family of near optimal stego-codes for arbitrarily chosen embedding rates, be it large or small.

Table 1. Distance between "SCF of LDGM2" (17) and the upper bound (14)

k	0	1	2	3	4	5	6	7	8	9	10
$\alpha_2(k)\%$	50.00	30.75	18.25	10.56	6.00	3.36	1.86	1.02	0.55	0.33	0.16
Distance	0.184	0.226	0.240	0.244	0.243	0.241	0.239	0.236	0.234	0.231	0.230

3.4   Computational Complexity

The proposed method increases embedding efficiency by combining previous stego-codes with wet paper codes, which costs more computational complexity, and the additional computational complexity comes from the wet paper coding.

For the SCF of $SC(R_a, N, n)$, computational complexity is determined by the complexity of implementing $SC(R_a, N, n)$ and coding on the Hamming wet paper channel. Usually implementation of stego-codes based on constructed covering codes is very simple. For random codes, a fast algorithm is proposed in [8]. To construct the Hamming wet paper channel, we only need an XOR of some binary vectors of length k to get the changing position, as shown in the example on $[7, 4]$ Hamming code in Subsection 3.1, which has negligible complexity.

A fast algorithm on binary wet paper coding has been presented in [15]. For length-M wet paper channel with m dry positions, we can embed messages with embedding rate m/M and computational complexity $O(M \ln(m/\delta))$ where δ is a constant [15]. For Hamming wet paper channel, computational complexity is mainly influenced by the length of the channel. As shown in Subsection 3.2, if the cover image consists of $LN2^k$ pixels, we can get a Hamming wet paper channel of length LNk. When using wet paper codes, we can divide this channel into disjoint segments with appropriate length M such as $M = 10^5$.

4   Modified SCFs for ± 1 Steganography

Coding for ± 1 steganography can be viewed as a problem of ternary codes. Ternary Hamming and Golay codes were proposed by Willems, who also obtained the upper bound at the embedding rate α of ± 1 steganography subject to the constraint of an average distortion D [9]:

$$C(D) = \begin{cases} G(D) & D \leq \frac{2}{3} \\ \log_2 3 & D > \frac{2}{3} \end{cases} , \tag{18}$$

where $G(D) = H(D) + D$. To evaluate embedding efficiency, we rewrite Equation (18) as an upper bound of the embedding efficiency e depending on a given embedding rate α:

$$e(\alpha) \leq \frac{\alpha}{G^{-1}(\alpha)}, \quad 0 \leq \alpha \leq \log_2 3 , \tag{19}$$

where G^{-1} is the inverse function of G.

To employing SCFs of binary codes to approach the bound (19), we only need to slightly modify the construction of Hamming wet paper channel in Subsection 3.2. Assume that the cover is a gray scale image. Denote the gray value of a pixel by g_i, $0 \leq g_i \leq 255$, whose LSB is represented with x_i. For a stego-code $SC(R_a, N, n)$, we still suppose that the image consists of L disjoint pixel blocks of length $N2^k$. Each block is arranged as a matrix with the form like (8). For simplicity, we only use the first column to explain the modification to the Hamming wet paper channel.

The first column of LSBs in (8) is $(x_{1,1}, \cdots, x_{2^k,1})$ and the corresponding column of gray value is $(g_{1,1}, \cdots, g_{2^k,1})$. $y_1 = x_{1,1} \oplus \cdots \oplus x_{2^k,1}$ is the first bit of the first embedding channel, and this column is mapped into k bits by

$$\mathbf{H}\mathbf{x}_1^T = \mathbf{H}(x_{1,1}, \cdots, x_{2^k-1,1})^T. \tag{20}$$

Let

$$z_1 = \left(\left\lfloor \frac{g_{11}}{2} \right\rfloor + \cdots + \left\lfloor \frac{g_{2^k,1}}{2} \right\rfloor \right) \bmod 2 . \tag{21}$$

If y_1 needs to be flipped, we can change any one component in $(x_{1,1}, \cdots, x_{2^k,1})$. Which one should be changed is determined by the k bits $\mathbf{H}\mathbf{x}_1^T$ that we want. For example, suppose that $x_{i,1}$, $1 \leq i \leq 2^k$, should be changed. This can be achieved by $g_{i,1} + 1$ or $g_{i,1} - 1$. The choice of adding or subtracting one can be used to control the value of $\lfloor g_{i,1}/2 \rfloor \bmod 2$, therefore control the value of z_1. This means that, when flipping y_1, we get a free bit z_1, or a dry position in terms

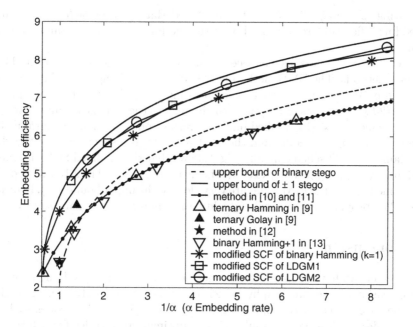

Fig. 2. Performance comparisons among modified SCFs and methods in [9,10,11,12,13]

of wet paper codes, by the same change. In other words, when changing y_1, we can map $(g_{1,1}, \cdots, g_{2^k,1})$ to any $k+1$ bits $(\mathbf{Hx}_1^T, z_1)$ by one change. Doing this to every column of (8), the Hamming wet paper channel (11) can be modified as follows:

$$\mathbf{Hx}_1^T, z_1, \mathbf{Hx}_2^T, z_2, \ldots, \mathbf{Hx}_N^T, z_N \; . \tag{22}$$

This is an embedding channel of length $N(k+1)$ with $R_a(k+1)$ dry positions. Therefore we can get stego-codes $SC(R_a, N2^k, n + R_a(k+1)), k \geq 0$. We call them the modified SCF of $SC(R_a, N, n)$.

Note that the above embedding process may fail when the pixel value $g_{i,1}$ is saturated, i.e., $g_{i,1} = 0$ or 255. In this case, change in only one direction is allowed. When $g_{i,1} = 0$, $g_{i,1} - 1$ is not allowed. We can use $g_{i,1} + 3$ instead to satisfy z_1. Similarly, when $g_{i,1} = 255$ while $g_{i,1} + 1$ is required to satisfy z_1, we use $g_{i,1} - 3$ instead. This of course will introduce larger distortion. But if the probability of gray value saturation is not too large, the effect on the overall performance is negligible.

For a stego-code $SC(R_a, N, n)$ with embedding rate $\alpha = n/N$, embedding efficiency $e = n/R_a$ and average distortion $D = R_a/N$, the modified SCF has the following performance:

$$\alpha(k) = \frac{\alpha + D(k+1)}{2^k}, \quad e(k) = e + k + 1, \quad D(k) = \frac{D}{2^k}, \quad k \geq 0 \; . \tag{23}$$

Comparing (23) and (12), it can be concluded that both embedding rate and embedding efficiency are improved with the modified SCF at the same average distortion.

Performance comparisons have been made between the modified SCFs and the previous methods. The EMD method in [10] and grid coloring method in [11] can provide the same family of schemes, embedding $\log_2(2d + 1)$ bits into d pixels with $2d/(2d+1)$ changes on average, which includes the ternary Hamming stego-codes. The method in [13] applied binary covering codes to ±1 steganography by extending the length of codes and the method in [12] is a special case of the "binary Hamming +1" scheme in [13]. Fig.2 shows that the modified SCF of binary Hamming ($k = 1$) significantly exceeds the methods in [9,10,11,12,13]. Moreover, the modified SCFs of LDGM codes are very close to the upper bound (19). In other words, they provide near optimal embedding schemes for ±1 steganography.

5   Conclusions

In this paper, we have proposed a new method to construct embedding schemes for applications in steganography, which can generate a family of stego-codes from one covering code. By combining this method with random codes such as LDGM codes, we can get a family of near optimal stego-codes for arbitrarily chosen embedding rates.

To resist detection, the sender can always reduce changes to the cover by embedding fewer messages into an image, i.e., use low embedding rate. However, recent advances in steganalysis have made LSB steganography with small embedding rates detectable. For example, the method in [16] can detect simple LSB steganography with embedding rate as low as 2%. Since embedding efficiency of simple LSB steganography is 2, detecting 2% embedding rate means detecting 1% changes. SCF of LDGM codes can provide embedding efficiency better than 10 for the embedding rate of 2%, that is, changes are reduced to 0.2%. That is why SCFs are used to resist steganalysis. Furthermore, it has been shown that ±1 steganography is more secure than LSB steganography because ±1 embedding can avoid the statistical imbalance introduced by LSB replacement. As shown in Section 4, larger embedding efficiency can be obtained with the modified SCFs, so ±1 steganography plus the modified SCFs will provide even better security.

On the other hand, relations between stego-coding and error-correcting codes have been studied in [6,17]. The duality between data embedding and source coding is shown in [8,18]. For example, LDGM codes can be very close to the rate-distortion bound of the source codes, which is just the reason that schemes based on LDGM codes in [8] can almost achieve the bound of embedding efficiency. All these results imply that the SCF is potentially applicable to both source coding and channel coding. Our further study will include applications of SCFs to other fields.

Acknowledgments. This work was supported by the Natural Science Foundation of China (60803155, 60502039), the China Postdoctoral Science

Foundation funded project (20070420096), the High-Tech Research and Development Program of China (2007AA01Z477), and Shanghai Rising-Star Program (06QA14022).

Special thanks go to Professor Jessica Fridrich and Dr. Tomáš Filler for the results of stego-coding based on LDGM codes. The authors would also like to sincerely thank the anonymous reviewers for their valuable comments.

References

1. Crandall, R.: Some notes on steganography. Posted on steganography mailing list (1998), http://os.inf.tu-dresden.de/westfeld/crandall.pdf
2. Galand, F., Kabatiansky, G.: Information hiding by coverings. In: Proceedings of the IEEE Information Theory Workshop 2004, pp. 151–154 (2004)
3. Bierbrauer, J., Fridrich, J.: Constructing good covering codes for applications in steganography. In: Transactions on Data Hiding and Multimedia Security. LNCS. Springer, Heidelberg (to appear, 2007), http://www.math.mtu.edu/jbierbra/
4. Tseng, Y.C., Chen, Y.-Y., Pan, H.-K.: A secure data hiding scheme for binary images. IEEE Transactions on Communications 50(8), 1227–1231 (2002)
5. Schönfeld, D., Winkler, A.: Embedding with syndrome coding based on BCH codes. In: Proc. ACM the 8th workshop on Multimedia and Security, pp. 214–223 (2006)
6. Munuera, C.: Steganography and error-correcting codes. Signal Processing 87, 1528–1533 (2007)
7. Fridrich, J., Soukal, D.: Matrix embedding for large payloads. IEEE Transactions on Information Security and Forensics 1(3), 390–394 (2006)
8. Fridrich, J., Filler, T.: Practical methods for minimizing embedding impact in steganography. In: Proc. SPIE Electronic Imaging, vol. 6050 (2007)
9. Willems, F., Dijk, M.: Capacity and codes for embedding information in gray-scale signals. IEEE Transactions on Information Theory 51(3), 1209–1214 (2005)
10. Zhang, X., Wang, S.: Efficient steganographic embedding by exploiting modification direction. IEEE Communications Letters 10(11), 781–783 (2006)
11. Fridrich, J., Lisoněk, P.: Grid coloring in steganography. IEEE Transactions on Information Theory 53(4), 1547–1549 (2007)
12. Mielikainen, J.: LSB matching revisited. IEEE Signal Processing Letters 13(5), 285–287 (2006)
13. Zhang, W., Wang, S., Zhang, X.: Improving embedding efficiency of covering codes for applications in steganography. IEEE Communications Letters 11(8), 680–682 (2007)
14. Zhang, W., Zhang, X., Wang, S.: A double layered "plus-minus one" data embedding scheme. IEEE Signal Processing Letters 14(11), 848–851 (2007)
15. Fridrich, J., Goljan, M., Lisonek, P., Soukal, D.: Writing on wet paper. IEEE Transactions on Signal Processing 53(10), 3923–3935 (2005)
16. Ker, A.D.: A General Framework for the Structural Steganalysis of LSB Replacement. In: Barni, M., Herrera-Joancomartí, J., Katzenbeisser, S., Pérez-González, F. (eds.) IH 2005. LNCS, vol. 3727, pp. 296–311. Springer, Heidelberg (2005)
17. Zhang, W., Li, S.: A coding problem in steganography. Designs, Codes and Cryptography 46(1), 67–81 (2008)
18. Barron, R.J., Chen, B., Wornell, G.W.: The duality between information embedding and source coding with side information and some applications. IEEE Transactions on Information Theory 49(5), 1159–1180 (2003)

Detecting Re-projected Video

Weihong Wang and Hany Farid

Department of Computer Science
Dartmouth College
Hanover, NH 03755
www.cs.dartmouth.edu/~{whwang,farid}

Abstract. A common and simple way to create a bootleg video is to simply record a movie from the theater screen. Because the recorded video is not generally of high quality, it is usually easy to visually detect such recordings. However, given the wide variety of video content and film-making styles, automatic detection is less straight-forward. We describe an automatic technique for detecting a video that was recorded from a screen. We show that the internal camera parameters of such video are inconsistent with the expected parameters of an authentic video.

Keywords: Digital Forensics, Digital Tampering.

1   Introduction

Often only hours after their release, major motion pictures can find their way onto the Internet. A simple and popular way to create such bootleg video is to simply record a movie from the theater screen. Although these video are certainly not of the same quality as their subsequent DVD releases, increasingly compact and high resolution video recorders are affording better quality video recordings.

We describe how to automatically detect a video that was recorded from a screen. Shown in Fig. 1, for example, is a scene from the movie *Live Free Or Die Hard*. Also shown in this figure is the same scene as viewed on a theater screen. Note that due to the angle of the video camera relative to the screen, a perspective distortion has been introduced into this second recording. We show that this re-projection can introduce a distortion into the intrinsic camera parameters (namely, the camera skew which depends on the angle between the horizontal and vertical pixel axes). We leverage previous work on camera calibration to estimate this skew and show the efficacy of this technique to detect re-projected video.

2   Methods

We begin by describing the basic imaging geometry from 3-D world to 2-D image coordinates for both arbitrary points (Section 2.1) and for points constrained to a planar surface (Section 2.2). See [3] for a thorough treatment. We then describe the effect of a re-projection: a non-planar projection followed by a planar projection (Section 2.3). Such a re-projection would result from, for example, video recording the projection of a movie.

K. Solanki, K. Sullivan, and U. Madhow (Eds.): IH 2008, LNCS 5284, pp. 72–86, 2008.
© Springer-Verlag Berlin Heidelberg 2008

Fig. 1. Shown on the right is a scene from the movie *Live Free Or Die Hard*, and shown on the left is the same scene as viewed on a movie screen. A recording of the projected movie introduces distortions that can be used to detect re-projected video.

2.1   Projective Geometry: Non-planar

Under an ideal pinhole camera model, the perspective projection of arbitrary points $\boldsymbol{X}$ (homogeneous coordinates) in 3-D world coordinates is given by:

$$\boldsymbol{x} = \lambda KM\boldsymbol{X}, \tag{1}$$

where $\boldsymbol{x}$ is the 2-D projected point in homogeneous coordinates, λ is a scale factor, K is the intrinsic matrix, and M is the extrinsic matrix.

The 3×3 intrinsic matrix K embodies the camera's internal parameters:

$$K = \begin{pmatrix} \alpha f & s & c_x \\ 0 & f & c_y \\ 0 & 0 & 1 \end{pmatrix}, \tag{2}$$

where f is the focal length, α is the aspect ratio, (c_x, c_y) is the principle point (the projection of the camera center onto the image plane), and s is the skew (the skew depends on the angle, θ, between the horizontal and vertical pixel axes: $s = f\tan(\pi/2 - \theta)$). For simplicity, we will assume square pixels ($\alpha = 1$, $s = 0$) and that the principal point is at the origin ($c_x = c_y = 0$) – these are reasonable assumptions for most modern-day cameras. With these assumptions, the intrinsic matrix simplifies to:

$$K = \begin{pmatrix} f & 0 & 0 \\ 0 & f & 0 \\ 0 & 0 & 1 \end{pmatrix}. \tag{3}$$

The 3×4 extrinsic matrix M embodies the transformation from world to camera coordinates:

$$M = (\, R \mid \boldsymbol{t}\,), \tag{4}$$

where R is a 3×3 rotation matrix, and $\boldsymbol{t}$ is a 3×1 translation vector.

2.2   Projective Geometry: Planar

Under an ideal pinhole camera model, the perspective projection of points Y constrained to a planar surface in world coordinates is given by:

$$y = \lambda K P Y, \tag{5}$$

where y is the 2-D projected point in homogeneous coordinates, and Y, in the appropriate coordinate system, is specified by 2-D coordinates in homogeneous coordinates. As before, λ is a scale factor, K is the intrinsic matrix, and P is the extrinsic matrix. The intrinsic matrix K takes the same form as in Equation (3). The now 3×3 extrinsic matrix P takes the form:

$$P = (\,p_1\ p_2\ t\,), \tag{6}$$

where p_1, p_2 and $p_1 \times p_2$ are the columns of the 3×3 rotation matrix that describes the transformation from world to camera coordinates, and as before, t is a 3×1 translation vector.

2.3   Re-projection

Consider now the effect of first projecting arbitrary points in 3-D world coordinates into 2-D image coordinates, and then projecting these points a second time. As described in Section 2.1, the first projection is given by:

$$x = \lambda_1 K_1 M_1 X. \tag{7}$$

The second planar projection, Section 2.2, is given by:

$$y = \lambda_2 K_2 P_2 x = \lambda_2 K_2 P_2 (\lambda_1 K_1 M_1 X) = \lambda_2 \lambda_1 K_2 P_2 (K_1 M_1 X). \tag{8}$$

The effective projective matrix $K_2 P_2 K_1 M_1$ can be uniquely factored (see Appendix A) into a product of an intrinsic, K, and extrinsic, M, matrix:

$$y = \lambda_2 \lambda_1 \lambda K M X. \tag{9}$$

Recall that we assumed that the camera skew (the $(1,2)$ entry in the 3×3 intrinsic matrix, Equation (2), is zero. We next show that that a re-projection can yield a non-zero skew in the intrinsic matrix K. As such, significant deviations of the skew from zero in the estimated intrinsic matrix can be used as evidence that a video has been re-projected.

We have seen that the re-projection matrix $K_2 P_2 K_1 M_1$ can be factored into a product of a scale factor and intrinsic and extrinsic matrices:

$$K_2 P_2 K_1 M_1 = \lambda K M. \tag{10}$$

Expressing each 3×4 extrinsic matrix M_1 and M in terms of their rotation and translation components yields:

$$K_2 P_2 K_1 (R_1 \mid t_1) = \lambda K (R \mid t)$$
$$K_2 P_2 K_1 R_1 = \lambda K R. \tag{11}$$

Reshuffling[1] a few terms yields:

$$K^{-1}K_2P_2K_1R_1 = \lambda R$$
$$K^{-1}K_2P_2K_1 = \lambda RR_1^T. \tag{12}$$

Note that the right-hand side of this relationship is an orthogonal matrix – this will be exploited later. On the left-hand side, the left-most matrix is the inverse of the effective intrinsic matrix in Equation (2):

$$K^{-1} = \begin{pmatrix} \frac{1}{\alpha f} & -\frac{s}{\alpha f^2} & \frac{sc_y - c_x f}{\alpha f^2} \\ 0 & \frac{1}{f} & -\frac{c_y}{f} \\ 0 & 0 & 1 \end{pmatrix}. \tag{13}$$

And the product of the next three matrices is:

$$K_2P_2K_1 = \begin{pmatrix} f_2 & 0 & 0 \\ 0 & f_2 & 0 \\ 0 & 0 & 1 \end{pmatrix} \begin{pmatrix} p_{11} & p_{21} & t_1 \\ p_{12} & p_{22} & t_2 \\ p_{13} & p_{23} & t_3 \end{pmatrix} \begin{pmatrix} f_1 & 0 & 0 \\ 0 & f_1 & 0 \\ 0 & 0 & 1 \end{pmatrix},$$
$$= \begin{pmatrix} f_1 f_2 p_{11} & f_1 f_2 p_{21} & f_2 t_1 \\ f_1 f_2 p_{12} & f_1 f_2 p_{22} & f_2 t_2 \\ f_1 p_{13} & f_1 p_{23} & t_3 \end{pmatrix}$$
$$= \begin{pmatrix} q_1^T \\ q_2^T \\ q_3^T \end{pmatrix}, \tag{14}$$

where f_2 and f_1 are the focal lengths of the original projections, p_{1i} and p_{2i} correspond to the ith element of p_1 and p_2, and t_i corresponds to i^{th} element of t_2 (the third column of matrix P_2). The product of the four matrices on the left-hand side of Equation (12) is then:

$$K^{-1}K_2P_2K_1 = \begin{pmatrix} \left(\frac{1}{\alpha f} q_1 - \frac{s}{\alpha f^2} q_2 + \frac{sc_y - c_x f}{\alpha f^2} q_3 \right)^T \\ \left(\frac{1}{f} q_2 - \frac{c_y}{f} q_3 \right)^T \\ q_3^T \end{pmatrix}. \tag{15}$$

Recall that $K^{-1}K_2P_2K_1 = \lambda RR_1^T$, Equation (12), and that R and R_1^T are each orthonormal. Since the product of two orthonormal matrices is orthonormal, $K^{-1}K_2P_2K_1$ is orthogonal (the rows/columns will not be unit length when $\lambda \neq 1$). This orthogonality constrains the above matrix rows as follows:

$$q_3^T \left(\frac{1}{f} q_2 - \frac{c_y}{f} q_3 \right) = 0 \tag{16}$$

$$\left(\frac{1}{f} q_2 - \frac{c_y}{f} q_3 \right)^T \left(\frac{1}{\alpha f} q_1 - \frac{s}{\alpha f^2} q_2 + \frac{sc_y - c_x f}{\alpha f^2} q_3 \right) = 0. \tag{17}$$

---

[1] Since the matrix R_1 is orthonormal $R_1^{-1} = R_1^T$.

Solving Equation (16) for c_y yields:

$$c_y = \frac{q_3^T q_2}{\|q_3\|^2}. \tag{18}$$

Substituting for c_y into Equation (17), followed by some simplifications, yields:

$$s = f \frac{q_2^T q_1 \|q_3\|^2 - (q_3^T q_2)(q_3^T q_1)}{\|q_2\|^2 \|q_3\|^2 - (q_3^T q_2)^2}. \tag{19}$$

Note that the skew, s, is expressed only in terms of the effective focal length f, the pair of intrinsic matrices K_1 and K_2, and the second transformation matrix P_2. We can now see under what conditions $s = 0$.

First, note that the denominator of Equation (19) cannot be zero. If $\|q_2\|^2 \|q_3\|^2 - (q_3^T q_2)^2 = 0$ then, $q_2 \propto q_3$, in which case $K_2 P_2 K_1$ is singular, which it cannot be, since each matrix in this product is full rank. And, since $f \neq 0$, the skew is zero only when the numerator of Equation (19) is zero:

$$q_2^T q_1 \|q_3\|^2 - (q_3^T q_2)(q_3^T q_1) = 0$$
$$f_1^2 p_{31} p_{32} - t_1 t_2 + p_{33}^2 t_1 t_2 + p_{31} p_{32} t_3^2 - p_{32} p_{33} t_1 t_3 - p_{31} p_{33} t_2 t_3 = 0, \tag{20}$$

where p_{3i} is the ith element of $p_3 = p_1 \times p_2$. Although we have yet to geometrically fully characterize the space of coefficients that yields a zero skew, there are a few intuitive cases that can be seen from the above constraint. For example, if the world to camera rotation is strictly about the z-axis, then $p_{31} = p_{32} = 0$ and $p_{33} = 1$, and the skew $s = 0$. This situation arises when the image plane of the second projection is perfectly parallel to the screen being imaged. As another example, if $t = \pm f_1 p_3$, then the skew $s = 0$. This situations arises when the translation of the second projection is equal to the third column of the rotation matrix scaled by focal length of the first projection – a perhaps somewhat unlikely configuration.

Although there are clearly many situations under which $s = 0$, our simulations suggest that under realistic camera motions, this condition is rarely satisfied. Specifically, we computed the skew, Equation (19), from one million randomly generated camera configurations. The relative position of the second camera to the planar projection screen was randomly selected with the rotation in the range $[-45, 45]$ degrees, X and Y translation in the range $[-1000, 1000]$, Z translation in the range $[4000, 6000]$, and focal length in the range $[25, 75]$. The average skew was 0.295, and only 48 of the $1,000,000$ configurations had a skew less than 10^{-5} (in a similar simulation, the estimated skew for a single projection is on the order of 10^{-12}).

2.4   Camera Skew

From the previous sections, we see that re-projection can cause a non-zero skew in the camera's intrinsic parameters. We review two approaches for estimating camera skew from a video sequence. The first estimates the camera skew from a known planar surface, while the second assumes no known geometry.

Skew Estimation I: Recall that the projection of a planar surface, Equation (5), is given by:

$$y = \lambda KPY = \lambda HY, \tag{21}$$

where y is the 2-D projected point in homogeneous coordinates, and Y, in the appropriate coordinate system, is specified by 2-D coordinates in homogeneous coordinates. The 3×3 matrix H is a non-singular matrix referred to as a homography. Given the above equality, the left- and right-hand sides of this homography satisfy the following:

$$y \times (HY) = 0$$

$$\begin{pmatrix} y_1 \\ y_2 \\ y_3 \end{pmatrix} \times \left(\begin{pmatrix} h_{11} & h_{21} & h_{31} \\ h_{12} & h_{22} & h_{32} \\ h_{13} & h_{23} & h_{33} \end{pmatrix} \begin{pmatrix} Y_1 \\ Y_2 \\ Y_3 \end{pmatrix} \right) = 0. \tag{22}$$

Note that due to the equality with zero, the multiplicative scalar λ, Equation (21), is factored out. Evaluating the cross product yields:

$$\begin{pmatrix} y_2(h_{13}Y_1 + h_{23}Y_2 + h_{33}Y_3) - y_3(h_{12}Y_1 + h_{22}Y_2 + h_{32}Y_3) \\ y_3(h_{11}Y_1 + h_{21}Y_2 + h_{31}Y_3) - y_1(h_{13}Y_1 + h_{23}Y_2 + h_{33}Y_3) \\ y_1(h_{12}Y_1 + h_{22}Y_2 + h_{32}Y_3) - y_2(h_{11}Y_1 + h_{21}Y_2 + h_{31}Y_3) \end{pmatrix} = 0. \tag{23}$$

This constraint is linear in the unknown elements of the homography h_{ij}. Re-ordering the terms yields the following system of linear equations:

$$\begin{pmatrix} 0 & 0 & 0 & -y_3 Y_1 & -y_3 Y_2 & -y_3 Y_3 & y_2 Y_1 & y_2 Y_2 & y_2 Y_3 \\ y_3 Y_1 & y_3 Y_2 & y_3 Y_3 & 0 & 0 & 0 & -y_1 Y_1 & -y_1 Y_2 & -y_1 Y_3 \\ -y_2 Y_1 & -y_2 Y_2 & -y_2 Y_3 & y_1 Y_1 & y_1 Y_2 & y_1 Y_3 & 0 & 0 & 0 \end{pmatrix} \begin{pmatrix} h_{11} \\ h_{21} \\ h_{31} \\ h_{12} \\ h_{22} \\ h_{32} \\ h_{13} \\ h_{23} \\ h_{33} \end{pmatrix} = 0$$

$$Ah = 0. \tag{24}$$

A matched set of points y and Y appear to provide three constraints on the eight unknowns elements of h (the homography is defined only up to an unknown scale factor, reducing the unknowns from nine to eight). The rows of the matrix, A, however, are not linearly independent (the third row is a linear combination of the first two rows). As such, this system provides only two constraints in eight unknowns. In order to solve for h, we require four or more points with known image, y, and (planar) world, Y, coordinates that yield eight or more linearly independent constraints. From four or more points, standard least-squares techniques, as described in [3,5], can be used to solve for h: the minimal eigenvalue eigenvector of $A^T A$ is the unit vector h that minimizes the least-squares error.

We next describe how to estimate the camera skew from the estimated homography H. This approach is a slightly modified version of [15]. Recall that H can be expressed as:

$$H = KP = K(p_1 \; p_2 \mid t). \tag{25}$$

The orthonormality of p_1 and p_2, yields the following two constraints:

$$p_1^T p_2 = 0 \qquad \text{and} \qquad p_1^T p_1 = p_2^T p_2, \tag{26}$$

which in turn imposes the following constraints on H and K:

$$\begin{pmatrix} h_{11} \\ h_{12} \\ h_{13} \end{pmatrix}^T K^{-T} K^{-1} \begin{pmatrix} h_{21} \\ h_{22} \\ h_{23} \end{pmatrix} = 0 \tag{27}$$

$$\begin{pmatrix} h_{11} \\ h_{12} \\ h_{13} \end{pmatrix}^T K^{-T} K^{-1} \begin{pmatrix} h_{11} \\ h_{12} \\ h_{13} \end{pmatrix} = \begin{pmatrix} h_{21} \\ h_{22} \\ h_{23} \end{pmatrix}^T K^{-T} K^{-1} \begin{pmatrix} h_{21} \\ h_{22} \\ h_{23} \end{pmatrix}. \tag{28}$$

For notational ease, denote $B = K^{-T} K^{-1}$, where B is a symmetric matrix parametrized with three degrees of freedom (see Equation (41) in Appendix B):

$$B = \begin{pmatrix} b_{11} & b_{12} & 0 \\ b_{12} & b_{22} & 0 \\ 0 & 0 & 1 \end{pmatrix}. \tag{29}$$

Notice that by parametrizing the intrinsic matrix in this way, we have bundled all of the anomalies of a double projection into the estimate of the camera skew. Substituting the matrix B into the constraints of Equations (27)-(28) yields the following constraints:

$$\begin{pmatrix} h_{11} h_{21} & h_{12} h_{21} + h_{11} h_{22} & h_{12} h_{22} \\ h_{11}^2 - h_{21}^2 & 2 (h_{11} h_{12} - h_{21} h_{22}) & h_{12}^2 - h_{22}^2 \end{pmatrix} \begin{pmatrix} b_{11} \\ b_{12} \\ b_{22} \end{pmatrix} = - \begin{pmatrix} h_{13} h_{23} \\ h_{13}^2 - h_{23}^2 \end{pmatrix}. \tag{30}$$

Each image of a planar surface enforces two constraints on the three unknowns b_{ij}. The matrix $B = K^{-T} K^{-1}$ can, therefore, be estimated from two or more views of the same planar surface using standard least-squares estimation. The desired skew can then be determined (see Appendix B) from the estimated matrix B as:

$$s = -f \frac{b_{12}}{b_{11}}. \tag{31}$$

Note that the estimate of the skew, s, is scaled by the focal length, f. Since a camera's skew depends on the focal length, it is desirable to work with this normalized skew.

Skew Estimation II: We showed in the previous section how to estimate a camera's skew from two or more views of a planar surface. This approach has the advantage that it affords a closed-form linear solution, but has the disadvantage that it only applies to frames that contain a known planar surface. Here we review a related approach that does not require any known world geometry, but requires a non-linear minimization.

Consider two frames of a video sequence with corresponding image points given by u and v, specified in 2-D homogeneous coordinates. It is well established [3] that these points satisfy the following relationship:

$$v^T F u = 0, \tag{32}$$

where F, the fundamental matrix, is a 3×3 singular matrix ($\text{rank}(F) = 2$). Writing the above relationship in terms of the vector and matrix elements yields:

$$(v_1 \quad v_2 \quad 1) \begin{pmatrix} f_{11} & f_{21} & f_{31} \\ f_{12} & f_{22} & f_{32} \\ f_{13} & f_{23} & f_{33} \end{pmatrix} \begin{pmatrix} u_1 \\ u_2 \\ 1 \end{pmatrix} = 0$$

$$u_1 v_1 f_{11} + u_2 v_1 f_{21} + v_1 f_{31} + u_1 v_2 f_{12} + u_2 v_2 f_{22} + v_2 f_{32} + u_1 f_{13} + u_2 f_{23} + f_{33} = 0.$$

Note that this constraint is linear in the elements of the fundamental matrix f_{ij}, leading to the following system of linear equations:

$$(u_1 v_1 \quad u_2 v_1 \quad v_1 \quad u_1 v_2 \quad u_2 v_2 \quad v_2 \quad u_1 \quad u_2 \quad 1) \begin{pmatrix} f_{11} \\ f_{21} \\ f_{31} \\ f_{12} \\ f_{22} \\ f_{32} \\ f_{13} \\ f_{23} \\ f_{33} \end{pmatrix} = 0$$

$$A f = 0. \tag{33}$$

Each pair of matched points u and v provides one constraint for the eight unknown elements of f (the fundamental matrix is defined only up to an unknown scale factor reducing the unknowns from nine to eight). In order to solve for the components of the fundamental matrix, f, we require eight or more matched pairs of points [6,2]. Standard least-squares techniques can be used to solve for f: the minimal eigenvalue eigenvector of $A^T A$ is the unit vector f that minimizes the least-squares error.

We next describe how to estimate the camera skew from the estimated fundamental matrix F. We assume that the intrinsic camera matrix K, Equation (3), is the same across the views containing the matched image points. The essential matrix E is then defined as:

$$E = K^T F K. \tag{34}$$

Since F has rank 2 and the intrinsic matrix is full rank, the essential matrix E has rank 2. In addition, the two non-zero singular values of E are equal [4]. This property will be exploited to estimate the camera skew. Specifically, as described in [8], we establish the following cost function to be minimized in terms of the camera focal length f and skew s:

$$C(f, s) = \sum_{i=1}^{n} \frac{\sigma_{i1} - \sigma_{i2}}{\sigma_{i2}}, \tag{35}$$

where σ_{i1} and σ_{i2} are, in descending order, the non-zero singular values of E from n estimated fundamental matrices (each computed from pairs of frames throughout a video sequence), and where K is parametrized as:

$$K = \begin{pmatrix} f & s & 0 \\ 0 & f & 0 \\ 0 & 0 & 1 \end{pmatrix}. \tag{36}$$

Note that since only the relative differences in the singular values of E are considered, the arbitrary scale factor to which E is estimated does not effect the estimation of the skew. As before, by parametrizing the intrinsic matrix in this way, we have bundled all of the anomalies of a double projection into the estimate of the camera skew. The cost function, Equation (35), is minimized using a standard derivative-free Nelder-Mead non-linear minimization.

3   Results

We report on a set of simulations and sensitivity analysis for each of the skew estimation techniques described in the previous sections. We then show the efficacy of these approaches on a real-video sequence. In each set of simulations we provide the estimation algorithm with the required image coordinates. For the real-video sequence we briefly describe a point tracking algorithm which provides the necessary image coordinates for estimating the camera skew.

3.1   Simulation (Skew Estimation I)

Recall that a minimum of four points with known geometry on a planar surface viewed from a minimum of two views are required to estimate the camera skew. We therefore randomly generated between 4 and 64 points on a planar surface and generated a video sequence of this stationary surface. In all of the simulations, the first projection was specified by the following camera parameters: the planar surface was 2000 units from the camera, between successive frames the rotation about each axis was in the range $[-2.5, 2.5]$ degrees and the translation in each dimension was in the range $[-50, 50]$, and the camera focal length was in the range $[25, 75]$ (but fixed for each sequence). For the second projection, the camera was placed a distance of 5000 units from the first projected image and underwent a motion in the same range as the first camera. We randomly generated $10,000$ such sequences as imaged through a single projection, and $10,000$ sequences as imaged through a double projection (re-projection).

In the first simulation, we tested the sensitivity to additive noise. As described above, 30 frames were generated each containing 4 points on a planar surface. Noise in the range of $[0, 1]$ pixels was added to the final image coordinates. The skew was estimated from 15 pairs of frames, where each frame at time t was paired with a frame at time $t + 15$. A sequence was classified as re-projected if one or more of the image pairs yielded an estimated skew greater than 0.1. While this type of voting scheme yields slightly higher false positive rates, it also significantly improves the detection accuracy. In the absence of noise, 0 of the $10,000$ singly projected sequences were classified as re-projected, and 84.9% of the re-projected sequences were correctly classified. With 0.5 pixels of noise, 17.2% of the singly

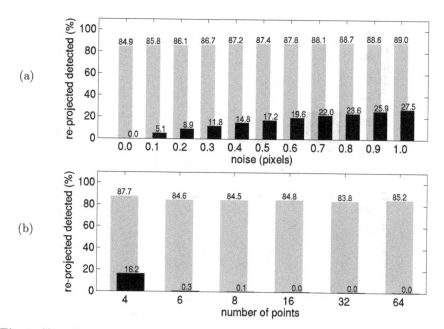

Fig. 2. Skew Estimation I: Detection accuracy (light gray) and false positives (dark gray) as a function of noise (top) and the number of points (bottom)

projected sequences were incorrectly classified as re-projected, and 87.4% of the re-projected sequences were correctly classified. Shown in Fig. 2(a) are the complete set of results for additive noise in the range of $[0, 1]$ pixels. Note that even with modest amounts of noise, the false positive rate increases to an unacceptable level. We next show how these results can be improved upon.

In this next simulation, we tested the sensitivity to the number of known points on the planar surface. The noise level was 0.5 pixels, and the number of known points was in the range $[4, 64]$. All other parameters were the same as in the previous simulation. With the minimum of 4 points, 16.2% of the singly projected sequences were incorrectly classified while 87.7% of the re-projected sequences were correctly classified (similar to the results in the previous simulation). With 6 points, only 0.33% of the single projection sequences were incorrectly classified, while the accuracy of the re-projected sequences remained relatively high at 84.6%. Shown in Fig. 2(b) are the complete set of results – beyond 8 points, the advantage of more points becomes negligible.

In summary, from 6 points, with 0.5 pixels noise, in 30 frames, re-projected video can be detected with 85% accuracy, and with 0.3% false positives.

3.2   Simulation (Skew Estimation II)

Recall that a minimum of eight points viewed from a minimum of two views are required to estimate the camera skew. We therefore generated between 8 and 128

(a)

(b)

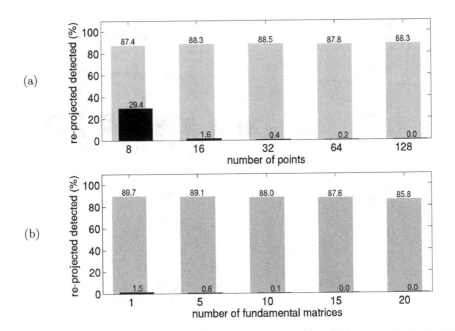

Fig. 3. Skew Estimation II: Detection accuracy (light gray) and false positives (dark gray) as a function of the number of points (top) and the number fundamental matrices (bottom)

points with arbitrary geometry and generated a video sequence of this stationary cloud of points. In all of the simulations, the first and second projection were generated as described in the previous section. We randomly generated 10, 000 sequences as imaged through a single projection, and 10, 000 sequences as imaged through a double projection (re-projection). As before, a sequence was classified as re-projected if the estimated skew was greater than 0.1.

In the first simulation with the minimum of 8 points, 2 frames, and with no noise, 0 of the 10, 000 singly projected sequences were classified as re-projected, and 88.9% of the re-projected sequences were correctly classified. With even modest amounts of noise, however, this minimum configuration yields unacceptably high false positives. We find that the estimation accuracy is more robust to noise when the skew is estimated from multiple frames (i.e., multiple fundamental matrices in Equation (35)). In the remaining simulations, we estimated the skew from 5 fundamental matrices, where each frame t is paired with the frame at time $t + 15$.

In the second simulation, the number of points were in the range $[8, 128]$, with 0.5 pixels of additive noise, and 5 fundamental matrices. With the minimum of 8 points the false positive rate is 29.4%, while with 32 points, the false positive rate falls to 0.4%. In each case, the detection accuracy is approximately 88%. Shown in Fig. 3(a) are the complete set of results for varying number of points.

In the third simulation, the number of points was 32, with 0.5 pixels of noise, and with the number of fundamental matrices (i.e., pairs of frames) in the range

original   re-projected

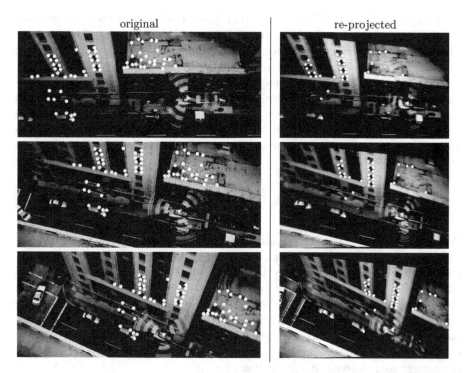

Fig. 4. Shown are the first, middle, and last frame of a 42-frame segment of the movie *Live Free or Die Hard*. On the left is the original digitized video, and on the right is the re-projected video. The white dots denote the tracked features used to estimate the camera skew using method II.

[1, 20]. As shown in Fig. 3(b), increasing the number of fundamental matrices reduces the false positives while the detection accuracy remains approximately the same.

In summary, from 32 points, with 0.5 pixels noise, in 5 fundamental matrices, re-projected video can be detected with 88% accuracy, and with 0.4% false positives. This is similar to the accuracy for the skew estimation from points on a planar surface. The advantage here, however, is that this approach does not require known geometry of points on a planar surface.

3.3   Real Video

Shown in Fig. 4 are three frames of a 42 frame segment from the movie *Live Free Or Die Hard*. These frames were digitized at a resolution of 720×304 pixels. Superimposed on each frame are 64 features tracked across all frames. We employed the KLT feature tracker [7,11,10] which automatically selects features using a Harris detector, and tracks these points across time using standard optical flow techniques. We manually removed any features with clearly incorrect tracking, and any points not on the buildings or street (the estimation of a fundamental matrix requires points with a rigid body geometry). These tracked features were then used to estimate the skew (method II). The 42 frames were grouped into 21 pairs from which the skew was estimated (each frame at time t was paired with the frame at time $t + 21$). The estimated skew was 0.029, well below the threshold of 0.1.

This 42-frame segment was then displayed on a 20 inch LCD computer monitor with 1600×1200 pixel resolution, and recorded with a Canon Elura video camera at a resolution of 640×480. As above, features were tracked in this video segment, from which the skew was estimated. The estimated skew was 0.25, an order of magnitude larger than the skew from the authentic video and well above our threshold of 0.1.

4 Discussion

We have described how to detect a re-projected video that was recorded directly from a projection on a movie or television screen. We have shown that such a re-projection introduces a skew into the camera's intrinsic parameters, which does not normally occur with authentic video. The camera skew can be estimated from two or more video frames from either four or more points on a planar surface, or eight or more arbitrary points. In addition, from four or more points, the camera skew can be estimated from only a single image. This technique can be applied to detect if a single image has been re-photographed (an often cited technique to circumvent some forensic image analysis, e.g., [9]).

Acknowledgments. This work was supported by a Guggenheim Fellowship, a gift from Adobe Systems, Inc., a gift from Microsoft, Inc., a grant from the National Science Foundation (CNS-0708209), a grant from the U.S. Air Force (FA8750-06-C-0011), and by the Institute for Security Technology Studies at Dartmouth College under grants from the Bureau of Justice Assistance (2005-DD-BX-1091) and the U.S. Department of Homeland Security (2006-CS-001-000001). Points of view or opinions in this document are those of the author and do not represent the official position or policies of the U.S. Department of Justice, the U.S. Department of Homeland Security, or any other sponsor.

References

1. Hartley, R.I.: Estimation of relative camera positions for uncalibrated cameras. In: European Conference on Computer Vision, pp. 579–587 (1992)
2. Hartley, R.I.: In defense of the eight-point algorithm. IEEE Transactions on Pattern Analysis and Machine Intelligence 19(6), 580–593 (1997)
3. Hartley, R.I., Zisserman, A.: Multiple View Geometry in Computer Vision, 2nd edn. Cambridge University Press, Cambridge (2004)
4. Huang, T.S., Faugeras, O.D.: Some properties of the E matrix in two-view motion estimation. IEEE Transactions on Pattern Analysis and Machine Intelligence 11(12), 1310–1312 (1989)

5. Johnson, M.K., Farid, H.: Metric measurements on a plane from a single image. Technical Report TR2006-579, Department of Computer Science, Dartmouth College (2006)
6. Longuet-Higgins, H.C.: A computer algorithm for reconstructing a scene from two projections. Nature (10), 133–135 (1981)
7. Lucas, B.D., Kanade, T.: An iterative image registration technique with an application to stereo vision. In: Proceedings of the 7th International Joint Conference on Artificial Intelligence, pp. 674–679 (1981)
8. Mendonça, P.R.S., Cipolla, R.: A simple technique for self-calibration. In: Computer Vision and Pattern Recognition (1999)
9. Popescu, A.C., Farid, H.: Exposing digital forgeries in color filter array interpolated images. IEEE Transactions on Signal Processing 53(10), 3948–3959 (2005)
10. Shi, J., Tomasi, C.: Good features to track. In: IEEE Conference on Computer Vision and Pattern Recognition, pp. 593–600 (1994)
11. Tomasi, C., Kanade, T.: Detection and tracking of point features. Technical Report CMU-CS-91-132, Carnegie Mellon University (1991)
12. Wang, W., Farid, H.: Exposing digital forgeries in video by detecting double MPEG compression. In: ACM Multimedia and Security Workshop (2006)
13. Wang, W., Farid, H.: Exposing digital forgeries in interlaced and de-interlaced video. IEEE Transactions on Information Forensics and Security 3(2), 438–449 (2007)
14. Wang, W., Farid, H.: Exposing digital forgeries in video by detecting duplication. In: ACM Multimedia and Security Workshop (2007)
15. Zhang, Z.: A flexible new technique for camera calibration. IEEE Transactions on Pattern Analysis and Machine Intelligence 22(11), 1330–1334 (2000)

Appendix A

In this appendix, we show that the product of matrices $K_2 P_2 K_1 M_1$ in Equation (8) can be uniquely factored into a product of an upper triangular matrix (intrinsic) and an orthonormal matrix augmented with a fourth column (extrinsic). We begin by expressing the second extrinsic matrix M_1 in terms of its rotation and translation components:

$$K_2 P_2 K_1 M_1 = K_2 P_2 K_1 \left(R_1 \mid t_1 \right). \tag{37}$$

Multiplying R_1 and t_1 each by the 3×3 matrix $(K_2 P_2 K_1)$ yields:

$$K_2 P_2 K_1 M_1 = \left(K_2 P_2 K_1 R_1 \mid K_2 P_2 K_1 t_1 \right) = \left(K_2 P_2 K_1 R_1 \mid t' \right). \tag{38}$$

Consider now the 3×3 matrix $K_2 P_2 K_1 R_1$. Since each of these matrices is non-singular, their product is non-singular. As such, this matrix can be uniquely factored (within a sign), using RQ-factorization, into a product of an upper triangular, U, and orthonormal, O, matrix:

$$K_2 P_2 K_1 M_1 = \lambda \left(UO \mid \tfrac{1}{\lambda} t' \right) = \lambda U \left(O \mid \tfrac{1}{\lambda} U^{-1} t' \right) = \lambda K M, \tag{39}$$

where $K = U$, $M = (O \mid \tfrac{1}{\lambda} U^{-1} t')$, and where λ is chosen so that the $(3,3)$ entry of U has unit value. Note that this factorization leads to a product of a scale factor, λ, an intrinsic matrix K, and an extrinsic matrix, M, as in Equation (9).

Appendix B

In this appendix, we show how to determine the skew, s, in Equation(31), from the estimated matrix $B = K^{-T} K^{-1}$. The intrinsic matrix is parametrized as:

$$K = \begin{pmatrix} f & s & 0 \\ 0 & f & 0 \\ 0 & 0 & 1 \end{pmatrix}. \tag{40}$$

Applying the matrix inverse and multiplication yields:

$$B = K^{-T} K^{-1} = \begin{pmatrix} \frac{1}{f^2} & -\frac{s}{f^3} & 0 \\ -\frac{s}{f^3} & \frac{s^2+f^2}{f^4} & 0 \\ 0 & 0 & 1 \end{pmatrix}. \tag{41}$$

from which:

$$-\frac{b_{12}}{b_{11}} = \frac{s}{f}, \tag{42}$$

where b_{ij} denotes the entries of the matrix B, Equation (29).

Residual Information of Redacted Images Hidden in the Compression Artifacts

Nicholas Zhong-Yang Ho and Ee-Chien Chang

School of Computing, National University of Singapore
iam@nicholasho.net, changec@comp.nus.edu.sg

Abstract. Many digital images need to be redacted before they can be disseminated. A common way to remove the sensitive information replaces the pixels in the sensitive region with black or white values. Our goal is to study the effectiveness of this simple method in purging information. Since digital images are usually lossily compressed via quantization in the frequency domain, each pixel in the spatial domain will be "spread" to its surroundings, similar to the Gibbs-effect, before it is redacted. Hence, information of the original pixels might not be completely purged by replacing pixels in the compressed image. Although such residual information is insufficient to reconstruct the original, it can be exploited when the content has low entropy. We consider a scenario where the goal of the adversary is to identify the original among a few templates. We give two approaches and investigate their effectiveness when the image is compressed using JPEG or wavelet-based compression scheme. We found that, if a redacted image is compressed in higher bit rate compared to the compression of the original image, then the correct template can be identified with noticeable certainty. Although the requirements are stringent, it will not be surprising that redacted images matching the requirements can be found in the public domain. Hence, our findings highlight a subtle attack that must be considered when declassifying images.

1 Introduction

Many digital images need to be redacted before they are disseminated. Consider a scenario where an archive of scanned documents is to be released to the public and some sub-regions in the scanned documents contain sensitive information, such as name, age or address of an individual. These information have to be removed before the whole image is released. In many cases, it is infeasible to redact the hard copies and re-digitize them, since the original hard copies may not be available, not be allowed to be damaged, or be simply too complicated to do so. A typical approach is to digitally redact the image by replacing each sensitive region with other values, for example white, black or some images indicating that this region has been redacted (Fig. 1(b)). Other examples are images of driver's license with sensitive information such as birth date, or images of road accidents with vehicle's plate numbers that needed to be redacted.

K. Solanki, K. Sullivan, and U. Madhow (Eds.): IH 2008, LNCS 5284, pp. 87–101, 2008.
© Springer-Verlag Berlin Heidelberg 2008

An interesting question now is, although the sensitive region has been replaced, can we deduce its content from the redacted image? Most images in the public domain are lossily compressed. Popular compression like JPEG and JPEG2000 quantized the coefficients in the transformed domain. Hence, information of a pixel will "spread" to other pixels in the spatial domain, creating compression artifacts like the Gibbs-effect. In other words, before an image is redacted, information in the sensitive region has already "spread" to surrounding. Hence, even if the sensitive region is replaced, some residual information might still remain in the surrounding regions. Thus, it is clear that there is information leakage through the compression artifacts. The next interesting question is whether such information is sufficient in deriving the content in the redacted region. Although it is unlikely that the original image can be reconstructed, the residual information might be useful when the content of the removed region has low entropy. The image in Fig. 1(a) & 6(a) are such examples. Each redacted region contains either the word "YES" or "NO". Furthermore, the fonts can be derived from other parts of the image. In such a situation, we can assume that an adversary has a few possible templates of the region removed, and his goal is to identify the template that is closest to the original.

Note that we do not consider information leakage that can be inferred from the semantic of the image. An example of such information is the size of the region, which revealed useful information[3, 10]. Another example is words that are not completely covered[10]. We are also not considering physical redaction like markings on the hard copies[10] or using a lower resolution optical device [2]. There are some techniques [14, 9, 1] on document redaction that works on the documents directly, like the tools available to redact PDF documents[8]. We also do not consider these techniques and tools, since they handle the documents directly before the documents are converted to images. Instead, in this paper, we are looking for artifacts that are generated as side-products of image processing. A digital image typically has to undergo a series of image processing operations before they are redacted and published. Many of these artifacts are not purged during redaction and residual information might be hidden in the artifacts. These are the types of information that we wish to exploit in recovering the secrets.

We propose two methods in recovering the secrets. The first method assumes that the adversary has a good estimate of the original raw image in the non-sensitive region, whereas the second method does not make such an assumption.

Note that the redacted image actually has been compressed at least twice: before redaction, and right after redaction. The quantization level applied in these two steps will affect the amount of information retained. Furthermore, it is unlikely that the exact original is one of the templates, due to noise like geometric distortion. In addition, the adversary may not know the exact compression parameters. In our experimental studies, we investigate the proposed methods under various types of noise and uncertainties.

Our experimental results show that the success rate of the adversary is noticeable when the second compression rate is of a much higher quality compared

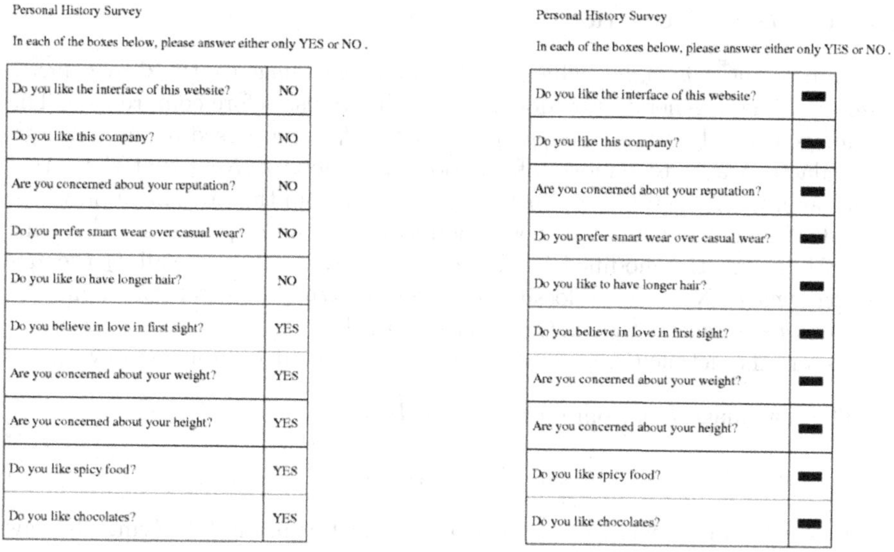

Personal History Survey

In each of the boxes below, please answer either only YES or NO.

Do you like the interface of this website?	NO
Do you like this company?	NO
Are you concerned about your reputation?	NO
Do you prefer smart wear over casual wear?	NO
Do you like to have longer hair?	NO
Do you believe in love in first sight?	YES
Are you concerned about your weight?	YES
Are you concerned about your height?	YES
Do you like spicy food?	YES
Do you like chocolates?	YES

(a)

Personal History Survey

In each of the boxes below, please answer either only YES or NO.

Do you like the interface of this website?	▬
Do you like this company?	▬
Are you concerned about your reputation?	▬
Do you prefer smart wear over casual wear?	▬
Do you like to have longer hair?	▬
Do you believe in love in first sight?	▬
Are you concerned about your weight?	▬
Are you concerned about your height?	▬
Do you like spicy food?	▬
Do you like chocolates?	▬

(b)

Fig. 1. (a) A document image. (b) A redacted version.

to the first compression, and the noise in the template is low. Such requirements are stringent. Nevertheless, it will not be surprising to find some redacted images meeting the requirements. Hence, this subtle attack must still be taken into consideration when redacting sensitive images.

YES   NO

(a)   (b)

Fig. 2. Two templates derived from the redacted image in Fig. 1 (b)

2   Problem Formulation

Let $C_\delta(I)$ be the lossily compressed I with quantization parameter δ in the transformed domain[1]. Given an image I, let $R(I, r, M)$ be the modified image where the pixels of I in the region r is replaced by the *mask* M. The region r is typically rectangular and can be represented by its corners. The mask can be all white, black, or image of symbols indicating that the region has been redacted. Let $T_{I,r}$ to be the sub-image of I in the region r. When it is clear in the context, for simplicity, we write $R(I, r, M)$ as $R(I)$, and the $T_{I,r}$ as T.

---

[1] The type of the parameter δ depends on the compression scheme, for example, it is the quantization table for JPEG.

2.1   Process of Redaction

Let I_0 to be the *raw image*, which can be document image captured by camera, scanner or image generated by document editing tools, before compression. The raw image is lossily compressed, giving $I_1 = C_{\delta_1}(I_0)$ and passed to the redactor. The redactor wants to remove information in a region r. Note that the actual intention of the redactor is to remove information from the raw image I_0, which the redactor does not have. Instead, the redactor replaces pixels in I_1 by some mask M, giving the modified image $I_2 = R(I_1, r, M)$. Let us call I_2 the *raw redacted image*. Next, I_2 is lossily compressed with parameter δ_2, giving the final *redacted image* I_3 that is to be disseminated.

Here are the detailed steps in obtaining the redacted I_3 from the raw I_0.

1. The raw image I_0 is compressed giving I_1.

$$I_1 = C_{\delta_1}(I_0). \tag{1}$$

2. The redactor replaces pixels in region r by the mask M, giving the raw redacted image I_2.

$$I_2 = R(I_1, r, M). \tag{2}$$

3. The raw redacted image is compressed with parameter δ_2, giving the final redacted image I_3.

$$I_3 = C_{\delta_2}(I_2) = C_{\delta_2}(R(C_{\delta_1}(I_0))). \tag{3}$$

2.2   Goal of the Adversary

The adversary has the redacted image I_3 in equation (3). We assume that the adversary knows the mask M and the region redacted r. In addition, he has two templates $\widetilde{T}_0$ and $\widetilde{T}_1$, where one of them is a noisy version of $T_{I_0, r}$. The adversary derives the templates from I_3 together with other background knowledge, for example, a font file. Hence, we write $\widetilde{T}_i = \texttt{Template}(I_3, i)$ for $i = 0, 1$ where $\texttt{Template}$ is the method the adversary employs in guessing the templates. Since it is unreasonable to assume that the algorithm $\texttt{Template}$ is able to output a template that is exactly same as $T_{I_0, r}$, we assume that there is noise like additive white noise and geometric deformation.

Let the *secret* $s = 0$ if $\widetilde{T}_0$ is the noisy version of $T_{I_0, r}$, and $s = 1$ otherwise. The secret can be viewed as a one-bit content that is removed from the image. Let us assume that the raw image is from a source such that the secret is equally likely to be 0 or 1. Thus, without seeing the redacted image I_3, the adversary can correctly guess the secret with probability 0.5.

The goal of the adversary, given I_3, is to correctly guess the secret s. If he succeeds with probability $0.5 + \epsilon$, we say that he achieves an advantage of ϵ in identifying the original. In other words, with the redacted image I_3, he can improve his chances by ϵ. If the adversary has non-zero advantage, the redacted image I_3 must still contain some information of the secret s. Note that this security notion is loosely inspired by the formulation of semantic security [7].

We assume that the adversary knows the redaction process, in particular, the compression scheme in used. He knows the parameter δ_2, which can be easily obtained from the header information in I_3. The adversary does not know δ_1. However, he can obtain an estimation of δ_1 by analyzing the distribution of the coefficients of I_3. There are a number of techniques that estimate the quantization in the studies of image forensic[5, 16, 13] and image steganography[6]. Let the estimated parameter be $\tilde{\delta}_1$.

Below is the summary of what the adversary knows.

- I_3, the redacted image.
- r, M, the region and the mask.
- $\tilde{T}_0, \tilde{T}_1$, two templates obtained using some background information and I_3.
- δ_2, the quantization parameter for the second compression.
- $\tilde{\delta}_1$, an estimation of the parameter δ_1 for the first compression.

In addition, the adversary may be able to reduce compression artifacts from I_3. That is, getting an approximation of $R(I_0, r, M)$. This is possible in some cases. For example, if the image is a document and the adversary is aware of the fonts library, he may attempt to reconstruct the document. If an accurate approximation of $R(I_0, r, M)$ is obtained, then the adversary can easily obtain the compression artifacts $R(I_0, r, M) - I_3$. On the other hand, the size of I_3 is generally much larger than the redacted region r. Thus, total error in estimating $R(I_0, r, M)$ could be significant. Nevertheless, such assumption is still reasonable when the compression scheme is JPEG, which divides the images into small 8×8 blocks. One of our proposed methods exploits this assumption.

- The adversary knows $\tilde{R}$, an approximation of $R(I_0, r, M)$.

The performance of an adversary will be affected by the noise in estimating the templates, the relationship between δ_1 and δ_2, and the noise in estimating δ_1. In addition, the accuracy of the approximation of $R(I_0, r, M)$ if the adversary chooses to exploit this information.

3   Proposed Methods

We will present two general methods. The first method requires and exploits the assumption that the adversary has an approximation of $R(I_0, r, M)$, whereas the second method does not require that. The first method is suitable for JPEG because each 8×8 block is relatively small, and it is feasible to estimate the raw image for the small block accurately. On the other hand, it is not easy to be applied on wavelet-based compression because each coefficient contains information from a large region.

Intuitively, the first method, starting from an estimate of the raw image, simulates the redaction process and then compares the differences between the actual redacted image I_3 and the simulated image in the spatial domain. The second method, starting from an estimate of the raw sub-image in the redacted region, obtains an estimate of the compressed (under the first compression) sub-image. Next the redaction process is simulated, and finally the actual image I_3 is compared with the simulated redacted image in the transformed domain.

3.1   First Method - Comparison in the Spatial Domain

Recall that, given the redacted image I_3 and background knowledge, the adversary can derive $\widetilde{R}$, an approximation of $R(I_0, r, M)$, and two templates T_0 and T_1. Let T_0^β and T_1^β be the geometrically distorted copy of the respective T_0 and T_1 under some parameter β. Let $\mathcal{T}$ be a collection of T_0^β and T_1^β for all β's. For example, $\mathcal{T}$ can be the collection of 18 templates that are translated horizontally, vertically by 1 pixel, and combinations of both.

The main idea is to find the $\widetilde{T} \in \mathcal{T}$ such that a composed image of $\widetilde{T}$ and $\widetilde{R}$ is most similar to I_3. The corresponding undistorted template of $\widetilde{T}$ (that is, either T_0 or T_1), is then declared as the revealed secret.

Here are the detailed steps: For a $\widetilde{T} \in \mathcal{T}$, the following are carried out.

1. A composed image $\widetilde{I}$ is obtained by replacing the redacted region in $\widetilde{R}$ by $\widetilde{T}$.
2. The redaction process described in Section 2.1 is performed on $\widetilde{I}$ using the parameters δ_1 and δ_2. Let the redacted image be $\widetilde{I_3}$.
3. Compute the difference of $\widetilde{I_3}$ and I_3. Let the difference be $d_1(\widetilde{T})$.

Finally, determine the $\widetilde{T}$ that minimizes $d_1(\widetilde{T})$. If $\widetilde{T}$ is derived from T_0, then declare the secret is 0, otherwise, declare the secret as 1.

3.2   Second Method - Comparison in the Transformed Domain

Unlike the previous section, $\widetilde{R}$ is not available. So, a straightforward comparison of the composed image and I_3 cannot be carried out. Instead, in this method, they are compared in the transformed domain. The main idea is as follows: Consider $T_{I_1,r}$, which is the sub image in the redacted region of I_1 (see Section 2 for the notations). The coefficients of the combined image of $T_{I_1,r}$ and I_3 should follow closely the distribution of coefficients quantized with parameter δ_1. Hence, given a $\widetilde{T} \in \mathcal{T}$, the adversary can try to obtain an estimate of $T_{I_1,r}$, which can then be filled into I_3. The distribution of the coefficients of the composed image is then examined. Note that the effect of the second compression is not taken into consideration and is treated as noise.

Here are the detailed steps: For a $\widetilde{T} \in \mathcal{T}$, the following are carried out.

1. An image $\widetilde{I}$ is obtained by replacing the redacted region in I_3 by $\widetilde{T}$.
2. The image $\widetilde{I}$ is compressed with quantization δ_1. Let the compressed image be I_{temp}. The sub-image of I_{temp} in the redacted region is treated as an approximation of $T_{I_1,r}$. Let us write this sub-image as $\widetilde{T}_{I_1,r}$.
3. Compose an image by replacing the redacted region in I_3 by $\widetilde{T}_{I_1,r}$. This can be viewed as an approximation of I_1 and let this image be $\widetilde{I_1}$.

4. Next, $\widetilde{I}_1$ is transformed and quantized one more time with parameter $\widetilde{\delta}_1$. Let $d_2(\widetilde{T})$ be the quantization error.

Finally, determine the $\widetilde{T}$ that minimizes $d_2(\widetilde{T})$. If $\widetilde{T}$ is derived from T_0, then declare that the secret is 0, otherwise, declare the secret as 1.

There are a few ways to measure quantization error in step 4. In our experiments, we employ a weighted Euclidean distance, where the weight is the inverse of the step size. That is, suppose $C = \{c_1, c_2, \ldots, c_k\}$ a set of k coefficients, and s_i is the quantization step size for the coefficient c_i, then the quantization error is:

$$\sqrt{\sum_i^k \frac{1}{s_i} \left| c_i - s_i \cdot round\left(\frac{c_i}{s_i}\right) \right|^2}$$

4   Experiment

Test Images.   We conduct experiments on two sets of images. The first set of images are uniformly randomly generated images, where each pixel is uniformly distributed in the range 0 to 255. The main purpose of using random images is to obtain a large number of images, so as to facilitate analysis of the attack effectiveness against different types and levels of noise.

The second set of images consists of a document image and a mobile phone image. The document image I_1 is shown in Fig. 1(a), and the redacted image shown in Fig. 1(b), where the sensitive information is covered by the black boxes. The size of I_1 is 1034×1494 pixels, and the size of each redacted region is 70×28 pixels. The two templates of "Yes" and "No" shown in Fig. 2 are derived from Fig. 1(b). The mobile phone image is (Fig. 6(a)) captured by a mobile phone with manufacturer recommended parameters.

Compression.   We focus on two image compression schemes - JPEG compression and Wavelet-based compression (used in JPEG2000)[12]. The JPEG quantization matrices used in our experiments are obtained from a Matlab JPEG Toolbox by Sallee [15]. Each quality value (ranging from 0 to 100) is assigned a quantization matrix. Appendix A shows some matrices and their corresponding quality values.

For the wavelet-based compression, we use the Cohen-Daubechies-Feauveau (CDF) 9/7 wavelet transform [4]. The lossy compression is done by applying scalar quantization on the coefficients. The subsequent lossless compression does not play a role in our problem.

4.1   Random JPEG Images

General setting.   Since JPEG divides an image into 8×8 blocks and lossily compresses the blocks independently, it is suffice to work on random images of size 8×8. The experiments are conducted with varying levels of noise parameters, and are designed to aid in the analysis of how the following affect the adversary's success rate:

1. The area redacted. Specifically, the number of columns redacted in a block.
2. The parameters of the two JPEG compression, δ_1 and δ_2.
3. Noise in the templates.
4. The uncertainty in obtaining the first compression parameter $\widetilde{\delta}_1$.
5. The noise in $\widetilde{R}$.

Generating the random images and templates. Without loss of generality, let the secret s be 0. Here are the steps in preparing the following information for the adversary: a redacted random image I_3, the templates T_0 and T_1, and the estimated redacted image $\widetilde{R}$.

1. Let I_0 be a uniformly and randomly generated 8×8 pixels block.
2. Extract template T_0 from image I_0. Extract template T_1 from another randomly generated 8×8 pixels block.
3. Compress image I_0 at JPEG compression quality δ_1 to get I_1.
4. Image I_1 is redacted and compressed at JPEG compression quality δ_2 to produce the redacted image I_3. (Equations (2) and (3))
5. Gaussian white noise is added to I_0, which in turn gives $\widetilde{R}$. Noise is also added to T_0 and T_1 to give $\widetilde{T}_0$ and $\widetilde{T}_1$.

Success rate. We call the variance of the white noise as the noise level. Given the randomly generated I_3, $\widetilde{T}_0$ and $\widetilde{T}_1$, the proposed method is carried out to produce a guess of the secret. For each set of parameters, the experiment is repeated for 1000 samples of randomly generated I_3, $\widetilde{T}_0$ and $\widetilde{T}_1$. The ratio of the correct guess is the estimated success rate. Note that the success rate is for a single block. If the image in question contains multiple blocks along the boundary of the redacted region, the adversary can make a decision using majority vote, which significantly improves the overall success rate.

Effect of the area redacted. Fig. 3(b) shows the success rate for various values of δ_2, with δ_1 fixed at 50. Gaussian white noise with variance = 50 has been added into the templates. We have repeated the experiment with $1, 2, \ldots, 7$ columns redacted. The results show that the larger the area of redaction, the lower the success rate near the larger δ_2 values.

Effect of the two JPEG compression parameters δ_1 and δ_2. Fig. 3(b) also shows that at higher δ_2 values, the success rate of the adversary improves almost linearly. However, at the smaller values of δ_2, success rate falls to 0.5.

Effect of noise in the templates. Fig. 3(c) shows the success rate of curves for various noise levels, where $\delta_1 = 50$ and $\delta_2 = 95$. Under the noise, each pixel in the template is corrupted by additive Gaussian white noise. The results show that as the amount of Gaussian white noise is added into the templates, the success rate decreases.

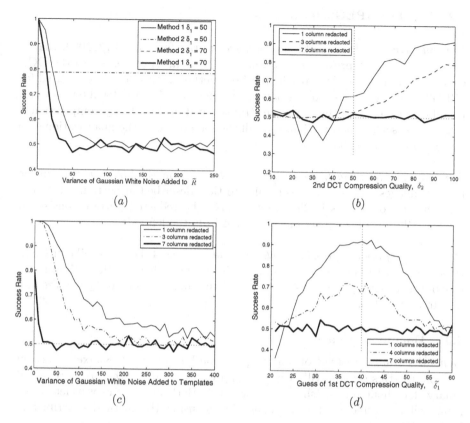

Fig. 3. (a) Success rate for image block, $\delta_1 = 50, 70$, $\delta_2 = 95$. All curves are results of redacting 3 columns. Both lines generated by the second method have Gaussian white noise (variance is 50 per pixel) added to templates. (b) Success rate of second method for image block, $\delta_1 = 50$ (indicated by the vertical line), Gaussian white noise (variance = 50) added to templates. (c) Success rate of second method for image block, $\delta_1 = 50$, $\delta_2 = 95$. (d) Success rate of second method for image against adversary's guess of first compression $\widetilde{\delta_1}$, The actual $\delta_1 = 40$ is indicated by the vertical line. The parameter $\delta_2 = 90$, and variance of Gaussian white noise added to templates is 50 (per pixel).

Effect of adversary guessing δ_1 wrongly. Fig. 3(d) shows the success rates for guessing δ_1, where actual $\delta_1 = 40$, $\delta_2 = 90$. The results in the figure shows that the closer the adversary's guess of δ_1 is to the actual δ_1, the better the success rates of the adversary to reveal the data hidden by redaction.

Effect of accuracy of approximating R on adversary success rate. Fig. 3(a) shows the success rate for both methods at two different values of $\delta_1 = 50, 70$ as accuracy of approximating $\widetilde{R}$ varies. In the figure, we can see that the first method's success rate is very sensitive to the accuracy of approximating $\widetilde{R}$. With noise level above 25 to 30, the first method fares worse than the second method.

4.2   Random JPEG2000 Images

General Setting.   Due to the use of wavelet transform in JPEG2000, the visual artifacts are "spread" over a much wider area, as compared to the DCT compression artifacts. As a result, the first method is unsuitable to be used for JPEG2000 images. Thus, in this paper, only the second method will be discussed for all experiments involving wavelet transformed images. Lossy compression is achieved by scalar quantization. We call the reciprocals of the quantization step the compression quality.

Generation of Random Images and Template.   The method of generation of the random images and template is similar to that described in Section 4.1 except that the size of images is 256×256 pixels. The redacted portion consists of vertical columns of the pixel block starting from the left side.

Parameters of the compression quality δ_1 and δ_2.   Fig. 4 shows a similar trend as those seen in JPEG experiments so far. That is, at higher δ_2 values, the success rate of the adversary improves. However, at the smaller values of δ_2, success rate falls to around 0.5.

4.3   Document Image

General setting.   Instead of applying the method on a 8×8 pixels block in Section 4.1, this section will deal with applying the 2nd method on a redacted binary document image (shown in Fig. 1(a)). Both JPEG and wavelet transform will be tested on the document image using the method described in Section 3.2.

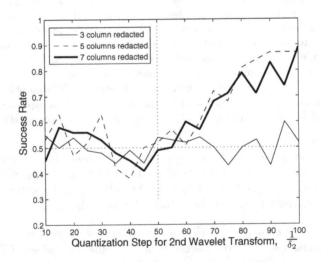

Fig. 4. Success rate for image JPEG2000 block using second method, $\delta_1 = 50$ (indicated by the vertical line), Gaussian white noise (variance = 10) added to templates

Let I_0 be the raw image shown in Fig. 1(a). The redacted image I_2 and templates T_0 and T_1 are prepared in the following way:

1. Compress image I_0 with quality δ_1 to give I_1.
2. Five "YES" and "NO" subimages are extracted from I_0, from which the two templates "YES" and "NO" are derived manually.
3. Image I_1 is redacted and compressed with quality δ_2 to produce image I_3 shown in Fig. 1(b). (Equations (2) and (3))
4. In addition, during guessing, in order to correct the geometric distortion, each template is translated horizontally and vertically by at most a pixel. Thus, there are a total of translated 9 copies for each template.

Since JPEG involves block-wise compression, the success rate in Fig. 5(a) is calculated by collectively comparing all the blocks intersecting the border of the redacted zone. As for JPEG2000, since it does not involve block-wise transformations, the whole document is compared to determine the success rate in Fig. 5(b).

Relationship of δ_1 and δ_2 for JPEG Compression. In Fig. 5(a), observe that when the second compression $\delta_2 < 65$, the chances of the adversary are only as good as guessing.

Relationship of δ_1 and δ_2 for Wavelet Transform. Fig. 5(b) shows the success rate for varying values of δ_1, where $\delta_2 = 1/100$. The values listed on the horizontal axis refers to the quantization step size of δ_1 from 1 to 1/100. When $\delta_1 = 1/50$ and 1/100, the percentage of zeros among all coefficients is 85.04% and 83.88% respectively. Note that these percentage reflect the compression rate [11]. As we can see from the figure, the success rate is fairly high when the compression parameter δ_2 is significantly more than δ_1. Note the interesting zig-zag

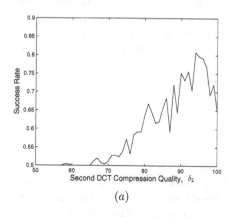
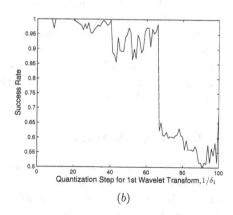

(a)   (b)

Fig. 5. (a) Success rate for binary image using second method with JPEG compression quality $\delta_1 = 50$ (b) Success rate for binary image using second method with wavelet transform quantization step $\delta_2 = 1/100$

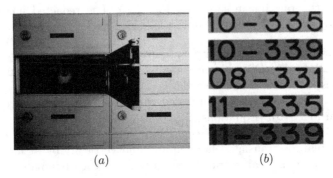

(a)   (b)

Fig. 6. (a) Image captured by a Nokia 6125 mobile phone and then redacted. (b) Templates of postal boxes.

shape of the curve. We suspect that the success rate depends on whether $(1/\delta_1)$ is an integer multiple of $(1/\delta_2)$. Further investigations are required.

4.4 Mobile Phone Camera Test

A postal box image was taken with a Nokia 6125 mobile phone ("normal" JPEG compression quality, image size at 640×480, grey scale effect). This image is then redacted and compressed with quality $\delta_2 = 90$ as shown in Fig. 6(a). The redacted text in the top and bottom left is "10-335" and "10-339" respectively. We assume that the adversary knows the first compression quality δ_1, and he knows that the text is one of the five candidates indicated in Fig. 7.

To prepare the templates, high quality 5 megapixels images of similar postal boxes were taken with a FujiFilm FinePix 31fd digital camera. The high quality images were then digitally adjusted to estimate the templates as shown in Fig. 6(b). Note that all the templates in Fig. 6(b) are derived from the images taken by the FujiFilm camera.

A test using the second method was carried out to recover the redacted information at the top and bottom left black boxes, and the results is tabulated in Fig. 7. From the left table in Fig. 7, the adversary can narrow the candidate down to "10-335" and "10-339". In the right table, the correct template "10-339" gives significantly lower errors.

5 Counter Measure

Since JPEG quantizes the block independently, by removing the whole 8×8 pixel block, all compression artifacts will be purged. If the above measures are not possible, then the image should be compressed in a lower bit rate after redaction. Alternatively, noise can be added to the redacted regions and its surrounding regions before the second compression. Additional studies are required to determine the level of noise required to prevent leakage of information in the redacted images.

Results for Top Left Box

Data Name	Quantization Error
Random Templates	123.0
10-335	92.6
10-339	92.2
08-331	95.0
11-335	96.9
11-339	97.3

Results for Bottom Left Box

Data Name	Quantization Error
Random Templates	104.9
10-335	69.1
10-339	67.1
08-331	71.7
11-335	72.8
11-339	73.7

Fig. 7. Results of second method on the redacted image in Fig. 6(a)

6 Conclusion

In this paper, we argue that information leftover in the compression artifacts may contain sufficient information to recover the redacted secret. We studied the redaction process and identified a few parameters that affect the success rate of the adversary. Experiment results show that it is possible to recover the secret hidden within the compression artifacts, albeit effective only under stringent conditions, in particular the redacted image is compressed in higher bit rate than the original image. Although the requirements are stringent, nevertheless, such subtle attack must still be taken into consideration when redacting sensitive images. Furthermore, as mobile camera phones are gaining popularity, there could be more publicly available images which are first compressed with lower quality before they are redacted. It would also be interesting to further explore other types of image processing artifacts to determine which of them can also be exploited to reveal hidden information.

References

[1] Anderson, G.B., Gross, B.P., Marlin, J.W., Tucker, V.D.: Method for storing and retrieving annotations and redactions in final form documents. US Patent (5581682) (1996)

[2] Berger, S., Kjeldsen, R., Pinhanez, C., Podlaseck, M., Narayanaswami, C., Raghunath, M.: Using symbiotic displays to view sensitive information in public. In: IEEE International Conference on Pervasive Computing and Communications, pp. 139–148 (2005)

[3] Butler, D.: US intelligence exposed as student decodes Iraq memo. Nature 429, 116 (2004)

[4] Daubechies, I.: Ten Lecture Notes on Wavelets. SIAM, Philadelphia (1992)

[5] Fan, Z., de Queiroz, R.: Identification of bitmap compression history: Jpeg detection and quantizer estimation. IEEE Transaction of Image Processing 12, 230–235 (2003)

[6] Fridrich, J., Goljan, M., Du, R.: Steganalysis based on jpeg compatibility. In: SPIE Multimedia Systems and Applications, pp. 275–280 (2001)

[7] Goldwasser, S., Micali, S.: Probabilistic encryption. Journal of Computer and System Sciences 28, 270–299 (1984)

[8] Johnson, D.: Redacting pdf files: A survey of tools. Adobe Acrobat User community Newsletter (2006), http://www.acrobatusers.com/

[9] Kelly, D., Foster, B.: A process for electronic document redaction. WO Patent (WO/2006/041318) (2006)

[10] Lopresti, D., Spitz, A.L.: Quantifying information leakage in document redaction. In: 1st ACM workshop on Hardcopy Document Processing, pp. 63–69 (2004)

[11] Mallat, S.: A Wavelet Tour of Signal Processing. Academic Press, London (1999)

[12] Marcellin, M.W., Gormish, M.J., Bilgin, A., Boliek, M.P.: An overview of JPEG-2000. In: IEEE Data Compression Conference, pp. 523–541 (2000)

[13] Popescu, A.C.: Statistical tools for digital image forensics (2004)

[14] Quaeler, L., Charnock, E., Dhakouani, N.: Method and apparatus to provide a unified redaction system. United States Patent and Trademark Office (Application number: 20070030528) (2007)

[15] Sallee, P.: Matlab JPEG toolbox,
http://www.philsallee.com/jpegtbx/index.html

[16] Ye, S., Sun, Q., Chang, E.-C.: Detecting digital image forgeries by measuring inconsistencies of blocking artifact. In: IEEE International Conference on Multimedia and Expo. (2007)

A   Quantization Matrices Used in JPEG Compressions

The matrices shown in Fig. 8 are some of the quantization matrices generated using the Matlab JPEG Toolbox by P. Sallee. The Matlab JPEG Toolbox was used because it adheres to the JPEG specification, section K.1, thus giving the closest lossy compression behavior to any generic JPEG image file.

80	55	50	80	120	100	255	305
60	60	70	95	130	290	300	275
70	65	80	120	200	285	345	280
70	85	110	145	255	435	400	310
90	110	185	280	340	545	515	385
120	175	275	320	405	520	565	460
245	320	390	435	515	605	600	505
360	460	475	490	560	500	515	495

(a)

27	18	17	27	40	67	85	102
20	20	23	32	43	97	100	92
23	22	27	40	67	95	115	93
23	28	37	48	85	145	133	103
30	37	62	93	113	182	172	128
40	58	92	107	135	173	188	153
82	107	130	145	172	202	200	168
120	153	158	163	187	167	172	165

(b)

16	11	10	16	24	40	51	61
12	12	14	19	26	58	60	55
14	13	16	24	40	57	69	56
14	17	22	29	51	87	80	62
18	22	37	56	68	109	103	77
24	35	55	64	81	104	113	92
49	64	78	87	103	121	120	101
72	92	95	98	112	100	103	99

(c)

1	1	1	1	1	1	1	1
1	1	1	1	1	1	1	1
1	1	1	1	1	1	1	1
1	1	1	1	1	1	1	1
1	1	1	1	1	1	1	1
1	1	1	1	1	1	1	1
1	1	1	1	1	1	1	1
1	1	1	1	1	1	1	1

(d)

Fig. 8. Quantization matrices used in JPEG compression according to the JPEG specifications: (a) Quality = 10% (b) Quality = 30% (c) Quality = 50% (d) Quality = 100%

Trusted Integrated Circuits: A Nondestructive Hidden Characteristics Extraction Approach

Yousra Alkabani[1], Farinaz Koushanfar[1,2], Negar Kiyavash[3], and Miodrag Potkonjak[4]

[1] Rice University CS Dept.
[2] Rice University ECE Dept.
[3] UIUC CS Dept.
[4] UCLA CS Dept.

Abstract. We have developed a methodology for unique identification of integrated circuits (ICs) that addresses *untrusted fabrication* and other security problems. The new method leverages *nondestructive gate-level characterization* of ICs post-manufacturing, revealing the hidden and *unclonable* uniqueness of each IC. The IC characterization uses the externally measured leakage currents for multiple input vectors. We have derived several optimization techniques for gate-level characterization. The probability of collision of IDs in presence of intra- and inter-chip correlations is computed. We also introduce a number of novel security and authentication protocols, such as *hardware metering*, *challenge-based authentication* and *prevention of software piracy*, that leverage the extraction of a unique ID for each IC. Experimental evaluations of the proposed approach on a large set of benchmark examples reveals its effectiveness even in presence of measurement errors.

1 Introduction

Recently, manufacturing variability (MV) emerged as a mechanism for providing IC security [11,12]. It was used for tasks such as authentication [4,10,19]. So far, the work in this area has relied on addition of new circuitry or specialized processes to achieve security. In order to address this limitation, we have developed a method for accurate characterization of an arbitrary IC at the gate level. Characterization is done in a nondestructive way, without the need for additional circuitry or special processes. The extracted characteristics can be translated in a unique and unclonable ID for each IC and form the starting point for the creation of variety of security protocols.

Probably the best way to introduce the new security approach is to consider a small example shown in Figure 1 that consists of 4 NAND gates with two inputs (NAND2). Table (b) shows the leakage current of a nominal NAND2 gate for different sets of inputs. However, in deep-submicron technologies, the current greatly varies from one IC to another due to MV. For example, in 65nm technology, the leakage currents of the same gate on two different ICs may scale by a factor of 20 [14]. Table (c) shows an example of possible scaling factors for

K. Solanki, K. Sullivan, and U. Madhow (Eds.): IH 2008, LNCS 5284, pp. 102–117, 2008.

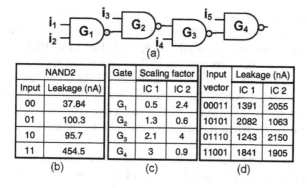

NAND2		Gate	Scaling factor		Input	Leakage (nA)	
Input	Leakage (nA)		IC 1	IC 2	vector	IC 1	IC 2
00	37.84	G_1	0.5	2.4	00011	1391	2055
01	100.3	G_2	1.3	0.6	10101	2082	1063
10	95.7	G_3	2.1	4	01110	1243	2150
11	454.5	G_4	3	0.9	11001	1841	1905
(b)		(c)			(d)		

Fig. 1. (a) A design consisting of 4 NAND2 gates, (b) leakage current vs. input for NAND2,(c) scaling factors of gates on two ICs, and (d) total leakages of ICs for different input vectors

the four gates in two circuits, denoted by IC1 and IC2. Table (d) shows leakage power in IC1 and IC2 for different input vectors.

It is easy to see that from these measurements, we can calculate the leakage power of each gate in both ICs. Once the scaling factor of each gate is extracted, we can use it as the circuit's ID. For instance, if we standardize that a scaling factor larger than 1 is denoted by one in the pertinent ID and zero otherwise, the ID of IC1 is 0111 and the ID of IC2 is 1010. For a more realistic IC with millions of gates, limited number of primary inputs and outputs, and a limited number of scanned flip-flops, the gate characterization task is much more challenging, but the chances for collision of IDs for any two ICs are much lower. In this paper, we introduce and analyze such characteristic extraction, ID assignment and uniqueness evaluation techniques.

We have two key conceptual and technical goals. The first is to demonstrate how nondestructive techniques for ICs can be used to extract unique and unclonable IDs from each chip for a given design. The second strategic objective is to introduce a new spectrum of security protocols that leverage the unique and irreproducible IDs by connecting them to the functionality of hardware or software executed on the IC. To achieve the two goals, one needs to address a system of demanding engineering, optimization, and modeling tasks. In the remainder of the manuscript, we show that the tasks can be solved in very elegant and efficient ways.

2   Related Work

The idea of adding circuitry that uses the manufacturing variability for generating a unique random ID for each IC with a single mask was proposed by a number of authors [11,12,18]. The IDs do not provide a measure of trust, as they are separated from the functionality and thus, are easy to tamper and remove.

A group of MIT researchers has focused on the idea of utilizing the variability-based delays for security and authentication purposes [4,10,19]. They add a circuitry that implements the physically unclonable function (PUF) which maps a set of challenges to a set of responses. PUFs are unique since the process variations result in significant fluctuations in delays of chips coming from the same mask. PUFs ensure that each IC has a unique set of outputs for each input vector. The method stores a database of the challenge-response pairs for each IC. An IC is authenticated when it correctly responds to the output of one or more challenge inputs.

Note that even though the PUF-based and other random ID generation circuits find usage in authentication devices and other security scenarios, they are radically different from the novel scheme proposed in this paper. Unlike the earlier approaches [11,12,18,4,10,19], the new method does not require addition of any circuitry, database of challenge-response sets, or special process technology. All what is needed is storing the unique ID for each chip. Furthermore, we will show how noninvasive ID extraction from the I/O measurements from the external pins can be used in new security and protection mechanisms.

In FPGA and other programmable platforms adding unique programmable fingerprints for each IC was proposed [9], but the techniques are not directly applicable to application specific integrated circuits (ASICs). In ASICs, giving a unique ID to each IC by adding a small programmable part to the control path of the design post-fabrication was pursued as well [8]. The technique does not exploit the manufacturing variability and only leverages the equivalence of various synthesized control paths to identify each circuit.

The prior work in trusted IC also consists of a number of watermarking schemes [21,15,7,16]. A comprehensive survey of fingerprinting and watermarking schemes can be found in [16]. Note that, watermarking is a radically different problem than unique identification. Watermarking addresses the problem of uniquely identifying each intellectual property (IP) core and not each IC.

3   Preliminaries

3.1   Background

Circuit model. The full specification of the circuit's functionality from input/output is assumed to be publicly available. The designer has post-synthesis design knowledge, including the exact mapping of the logic to gates in the technology library. The table that specifies leakage current values for each library gate versus the input state is also available.

Model of variations. Intensive scaling of CMOS to its physical limitations results in high variability of circuit-level parameters such as delay and leakage. Variations may be temporal or spatial. Our method leverages the spatial variations while it alleviates the temporal ones by introducing robust measures. Spatial variations are divided into two categories: (i) inter-chip variations, or the chip-to-chip fluctuations; and (ii) intra-chip variations, present inside one chip. We employ the variation model described in [17] where the multivariate normal distribution (MVN) is used for modeling all random components across the chip and intra-chip correlations. Furthermore, the grid model that partitions the space into grids is used; devices within the same grid are highly correlated and devices in further grids are correlated proportional to their distances.

Model of the leakage current. Leakage current is also a function of the process fluctuations. The leakage model we use here was proposed in [1]: the model considers the subthreshold leakage (I_{sub}) and the gate tunneling leakage (I_{gate}) for each gate. Both currents are modeled as exponential functions that can be approximated by a lognormal distribution. The full-chip leakage distribution is the sum of the lognormal distributions of all gates considering spatial correlations. The sum is not theoretically known to have a closed form, but can be well approximated as a lognormal distribution using Wilkinson's method [1].

3.2 Flow

The proposed unique chip identification has three phases: (i) gate-level characterization method and improving its performance; (ii) translation of gate characteristics into IDs.

Phase (i). The gate level characteristics that are subject to variations are extracted, e.g., such as the gate delays on a specific IC or its leakage current. In this paper we use the leakage current because of its properties such as high variability, coverage of all gates in each measurements, and suitability for treatment using provably optimal optimization techniques of polynomial complexity such as linear programming. It is also possible to add interconnect leakages but we did not include it since it has much less visible fluctuations.

The first phase itself has four steps: (i) input vector generation applying multiple inputs to the circuit; (ii) execution and analysis of measurements where the goal is to conduct measurements in the most effective way and to characterize errors; (iii) solving the systems of equations obtained by using the measurements. Depending on the error model and the structure of equations formed, different methods may be used;and (iv) statistical analysis to evaluate results' stability.

A key observation is that not all gate scaling factors have to be extracted for ID creation. In a number of relatively common designs, it is impossible to extract the characteristics of all gates. Note that there are a few techniques that indirectly alleviate requirements for very accurate measurements. For instance, if one increases the supply voltage or temperature, the leakage increases making the relative errors of measurements lower for the same measurement equipment.

Phase (ii). In this phase, the gate characteristics are translated (coded) into the corresponding IDs. We have developed two techniques that emphasize different trade-offs between the resiliency against measurement errors and circuit variations on one side and probability of collision on the other side.

Phase (iii). Once we have gate level characteristics for a sufficiently large number of gates and the coded IDs, we address potential security attacks by analyzing the technique with respect to the likelihood of ID collision.

Note that many new cryptographical, security, IPP and DRM protocols are enabled by the proposed method. The main idea is to leverage intrinsic and unclonable unique chip ID to create a task that can be easily completed in a short period of time on the IC, and requires many orders of time longer if one does not have access to the IC. In interest of brevity, we omit the discussion in this paper.

4   Nondestructive Extraction of IC Characteristics

The goal is to extract the gate-level properties of an IC in a noninvasive way (by external I/O measurement) such that the overhead in terms of the time and resources is minimized, while the method does not require a specific instrumentation other than the classical test equipment. Note that the destructive measurement of ICs for the purpose of characteristics extraction is done in industrial practice, but the method renders the IC unusable after testing [3]. Other noninvasive methods such as X-ray imaging are nonefficient and slow.

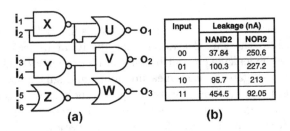

Input	Leakage (nA)	
	NAND2	NOR2
00	37.84	250.6
01	100.3	227.2
10	95.7	213
11	454.5	92.05

(a)   (b)

Fig. 2. (a) A small circuit consisting of NAND2 and NOR2 gates, (b) leakage current vs. input of the gates

Perhaps an example would be the best way to illustrate the nondestructive extraction method by using the leakage current measurements. In Figure 2(a) we show a small circuit consisting of 6 NAND2 and NOR2 gates X, Y, Z, U, V, and W. The circuit has 6 primary inputs and three primary outputs. The table in Figure 2(b) presents the leakage current of the two gate types versus the input to the gate, where the gate leakage has a strong dependence on its inputs [1].

Assume that all the gate inputs are set to 0, i.e., $\{i_1,i_2,i_3,i_4,i_5,i_6\}$=000000. On each chip one can measure the leakage current resulting from this input, denoted by $I_{leak}(000000)$. The error in this measurement is denoted by e_1. The leakage current of the circuit can be written in terms of the individual gates. Let us denote the leakage currents of the nominal-sized 2-input NOR and NAND gates by $I_{NAND}(.)$ and $I_{NOR}(.)$ respectively, where the arguments inside the parentheses are the inputs to the gate. Because of MV the exact gate leakage

---

[1] Such tables are standard and readily available. The table in Figure 2(b) is directly taken from the leakage current measurements by Yuan and Qu [22].

values deviate from the nominal value. We use a scaling coefficient times the nominal value to express the exact leakage of the gate. For the gates in Figure 2(a), we denote the scaling factors by s_X, s_Y, s_Z, s_U, s_V, and s_W.

$$
\begin{aligned}
I_{leak}(000000) + e_1 &= s_X I_{NAND}(00) + s_Y I_{NAND}(00) \\
&\quad + s_Z I_{NOR}(00) + s_U I_{NOR}(01) \\
&\quad + s_V I_{NAND}(11) + s_W I_{NOR}(11); \\
I_{leak}(010101) + e_2 &= s_X I_{NAND}(01) + s_Y I_{NAND}(01) \\
&\quad + s_Z I_{NOR}(01) + s_U I_{NOR}(01) \\
&\quad + s_V I_{NAND}(00) + s_W I_{NOR}(01); \\
I_{leak}(\ldots) + e_i &= \ldots; \qquad i = 4\ldots, M
\end{aligned}
\tag{1}
$$

Similarly, one can apply M different inputs to the circuit and write M linear relationships for the measured leakage as demonstrated in the Equation Set 1. To find the unknown scaling factors, we form an optimization framework, where the equations are the constraints of the optimization and the objective function (OF) is to optimize a specific norm of the measurement error. Let $f(E)$ denote a function for measuring a metric of errors, where $E=\{e_i\}_{i=1}^{M}$. The OF is written as min $f(E)$. Common forms of the f that are used in minimization are the L_p norms of error that are defined as: $L_p=(\sum_{m=1}^{M} w_m |e_m|^p)^{1/p}$ for $1 \leq p < \infty$; and $L_p=\max_{m=1}^{M} w_m |e_m|$ if $p = \infty$.

Independence of the Equations. While in principle one would be able to solve for and to find the scaling factor of each gate, it is possible to have ambiguous gates. The ambiguous gates are those whose combination always gets the same ratio of coefficients and are indistinguishable. As a simple example for an ambiguous combination take three inverters A, B, and C with scaling factors s_A, s_B, and s_C that are placed in series in the middle of the circuit. No matter which input combination is used, the term $s_A I_{inv}(0) + s_B I_{inv}(1) + s_C I_{inv}(0)$ or the term $s_A I_{inv}(1) + s_B I_i nv(0) + s_C I_{inv}(1)$ would be present in the circuit. It is impossible to distinguish between s_A and s_C since they always have the same coefficient. Even though the three inverter example is an extreme case, in real circuits, ambiguous cases occur (largely because of reconvergent fanout) and should be taken into account. We add a check that scans the equations and figures out the gate combinations that are ambiguous and consolidates them into one entity. The characteristics of the ambiguous gates will not be used in the final identification scheme.

Solving the Optimization Problem. The optimization problem may take many different formats depending on the form of the objective function. Generally speaking, the L_p error norms and the maximum likelihood determine a nonlinear OF with linear constraints which requires a nonlinear optimization method. Although many nonlinear solvers exist, it is well-known that the general non-linear optimization with uncertainty is prone to get stuck at local minima and may not be optimally solved. However, for a common class of the nondestructive extraction problems it is possible to cast the problems as linear, quadratic, or convex optimization that are easier to solve:

1. In case of minimizing L_1 norm, the optimization problem can be written in form of a linear program as follows: $\min \sum_{m=1}^{M} |e_m|$, subject to the M constraints presented in Equation Set 1. The absolute function is nonlinear, but we convert it to a linear one by introducing m auxiliary variables e_m^+ and adding $2m$ constraints, i.e., for each m, $e_m^+ \geq e_m$ and $e_m^+ \geq -e_m$. The linear objective function is: $\min \sum_{m=1}^{M} e_m^+$.

2. In case of the L_2 norm, the OF is: $\min \sqrt{\sum_{m=1}^{M} e_m^2}$, whose minimization is equivalent to $\min \sum_{m=1}^{M} e_m^2$. The optimization is a quadratic program.

3. To minimize the L_∞ norm, we define a new variable e_{max}. The OF is then $\min e_{max}$. We also add constraints that satisfy the L_∞ requirements, i.e., $e_{max} \leq e_m$ for $m=1, \ldots, M$ that can be also solved by a linear program.

4. If one assumes the errors are i.i.d Gaussian distribution $\mathcal{N}(0, \sigma^2)$, The log-likelihood function would be: $\max \sum_{m=1}^{M} log(\exp - \frac{e_m^2}{2\sigma^2}) \equiv \max \sum_{m=1}^{M} -e_m^2 \equiv \min \sum_{m=1}^{M} e_m^2$. This is equivalent to the quadratic program that minimizes the L_2 norm of the errors.

5   Formation and Analysis of IDs

5.1   Robust Coding for IDs

We form digital IDs using the extracted characteristics of the gates in the following way. The starting points are the analog values of the scaling factors. The values are quantized and concatenated to form digital IDs. We enforce a number of desiderata on this process, including low computational requirement, low probability of collision of two IDs, and stability and robustness against IC aging [6] and change in environmental conditions such as supply voltage and temperature. Note that the gate ordering and the coding methods must be easy to check and standardized. To have a suitable and standard notation, we introduce an *indicator string* for each IC. The length of the indicator string is equal to the number of gates in the design's netlist. The order of the gates in the netlist corresponds to their x and y placement coordinates. If a gate has a lower x coordinate, it has a lower position. If two gates have equal x coordinates, the gate with the smaller y, has a lower position. We observed that not all the characteristics of all ICs were extractable. Luckily, not all of them are needed for identifying one IC because on modern designs there are many gates. If a gate is used for identification, its corresponding indicator bit would be 1. Otherwise, it is 0. To improve stability and robustness, we calculate the normalized characteristics against leakage power of all gates on the pertinent IC. It has been experimentally proven that the environmental variations mostly change the characteristics of all the affected gates in the same way [20].

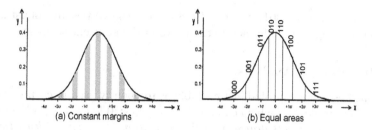

Fig. 3. Selecting identification codes that are robust: (a) margin coding with constant margins, and (b) equiareal coding with equal areas

Robust Translation into Codes. When converting the analog values into binary, it is important to consider the distribution of the analog values. After extracting the IC characteristics, we create a histogram of of the extracted values. We use two different methods for binary coding: (i) margin coding, and (ii) equiareal coding. Both schemes use the probability density function (PDF) of the extracted characteristics, obtained by smoothing of the histogram.

Margin coding. This scheme is illustrated in Figure 3(a). It finds a robust binary conversion of the analog codes by partitioning the PDF into regions. The regions are either approved (shown as white on the figure) or banned (shown as dark). The white and dark regions are interleaved. If the characteristics of a gate falls into the banned region, it will not be considered in the ID formation and its corresponding bit would be set to zero in the indicator string. If an analog value falls in the approved region, the corresponding value in the indicator string is 1. Each approved analog value obtains a binary code of its partition. The length of the margin codes depend on the number of partitions. The large number of partitions increases the length of IDs and decreases the robustness of margins. Thus, the number of partitions should provide a good trade-off between the length of the IDs and robustness. Note that, the dark partitions have uniform size as shown in Figure 3(a). If we denote the width of one partition by w, then we can detect any changes in the characteristics of amplitude w or less and correct the changes of the maximum size $\frac{w}{2}$.

Equiareal coding. This coding scheme partitions the region into segments so that the area under the PDF curve of all segments are equal. Thus, the probability of having a characteristic belonging to one area is the same for all segments in order to maximize the entropy of IDs. An example is shown in Figure 3(b) where the PDF is partitioned into 8 segments and thus, a 3-bit code can be used to identify each segment. All segments are used for ID creation. The robustness is achieved by taking into account the order of segments. Hence, changing the value by a relatively small amount translates into shifting to previous or the next segment. The encoding scheme takes into account such changes. For example, assume that in Figure 3(b), the scale factor of a gate was encoded as 011. For ID verification, the scale factor of the same gate is considered to be equal to any gate that has code 001, 011, or 010. So, the assigned IDs are robust against variations as long as the characteristics stays in the adjacent segment.

5.2 Probabilistic Analysis

One of the best-known probabilistic problems frequently used in cryptography is the birthday problem [2] which can be abstracted as: *What is the probability that among K possible objects drawn from the population $\{1,\ldots,n\}$ at least two have the same value.* Our problem requires solving generalized version of birthday problem with non-uniform probabilities that is defined as: *Given a collection of K binary sequences, each of length M; what is the probability of collision among the K strings?*

The above problem is a generalization of the birthday problem in the sense that, the strings are not required to be equally likely. There are total of $n = 2^M$ binary length M sequences. Let P_i denote the probability that the ID of the IC is sequence i and let $\mathbf{P} = (P_1,\ldots,P_n)$ be the collection of probabilities of all $n = 2^M$ sequences. In case of birthday problem all the probabilities P_i are equally likely and we can represent them by $\mathbf{n}^{-1} = (\frac{1}{n},\ldots,\frac{1}{n})$. Then probability of no match between K sequences is given by $P(M,K,\mathbf{n}^{-1}) = \frac{2^M!}{K^{2M}(2^M-K)!}$, and the probability of collision is $P(collision) = 1 - \frac{2^M!}{K^{2M}(2^M-K)!}$. When the sequences are not equally likely, probability of collision is given by

$$P(collision) = 1 - P(M,K,\mathbf{P})$$
$$= 1 - K! \sum_{1\leq\nu_1<\ldots<\nu_K\leq n} P_{\nu_1}P_{\nu_2}\ldots P_{\nu_K}, \qquad (2)$$

where $P(M,K,\mathbf{P})$ is the complimentary probability that no collision occurs.

As long as probability of the sequences $\mathbf{P}$ is specified, (2) gives the collision probability of the IDs. Depending on the problem formulation, we consider the following three cases for specifying $\mathbf{P}$:

- **Case 1:** The bits in each sequence are independent and identically distributed (i.i.d.) with P(any bit is 1)$= \pi$, P(any bit is 0)$= 1-\pi$. Then, P_i is $P_i = (1-\pi)^{n_{0i}}\pi^{n_{1i}}$, where n_{0i} denotes the total number of zeros in sequence i and n_{1i} denotes the total number of its ones.
- **Case 2:** The bits in each sequence are independent but not identically distributed with P(bit m is 1)$= \pi_m$, Prob (bit m is 0)$= 1-\pi_m$. Let us define the following function

$$I(b_m) = \begin{cases} \pi_m, & b_m = 1 \\ 1 - \pi_m, & b_m = 0 \end{cases},$$

  then P_i is $P_i = \prod_{m=1}^{M} I(b_m)$.
- **Case 3:** The bits in each sequence are correlated and their Cumulative Distribution Function (CDF) is $\mathbf{P}$.

The problem with (2) is that it involves sums of exponential number of terms. For a large number unique IDs, the exact solution of (2) is intractable. Hence, we suggest Nunnikhoven's approximation [13] details of which are omitted in interest of brevity for calculating the collision probability of (2).

5.3   Statistical Analysis

While the analysis of Section 5.2 takes into account the situations where the probability of IDs are related because of inter-chip correlations, it ignores the existence of the intra-chip correlations. In general, modeling the intra-chip spatial correlation is a complex problem. Hence, we perform nonparametric statistical Monte Carlo (MC) simulations to estimate the collision probability.

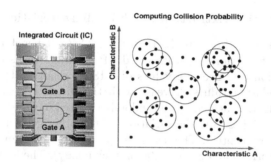

Fig. 4. An example of using 2 gates to identify the IC characteristics. The probability of collision between the ICs is calculated using the MC simulation on the 2D plot.

Figure 4 illustrates the MC-based simulations when only characteristics of two gates are used. The extracted analog characteristic (scaling factor) of each gate is used as one dimension of our analysis. Thus, we have a 2D space in this example. In the general case of using M' characteristics, we have a M'-dimensional space. Now, assume that we take K such ICs, and we would like to calculate the probability of collision. For computing the probability, we randomly position a sphere in the M' dimensions multiple times.

The center of each sphere is selected at the position of a new IC. Assuming that the coding that is done on the analog characteristics is robust, the points that fall within one circle will be assigned the same IDs. Since we repeat the MC experiment (i.e., circle generation) multiple times, we can count the number of possible points inside each circle because of the finite resolution of the measurements. Using the assumption and the multiple measurements, one can easily calculate the probability of collision for the whole space as follows,

$$P(collision) = \sum_{n=1}^{N_{MC}} P(collision|C_n)P(C_n) \qquad (3)$$

where N_{MC} denotes the number of MC-simulation runs, n is the index of each simulation, and C_n is the generated spheres for one experiment. The parameters of the MC analysis are the radius of the sphere and the number of random runs (N_{MC}) that must be carefully selected. In our experiments, we select the radius to be equal to the robust margin of the codes.

6   Experimental Results

In this section, we present the experimental evaluations of the new approach. We first show the results for the nondestructive extraction of chip characteristics and in the second subsection shows the probabilistic and statistical analysis of the collision of keys and robustness.

6.1   Nondestructive Extraction of Chip Characteristics

Our approach was tested on circuits from the MCNC'91 benchmarks. We used SIS and CPLEX to perform synthesis and LP solving. We used the variation model from Section 3.1. Leakage values of $0.18\mu m$ reported by [22] are used. The spatial correlation values decrease with the distance between the grids. There are 20 grids. On each chip, we randomly selected 5 center grids where the variations are the highest and the variations of the other grids are computed by correlations to those centers. The 3σ of the parameter variations of T_{ox} and L was set to 25% (corresponding to the 90nm technology). The levels of inter-chip and intra-chip variations were equal.

Table 1. The characterization error for different error distributions

error	characterization error (%)		
	Uniform	Triangle	Gaussian
0%	0	0	0
5%	0.99	0.75	0.11
10%	2.03	1.48	0.23
15%	3.25	2.34	0.35
20%	4.32	2.92	0.47
25%	5.21	3.7	0.6
30%	6.04	4.46	0.74
35%	7.49	5.2	0.86
40%	8.4	5.63	0.93
45%	9.34	6.06	1.06
50%	9.42	7.62	1.24

Table 1 shows the characterization error when we consider Uniform, Triangular, and Gaussian error measurement distributions for the alu2 circuit. The first column shows the absolute value of relative measurement error (percentage). The next three columns show the average extracted characterization error (percentage) for a measurement error of Uniform, Triangular, and Gaussian distributions respectively. We see that the characterization error is the smallest when the measurement error has a Gaussian distribution, and largest the for a Uniform distribution. For 25% relative absolute error, the Gaussian distribution leads to 0.6% error in characterization, whereas, Uniform and Triangular distributions yield 5.21% and 3.7% respectively.

Table 2 presents the characterization errors for 15 MCNC'91 benchmarks. The measurement error distribution is Gaussian. The first column shows the benchmark, the next two columns show the number of primary inputs and the number of gates after technology mapping to a subset of the MCNC library. The next two sets of three columns show the error when we optimized the average and the sum of squares of the measurement errors.

For every circuit, we generate a number of equations that is equal to the $\min\{2^{PI}, 3G\}$, where PI is the number of primary inputs, and G is the number of gates in the benchmark. We also tried minimization of the maximum error (L_∞) and it gave similar results.

Table 2. The characterization error for different benchmarks and different absolute relative errors

BM	PI	gates	$L_1(\%)$			$L_2(\%)$		
			1%	5%	10%	1%	5%	10%
9symml	9	166	0.03	0.14	0.26	0.03	0.13	0.24
alu2	10	356	0.02	0.12	0.25	0.02	0.12	0.24
C1908	33	615	0.01	0.05	0.09	0.01	0.04	0.09
C432	36	200	0.01	0.07	0.12	0.01	0.05	0.11
C8	28	164	0.01	0.04	0.07	0.01	0.04	0.08
C880	60	354	0.01	0.05	0.07	0.01	0.04	0.07
f51m	8	136	0.02	0.09	0.17	0.02	0.1	0.21
i6	138	340	0.01	0.04	0.06	0.01	0.04	0.06
i7	199	405	0.01	0.03	0.05	0	0.03	0.05
lal	26	116	0.01	0.05	0.1	0.01	0.07	0.13
term1	34	363	0.01	0.04	0.06	0.01	0.05	0.09
too_lrg	38	582	0.01	0.04	0.07	0.01	0.04	0.09
ttt2	24	207	0.01	0.03	0.05	0.01	0.04	0.08
x1	51	295	0.01	0.05	0.1	0.01	0.06	0.13
x3	135	742	0.01	0.03	0.05	0.01	0.02	0.05

To study the effect of the number of constraints used for characterization, we generate four different sets of constraints. Figure 5 shows the percentage error in characterization when considering different number of constraints for benchmark lal. The first column shows the relative absolute error used. The rest of the columns show the error in characterization for 500, 1000, 1500, and 2000 constraints. It can be seen that although the error in characterization is very small in the case of using 500 constraints, the error is reduced by going from 500 constraints to 1000 constraints. However, there is almost no improvement for constraints more than 1000.

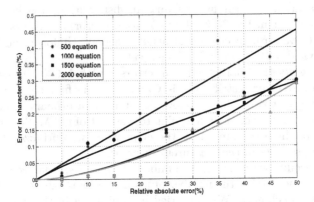

Fig. 5. Percentage characterization error for different number of constraints (la1 benchmark)

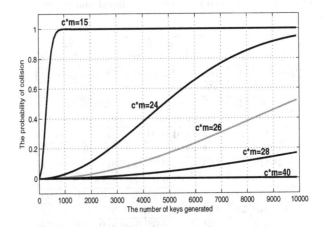

Fig. 6. The probability of collision of different number of keys for different values of code length (c) and number of circuit characteristics (m)

6.2 Evaluation of the Collision Probability

Figure 6 shows the probability of collisions for equiareal coding. The probability of collision is decreased when we increase the product $M = c.m$, where c is the number of code bits and m is the number of gates used for the key generation. In the case of margin coding the probability of the assigned codes were nonuniform and we used the Nunnikhoven's approximation to compute the probabilities. Our studies revealed that for a larger value of $c.m$ this distribution approached the Uniform distribution where the various codes have the same probabilities. Thus, the curves are similar to those in Figure 6 for large $c.m$. The only difference is that in margin coding for c bits codes the corresponding equiareal code with the equal number of partitions will have $c + 1$ bits.

Table 3. Robustness for the equiareal and equidistance (margin) coding schemes

	EQ-AREA			EQ-DIST		
BM	1 bit	2 bits	3 bits	1 bit	2 bits	3 bits
alu2	0.76	0.18	0.09	3.5	1.75	0.86
c8	0.77	0.17	0.08	3.7	1.87	0.93
lal	0.71	0.15	0.07	4.23	2.11	1.06
too_large	0.71	0.2	0.08	3.65	1.82	0.92
x1	0.75	0.23	0.09	3.84	1.92	0.96

Table 3 shows the robustness for the margin coding and equiareal coding for 5 benchmarks. The first column shows the benchmark. The next three columns show the robustness for equiareal codes (EQ-AREA). The last three columns show the robustness for using margin codes (EQ-DIST). We see that the second method increases the robustness at the expense of having shorter IDs.

For the statistical analysis of the probability of collision, we performed the MC simulations on five benchmarks. The number of runs was determined using bootstrapping techniques [5]: for each run number, we did multiple random MC simulations for calculating the probability of collisions. If the results were similar over multiple random instances we stopped increasing the run number since the confidence over the bootstrapped results was high. Table 4 presents the results. The first column shows the benchmark, and the remaining columns show the probability of collisions when considering 25, 50, 75, and 100 gates. For 100 characteristics, the probability of collision was always less than 0.005. It is interesting to compare the results from the statistical analysis to that of the probabilistic, even though one is for the collision of the analog characteristics and the other one for the coded characteristics. For example, for c.m=26 that is comparable to 25 characteristics and 1000 ICs, the probability of collision is much lower in number for Figure 6, as expected.

Table 4. Statistical analysis of collision probability

	Number of characteristics			
BM	25	50	75	100
alu2	0.027	0.011	0.005	0.002
c8	0.014	0.003	0.001	0
lal	0.007	0.001	0	0
too_large	0.032	0.015	0.008	0.0046
x1	0.023	0.007	0.002	0.001

7 Conclusions

We have developed a method for extraction of unique unclonable IDs from each IC of a given design by exploiting deep submicron manufacturing variability. The approach is applicable to legacy designs, and induces no power, area and timing overhead while enabling a spectrum of novel security and IPP protocols. Experimental results on a large set of industrial benchmark instances demonstrate the efficiency of the proposed methods. The characteristics of an IC could be extracted within 2% accuracy in presence of 50% relative measurement errors. We also demonstrated that for all industrial design, the probability of collision rapidly approached zero.

Acknowledgment

This work is partly supported by the DARPA/MTO Young Faculty Award W911NF-07-1-0198, NSF CT-0716674, and NSF CCF-0729061.

References

1. Chang, H., Sapatnekar, S.: Full-chip analysis of leakage power under process variations, including spatial correlations. In: DAC, pp. 523–528 (2005)
2. Coppersmith, D.: Another birthday attack. In: Williams, H.C. (ed.) CRYPTO 1985. LNCS, vol. 218, pp. 14–17. Springer, Heidelberg (1986)
3. Friedberg, P., et al.: Modeling within-die spatial correlation effects for process-design co-optimization. In: ISQED, pp. 516–521 (2005)
4. Gassend, B., et al.: Identification and authentication of integrated circuits. In: Concurrency and Computation: Practice and Experience, vol. 16, pp. 1077–1098. John Wiley & Sons, Chichester (2004)
5. Hastie, T., et al.: The Elements of Statistical Learning. Springer, Heidelberg (2001)
6. Bernstein, K., et al.: High-performance CMOS variability in the 65-nm regime and beyond. IBM Journal of Research and Development 50(4/5), 433–450 (2006)
7. Kirovski, D., Potkonjak, M.: Local watermarks: methodology and application to behavioral synthesis. IEEE Trans. CAD 22(9), 1277–1283 (2003)
8. Koushanfar, F., et al.: Intellectual property metering. In: IHW, pp. 81–95 (2001)
9. Lach, J., et al.: Fingerprinting digital circuits on programmable hardware. In: IHW, pp. 16–32 (1998)
10. Lee, J., et al.: A technique to build a secret key in integrated circuits for identification and authentication applications. In: Symposium of VLSI, pp. 176–179 (2004)
11. Lofstrom, K., et al.: IC identification circuits using device mismatch. In: ISSCC, pp. 372–373 (2000)
12. Maeda, S., et al.: An artificial fingerprint device (AFD): a study of identification number applications utilizing characteristics variation of polycrystalline silicon TFTs. IEEE Trans. Electron. Devices 50(6), 1451–1458 (2003)
13. Nunnukhoven, T.: A birthday problem solution for nonuniform birthday frequencies. The American Statistician 46(4), 270–274 (1992)
14. Vijaykrishnan, N., Xie, Y.: Reliability concerns in embedded system designs. IEEE Computer 39(1), 118–120 (2006)
15. Oliveira, A.: Techniques for the creation of digital watermarks in sequential circuit designs. IEEE Trans. on CAD 20(9), 1101–1117 (2001)
16. Qu, G., Potkonjak, M.: Intellectual Property Protection in VLSI Design. Kluwer Academic Publishers, Dordrecht (2003)

17. Srivastava, A., et al.: Statistical Analysis and Optimization for VLSI: Timing and Power. Series on Integrated Circuits and Systems. Springer, Heidelberg (2005)
18. Su, Y., et al.: A 1.6 J/bit stable chip ID generating circuit using process variations. In: ISSCC, 406–407 (2007)
19. Suh, G., et al.: Design and implementation of the aegis single-chip secure processor using physical random functions. In: ISCA, pp. 25–36 (2005)
20. Thompson, A., Layzell, P.: Evolution of robustness in an electronics design. In: ICES, pp. 218–228 (2000)
21. Torunoglu, I., Charbon, E.: Watermarking-based copyright protection of sequential functions. JSSC 35(3), 434–440 (2000)
22. Yuan, L., Qu, G.: A combined gate replacement and input vector control approach for leakage current reduction. IEEE Trans. on VLSI 14(2), 173–182 (2006)

Reversible Watermarking with Subliminal Channel

Xianfeng Zhao and Ning Li

State Key Laboratory of Information Security, Institute of Software,
Chinese Academy of Sciences, Beijing 100190, China
{xfzhao,lining}@is.iscas.ac.cn

Abstract. With some difficulty in making more redundant capacity, only a symmetrically encrypted hash code is embedded in some reversible watermarking schemes, which makes it possible that a dishonest verifier fabricates legal contents. This paper shows that for reversible watermarking, by exploiting a subliminal channel, only a capacity of several more bytes than the length of a hash code is needed to embed a longer public-key signature. Only 4 bytes more suffices in the research. To exemplify the idea, the paper gives a variant of the R-S watermarking scheme. The variant adopts the broad-band subliminal channel in RSA-PSS signature scheme. The analysis and experiments show that with the aid of the channel it is easier to implement the reversibility, localize the tampering, and so forth.

1 Introduction

Fragile watermarking has long been used to authenticate the origin and integrity of multimedia. It has also adopted the public-key signature scheme and provided users with asymmetric security and feasible key management [1]. Usually watermark embedding introduces some distortion to the distributed copy. Although the distortion can be imperceptible, it is not wanted for many cases [2, 3]. For instance, for the image which is used as legal evidence, or already has great quality degradation, even very slight change may not be allowed. Therefore the *reversible watermarking*, which can reverse a watermarked copy back to the exact original, has been studied and developed since the birth of watermarking.

Many techniques of reversible watermarking [4-13] have been proposed but most of them take a symmetric way for authentication which makes it possible for a dishonest verifier to fabricate legal contents. An important reason for it is that it is difficult to stably acquire a *redundant capacity* which can losslessly hold a signature and other possible data under various technical restrictions. As we know, a 1024 or 2048-bit length is common for a signature [14-16], whereas the length of a hash code or message authentication code (MAC) is much shorter, for example, 128 or 256 bits [17]. In many existing schemes [4-8] the capacity is made by lossless compression of a perceptually insignificant part of a host signal. However, the distribution of the part is often so random as to make it impossible to acquire a satisfactory capacity. For all the ways of making capacity, the requirement of imperceptibility, tampering localizability, etc. can produce new restrictions. For example, better perceptual quality can be kept by diminishing the energy of an embedded signal, thus decreasing the capacity

K. Solanki, K. Sullivan, and U. Madhow (Eds.): IH 2008, LNCS 5284, pp. 118–131, 2008.

severely [5-13]. And to localize the tampering an original is often partitioned into small blocks which can hold less embedded data each. In addition, sending a message by watermarking produces a direct need for capacity.

Apparently, it is important to further enlarge the redundant capacity for the introduction of public-key signature to many reversible watermarking schemes. For doing so, this paper reviews current techniques of the capacity making as follows.

– *Lossless Compression*. In J. M. Barton's invention [4] the least significant bits (LSBs) or some scattered pixels of a host signal are compressed, and an authorization tag or a signature is embedded in the acquired capacity. In his case 1024 bits must be provided for a signature. But the independence among the LSBs or pixels can prevent a high compression ratio. J. Fridrich et al. [5-7] studied the capacity making with lossless compression systematically. Their results show that in a typical case only the 5th spatial LSB plane of a noisy image can provide a space larger than 128 bits [5] while the LSB plane of the same components in the DCT blocks can give the space [6]. The R-S scheme [7] compresses the vector of R-S (regular-singular) attribute of pixel groups, and embeds data by flipping the pixels. In the scheme a watermarking rate ranging from 0.019 to 0.12 bits per pixel (bpp) is acquired, but sometimes some perceptible distortion is introduced [3]. By exploiting the larger bias between 1 and 0 in the bit-plane of integer wavelet transform (IWT) domain, G. Xuan et al. [8] acquired a watermarking rate ranging from 0.1 to 0.4 bpp.

– *Modulo Addition and Spread Spectrum Communication*. C. W. Honsinger et al. [9] invented a method for embedding the encrypted hash code or signature which can be retrieved by spread spectrum communication and removed by modulo addition. However, it is not suitable that a signature is defined as a hash code encrypted by stream cipher in [9], and the modulo addition makes some striking pepper noises [3]. Since the embedded data is retrieved by the computation of the correlation between a received image and a pseudo-random carrier, the interference of an original signal can prevent a large channel capacity.

– *Difference Expansion*. The scheme proposed by J. Tian [10] employs 2 pixels to embed a bit through an invertible integer transform. The bit is represented by an expansion of the difference between the 2 pixels. However, because the value of an embedded pixel may overflow or underflow, not all pixel pairs can be embedded. In practice, a threshold is used to avoid the overflow and underflow, and in this case some additional information, called location map, must also be embedded to indicate whether a pixel has been used. By elaborate design, A. M. Alattar [11] generalized Tian's method to using difference expansion of vectors.

– *Histogram Operation*. To enhance the robustness and provide the semi-fragility, some reversible schemes [12, 13] embed a watermark bit by modifying the histogram of an image block, and invert the modification with some patchwork skills. Since only one bit is embedded in one block, the capacity made this way is less impressive.

While it is thought that most reversible schemes have to make more capacity if the use of public-key signature and the realization of more functions are mandatory, it is neglected that a signature itself can convey more information than just an authentication code. We found that a *subliminal channel* [18-22] is helpful to provide capacity for reversibly embedding a signature and other needed data. Subliminal channels, first found by G. J. Simmons [18], can be defined as the covert communication in a public-key signature scheme. Specifically, disposable pseudo-random numbers, padding data, etc. can be used to convey information in the generation and verification of a signature. When a signature is reversibly embedded, intuitively, such a channel can provide more capacity to be needed. This paper is intended to investigate the issue. The research results show that for reversible watermarking, with the aid of a subliminal channel only a redundant capacity several bytes more than the length of an encrypted hash code is needed in embedding a public-key signature. To exemplify the idea, the paper gives a variant of R-S scheme, which takes the subliminal channel in the RSA-PSS signature scheme as a part of the capacity of holding the compressed data and some needed information. In this paper the acquired space can be as large as 880 bits in a 1024-bit RSA-PSS signature and 1904 bits in a 2048-bit RSA-PSS signature. And the result also makes it possible to partition an image into several tens of blocks so that the tampering can be localized.

The paper is organized as follows. In Sect. 2, the subliminal channel in RSA-PSS signature scheme is tailored for composing a part of the capacity needed in reversible embedding. Sect. 3 gives a variant of R-S scheme to exemplify the use of the channel. Sect. 4 analyzes some properties of the scheme, and Sect. 5 brings out the experimental results. Finally, Sect. 6 draws the conclusions.

2   Subliminal Channel in RSA-PSS

This section surveys the existing subliminal channels, and explains why we choose the channel of RSA-PSS in the reversible watermarking.

2.1   Various Subliminal Channels

G. J. Simmons [18,19] classified subliminal channels in bandwidth and security setting. He first divided them into the broad-band and the narrow-band ones. Suppose that a signature is α bits long and that a hash code or other data that provides the security against forgery and tampering is β bits long, where $\beta < \alpha$. A broad-band channel means that all or most of the $\alpha - \beta$ bits can be used in the channel. Notably, the *probabilistic signature* scheme (PSS) [23, 24] plays an important role in the making of the channels since disposable pseudo-random data is adopted in computing a signature. If the data is used for representing specific meanings, a subliminal channel is built. The channels can also be categorized into type I and type II [18]. When a sender unconditionally trusts a receiver, or even they share a private key, the channel between them is type I. When the trust cannot be established, the channel is type II. A type I channel is broad-band but insecure because a receiver may fabricate signatures. R. Anderson et al. [20] demonstrated that a type II channel can be either narrow or broad-band. Actually, there is always a tradeoff among security, bandwidth, and complexity.

A type II broad-band subliminal channel is apparently more suitable for reversible watermarking because of its larger capacity and more secure setting. And for practical reasons, the channel provided by a standardized or widely used signature scheme is more preferable. G. J. Simmons [18] only constructed type I broad-band subliminal channels in ElGamal and DSA signature schemes. R. Anderson et al. [20] found that DSA restricts the secure use of a broad-band channel. So they resorted to constructing the so-called Newton channel from ElGamal. It is broad-band and type II, but a receiver can compute a part of the private key, i.e. a number congruent to the key modulo a known integer. In [21] and [22], where more type II broad-band subliminal channels are given, such a part is even directly shared. However, the crucial drawback of the channels in an ElGamal or DSA scheme might be that only half of signed data, which is the pseudo-random data, can be exploited. Intuitively, an RSA-like signature scheme can be more useful because the padding of a data block is directly sent by encryption and received by decryption. Unfortunately, the RSA signature scheme early standardized by [14] is deterministic. A data block EB to be encrypted is taken as an octet (8-bit byte) string, and must be formatted by

$$EB = 00 \parallel BT \parallel PS \parallel 00 \parallel D, \tag{1}$$

where "$\parallel$" means concatenation, and 00 represents an octet of all zero bits, i.e. 0x00. PS denotes the padding, and D a hash code. The octet BT, which is only 00 and 01, indicates a block type. If $BT = 01$, PS contains only 00; otherwise PS contains only FF. Of course, one can pad messages into PS. But the standard [14] requires a verification process to check the validity of the format, thus closing the potential channel. As an asymmetric encryption scheme RSA allows disposable pseudo-random padding in the public key operation but as for reversible watermarking it is a private key operation that sends subliminal messages. It implies that for those who insist on complying with the standard RSA is not fit for enlarging the capacity. However, things have been changed since the standardization of RSA-PSS [15]. [25] and [26] have constructed a subliminal channel in RSA-PSS. We shall further introduce it and try to explain that it is an easy-to-use and secure channel for reversible watermarking.

2.2 Tailored Subliminal Channel in RSA-PSS

A broad-band subliminal channel in RSA-PSS has been constructed in [25] and [26]. We depict the use of the channel in Fig. 1. Suppose that s, called $salt$ in [15], is the pseudo-random number one-time used in producing the signature Sig for the hash code $h = \mathrm{Hash}(C)$. Let $\mathrm{MGF}(a, b)$ be a masking generating function (MGF) for one-way computation of a b-long pseudo-random string with a. Then a data block to be signed is constructed through

$$EM = (p \parallel 01 \parallel s) \oplus \mathrm{MGF}(H, |EM| - |H| - 1) \parallel H \parallel \mathrm{bc}, \tag{2}$$

where "$|\cdot|$" denotes the length in octets. In (2), p is a padding of zero octets, and $H = \mathrm{Hash}(M)$, where

$$M = \underbrace{00 \cdots 00}_{8\,\mathrm{octets}} \parallel \mathrm{Hash}(C) \parallel s. \tag{3}$$

Then RSA encryption gives the signature $Sig = E(K_S, EM)$, where K_S is a private key. With the RSA public key Sig is first decrypted in the verification of the signature, and H and mDB are obtained. Then the verification calculates

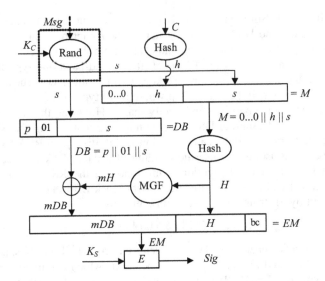

Fig. 1. Embedding subliminal message *Msg* in an RSA-PSS signature *Sig*: *C* is the signed data. The randomized *s* is the salt. K_C is an optional parameter controlling the randomization. K_S is an RSA private key. MGF is a masking generating function, and $\oplus$ denotes the exclusion OR.

$DB = p \parallel 01 \parallel s = mDB \oplus \text{MGF}(H, |EM| - |H| - 1)$ and retrieves the salt s. To authenticate the data, it computes a hash code h' of the data, and acquires $M' = 00\cdots00 \parallel h' \parallel s$. Only if $\text{Hash}(M') = H$, the authenticity of *Sig* is verified. Since s can convey messages, apparently there is a subliminal channel. And as $|p| = 0$ is allowed in [15], we can see that the channel capacity in octets is

$$Cap_{\text{Sub-Ch}} = \max(|Msg|) = |EM| - |H| - 2 \text{ octets} . \qquad (4)$$

Since $|EM|$ is also the length of an RSA modulus, we can calculate the capacity easily. For example, for a 1024-bit modulus and 128-bit hash code, the capacity is 880 bits (110 octets), and for a 2048-bit modulus and 256-bit hash code, 1776 bits (222 octets).

3   R-S Scheme Using Subliminal Channel

To exemplify the use of a subliminal cannel in the reversible watermarking adopting a public-key signature scheme, in this section we change the well-known R-S water-marking scheme [2, 7] into its asymmetric counterpart.

3.1   R-S Scheme

An R-S scheme embeds watermark bits by modifying R-S attribute of grouped samples. Suppose that an original signal has been partitioned into disjoint groups. First a discrimination function must be defined to compute the attribute. If $G = (x_1, \cdots, x_n)$ is one of the groups, the function can be

$$f(x_1, \cdots, x_n) = \sum_{i=1}^{n-1} | x_{i+1} - x_i |. \tag{5}$$

It reflects the variation of nearby samples. To change and restore the R-S attribute, an invertible operation must also be employed. Flipping the bits on LSB or higher bit planes serves as the operations in [2, 7]. For instance, 2 of them are

$$F_{\text{LSB}} \quad : \quad 0 \leftrightarrow 1, 2 \leftrightarrow 3, \cdots, 254 \leftrightarrow 255 \text{, and}$$
$$F_{\text{2nd LSB}} : \quad 0 \leftrightarrow 2, 1 \leftrightarrow 3, \cdots, 254 \leftrightarrow 252 \text{.}$$

Other flipping operations are also allowable. Apparently their inverses are themselves so that $F(F(G)) = G$. Let $P = \{0, 1, \cdots, 255\}$ denote the set of all possible values of samples. The distortion introduced by F can be evaluated by the *flipping amplitude*

$$A = \frac{1}{|P|} \sum_{x \in P} | x - F(x) |. \tag{6}$$

Finally the R, S and U attribute of G can be respectively defined by

regular, i.e. $G \in \mathbf{R}$, if and only if $f(F(G)) > f(G)$,

singular, i.e. $G \in \mathbf{S}$, if and only if $f(F(G)) < f(G)$, and

unusable, i.e. $G \in \mathbf{U}$, if and only if $f(F(G)) = f(G)$,

where $\mathbf{R}$, $\mathbf{S}$, and $\mathbf{U}$ are respectively the sets of all regular, singular, and unusable groups. And $G \in \mathbf{R} \Leftrightarrow F(G) \in \mathbf{S}$, $G \in \mathbf{S} \Leftrightarrow F(G) \in \mathbf{R}$, and $G \in \mathbf{U} \Leftrightarrow F(G) \in \mathbf{U}$ holds. If we use 1 and 0 to express $G \in \mathbf{R}$ and $G \in \mathbf{S}$ respectively, the attribute can be changed where necessary to embed bits on R and S groups. Since most $f(F(G))$ are larger than $f(G)$, the bias makes the compression of a sequence of the above 0s and 1s, called *R-S vector*, more effective than the direct treatment of the bit planes [2, 7].

3.2   R-S Scheme with Subliminal Channel

Due to the probable lack of capacity, the function of the R-S scheme in [2, 7] is limited. It embeds a hash code or such a code encrypted by a symmetric key, enabling a dishonest verifier to fabricate signatures and legal contents. It might have to do so since sometimes the capacity acquired from an image is smaller than the size of a signature, especially when the above A is small. For image sizes ranging from 128×128 to 512×512 pixels, the capacity is often less than 200 bits when $A = 1$, and less than 750 bits when $A = 2$. When $A = 6$, the distortion becomes obtrusive [3]. It prevents the capacity from being further enlarged by increasing A. And since the localization of tampering often needs to operate on small blocks [1], the implementation of it can additionally downsize the capacity.

However, the authentication of an R-S scheme can be made asymmetric more effortlessly if it adopts RSA-PSS and makes use of the subliminal channel. By (4) we know that $Cap_{\text{Sub-Ch}}$ is only $|H| + 2$ octets shorter than $|EM|$, which is actually the size of a signature. Because the subliminal capacity can also hold the compressed data, it is surprising that introducing a public-key signature scheme in reversible watermarking only needs a redundant capacity several octets more than the size of a hash code which has already been provided. Among the several octets, we have seen in Fig. 1 that the required 0xbc and 0x01 constitutes two, and the others are often 14~16 bits for recording the length of compressed data and the number of blocks that must be processed as a whole. Typical need of the redundant capacity follows:

- when $|H|=128$ bits as in MD5, $128 + 4\times8$ bits are needed,
- when $|H|=160$ bits as in SHA-1, $160 + 4\times8$ bits are needed, and
- when $|H|=256$ bits as in SHA-256, $256 + 4\times8$ bits are needed.

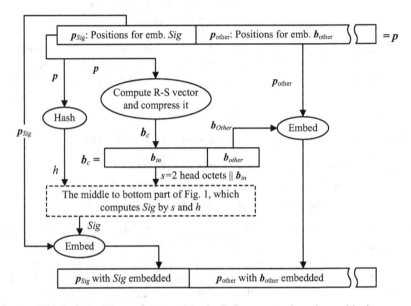

Fig. 2. Embedding a signature into the R-S vector p of one image block

In most reversible watermarking schemes, the acquired capacity has been larger than the mere $|H|+4$ octets. Even over a block of 80×80 pixels, the capacity can usually be ensured. It implies that they may become asymmetric and keep the tampering localizability by using a subliminal channel. To exemplify the idea, we introduce RSA-PSS to the R-S scheme, and give a variant of it. The variant is described by Fig. 2 and the algorithm following the paragraph. For simplicity the algorithm only provides the scheme with the functions of asymmetric authentication and tampering localizability, where the localizability is based on adaptive partition that can avoid lack of capacity on a block. Some other potential will be discussed in the next section.

Suppose that $|Sig|$ and $|H|$ bits are still the respective sizes of a signature and a hash code, and 4 pixels constitute a group. The embedding input by an image I and a private key K_S in the variant of an R-S scheme can be described as follows.

a) *Partitioning and Grouping.* Partition I into M *original blocks*, each having $N\times N$ pixels except the larger last one which annexes the oddment. In row order, each 4 pixels are taken for one group. For each block p, do the following steps.

b) *Lossless Compression.* Compute the type of each group, i.e. R, S, or U. Let the bit 1 and 0 represent R and S respectively. Record all the occurrences of R and S, and acquire the R-S vector b. Let N_R and N_S denote the respective numbers of R and S groups. Then $|b| = N_R + N_S$ is the number of bits which can be embedded. If $d_1 = |b| - |Sig| < 0$, continually annex the next original block until $d_1 \geq 0$. Compress b to b_c by Huffman coding.

c) *Capacity Evaluation.* A signature can be reversibly embedded in the block if

$$|b| - |b_c| \geq |H| + 32 \quad \text{bits.} \tag{7}$$

If it holds, let $Cap \leftarrow |b| - |b_c|$; otherwise, keep annexing the next block and re-compressing the R-S vector until it is satisfied. Let $d_2 \leftarrow |Sig| - |H| - 32$ bits. Then $d_1 + d_2$ is the size of the space that can be used to hold the compressed data, where d_2 bits of it are in the subliminal channel. By

$$m = d_1 + d_2 - |b_c| = Cap - |H| - 32 \geq 0, \tag{8}$$

even m bits of the space may not be used.

d) *Signing and Embedding.* Compute a hash code h of the current block. Divide b_c into b_{other} and b_{in}, where b_{in} is the first d_2 bits of b_c, or all bits of it if $d_2 \geq |b_c|$. The 16-bit header data and b_{in} are prepared as the salt. The former re-cords the value of $|b_c|$ and the number of original blocks that must be treated as a whole. After then, produce a signature Sig by the salt s and hash code h, and em-bed it in p_{Sig}. No matter how many bits b_{other} contains, if it is not empty, embed it in p_{other}. All the positions for embedding are fixed in one block. If some origi-nal blocks are treated as a whole, the embedding starts from the first one, i.e. p_{Sig} has a fixed length of $|Sig|$ and always precedes p_{other}.

For the above embedding, the corresponding authentication, input by an image $\tilde{I}$ and a public key K_p, can be described by:

a) *Partitioning and Grouping.* The same as the above a).

b) *Image Recovery and Signature Verification.* Extract the signature, and decrypt it by K_p to get H and the salt s. By the header data in s, acquire how large the current block is and how long the compressed data is. Retrieve all compressed data embedded in p_{other} and contained in s. Decompress it by Huffman decoding and acquire the original R-S vector. Restore the R or S attribute of all R and S groups over the current block by it. Then compute a hash code h' of the restored block, and by (3) let $M' = 00\cdots00 \parallel h' \parallel s$. If $\text{Hash}(M') = H$, the signature is verified. Otherwise, just alarm that the first original block in the current block has been tampered with, and then go to process the next original block.

Our experimental results show that the above scheme is practical when an original block has 80×80 pixels. More than 89.6 % of original blocks provide the needed redundant capacity of $|H| + 32$ bits alone. Next we shall give more discussion on the properties and possible improvement of the new scheme.

4 Analysis of the New Scheme

Besides the newly acquired features of asymmetric authentication and tampering localization, the above variant of R-S watermarking with the subliminal channel in RSA-PSS has or can have the following properties.

- *Minor capacity additionally needed.* Suppose that an existing reversible scheme embeds an $|H|$-bit hash code, and the symmetric encryption dose not change its size. Then transforming it into its asymmetric counterpart needs $|Sig|-|H|$ more bits of capacity if the new scheme does not exploit a subliminal channel. It implies that more than 900 bits or much more bits of redundant capacity must be acquired from the processing of an original, or one of its blocks or segments which is to be signed alone. For the scheme proposed in Sect. 3, however, only a 32-bit additional redundant capacity is needed while $|Sig|$ can be 1024, 2048, or more bits long. In practice, such mere 32 bits of capacity often have already been provided.
- *Even decreasing the need for capacity.* In many cases, the block size of a symmetric cipher is larger than the size of a hash code. For examples, when SHA-1 and AES-256 is used, a 160-bit hash code is extended to a 256-bit encrypted block. Suppose that the block size of a symmetric cipher is $|B|$. For the above scheme using the subliminal channel, if

$$|H|+32 < |B| \quad \text{bits},\tag{9}$$

it even decreases the need for redundant capacity by $|B|-|H|-32$ bits.
- *Adaptive capacity making.* The way of partition in the scheme proposed in Sect. 3 is adaptive. At the beginning the embedding only partitions an original into the so-called original blocks. To decrease the block size, they are designed not each to ensure providing a redundant space big enough for reversibly embedding a signature. If the needed capacity cannot be made, two or more blocks are combined. The treatment, on one hand, downsizes the grain of tampering localization, and on the other hand, reliably provides the sufficient capacity. Our experimental results show that when about 90 % of original blocks need not annex the nearby blocks, the size of an original block is around 80×80 pixels. We shall call the percentage OSP (*one-time sufficient percentage*).
- *More than type II security.* A receiver of the subliminal message has no possession of the private key. Thus the subliminal channel in the RSA-PSS is at least type II. Furthermore, it can be considered more secure in the sense that only more unimportant knowledge, i.e. the meaning of a salt, is shared between a sender and a receiver. However, the knowledge is not in any sense related to an RSA private key. In actuality such a salt is still one-time-use since it is rare that the compressed data can collide with each other. And the salt is also sufficiently random by primarily containing compressed data. Although the 16-bit header data somewhat diminishes the space of a salt, slightly increasing the size of RSA modulus enlarges it immediately. In contrast, a sender and a receiver of type II broad-band subliminal channels often share the knowledge directly related to the private key. In [21, 22], a sender and a receiver of the channel in ElGamal signature scheme share a part of the private key. If $p-1$ denotes the order of the multiplication group $GF(p)^*$ used by ElGamal, typically the part can be expressed by

$$x_q = x \,(\bmod\ q),\tag{10}$$

where q is a factor of $p-1$, and x is the private key. Although the setting of a Newton channel [20] does not directly gives the data, a similar $x_t = x \,(\bmod t)$ can be computed by solving

$$y^q = \left(g^q\right)^x \ (\bmod\ q), \quad tq = p-1,$$ (11)

where y is the public key and g is a generator of $GF(p)^*$. The computation is actually executed in the same way of extracting a subliminal message.

- *Improved imperceptibility.* Compared with other reversible watermarking also using a signature scheme, adopting a subliminal channel directly decreases the distortion resulting from the embedding. The compressed and other kind of data, or part of it, can be combined in a signature such that the amount of data to be embedded decreases.

The scheme proposed in Sect. 3 can be further improved. To prevent an attacker from copying a block somewhere and pasting it elsewhere, the coordinates of blocks can also be hashed with content. By (8), we see that some redundant capacity is not used. One can make use of it in many ways. For example, some message can be conveyed. Or it can be used to hold additional information about the pixels to further downsize the grain of tampering localization. In addition, the code book of Huffman coding can be tailored to R-S vectors.

5 Experimental Results

To avoid too many occurrences of annexing a nearby block, the first goal of our experiments is to find a proper size of original blocks, most of which provide a sufficient large redundant capacity alone. However, the OSP cannot be too large because it can leads to a coarser grain of tampering localization. Our experiment determines a proper size of original blocks respectively for the use of 128, 160, and 256-bit hash codes. Then it examines the properties and chooses other parameters. The images of different sizes (Fig. 3) are used in the experiments.

Fig. 4 displays some distributions of the number of all R and S groups, and the redundant capacity made over the image blocks. It shows that some original blocks such as those in Plane are more likely to have smaller numbers of all R and S groups. However, since the bias between the number of R groups and that of S groups is at the same level of other images, the blocks provide similar sizes of redundant capacity. In any case, the choice of block sizes must first let most of them be capable of holding a RSA-PSS signature with a secure length such as 1024 bits.

(a) Plane   (b) Lena   (c) Peppers

Fig. 3. Three of the experimented images with sizes ranging from 180×180 to 512×512 pixels

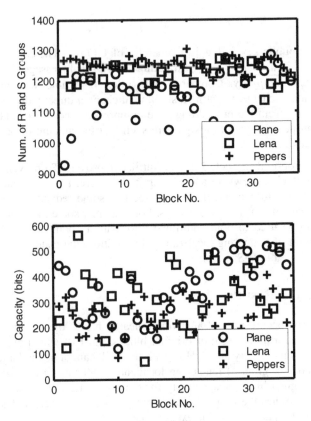

Fig. 4. The number of all R and S groups, and redundant capacity over the original blocks, where the flipping amplitude A is 4, and the 480×480 images are partitioned into 36 80×80 blocks

Table 1. The sizes of an original block for the hash codes, and the properties when $A=2$

Hash code length $|H|$ (bit)	128	160	256
Sizes of original block (pix)	84×84	98×98	112×112
Mean OSP (%)	84.40	81.14	81.25
Mean $N_R + N_S$ (group)	1542.2	2070.8	2727.8
Preferable $|Sig|$ (bit)	1024~1300	1024~1700	1024~2400
Mean redundant capacity (bit)	199.53	251.27	322.19
Min grain of localization (pix)	84×84	98×98	112×112
Max grain of localization (pix)	84×84×3	98×98×2	112×112×2

Our major results are listed in Tables 1 and 2. They show that the mean number of all R and S groups $N_R + N_S$ is always much larger than 1024 over a original block larger than 80×80 pixels. Then the block size is primarily determined by the hash code length and the redundant capacity that such a block can provide. The experimental results reveal that a block significantly smaller than a common image, such as

Table 2. The sizes of an original block for the hash codes, and the properties when $A=4$

Hash code length $|H|$ (bit)	128	160	256
Sizes of original block (pix)	80×80	80×80	90×90
Mean OSP (%)	93.22	89.69	89.13
Mean $N_R + N_S$ (group)	1345.1	1345.1	1721.9
Preferable $|Sig|$ (bit)	1024	1024	1024~1300
Mean redundant capacity (bit)	322.08	322.08	403.30
Min grain of localization (pix)	80×80	80×80	90×90
Max grain of localization (pix)	80×80×2	80×80×2	90×90×2

Fig. 5. Watermarked images: In 1st row, $A = 2$, PSNRs are 45.12, 45.14, and 45.11dB; in the 2nd row, $A = 4$, and PSNRs are 39.23, 39.20, and 39.19 dB

a block of more than 80×80 pixels, can already provide the capacity needed by the variant of R-S scheme. The situation also implies that the grain of tampering localizability is also of the size in the new scheme.

It is worth mentioning that the block sizes in Tables 1 and 2 are even comparable with the lossy fragile watermarking using RSA. A block size of 8×8 pixels is claimed by the LSB-based fragile watermarking in [1]. However, the security of RSA requires that a signature is at least 1024 bits long. It implies that the block size in [1] must be at least 32×32 pixels [27].

By the results in Tables 1 and 2, we see that under the setting of $A = 4$ and $|H| = 160$ the scheme can be both secure and practical in that it uses a hash code enough long and still keeps using the 80×80-pixel original blocks. And the distortion introduced by watermarking is acceptable under the setting. When $A = 4$, the PSNR of the embedded images are at a level of about 39.2 dB (Fig. 5), and they are often around 45.1 dB when $A = 2$.

6 Conclusions

To prevent a dishonest verifier from fabricating legal contents, fragile watermarking for content authentication is often required to combine an asymmetric signature scheme. For some reversible watermarking schemes, the difficulty in making more redundant capacity makes it more infeasible to do so. However, by giving and investigating a variant of the R-S scheme this paper has demonstrated that the introduction of an RSA-PSS signature scheme to reversible watermarking needs only 4 bytes more redundant capacity in the case of the subliminal channel. Since such a channel is at least of type II and broad-band, it is fit for securely storing the compressed data in a signature. Tampering localization can also be implemented since only an 80×80-pixel block can provide the capacity. And one can make use of the channel to further improve the new scheme.

Acknowledgements

This work is partly supported by the National Natural Science Foundation of China under the Grant No. 60573049 and 60633030.

References

1. Wong, P.W.: A public key watermarking for image verification and authentication. In: Proc. of ICIP, Chicago, Illinois, vol. 1, pp. 455–459 (October 1998)
2. Fridrich, J., Goljian, M., Du, R.: Lossless data embedding—New paradigm in digital watermarking. EURASIP J. on Applied Signal Processing (2), 185–196 (2002)
3. Shi, Y.Q.: Reversible data hiding. In: Cox, I., Kalker, T., Lee, H.-K. (eds.) IWDW 2004. LNCS, vol. 3304, pp. 1–12. Springer, Heidelberg (2005)
4. Barton, J.M.: Method and apparatus for embedding authentication information within digital data, U. S. Patent: 5646997, August 7 (1997)
5. Fridrich, J., Goljian, M., Du, R.: Invertible authentication. In: SPIE Conf. Security and Watermarking of Multimedia Contents III. Proceedings of SPIE, San Jose, CA, vol. 3971, pp. 197–208 (January 2001)
6. Fridrich, J., Goljian, M., Du, R.: Invertible authentication watermark for JPEG images. In: Proc. of IEEE ITCC 2001, Las Vegas, Nevada, pp. 223–227 (April 2001)
7. Goljan, M., Fridrich, J., Du, R.: Distortion-free data embedding for images. In: Moskowitz, I.S. (ed.) IH 2001. LNCS, vol. 2137, pp. 27–41. Springer, Heidelberg (2001)
8. Xuan, G., Zhu, J., Chen, J., Shi, Y.Q., Ni, Z., Su, W.: Distortionless data hiding based on integer wavelet transform. IEE Electronics Letters 38(25), 1646–1648 (2002)
9. Honsinger, C.W., Jones, P., Rabbani, M., Stoffel, J.C.: Lossless recovery of an original image containing embedded data, U. S. Patent: 6278791, August 21 (2001)
10. Tian, J.: Reversible data embedding using a difference expansion. IEEE Trans. Circuits and Systems for Video Technology 13(8), 890–896 (2003)

11. Alattar, A.M.: Reversible watermark using the difference expansion of a generalized integer transform. IEEE Trans. Image Processing 13(8), 1147–1156 (2004)
12. Vleeschouwer, C.D., Delaigle, J.F., Macq, B.: Circular interpretation of bijective transformations in lossless watermarking for media asset management. IEEE Trans. Multimedia 5(1), 97–105 (2003)
13. Ni, Z., Shi, Y.Q., Ansari, N., Wei, S.: Reversible data hiding. In: Proc. of Intern. Symp. on Circuits and Systems, Bangkok, Thailand, May 25-28, vol. 2, pp. 912–915 (2003)
14. RSA Laboratories. RSA Cryptography Standard, PKCS #1 v. 1.5, November 1 (1993)
15. RSA Laboratories. RSA Cryptography Standard, PKCS #1 v. 2.1 June 14 (2002)
16. NIST. Digital Signature Standard (DSS), FIPS PUB 186-2, January 27 (2000)
17. NIST. Secure Hash Standard, FIPS PUB 180-2, August 1 (2002)
18. Simmons, G.J.: Subliminal channels: past and present. European Transactions on Telecommunications 4(4), 459–473 (1994)
19. Simmons, G.J.: The history of subliminal channels. IEEE J. Selected Areas in Communication 16(4), 452–462 (1998)
20. Anderson, R., Vandeney, S., Preneel, B., Nyberg, K.: The Newton channel. In: Anderson, R. (ed.) IH 1996. LNCS, vol. 1174, pp. 151–156. Springer, Heidelberg (1996)
21. Harn, L., Gong, G.: Digital signature with a subliminal channel. IEE Proceedings - Computers and Digital Techniques 144(6), 387–389 (1997)
22. Jan, J.-K., Tseng, Y.-M.: New digital signature with subliminal channels based on the discrete logarithm problem. In: Proc. of 1999 Int. Workshops on Parallel Processing, Aizu-Wakamatsu, Japan, September 21-24, pp. 198–203 (1999)
23. Bellare, M., Rogaway, P.: The exact security of digital signatures: How to sign with RSA and Rabin. In: Maurer, U.M. (ed.) EUROCRYPT 1996. LNCS, vol. 1070, pp. 399–416. Springer, Heidelberg (1996)
24. Coron, J.-S.: Optimal security proofs for PSS and other signature schemes. In: Knudsen, L.R. (ed.) EUROCRYPT 2002. LNCS, vol. 2332, pp. 272–287. Springer, Heidelberg (2002)
25. Bao, F., Wang, X.: Steganography of short messages through accessories. In: Proc. of 2002 Pacific Rim Workshop on Digital Steganography (STEG 2002) (2002)
26. Bohli, J.-M., Steinwandt, R.: On subliminal channels in deterministic signature schemes. In: Park, C.-s., Chee, S. (eds.) ICISC 2004. LNCS, vol. 3506, pp. 182–194. Springer, Heidelberg (2005)
27. Barreto, P.S., Kim, H.Y.: Pitfalls in public key watermarking. In: Proc IEEE XII Brazilian Symp. on Comp. Graphics and Image Processing, pp. 241–242. IEEE Press, Los Alamitos (1999)

Watermarking Security Incorporating Natural Scene Statistics

Jiangqun Ni[1,2,*] , Rongyue Zhang[3], Chen Fang[1], Jiwu Huang[1,2], Chuntao Wang[1],
and Hyoung-Joong Kim[3]

[1] School of Information Science and Technology,
Sun Yat-Sen University, Guangzhou, 510275, P. R. China
[2] Guangdong Key Laboratory of Information Security Technology,
Guangzhou, 510275, P.R. China
[3] Graduate School of Information Security, Korea University, Seoul 136-701, Korea

Abstract. Watermarking security has emerged as the domain of extensive research in recent years. This paper presents both information theoretic analysis and practical attack algorithm for spread-spectrum based watermarking security incorporating natural scene statistics (NSS) model. Firstly, the Gaussian scale mixture (GSM) is introduced as the NSS model. The security is quantified by the mutual information between the observed watermarked signals and the secret carriers. The new security measures are then derived based on the GSM model, which allows for more accurate evaluation of watermarking security. Finally, the practical attack algorithm is developed in the framework of variational Bayesian ICA, which is shown to increase the performance and flexibility by allowing incorporation of prior knowledge of host signal. Extensive simulations are carried out to demonstrate the feasibility and effectiveness of the proposed algorithm.

1 Introduction

Robustness, capacity and imperceptibility have long been considered as the three main constraints in the development of watermarking algorithm [1]. Recently, more attentions have been paid on the issue of security [2][3][5] after the pioneering works of [6], which appears to be another fundamental constraint to respect for watermarking. Unlike the concept of robustness which deals with blind attacks, the security is more critical for watermarking as it deals with the intentional attacks where the information about watermarking scheme is known by the attacker, therefore offering complete break. In [3] Furon *et al* employ the Kerckhoff's principle [4] from cryptography to describe the model of watermarking security, i.e., each unit of the watermarking system (encoding/embedding, decoding/detection ...) should be declared public except for the secret key. And the objective for attacks to security is gaining the knowledge about the secret keys of the system. Based on the knowledge available to the attacker, three different attacks are defined, i.e., watermarked only attack (WOA), known message attack (KMA) and known original attack (KOA).

---

* Corresponding author, Phn.: 86-20-84036167, issjqni@mail.sysu.edu.cn

K. Solanki, K. Sullivan, and U. Madhow (Eds.): IH 2008, LNCS 5284, pp. 132–146, 2008.

With the Fisher information, Cayre *et al* in [6] quantified for the first time the security of the well-known class of spread spectrum (SS) watermarking schemes. While in [7], Comesaña *et al* employed another measure for information leakage, i.e., the mutual information between the observed watermarked signals and the secret carriers, whose suitability for evaluating watermarking security is justified. The information-theoretic approach for watermarking security requires a statistical modeling of the signals involved in the problem: the host signal and the spreading carriers. Usually Gaussian distributions are assumed for the involved signals in the interest of mathematical tractability [6][7]. In this paper, the same issue is further investigated based on the NSS model. Images and videos of the visual environment are classified as natural scenes, which are the main carriers for watermark. Both the models of generalized Gaussian (GG) and mixture of Gaussian (MoG) are used to characterize the behavior of natural images in transformed domain. However, the security analysis with the aforementioned models still suffers from the difficulty of mathematical manipulation. Recently, the Gaussian scale mixture (GSM) has been proposed and proved to be capable of accurately model the natural image in wavelet domain [8][9] (we use the terms of NSS and GSM interchangeably throughout the paper). Although the marginal distribution of natural scenes in wavelet domain may be sharply peaked and heavy-tailed, according to the GSM model, the coefficient in a particular position is Gaussian distributed, conditioned on its scale [8]. Consequently, the GSM model is easily adopted in an information-theoretic setting for evaluation of watermarking security. And a more accurate security bound is expected to be obtained. Actually, it is proved in the subsequent section that the mutual information between the observed watermarked signals and the secret carriers, when taking into account the NSS model of host, is consistently greater than the one when the host signal is assumed to be Gaussian distributed. It is then motivated the development of more efficient practical algorithm for attacks to security by incorporation of NSS model.

The objective of attacks to the security of spread-spectrum (SS) watermarking system is to estimate the spread carriers derived from the secret key, based on the knowledge available to the attacker. Usually the BSS techniques, namely PCA and ICA are utilized to design the attack algorithm [6]. The conventional ICA method, such as FastICA, can only take the advantage of the independence between SS carriers, and the host signal is assumed to be Gaussian distributed. An efficient practical algorithm for attack to security is developed based on the variational Bayesian ICA approach [12], which is shown to increase the performance and flexibility by allowing the ready incorporation of prior knowledge of host signal with GSM model, and imposition of constraints to spreading carriers. Extensive simulation results demonstrate that the proposed attack algorithm has significant improvements in performance compared to conventional one.

The reminder of the paper is organized as follows. The GSM model and its performance are presented in section 2. The security analysis of Add-SS watermarking based on NSS model is given in section 3. The derivation of VB ICA based efficient algorithm of attack to security is described in section 4. Simulation results and analysis are included in section 5. Finally, the concluding remarks are provided in section 6.

2 The Gaussian Scale Mixture Model and Its Performance

As mentioned in the previous section, the NSS model we employ is the Gaussian scale mixture model (GSM) in wavelet domain. The wavelet coefficient in one sub-band is modeled as the GSM RF (Random Field), i.e., $\mathbf{X} = \{X_i : i \in \mathbf{I}\}$, where $\mathbf{I}$ denotes the set of spatial indices for the RF. The GSM RF $\mathbf{X}$ is formed as the product of two stationary RFs that are independent of each other [8], i.e.,

$$\mathbf{X} = \mathbf{S} \cdot \mathbf{U} = \{S_i \cdot U_i : i \in \mathbf{I}\} \tag{1}$$

where the symbol "$=$" in (1) denotes the equality in distribution, $\mathbf{U} = \{U_i : i \in \mathbf{I}\}$ is a Gaussian scalar RF with mean zero and variance σ_U^2, and $\mathbf{S} = \{S_i : i \in \mathbf{I}\}$ is a RF of positive multipliers that control the variances of local coefficients. For the GSM defined in (1), when conditioned on S_i, X_i are Gaussian distributed, i.e.,

$$p_{X_i|S_i}(x_i \mid s_i) \sim N\left(0, s_i^2 \sigma_U^2\right) \tag{2}$$

Another observation that can be concluded from GSM model is that given S_i, X_i are independent of S_j $\forall j \neq i$, implying that the variance of the coefficient X_i specifies its distribution completely. The GSM framework can be used to model the marginal statistics of wavelet coefficients of natural images, the joint distributions between the coefficients, as well as the space-varying localized statistics through appropriate modeling of the RF $\mathbf{S}$. For the scalar GSM model, the estimates of s_i^2 can be obtained through localized sample variance estimation since for natural images, $\mathbf{S}$ is known to be a spatially correlated field, and σ_U^2 can be assumed to be unity without loss of generality. Fig.1 shows the empirical histograms of the HL1 subband from 2 different natural images Barb and Lena (blue dot-dashed line), and those of the synthesized GSM RF samples learned from each corresponding subband (red solid line). A Gaussian with the same standard deviation as the image subband is also given for comparison (green dashed line). Note that the GSM model can accurately capture the non-Gaussian characteristics exemplified by the high peak and heavy tails in the marginal distribution of the subband.

A more efficient implementation of GSM model is the vector GSM as adopted in the subsequent section, where the image subband is partitioned into nonoverlapping block-neighborhoods. Assume that $\vec{X}_j = \left(X_{j,i}, i = 1 \ldots M\right)$ is a vector of M wavelet coefficients that form the jth neighborhood. All such vectors, corresponding to the nonoverlapping neighborhoods, are assumed to be uncorrelated with each other. Follow the definition of scalar GSM RF, the vector RF $\mathbf{X} = \left\{\vec{X}_i : i \in \mathbf{I}\right\}$ on lattice $\mathbf{I}$ is a product of scalar RF $\mathbf{S}$ and mean zero Gaussian vector RF $\mathbf{U} = \left\{\vec{U}_i : i \in \mathbf{I}\right\}$ with covariance $C_{\vec{U}}$. For the vector GSM model, the maximum-likelihood estimate of s_j^2 can be determined as follows [9]:

$$s_j^2 = \frac{\vec{X}_j^T C_U^{-1} \vec{X}_j}{M} \qquad (3)$$

where M is the dimensionality of vector $\vec{X}_j$. The estimation of covariance matrix $C_{\vec{U}}$ is also straightforward from the image wavelet coefficients [9]:

$$C_{\vec{U}} = \frac{M}{N} \sum_{j=1}^{N/M} \vec{C}_j \vec{C}_j^T \qquad (4)$$

where N is the dimensionality of $\mathbf{X}$, and in (3) and (4), $(1/N)\sum_{i=1}^{N} s_i^2$ is assumed to be unity without loss of generality [9].

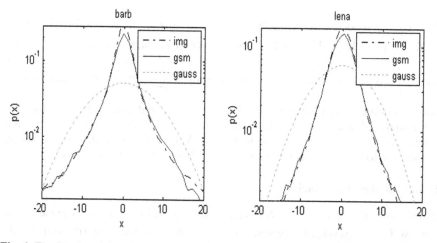

Fig. 1. Empirical marginal distribution of coefficients from LH1 subband of 2 different natural images (blue dot-dashed line), synthesized GSM RF samples from the same subband (red solid line), and a Gaussian with the same standard deviation (green dashed line)

3   Security Analysis of Add-SS Watermarking Based on NSS Model

3.1   Notation and Mathematical Model

Let us first give the notations and conventions used in the current and subsequent sections. Vectors, matrix and sets are represented in bold fonts. Data are written in small letters, and random variables in capital ones. The key notations are listed as follows:

$\mathbf{Y}^j$ and $\mathbf{X}^j$: L_1-dimensional vectors that represent the jth observed water-marked and host signal, respectively.

$\mathbf{Z}^i$:   The L_1-dimensional vector that represent the ith secret spreading vector. Totally L_b spreading vectors are assumed.

$\mathbf{S}$:   The L_1-dimensional vector which is a RF of positive multipliers controlling the local coefficient variances.

B_i^j :   The ith message bit in the jth observed watermarked signal

For the Add-SS watermarking system, the embedding is the addition of the watermark signal which is the modulation of private carriers $\mathbf{Z}^i$ generated depending on the secret key Θ. Without loss of generality, L_b spreading vectors $\mathbf{Z}^i$ are assumed, one for each message bit to be hidden. Therefore the process of embedding can be expressed as [7]:

$$\mathbf{Y}^j = \mathbf{X}^j - \frac{1}{\sqrt{L_b}} \sum_{i=1}^{L_b} \mathbf{Z}^i (-1)^{B_i^j}, \quad 1 \le j \le N_0 \tag{5}$$

The host is modeled as the GSM RF, and the carrier is assumed to be Gaussian, $\mathbf{Z}^i \sim N\left(\mathbf{0}, \sigma_Z^2 \mathbf{I}_{L_1}\right)$. The relative power document/watermark is defined as the Document to Watermark Ratio, i.e., $DWR = 10\log_{10}\left(\dfrac{\sigma_X^2}{\sigma_Z^2}\right)$, where σ_X^2 is the average variance of content. By taking into account the NSS model, the security for the scenarios introduced in the section 1 is assessed in the next section. It should be pointed out that only the results for cases of KMA and WOA are investigated in this paper. The result for KOA is similar to the one in [7], although the NSS model is considered.

3.2 Known Message Attack

The objective of KMA for Add-SS watermarking system is to gain knowledge of secret key Θ (or equivalently the spreading vector $\mathbf{Z}^i$) when the watermarked signals and corresponding messages are known to the attacker. The information theoretic security is measured by the mutual information between the observed watermarked signals and the secret carriers as follows:

$$I\left(\mathbf{Y}^1, \mathbf{Y}^2, \cdots, \mathbf{Y}^{N_0}; \mathbf{Z}^1, \mathbf{Z}^2, \cdots, \mathbf{Z}^{L_b} \mid \mathbf{B}^1, \mathbf{B}^2, \cdots, \mathbf{B}^{N_0}\right) \tag{6}$$

Taking into account the GSM model of host signal, the mutual information in (6) can be further expressed as

$$I\left(\mathbf{Y}^1, \mathbf{Y}^2, \cdots, \mathbf{Y}^{N_0}; \mathbf{Z}^1, \mathbf{Z}^2, \cdots, \mathbf{Z}^{L_b} \mid \mathbf{S}^1, \mathbf{S}^2, \cdots, \mathbf{S}^{N_0}, \mathbf{B}^1, \mathbf{B}^2, \cdots, \mathbf{B}^{N_0}\right) \tag{7}$$

where $\mathbf{S}^i$ and $\mathbf{B}^i$ represents the positive RF and the embedding messages for the ith observation, respectively.

Consider KMA for the scenario of a single observation. When the sent message is known to the attacker, for a single observation ($N_0 = 1$) and single spreading vector ($L_b = 1$), we have

$$I\left(\mathbf{Y};\mathbf{Z}^1 \mid \mathbf{S},\mathbf{B}\right) = \sum_{i=1}^{L_s}\sum_{j=1}^{L_s} I\left(Y_i;Z_j^1 \mid \mathbf{S},\mathbf{B},Y_{i-1},\cdots Y_1,Z_{j-1}^1,\cdots Z_1^1\right) \tag{8-1}$$

$$= \sum_{i=1}^{L_s} I\left(Y_i;Z_i^1 \mid s_i,\mathbf{B}\right) = \sum_{i=1}^{L_s} I\left(Y_i;Z_i^1 \mid s_i,\mathbf{B}=0\right) \tag{8-2}$$

$$= \sum_{i=1}^{L_s}\left[h\left(Y_i \mid s_i,\mathbf{B}=0\right) - h\left(Y_i \mid s_i,\mathbf{B}=0,Z_i^1\right)\right] \tag{8-3}$$

$$= \sum_{i=1}^{L_s}\left[h\left(X_i + Z_i^1 \mid s_i\right) - h\left(X_i \mid s_i\right)\right] \tag{8-4}$$

$$= \sum_{i=1}^{L_s}\left[h\left(N\left(0,s_i^2\sigma_U^2 + \sigma_Z^2\right)\right) - h\left(N\left(0,s_i^2\sigma_U^2\right)\right)\right] \tag{8-5}$$

$$= \frac{1}{2}\sum_{i=1}^{L_s}\log\left(1 + \frac{\sigma_Z^2}{s_i^2\sigma_U^2}\right) \tag{8-6}$$

where we get (8-1) by the chain rule [11], and (8-2) by the fact that Y_i is independent of $Z_j^1, \forall i \neq j$, and (8-4) by the fact that given s_i, X_i is independent of s_j, $\forall i \neq j$. The $h(X)$ in (8) denotes the differential entropy of continuous random variable X, and for $X \sim N(\mu,\sigma^2)$, $h(X) = \frac{1}{2}\log\left(2\pi e\sigma^2\right)$ [11].

When there are multiple carriers, i.e., $L_b > 1$, we have

$$I\left(\mathbf{Y};\mathbf{Z}^1,\mathbf{Z}^2,\cdots,\mathbf{Z}^{L_b} \mid \mathbf{S},\mathbf{B}\right) = \sum_{i=1}^{L_s} I\left(Y_i;Z_i^1,Z_i^2,\cdots,Z_i^{L_b} \mid s_i,\mathbf{B}\right) \tag{9-1}$$

$$= \sum_{i=1}^{L_s}\left\{h(Y_i \mid s_i,\mathbf{B}) - h\left(Y_i \mid s_i,Z_i^1,\cdots,Z_i^{L_b},\mathbf{B}\right)\right\} \tag{9-2}$$

$$= \sum_{i=1}^{L_s}\left\{h\left(X_i + \sum_{j=1}^{L_b}(L_b)^{-1/2} Z_i^j \mid s_i\right) - h\left(X_i \mid s_i\right)\right\} \tag{9-3}$$

$$= \sum_{i=1}^{L_s}\left\{h\left(N\left(0,s_i^2\sigma_U^2 + \sigma_Z^2\right)\right) - h\left(N\left(0,s_i^2\sigma_U^2\right)\right)\right\} \tag{9-4}$$

$$= \frac{1}{2}\sum_{i=1}^{L_s}\log\left(1 + \frac{\sigma_Z^2}{s_i^2\sigma_U^2}\right) \tag{9-5}$$

Therefore the residual entropy after a single observation will be

$$h\left(\mathbf{Z}^1,\mathbf{Z}^2,\cdots,\mathbf{Z}^{L_b}\mid\mathbf{S},\mathbf{Y},\mathbf{B}\right)=\frac{1}{2}\sum_{i=1}^{L_1}\log\left[\left(2\pi e\frac{\sigma_z^2}{L_b}\right)^{L_b}\cdot\frac{s_i^2\sigma_U^2}{s_i^2\sigma_U^2+\sigma_z^2}\right]\qquad(10)$$

The result in (9-5) implies that the information leakage to an attacker is the same whatever the number of carriers.

Comesaña *et al* in [7] give the mutual information for KMA when host is assumed to be Gaussian. The proposition below states that, when taking into account the GSM model, the information leakage is consistently greater than the one obtained in [7], which allows to design more efficient attacking algorithm as described in next section.

Proposition: For the KMA of Add-SS watermarking system and single observation, when the host is modeled as GSM RF, the mutual information between the observed watermarked signals and the spreading vectors is consistently greater than the one when host is assumed to be Gaussian, i.e.,

$$\frac{1}{2}\sum_{i=1}^{L_1}\log\left(1+\frac{\sigma_z^2}{s_i^2\sigma_U^2}\right)\geq\frac{L_1}{2}\log\left(1+\frac{\sigma_z^2}{\sigma_X^2}\right)\qquad(11)$$

Proof: Without loss of generality, take σ_U^2 in (11) to be unity.

Let $I=\frac{1}{2}\sum_{i=1}^{L_1}\log\left(1+\frac{\sigma_z^2}{s_i^2\sigma_U^2}\right)=\frac{1}{2}\sum_{i=1}^{L_1}\log\left(1+\frac{\sigma_z^2}{s_i^2}\right)$, and $\sum_{i=1}^{L_1}s_i^2=E$ (finite Constant)

Denote $p_i=\frac{s_i^2}{E}>0,\quad i=1,\cdots,L_1$, and note that $\sum_{i=1}^{L_1}p_i=1$, we have

$I=\frac{1}{2}\sum_{i=1}^{L_1}\log\left(1+\frac{\sigma_z^2}{p_iE}\right)$, where σ_z^2 is also positive constant.

Let $f(x)=\log\left(1+\frac{\sigma_z^2}{Ex}\right)$, then $f(x)$ is convex due to $f''(x)>0$ [11]

By making use of the convexity of $f(x)$ and Jensen's inequality [11], we can write

$$I=\frac{1}{2}\sum_{i=1}^{L_1}f(p_i)=\frac{L_1}{2}\sum_{i=1}^{L_1}\left[\frac{1}{L_1}f(p_i)\right]\geq\frac{L_1}{2}f\left[\sum_{i=1}^{L_1}\frac{1}{L_1}p_i\right]=\frac{L_1}{2}f\left(\frac{1}{L_1}\right)=\frac{L_1}{2}\log\left(1+\frac{\sigma_z^2}{E/L_1}\right)$$

In view of the fact $\frac{E}{L_1}=\sigma_X^2$, we can conclude the proposition:

$$I=\frac{1}{2}\sum_{i=1}^{L_1}\log\left(1+\frac{\sigma_z^2}{s_i^2}\right)\geq\frac{L_1}{2}\log\left(1+\frac{\sigma_z^2}{E/L_1}\right)=\frac{L_1}{2}\log\left(1+\frac{\sigma_z^2}{\sigma_X^2}\right)$$

By employing the vector GSM model mentioned in section 2, a more efficient security analysis for KMA is developed. The observed watermarked signal is partitioned into non-overlapping blocks with length M, which are assumed to be uncorrelated with each other. For the KMA of single observation and single spreading vector, (8) can be rewritten as:

$$I\left(\mathbf{Y};\mathbf{Z}^1 \mid \mathbf{B},\mathbf{S}\right) \le \sum_{j=1}^{L_t/M} I\left(\vec{Y}_j;\vec{Z}_j^1 \mid s_j,\mathbf{B}\right) = \frac{1}{2}\sum_{j=1}^{L_t/M} \log\left(\frac{\left|s_j^2 C_{\vec{U}} + C_{\vec{Z}}\right|}{\left|C_{\vec{Z}}\right|}\right) \tag{12-1}$$

$\vec{Y}_j$ and $\vec{Z}_j^1$ in (12) are j^{th} vector with length M of observed signal and spreading carrier, respectively. While $C_{\vec{U}}$ and $C_{\vec{Z}}$ are covariance matrix for vector $\vec{U}_i$ and $\vec{Z}_i$ as defined in section 2. In view of the fact that, for n-D continues Gaussian random vector $\vec{X} \sim N\left(\vec{\mu},\Sigma\right)$, $h\left(\vec{X}\right) = 1/2\log(2\pi e)^n |\Sigma|$. And considering that $C_{\vec{U}}$ is symmetric and can be factorized as $\mathbf{Q}\Lambda\mathbf{Q}^T$ with orthonormal $\mathbf{Q}$ and eigenvalues λ_k. (12-1) can be further simplified as

$$I\left(\mathbf{Y};\mathbf{Z}^1 \mid \mathbf{B},\mathbf{S}\right) \le \frac{1}{2}\sum_{j=1}^{L_t/M} \log\left(\frac{\left|s_j^2 C_{\vec{U}} + C_{\vec{Z}}\right|}{\left|C_{\vec{Z}}\right|}\right) = \frac{1}{2}\sum_{j=1}^{L_t/M} \log\left(\frac{\left|s_j^2 \mathbf{Q}\Lambda\mathbf{Q}^T + \sigma_Z^2 \mathbf{I}\right|}{\sigma_Z^{2M}}\right) \tag{12-2}$$

$$= \frac{1}{2}\sum_{j=1}^{L_t/M} \log\left(\frac{\left|s_j^2 \Lambda + \sigma_Z^2 \mathbf{I}\right|}{\sigma_Z^{2M}}\right) = \frac{1}{2}\sum_{j=1}^{L_t/M}\sum_{k=1}^{M} \log\left(1 + \frac{s_j^2 \lambda_k}{\sigma_Z^2}\right) \tag{12-3}$$

We have the similar result for the case of multicarriers when the vector GSM model is used.

3.3 Watermark Only Attack

For the scenario of WOA, the attacker has access only to the watermarked signals. By taking into account the GSM model of host, the security is also quantified by the mutual information between the observed watermarked signals and secret carriers. For WOA of single observation ($N_0 = 1$) and single spreading vector ($L_b = 1$), we have

$$I\left(\mathbf{Y};\mathbf{Z}^1 \mid \mathbf{S}\right) = \sum_{i=1}^{L_t} I\left(Y_i;Z_i^1 \mid s_i\right) = \sum_{i=1}^{L_t}\left(h(Y_i \mid s_i) - h\left(Y_i \mid s_i,Z_i^1\right)\right) \tag{13-1}$$

$$= \sum_{i=1}^{L_t}\left(h(Y_i \mid s_i,\mathbf{B}=0) - h\left(Y_i \mid s_i,Z_i^1\right)\right) \tag{13-2}$$

$$= \sum_{i=1}^{L_t}\left(h\left(X_i + Z_i^1 \mid s_i\right) - h\left(Y_i \mid s_i,Z_i^1\right)\right) \tag{13-3}$$

$$= \sum_{i=1}^{L_b} \left(h\left(N\left(0, s_i^2 \sigma_U^2 + \sigma_Z^2\right)\right) - h\left(Y_i \mid s_i, Z_i^1\right)\right) \tag{13-4}$$

$$= \sum_{i=1}^{L_b} \left(\frac{1}{2} \log\left(2\pi e\left(s_i^2 \sigma_U^2 + \sigma_Z^2\right)\right) - h\left(Y_i \mid s_i, Z_i^1\right)\right) \tag{13-5}$$

We get (13-2) by the independence between Y_i and **B**. And the rightmost term of (13-5) must be numerically computed.

For WOA of single observation and multiple carriers ($N_0 = 1$ and $L_b > 1$), we have

$$I\left(\mathbf{Y}; \mathbf{Z}^1, \mathbf{Z}^2, \cdots, \mathbf{Z}^{L_b} \mid \mathbf{S}\right) = \sum_{i=1}^{L_b} I\left(Y_i; Z_i^1, \cdots, Z_i^{L_b} \mid s_i\right) \tag{14-1}$$

$$= \sum_{i=1}^{L_b} \left(h\left(Y_i \mid s_i\right) - h\left(Y_i \mid s_i, Z_i^1, \cdots, Z_i^{L_b}\right)\right) \tag{14-2}$$

$$= \sum_{i=1}^{L_b} \left[\frac{1}{2} \log\left(2\pi e\left(s_i^2 \sigma_U^2 + \sigma_Z^2\right)\right) - h\left(Y_i \mid s_i, Z_i^1, \cdots, Z_i^{L_b}\right)\right] \tag{14-3}$$

The rightmost term of (14-3) must also be numerically computed.

4 Development of Efficient Attack Algorithm with VB ICA

The algorithm development of attacks to security of Add-SS watermarking system is aimed at estimating the spreading vectors derived from the secret key. Cayre *et al* in [6] proposed a maximum likelihood watermark estimator for KMA, while the ICA is employed for WOA. The conventional ICA method, such as the FastICA [13] adopted in [6], can only take the advantage of the independence among sources (the spreading vectors), the host is assumed to be Gaussian. In this section, we try to develop an efficient algorithm for attack to security based on the framework of variational Bayesian ICA, which allows the incorporation of NSS model of host, and imposition of constraints to spreading vectors.

4.1 Problem Formulation and Model

In view of (5), the process of watermark embedding for Add-SS can be described with (15)

$$\mathbf{Y}_n = \mathbf{H}\mathbf{Z}_n + \mathbf{X}_n, \qquad n = 1, 2, \cdots, L_1 \tag{15}$$

where $\mathbf{Y}_n = \begin{bmatrix} Y_n^1 \\ \vdots \\ Y_n^{N_0} \end{bmatrix}$, $\mathbf{X}_n = \begin{bmatrix} X_n^1 \\ \vdots \\ X_n^{N_0} \end{bmatrix}$ and $\mathbf{Z}_n = \begin{bmatrix} Z_n^1 \\ \vdots \\ Z_n^{L_b} \end{bmatrix}$ are N_0-D observed vector, N_0-D

host and L_b-D carrier vector at interval n, respectively. The $N_0 \times L_b$ **H** is the mixing matrix which is determined by the embedding messages.

With model given in (15), the VB ICA based attacking algorithm is developed to recover the spreading vector $\mathbf{Z}$, which is the one for WOA when only $\mathbf{Y}$ is available, and KMA when both $\mathbf{Y}$ and $\mathbf{H}$ (the embedding messages) are given.

4.2 The Models for Host and Spreading Vector

Instead of the Gaussian, the NSS model GSM is utilized to characterize the behavior of host vector. Given $\mathbf{S}_n$, $\mathbf{X}_n$ is Gaussian distributed, with zero mean and diagonal covariance matrix Σ_n (or precision matrix Λ_n, $\Lambda_n = \Sigma^{-1}$), i.e.,

$$p(\mathbf{X}_n \mid \mathbf{S}_n) \sim N(\mathbf{0}, \Sigma_n) = N(\mathbf{0}, \Lambda_n) \tag{16}$$

where $p(x_n^i \mid s_n^i) \sim N(0, s_n^{i2} \sigma_U^{i2})$, $\mathbf{X}_n = \begin{bmatrix} X_n^1 & \cdots & X_n^{N_0} \end{bmatrix}^T$.

Each spreading vector Z_n^i is modeled by a mixture of Gaussian (MoG), and the Gaussian distribution is a special case of MoG.

$$p(Z_n^i \mid \theta) = \sum_{q_i=1}^{m_i} \pi_{i,q_i} N(Z_n^i; \mu_{i,q_i}, \beta_{i,q_i}) \tag{17}$$

where μ_{i,q_i} and β_{i,q_i} are the mean and precision of q_i th Gaussian of Z^i, respectively.

4.3 The Generative Model

The probability of observing vector given spreading vectors and parameters is

$$p(\mathbf{Y}_n \mid \mathbf{Z}_n, \mathbf{H}, \Lambda_n) = \left| \det\left(\frac{1}{2\pi}\Lambda_n\right) \right|^{\frac{1}{2}} \exp\left(-\frac{E_d}{2}\right) \tag{18}$$

where $E_d = (\mathbf{Y}_n - \mathbf{HZ}_n)^T \Lambda_n (\mathbf{Y}_n - \mathbf{HZ}_n)$.

The sources, i.e., the spreading vectors can be further factorized as

$$p(\mathbf{Z}_n) = \prod_{i=1}^{L_h} p(Z_n^i) \tag{19}$$

With the generative model, the likelihood of the IID data $D = \{\mathbf{Y}_1, \mathbf{Y}_2, \cdots, \mathbf{Y}_{L_1}\}$ is then

$$p(D \mid \mathbf{H}, \Lambda, \theta) = \prod_{n=1}^{L_1} \sum_{q=1}^{m} \int p(\mathbf{Y}_n, \mathbf{Z}_n, q \mid \mathbf{H}, \Lambda_n, \theta) d\mathbf{Z} \tag{20}$$

The model parameters $\{\mathbf{H}, \Lambda, \theta\}$ can be learnt through EM algorithm.

4.4 The Development Efficient Attack Algorithm with VB ICA

Let $\Theta = \{\mathbf{H}, \Lambda, \theta\}$, then the evidence for model M is

$$p(D \mid M) = \sum_{q=1}^{m} \iint p(D, \mathbf{Z}, q, \Theta \mid M) d\Theta d\mathbf{Z} \tag{21}$$

The log-evidence L is

$$L = \log \sum_{q=1}^{m} \iint p'(\mathbf{Z}, q, \Theta) \frac{p(D, \mathbf{Z}, q, \Theta \mid M)}{p'(\mathbf{Z}, q, \Theta)} d\Theta d\mathbf{Z} \qquad (22)$$

This can be further simplified as

$$L = F(M) + KL\left[p'(\mathbf{Z}, q, \Theta), p(\mathbf{Z}, q, \Theta \mid D, M)\right] \qquad (23)$$

where $F(M) = \langle \log p(\mathbf{D}, \mathbf{Z}, q, \Theta \mid M) \rangle_{p'(\mathbf{Z}, q, \Theta)}$ is the negative variational free energy and KL is the Kullback-Liebler Divergence.

Maximizing F in (23) makes the $p'(\mathbf{Z}, q, \Theta)$ approximate the true posterior. Due to space restriction, only the key steps and incorporation of NSS model in the algorithm development are given in this section. The detail derivation and development of the proposed VB ICA based attack algorithm can follow that of [14].

5   Simulation Results and Analysis

This section demonstrates the performance of the proposed attack algorithm in the framework of VB ICA, which incorporates the NSS model. We test multiple 512×512 natural images with different texture characteristics. The images are decomposed with biorthogonal 9/7 wavelet into 2-level pyramid, among which the coarsest subbands, i.e., HL2, LH2 and HH2, are used to embed the watermarks. In our simulation, L_b spreading carriers with length L_1 are used ($L_b = 2$ or 4 , $L_1 = 512$ or 1024), one for each message bit to be sent. The spreading carriers with both Gaussian and MoG distributions are employed. Consequently at most 96 and 48 observed watermarked signals are available from each test image, when the lengths of spreading vector are 512 and 1024, respectively. The GSM is only a statistical characterization of host and can be obtained through watermarked signal directly, considering the fact that sufficient large DWR is always taken for practical watermark application. The algorithm is implemented with observed watermarked signal from both single and multiple images. The performance is measured by the average normalized correlation between the recovered spreading vector and the original one vs. the number of observations. If there are L_b spreading vectors and $\mathbf{Z}^i$ and $\hat{\mathbf{Z}}^i$ denote the ith original and recovered one, respectively, the average correlation is defined as

$$\eta = \frac{1}{L_b} \sum_{i=1}^{L_b} \frac{\hat{\mathbf{Z}}_i^T \mathbf{Z}_i}{\|\hat{\mathbf{Z}}_i\| \cdot \|\mathbf{Z}_i\|} \qquad (24)$$

Case 1: WOA for Single Image

Four 512×512 test images, namely Barb, F16, Fishing boat and Lena, are used in our simulation. Each spreading vector $\mathbf{Z}^i$ is generated with Gaussian or MoG model, which is then modulated with 1 message bit. The length of spreading vector L_1 is set to 512. And the number of spreading carriers L_b is set to 2 or 4. The mixing matrix

H in (15) is determined by the hidden messages, which is unknown to the attacker for WOA. The ith watermarked signal is generated with $\mathbf{Y}^i = \lambda_i \mathbf{Z}^i \mathbf{H} + \mathbf{X}^i$, where the λ_i is the embedding factor to control the *DWR* and $\mathbf{X}^i$ is modeled with GSM. The GSM model can be obtained through the observed watermarked signal directly or learnt with the EM algorithm during the implementation of VB ICA. For simulation in case 1, the observed watermarked signals are obtained from the single image, and 96 observations are available for each image. The attacking algorithm with FastICA as used in [6], is also implemented and compared with the proposed attack algorithm. Fig.2 gives the performances of both FastICA and the proposed VB ICA based algorithm for WOA. Fig.2 (a) shows the situation with image Barb, where the 2 spreading vectors are generated with Gaussian model ($L_b = 2$ and $L_1 = 512$). It is observed that,

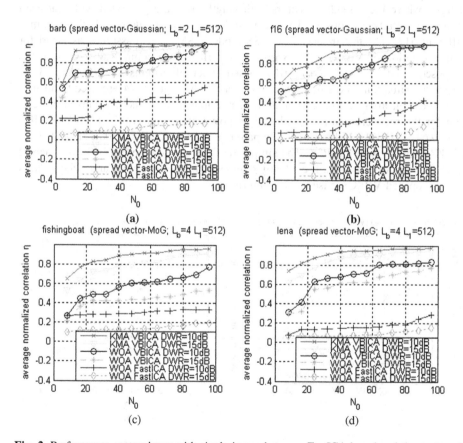

Fig. 2. Performance comparisons with single image between FastICA based and the proposed VB ICA based attack algorithms for WOA. (a) image Barb; spreading vector- Gaussian; $L_b = 2$ and $L_1 = 512$; (b) image F16; spreading vector- Gaussian; $L_b = 2$ and $L_1 = 512$; (c) image Fishing boat; spreading vector-MoG; $L_b = 4$ and $L_1 = 512$; (d) image Lena; spreading vector-MoG; $L_b = 4$ and $L_1 = 512$.

with the 96 observed watermarked signals from Barb image, the normalized correlation η for the recovered carriers with the proposed algorithm is 0.98 ($DWR = 10dB$)and 0.95 ($DWR = 15dB$) as compared to 0.52 ($DWR = 10dB$) and 0.18 ($DWR = 15dB$) with FastICA. The similar situations are observed with F16 image (Fig.2(b)) and other images. Fig.2 (c) and (d) shows the performance comparisons of the two algorithms with images Fishing boat and Lena, where the 4 spreading vectors are generated with MoG models ($L_b = 4$ and $L_1 = 512$). Significant performance improvements are also observed with the proposed VB ICA algorithm.

Case 2: WOA for Multiple Images
The proposed VB ICA based attack algorithm is also implemented with multiple images, where the spreading vectors with length 1024 are generated with Gaussian model and totally 336 observed watermarked signals are randomly obtained from 7 different 512×512 test images. The NSS model GSM is also assumed as priori for implementation of VB ICA. Fig.3 gives the performance comparisons between the proposed VB ICA based and FastICA based attack algorithms for WOA. Fig.3 (b) shows the situation where 4 spreading vectors with length 1024 are used. And it is observed that, after 336 observations from multiple images, the normalized correlation for the recovered carriers with the proposed algorithm is 0.76 ($DWR = 10dB$) and 0.64 ($DWR = 15dB$), as compared to 0.53 ($DWR = 10dB$) and 0.28 ($DWR = 15dB$) with FastICA. The similar result is also shown in Fig.3 (a), where 2 spreading carriers are used. It evidently demonstrates the feasibility and effectiveness of the proposed VB ICA based attack algorithm.

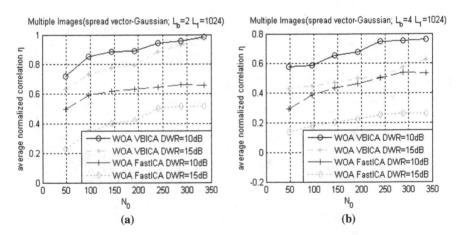

Fig. 3. Performance comparisons with multiple images between FastICA based and the proposed VB ICA based attack algorithms for WOA. (a) multiple images; spreading vector- Gaussian; $L_b = 2$ and $L_1 = 1024$; (b) multiple images; spreading vector-Gaussian; $L_b = 4$ and $L_1 = 1024$.

Case 3: KMA
The same framework of VB ICA for WOA can be reformulated for KMA. In case of KMA, the embedded messages for each observation are known to attacker, therefore the mixing matrix **H** is determined. Fig.2 shows the performance of the proposed VB ICA attack algorithm for KMA, which allows the incorporation of NSS model of host. The spreading vectors with length 512 are generated with both Gaussian and MoG models, and number of carriers is set to be 2 or 4. In all the situations of Fig.2, the performance of the proposed algorithm is satisfactory and normalized correlation for recovered spreading vectors is consistently near 1 after 96 observations.

6 Conclusions

This paper presents both information theoretic analysis and practical attack algorithm for spread-spectrum based watermarking security incorporating natural scene statistics (NSS) model. The security is quantified by the mutual information between the observed watermarked signals and the secret carriers. The new security measures are derived based on the NSS model GSM, which allows for more accurate evaluation of watermarking security. The practical attack algorithm is also developed in the framework of variational Bayesian ICA, which is shown to increase the performance and flexibility by allowing incorporation of prior knowledge of host and taking full advantages of the potentials suggested by information-theoretic evaluations. Extensive simulations are carried out to demonstrate the feasibility and effectiveness of the proposed attack algorithm.

Acknowledgment

The authors appreciate the supports received from NSFC (60773200, 90604008, 60633030), NSF of Guangdong (7003722, 04205407, 06023191), and 973 Program (2006CB303104)

References

1. Cox, I.J., Miller, M.L., Bloom, J.A.: Digital Watermarking. Elsevier Science, Amsterdam (2002)
2. Kalker, T.: Consideration on watermarking security. In: Proc. MMSP, Cannes, France, pp. 201–206 (October 2001)
3. Furon, T., et al.: Security Analysis, European Project IST-1999-10987 CERTIMARK, Deliverable D.5.5 (2002)
4. Kerckhoffs, A.: La cryptographie militaire. Journal des militaries 9, 5–38 (1983)
5. Pérez-Freire, L., Comesaña, P., Troncoso-Pastoriza, J.R., Pérez-González, F.: Watermarking security: a survey. In: Shi, Y.Q. (ed.) Transactions on Data Hiding and Multimedia Security I. LNCS, vol. 4300, pp. 41–72. Springer, Heidelberg (2006)
6. Cayre, F., Fontaine, C., Furon, T.: Watermarking security: Theory and practice. IEEE Trans. Signal Processing 53, 3976–3987 (2005)

7. Comesaña, P., Pérez-Freire, L., Pérez-Gonzále, F.: Fundamentals of data hiding security and their application to spread-spectrum analysis. In: Barni, M., Herrera-Joancomartí, J., Katzenbeisser, S., Pérez-González, F. (eds.) IH 2005. LNCS, vol. 3727, pp. 146–160. Springer, Heidelberg (2005)
8. Lyu, S., Simoncelli, E.P.: Statistical modeling of images with fields of Gaussian scale mixtures. Advances in Neural Information Processing Systems 19 (May 2007)
9. Wainwright, M.J., Simoncelli, E.P., Wilsky, A.S.: Random cascades on wavelet trees and their use in analyzing and modeling natural images. Appl. Comput. Harmon. Anal. 11, 89–123 (2001)
10. Sheikh, H.R., Bovik, A.C., Veciana, C.: An information fidelity criterion for image quality assessment using natural scene statistics. IEEE Trans. Image Processing 14(12), 2117–2128 (2005)
11. Cover, T.M., Thomas, J.A.: Elements of Information Theory. John Wiley & Sons, Chichester (1991)
12. Hyvarinen, A., Oja, E.: Independent component analysis: Algorithms and Applications. Neural Networks 13, 411–430 (2000)
13. Hyvarinen, A.: Fast and robust fixed-point algorithms for independent component analysis. IEEE Trans. Neural Networks 10(3), 626–634 (1999)
14. Choudrey, R.A.: Variational Method for Bayesian Independent Component Analysis, Ph.D. Thesis, Oxford University (2002)
15. Choudrey, R.A., Robert, S.J.: Variational mixture Bayesian independent component analysis. Neural Computation 15(1) (2003)

Block-Chain Based Fragile Watermarking Scheme with Superior Localization

Hong-Jie He[1], Jia-Shu Zhang[1], and Heng-Ming Tai[2]

[1] Sichuan Key Lab of Signal and Information Processing, Southwest Jiaotong University, Chengdu 610031, China
[2] Department of Electrical Engineering, University of Tulsa, Tulsa, OK 74104, USA

Abstract. This paper proposes a block-chain based fragile watermarking scheme to address the issue of security and accuracy of tamper localization. The relationship between the security strength and block size is also discussed. In the proposed scheme, all blocks in the original image randomly form a linear chain based on the secret key in such a manner that the watermark of an image block is hidden in the next block in the block-chain. In the tamper detection process, the legitimacy of image block is determined by the adjacent blocks of the block and the following block in the block-chain. Compared with conventional block-wise fragile watermarking techniques, the proposed block-chain based scheme not only satisfactorily resists the VQ and collage attacks, but also improves the localization accuracy without sacrificing security. Moreover, the security strength is proposed to quantitatively evaluate the security ability of fragile watermarking techniques.

Keywords: fragile watermarking, block-chain, security strength, false rejection rate, false acceptance rate.

1 Introduction

Security and accuracy of tamper localization are two critical requirements for the fragile watermarking techniques. In the existing block-wise fragile watermarking techniques, the security completely dependents on the cryptographic hash or the encryption mechanism. The more the bits of hash-code are, the higher the security is. As a consequence, the accuracy of tamper localization will be sacrificed in that the block size is also enlarged with the constant embedding payload. In this paper, a block-chain based fragile watermarking algorithm is proposed to provide a graceful balance between the security and the block size in terms of the accuracy of localization.

Nowadays, the authenticity of digital images is of great threat in that it is not difficult to modify or forge the image content without leaving detectable traces by publicly available image processing software packages, such as Adobe Photoshop. Therefore, authentication techniques are required in applications where verification of integrity and authenticity of an image is essential [1]. Digital watermarking provides a possible solution to the above issue. In 1997, Wong

K. Solanki, K. Sullivan, and U. Madhow (Eds.): IH 2008, LNCS 5284, pp. 147–160, 2008.
© Springer-Verlag Berlin Heidelberg 2008

[2] proposed the block-wise fragile water-marking scheme. It was capable to detect and localize any unauthorized tamper block, but vulnerable to vector quantization (VQ) codebook attack [3] and collage attack [4]. Investigations have been performed to improve this drawback and some feasible countermeasures have been proposed [5-10]. These schemes were mainly to introduce the block-wise dependency by adding new parameters in the hash function, for example, the distinct image index [5, 6], the previous block and hash-code [8], and the gradient image block [9] etc.

In these techniques, the watermark of an image block is embedded into the LSB of the same block. The contents (7 MSBs: most significant bits) of the image blocks and the corresponding watermarks are in the public domain, and the security is only based on the cryptographic hash or the encryption mechanism. Wong [2, 5] believed that the 64-bit hash code is secure, because it would take 2^{64} tries to find an input resulting into a given hash-code via the exhaustive search (ES) attack. While some researchers [6, 10] pointed out that at least 128 bits hash-code should be used to defeat the cryptographic attacks such as Birthday Attack. If the watermark's embedding payload is 1 bpp (bit per pixel) [11], the block size should contain at least 64 pixels. This implies that the accuracy of tamper localization is no less than 64 pixels. It is known that good localization property is a desired feature for fragile watermarking techniques. To achieve it, the embedding payload is extended from 1 bpp to 2 bpp [12] or 3 bpp [13]. Apparently, increasing the watermark payload alone is not adequate to improve the localization accuracy.

In this paper, an effective block-wise fragile watermarking method is developed for image tamper localization. It provides a superior localization property compared to the existing block-wise fragile watermark algorithms with the same security and the same watermark payload. The proposed scheme first form a linear circle chain, called the block-chain, from all blocks in an image based on the secret key k_1. Then the watermark of the image block is hidden in the subsequent block in the block-chain based on another secret key k_2. These strategies make the content and the embedded watermark of image block secret. In the tamper detection process, we take the block and all its adjacent blocks and the following block into account for consistency. The legitimacy of the test block is determined by comparing the number of inconsistent adjacent blocks of the test block with that of the subsequent one. The localization accuracy of this method is compared with that of the existing block-wise fragile watermarking schemes by examining the relationship between the security strength and the block size. Theoretical analysis and experimental results demonstrate that the proposed method sufficiently resists the VQ and collage attacks, and improves the localization accuracy without sacrificing the security when the block size is decreased from 8×8 pixels to 4×4 pixels.

2   Block-Chain Based Fragile Watermarking Scheme

We assume that the watermark payload of the proposed block-chain based fragile watermarking scheme is 1 bpp, the same as current block-wise fragile watermarking techniques [2, 5-9]. The invisible watermark image W of the same size as the original image is formed by periodically replicating the bi-level logo. For convenient description, we introduce some notations.

- k_1, k_2: secret keys;
- X, W, Y, Y^*: Original image, watermark, the watermarked image, and the tested image;
- X_i, W_i, Y_i, Y_i^*: the ith image block of the corresponding image;
- $\widetilde{X}_i, \widetilde{Y}_i\ \widetilde{Y}_i^*$: the contents (7 MSBs) of the corresponding image block;
- $N(= m \times n)$: number of blocks in an image;
- $N_b(= m_b \times n_b)$: number of pixels in an image block;
- $A_8(X_i)$: the neighborhood set consisting of eight adjacent blocks of block X_i.

In general, an image can be viewed as an ordered set formed by all blocks, i.e., $X = \{X_i \mid i = 1, 2, ..., N\}$. Suppose that the blocks are numbered from top-to-bottom and left-to-right. As depicted in Fig. 1, the neighborhood set $A_8(X_i)$ is,

$$A_8(X_i) = \{X_{i+1}, X_{i+n}, X_{i+n+1}, X_{i-n+1}, X_{i-1}, X_{i-n}, X_{i+n-1}, X_{i-n-1}\} \quad (1)$$

Note that the periodic boundary condition (torus topology) is used to ensure that all blocks in $A_8(X_i)$ are inside the image.

2.1   Block-Chain Generation

In our work, the watermark derived from a block is not embedded into the same block; rather, it is hidden in other block. Fig. 2 depicts the position at which the watermark is placed and the structure of a watermarked block. Here, the watermark information of the block X_{i0} is embedded in the block X_{i1}, the watermark of block X_{i1} is embedded in the block X_{i2}, and the watermark of block X_{i2} is embedded in the block X_{i3}, and so on. In other words, watermark embedding enables all blocks in an image to form a linear chain $\{X_{i0}, X_{i1}, X_{i2}, X_{i3}, ..., X_{iN}\}$,

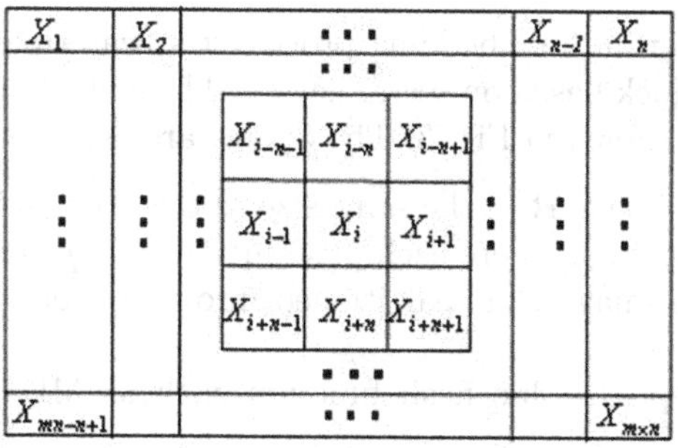

Fig. 1. Neighborhood set of X_i

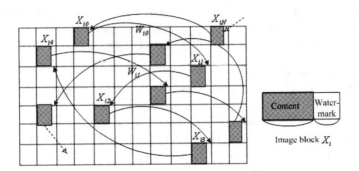

Fig. 2. Block-chain and structure of watermarked image block

which we call it the block-chain. Hence, we generate the block-chain prior to the watermark embedding. The block-chain of an image $X = \{X_i \mid i = 1, 2, ..., N\}$ is formulated as,

$$X_{\_BC} = \{(X_i, X_{i'}) \mid i, i' \in [1, N]\} \tag{2}$$

where $X_{i'}$ is the next block of X_i, That is, the watermark of X_i is hidden in its next block $X_{i'}$.

To satisfy the security and tamper localization [14], the next block $X_{i'}$ of each block X_i should be randomly distributed in the whole image. Moreover, the watermark derived from different blocks must not be inserted into the same block; specifically, $i' \neq j'$ for $\forall i, j \in [1, N]$, and $i \neq j$. Thus the random sequence is used for the block-chain generation. For each image block X_i, the process of generating its next block $X_{i'}$ is described as follows.

Step1: Based on the secret key k_1, a random sequence $R^1 = (r_1^1, r_2^1, ..., r_N^1)$ of length N is generated.
Step2: An ordered index sequences $(a_1, a_2, ..., a_N)$ such that $r_{a_1}^1 \leq r_{a_2}^1 \leq ... \leq r_{a_N}^1$ is obtained by sorting out the random sequence R^1.
Step3: For each block X, assign the index of its next block $X_{i'}$ be $i' = a_i$, i.e., $X_{i'} = X_{a_i}$.

2.2   Watermark Embedding

In the proposed watermark embedding process, the watermark of each block is hidden in the next block based on secret key k_2. The embedding process consists of six operations, as shown in Fig. 3. The details are described as follows.

Step1: The random image $\mathbf{R}$ of the same size as the original image is generated based on the secret key k_2, where each pixel in $\mathbf{R}$ is an integer in interval $[0, 3]$;
Step2: The random image $\mathbf{R}$ is partitioned into non-overlapping blocks $\{R_i \mid i = 1, 2, ..., N\}$;
Step3: Using a cryptographic hash function such as MD5, we compute the hash-code of block X_i,

$$H(m, n, \tilde{X}_i) = (d_1, d_2, ..., d_p) \tag{3}$$

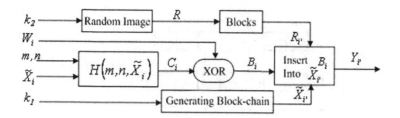

Fig. 3. Block diagram of the embedding procedure to each image block

Note that, we take the first N_b bits to form C_i in the case where $p > N_b$. **Step4:** The binary data block, B_i, is formed by combining W_i with C_i using a pixel by pixel exclusive OR operation,

$$B_i = C_i \oplus W_i \qquad (4)$$

Step5: According to the method described in sub-section 2.1, the block-chain can be generated by the secret key k_1. The next block $X_{i'}$ of block X_i and the corresponding random block $R_{i'}$ generated by the secret key k_2 are obtained; **Step6:** The watermarked block $Y_{i'} = \{Y_{i'j} \mid j = 1, 2, ..., N_b\}$ is obtained using the corresponding original image block $X_{i'}$, binary data block B_i, and random block $R_{i'}$. For each pixel $x_{i'j}$ in the block $X_{i'}$, the position at which b_{ij} is hidden is decided by the value of the corresponding $r_{i'j}$. Fig. 4 illustrates the process of watermark embedding for pixel $x_{i'j}$ as $r_{i'j=2}$. This situation can be expressed generally in the form,

$$y_{i'j} = \lfloor \tilde{x}_{i'j}/t \rfloor \times 2t + b_{ij} \times t + v \qquad (5)$$

where $\tilde{x}_{i'j} = \lfloor x_{i'j}/2 \rfloor, t = 2^{r_{i'j}}$,and $v = mod(\tilde{x}_{i'j}, t)$.The symbol $\lfloor x \rfloor$ denotes the largest integer less than or equal to x and mod denotes the modulo operation.

In the above procedure, two user keys k_1 and k_2 are adopted to embed the fragile watermarks in a more secure way. This makes it difficult to obtain the content and the embedded watermark of image block without secret keys, which the security of the presented method depends on. In the following, we examine the quality of the watermarked image using the peak-signal-to-noise-ratio (PSNR) value [1]. We can obtain the difference between the watermarked pixel $y_{i'j}$ and the original one $x_{i'j}$,

$$\begin{aligned} |x_{i'j} - y_{i'j}| &= |(2v + l_{i'j}) - (b_{ij} \times t + v)| \\ &= |v + l_{i'j} - b_{ij} \times t| \end{aligned} \qquad (6)$$

where $b_{ij}, l_{i'j} \in \{0, 1\}$. Assume that the probability when b_{ij} and $l_{i'j}$ equal to 0 or 1 is identical. We compute the average energy of distortion for each given $r_{i'j}$ as,

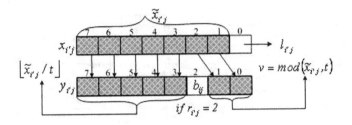

Fig. 4. Watermark hiding based on the user key k_2

$$E\left(|x_{i'j} - y_{i'j}|^2\right) = \sum_{b_{ij}=0}^{1} \sum_{l_{i'j}=0}^{1} |x_{i'j} - y_{i'j}|^2$$

$$= \sum_{b_{ij}=0}^{1} \sum_{l_{i'j}=0}^{1} |v + l_{i'j} - b_{ij} \times t|^2 \qquad (7)$$

$$= v^2 + (v+1)^2 + (v-t)^2 + (1+v-t)^2$$

Also assume that the distribution of both the original 4 LSBs and r_{ij} are uniform, then the average energy of distortion caused by watermarking on each pixel is,

$$E_D = \sum_{r_{i'j}=0}^{3} E\left(|x_{i'j} - y_{i'j}|^2\right)$$

$$= \sum_{r_{i'j}=0}^{3} \left(v^2 + (v+1)^2 + (v-t)^2 + (1+v-t)^2\right) \qquad (8)$$

$$= \sum_{t=1,2,4,8} \sum_{v=0}^{2t-1} (1/t)\left(v^2 + (v+1)^2 + (v-t)^2 + (1+v-t)^2\right)$$

This yields $E_D = 7.5$. Then PSNR is approximately [13],

$$PSNR = 10 \times log_{10}\left(255^2/E_D\right) = 39.53dB \qquad (9)$$

2.3   Image Verification

The watermark of an image block is inserted in the other block, which makes it difficult to detect and localize the possible tampering [15]. In this paper, the test block and all adjacent blocks of it and its next block are taken into account for consistency to determine the legitimacy of it. The proposed process of image verification includes two parts: watermark extraction and watermark verification.

(1)Watermark Extraction. Let Y^* represents the tested image, which can be a distorted watermarked image or unaltered one. Watermark extraction can be considered as the inverse process of watermark embedding. For each tested block

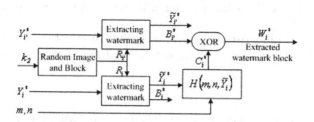

Fig. 5. Block diagram of the watermark extraction procedure for each block

Y_i^*, its next block $Y_{i'}^*$ can be obtained according to the block-chain generated by the secret key k_1. Fig.5 depicts the proposed procedure of watermark extraction for each block. It consists of five functional blocks.

step 1: Followed by the stage 1 & 2 in watermark embedding algorithm, the random image is generated and divided into blocks R_i based on the secret key k_2.

step 2: For an image block Y_i^*, the binary data B_i^* hidden in it and its content $\widetilde{Y}_i^*$ can be extracted according to the corresponding random block R_i, respectively. Specifically, each pixel in B_i^* and $\widetilde{Y}_i^*$ is computed by the following expressions.

$$b_{ij}^* = mod\left(\lfloor y_{ij}^*/2^{r_{ij}}, 2 \rfloor\right) \tag{10}$$

$$\widetilde{y}_{ij}^* = \lfloor y_{ij}^*/2^{r_{ij}+1} \rfloor \times 2^{r_{ij}} + mod(y_{ij}^*, t) \tag{11}$$

step 3: According to formula (10), the binary data $B_{i'}^*$ embedded in $Y_{i'}^*$ can also be obtained using the corresponding random block $R_{i'}$.

step 4: Followed by the step 3 in watermark embedding algorithm, the value of C_i is formed by $H\left(m, n, \widetilde{Y}_i^*\right)$.

step 5: The watermark W_i^* extracted from the block Y_i^* can be achieved by the following expression,

$$W_i^* = C_i^* \oplus B_{i'}^* \tag{12}$$

The extracted watermark W_i^* is dependent on both the test block Y_i^* and its next block $Y_{i'}^*$.

(2)Watermark Verification. We use a binary sequence $T = \{t_i \mid i = 1, 2, ..., N\}$, which we call the tamper detection mark (TDM), to depict the validity of each block. If $t_i = 1$, the corresponding block Y_i^* is invalid; otherwise, the block Y_i^* is authentic. The following verification procedure is used to obtain the TDM.

Step 1 - Consistency inspection: The block consistency mark $D = \{d_i \mid i = 1, 2, ..., N\}$ is constructed by comparing the original watermark with the extracted one. That is,

$$d_i = \begin{cases} 1 & , \quad W_i \neq W_i^* \\ 0 & , \quad W_i = W_i^* \end{cases} \tag{13}$$

Obviously, the block Y_i^* is inconsistent if $d_i = 1$; otherwise, it is a consistent block.

Step 2 - Consistency statistic: Form the sequence $\Gamma = \{\tau_i \mid i = 1, 2, ..., N\}$, where τ_i denotes the number of nonzero d_j in $A_8(d_i)$ obtained from (1), that is,

$$\tau_i = \sum_{\forall d_j \in A_8(d_i)} d_j \tag{14}$$

Step 3 - Legitimacy inspection: The TDM can be initialized by the following expressions.

$$d_i = \begin{cases} 1 & , \quad (d_i \neq 0)\&(\tau_i \geq \tau_{i'}) \\ 0 & , \quad otherwise \end{cases} \tag{15}$$

where $\tau_{i'}$ is the consistency statistic of the next block $Y_{i'}^*$ of block Y_i^*.

Step 4 - Post-processing: Let $\delta_i = \sum_{\forall t_j \in A_8(t_i)} t_j$, the value t_i in the TDM is rechecked by the following,

If $t_i = 0$ and $\delta_i \geq 5$, set $t_i = 1$;
If $t_i = 1$ and $\delta_i \leq 1$, set $t_i = 0$;

It can be seen from (15) that the legitimacy of the image block Y_i^* is determined by d_i, τ_i, and $\tau_{i'}$. According to (14), the value of τ_i is computed using the consistency of the eight neighboring blocks of Y_i^*. To obtain the consistency of a block, two blocks, i.e., itself and its next block are visited. Thus the proposed scheme takes $(1 + 2 \times 8) \times 2 = 34$ blocks into consideration to determine the validity of an image block. This approach effectively lifts the block-wise independency and makes the proposed scheme less vulnerable to the VQ and collage attacks.

Another concern is the ability of tamper detection of the proposed method. The full in-depth theoretical analysis of the tamper localization performance of the proposed method will be another important and involved research topic. In this paper, we will demonstrate the effectiveness of tamper detection of the proposed scheme by experimental and statistical results in section 4.

3   Relationship between the Security Strength and the Block Size

Security is an important aspect of fragile watermarking techniques. Recent literature on fragile watermarking indicated that security refers to "the inability by unauthorized users to manipulate the watermarked authentic image without being detected" [1]. For quantitative evaluation, we adopt the measure of the success forgery probability (SFP) introduced in [16]. The SFP represents the probability that a manipulated pixel is undetected by the verification system, and such manipulation refers to various possible attacks. The smaller the SFP of the verification system is, the stronger the security strength (SS). Here we define the security strength of the verification system as,

$$SS = min \left\{ log_2 \left(\frac{1}{P_{|\alpha A}} \right) \right\} \tag{16}$$

where $P_{|\alpha A}$ is the SFP of the verification system for a given attack, and $min\{.\}$ is the smallest element in all elements. The unit of the SS is bit.

In the following, we discuss the security of the proposed method using SS. Assume that the attackers already know every detail of the watermarking method, including the Hash function, watermark logo, size of the image block, and image size, except the two secret keys k_1 and k_2. For simplicity and without loss of generality, let the block size be N_b pixels and the embedding capacity 1 bpp (bit per pixel). The number of watermarks for each image block is N_b bits.

In our block-chain watermarking scheme, two keys k_1 and k_2 are employed to securely insert the fragile watermarks. From the watermarked image, it is difficult to find out the content (one of the input parameters of the Hash function) and the corresponding watermark information (the output of Hash function) of an image block without secret keys, thus both the input and the output of the Hash function are not known in public. This makes the proposed scheme less vulnerable to the cryptographic attacks such as Birthday Attack proposed in [10].

It can be seen from Fig. 4 that the watermark bit in a watermarked pixel has four possible positions. As a result, without the secret keys, the probability that the content or embedded watermark is correctly extracted from a watermarked image block is $\frac{1}{4^{N_b}}$. Then the SFP of the proposed scheme under the ES attack is,

$$
\begin{aligned}
P_{our|ESA} &= N_b/(4^{N_b} \times N \times 4^{N_b}) \\
&= N_b/(N \times 2^{4N_b})
\end{aligned} \tag{17}
$$

Accordingly, the security strength is,

$$
S_{our|ESA} = 4N_b + \log_2 N - \log_2 N_b \tag{18}
$$

On the other hand, for conventional block-wise fragile watermarking schemes, the watermark of an image block is publicly embedded in the LSB of the same block. For each original image block, the number of watermarked one is determined by the number of watermark bits and expressed as 2^{N_b}. Thus the SFP of conventional block-wise watermarking schemes under the ES attack is,

$$
P_{conv|ESA} = N_b/2^{N_b} \tag{19}
$$

and its SS is,

$$
S_{conv|ESA} = N_b - \log_2 N_b \tag{20}
$$

It follows from (18) and (20) that the security strength of our method is about four times that of conventional fragile watermarking schemes when the number of pixels in each image block is identical. Note that the security strength of the proposed method increases with image size. One important point to notice is that the security strength of fragile watermarking techniques generally goes up with the number of pixels in an image block. Therefore, the block size can be adjusted to the specific requirement of an application for a given embedding capacity.

As pointed out in [10], 64 bits watermark can be considered secure, because an exhaustive search would take $2^{64} \approx 1.84 \times 10^{19}$ tries. According to (18), the proposed scheme selects the block size of 4×4 pixels. This results in the SS of our scheme to be better than 64 bit. For example, for an image of size 256×256, the SS of the proposed scheme is 72 bit.

4   Experimental Results

In all experiments, the grayscale images are used as test images, and the MATLAB function $rand(.)$ is used to generate the random sequence based on the secret keys. For quantitative evaluation, three measures were introduced to evaluate the performance of tamper detection. They are the tampering ratio (TR), the false acceptance rate (FAR), and the false rejection rate (FRR)

$$\textbf{TR:} R_t = N_t/N \times 100\% \tag{21}$$

$$\textbf{FAR:} R_{fa} = (1 - N_{td}/N_t) \times 100\% \tag{22}$$

$$\textbf{FRR:} R_{fr} = N_{vd}/(N - N_t) \times 100\% \tag{23}$$

where N_t the number of the tampered blocks, N_{td} the number of tampered blocks which are correctly detected, N_{vd} the number of valid blocks which are falsely detected. In the ideal situation, the values of both FAR and FRR should be zero with different tamper ratio [17].

First experiment considers the ordinary tampering. The original image of size 512×512, as shown in Fig. 6(a), is used. Fig. 6(b) is the watermark logo of size 64×80. Using the proposed scheme, the watermarked image is generated and shown in Fig. 6(c). The PSNR is 39.64 dB, which accords with the value obtained by (9). The watermarked image was modified, as shown in Fig. 6(d) via four different modifications: (1) a tortoise pasted in the right-bottom, (2) the letters "ABC" in the left-top, (3) a small stone pasted on between two feet of woman, and (4) a small grass pasted in the bottom. The modifications are so natural that one can hardly suspect any changes that had been made to this picture. The tampering ratio (TR) is about 2.31% in Fig. 6(d). With the correct keys, the watermark can be extracted from Fig. 6(d). Fig. 6(e) shows the watermark difference, which represents the difference between the original watermark W and the extracted one W^*. It can be seen that some valid blocks are detected. Using the proposed watermark verification, TDM is obtained and displayed in Fig. 6(f). It clearly shows the tampered blocks. The values of FAR and FRR are 0.53% and 0.45%, respectively.

Next we consider the effect against collage attack. The one considered here is an improved variation of the VQ attack. This attack creates a new image from multiple authenticated images by combining portions of several images while preserving their relative spatial location within the image. Two images, $MonaLisa$ and $Napoleon$, both of size 372×288, were watermarked with the same key. Fig. 7(a) and 7(b) show the watermarked images of $Napoleon$ and $MonaLisa$, which have PSNR of $39.59dB$ and $39.53dB$,respectively. We constructed the counterfeited image, Fig. 7(c), by copying the face of $MonaLisa$ and pasting it onto the $Napoleon$ image. The tampering ratio of the counterfeited image is 18%.

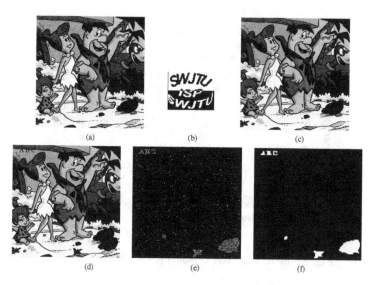

Fig. 6. Tamper detection by ordinary tampering (a) original image, (b) watermark logo, (c) watermarked image, (d) tampered image, (e) watermark difference, and (f) tamper detection mark, white spots denote invalid blocks

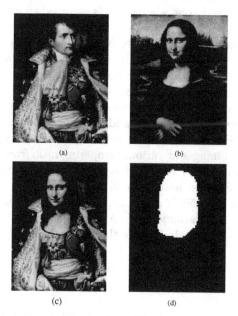

Fig. 7. Tamper detection by collage attack. (a) Watermarked Napoleon image, (b) Watermarked Mona Lisa image, (c) tampered image, (d) detection results (TDM).

Fig. 6(d) shows the TDM of the counterfeited image, where the FAR and FRR are 0.66% and 0.7%, respectively. The low FAR and FRR imply that the proposed method effectively resist the collage attack.

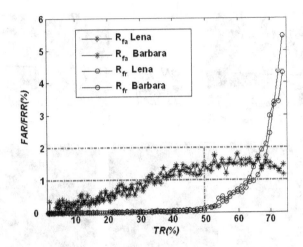

Fig. 8. FAR and FRR versus TR for different images

To verify the tamper localization performance of the proposed scheme, the experiments were carried out using the different images (*Lena* and *Barbara*) and taking a square tampered region for instance. Let N_t denote the number of the blocks in the tampered area, where $\sqrt{N_t}$ is assumed an integer in the interval $[2, min[m, n] - 20]$. In testing, the tampered image, Y^t, is obtained by replacing every pixel in the chosen area of size $4\sqrt{N_t} \times 4\sqrt{N_t}$ with a random integer in the interval $[0, 255]$. According to the detection results of the tampered image, we can obtain the following statistical values:

N_{td}: the number of the detected blocks in the tampered region;

N_{vd}: the number of the detected blocks out of the tampered region.

According to the formulas (21), (22) and (23), the experimental values of TR, FAR and FRR can be achieved, respectively. Fig. 8 shows the FAR and FRR of the different tampered images at various tampering ratio from 0.01% up to 75%. As shown in Fig. 8, the FAR is less than 2% at various tampering ratio from 0.01% to 75%. The FRR is quite perfect (close to zero) at low and moderate tampering ratio (less than 50%) and is acceptable (not more than 6%) even at very high tampering ratio around 70%. As a result, we can conclude that the proposed scheme can accurately localize the tampered blocks.

5   Conclusion

In this paper, we have presented a fragile watermarking scheme based on the block-chain strategy to address the issues of security and localization accuracy. We have also examined the relationship between the security strength and block size. Our investigation demonstrates that the security strength of block-wise fragile watermarking techniques generally goes up with the number of pixels in an image block. The main features of the proposed method are summarized below:

(1) Security of the algorithm relies on the secrecy of the content and corresponding watermark information of the image block;

(2) The proposed method can effectively thwart the VQ and collage attacks due to its block-dependence feature;

(3) The block size can be reduced from 8×8 pixels to 4×4 pixels with the same embedding watermark payload. The FAR and FRR is close to zero at low and moderate tampering ratio (less than 50%).

Future research includes extending this approach to resist mild distortion such as random noise and JPEG compression, and analytic investigation on the tamper detection performance of the watermarking-based authentication techniques.

Acknowledgments

This work was supported in part by the National Natural Science Foundation of China (Grant $No.60572027$), by the Program for New Century Excellent Talents in University of China ($NCET - 05 - 0794$), and by the Southwest Jiaotong University Doctors Innovation Funds ($No.2007$).

References

1. Yuan, H., Zhang, X.-P.: Multiscale fragile watermarking based on the Gaussian mixture model. IEEE Trans. Image process 15(10), 3189–3200 (2006)
2. Wong, P.: A public key watermark for image verification and authentication. In: Proc. IEEE Int. Conf. Image Process., Chicago, IL, pp. 425–429 (1998)
3. Holliman, H., Memon, N.: Counterfeiting attacks on oblivious block-wise independent invisible watermarking schemes. IEEE Trans. Image Process 9(3), 432–441 (2000)
4. Fridrich, J., Goljan, M., Memon, N.: Cryptanalysis of the Yeung-Mintzer fragile watermarking technique. J. Electronic Imaging 11, 262–274 (2002)
5. Wong, P., Memon, N.: Secret and public key image watermarking schemes for image authentication and ownership verification. IEEE Trans. Image Process. 10, 1593–1601 (2001)
6. Fridrich, J.: Security of fragile authentication watermarks with localization. In: Proc. SPIE. Security and Watermarking of Multimedia Contents, San Jose, CA, vol. 4675, pp. 691–700 (January 2002)
7. Celik, M., Sharma, G., Saber, E., Tekalp, A.M.: Hierarchical watermarking for secure image authentication with localization. IEEE Trans. Image Process. 11(6), 585–595 (2002)
8. Barreto, P., Kim, H., Rijmen, V.: Toward secure public-key block-wise fragile authentication watermarking. IEE Proc. -Vision, Image and Signal Process. 149(2), 57–62 (2002)
9. Suthaharan, S.: Fragile image watermarking using a gradient image for improved localization and security. Pattern Recognition Letters 25, 1893–1903 (2004)

10. Deguillaume, F., Voloshynovskiy, S., Pun, T.: Secure hybrid robust watermarking resistant against tampering and copy attack. Signal Process 83, 2133–2170 (2003)
11. Lee, S., Yoo, C.D., Kalker, T.: Reversible image watermarking based on integer-to-integer wavelet transform. IEEE Trans. Inf. forensics security 2(3), 321–330 (2007)
12. Lin, P.L., Hsieh, C.K., Huang, P.W.: A hierarchical digital watermarking method for image tamper detection and recovery. Pattern Recognition 38(12), 2519–2529 (2005)
13. Zhang, X., Wang, S.: Statistical fragile watermarking capable of locating individual tampered pixels. IEEE Signal Process. Lett. 14(10), 727–731 (2007)
14. He, H.J., Zhang, J.S., Wang, H.X.: Synchronous counterfeiting attacks on self-embedding watermarking schemes. Intern. J. Comput. Sci. Network Security 6(1), 251–257 (2006)
15. Fridrich, J., Goljan, M.: Images with self-correcting capabilities. In: Proc. ICIP 1999, Kobe, Japan, October 25-28 (1999)
16. Wu, Y., Deng, R.H.: Security of an ill-posed operator for image authentication. IEEE Trans. Circuits Syst. Video Technol. 15(1), 161–163 (2005)
17. He, H., Zhang, J., Tai, H.-M.: A wavelet-based fragile watermarking scheme for secure image authentication. In: Shi, Y.Q., Jeon, B. (eds.) IWDW 2006. LNCS, vol. 4283, pp. 422–432. Springer, Heidelberg (2006)

Generic Adoption of Spatial Steganalysis to Transformed Domain

Andreas Westfeld

Technische Universität Dresden
Faculty of Computer Science
Institute of Systems Architecture
01062 Dresden, Germany
`mailto:westfeld@inf.tu-dresden.de`

Abstract. There are several powerful steganalytic methods for images in the spatial domain, which are based on higher order statistics. We propose a generic methodology to prepare higher order steganalytic methods from spatial domain for application in the transformed domain. This paper presents 72 new systematically designed methods that are derived from the spatial domain. Their reliability and the precision of their length estimation is evaluated based on 1700 million attacks. We present the contribution of the proposed methods in terms of detection power and precision compared to prior art and determine how properties like image size and JPEG quality influence the ranking of the proposed attacks.

1 Steganography in JPEG Files

Steganography is the art and science of invisible communication. Its aim is the transmission of information embedded invisibly into carrier data. The goal of *steganalysis* is to discover steganographic alterations to carrier data. We can distinguish *targeted* attacks, which are fine-tuned to one particular embedding method, and *blind* (or universal) attacks, which detect steganographic changes using a classifier that is trained with features from known steganograms and carrier media. Targeted methods are often used to extract features for the training. The distinction of blind and targeted attacks is blurred in this respect.

The most simple embedding methods are at the same time the most widely used. Common carrier data include digitised images or audio files. In many cases the image data are stored in the spatial domain (e.g., in BMP or PNM format). The message is embedded by replacing the least significant bits of the colour or brightness values by the (encrypted) message bits. The human eye will usually not notice the changes that are caused by the embedding in the image.

Sometimes, however, the embedding can still be detected by statistical means. One of the first steganalytic attacks was based on the global histogram of the colour or brightness values and is also applicable to DCT values in JPEG files [1]. JPEG files are more common as e-mail attachments than spatial domain images. As such, they are a more important carrier medium for steganography.

K. Solanki, K. Sullivan, and U. Madhow (Eds.): IH 2008, LNCS 5284, pp. 161–177, 2008.

All previous targeted attacks to Jsteg embedding [2] only evaluated global frequencies of DCT values. They ignored the location of these values and the spatial frequency in the context in which they occurred. This is also called marginal distributions or first order statistics. Part of this concept are, e.g., the attack by Zhang and Ping [3] (ZP, cf. Sect. 3.1), the attack by Yu et al. [4] (Yu, cf. Sect. 3.2), and the category attack by Lee et al. [5] (CA, cf. Sect. 3.3) together with its generalisation (GCA) [6]. Blind attacks also employ *higher* order statistics, however, unlike the aforementioned attacks, they are rarely used to estimate the length of the embedded message [7,8,9]. A recent evaluation concluded that blind attacks to JPEG images are less reliable than the CA, at least for heterogeneous sources of images [6].

There are several steganalytic techniques for the spatial domain that use higher order statistics, e.g., RS [10], WS [11], SPA [12,13], and Pairs [14]. To our knowledge, they have never been applied directly to coefficients of the frequency domain before, while this was done from the beginning with the histogram based chi-square attack. It seems not very obvious how to extract the sample sequences from the DCT frequency domain to use them with spatial domain higher order statistical attacks. It is even doubtful because the goal of the JPEG compression is to remove irrelevance, i.e., to reduce the local dependency that is inherent to images and exploited by the higher order attacks. We tried it, though, contributing partly considerable improvements in terms of reliability and precision.

Although we think the proposed methodology is applicable in general to exploit local dependencies in JPEG files, there is essentially only one steganographic algorithm used for both, spatial *and* DCT domain: LSB replacement. At the same time this is the most completely analysed algorithm in the spatial domain, which offers a wide range of different steganalytical approaches for testing our methodology. While we apply these approaches to Jsteg [2] in our evaluation, an adaption to JPhide [15] is easy, however, the ranking of attacks could be different.

This paper is organised as follows: Section 2 looks at several scanpaths (intra block and inter block) to exploit local dependencies in the DCT domain. Section 3 briefly describes histogram-based attacks to JPEG files. In Sect. 4 we derive 72 new attacks for JPEG media (6 fundamental attacks × 6 scanpaths × with and without DC coefficients) from the spatial domain attacks mentioned at the beginning (RS, WS, SPA, and Pairs). The new attacks are evaluated in Sect. 5. All in all we produced 1700 million length estimations for a variety of different messages of several lengths in a set of images with different quality and size to pick the best scanpath and the most suitable attack from the spatial domain. The paper is concluded in Sect. 6.

2   Methods

2.1   Local Correlation

A well-known feature of spatial domain images is the dependency between neighbouring pixels. This has been exploited for steganalysis using fractal scanpaths [16].

Correlations of DCT coefficients have been studied in the context of entropy coding in JPEG images. Tu and Tran distinguish three kinds of correlations [17]:

Intrablock or intersubband correlation. The magnitudes of (unquantised) AC coefficients decrease as the frequency increases. This results in a dependency between neighbouring coefficients. However, the intrablock dependency is limited to a small block of 8×8 pixels only. It is also weak, since the coefficients of one block belong to different, (nearly) orthogonal subbands. Most coefficients are quantised to zero and do not carry much information.

Interblock or intrasubband correlation. Low frequency coefficients and their neighbours are mutually dependent on each other within the same subband. Generally, the interblock dependency is much stronger than the intrablock dependency. However, it is limited especially for higher frequencies because, compared to the raster of pixels, their distance is increased to the block raster (e.g., factor 8).

Sign correlation. Deever and Hemami analysed the sign behaviour of wavelet coefficients [18]. A similar intrasubband dependency can be found for low frequency coefficients in JPEG images.

Fridrich uses co-occurrence matrices of neighbouring coefficients in the same subband in her blind attack using 23 DCT features [7]. Even individual co-occurrence features very reliably detect F5, Outguess, and MB1 [19,20,21] for full embedding rate.

Fu et al. rearrange the DCT coefficients to exploit both, intrablock and interblock dependency for their blind attack based on Markov empirical transition matrices [22]. They apply a zigzag scan for intrablock dependency as well as a slalom scan for interblock dependency.

2.2   Scanning Orders for DCT Coefficients

The JPEG compression reorders the DCT coefficients of one 8×8 block from their natural order to zigzag order (cf. Fig. 1) to take advantage of the intrablock dependency. We scan DCT coefficients in natural and zigzag order to exploit intrablock dependency by our attacks.

The dependency in different subbands may have different orientation. From spatial domain we know that recursive scanning paths increase the dependency between pixel values [16]. This is also valid for DC coefficients. AC coefficients might favour the interblock dependency in vertical or horizontal lines. We apply recursive and linear scanning paths (cf. Fig. 2) to evaluate the interblock dependency by the attacks that we propose in the sequel.

3   Prior Attacks to Jsteg-Like Embedding

Jsteg is probably the first algorithm that was developed for JPEG images [2]. It overwrites the least significant bits of the quantised DCT coefficients with secret message bits. Jsteg is detectable by the chi-square attack [1]. However, the attack

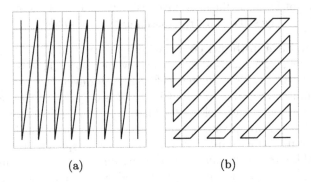

Fig. 1. Intrablock scanpath in natural order (a) and zigzag order (b)

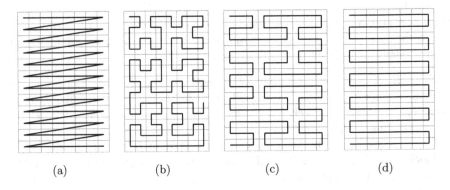

Fig. 2. Row by row scan (a), fractal scan along Hilbert 1 curve (b) and Hilbert 2 curve (c), slalom scan (d)

fails if the message is pseudo-randomly straddled over all DCT coefficients, which is called "randomised Jsteg." While there exist several powerful steganalytic techniques for the spatial domain [10,11,12,14], which *can* detect such straddled messages and even estimate their length, there are only a few techniques for randomised Jsteg, which consider merely the marginal statistics of the DCT coefficients, but can also estimate lengths.

In the following subsections we will consider three known detection methods for randomised Jsteg as far as it is essential for the implementation used here. The Method of Zhang and Ping divides the histogram into two interleaved groups, the attack of Yu et al. estimates the density function of the quantised values on a steganographically invariant basis, and the category attack compares equalising and complementary pairs of values with each other. All three can estimate the length of the embedded message. For further details please refer to the description in the respective original publications. The methods start the detection based on the histogram $h(k)$ of the quantised DCT coefficients $k \in \mathbb{Z}$ from a JPEG image.

3.1 Method by Zhang and Ping

We define two sets of values

$$L = \{i > 0 | i \text{ even}\} \cup \{i < 0 | i \text{ odd}\} \text{ and} \tag{1}$$
$$R = \{i > 0 | i \text{ odd}\} \cup \{i < 0 | i \text{ even}\}. \tag{2}$$

The proportion p of the capacity used by randomised Jsteg is estimated by

$$p = \frac{1}{h(1)} \cdot \left(\sum_{r \in R} h(r) - \sum_{l \in L} h(l) \right). \tag{3}$$

3.2 Method by Yu et al.

Inspired by Sallee [21], Yu et al. model the density of quantised JPEG coefficients by a modified, generalised Cauchy distribution

$$f(k, \pi, s) = \frac{\pi - 1}{2s} \left(\left| \frac{k}{s} \right| + 1 \right)^{-\pi}. \tag{4}$$

Its scale parameter s and location parameter π are computed for all DCT coefficients (globally, for all subbands together) by a maximum likelihood estimation over $h(0)$, $h(1)$, and the low precision bins $H(i) = h(2i) + h(2i + 1)$ for $i \neq 0$. First we estimate the histogram of the carrier image:

$$\hat{h}(i) = \begin{cases} h(i) & \text{for } i \in \{0, 1\}, \\ (h(2i) + h(2i+1)) \frac{\int_{i-0.5}^{i+0.5} f(x,\pi,s)\mathrm{d}x}{\int_{i-0.5}^{i+1.5} f(x,\pi,s)\mathrm{d}x} & \text{otherwise.} \end{cases} \tag{5}$$

The proportion p of the capacity used by randomised Jsteg is estimated by

$$p = \frac{\sum_{i \neq 0} (h(2i) - \hat{h}(2i)) \cdot (\hat{h}(2i) - \hat{h}(2i+1))}{\sum_{i \neq 0} (\hat{h}(2i) - \hat{h}(2i+1))^2}. \tag{6}$$

3.3 Category Attack

We renumber the bins and create an adjusted version of the histogram that excludes the values 0 and 1, which are not changed by Jsteg:

$$h'(k) = \begin{cases} h(k) & \text{for } k < 0, \\ h(k - 2) & \text{for } k > 1. \end{cases} \tag{7}$$

The proportion p of the capacity used by randomised Jsteg is estimated using the statistics s for *shifted* categories that are not equalised and *induced* categories that are equalised by Jsteg embedding:

$$s(k) = \frac{(h'(k) - h'(k+1))^2}{h'(k) + h'(k+1)}, \tag{8}$$

$$p = \frac{\sum_i s(2i) - \sum_i s(2i - 1)}{\sum_i s(2i) + \sum_i s(2i - 1)}. \tag{9}$$

4   Attacks Derived from Prior Spatial Domain Methods

While there have been several proposals to use higher order statistics in the spatial domain, no specific method exists to the best of our knowledge for the DCT domain. There are only some blind detection methods, which work less reliably than the best histogram based attack [6], require training, and furthermore are no precise estimators for the length of the embedded message.

In the following we will apply several techniques that are known from the spatial domain to (selected) DCT coefficients, which have been scanned along different paths (intrablock and interblock).

Firstly we describe how to prepare DCT coefficients "palatable" for attacks that have only been applied to brightness or colour values so far. In the subsequent subsections we describe the adaptation of the spatial domain attacks RS, Pairs, SPA, and WS to DCT coefficients, as far as this is essential for the implementation used here. For further details please refer to the detailed description in the respective original publications.

4.1   Preprocessing of Coefficients

Let $\mathbf{x}$ be a sequence of DCT coefficients, scanned from a JPEG file in one of the orders described in Sect. 2.2. To ease the application of spatial domain attacks, we delete all elements in $\mathbf{x}$ that are 0 or 1 (i.e., steganographically unused by Jsteg), yielding $\mathbf{x}'$. Then we change all coefficients to be non-negative and get the normalised sequence $\mathbf{d}$ with the elements:

$$d_i = \begin{cases} x_i' - x_{\min} & \text{if } x_i' < 0, \\ x_i' - x_{\min} - 2 & \text{if } x_i' > 1, \end{cases} \tag{10}$$

$$\text{where} \quad x_{\min} = \begin{cases} \min \mathbf{x} & \text{if } \min \mathbf{x} \text{ is even,} \\ \min \mathbf{x} - 1 & \text{otherwise.} \end{cases} \tag{11}$$

Lee et al. reported that the CA and the ZP attack showed increased reliability when only AC coefficients were used in the histogram [6]. Therefore, we derive another sequence $\mathbf{d}_{\text{AC}}$ from the sequence $\mathbf{d}$ of all normalised coefficients, in which we delete all DC coefficients.

4.2   JRS

The RS attack by Fridrich et al. [10] counts the number of regular and singular groups of pixels before and after flipping operations. There are several types of flipping operations: One flips induced pairs like LSB embedding, $f_1: 0 \leftrightarrow 1$, $2 \leftrightarrow 3$, $4 \leftrightarrow 5$, ..., another one flips shifted pairs, $f_{-1}: -1 \leftrightarrow 0$, $1 \leftrightarrow 2$, $3 \leftrightarrow 4$, ..., the third one is the identity $f_0(x) = x$. These flipping functions add typical steganographic noise (f_1) and noise that is atypical for steganography (f_{-1}). JRS, the derived version of the attack for JPEG, works in the same manner as RS except that it considers normalised coefficients d_k instead of pixels. The noise is measured in a group of coefficients $\mathbf{d}_k = (d_{nk}, d_{nk+1}, \ldots, d_{nk+n-1})$ with a default length $n = 4$ for $k \in \mathbb{N}$:

$$r(\mathbf{d}_k) = |d_{nk+1} - d_{nk}| + |d_{nk+2} - d_{nk+1}| + \cdots + |d_{nk+n-1} - d_{nk+n-2}|. \quad (12)$$

In a typical image, the noise will increase rather than decrease. We define sets of regular groups R and singular groups S for mask m before and after flipping the LSB of all normalised coefficients:

$$R_m = \{k | r(\mathbf{f}_m(\mathbf{d}_k)) > r(\mathbf{d}_k)\}, \quad (13)$$
$$S_m = \{k | r(\mathbf{f}_m(\mathbf{d}_k)) < r(\mathbf{d}_k)\}, \quad (14)$$
$$R'_m = \{k | r(\mathbf{f}_m(\mathbf{d}'_k)) > r(\mathbf{d}'_k)\}, \quad (15)$$
$$S'_m = \{k | r(\mathbf{f}_m(\mathbf{d}'_k)) < r(\mathbf{d}'_k)\}, \quad (16)$$
$$\mathbf{d}'_k = (f_1(d_{4k}), f_1(d_{4k+1}), f_1(d_{4k+2}), f_1(d_{4k+3})), \quad (17)$$
$$m = (0, 1, 1, 0), \quad (18)$$
$$\mathbf{f}_m(\mathbf{d}_k) = (d_{4k}, f_1(d_{4k+1}), f_1(d_{4k+2}), d_{4k+3}). \quad (19)$$

The cardinality of these sets is used to formulate the following quadratic equation:

$$2(q_0 + q'_0)x^2 + (q_1 - q'_1 - q'_0 - 3q_0)x + q_0 - q_1 = 0, \quad (20)$$

where $q_0 = |R_m| - |S_m|$, $q'_0 = |R'_m| - |S'_m|$, $q_1 = |R_{-m}| - |S_{-m}|$, and $q'_1 = |R'_{-m}| - |S'_{-m}|$. The estimated proportion p of the capacity used by randomised Jsteg is derived from the root x with the smaller absolute value:

$$p = \frac{x}{x - \frac{1}{2}}. \quad (21)$$

We studied all possible masks for group size $n = 2 \ldots 10$ in the spatial domain using a set of 500 images. Smaller masks lead to higher detection reliability and produced less failures.[1] Therefore two versions of the attack will be evaluated: One with the standard mask (cf. Eq. 18) and another one with the mask $(0, 1)$ and group size $n = 2$.

4.3   JPairs

The Pairs Analysis by Fridrich et al. [14] evaluates the number of homogeneous (00 or 11) and inhomogeneous pairs (01 or 10) in a binary sequence. After preprocessing (cf. Sect. 4.1) these binary sequences can be derived also from a sequence of DCT coefficients. Let $d_{\max}$ be the maximum even coefficient increased by one:

$$d_{\max} = \begin{cases} \max \mathbf{d} + 1 & \text{if } \max \mathbf{d} \text{ is even,} \\ \max \mathbf{d} & \text{otherwise.} \end{cases} \quad (22)$$

---

[1] Failures occur if Eq. 20 has no real solution.

The JPairs attack creates a binary sequence z for all pairs of normalised DCT values $(0, 1), (2, 3), \ldots, (d_{max} - 1, d_{max})$. To construct these sequences, sequence $\mathbf{d}$ is scanned $\lceil d_{max}/2 \rceil$ times. In the first scan, 0 is appended to the initially empty sequence z whenever the value 0 is encountered in $\mathbf{d}$, and 1 if the value 1 is encountered. In the next scan, 0 is appended to z whenever the value 2 occurs in $\mathbf{d}$, and 1 if the value 3 is encountered. This is continued for all pairs. Likewise another sequence z' is created for the shifted pairs $(1, 2), (3, 4), \ldots, (d_{max}, 0)$. Let ℓ be the length of $\mathbf{d}$. The proportion p of the capacity used by randomised Jsteg is estimated by

$$p = 1 - \sqrt{1 - \frac{q - q'}{\frac{\ell - 1}{2} - \bar{q}}} \quad , \tag{23}$$

$$\text{where} \quad q = \sum_{i=1}^{\ell-1} |z_i - z_{i+1}|, \tag{24}$$

$$q' = \sum_{i=1}^{\ell-1} |z_i' - z_{i+1}'|, \quad \text{and} \tag{25}$$

$$\bar{q} = \sum_{j=1}^{\ell} \frac{1}{2^j} \sum_{i=1}^{\ell-j} |z_i' - z_{i+j}'|. \tag{26}$$

In our implementation, Eq. 26 is evaluated for $j = 1 \ldots 24$ only, because there is no practical contribution for $j > 24$ due to the limited precision of the CPU.

4.4   JSPA

The sample pairs attack (SPA), developed by Dumitrescu et al. [12,13], is directly applicable to a sequence of normalised DCT coefficients. Let d_{max} be the maximum even coefficient, increased by one (cf. Eq. 22). The following two sets classify the sample pairs (u, v), which originate (non overlapping) from each two consecutive elements of the sequence of coefficients $\mathbf{d}$:

$$A = \{(u, v) | u \geq v, \ u \text{ even}\} \cup \{(u, v) | u < v, \ u \text{ odd}\}, \tag{27}$$
$$B = \{(u, v) | u < v, \ u \text{ even}\} \cup \{(u, v) | u \geq v, \ u \text{ odd}\}. \tag{28}$$

We define two histograms

$$h_0(|u_0 - v_0|) \text{ for } (u_0, v_0) \in A \quad \text{and} \tag{29}$$
$$h_1(|u_1 - v_1|) \text{ for } (u_1, v_1) \in B. \tag{30}$$

The estimated proportion p of the capacity used by randomised Jsteg is the larger of the two roots of the following quadratic equation:

$$0 = ap^2 + bp + c, \quad \text{where} \tag{31}$$

$$c = \sum_{i=0}^{j-1} h_0(2i) - h_1(2i+1), \tag{32}$$

$$b = h_0(0) + h_1(0) - \frac{h_0(2j+2) + h_1(2j+2)}{2} + \frac{c}{2}, \quad \text{and} \tag{33}$$

$$a = \sum_{i=0}^{1} \frac{h_0(i) + h_1(i)}{2} - \frac{h_0(2j+2+i) + h_1(2j+2+i)}{4}. \tag{34}$$

The upper limit j was determined experimentally. In the implementation used here, it was $j = 30$.

4.5 JWS

The WS attack by Fridrich and Goljan [11] is also directly applied to a sequence $\mathbf{d}$ of ℓ normalised JPEG coefficients. The proportion p of the capacity used by randomised Jsteg is estimated by

$$p = \frac{2 \sum_{i=3}^{\ell-2} q_i}{\sum_{i=3}^{\ell-2} \frac{1}{1+v_i}} \quad \text{with} \tag{35}$$

$$v_i = \frac{1}{3}((d_{i-2} - \mu_i)^2 + (d_{i-1} - \mu_i)^2 + (d_{i+1} - \mu_i)^2 + (d_{i+2} - \mu_i)^2), \tag{36}$$

$$\mu_i = \frac{1}{4}(d_{i-2} + d_{i-1} + d_{i+1} + d_{i+2}), \quad \text{and} \tag{37}$$

$$q_i = \begin{cases} \frac{1}{1+v_i}(\mu_i - d_i) & \text{if } d_i \text{ is even,} \\ \frac{1}{1+v_i}(d_i - \mu_i) & \text{otherwise.} \end{cases} \tag{38}$$

The JWS attack estimates the original value of the coefficient q_i as the mean μ_i of a local environment of four values (cf. Eq. 37). Original values could be even more precisely estimated from steganographically unchanged neighbours. However, all those unchanged values have been removed in the sequence $\mathbf{d}$ of normalised JPEG coefficients.

4.6 Weighted Nonsteganographic Borders Attack (WB)

WB is a variant of the JWS attack, which estimates the original values directly from the sequence $\mathbf{x}$ of ℓ_0 JPEG coefficients (cf. Eq. 40). The values 0 and 1 are not used by randomised Jsteg. If they occur among the four elements forming the environment used for estimation, we can expect a higher precision of the estimated value. Consequently, this estimated value should have a larger weight in the attack. Apart from that, the mean distance of two consecutive coefficients is smaller in the sequence $\mathbf{x}$ since no elements are skipped. Consequently, the mean dependency between consecutive elements in $\mathbf{x}$, which is exploited by the attack, is larger than in $\mathbf{d}$. Note that the weight w_i (cf. Eq. 41) consists of three factors with the following features: The first factor excludes all $x_i \in \{0, 1\}$ ($w_i = 0$ for values that are not used by Jsteg), the second factor is the weight based on the variance as proposed for WS [11], and the third factor increases the weight if there are steganographically unused values in the estimation environment ($x_{i-2}, x_{i-1}, x_{i+1}, x_{i+2} \in \{0, 1\}$). The proportion p of the capacity used by randomised Jsteg is estimated by

$$p = \frac{3 + 4 \sum_{i=3}^{\ell_0 - 2} w_i (\mu_i - x_i)(-1)^{x_i}}{5 \sum_{i=3}^{\ell_0 - 2} w_i} \quad \text{with} \tag{39}$$

$$\mu_i = \frac{1}{4}(x_{i-2} + x_{i-1} + x_{i+1} + x_{i+2}), \tag{40}$$

$$w_i = (1 - f(x_i)) \cdot \frac{1}{1 + v_i} \cdot \frac{1}{1 - \frac{1}{9}\sum_{j=-2}^{2} f(x_{i+j})(2 - x_{i+j})}, \tag{41}$$

$$f(x) = \begin{cases} 1 & \text{if } x \in \{0, 1\}, \\ 0 & \text{otherwise, and} \end{cases} \tag{42}$$

$$v_i = \frac{1}{3}((x_{i-2} - \mu_i)^2 + (x_{i-1} - \mu_i)^2 + (x_{i+1} - \mu_i)^2 + (x_{i+2} - \mu_i)^2). \tag{43}$$

5   Results and Discussion

5.1   Reliability

For meaningful experimental validation we use scanned images from a public database, which never have been lossy compressed before. We follow the tradition to apply the attacks to greyscale images. Of course the attacks can be applied to colour images as well by treating the colour components the same way as the brightness component. On the one hand it is not really advisable to steganographically use the colour components of a JPEG file since there are mutual dependencies between the components. On the other hand steganalysis could be improved to exploit these dependencies for more reliable detection of steganography in colour components. Steganographic messages with the same embedding rate are harder to detect in small images than in larger ones. Firstly, we choose an embedding rate with strongest possible distinction between the particular attacks in terms of reliability.

For the comparison in Fig. 3 we downloaded 2300 large TIFF images (2100 × 1500 pixels) from the NRCS database [23]. These images have been downsized to 840 × 600 pixels by pnmscale's default method, converted to greyscale, and JPEG compressed with quality $q = 0.8$. We applied randomised Jsteg to use 1 % of the image capacity. Figure 3 shows 39 bars that stand each for two readings of the area under the ROC curve (AUC). The solid lines give the result for all coefficients (AC and DC), while the dashed, which end with a small ring, indicate the case where DC coefficients—though used by randomised Jsteg—have been excluded (cf. coefficient sequence $\mathbf{d}_{AC}$ in Sect. 4.1). The first three bars from the left represent the known Jsteg attacks with first order statistics (cf. Sect. 3). The

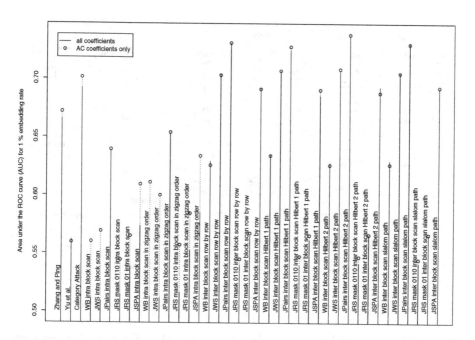

Fig. 3. Area under the ROC curve to compare the reliability of attacks for 3 known and 36 proposed attacks, each in two variants: with and without exclusion of DC coefficients

adjacent bars to the right give the two values for 36 combinations of 6 fundamental methods and 6 scanpaths.

Altogether the results of 78 different steganalytic methods are shown for a very low embedding rate, i.e., for adverse and meaningful, differentiating conditions (for maximum embedding rate all methods that are presented here separate perfectly). The longer the line in the diagram, the larger the area under the ROC curve (receiver operating characteristic). An area 1 means perfect separation. If the area is 0.5, the detector is not better than a random decision. In general, the area under the curve is more meaningful than a single point on the ROC curve (i.e., a pair of false positive rate and detection rate, which is valid for a particular threshold only). As mentioned earlier, the category attack has a small gain in reliability if only AC coefficients are considered. Apart from JPairs, this gain is more pronounced for the methods with intrablock scanpath. However, the intrablock methods perform worse than the leftmost histogram based methods (ZP and CA). Almost independent on the scanpath, the interblock methods score best. Merely the RS attack improves for the intrablock scan of AC coefficients. The JPairs attack is the obvious favourite for low embedding rates in small images. It is solely the reliability of JPairs that clearly tops the histogram based category attack by Lee et al. However, this result is only a snapshot for a particular pair of size and embedding rate. As we will see in Sect. 5.2, the ranking could severely change for smaller image sizes.

It is already known that recursive scanpaths (Hilbert 1, Hilbert 2) lead to noticeable improvements of the reliability for the Pairs Analysis in the spatial

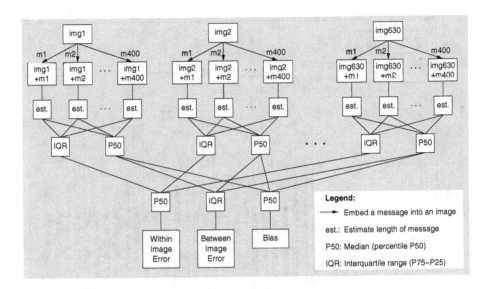

Fig. 4. Separation of within-image error, between-image error, and bias

domain [16]. One could argue that the advantage in the DC subband is equalised by a disadvantage in other subbands. Future work can clarify if different scan-paths in different subbands can still achieve an overall advantage.

5.2   Precision

All proposed methods estimate the length of the embedded message. In this section we will evaluate the precision of these DCT domain methods. Böhme and Ker evaluated the precision for spatial domain methods [24]. They separated different sources of errors by averaging. We will apply this principle also here, to evaluate three error-measures. A *cell* is a set of steganograms, produced by embedding different messages of the same length in one particular carrier medium. To separate the error sources we measure the statistical dispersion (interquartile range, IQR, difference between 0.75- and 0.25-quantile) and the central tendency (median, 0.5-quantile) of length estimations for each cell. From these two measures we derive three kinds of error (cf. Fig. 4).

The *within-image error* is the median of all cell IQRs. This kind of error is induced by the message and the secret key that is used for embedding. The distribution of the cell IQRs passed tests of normality. The *between-image error* is the IQR of all cell medians. This is an image-specific error. The cell medians are rather Student-t distributed with $\nu = 1 \ldots 10$ degrees of freedom for the proposed set of attacks. Finally, the *bias* is the median of the cell medians. This error can be pre-computed for a given source of images and a particular length estimating attack.

We downloaded another 630 large TIFF images (1500×2100 pixels) from the NRCS database [23]. These images have been downsized (using pnmscale) to five different sizes (600×840, 400×560, 200×280, 80×112, and 40×56 pixels), converted to greyscale, and JPEG compressed with quality $q = 0.8$. The medium sized images (200×280) have been compressed at seven different qualities ($q = 0.5, 0.6, 0.7, 0.8, 0.9, 0.95, 0.99$). We applied randomised Jsteg at 8 different rates (1%, 5%, 10%, 20%, 40%, 60%, 80%, and 100% of the image capacity). We repeat the embedding with 400 random messages for over 600 images, at 11 combinations of size and quality, and at 8 embedding rates, detecting the result with 78 attacks. This results in about 1700 million length estimations.

Figures 5 and 6 present some views on these results. In abundance of results we highlight only the best representative for each fundamental estimation method. This selection is based on the between-image error at embedding rate 0.01 (600×840, JPEG quality 0.8, cf. Fig. 5(b)), which is related to the detection power, since this kind of error dominates at low embedding rates, while the within-image error is negligible (cf. Fig. 5(a)) and the bias is without influence to reliability. The representatives are the JPairs attack applied to AC coefficients only, scanned interblock along a Hilbert 1 path (cf. Sect. 4.3 and Fig. 2(b)), the JSPA attack applied to AC coefficients only, scanned interblock row by row (cf. Sect. 4.4 and Fig. 2(a)), the attack by Zhang and Ping [3], the category attack by Lee et al. [5], the JWS attack applied to AC coefficients only, scanned interblock row by row (cf. Sect. 4.5 and Fig. 2(a)), the WB attack applied to both AC and DC coefficients, scanned interblock along a slalom path (cf. Sect. 4.6 and Fig. 2(d)), the JRS attack with mask $(0, 1)$ applied to AC coefficients only, scanned intrablock in zigzag order (cf. Sect. 4.2 and Fig. 1(b)), and finally the attack by Yu et al. [4]. The pale curves in the diagrams show the remaining 70 attack variants. Apparently, the 8 representatives that have been selected based on their small between-image error have also a small within-image error. The within-image error grows with the embedding rate, but also for high JPEG qualities above 0.9 (cf. Fig. 5(c)). It decreases with increasing image size (not shown). This is also true for the between-image error (cf. Fig. 5(d)). While the between-image error of the JPairs attack is smallest for images larger than 200×280, there are more suitable candidates for thumbnail images (40×56): WB attack, category attack, and the attack by Yu et al. Interestingly, the JWS attack, which is closely related to the front runner WB, has the biggest problem with thumbnail images. One possible explanation could be the increased variance in downscaled images. The anonymous curves with the insignificantly lower error rates for small images belong to other variants of the WB attack.

Figure 5(e) shows the between-image error as a function of the JPEG quality. Apart from the category attack and the attack by Zhang and Ping, this kind of error is increased for qualities above 0.9.

The detector specific bias is shown in Fig. 5(f). We can distinguish several types of bias: (1) linearly decreasing (e.g., attack by Yu et al.), (2) arc with zero ends (e.g., JWS and category attack), (3) arc with zero left and negative right end (e.g., JRS, JPairs and JSPA), and (4) bias-free and bias-corrected types, which are close to zero over the whole range of embedding rates (e.g., the attack

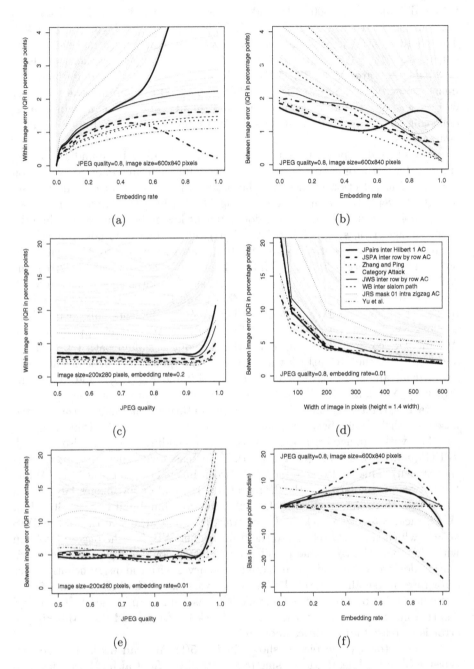

Fig. 5. Separated within- (a) and between-image error (b), within-image error as a function of quality (c), between-image error as a function of size (d) and quality (e), and detector-specific offset (f)

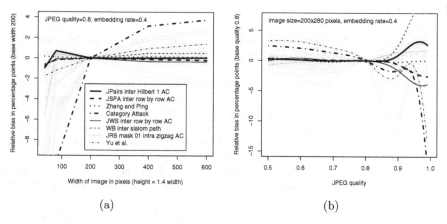

Fig. 6. Bias as a function of image size (a) and JPEG quality (b)

by Zhang and Ping as well as the WB attack). Note that the constants in Eq. 39 are adjusted based on a small, disjoint set of images in order to correct the bias that appears for the JWS attack. In Fig. 6 the bias of both, JWS and WB, appears invariant to changes of the image size. For JPEG qualities above 0.8, the relative bias curves of JWS and WB run in opposite directions. Despite its simple structure (or even because of it) the method of Zhang and Ping remains bias-free also for changes in size and JPEG quality.

6   Conclusion and Further Work

We developed a methodology to apply higher order steganalytic attacks from the spatial domain in the transformed domain. Based on 1700 million attacks, we evaluated the performance of the proposed attacks, and determined the most advisable schemes (WB for small images, JPairs for larger ones). Further work is needed regarding subband-specific scanpaths and an improved model for the estimation of original carrier values.

Acknowledgements

The work on this paper was supported by the Air Force Office of Scientific Research, Air Force Material Command, USAF, under the research grant number FA8655-06-1-3046. The U. S. Government is authorised to reproduce and distribute reprints for Governmental purposes notwithstanding any copyright notation there on. Travel to the ACM Multimedia and Security Workshop was supported in part by the European Commission through the IST Programme under contract IST-2002-507932 ECRYPT.

References

1. Westfeld, A., Pfitzmann, A.: Attacks on steganographic systems. In: Pfitzmann, A. (ed.) IH 1999. LNCS, vol. 1768, pp. 61–76. Springer, Heidelberg (2000)
2. Upham, D.: Jsteg (1993),
   http://www.nic.funet.fi/pub/crypt/steganography/jpeg-jsteg-v4.diff.gz
3. Zhang, T., Ping, X.: A new approach to reliable detection of LSB steganography in natural images. Signal Processing 83, 2085–2093 (2003)
4. Yu, X., Wang, Y., Tan, T.: On estimation of secret message length in Jsteg-like steganography. In: Proceedings of the 17th International Conference on Pattern Recognition (ICPR 2004), pp. 673–676 (2004)
5. Lee, K., Westfeld, A., Lee, S.: Category Attack for LSB steganalysis of JPEG images. In: Shi, Y.Q., Jeon, B. (eds.) IWDW 2006. LNCS, vol. 4283, pp. 35–48. Springer, Heidelberg (2006)
6. Lee, K., Westfeld, A., Lee, S.: Generalised Category Attack—improving histogram-based attack on JPEG LSB embedding. In: Furon, T., Cayre, F., Doërr, G., Bas, P. (eds.) IH 2007. LNCS, vol. 4567, pp. 378–391. Springer, Heidelberg (2008)
7. Fridrich, J.: Feature-based steganalysis for JPEG images and its implications for future design of steganographic schemes. In: Fridrich, J. (ed.) IH 2004. LNCS, vol. 3200, pp. 67–81. Springer, Heidelberg (2004)
8. Shi, Y.Q., Chen, C., Chen, W.: A Markov process based approach to effective attacking JPEG steganography. In: Camenisch, J.L., Collberg, C.S., Johnson, N.F., Sallee, P. (eds.) IH 2006. LNCS, vol. 4437, pp. 249–264. Springer, Heidelberg (2007)
9. Pevný, T., Fridrich, J.: Merging Markov and DCT features for multi-class JPEG steganalysis. In: Delp III, E.J., Wong, P.W. (eds.) Security, Steganography and Watermarking of Multimedia Contents IX (Proc. of SPIE), San Jose, CA (2007)
10. Fridrich, J., Goljan, M., Du, R.: Detecting LSB steganography in color and grayscale images. IEEE Multimedia 8(4), 22–28 (2001)
11. Fridrich, J., Goljan, M.: On estimation of secret message length in LSB steganography in spatial domain. In: Delp III, E.J., Wong, P.W. (eds.) Security, Steganography and Watermarking of Multimedia Contents VI (Proc. of SPIE), San Jose, CA (2004)
12. Dumitrescu, S., Wu, X., Wang, Z.: Detection of LSB steganography via sample pair analysis. In: Petitcolas, F.A.P. (ed.) IH 2002. LNCS, vol. 2578, pp. 355–372. Springer, Heidelberg (2003)
13. Dumitrescu, S., Wu, X., Wang, Z.: Detection of LSB steganography via sample pair analysis. IEEE Trans. of Signal Processing 51, 1995–2007 (2003)
14. Fridrich, J., Goljan, M., Soukal, D.: Higher-order statistical steganalysis of palette images. In: Delp III, E.J., Wong, P.W. (eds.) Security, Steganography and Watermarking of Multimedia Contents V (Proc. of SPIE), San Jose, CA, pp. 178–190 (2003)
15. Latham, A.: JPhide and JPseek (1998),
    http://packetstormsecurity.org/crypt/stego/jphs/
16. Westfeld, A.: Space filling curves in steganalysis. In: Delp III, E.J., Wong, P.W. (eds.) Security, Steganography and Watermarking of Multimedia Contents VII (Proc. of SPIE), San Jose, CA, pp. 28–37 (2005)
17. Tu, C., Tran, T.D.: Context-based entropy coding of block transform coefficients for image compression. IEEE Transactions on Image Processing 11, 1271–1283 (2002)
18. Deever, A., Hemami, S.S.: What's your sign? Efficient sign coding for embedded wavelet image coding. In: Data Compression Conference, pp. 273–282 (2000)

19. Westfeld, A.: F5—a steganographic algorithm: High capacity despite better steganalysis. In: Moskowitz, I.S. (ed.) IH 2001. LNCS, vol. 2137, pp. 289–302. Springer, Heidelberg (2001)
20. Provos, N.: Outguess (2001), http://www.outguess.org
21. Sallee, P.: Model-based steganography. In: Kalker, T., Cox, I., Ro, Y.M. (eds.) IWDW 2003. LNCS, vol. 2939, pp. 154–167. Springer, Heidelberg (2004)
22. Fu, D., Shi, Y.Q., Zou, D., Xuan, G.: JPEG steganalysis using empirical transition matrix in block DCT domain. In: IEEE 8th Workshop on Multimedia Signal Processing, pp. 310–313 (2002)
23. NRCS: Photo gallery of the USDA Natural Resources Conservation Service (2006), http://photogallery.nrcs.usda.gov/
24. Böhme, R., Ker, A.D.: A two-factor error model for quantitative steganalysis. In: Delp III, E.J., Wong, P.W. (eds.) Security, Steganography and Watermarking of Multimedia Contents VIII (Proc. of SPIE), San Jose, CA, vol. 6072, pp. 59–74 (2006)

Weighted Stego-Image Steganalysis for JPEG Covers

Rainer Böhme

Technische Universität Dresden
Institute of Systems Architecture
01062 Dresden, Germany
rainer.boehme@tu-dresden.de

Abstract. This paper contains two new results for the quantitative detector of LSB replacement steganography based on a weighted stego-image (WS). First, for spatial domain steganalysis, a variant of the WS method is known to be highly accurate only when cover images have never been subject to lossy compression. We propose a new variant of WS which increases the accuracy for JPEG pre-processed covers by one order of magnitude, thus leaving behind the best structural detectors which were known to be more robust on JPEG pre-compressed covers than WS. Second, we explain why WS-like estimators can also detect LSB replacement steganography in the transformed domain, and derive a reduced-form estimator for JSteg steganography which has equal or slightly better performance than the currently best JSteg detectors.

1 Introduction

The steganalysis method using a weighted stego-image (WS) proposed in 2004 by Fridrich and Goljan [1] is a mathematically well-founded, modular, and computationally fast estimator for the secret message length of *least significant bit* (LSB) replacement steganography in the spatial domain. In its original form, its performance is competitive with alternative methods only at high embedding rates, where high accuracy is less relevant in practice. Thus the method resided in the shade for years. Only recently, this turned out to be unjustified: An evaluation of an improved variant of WS concludes that for never-compressed covers, the performance of enhanced WS is (almost always) superior to any other detector, while its computational complexity is comparatively low [2]. However, enhanced WS still does not match the performance of methods from the class of *structural detectors* (see [3] for an overview of structural LSB steganalysis) if the cover image has been compressed with JPEG at some stage before embedding [4]. This is a substantial drawback because many image acquisition devices, foremost digital cameras in the consumer segment, store JPEG images by default. To close this gap, a modification of WS optimised for JPEG covers will be presented and benchmarked in the first part of this paper (Sect. 3).

The second part of this paper (Sect. 4) investigates ways to apply the WS method directly in the transformed domain; more precisely to detect LSB

K. Solanki, K. Sullivan, and U. Madhow (Eds.): IH 2008, LNCS 5284, pp. 178–194, 2008.
© Springer-Verlag Berlin Heidelberg 2008

replacement of JPEG coefficients as implemented in the popular JSteg [5] embedding function. We will show that WS-like detectors actually work in the JPEG domain, and their performance matches the best of all known detectors, despite some elements of the WS method seem completely inappropriate for this purpose! Aside from introducing yet another improved JSteg detector, we see our main contribution in the analysis *why* WS works in the transformed domain, and provide further tentative generalisations on the minimal cover assumptions required for the estimation of LSB replacement steganography.

Two more remarks on the organisation of this paper: Ahead of the main parts, the next section recapitulates the WS method, its recent enhancements, and briefly describes the image source for the experiments used to back our claims in the following sections. Due to space constraints, we omit a detailed review of related techniques and conclude our paper only tersely in Section 5.

2   Preliminaries

Let $\mathbf{x} = (x_1, \ldots, x_n), x_i \in \{0, \ldots, 2^\ell - 1\}$ be a vector of pixel intensity values, function $\mathcal{F} : \mathbb{Z}^n \to \mathbb{R}^n$ a local predictor for pixels from their spatial neighbourhood, and $\mathcal{V} : \mathbb{Z}^n \to \mathbb{R}^{+n}$ a measure of local predictability with respect to $\mathcal{F}$. We further define $\bar{x} = x + (-1)^x$ as the intensity with inverted LSB. Embedding rate p is the proportion of LSBs in $\mathbf{x}$ overwritten with random message bits, hence $p = 0$ for covers and $0 < p \leq 1$ for stego images. According to Theorem 3 in [1], p can be estimated by minimising the weighted L2-norm between the estimated cover, using local predictor $\mathcal{F}$, and a *weighted stego-image* with parameter α:

$$\hat{p} = 2 \arg\min_\alpha \sum_{i=1}^n w_i \big(\underbrace{\alpha \bar{x}_i + (1-\alpha)x_i}_{\text{weighted stego-image}} - \mathcal{F}(\mathbf{x})_i \big)^2 = \frac{2}{n} \sum_{i=1}^n w_i (x_i - \bar{x}_i)(x_i - \mathcal{F}(\mathbf{x})_i)$$

(1)

where $\mathbf{w} = (w_1, \ldots, w_n)$ is a vector of weights of the form

$$w_i \propto \frac{1}{\theta + \mathcal{V}(\mathbf{x})_i} \quad \text{with} \quad \theta = \begin{cases} 1 & \text{for standard WS} \\ 5 & \text{for enhanced WS} \end{cases}, \text{ and } \sum_{i=1}^n w_i = 1.$$

For *standard WS*, function $\mathcal{F}$ is the unweighted mean of the four directly adjacent pixels (in horizontal and vertical direction, ignoring diagonals) [1], and for *enhanced WS*, $\mathcal{F}$ is the result of a linear filter of dimension 5×5, excluding centre pixels, with coefficients estimated to minimise the squared prediction error in the entire image using the ordinary least squares method [2]. Function $\mathcal{V}$ measures predictability by the empirical variance of all pixels in the local predictor.

Note that $\hat{p}$ in (1) can be further improved with an additive bias correction term (which also exists in a standard and enhanced version) to compensate for *parity co-occurrence* (spatial neighbourhoods of pixels with equal parity) in cover images [1,2]. We will omit bias correction in this paper for brevity as it is most useful for denoised and saturated images, and not relevant in our image set.

The reference set for the experimental parts in this paper contains 1600 images. All images were obtained from a digital camera in raw format, down-scaled to 640×480 using Photoshop bilinear interpolation, and then converted to 8 bit greyscale. Although down-scaling alters local statistics and might affect steganalysis results in general [6], we conjecture that the results in this paper are less sensitive to such influence because compression artifacts largely erase the more subtle traces of resampling. All JPEG compression and pre-compression operations were conducted with `libjpeg`, the Independent JPEG Group's reference implementation, using default ('slow') settings for the DCT method.

3   Results for Spatial Domain Steganalysis

This section deals with the scenario, in which the steganalyst examines suspect images transmitted as uncompressed or loss-less compressed spatial domain representations. But the covers used for embedding had previously been subject to lossy JPEG compression, so that JPEG compression artefacts are still present in the data and might hinder standard and enhanced WS steganalysis.

3.1   Improved Local Predictor for JPEG Covers

Before we propose a specialised local predictor for JPEG pre-compressed covers, let us recapitulate the key elements of JPEG compression. The *discrete cosine transformation* (DCT) of column vector $\mathbf{x}$ of length N is defined as $\mathbf{y} = \mathbf{D}\mathbf{x}$ with elements of the orthogonal matrix $\mathbf{D}$ given as

$$D_{ij} = \sqrt{\frac{2}{N}} \cdot \cos\left(\frac{(2j-1)(i-1)\pi}{2N}\right)\left(1 + \frac{\delta_{i,1}}{2}(\sqrt{2}-2)\right), \quad 1 \le i,j \le N.$$

Operator δ_{ij} is the Kronecker delta. The 2D-DCT transformation of image blocks of dimension $N \times N$ serialised in columns of matrix $\mathbf{X} \in \{0, \ldots, 2^\ell - 1\}^2$ can be written as

$$\mathbf{Y} = \mathbf{S}\mathbf{X} \quad \text{with} \quad \mathbf{S} = \left(\mathbf{1}^{N\times 1} \otimes \mathbf{D} \otimes \mathbf{1}^{1\times N}\right) \odot \left(\mathbf{1}^{1\times N} \otimes \mathbf{D} \otimes \mathbf{1}^{N\times 1}\right) \quad (2)$$

where $\otimes$ is the Kronecker product, $\odot$ denotes element-wise multiplication, and $\mathbf{1}^{i\times j}$ is a matrix of ones with dimension $i \times j$. Matrix $\mathbf{S}$ is orthogonal. $\mathbf{Y} \in \mathbb{R}^2$ contains coefficients for N^2 subbands in rows, one column per transformed block. Constants are fixed to $N = \ell = 8$ in this work. During JPEG compression, DCT coefficients are divided by subband-specific quantisation factors and then rounded to the nearest integer.

$$\mathbf{Y}^* = \lfloor \bar{\mathbf{q}}\,\mathbf{Y} + 1/2 \rfloor \quad \text{with} \quad \bar{q}_i = 1/q_i = 1/\mathcal{Q}(q,i)$$

Function $\mathcal{Q} : \mathbb{R}^+ \times \{1, \ldots, N\} \to \mathbb{Z}^+$ is a publicly known method to calculate subband-specific quantisation factors for a given JPEG compression quality q.

We will now describe a new local predictor $\mathcal{F}$ for WS targeted for covers resulting from JPEG decompression. Our predictor works on former JPEG blocks

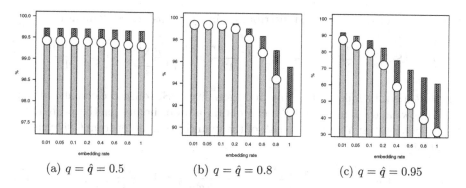

Fig. 1. JPEG predictor accuracy: percentage of embedding changes reverted to cover values after re-quantisation (grey bars), percentage of non-embedding positions altered after re-quantisation (hatched bars), total accuracy measured as difference between the two (white disks); note the different scales

and exploits the constraints imposed on possible realisations in $\mathbb{R}^N$ through quantisation with factors greater than one.

$$\mathcal{F}(\mathbf{X}, \hat{q}) = \mathbf{S}^\top \mathbf{q} \lfloor \bar{\mathbf{q}} \mathbf{S} \mathbf{X} + 1/2 \rfloor \tag{3}$$

To show why and under which conditions (3) is a good predictor, let us decompose the image under analysis as the cover plus an additive stego signal.

$$\mathbf{X} = \mathbf{X}_{\text{cover}} + \mathbf{X}_{\text{stego}}^{(p)} = \mathbf{S}^\top \mathbf{q} \mathbf{Y}^* + \boldsymbol{\epsilon} + \mathbf{X}_{\text{stego}}^{(p)}$$
$$= \mathbf{S}^\top \left(\mathbf{q} \mathbf{Y}^* + \mathbf{S} \left(\boldsymbol{\epsilon} + \mathbf{X}_{\text{stego}}^{(p)} \right) \right) = \mathbf{S}^\top \left(\mathbf{q} \mathbf{Y}^* + \tilde{\mathbf{Y}} \right)$$

The second identity rewrites $\mathbf{X}_{\text{cover}}$ as a result from a JPEG decompression operation with additive rounding error $\boldsymbol{\epsilon}$ due to the cast of real intensity values to integers in the spatial domain. Equation (3) is a good predictor for $\mathbf{X}_{\text{cover}}$, on average, if the DCT transformation $\tilde{\mathbf{Y}}$ of the sum of stego signal and pixel rounding error is below half of one quantisation factor with high probability.

We can approximate this probability for each subband as sum of independent random variables with known variance. The pixel rounding error is assumed to follow a uniform distribution in the interval $[-0.5, +0.5)$.[1] The stego signal is a random variable with three possible realisations 0 (with probability $(1 - p/2)$), -1, and $+1$ (each with probability $p/4$).[2] The distribution of the sum of pixel rounding error and stego signal has zero mean and variance $(1 + 6p)/12$. Each coefficient in $\tilde{\mathbf{Y}}$ is the weighted sum of N^2 (=64) independent realisations, so

---

[1] This assumption may be violated for saturated pixels, which need are special treatment in WS anyhow. Our test images exhibit comparatively little saturated areas.

[2] Here we can ignore the structural dependence typical for LSB replacement between the sign of the stego signal and the parity of the cover.

the variance of the compound distribution in the transformed domain is

$$\tilde{\sigma}^2 = (S_{i,1})^2 \frac{1+6p}{12} + \ldots + (S_{i,N})^2 \frac{1+6p}{12} = \frac{1+6p}{12} \sum_{j=1}^{N} (S_{ij})^2 = \frac{1+6p}{12} .$$

The last identity follows from the orthogonality of $\mathbf{S}$: squared elements add up to one row- and column-wise. We can obtain a lower bound for the probability that coefficients in $\tilde{\mathbf{Y}}$ are below half of the quantisation factor from Chebychev's inequality:

$$\text{Prob}\left(|\tilde{Y}_{ij}| < \frac{\mathcal{Q}(q,i)}{2}\right) \geq 1 - \frac{4\,\tilde{\sigma}^2}{\mathcal{Q}(q,i)^2} = 1 - \frac{(1+6p)}{3\,\mathcal{Q}(q,i)^2} \tag{4}$$

For example, the lowest quantisation factor at $q = 0.8$ is 4, so that at least 97 % of the cover pixels can be correctly predicted for embedding rates up to $p = 0.05$, 92 % for $p = 0.5$, and still 85 % for maximum capacity $p = 1$. Note that these estimates are very conservative, both because (4) is a rather loose bound and quantisation factors for higher subbands are up to ten times larger than the lowest. In practice, the chances of predicting cover pixels correctly are even higher, as can be seen from the results of experiments on real images displayed in Fig. 1. Observe that the predictor accuracy depends on both p and q in the theoretically founded way.

It is difficult to derive analytical results for the accuracy of (3) if $|\tilde{Y}_{ij}| > \mathcal{Q}(q,i)/2$ for a non-negligible number of coefficients in a block, because hardly tractable interdependencies between pixels emerge. Even if the predictor properties do not degrade severely on average, we have to raise an important assumption of the WS method, namely that the prediction error $\mathcal{F}(\mathbf{x})_i - x_i$ is independent of the stego signal at position i. Another source of deviations from the theoretical results could be error correlation due to propagation in efficient DCT implementations, such as the common 'fast' F-DCT.

3.2 Performance Evaluation

The performance of WS with improved predictor for JPEG covers (3), weighted and unweighted ($w_i = 1/n \; \forall i$), has been benchmarked against standard WS [1], enhanced WS [2], and SPA [7], which is a representative of structural detectors known for its robustness against cover pre-compression [4]. The predictor accuracy, measured as mean absolute error (MAE), is shown in the top four graphs of Fig. 2. For moderate compression factors, as expected, SPA is largely more accurate than the known variants of WS (standard and enhanced). The proposed JPEG WS, however, has an additional advantage over SPA, by up to one order of magnitude for $q = 0.5$. This advantage decreases gradually for higher pre-compression qualities and more so for large embedding rates. Note that weighting does not improve the accuracy of JPEG WS, a finding which resembles the situation for denoised covers in [2]. Unweighted JPEG WS turns out to be the most accurate quantitative stego-detector for pre-compressed covers up to JPEG qualities $q = 0.8$. Above this threshold it remains, by a large

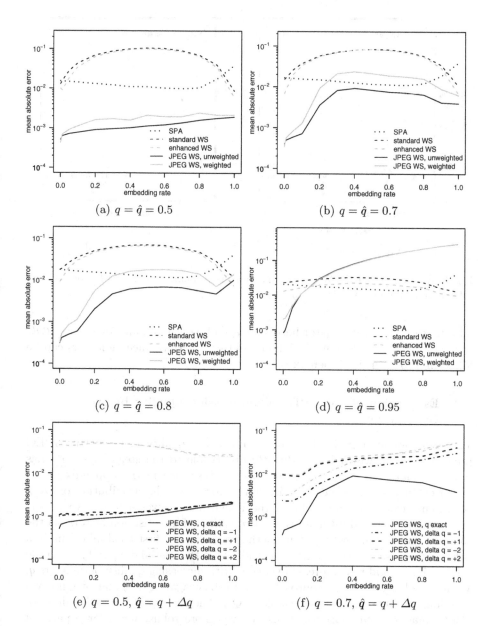

Fig. 2. Spatial domain WS for JPEG covers: Mean absolute estimation error for different JPEG qualities q. Graphs (a)–(d) assume perfect knowledge of q, graphs (e) and (f) display the estimator sensitivity to small deviations between the predictor parameter $\hat{q}$ and the actual pre-compression quality q.

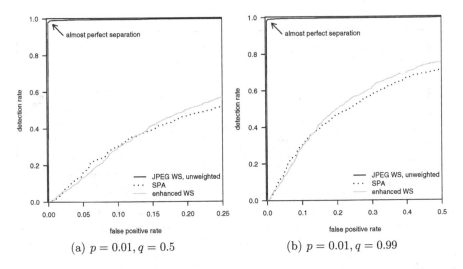

(a) $p = 0.01, q = 0.5$　　　　　　(b) $p = 0.01, q = 0.99$

Fig. 3. ROC curves: JPEG WS has unmatched discriminatory power for low embedding rates even at high quality factors q

margin, the best discriminator between stego objects and plain covers (see ROC curves in Fig. 3). A documentation of additional performance indicators can be found in Tab. 2 in the appendix.

3.3 Estimation of the JPEG Compression Quality before Embedding

The local predictor $\mathcal{F}$ in (3) depends on $\hat{q}$, the quality factor of the JPEG pre-compression, which is not directly observable to the steganalyst and has to be estimated. One option is the method described in the appendix of [8], which estimates *individual* quantisation factors from the distribution of DCT coefficients calculated from the of the image under investigation. We pursue another approach and estimate the *entire matrix* of quantisation factors via the common quality parameter q. Our method searches the first local minimum in a series of mean square errors (MSE) calculated in the spatial domain between the original image and re-compressed versions with increasing quality parameters q. We acknowledge that our approach is less robust against irregular or unknown functions $\mathcal{Q}$, but much more reliable if $\mathcal{Q}$ is known (as for the lion's share of JPEG images in circulation). It also proved more robust when large parts of the image under investigation have been modified with LSB replacement after decompression. Tab. 1 summarises the success rate ($\hat{q} = q$) for varying qualities q and embedding rates p. Observe that the method fails in precisely those cases where JPEG WS is not the optimal detector anyway. Since wrong estimates of $\hat{q}$ appear as never-compressed, this method is a safe decision criterion for the subsequent steganalysis method, namely enhanced WS for seemingly never-compressed images and JPEG WS if $\hat{q}$ exists.

Table 1. Success rate for correct estimation of pre-compression quality q

embedding rate p	raw covers	JPEG covers with quality q						
		0.5	0.6	0.7	0.8	0.9	0.95	0.99
0.00	100.0	100.0	100.0	100.0	100.0	100.0	100.0	0.0
0.01	100.0	100.0	100.0	100.0	100.0	100.0	100.0	0.0
0.05	100.0	100.0	100.0	100.0	100.0	100.0	100.0	0.0
0.10	100.0	100.0	100.0	100.0	100.0	100.0	89.9	0.0
0.20	100.0	100.0	100.0	100.0	100.0	100.0	0.0	0.0
0.40	100.0	100.0	100.0	100.0	100.0	100.0	0.0	0.0
0.60	100.0	100.0	100.0	100.0	100.0	100.0	0.0	0.0
0.80	100.0	100.0	100.0	100.0	100.0	96.6	0.0	0.0
1.00	100.0	100.0	100.0	100.0	99.2	51.7	0.0	0.0

All misclassified images were mistaken for raw covers.

Experimental results on the robustness of JPEG WS in the hypothetical case when $\hat{q}$ is estimated close but not equal to actual q are printed in the bottom two charts of Fig. 2. For low qualities ($q = 0.5$), a discrepancy of ± 1 is tolerable, whereas larger deviations are penalised with a drop in performance. With increasing q, it becomes more important to get $\hat{q}$ right. However, when in doubt between two subsequent values, a slight underestimation of $\hat{q}$ retains higher performance than overestimation.

4   Results for Transformed Domain Steganalysis

Unlike in the previous section, we now consider a scenario in which the steganalyst examines suspect images transmitted in JPEG format. We will explain how WS-like methods can reliably detect LSB replacement steganography even in the transformed domain. In particular, we will target our estimator to the JSteg [5] embedding function, which overwrites LSBs of quantised DCT coefficients at random positions except those with values 0 and 1.

4.1   Why WS-Like Detectors Work in the Transformed Domain

Following the notation for the spatial domain, let $\mathbf{c} = (c_1, \ldots, c_n), c_i \in \mathbb{Z}$ be a vector of quantised JPEG AC coefficients, function $\mathcal{F}_{\mathrm{DCT}} : \mathbb{Z}^n \to \mathbb{R}^n$ a local predictor for JPEG AC coefficients, and $\mathcal{V}_{\mathrm{DCT}} : \mathbb{Z}^n \to \mathbb{R}^{+n}$ a measure of local predictability with respect to $\mathcal{F}_{\mathrm{DCT}}$. We further define $\bar{c} = c + (-1)^c$ as the coefficient with inverted LSB.

A crude WS-like detector for Jsteg steganography is given as

$$\hat{p} \propto \sum_{i=1}^{n} w_i \big(c_i - \bar{c}_i \big) \big(c_i - \mathcal{F}_{\mathrm{DCT}}(\mathbf{c})_i \big) = \check{p} \qquad (5)$$

where $\mathbf{w} = (w_1, \ldots, w_n)$ is a vector of weights of the form

$$w_i \propto \frac{1 - \delta_{c_i,0} - \delta_{c_i,1}}{1 + \mathcal{V}_{\mathrm{DCT}}(\mathbf{c})_i} = \breve{w}_i \qquad \text{and} \qquad \sum_i w_i = 1. \tag{6}$$

The Kronecker deltas appear in the numerator to exclude coefficients of value 0 and 1 from the estimation. This is specific to JSteg detection. For the same reason, $\breve{p}$ in (5) must be adjusted to ensure that $\hat{p}$ is in the domain $[0,1]$:

$$\hat{p} = \breve{p} + W_1^* = \breve{p} + \left(\sum_i \breve{w}_i\right)^{-1} \sum_i \frac{\delta_{c_i,1}}{1 + \mathcal{V}_{\mathrm{DCT}}(\mathbf{c})_i} \tag{7}$$

Offset W_1^* is the 'virtual' weight of all coefficients with value $+1$, if they were not excluded in (6), normalised to the scale of the actual weights.

One possible implementation for $\mathcal{F}_{\mathrm{DCT}}$ is taking the mean of the same JPEG AC coefficient in the four adjacent blocks (excluding border blocks from the analysis). $\mathcal{V}_{\mathrm{DCT}}$ can be measured as empirical variance of the coefficients used to calculate the value of $\mathcal{F}_{\mathrm{DCT}}$. Note that in (5) and (7), quantised AC coefficients for all 63 subbands are taken together. Surprisingly, $\hat{p}$ is a quite good estimator for the true embedding rate p. This is puzzling since it is known that AC coefficients are hardly predictable from spatial relations between blocks. In fact, the performance of the local predictor $\mathcal{F}_{\mathrm{DCT}}$ measured as weighted share of explained variance R^2, compared to an unconditional mean benchmark, is extremely poor. R^2 is calculated as

$$R^2 = \left(1 - \frac{\sum_i w_i (\mathcal{F}_{\mathrm{DCT}}(\mathbf{c})_i - c_i)^2}{\sum_i w_i (\mu - c_i)^2}\right) \times 100\% \qquad \text{with} \qquad \mu = \sum_i w_i c_i .$$

We found that R^2 is *negative* in the large majority of cases. This means the unconditional mean μ is a *better* predictor than using information from adjacent blocks. We have also experimented with alternative predictors calculated from 'calibrated' versions of the image, similar to the calibration procedure used for universal JPEG steganalysis [9], but without much success.

As μ is very close to zero in typical images (in line with the zero-mean Laplace distribution model for AC coefficients), it is not surprising that we can omit the local predictor in (5) without compromising estimation accuracy.

$$\hat{p} = \sum_{i=1}^n w_i(c_i - \bar{c}_i)\, c_i + W_1^* \tag{8}$$

We will refer to detectors of this type as *reduced form estimators* and, in the following, sketch a proof that (8) is, in principle, a JSteg detector.

Lemma 1. *For $p = 0$ (plain covers), $\hat{p}$ in (8) converges to 0.*

Proof. After elimination of $\mathcal{F}_{\mathrm{DCT}}(\mathbf{c})_i$ in (5), we can rewrite (8) as weighted histogram-based detector. Let W_k be the weighted fraction of coefficients with value k, $W_k = \sum_{i \in \{i | c_i = k\}} w_i$. Then,

$$\hat{p} = \sum_k W_k(k - \bar{k})k + W_1^*$$

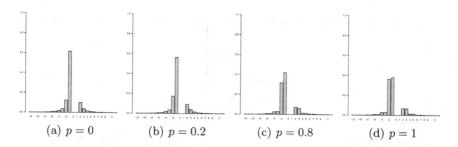

Fig. 4. Histogram of W_k for images with varying embedding rates ($q = 0.8$)

$$= \sum_{k \geq 2 \, \wedge \, k \text{ even}} \left[\overbrace{W_k(-1)k}^{\text{positive, even}} + \overbrace{W_{k+1}(+1)(k+1)}^{\text{positive, odd}} + \right.$$

$$\left. \underbrace{W_{-k}(-1)(-k)}_{\text{negative, even}} + \underbrace{W_{-k-1}(+1)(-k-1)}_{\text{negative, odd}} \right] - W_{-1} + W_1^*$$

Using the symmetry of AC coefficient frequencies in cover images, $W_k \approx W_{-k}$ for $k \geq 2$ and $W_{-1} \approx W_1^*$

$$\hat{p} \approx \sum_{k \geq 2 \, \wedge \, k \text{ even}} \left[-W_k k + W_{k+1}(k+1) + W_k k - W_{k+1}(k+1) \right] \approx 0$$

$\square$

Lemma 2. *For $p = 1$ (full embedding), $\hat{p}$ converges to $1 + b$, where estimation bias b is bound by $|b| \leq 1/2$.*

Proof. We use the same conventions as before and rewrite (8) as weighted histogram-based detector.

$$\hat{p} = \sum_{k \text{ even}} W_k(-1)k - \sum_{k \text{ odd}} W_k(+1)k + W_1^*$$

$$= \sum_{k \text{ even}} \left[W_{k+1}(k+1) - W_k k \right] + W_1^*$$

Due to the formation of pairs of values for $p = 1$, $W_k \approx W_{k+1} + \Delta_k$ (for k even). In contrast to detectors using the unweighted histogram, the expected values of W_k and W_{k+1} for pairs of values (k even) are not exactly equal, because coefficients with higher absolute value tend to get lower weight per coefficient even for $p = 1$ (see Fig. 4). However, difference $\Delta_k \approx -\Delta_{-k}$, so that $\sum_{k \text{ even}} \Delta_k \approx 0$ and $\sum_{k \text{ even}} W_k \approx 1/2$. Hence,

$$\hat{p} \approx \sum_{k \text{ even}} W_k(k+1-k) + W_1^* \approx \frac{1}{2} + W_1^* = 1 + b$$

$$b = W_1^* - \frac{1}{2}$$

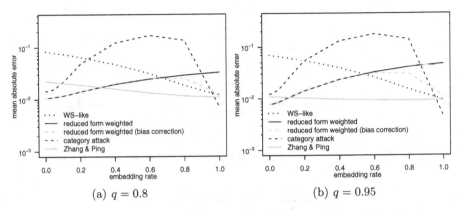

(a) $q = 0.8$ (b) $q = 0.95$

Fig. 5. Mean absolute estimation errors in the transformed domain

From $0 \leq W_1^* \leq 1$ follows $|b| \leq 1/2$.   □

In practice, we found that $W_1^* \approx 1/2$ with mean absolute deviation between images about $1/20$, so that (8) has lower average errors towards $p = 1$. Incidentally, this happens to hold approximately independent of q.

From Lemma 1 and Lemma 2 follows immediately that (8) is a JSteg detector. It is not straight-forward to show that (8) is a *quantitative* detector, that is $\hat{p} \approx p$ for all $0 \leq p \leq 1$. The reason is that increasing embedding rates change both histogram and inter-block variance and thus the distribution of weight per coefficient value as function of p is intractable.

Before we proceed with the experimental results, we introduce a variant of the reduced form estimator including bias correction if $|b| = |1/2 - W_1^*| > 0$.

$$\hat{p}^* = \hat{p} + \left(\hat{p} + \hat{p} \left(\frac{1}{2} - W_1^* \right) \right)^4 \left(\frac{1}{2} - W_1^* \right) \qquad (9)$$

Bias correction starts from an initial estimate $\hat{p}$, which is refined in two iterations. We expect that (9) shows comparable performance to (8) for small embedding rates and is more accurate for p close to 1. The exponent 4 has been determined experimentally to deal with a non-linearity of $|b|$ as function of p.

4.2   Performance Evaluation

Since WS-like detectors in the JPEG domain are merely variants of histogram-based detectors (i.e. no spatial relation of coefficients in subbands or blocks is exploited), we should also expect similar performance. As fair benchmarks, we have selected from the literature the most accurate estimator, Zhang & Ping's method [10], and the most reliable discriminator, the so-called *category attack* by Lee et al. [11].[3] Predictor accuracy, as function of the embedding rate, is

---

[3] Its generalised variant [12] performs better on double-compressed images only.

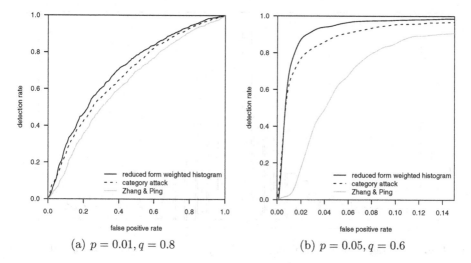

(a) $p = 0.01, q = 0.8$ (b) $p = 0.05, q = 0.6$

Fig. 6. ROC curves: the proposed methods' discriminatory power matches or marginally exceeds known schemes. Bias correction is not relevant for $p < 1/2$.

displayed in Fig. 5. The dotted line labelled 'WS-like' refers to (7), and 'reduced form weighted' to (8) without and (9) with bias correction, respectively. Observe that the reduced form estimators exhibit lower MAE for small embedding rates, whereas Zhang & Ping's method becomes more accurate for medium and high p. Further, the advantage of Zhang & Ping's method expands with increasing q. The category attack is less accurate except for $p = 1$. As expected, bias correction helps substantially for high embedding rates.

Turning to the performance as discriminator, the ROC curves in Fig. 6 demonstrate that our reduced form estimators are at least as good as established JSteg detectors. Hence, spatial domain WS not only happens to work as detector for LSB replacement in AC coefficients, but – with some theoretically justified tweaks – also constitutes a highly reliable detector.

Again, additional performance indicators are printed in Tab. 3 in the appendix. This table also shows the unmatched low deviation between images of the reduced form methods for $p < 1$ compared to the alternatives tested in the experiments.

4.3 The Role of Weights

We have argued that the correctness of WS in the JPEG domain *does not* depend on the choice of $\mathcal{F}_{\mathrm{DCT}}$ (as long as $E(\mathcal{F}_{\mathrm{DCT}}(\mathbf{c})) \approx 0$) nor on the weights as measure of predictability. However, results from experiments with unweighted versions of WS-like detectors were dissatisfactory. Weights are important for two reasons. First, for $p = 1$, to ensure that $W_1^* \approx 1/2$ for good initial estimates $\hat{p}$ in (8). Second, for $p = 0$, to suppress deviations from the histogram symmetry $W_k \approx W_{-k}$ for (sparsely populated but otherwise highly influential)

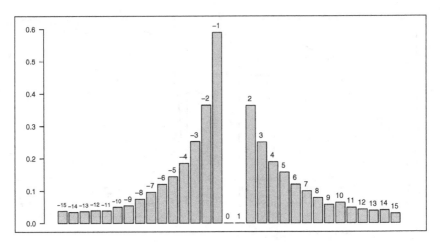

Fig. 7. Average weight by value: $|\mathcal{S}|^{-1} \cdot \sum_{i \in \mathcal{S}} w_i$ with $\mathcal{S} = \{i | c_i = k\}$, $q = 0.8$

coefficients with large absolute value. So we conjecture that a weighing scheme which amplifies the low value AC coefficients in the joint histogram, as shown in Fig. 7, is crucial to suppress image-specific dispersion. The empirical variance criterion works because, as a side effect, those AC subbands which are quantised to smaller magnitudes exhibit lower absolute differences between adjacent blocks even though their sign may be fully uncorrelated. The weights also help to make WS-like estimators less sensitive to variations in the JPEG quality q, as subbands with lots of decisive coefficients (with low absolute value after quantisation) are assigned over-proportional weight (see Fig. 8). It is up to further research if the weighting function $\mathcal{V}_{\mathrm{DCT}}$ can be replaced by one that does not depend on the spatial relations between adjacent blocks. This would allow to implement WS-like methods equally fast as other histogram-based detectors.

4.4 Lessons Learned and Generalisation

The finding that WS-like detectors, which were designed to exploit – via function $\mathcal{F}$ – spatial correlation between samples, also work in a domain of uncorrelated samples, such as after an orthogonal transformation, is not as unexpected as it seems. This is so because WS, as well as most other LSB detectors, are effectively built on assumptions of dependence between *first differences of samples*, not primarily of their levels. This condition can be roughly formulated as

$$\mathrm{Prob}(x_i | x_{i+1} = x_i + k) \approx \mathrm{Prob}(x_i | x_{i+1} = x_i + \beta k) - \varepsilon \quad \text{for} \quad \beta > 1, \varepsilon > 0.$$

Some detectors, including WS, also need an approximate symmetry condition:

$$\mathrm{Prob}(x_i | x_{i+1} = x_i + k) \approx \mathrm{Prob}(x_i | x_{i+1} = x_i - k)$$

These conditions are met by a wide range of cover models, including i. i. d. signals with various marginal distributions. In fact, if correctness of a stego-estimator

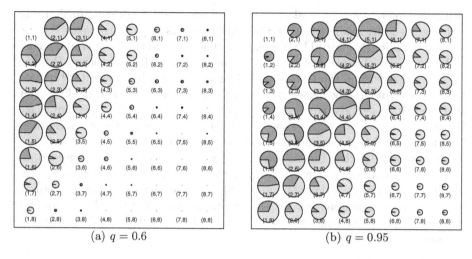

(a) $q = 0.6$ (b) $q = 0.95$

Fig. 8. Cumulative weight by DCT subband. The area is proportional to the total weight of all coefficients in a subband. The bright segment is the (unweighted) fraction of coefficients $c_i \in \{0, 1\}$ excluded from the analysis.

is defined in terms of consistency of a point estimate, i.e. $\hat{p}$ converges to p with increasing n, then WS, SPA, and other spatial domain detectors 'work' on i.i.d. covers (also confirmed by experiments and noted in [7, p. 1997] for SPA). Spatial dependence as well as leptocurtic marginal distributions (like for JPEG AC coefficients) can strengthen the above-stated relationship, but are not required for the *consistency* of the estimator. What matters for steganalytic *performance*, however, is the size and the distribution of errors around the expected value; in brief, the estimator *efficiency*. In that sense, it is indeed a coincidence, that the WS-like weighting scheme yields so favourable asymptotics for JSteg detection. Unfortunately, the deviation of asymptotics of secret message length estimators is largely under-developed ([13] being a commendable exception), and impeded by the lack of tractable image models. Maybe the way forward goes via estimators in the transformed domain, where reasonable assumptions can be made for the marginal distribution of AC coefficients, leaving spatial domain asymptotics a longer-term goal.

5 Concluding Remarks

This paper contributes two rather distinct results, which have in common the relation to the weighted stego-image (WS) method and JPEG covers. First, we have optimised spatial domain WS for cases when the cover has been pre-compressed with the JPEG algorithm, a scenario in which known variants of WS were less reliable than other detectors build on the structural paradigm. Our proposed method could improve the performance up to one order of magnitude, thus leaving behind state-of-the-art structural detectors particularly in those situations where standard and enhanced WS are worst (high compression rate or low embedding rate). Together with earlier results in [2], this makes WS the method of choice for general LSB replacement steganalysis in the spatial domain.

The second contribution of this paper is an analysis in the reasons why WS-like detectors also work in the transformed domain. The resulting detector targeted to JSteg steganography turned out to be comparable to (or marginally better than) existing methods. Some reflections on the fundamental causes that make WS work in uncorrelated covers shed new light on the minimal cover assumptions for current (LSB replacement) steganalysis techniques.

We acknowledge that further theoretical work in this direction is needed, as well as additional experiments concerning the robustness of the proposed methods to saturation, variations of the JPEG implementation and DCT method, as well as double-compressed covers. For practitioners, optimised detectors for more exotic pre-processing sequences, such as subtle resizing after JPEG decompression, might be of interest.

Acknowledgements

We are grateful to Andrew Ker for sharing the test images. Andreas Westfeld recommended the benchmark attacks for the transformed domain experiments. Thomas Gloe, Matthias Kirchner and the anonymous reviewers provided useful comments.

References

1. Fridrich, J., Goljan, M.: On estimation of secret message length in LSB steganography in spatial domain. In: Delp, E.J., Wong, P.W. (eds.) Security, Steganography and Watermarking of Multimedia Contents VI (Proc. of SPIE), San Jose, CA (2004)
2. Ker, A.D., Böhme, R.: Revisiting weighted stego-image steganalysis. In: Delp, E.J., et al. (eds.) Security, Forensics, Steganography and Watermarking of Multimedia Contents X (Proc. of SPIE), San Jose, CA, vol. 6819 (2008)
3. Ker, A.D.: A general framework for the structural steganalysis of LSB replacement. In: Barni, M., Herrera-Joancomartí, J., Katzenbeisser, S., Pérez-González, F. (eds.) IH 2005. LNCS, vol. 3727, pp. 296–311. Springer, Heidelberg (2005)
4. Böhme, R., Ker, A.D.: A two-factor error model for quantitative steganalysis. In: Delp, E.J., Wong, P.W. (eds.) Security, Steganography and Watermarking of Multimedia Contents VIII (Proc. of SPIE), San Jose, CA, vol. 6072, pp. 59–74 (2006)
5. Upham, D.: JSteg, Version 4 (1992), http://zooid.org/~paul/crypto/jsteg/
6. Böhme, R.: Assessment of steganalytic methods using multiple regression models. In: Barni, M., Herrera-Joancomartí, J., Katzenbeisser, S., Pérez-González, F. (eds.) IH 2005. LNCS, vol. 3727, pp. 278–295. Springer, Heidelberg (2005)
7. Dumitrescu, S., Wu, X., Wang, Z.: Detection of LSB steganography via sample pair analysis. IEEE Trans. on Signal Processing 51, 1995–2007 (2003)
8. Fridrich, J., Goljan, M., Du, R.: Steganalysis based on JPEG compatibility. In: Tescher, A.G., Vasudev, B., Bove Jr., V.M. (eds.) Multimedia Systems and Applications IV (Proc. of SPIE), Denver, CO, pp. 275–280 (2001)

9. Fridrich, J.: Feature-based steganalysis for JPEG images and its implications for future design of steganographic schemes. In: Fridrich, J. (ed.) IH 2004. LNCS, vol. 3200, pp. 67–81. Springer, Heidelberg (2004)

10. Zhang, T., Ping, X.: A fast and effective steganalytic technique against JSteg-like algorithms. In: Proc. of ACM Symposium on Applied Computing, Melbourne, Florida, pp. 307–311. ACM Press, New York (2003)

11. Lee, K., Westfeld, A., Lee, S.: Category attack for LSB steganalysis of JPEG images. In: Shi, Y.Q., Jeon, B. (eds.) IWDW 2006. LNCS, vol. 4283, pp. 35–48. Springer, Heidelberg (2006)

12. Lee, K., Westfeld, A., Lee, S.: Generalised category attack – improving histogram-based attack on JPEG LSB embedding. In: Furon, T., Cayre, F., Doërr, G., Bas, P. (eds.) IH 2007. LNCS, vol. 4567, pp. 378–391. Springer, Heidelberg (2008)

13. Ker, A.D.: Derivation of error distribution in least squares steganalysis. IEEE Trans. on Information Forensics and Security 2, 140–148 (2007)

Appendix

Table 2. Performance indicators for spatial domain estimators

indicator	MAE[a]				IQR[b]				median err.[c]				FP$_{50}$[d]
emb. rate	0.0	0.1	0.4	1.0	0.0	0.1	0.4	1.0	0.0	0.1	0.4	1.0	0.01
q = 0.5													
JPEG WS, unw.	0.1	0.1	0.1	0.2	0.0	0.1	0.2	0.3	0.0	0.0	0.0	−0.0	0.6
JPEG WS, w.	0.0	0.1	0.2	0.2	0.0	0.1	0.2	0.3	0.0	0.0	0.0	0.0	0.8
enhanced WS	1.0	3.5	9.6	0.6	1.0	4.1	12.5	0.7	−0.3	3.1	9.2	−0.1	5.3
SPA[e]	1.5	1.4	1.1	3.9	1.1	1.1	0.9	2.5	0.3	0.3	0.2	−3.6	22.8
q = 0.8													
JPEG WS, unw.	0.0	0.1	0.6	1.0	0.0	0.1	0.8	0.7	0.0	0.0	0.2	−0.9	0.1
JPEG WS, w.	0.0	0.1	1.6	1.4	0.0	0.2	2.2	1.3	0.0	0.0	0.5	−1.2	0.3
enhanced WS	0.9	3.0	6.5	0.7	0.8	3.7	9.9	0.9	0.1	2.5	5.3	−0.1	12.4
SPA[e]	1.8	1.6	1.3	4.2	1.4	1.3	1.2	2.9	0.3	0.2	0.2	−3.9	24.4
q = 0.95													
JPEG WS, unw.	0.1	1.1	8.2	30.5	0.1	0.2	0.3	0.5	0.0	−1.1	−8.2	−30.5	0.4
JPEG WS, w.	0.2	1.1	8.0	30.9	0.2	0.3	0.5	0.9	0.0	−1.1	−8.2	−30.9	4.0
enhanced WS	1.3	1.6	2.3	1.0	1.3	1.6	2.4	1.3	0.2	0.6	1.0	−0.1	19.9
SPA[e]	2.0	1.9	1.6	4.4	1.8	1.7	1.6	2.9	0.3	0.3	0.2	−4.2	26.0
never-compressed													
enhanced WS	2.2	2.1	1.8	1.1	1.7	1.6	1.8	1.6	0.2	0.3	0.2	0.0	23.8
SPA[e]	2.7	2.5	2.0	4.5	2.3	2.2	2.1	2.7	0.4	0.4	0.3	−4.3	31.6

a) mean absolute error (in percentage points); a summary measure
b) inter-quartile range (in p. p.); a robust measure of dispersion
c) median error (in p. p.); a robust measure of bias
d) false positive rate at 50 % detection rate (in %)
e) SPA failures omitted (no real root of the estimation equation)

Table 3. Performance indicators for transformed domain estimators

indicator	MAE[a]				IQR[b]				median err.[c]				FP$_{50}$[d]
emb. rate	0.0	0.1	0.4	1.0	0.0	0.1	0.4	1.0	0.0	0.1	0.4	1.0	0.01
q = 0.8													
WS-like	8.3	7.4	4.7	1.2	3.0	2.8	2.4	1.9	−8.0	−7.1	−4.5	−0.3	29.8
reduced form	1.1	1.2	1.9	3.3	1.7	1.7	1.9	2.5	−0.1	−0.6	−1.8	−3.1	21.6
−″− bias corr.	1.1	1.2	2.0	1.3	1.7	1.7	1.9	2.0	−0.1	−0.6	−1.8	−0.4	21.6
category attack	1.5	2.1	12.2	0.7	2.3	2.4	2.6	0.3	−0.1	1.7	12.3	−0.7	26.5
Zhang & Ping	2.2	2.1	1.6	1.1	2.7	2.5	2.1	1.8	0.2	0.1	−0.1	−0.4	30.3

a) mean absolute error (in percentage points); a summary measure
b) inter-quartile range (in p. p.); a robust measure of dispersion
c) median error (in p. p.); a robust measure of bias
d) false positive rate at 50 % detection rate (in %)

Practical Insecurity for Effective Steganalysis

Johann Barbier[1,2] and Stéphanie Alt[1]

[1] Centre d'Électronique de l'ARmement, Département de Cryptologie,
La Roche Marguerite, BP 57419,
35174 Bruz Cedex, France
[2] École Supérieure et d'Application des Transmissions,
Laboratoire de Virologie et Cryptologie,
BP 18, 35998 Rennes Cedex, France
{johann.barbier,stephanie.alt}@dga.defense.gouv.fr

Abstract. In this paper, we propose to link practical steganalysis and classical security models. In one hand, some steganography schemes are proved to be secure in some security models but in practice, they cannot be used in real-life because of too many constrains. In the other hand, lots of practical steganography algorithms have been broken by effective steganalysis but without any connection with standard models of attackers. So, we introduce two new types of adversaries to simulate real attackers, the IND-SSA adversary and the IND-USA adversary. The IND-SSA adversary emulates specific steganalysis whereas the IND-USA attacker stands for universal steganalysis. We also define the games and the security models associated with and formalize discrimination attacks and discriminant steganalysis. Then, we connect these new models with the hierarchy of classical security models. Using models introduced by C. Cachin, S. Katzenbeisser and F. Petitcolas, and finally by N. Hopper, we show how effective steganalysis gives us a lower bound on the insecurity of the steganalyzed steganography schemes. We also point out that steganography schemes which are not secure in these new models are also not secure in the classical models of security.

Keywords: security models, practical steganalysis.

1 Introduction

If we considered a steganography algorithm as a particular channel for communication, its security can be related to the transmission security (TRANSEC) which is traditionally defined for physical communication channels. As in cryptography, the evaluation of such a security is mandatory to compare the robustnesses of the steganography algorithms all together but also to compare the efficiencies of steganalysis. To deeply understand the TRANSEC adapted to steganography, we consider that hiding information into a cover medium is an equivalent process to emit a numerical signal into a physical channel. This point of view maps the hidden message to the emitted signal, the cover medium to the channel itself, the embedding algorithm to the channel coding step (including the

K. Solanki, K. Sullivan, and U. Madhow (Eds.): IH 2008, LNCS 5284, pp. 195–208, 2008.

modulation) and finally, the extraction algorithm to the reception and channel decoding steps (signal demodulation and decoding). Moreover, the Shannon's bound implies that the capacity of the channel is limited and that this limit depends on the way to encode the information. In the same way, the capacity of a cover medium is bounded and this bound depends on the cover medium itself but also on the embedding algorithm. This strong analogy between steganography and the world of the communication channels let us foresee an easy adaptation of the concepts of the information theory to model steganography mechanisms. C. Cachin [1,2,3] followed by R. Chandramouli [4,5,6] dealt with the security and the capacity of steganography algorithms through this scope. C. Cachin was the first one to define the concept of security for a steganography algorithm. Let $\mathcal{C}$ be the set of all the cover media, of distribution $P_{\mathcal{C}}$ and $\mathcal{S}$, the set of stego media, of distribution $P_{\mathcal{S}}$, then the security of a steganography scheme is given by the *mutual entropy* $D_0(P_{\mathcal{C}}||P_{\mathcal{S}})$ between $P_{\mathcal{C}}$ and $P_{\mathcal{S}}$. A steganography scheme is then said to be ε-*secure* against a passive adversary, if and only if

$$D_0(P_{\mathcal{C}}||P_{\mathcal{S}}) = \sum_{c \in \mathcal{C}} P_{\mathcal{C}}(c) \log \frac{P_{\mathcal{C}}(c)}{P_{\mathcal{S}}(c)} \leq \varepsilon.$$

Moreover, if $\varepsilon = 0$ then the scheme is said to be *perfectly secure*. This pseudo-distance is also called *Kullbak-Liebler distance*. In other words, the security of a steganography scheme depends on the incapacity of the adversary to distinguish between two probability density functions, $P_{\mathcal{C}}$ and $P_{\mathcal{S}}$. Numerous security models for steganography have been proposed so far. Some of them are dedicated to private keys schemes [2,7,8,9] and other ones fit to public keys schemes [10,3,11]. Moreover, different types of adversaries have also been considered like passives ones [2,8,11,10] or active ones [3,12]. N. Hopper's PhD. thesis [13] is perhaps one of the most complete work dealing with the security of steganography schemes. Different models and notations are rigorously defined and compared with the security of cryptography schemes.

Two aims are considered in this paper. The first one is to rigorously model the real-life steganographic adversary which is commonly used. The second one is to point out a lower bound on the insecurity of the attacked scheme directly from practical steganalysis performances. The traditional approach in security proofs is to take the designer's point of view and prove with a strong adversary, the security of a designed scheme, in a given model by using reductions to hard problems. Our approach is a little bit different. We deal with a steganalysis of a given steganography scheme and we want to study the insecurity of the scheme in a model that fits the best the real-life attacker. As the real-life adversary is very weak, he is never taken into account in the design of security models. Recently, A.D. Ker [14] went to the same direction and proposed a methodology to benchmark practical steganalysis.

This paper is organized as follows. First, using models proposed by C. Cachin [2], S. Katzenbeisser and F. Petitcolas [9] and N. Hopper [13], we formalize the concepts of *discrimination attacks*, classifier and *discriminant steganalysis*; then we summarize the last one as a statistical discrimination problem. In the second section, we recall the classical indistinguishability-based security models and weaken them, in the third section, to simulate real-life specific but also universal steganalysis. We propose two new models of security, IND-SSA and IND-USA and link them to the hierarchy of classical ones. Finally, we lower bound the insecurity using the probabilities of false positive and false negative of effective steganalysis and show how this bound also holds for classical models. In conclusion, we discuss about the need to have a common methodology to evaluate the security of a given steganography algorithm or to compare the performances of steganalysis.

2   Notations and Definitions

We now take the adversary's point of view and blindly intercept media exchanged by Alice and Bob. First, we recall the formal definition of a private keys steganography scheme.

Definition 1. [9] *A private keys steganography scheme Σ is defined by a set $\mathcal{C}$ of cover media and by three polynomial algorithms :*

- *A probabilistic algorithm $\mathcal{K}$, which generates the keys. Its input is a security parameter k and its ouput is a private key K.*
- *A probabilistic embedding algorithm Emb. Its inputs are the key K, a plain text $m \in \mathcal{M} \subset \{0,1\}^*$, a cover medium $C \in \mathcal{C}$ and its output is a stego medium $C' \in \mathcal{S}$, the set of stego media.*
- *A deterministic extraction algorithm Ext. Its inputs are the private key K, a medium C' and outputs the plain text m if C' has been embedded using K or $\perp$, an error message.*

Remark 1. As in cryptography, this definition can be easily adapted to public keys schemes. In the scope of this paper, we only deal with private keys schemes. Nevertheless, all that is presented here remains true for public keys schemes. In a more general context, such adaptations are not always so straight forward and should be done with lots of precautions.

In this context, the attacker is passive and given a medium C, he must answer the question *"Is C a stego medium ?"*. This question is equivalent to distinguish a cover medium $c \in \mathcal{C}$, knowing $P_{\mathcal{C}}$ from a stego medium $s \in \mathcal{S}$, knowing $P_{\mathcal{S}}$. To distinguish these probability density laws, we use the statistical distance $D(.,.)$ introduced by N. Hopper [13], and defined by

$$D(P_{\mathcal{C}}, P_{\mathcal{S}}) = \frac{1}{2} \sum_{I \in \mathcal{C} \cup \mathcal{S}} |P_{\mathcal{C}}(I) - P_{\mathcal{S}}(I)| .$$

A steganography scheme is said to be ε-secure if and only if

$$D(P_{\mathcal{C}}, P_{\mathcal{S}}) \leq \varepsilon ,$$

and perfectly secure if and only if $\varepsilon = 0$. Most of times it is impossible, in practice, to evaluate P_C and P_S but we are able to obtain a partial estimation of them through real attacks. In this paper, we propose to link the security of steganographic schemes to the probabilities of detection and false alarm obtained by a real-life adversary which implements a given attack. This is achieved by defining the appropriate models of security and the associated games. Moreover, it exists different statistical distances, like the *Kulbak-Liebler distance* (KL), but $D(.,.)$ is the most adapted to define the security of a scheme with the probability of success of an effective steganalysis. This point is clearly illustrated in the proof of theorem 2. First, we need to introduce *discrimination attacks*.

Definition 2. *Let Σ a steganography scheme. We call discrimination attack a function defined by*

$$V: \quad \mathcal{I} = \mathcal{C} \cup \mathcal{S} \longrightarrow \mathcal{V}_1 \times \ldots \times \mathcal{V}_n$$
$$I \longrightarrow V(I) = (V_1(I), \ldots, V_n(I)) \ ,$$

where V_i is a random variable from $\mathcal{I}$ to $\mathcal{V}_i$ computable in a polynomial time.

Such an attack is equivalent to n measures onto the medium considered as coordinates of a statistical vector, that is also known as *features extraction*. Moreover, we say that such an attack is *efficient* if and only if we are able to distinguish $\mathcal{C}$ from $\mathcal{S}$ using V. To be efficient, an attack must verify at least of the following criteria: It exists $j \in [1, n]$ such that $P_{V_j(\mathcal{C})} \neq P_{V_j(\mathcal{S})}$ or it exists $j \in [1, n]$ such that $P_{(V_j | \{V_k, k \neq j\})(\mathcal{C})} \neq P_{(V_j | \{V_k, k \neq j\})(\mathcal{S})}$. The first criteria implies that $I \longrightarrow V_j(I)$ is also an efficient discrimination attack, that is not the case for the second one. If $V_j(I)$ is not efficient, that means we also need to observe more coordinates of V to get information about I, using V_j.

This definition is not constraining as many powerful attacks, like chi-square attacks, pair analysis [15] or RS analysis [16], can easily be adapted to fit it; this gives us a framework to compare all types of attacks. Finding an efficient attack only gives us the proof of the capability to discriminate cover media and stego media using V. To achieve this, we also need a detector which discriminates $P_{V(\mathcal{C})}$ and $P_{V(\mathcal{S})}$ using the marginal distributions P_{V_i}, and the conditional ones, $P_{V_i | \{V_k, k \neq i\}}$. We adapt C. Cachin's [2] definition. Let Σ be a steganography scheme and V a discrimination attack against Σ. A function defined by

$$D_V : \mathcal{V}_1 \times \ldots \times \mathcal{V}_n \longrightarrow \{0, 1\} \ ,$$

and computable in a polynomial time, is called a *classifier compatible with V*. Traditionally, 0 stands for cover medium and 1 for stego medium.

This gives us a natural definition of the discriminant steganalysis, which is perhaps one of the most implicitly used by the community.

Definition 3. *Let Σ be a steganography scheme. We call discriminant steganalysis against Σ, every pair (V, D_V), where V is a discrimination attack against Σ and D_V a classifier compatible with V.*

This formal definition that we propose well simulates the behavior of a real-life adversary. Indeed, an effective adversary processes two steps. First, he points out a set a measures such that at least one of them does not follow the same marginal or conditional probability density functions for cover media and for stego media. This first step is the features extraction. In a second step, he designs a classifier using discrimination analysis tools. For a given discrimination attack V, it exists different ways of designing a classifier compatible with V. For instance, using Fisher discrimination, Principal Component Analysis, Support Vector Machines... V comes from the steganalyst's experiments whereas D_V comes from hypothesis testing methods. Practically, with enough observations, it is possible to obtain a good approximation of $P_{V(C)}$ and $P_{V(S)}$. The definition of discriminant steganalysis leads us naturally to enlarge the definition of the unconditional security to a *security against a given discriminant steganalysis*.

Definition 4. *Let Σ a steganography scheme and (V, D_V) a discriminant steganalysis. Σ is said to be ε-secure against (V, D_V) if and only if*

$$D(P_{D_V \circ V(C)}, P_{D_V \circ V(S)}) \leq \varepsilon.$$

Moreover, if $\varepsilon = 0$ then the scheme is said to be perfectly secure against (V, D_V).

The following proposition links the security against a given discriminant steganalysis with the classical concept of security of steganographic schemes.

Proposition 1. *Le Σ a steganography scheme. Then*

$$\Sigma \text{ is } \varepsilon\text{-secure} \implies \Sigma \text{ is } \varepsilon\text{-secure against } (V, D_V),$$

$\forall (V, D_V)$ *discriminant steganalysis.*

Proof :
From [13, p. 12], for all functions f defined on $\mathcal{I}$ we have

$$D\left(P_{f(C)}, P_{f(S)}\right) \leq D(P_C, P_S) \qquad \blacksquare$$

The unconditional security of a steganography scheme is a then an upper bound over the set of the discriminant steganalysis. Moreover, if Σ is perfectly secure, then it is perfectly secure against all the discriminant steganalysis. In that case, it implies that it does not exist any efficient discriminant attack against Σ.

3   Overview of Traditional Models of Security

From the designer's point of view, a steganography scheme is evaluated through the scope of its unconditional security. To show that a scheme is ε-secure in a given adversary model, he has to prove that $\forall (V, D_V)$, the scheme is ε-secure against (V, D_V). On the contrary, through the adversary's point of view, we prefer to quantify the *insecurity* of the analyzed scheme. In that context, we have to point out a lower bound for the insecurity, *i.e.* to find an efficient discrimination attack and a compatible classifier. Obviously, bigger is that bound, higher is the insecurity and so weaker is the security of the scheme.

We present now the classical security models. Such models are based on well-known security models in cryptography which have been introduced first by S. Goldwasser et S. Micali [17] for public keys cryptography schemes, then adapted by M. Bellare *et al.* [18] for private keys schemes. Here, we consider a private keys steganography scheme. The adversary A is couple of polynomial probabilistic algorithms (A_1, A_2). Each algorithm A_i has access to an oracle $\mathcal{O}_i$. At the beginning of the experiment, the challenger randomly chooses a secret key K with the generation keys algorithm $\mathcal{K}$. During the first step, A_1 can make as many queries to $\mathcal{O}_1$ he wants. At the end of this step, it stores its internal state in a variable s and generates a message m. In the second step, the challenger randomly chooses a bit b and a cover medium $C \in \mathcal{C}$. Then, it gives the adversary back either C embedded with m and K if $b = 1$ or C otherwise. During this step, A_2 is allowed to make as many queries to $\mathcal{O}_2$ he wants excepted the extraction query with the challenge. Finally, using s and m he must guess if the challenge is a stego medium or not and returns b'. $\mathcal{O}_1$ is an insertion and/or extraction oracle and $\mathcal{O}_2$ is only an insertion oracle. Insertion oracles are parametrized by K, take a cover medium and a message as inputs and return a stego medium or nothing. Extraction oracles are parametrized by K, take a stego medium and return *failure* or the embedded message, or nothing. Three types of adversary are considered depending on their power.

- IND-PA (Passive Attack) adversary. $\mathcal{O}_1$ and $\mathcal{O}_2$ always return nothing. This is a passive adversary.
- IND-CMA (Chosen Message Attack) adversary. $\mathcal{O}_1$ and $\mathcal{O}_2$ are an insertion oracles. During the first step, the adversary is allowed to choose the embedded message.
- IND-CHA (Chosen Hidden text Attack) adversary. $\mathcal{O}_1$ is an extraction and insertion oracle and $\mathcal{O}_2$ is an insertion one. During the first step, the adversary is allowed to have hidden text extracted with a chosen stego media.

Let $ATK \in \{PA, CMA, CHA\}$, then the indistinguishability game previously described, with an adversary A playing ATK against Σ and a security parameter 1^k, is denoted $\mathbf{Exp}_{\Sigma}^{\mathbf{IND\text{-}ATK}}(\mathbf{A}, \mathbf{k})$ and is summarized in the figure 1.

Definition 5. [13] *We traditionally define the efficiency of the adversary by his advantage $Adv_{\Sigma}^{IND\text{-}ATK}(A, k)$ such that*

$$Adv_{\Sigma}^{IND\text{-}ATK}(A, k) = 2|\mathcal{P}r\left(Exp_{\Sigma}^{IND\text{-}ATK}(A, k) = 1\right) - \frac{1}{2}|,$$

where $ATK \in \{PA, CMA, CHA\}$.

The advantage measures the gain that the adversary obtains compared with tossing up for it. As the security is evaluated from the designer's point of view, the insecurity $InSec_{\Sigma}^{IND\text{-}ATK}(k)$ is preferred to measure the weakness of a steganography scheme. One definition of the insecurity can be found in [13].

$$InSec_{\Sigma}^{IND\text{-}ATK}(k) = \max_{A \in \mathcal{A}}\{Adv_{\Sigma}^{IND\text{-}ATK}(A, k)\},$$

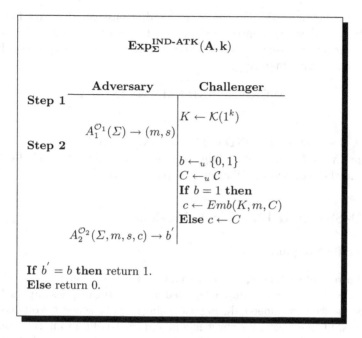

Fig. 1. Game for an IND-ATK adversary against Σ

where $\mathcal{A}$ is the set of polynomial attackers. These security models are just a translation of the cryptographic ones. For cryptographic schemes, a stronger model exists, where $\mathcal{O}_1$ and $\mathcal{O}_2$ are both encryption and decryption oracles. This is the most commonly used in cryptography but it requires a non malleability property for the ciphertexts, that is the difficulty for an adversary to produce a new ciphertext for which the plaintext is correlated with the one of a given ciphertext (typically the challenge). This is a very strong property for most steganography schemes since given a medium C, an adversary may randomly change one bit b_i in C, and submit the result to the extraction oracle. The adversary processes this step q times. If c is not a stego medium then the oracle always outputs an error message. On the contrary, if b_i has not been used by the Emb algorithm, then the oracle outputs m. If b_i has been used by Emb, but is not critical for the extraction, then the oracle outputs m' eventually different from m, otherwise, it outputs an error message. In most steganography schemes, the proportion p of critical bits is very low. Finally, the adversary returns $b' = 0$ if $\mathcal{O}_2$ outputs q error messages and $b' = 1$ otherwise. In that context, he fails only when the challenge is a stego medium and $\mathcal{O}_2$ outputs q error messages, *i.e.* he flipped q times a critical bit. The probability of such an event is

$$\mathcal{P}r(A \text{ fails }) = p^q ,$$

and the advantage of A is then

$$Adv_\Sigma^{\text{IND-CHA}}(q) = 1 - p^q .$$

This model is not realistic. On the other hand, a passive adversary fits well to the real-life attacker who controls neither the key nor the medium. To simulate such an adversary, we use the IND-PA attacker under certain hypothesis keeping in mind the following hierarchy.

$$\text{IND-CHA} \implies \text{IND-CMA} \implies \text{IND-PA}.$$

Remark 2. The notation " IND-CHA $\implies$ IND-CMA " means Σ *is secure against an IND-CHA adversary implies* Σ *is secure against an IND-CMA adversary and the reduction is efficient (i.e. polynomial).*

4   IND-SSA and IND-USA Models

4.1   Specific Steganalysis

To model a real-life attacker, we need to add some more constrains to the IND-PA adversary. The adversary implicitly used in most steganalysis papers does not choose the message m. Indeed, during a learning step, he generates on his own his private keys, his messages, his cover media and try to obtain information about P_C and P_S. Then, he designs a classifier for these two density probability laws. During the challenge step, he only intercepts media exchanged between Alice and Bob and should guess for each medium if it is stego or not. In that context, the adversary has no access to any oracle with the private key K shared by Alice and Bob. For such an attacker, $\mathcal{O}_1$ and $\mathcal{O}_2$ output nothing. Moreover, as he cannot choose the message, m is fixed by the challenger. The common sense of effective steganalysis relies on such hypothesis. This model of adversary represents basic specific steganalysis and is called an IND-SSA (Specific Steganalysis Attack) adversary. The game that the attacker plays is summarized in figure 2.

In that game, the attacker is not restricted to a given steganalysis. Practically, we want to evaluate the insecurity of a steganography scheme against a given attack. To achieve this, we introduce the IND-SSA(V, D_V) adversary who is restricted to use a given discrimination attack (V, D_V), *i.e.* he outputs $b' = D_V(V(c))$. We enlarge definition 5, considering $ATK \in \{SSA(V, D_V), SSA, PA, CMA, CHA\}$ and deduce the following proposition.

Proposition 2. *Let Σ a steganography scheme and (V, D_V) a discriminant steganalysis against Σ. Then, Σ is ε-secure against an adversary A in the model IND-SSA(V, D_V) if and only if*

$$Adv_{\Sigma}^{IND\text{-}SSA(V,D_V)}(A, k) \leq \varepsilon.$$

Proof
This is equivalent to prove that the advantage of an attacker playing the previous game is exactly $D\left(P_{(D_V \circ V)(C)}, P_{(D_V \circ V)(S)}\right)$.

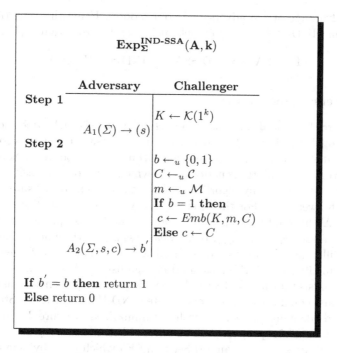

Fig. 2. Game for and IND-SSA attacker against Σ

$$Adv_{\Sigma}^{\text{IND-SSA}(V,D_V)}(A,k)$$

$$= 2\left|\mathcal{P}r\left(Exp_{\Sigma}^{\text{IND-SSA}(V,D_V)}(A,k)=1\right)-\frac{1}{2}\right|,$$

$$= 2\left|\,P_r(b'=1|b=1)P_r(b=1)+P_r(b'=0|b=0)P_r(b=0)-\frac{1}{2}\,\right|,$$

$$= \left|\,P_r(b'=1|b=1)+P_r(b'=0|b=0)-1\,\right|,$$

$$= \left|\,P_{(D_V \circ V)(\mathcal{S})}(1)-P_{(D_V \circ V)(\mathcal{C})}(1)\,\right|.$$

In the same way,

$$2\left|\mathcal{P}r\left(Exp_{\Sigma}^{\text{IND-SSA}(V,D_V)}(A,k)=1\right)-\frac{1}{2}\right| = \left|\,P_{(D_V \circ V)(\mathcal{S})}(0)-P_{(D_V \circ V)(\mathcal{C})}(0)\,\right|.$$

Finally,

$$Adv_{\Sigma}^{\text{IND-SSA}(V,D_V)}(A,k) = \frac{1}{2}\left(\left|\,P_{(D_V \circ V)(\mathcal{S})}(1)-P_{(D_V \circ V)(\mathcal{C})}(1)\,\right|\right.$$
$$\left. + \left|\,P_{(D_V \circ V)(\mathcal{S})}(0)-P_{(D_V \circ V)(\mathcal{C})}(0)\,\right|\right). \qquad \blacksquare$$

The choice of the statistical measure $D(.,.)$ rather than the KL distance is justified by the definition of the adversary's advantage. Indeed, such a distance allows us to link easily the security against a given discriminant steganalysis with the advantage of the adversary in our models. Using the definition of the IND-SSA and IND-SSA(V, D_V) models, it is easy to prove that $\forall\, (V, D_V)$,

$$\text{IND-PA} \implies \text{IND-SSA} \implies \text{IND-SSA}(V, D_V).$$

4.2 Universal Steganalysis

In steganography, one also considers a particular attacker who does not respect the Kerckhoffs' principles [19]. Obviously, this adversary is never taken into account when designing a steganography algorithm as he is too weak. Nevertheless, such an adversary simulates generic attacks which point out intrinsic weaknesses of a class of steganography algorithms. The goal is then to measure how much generic is the weakness. For this, the adversary has access to all steganography algorithms Σ_i he wants, excepted Σ_j. During the first step, he tries to obtain information about P_C and $P_{S_{i \neq j}}$. If the weakness is generic enough then P_{S_j} will not be so different from at least one P_{S_i}. Then, the challenge is forged with Σ_j. If it exists an efficient discrimination attack against Σ_j then it exists a discriminant steganalysis that may detect unknown steganography schemes using Σ_i for training. This model is called *universal*, noted IND-USA (Universal Steganalysis Attack), and the game associated with is summarized in figure 3. For instance, J. Barbier *et al.* [20,21] propose such an universal steganalysis against implementations of Outguess, JPHide and JPSeek and F5 which force by default certain coding patterns of the JPEG.

As previously, we introduce an IND-USA(V, D_V) adversary who is restricted to the discrimination attack (V, D_V), *i.e.* he outputs $b' = D_V(V(c))$. We enlarge definition 5, considering $ATK \in \{USA(V, D_V), USA, SSA(V, D_V), SSA, PA, CMA, CHA\}$ and deduce the following proposition.

Proposition 3. *Let Σ be a steganography scheme and (V, D_V) a discriminant steganalysis against Σ. Then Σ is ε-secure against an adversary A in the model IND-USA(V, D_V) if and only if*

$$Adv_\Sigma^{IND\text{-}USA(V,D_V)}(A, k) \leq \varepsilon.$$

Proof
Identical to the proof of the proposition 2 ∎

Definition 6. *Under the previous hypothesis, if*

$$Adv_\Sigma^{IND\text{-}USA(V,D_V)}(A, k) > 0,$$

then (V, D_V) is a universal discriminant steganalysis.

Moreover, using the definition of the IND-USA and IND-USA(V, D_V) models, it is easy to show that $\forall\, (V, D_V)$

$$\text{IND-SSA} \implies \text{IND-USA} \implies \text{IND-USA}(V, D_V).$$

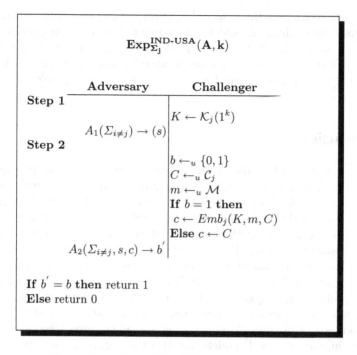

Fig. 3. Game for an IND-USA attacker against Σ_j

4.3 Practical Bound on the Insecurity

IND-SSA and IND-USA represent real-life adversaries who are implicitly considered in effective steganalysis papers. In that context, the efficiency of practical steganalysis is evaluated through the scope of the detection, false positive and false negative rates of the classifier. Let (V, D_V) be a discriminant steganalysis, and an IND-ATK(V, D_V) attacker who performs a false positive rate α and false negative rate β playing his associated game. $P_{(D_V \circ V)(\mathcal{C})}$ and $P_{(D_V \circ V)(\mathcal{S})}$ are uniform distributions of parameters $(1 - \beta)$ and $(1 - \alpha)$. From the proof of proposition 2, we deduce the following proposition.

Proposition 4. *Let Σ be a steganography scheme and ATK be in $\{SSA, USA\}$ then*

$$|1 - (\alpha + \beta)| \leq InSec_\Sigma^{IND\text{-}ATK}(k) \ .$$

This proposition gives us the first link between practical steganalysis and the insecurity of steganography schemes in IND-SSA and IND-USA models. Moreover, it is easy to show that

Proposition 5. $\forall (V, D_V)$,

$$IND\text{-}CHA \Longrightarrow IND\text{-}CMA \Longrightarrow IND\text{-}PA \Longrightarrow IND\text{-}SSA \Longrightarrow IND\text{-}SSA(V, D_V),$$

and

$$IND\text{-}SSA \Longrightarrow IND\text{-}USA \Longrightarrow IND\text{-}USA(V, D_V).$$

This proposition connects the practical insecurity of steganography schemes with the insecurity in traditional models and implies that a steganography scheme which is not secure in IND-SSA, or IND-USA models is not secure in classical ones. That is the case of all steganography algorithms broken by effective steganalysis. Moreover, the lower bound $|1 - (\alpha + \beta)|$ holds in classical models.

5   Conclusion

In this paper we formally define the notion of discriminant steganalysis and split it into two main parts according to the real-life attacker. The first one is the discrimination attack which is n measures onto a medium. This discrimination attack is often called the *features extraction* and comes from the adversary experience. The second one is the classifier which is a statistical mean to solve hypothesis testing problems. It is also called a *steganographic detector*. Then, we recall classical steganography security models and introduce two new attackers to model real-life adversaries. The IND-SSA adversary simulates the common specific steganalysis and the IND-USA adversary simulates the universal steganalysis. The second one measures the ability of a steganalysis to detect unknown algorithms. We show that steganographic schemes which are not secure in the proposed models are also not secure in the classical ones. Moreover, in these models, we are able to compute a lower bound on the insecurity using practical measures of false negative and false positive rates. These new models link theoretical models, in which some steganography schemes are provably secure but are difficult to use in practice, and the effective steganalysis which gives us a lower bound on the practical insecurity of steganography schemes.

This paper aims to propose a general framework to compare the security of steganography schemes faced to real attacks but mainly to compare practical steganalysis. It is often difficult to compare experimental results for mainly reasons. Most of times, sets of challenges come from very different databases, their sizes and their compositions are different from a paper to the others and source codes are mainly not available. Designing models for evaluation is the first piece for a common methodology which should be the only way to rigorously compare and evaluate practical steganalysis.

We are now looking for two main directions. First, we start with robust steganographic schemes in the weakest model and try to find criteria of design to insure the security in a stronger model. For instance, if we find a generic way to conceive non-malleable schemes, then all the schemes which are secure in the IND-CHA model would also be secure in a stronger model which would consider an adaptive adversary. The second direction consists in trying to make provably secure schemes usable and control the loss of security in the same way.

References

1. Cachin, C.: An information-theoretic model for steganography. In: Aucsmith, D. (ed.) IH 1998. LNCS, vol. 1525, pp. 306–318. Springer, Heidelberg (1998)
2. Cachin, C.: An information-theoretic model for steganography. Information and Computation 192(1), 41–56 (2004)
3. Cachin, C.: Digital steganography. In: van Tilborg, H. (ed.) Encyclopedia of Cryptography and Security. Springer, Heidelberg (2005)
4. Chandramouli, R.: Mathematical theory for steganalysis. In: Proc. SPIE Security and Watermarking of Multimedia Contents IV (2002)
5. Chandramouli, R., Kharrazi, M., Memon, N.: Image steganography and steganalysis: Concepts and practice. In: Kalker, T., Cox, I., Ro, Y.M. (eds.) IWDW 2003. LNCS, vol. 2939, pp. 35–49. Springer, Heidelberg (2004)
6. Chandramouli, R., Memon, N.: Steganography capacity: A steganalysis perspective. In: Proc. SPIE, Security and Watermarking of Multimedia Contents V, Santa Clara, CA, USA, vol. 5020, pp. 173–177 (2003)
7. Dedić, N., Itkis, G., Reyzin, L., Russel, S.: Upper and lower bounds on blackbox steganography. In: Kilian, J. (ed.) TCC 2005. LNCS, vol. 3378, pp. 227–244. Springer, Heidelberg (2005)
8. Hopper, N., Langford, J., von Ahn, L.: Provably secure steganography. In: Yung, M. (ed.) CRYPTO 2002. LNCS, vol. 2442, pp. 77–92. Springer, Heidelberg (2002)
9. Katzenbeisser, S., Petitcolas, F.: Defining security in steganographic systems. In: Proc. SPIE Security and Watermarking of Multimedia contents IV, vol. 4675, pp. 50–56 (2002)
10. von Ahn, L., Hopper, N.J.: Public-key steganography. In: Cachin, C., Camenisch, J.L. (eds.) EUROCRYPT 2004. LNCS, vol. 3027, pp. 323–341. Springer, Heidelberg (2004)
11. Levan, T., Kurosawa, K.: Efficient public key steganography secure against adaptative chosen stegotext attacks. In: Proc. Information Hiding, 8th International Workshop, Old Town Alexandria, Virginia, USA (2006)
12. Hopper, N.: On steganographic chosen covertext security. In: Caires, L., Italiano, G.F., Monteiro, L., Palamidessi, C., Yung, M. (eds.) ICALP 2005. LNCS, vol. 3580, pp. 311–323. Springer, Heidelberg (2005)
13. Hopper, N.: Toward a Theory of Steganography. PhD thesis, School of Computer Science, Carnegie Mellon University, Pittsburgh, PA, USA (2004)
14. Ker, A.: The ultimate steganalysis benchmark? In: MM&Sec 2007: Proceedings of the 9th workshop on Multimedia & security, Dallas, Texas, USA, pp. 141–148. ACM, New York (2007)
15. Westfeld, A., Pfitzmann, A.: Attacks on steganographic systems. In: Pfitzmann, A. (ed.) IH 1999. LNCS, vol. 1768, pp. 61–76. Springer, Heidelberg (2000)
16. Fridrich, J., Goljan, M., Hogea, D.: New methodology for breaking steganographic techniques for JPEGs. In: Proc. SPIE, Security and Watermarking of Multimedia Contents V, Santa Clara, CA, USA, vol. 5020, pp. 143–155 (2003)
17. Goldwasser, S., Micali, S.: Probabilistic encryption. Journal of Computer and System Science 28, 270–299 (1984)
18. Bellare, M., Desai, A., Jokipii, E., Rogaway, P.: A concrete security treatment of symmetric encryption: Analysis of the DES modes of operation. In: Proc. 38th Symposium on Foundations of Computer Science FOCS. IEEE, Los Alamitos (1997)
19. Kerckhoffs, A.: La cryptographie militaire. Journal des Sciences Militaires (1883)

20. Barbier, J., Filiol, E., Mayoura, K.: Universal detection of JPEG steganography. Journal of Multimedia 2(2), 1–9 (2007)
21. Barbier, J., Filiol, E., Mayoura, K.: Universal JPEG steganalysis in the compressed frequency domain. In: Shi, Y.Q., Jeon, B. (eds.) IWDW 2006. LNCS, vol. 4283, pp. 253–267. Springer, Heidelberg (2006)

Authorship Proof for Textual Document

J. Wu* and D.R. Stinson**

David R. Cheriton School of Computer Science
University of Waterloo
Waterloo, Ontario, N2L 3G1, Canada
{j32wu,dstinson}@uwaterloo.ca

Abstract. In this paper, we investigate the problem of how to prove the authorship of textual documents. We propose to use natural language watermarks to solve the problem. We identify two essential requirements for an authorship proof scheme (APS) to be secure against watermark erasing attacks. We evaluate the security of existing natural language watermarking schemes, and we propose two new APS with improved security.

1 Introduction

The Internet has provided a new publishing channel for writers. Now many writers put their work online before officially publishing them in traditional media. Such practice benefits the writers by allowing feedback from readers and by promoting their works to publishers. This creates a new problem about protecting authors' rights, specifically, their authorship. Usually authors do not care if their work is reprinted online elsewhere, as long as the correct authorship is stated. However, someone may copy a text and reprint it online, or publish it in official channels, in his or her own name. Such cases have been observed. When this happens, it is difficult for the true authors to dispute their authorship.

A straightforward solution to this problem is to use a trusted register service. The author submits the "fingerprint", i.e., the hash value of the document, to the service provider, who records the fingerprint and the time of registration. For example, in Surety LLC's AbsoluteProof [21], a fingerprint is published in the Public Notices section of the New York Times. Alternatively, the service provider may digitally sign the fingerprint and the time of signature. The publication of the fingerprint in the New York Times or the signature on the fingerprint serves as evidence that the fingerprint (and thus the document from which the fingerprint was generated) was generated before the time of publication or signature. A drawback of such a solution is that it relies on a trusted third-party.

Another possible solution is to hide the authorship information in the text. The similar problem for digital multimedia such as image, audio, and video can be solved by using digital watermarking techniques. Some researchers have tried

---

* Research supported by an NSERC post-graduate scholarship.
** Research supported by NSERC discovery grant 203114-06.

K. Solanki, K. Sullivan, and U. Madhow (Eds.): IH 2008, LNCS 5284, pp. 209–223, 2008.

to solve the problem for textual documents with similar approaches. One approach is to transform a textual document to an image, and then apply image watermarks [5], [4], [9]. Another approach embeds information in a text by modifying the appearance of its elements such as the fonts, space between lines and words, etc. (see [7], [6], [11], [13]). A common problem of the above two approaches is that the watermark can be erased by reformatting or re-typing the text document.

An approach immune to reformatting or re-typing is natural language watermarking. It embeds a bitstream as a watermark in a text document using linguistic transformations such as synonym substitution, syntactic transformations and semantic transformations. There have been some research on natural language watermarks (see [18], [17], [2], [19], [1], [8], [10]). With natural language watermarks, it is possible to embed the authorship information in the text, and use the information to prove the authorship.

1.1   Our Contributions

Our contributions in this paper are two-fold. First, we identify the requirements and evaluation criteria to authorship proof schemes (APS) for textual documents. Although using watermarks to prove the authorship (along with other copyright information) of a textual document is not a new idea, how to evaluate the performance of an APS has not been closely investigated. Without an established criteria, it is difficult to evaluate how well a scheme works, or to compare the performance of different schemes.

Second, we design new APS more robust than existing natural language watermarks used as APS. An important attribute of a natural language watermark is its robustness against erasing attacks. An adversary may alter the text to erase the embedded watermark. Robustness is the main challenge in designing a watermark embedding and detecting scheme for authorship proof, as well as for general purpose watermarks. Roughly speaking, our improvement in robustness is obtained from two new techniques: text meaning representation is used to locate the watermark bits in a text document, and edit distance is used to evaluate the extent of the damage to a watermark.

The remainder of this paper is organized as follows. In Section 2, we formally identify and define the requirements and evaluation criteria to APS for textual documents. In Section 3, we investigate existing natural language watermark schemes and evaluate their performance when used as APS. In Section 4, we propose two new APS with improved robustness. In Section 5, we discuss remaining problems and further improvements.

2   Authorship Proof Scheme

2.1   Functionalities and Security

First we identify the basic functionalities of an APS, the components it must have, the attacks it may be confronted with, and the security properties it has to provide. We assume that an author has several texts to protect, and the author has one master key, K. For each of the texts T, the author can generate a secret key K_T from K and T, e.g., $K_T = h(K\|T)$ where $h()$ is a cryptographic hash function and $K\|T$ is the concatenation of K and T. An APS enables the author to watermark T and prove his or her authorship on the watermarked text. The APS consists of two processes:

1. $E(K_T, T)$, the *embedding process*, which takes the *text* T and the *secret key* K_T as inputs, and outputs the *watermarked text* T_w which is embedded with information about K_T;
2. $V(K_T, T_w)$, the *verification process*, which takes T_w and K_T as inputs, and outputs *true* if T_w is generated by $E()$ using the same K_T, otherwise it outputs *false*.

Given the above APS, we identify several possible attacks. We assume an adversary with polynomially bounded computational ability, i.e., the adversary cannot break secure cryptographic hash functions. The adversary has several copies of watermarked texts from one author. The attacks are as follows.

1. The adversary may try to find out the author's master key, K.
2. The adversary may try to extract a specific secret key, K_T.
3. The adversary may try to declare authorship on a T_w by computing a K' such that $V(K', T_w) = true$ while $K' \neq K_T$ (we call this an *impersonation attack*).
4. The adversary may try to erase the watermark in T_w by making some changes on T_w to produce T_w' which has essentially the same content as T_w, but where $V(K_T, T_w') = false$ (we call this an *erasure attack*).
5. The adversary may watermark a text T_w with his or her own key to produce a T_w' and declare authorship on T_w' (we call this a *double watermark attack*).

For the above APS, K is secure since it is only used as a seed to compute some hash values K_T using a cryptographic hash function. Since each text T will be different, the keys $K_T = h(K\|T)$ can be regarded random and independent of each other. It is not difficult to show that knowing some other watermarked texts does not help to attack a certain T_w or its K_T. Therefore we only need to analyze, when an adversary is given one T_w, if he or she is able to find out the corresponding K_T, or succeed in an impersonation attack, erasure attack, or double watermark attack on the given T_w.

Next we show that if an APS satisfies the following two basic security requirements, then it is secure against all the attacks described above:

1. Low false negative probability
   A false negative occurs if an adversary can edit T_w by inserting, deleting, and/or modifying some sentences to produce T_w' such that $V(K_T, T_w') = false$. False negative probability indicates robustness of the embedded watermark.

2. Low false positive probability

A false positive is the event that $V(K', T_w) = true$, while $T_w = E(K_T, T)$ and $K' \neq K_T$.

False positive probability must be very small to prevent impersonation attacks. In this paper, we stipulate that false positive probability is less than $\epsilon = 1/2^{56}$, which is the security level of a well-chosen password consisting of eight ASCII characters.

Low false negative probability implies the embedded watermark is secure (otherwise the adversary can easily erase the watermark with certainty), which in turn implies K_T is secure (otherwise the adversary can find out the watermark using K_T). In the case of a double watermark attack, the adversary produces $T'_w = E(K', T_w)$ using his or her own K'. The adversary can prove authorship on T'_w but not on T_w (because of the low false positive probability), while the true author can prove authorship on both T_w and T'_w (because of the low false negative probability). This indicates that T'_w is produced by modifying T_w, which resolves the dispute.

Since low false negative probability and low false positive probability indicate the security of an APS against all the attacks we have identified, in the following parts, we only need to analyze these two properties of an APS.

2.2 APS Evaluation

For an APS, its false positive probability must be lower than the pre-defined security level ϵ, but we do not mind if the false positive probability of one scheme is lower than that of another, as long as they are both lower than ϵ. That is, as long as the schemes are secure, it does not matter so much if one is more secure. For false negative probability, we hope that it is as low as possible. Therefore, to compare two schemes, first we tune their settings so that their false positive probabilities are all close to and lower than ϵ, then we compare their false negative probabilities to see which one is more robust.

3   Related Works

3.1   Natural Language Watermarking

Natural language watermarking embeds information using linguistic transformations such as synonym substitution, syntactic transformations and semantic transformations (see [18], [17], [2], [19], [1], [8], [10]). It embeds a bitstream as a watermark in a text document, while preserving the meaning, context, and flow of the document. Ideally, the modifications to the text are hardly perceptible to human readers. A natural language watermark scheme consists of two processes, a watermark embedding process and a watermark extraction process. The rightful owner has the original text and a secret key. The embedding process takes the text, the key, and some watermark information as inputs and produces a watermarked text, which is published. The watermark can be extracted from the watermarked text only with the knowledge of the key. The basic requirement of these schemes is that the watermark should not be perceivable, otherwise an adversary can easily erase the the watermark. As general-purpose watermark schemes, some other requirements, e.g., resistance to collusion attacks, are also considered in such schemes.

3.2   Previous Schemes

We briefly analyze the robustness of existing natural language watermarking schemes that can be used for authorship proof. There have only been a few such schemes, e.g., [2], [1] and [8], that are suitable for this purpose. In [2] Atallah *et al.* treat a text as a collection of sentences. The syntactic structure of a sentence is used to embed the watermark. Suppose a text T consists of m sentences, and an n-bit watermark is to be embedded in n sentences (i.e., we have one watermark bit for each of the *watermarked* sentences). A secret *rank* is computed for each sentence in T. The n sentences with least ranks are chosen as *markers*. Each sentence following a marker is transformed to carry one bit of the watermark. Both rank computing and watermark insertion are based on a secret key. Without the key, the probability that an adversary can forge a text with a valid n-bit watermark is 2^{-n}, i.e., the false positive probability of this scheme is 2^{-n}. When the adversary tries to erase the watermark, he or she cannot locate the markers or the watermarked sentences without the key. So the adversary can only randomly insert/delete/modify some sentences. When an inserted sentence happens to have a small rank, or it happens to be inserted right after a marker, the watermark will be damaged. When a deleted sentence happens to be a marker or a watermarked sentence, the watermark will also be damaged. When a modified sentence is a marker or a watermarked sentence, or the rank of the modified sentence becomes one of the n least ranks, the watermark will be damaged too. The probability that one random sentence insert/delete/modify operation can destroy the watermark is no more than $3n/m$. Therefore, when c sentences are inserted/deleted/modified, the false negative probability is $1 - (1 - \frac{3n}{m})^c$. For example for $n = 56$, $m = 2000$, when the adversary randomly edits eight sentences, the false negative probability is 0.5, i.e., there is a 50% chance the watermark will be erased.

A follow-up paper [1] improves upon [2] in terms of the number of watermark bits embedded in one sentence. The algorithms used in [1] are the same as in [2], but the algorithms are applied to the sematic structure of a sentence, instead of the syntactic structure, to embed the watermark bits. Since the semantic structure is much larger and richer than the syntactic structure, this allows transformations of a large number of elements they contain, and therefore it achieves more watermark bits in one sentence. In view of robustness, the probability that one sentence insert/delete/modify can destroy the watermark in [1] is the same as [2], therefore its false negative probability is also the same as [2].

In [8] Gupta *et al.* proposed a scheme to improve the robustness. The scheme treats the text as a collection of paragraphs, each of which consists of number of sentences. In the scheme, the paragraphs are ordered according to the number of the sentences in it. Although the scheme is robust against various possible attacks, these attacks do not cover all possible attacks (from a cryptanalyst's point of view) which can effectively erase the watermark, e.g., insert/delete a paragraph, or insert/delete sentences in a paragraph such that its order is changed. In such cases, the false negative probability is rather high.

To the best of our knowledge, the most robust APS we can find in previous works are the ones from [2] or [1]. We use the scheme in [2] as an example and refer to it as APS1 hereafter.

4   Proposed Schemes

In this section we propose two new robust authorship proof schemes, APS2 and APS3. The building blocks of our schemes include:

- **Cryptographic hash functions**
  A cryptographic hash function takes a variable length input and produces a fixed length output which can be considered to be randomly uniformly distributed on the function domain.
- **Text-meaning representation**
  A *text meaning representation* (TMR) is a language-independent description of the information conveyed in natural language text. The theory and methodology of TMR have been studied and applied in machine translation systems. For more about TMR, we refer to [15], [14], [3], [16]. In this paper, we do not go into the details of TMR. We simply assume the existence of a TMR system $M()$ which takes as input a sentence s and outputs its *meaning representation* $M(s)$. For literally different sentences which have the same meaning, their meaning representations are the same, so when s is rewritten to s', which is literally different but has the same meaning, its meaning representation does not change, i.e., we have $s' \neq s$, but $M(s) = M(s')$.
- **Edit distance**
  The *edit distance*, also named *Levenshtein Distance*, between two strings is the minimum number of character insert/delete/modify operations on one string to produce the other string. We use $D_{Lev}(S_1, S_2)$ to denote the edit distance between the strings S_1 and S_2. Given two strings, their edit distance can be computed using dynamic programming algorithms [12].

4.1   APS2

Following are the parameters and functions defined in APS2:

T: a text document consisting of m sentences $s_0, \cdots, s_{m-1}$.
$\mathcal{K} = \{0,1\}^k$: the key set.
$h_0 : \{0,1\}^* \to \mathcal{K}$, a hash function to generate a key.
$h_1 : \mathcal{K} \to \{0,1\}^n$, a hash function with n-bit output.
$h_2 : \mathcal{K} \times \{0,1\}^* \to \{0,1\}^{160}$, a keyed hash function with 160-bit output.
$h_3 : \{0,1\}^* \to \{0,1\}$, a hash function with 1-bit output.

d_{max}: a pre-defined threshold. If the edit distance between a damaged water-mark and the original watermark is no greater than d_{max}, then the damaged one is considered valid.

We note that h_0, h_1, h_2 and h_3 can be easily constructed from standard crypto-graphic hash functions such as SHA-1.

APS2 Watermark Embedding. Given an original text document T, the author computes $K_T = h_0(K||T)$ where K is the master key, then performs the following embedding process:

1. Compute an n-bit pseudo-random string $W = h_1(K_T)$. $W = w_0 \cdots w_{n-1}$ is the watermark to be embedded.
2. Compute $o_i = h_2(K_T, M(s_i))$ for each sentence s_i. Here o_i is used as a secret *rank* of s_i. For simplicity, we assume each sentence has a different meaning, and therefore there will not be conflicting o_i values.
3. In the text T, rewrite the n sentences $\{s_{j_0}, \cdots, s_{j_i}, \cdots, s_{j_{(n-1)}}\}$ with least rank to $\{s'_{j_0}, \cdots, s'_{j_i}, \cdots, s'_{j_{(n-1)}}\}$ such that $h_3(s'_{j_i}) = w_{j_i}$ and $M(s_{j_i}) = M(s'_{j_i})^1$. The produced textual document T_w is then made public. After s_{j_i} is rewritten to s'_{j_i}, its literal expression is changed such that the water-mark bit w_{j_i} is "embedded", meanwhile, its meaning does not change, and hence ranks of the rewritten sentences do not change, either.

APS2 Authorship Verification. To prove the authorship of T_w, the author presents K_T and runs the verification process $V(K_T, T_w)$ as follows:

1. compute $o_i = h_2(K_T, M(s_i))$ for each sentence in T_w.
2. compute an $(n+d_{max})$-bit string W' by hashing the $n+d_{max}$ sentences with least o_i values using h_3.
3. If there is a prefix W'' of W' such that $D_{Lev}(W'', h_1(K)) \leq d_{max}$, then output *true*, otherwise output *false*. Clearly $n - d_{max} \leq |W''| \leq n + d_{max}$.

The prefix search in step 3 guarantees that if the watermark is damaged by at most d_{max} insert/delete/modify bit operations, the verification process outputs *true*, otherwise it outputs *false*.

APS2 Watermark and Key Secrecy. Given T_w, the adversary can compute $h_3(s_i)$ for each sentence. The string $\{h_3(s_i)\}$ includes the watermark which is a pseudo-random string generated by $h_1(K_T)$. For the sentences not rewritten in the watermark embedding process, their h_3 values can be regarded as random bits. It is not difficult to show that, given T_w, it is infeasible for the adversary to tell what is the watermark, which sentences carry the watermark, nor can the adversary infer any information about the key K_T.

---

[1] The rewriting can be done manually or by an automated process such as synonym substitution.

APS2 False Positive Probability. Since the adversary cannot infer any information about K_T, when trying to impersonate the true author, he or she cannot do better than present a randomly chosen K'. The adversary wins if $V(K', T_w) = true$.

Now we consider if the adversary presents a random K', when $K' \neq K_T$, what the probability is that $\Pr[V(K', T_w) = true]$. Let $\mathcal{A}_l = \{S : |S| = l, D_{lev}(S, W) \leq d_{max}\}$, the set of strings whose lengths is l, and whose edit distances from $W = h_1(K')$ are at most d_{max}. Any string in $\mathcal{A}_l$ can be produced by applying $d \leq d_{max}$ insertion/deletion/modifcation operations on W. We can assume these operations affect disjoint bits. Also it is easy to check that the order of the operations does not affect the result. Given n, l, and d_{max}, we have

$$|\mathcal{A}_l| \leq \sum_{d_i - d_d = l - n, d_i + d_d + d_m \leq d_{max}} \binom{n}{d_m + d_d} \binom{n - d_d + d_i}{d_i} 2^{d_i + d_d + d_m}. \quad (1)$$

In the above inequality, d_i can be interpreted as the number of insertions, d_d the number of deletions, and d_m the number of modifications. $\binom{n}{d_m + d_d} 2^{d_m + d_d}$ is the number of ways to delete d_d bits and modify d_m bits in an n-bit string. $\binom{n - d_d + d_i}{d_i} 2^{d_i}$ is the number of ways to insert d_i bits into an $(n - d_d + d_i)$-bit string.

If T_w is not produced by using K', then we can assume that $W = h_1(K')$ and the $n + d_{max}$ bits W' generated from T_w and K' are independent random strings. In the verification process, if any prefix of W' is in $\mathcal{A}$, the verification process will output $true$, and a false positive event happens. There are $2d_{max} + 1$ different prefixes of W' whose edit distances from W are possibly no more than d_{max}. The lengths of these prefixes range from $n - d_{max}$ to $n + d_{max}$. Therefore, the false positive probability is

$$P_{fp} \leq \sum_{n - d_{max} \leq l \leq n + d_{max}} \frac{|\mathcal{A}_l|}{2^l}. \quad (2)$$

APS2 False Negative Probability. Since given T_w, the adversary does not know which sentences carry the watermark nor what is the watermark, when the adversary changes T_w in order to erase the watermark, he or she can do it only in a random way . When the adversary inserts a new sentence, the probability that one bit is inserted into the watermark, which is the same as the probability that the rank of the new sentence is among the n least ranks of all the m ranks, is n/m. When the adversary modifies (without change the meaning[2]) or delete a sentence, the probability that one bit in the watermark is changed or deleted is n/m. So when c sentences are inserted/deleted/modified in T_w, the false negative probability of APS2 is

$$P_{fn} \leq 1 - \sum_{d=0}^{d_{max}} \binom{c}{d} \left(\frac{n}{m}\right)^d \left(1 - \frac{n}{m}\right)^{c-d}. \quad (3)$$

---

[2] If a modification changes the meaning a sentence, it can be considered as one delete operation plus one insert operation: the old sentence is replaced by a new sentence.

$\longrightarrow$

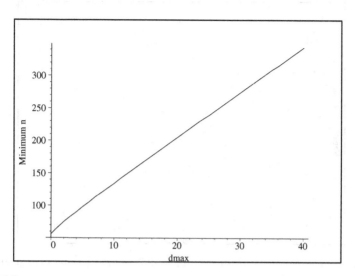

Fig. 1. APS2: minimum n that satisfies false positive probability $\leq \epsilon = 2^{-56}$ under different d_{max} when $m = 2000, c = 200$

Other edit operations, such as moving/switching sentences, do not damage the watermark.

APS2 Parameters. In this part we use some concrete parameters to check the performance of APS2. Suppose $k = 100$ is fixed first. The false positive probability of APS2 is determined by n and d_{max}. Given m and c, the false negative probability of APS2 is determined by n and d_{max} too. Different pairs (n, d_{max}) may result in the same false positive probability and different false negative probability. So we hope to find the (n, d_{max}) such that false positive probability $\leq \epsilon$, while the false negative probability is the least.

We set $m = 2000, c = 200$, and compute the minimum n such that the false positive probability $\leq \epsilon = 2^{-56}$, and the corresponding false negative probability. The results are shown in Figures 1 and 2 respectively.

The results suggest that a large value of d_{max} is beneficial. In the above example, such an (n, d_{max}) pair, say $(321, 40)$, results in both small false negative probability (0.06) and false positive probability $(< \epsilon)$. We can use bigger d_{max} to achieve smaller false negative probability. The cost is a longer watermark, which means more effort is required to embed the watermark.

Now we set $n = 321, d_{max} = 40$ for APS2, and $n = 56$ for APS1. In such a setting, the false positive probabilities of both APS1 and APS2 are close and no more than ϵ. We compare their false negative probabilities as a function of c in Figure 3, which shows a significant improvement of APS2, as compared to APS1, in robustness.

Remarks on Design of APS2. The design of APS2 uses two approaches to improve the work in [2] and [1]. First, in the previous schemes, two sentences, a

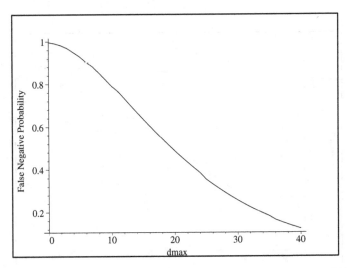

Fig. 2. APS2: false negative probabilities under different d_{max} when $m = 2000, c = 200$

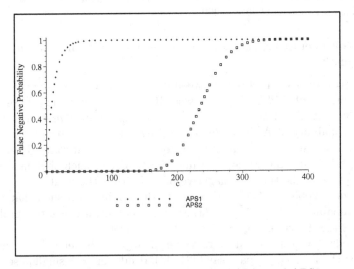

Fig. 3. False negative probabilities of APS1 and APS2

marker and a carrier, are necessary to carry one watermark bit. The reason that a marker itself cannot carry a watermark bit is that if it is changed to carry the watermark, its rank will be changed and is no longer a valid marker. We solve this dilemma by using TMR to compute the rank, and inserting the watermark bits in the marker sentences by changing their literal expression without changing their TMR. Thus, we not only lower the probability that the watermark is damaged when one sentence is inserted/deleted/modified (from $\frac{3n}{m}$ to $\frac{n}{m}$), but we also get rid of the watermark damage caused by moving/switching the sentences.

Another approach used in APS2 to improve the robustness is based on the simple idea of error-tolerance: when a small number of bits are damaged in a long watermark, the damaged watermark should still be regarded as valid. We use edit distance to quantify the extent to which a watermark is damaged. It turns out that this measure significantly improves the robustness of the scheme.

4.2   APS3

APS2 relies on TMR systems. In this section, we design a lightweight scheme, denoted APS3, without using TMR systems. APS3 uses the same building blocks as APS2, except that it does not use the functions $M()$ or $h_2()$.

APS3 Watermark Embedding. In APS3, the author first computes $K_T = h_0(K||T)$, then performs the following embedding process:

1. Compute an n-bit pseudo-random string $W = h_1(K_T)$, and choose a random number $p \in [0, m - 1]$. $W = w_0 \cdots w_{n-1}$ is the watermark and p indicates where in T to insert W.
2. In T, starting from the pth sentence s_p, rewrite the following n sentences such that $h_3(s_{p+i}) = w_i, 0 \leq i \leq n - 1$. The resulting text T_w is then published.

Authorship Verification. To prove authorship on T_w, the author presents K_T and runs the verification process $V(K_T, T_w)$ as follows:

1. Compute an m-bit string S by hashing each sentence in T_w using h_3.
2. If S has a contiguous substring whose edit distance from $W = h_1(K_T)$ is no more than d_{max}, then output *true*, otherwise output *false*.

   Note that the value of p is not used in the verification process.

APS3 Watermark and Key Secrecy. When an adversary applies h_3 to each sentence in T_w, he or she gets an m-bit string S which contains the watermark W starting from the pth bit in S. S consists of three parts: a p-bit random string (from bit 0 to bit $p - 1$), followed by an n-bit pseudo-random string W, followed by an $m - p - n$ bit random string (from bit $p + n$ to bit $m - 1$). Given such a string, assume h_1 is a secure pseudo-random bit generator, then it is infeasible for the adversary to determine which part is W, i.e., the watermark is imperceptible to the adversary.

In APS3, the watermark will be damaged only when the adversary deletes and/or modifies sentences in the n-sentence block that carries the watermark, or inserts sentences in that block. Since the adversary does not know where in T_w the block is, when the adversary tries to erase the watermark by editing T_w, he or she cannot do better than rewrite/delete randomly chosen sentences in T_w, or insert new sentences at random locations in T_w.

Note that unlike APS2, APS3 is not immune to sentence move/switch. Such attacks can be regarded as combination of multiple sentence insert/delete.

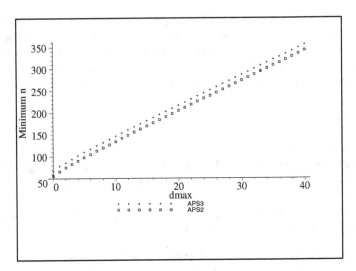

Fig. 4. Comparison of minimum n of APS2 and APS3 that satisfies false positive probability $\leq \epsilon = 2^{-56}$ under different d_{max} when $m = 2000, c = 200$

Since the adversary cannot find the watermark in T_w, he or she can compute nothing about the secret key K_T which is used to generate T_w (in fact, since h_1 is a secure hash function, even given the watermark $W = h_1(K_T)$, the adversary cannot find K_T).

APS3 False Positive Probability. Since the adversary knows nothing about K_T, to prove he or she is the true author of T_w, the adversary cannot do better than choosing a random K'. If $V(K', T_w)$ happens to output *true*, a false positive event happens and the adversary wins. Next we analyze the false positive probability of APS3.

In (1) we have computed $|\mathcal{A}_l|$, the number of strings whose lengths are l, and whose edit distances from W are at most d_{max} where $W = h_1(K')$. If any of the contiguous substrings of the m-bit string S is in any $\mathcal{A}_l$, a false positive event happens. Since there are at most m different contiguous substrings of any given length l in S, and only the substrings of length $n - d_{max} \leq l \leq n + d_{max}$ can possibly be in an $\mathcal{A}_l$, the false positive probability is

$$P_{fp} \leq \sum_{n-d_{max}\leq l\leq n+d_{max}} \frac{m|\mathcal{A}_l|}{2^l}. \tag{4}$$

APS3 False Negative Probability. As we have analyzed, the best way an adversary can damage the watermark is to delete/modify sentences randomly chosen from T_w, or insert new sentences at randomly chosen locations in T_w. Given m, n, d_{max}, and c, the false negative probability of APS3 is the same as that of APS2, i.e.,

$$P_{fn} \leq 1 - \sum_{d=0}^{d_{max}} \binom{c}{d} \left(\frac{n}{m}\right)^d \left(1 - \frac{n}{m}\right)^{c-d}. \tag{5}$$

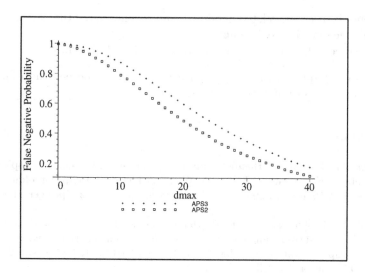

Fig. 5. Comparison of false negative probabilities of APS2 and APS3 under different d_{max} when $m = 2000, c = 200$

APS2 and APS3 Comparison. We compare the minimum n to achieve false positive probabilities $\leq \epsilon$, and corresponding false negative probabilities of APS2 and APS3 in Figure 4 and 5 respectively. It shows with the same d_{max}, APS3 needs a larger value of n to achieve the same false positive probability, and the corresponding false negative probability is higher. It is consistent with the intuition that, since APS3 searches the watermark in a wider range, it needs a smaller d_{max} or a larger n to keep the same false positive probability. Then the smaller d_{max} or larger n results in a higher false negative probability.

Although APS3 is not as robust as APS2, it does not rely on TMR and is much simpler. It may be an alternative to APS2 in occasions where simplicity is more important.

5   Conclusion

In this paper, we investigated the problem of how to prove the authorship of a textual document. We identified and defined the general requirements for authorship proof schemes (APS). We studied existing natural language watermark techniques to solve the problem, and we proposed two new schemes which are more robust than the previous ones.

There are two techniques in our schemes which improved the robustness:

1. We used the meaning representation of a sentence to generate the rank, and we used the literal representation to embed the watermark bit. With this approach, we can use a sentence as both a marker and as a watermark carrier. Thus we reduced the probability that the watermark is damaged when one

sentence is inserted/deleted/modified, and we eliminated the damage caused by sentence moving/switching.

2. We used edit distance for error-tolerant watermark search.

These two techniques can also be applied to general purpose natural language watermark schemes to improve their robustness.

References

1. Atallah, M., Raskin, V., Hempelmann, C.F., Karahan, M., Sion, R., Topkara, U., Triezenberg, K.E.: Natural Language Watermarking and Tamperproofing. In: Petitcolas, F.A.P. (ed.) IH 2002. LNCS, vol. 2578, pp. 196–212. Springer, Heidelberg (2003)
2. Atallah, M., Raskin, V., Crogan, M., Hempelmann, C., Kerschbaum, F., Mohamed, D., Naik, S.: Natural language watermarking: design, analysis, and a proof-of-concept implementation. In: Moskowitz, I.S. (ed.) IH 2001. LNCS, vol. 2137, pp. 185–199. Springer, Heidelberg (2001)
3. Beale, S., Nirenburg, S., Mahesh, K.: Semantic Analysis in the MikroKosmos Machine Translation Project. In: Proc. of the 2nd SNLP 1995, Bangkok, Thailand (1995)
4. Brassil, J., Low, S., Maxemchuk, N., O'Gorman, L.: Marking text features of document images to deter illicit dissemination. In: Proc. of the 12th IAPR International Conference on Computer Vision and Image Processing, Jerusalem, Israel, vol. 2, pp. 315–319 (1994)
5. Brassil, J., Low, S., Maxemchuk, N.F., O'Gorman, L.: Hiding information in documents images. In: Conference on Information Sciences and Systems (CISS 1995) (1995)
6. Chotikakamthorn, N.: Electronic document data hiding technique using inter-character space. In: Proc. of The 1998 IEEE Asia-Pacific Conference on Circuits and Systems, IEEE APCCAS 1998, Chiangmai, Thailand, pp. 419–422 (1998)
7. Chotikakamthorn, N.: Document image data hiding techniques using character spacing width sequence coding. In: Proc. IEEE Intl. Conf. Image Processing, Japan (1999)
8. Gupta, G., Pieprzyk, J., Wang, H.X.: An attack-localizing watermarking scheme for natural language documents. In: Proceedings of the 2006 ACM Symposium on Information, computer and communications security, Taipei, Taiwan (2006)
9. Ji, H., Sook, J., Young, H.: A new digital watermarking for text document images using diagonal profile. In: Shum, H.-Y., Liao, M., Chang, S.-F. (eds.) PCM 2001. LNCS, vol. 2195, p. 748. Springer, Heidelberg (2001)
10. Kankanhalli, M.S., Hau, K.F.: Watermarking of electronic text documents. Electronic Commerce Research 2(1-2), 169–187 (2002)
11. Kim, Y., Moon, K., Oh, I.: A text watermarking algorithm based on word classification and inter-word space statistics. In: Conference on Document Analysis and Recognition (ICDAR 2003) (1995)
12. Levenshtein, V.I.: Binary codes capable of correcting deletions, insertions, and reversals. Dokl. Akad. Nauk SSSR 163, 845–848 (Russian); Translated as Soviet Physics Dokl. 10, 707–710 (1965)

13. Low, S., Maxemchuk, N., Brassil, J., O'Gorman, L.: Document marking and identification using both line and word shifting. In: Fourteenth Annual Joint Conference of the IEEE Computer and Communications Societies. Bringing Information to People, INFOCOM 1995, Boston, USA, vol. 2, pp. 853–860 (1995)
14. Mahesh, K., Nirenburg, S.: Meaning Representation for Knowledge Sharing in Practical Machine Translation. In: Proc. the FLAIRS 1996 Track on Information Interchange. Florida AI Research Symposium (1996)
15. Nirenburg, S.: Application-Oriented Computational Semantics. In: Johnson, R., Rosner, M. (eds.) Computational Linguistics and Formal Semantics (1991)
16. Onyshkevych, B.: An Ontological- Semantic Framework for Text Analysis. Ph.D. Diss., School of Computer Science, Carnegie Mellon University (1997)
17. Sun, X., Luo, G., Huang, H.: Component-based digital watermarking of Chinese texts. In: Proceedings of the 3rd international conference on Information security, Shanghai, China (2004)
18. Topkara, M., Riccardi, G., Hakkani-Tur, D., Atallah, M.J.: Natural Language Watermarking: Challenges in Building a Practical System. In: Proceedings of the SPIE International Conference on Security, Steganography, and Watermarking of Multimedia Contents, San Jose, CA (2006)
19. Topkara, M., Taskiran, C., Delp, E.J.: Natural Language Watermarking. In: Proceedings of the SPIE International Conference on Security, Steganography, and Watermarking of Multimedia Contents, San Jose, CA (2005)
20. Helmreich, S., Farwell, D.: Text Meaning Representation as a Basis for Representation of Text Interpretation. In: White, J.S. (ed.) AMTA 2000. LNCS (LNAI), vol. 1934, pp. 179–188. Springer, Heidelberg (2000)
21. http://www.surety.com/

Linguistic Steganography Detection Using Statistical Characteristics of Correlations between Words

Zhili Chen*, Liusheng Huang, Zhenshan Yu, Wei Yang,
Lingjun Li, Xueling Zheng, and Xinxin Zhao

National High Performance Computing Center at Hefei,
Department of Computer Science and Technology,
University of Science and Technology of China,
Hefei, Anhui 230027, China
zlchen3@mail.ustc.edu.cn

Abstract. Linguistic steganography is a branch of Information Hiding (IH) using written natural language to conceal secret messages. It plays an important role in Information Security (IS) area. Previous work on linguistic steganography was mainly focused on steganography and there were few researches on attacks against it. In this paper, a novel statistical algorithm for linguistic steganography detection is presented. We use the statistical characteristics of correlations between the general service words gathered in a dictionary to classify the given text segments into stego-text segments and normal text segments. In the experiment of blindly detecting the three different linguistic steganography approaches: Markov-Chain-Based, NICETEXT and TEXTO, the total accuracy of discovering stego-text segments and normal text segments is found to be 97.19%. Our results show that the linguistic steganalysis based on correlations between words is promising.

1 Introduction

As text-based Internet information and information dissemination media, such as e-mail, blog and text messaging, are rising rapidly in people's lives today, the importance and size of text data are increasing at an accelerating pace. This augment of the significance of digital text in turn creates increased concerns about using text media as a covert channel of communication. One of such important covert means of communication is known as linguistic steganography. Linguistic steganography makes use of written natural language to conceal secret messages. The whole idea is to hide the very presence of the real messages. Linguistic steganography algorithms embed messages into a cover text in a covert manner such that the presence of the embedded messages in the resulting stego-text cannot be easily discovered by anyone except the intended recipient.

Previous work on linguistic steganography was mainly focused on how to hide messages. One method of modifying text for embedding a message is to substitute selected words by their synonyms so that the meaning of the modified

K. Solanki, K. Sullivan, and U. Madhow (Eds.): IH 2008, LNCS 5284, pp. 224–235, 2008.

sentences is preserved as much as possible. A steganography approach that is based on synonym substitution is the system proposed by Winstein [1]. There are some other approaches. Among them NICETEXT and TEXTO are most famous.

NICETEXT system generates natural-like cover text by using the mixture of word substitution and Probabilistic Context-free Grammars (PCFG) ([2], [3]). There are a dictionary table and a style template in the system. The style template can be generated by using PCFG or a sample text. The dictionary is used to randomly generate sequences of words, while the style template selects natural sequences of parts-of-speech when controlling generation of word, capitalization, punctuation, and white space. NICETEXT system is intended to protect the privacy of cryptograms to avoid detection by censors.

TEXTO is a linguistic steganography program designed for transforming uuencoded or PGP ascii-armoured ASCII data into English sentences [4]. It is used to facilitate the exchange of binary data, especially encrypted data. TEXTO works just like a simple substitution cipher, with each of the 64 ASCII symbols used by PGP ASCII armour or uuencode from secret data replaced by an English word. Not all of the words in the resulting text are significant, only those nouns, verbs, adjectives, and adverbs are used to fill in the preset sentence structures. Punctuation and "connecting" words (or any other words not in the dictionary) are ignored.

Markov-Chain-Based is another linguistic steganography approach proposed by [5]. The approach regards text generation as signal transmission from a Markov signal source. It builds a state transfer chart of the Markov signal source from a sample text. A part of state transfer chart with branches tagged by equal probabilities that are represented with one or more bit(s) is illustrated by Fig. 1. Then the approach uses the chart to generate cover text according to secret messages.

The approaches described above generate innocuous-like stego-text to conceal attackers. However, there are some drawbacks in them. For example, the first approach sometimes replaces word synonyms that do not agree with correct English usage or the genre and the author style of the given text. And the later three approaches are detectable by a human warden, the stego-text generated by which doesn't have a natural, coherent and complete sense. They can be used in communication channels where only computers act as attackers.

A few detection methods have been proposed making use of the drawbacks discussed. The paper [6] brought forward an attack against systems based on synonym substitution, especially the system presented by Winstain. The 3-gram language model was used in the attack. The experimental accuracy of this method on classification of steganographically modified sentences was 84.9% and that of unmodified sentences was 38.6%. Another detection method enlightened by the design ideas of conception chart was proposed by the paper [7] using the measurement of correlation between sentences. The accuracy of the simulation detection using this method was 76%. The two methods fall short of accuracy that the practical application of detection requires. In addition, the first method

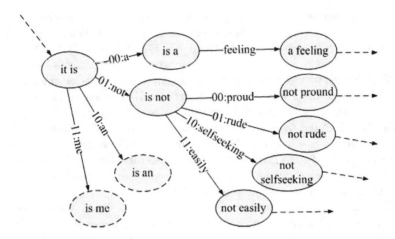

Fig. 1. A part of tagged state transfer chart

requires a great lot of computation to calculate a large number of parameters of the 3-gram language model and the second one requires a database of rules consuming a lot of work.

Our research examines drawbacks of the last three steganography approaches, aiming to accurately detect the application of the three approaches in given text segments and bring forward a blind detection method for linguistic steganography generating cover texts. We have found a novel, efficient and accurate detection algorithm that uses the statistical characteristics of the correlations between the general service words that are gathered in a dictionary to distinguish between stego-text segments and normal text segments.

2   Important Notions

2.1   N-Window Mutual Information (N-WMI)

In the area of statistical Natural Language Processing (NLP), an information-theoretically measurement for discovering interesting collocation is Mutual Information (MI) [8]. MI is originally defined between two particular events x and y. In case of NLP, the MI of two particular words x and y, as follows:

$$MI(x,y) = \log_2 \frac{P(x,y)}{P(x)P(y)} = \log_2 \frac{P(x|y)}{P(x)} = \log_2 \frac{P(y|x)}{P(y)} \qquad (1)$$

Here, $P(x,y)$, $P(x)$ and $P(y)$ are the occurrence probabilities of "xy", "x" and "y" in given text. In our case, we regard these probabilities as the occurrence probabilities of the word pairs "xy", "x?" and "?y" in given text, respectively, and "?" represents any word.

In natural language, collocation is usually defined as an expression consisting of two or more sequential words. In our case, we will investigate pairs of words

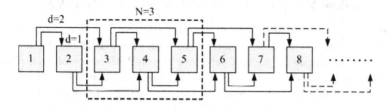

Fig. 2. An illustration of 3-WWP

within a certain distance. With the distance constraint, we introduce some definitions as follows.

N-Window Word Pair (N-WWP): Any pair of words in the same sentence with a distance less than N (N is an integer greater than 1). Here, the distance of a pair of words equals to the number of words between the words in the pair plus 1. Note that N-WWP is order-related. In Fig. 2, the numbered boxes represent the words in a sentence and the variable d represents distance of the word pair. The 3-WWPs in the sentence are illustrated in the figure by arrowed, folded lines. Hereafter, we will denote N-WWP "xy" as $\langle x, y \rangle$.

N-Window Collocation (N-WC): An N-WWP with frequent occurrence. In some sense, our detection results are partially determined by the distribution of N-WCs in given text segment and later we can see it.

N-Window Mutual Information (N-WMI): We use the MI of an N-WWP to measure its occurrence. This MI is called N-Window Mutual Information (N-WMI) of the words in the word pair. Therefore, an N-WWP is an N-WC if its N-WMI is greater than a particular value.

With the definition of N-WMI, we can use equation (1) to evaluate the N-WMI of words x and y in a particular text segment. Given a certain text segment, the counts of occurrences of any N-WWP, N-WWP $\langle x, y \rangle$, $\langle x, ? \rangle$ and $\langle ?, y \rangle$ are C, C_{xy}, C_x and C_y , respectively, the N-WMI value is denoted by MI_N, then the evaluation as follows:

$$MI_N(x, y) = \log_2 \frac{P(x, y)}{P(x)P(y)} = \log_2 \frac{C_{xy}/C}{(C_x/C)(C_y/C)} = \log_2 \frac{CC_{xy}}{C_xC_y} \quad (2)$$

Because of the signification of N-WMI in our detection algorithm, we will make a further explanation with an example. Given a sentence "We were fourteen in all, and all young men." let us evaluate the 4-WMI of $\langle in, all \rangle$. All 4-WWPs in the sentence are as follows: $\langle we, were \rangle$, $\langle we, fourteen \rangle$, $\langle we, in \rangle$, $\langle were, fourteen \rangle$, $\langle were, in \rangle$, $\langle fourteen, in \rangle$, $\langle were, all \rangle$, $\langle fourteen, all \rangle$, $\langle in, all \rangle$, $\langle fourteen, and \rangle$, $\langle in, and \rangle$, $\langle all, and \rangle$, $\langle in, all \rangle$, $\langle all, all \rangle$, $\langle and, all \rangle$, $\langle all, young \rangle$, $\langle and, young \rangle$, $\langle all, young \rangle$, $\langle and, men \rangle$, $\langle all, men \rangle$, $\langle young, men \rangle$. We get $C = 21$, $C_{in,all} = 2$, $C_{in} = 3$, $C_{all} = 6$. Then we have:

$$MI_4(in, all) = \log_2 \frac{CC_{in,all}}{C_{in}C_{all}} = \log_2 \frac{21 \times 2}{3 \times 6} = 1.2224$$

2.2 N-Window Variance of Mutual Information (N-WVMI)

Suppose D is the general service word dictionary and M is the count of words in D, then we can get $M \times M$ different pairs of words from the dictionary D. In any given text segment, we can calculate the N-WMI value of each different word pair in dictionary D, and get an N-WMI matrix. However, it is probably that some items of the matrix have no values because of the absence of their corresponding pairs of words in the given text segment, that is to say, these items are not present. We denote the N-WMI matrix of the training corpus as $T_{M \times M}$, and that of a sample text segment as $S_{M \times M}$. Therefore, when all items of both $T_{M \times M}$ and $S_{M \times M}$ are present, we define the N-Window Variance of Mutual Information (N-WVMI) as:

$$V = \frac{1}{M \times M} \sum_{i=0}^{M} \sum_{j=0}^{M} (S_{ij} - T_{ij})^2 \tag{3}$$

When either an item of $S_{M \times M}$ or its corresponding item of $T_{M \times M}$ dose not exist, we say that the pair of items is not present, otherwise it is present. For example, if either S_{ij} or T_{ij} dose not exist, we say the pair of items in position (i, j) is not present. Suppose I pairs of items are present, we evaluate N-WVMI as:

$$V = \frac{1}{I} \sum_{i=0}^{M} \sum_{j=0}^{M} (S_{ij} - T_{ij})^2 \delta(i,j) \tag{4}$$

Here, $\delta(i,j) = 1$ if both S_{ij} and T_{ij} are present, $\delta(i,j) = 0$ otherwise. When $I = M \times M$, equation (4) turns into equation (3).

2.3 Partial Average Distance (PAD)

The N-WVMI is defined to distinguish between the statistical characteristics of normal text segments and stego-text segments in principle. But a more precise statistical variable is necessary for the accurate detection. Therefore, the Partial Average Distance (PAD) of the two N-WMI matrixes $S_{M \times M}$ and $T_{M \times M}$ is defined as follows:

$$D_{\alpha,K} = \frac{1}{K} \sum_{i=0}^{M} \sum_{j=0}^{M} |S_{ij} - T_{ij}| [|S_{ij} - T_{ij}| > \alpha] \lambda_K(i,j) \tag{5}$$

In this equation, α represents a threshold of the distance of two N-WMI values, K represents that only the first K greatest items of $S_{M \times M}$ are calculated. As we can see, equation (5) averages the differences of items of $S_{M \times M}$ and $T_{M \times M}$ with great N-WMI values and great distances, as these items well represent the statistical characteristics of the two type of text segments. The expressions $[|S_{ij} - T_{ij}| > \alpha]$ and $\lambda_K(i,j)$ are evaluated as:

$$[|S_{ij} - T_{ij}| > \alpha] = \begin{cases} 1 & \text{if } |S_{ij} - T_{ij}| > \alpha \\ 0 & \text{otherwise} \end{cases}$$

$$\lambda_K(i,j) = \begin{cases} 1 & \text{if } S_{ij} \text{ is the first } K \text{ greatest} \\ 0 & \text{otherwise} \end{cases}$$

3   Method

In natural language, normal text has many inherent statistical characteristics that can't be provided by text generated by linguistic steganography approaches we investigate. Here is something we have observed: there is a strong correlation between words in the same sentence in normal text, but the correlation is weakened a lot in the generated text. The reason is a normal sentence has a natural, coherent and complete sense, while a generated sentence doesn't. For example, for a sentence leading with "She is a . . .", it reads more likely "She is a woman teacher", or "She is a beautiful actress", or "She is a mother" and so on in the normal text. But "She is a man", or "She is a good actor", or "She is a father" only possibly exists in the generated text. This shows that the word "she" has a strong correlation with "woman", "actress" and "mother", but it has a weak correlation with "man", "actor" and "father". Therefore, we probably evaluate the N-WMI of "she" and "woman" or "actress" or "mother" with a greater value than that of "she" and "man" or "actor" or "father". In our research, we use N-WMI to measure the strength of correlation between two words.

In our experiment, we build a corpus from the novels written by Charles Dickens, a great English novelist in the Victorian period. We name this corpus Charles-Dickens-Corpus. We build another corpus from novels written by a few novelists whose last name begin with letter "s" and name it S-Corpus. Finally, we build a third corpus from the cover text generated by the linguistic steganography algorithms we investigated: NICETEXT, TEXTO and Markov-Chain-Based, calling it Bad-Corpus. We then build the training corpus from Charles-Dickens-Corpus, the good testing sample set from S-Corpus and the bad testing sample set from Bad-Corpus. The training corpus consists of about 400 text documents amounting to a size of more than 10MB. There are 184 text documents in the good testing sample set and 422 text documents in bad testing sample set. The commonly used word dictionary D collects 2000 words (that is $M = 2000$) most widely used in English. We let $N = 4$, that is, we use 4-WMI. Thereafter, the following procedure has been employed.

First, we process the training corpus as a large text segment to get the training N-WMI matrix $T_{M \times M}$ using dictionary D. Our program reads every text document, splits it into sentences, counts the numbers of occurrences of all the N-WWP in D that were contained in the training corpus and gets C. Furthermore, for every N-WWP, we can get its C_{xy}, C_x and C_y incidentally. Then we can evaluate the N-WMI of every N-WWP with equation (2), and obtain the training N-WMI matrix $T_{M \times M}$. In the step, we can store $T_{M \times M}$ to disk for later use. So if the related configuration parameters are not altered, we can just read $T_{M \times M}$ from the disk in this step for the sequent sample text segment detection.

Second, we process a sample text segment to get the sample N-WMI matrix $S_{M \times M}$. The procedure is similar with the first step, but in this step our program just read a text segment of a certain size, such as 10kB from every sample text document. In this way, we can control the size of the sample text segment.

Third, we evaluate N-WVMI value V of the sample text segment using $S_{M \times M}$ and $T_{M \times M}$ with equation (3) or (4). Some attentions have to be paid to this step. If there are some pairs of items absent in matrix $S_{M \times M}$ and $T_{M \times M}$, we use equation (4). That is to say, we just calculate variance of the I pairs of items when I pairs of items are present in the matrixes $S_{M \times M}$ and $T_{M \times M}$. Otherwise, equation (4) turns to equation (3). In this step, another variable, the PAD value $D_{\alpha,K}$ is calculated by equation (5). The variable is a useful assistant classification feature in addition to N-WVMI value V. In the experiment, we let $= 2$ and K=100, so we calculate $D_{2,100}$.

Finally, we use SVM classifier to classify the sample text segment as stego-text segment or normal text segment according the values V and $D_{2,100}$.

Fig. 3 shows the flow of the detection procedure. The real line arrowhead represents the flow of data, while the dashed line arrowhead represents that nothing will be transferred or processed if $T_{M \times M}$ has already been stored. The thick dashed rectangle indicates the whole detection system. Obviously, there are two key flows in the system: training and testing. The training process is not always required before the testing process. Once the training process is completed, it does not need to repeat in sequent detection unless the some configuration parameters are changed. The testing process contains two steps to evaluate sample N-WMI matrix, classification features N-WVMI and PAD values respectively, ending with an output that indicates whether the testing sample text segment is stego-text using a SVM classifier [9].

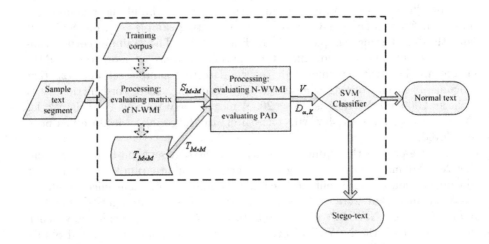

Fig. 3. Flow of the detection procedure

Table 1. Sample text set and detection results

Type	Generator	Sample	Success	Failure	Accuracy
Good Set		184	178	6	
Bad Set	Markov-Chain-Based	100	89	11	94.01%
	NICETEXT	212	212	0	98.48%
	TEXTO	110	110	0	97.96%
Total		606	589	17	97.19%

4 Results and Discussion

In our experiment, totally 606 testing sample text segments with a size of 20kB are detected by using their 4-WVMIs. The composing of the sample text set is present in Table 1. Using a SVM classifier, we can get a total accuracy of 97.19%.

Note that the accuracy of each linguistic steganography method (denoted by *LSMethod*) is computed as follows:

$$Accuracy(LSMethod) = \frac{SUC(GoodSet) + SUC(LSMethod)}{SAM(GoodSet) + SAM(LSMethod)}$$

Where SUC represents the number of success text segments, and SAM represents the number of sample text segments.

In Table 1, we can see that the accuracy of detecting stego-text segments generated by Markov-Chain-Based is obviously lower than that generated by the other two algorithms. The probable reason is that Markov-Chain-Based method sometimes embeds secret messages by adding white space between sequent words in sample text, copying these words as generated words, other than generating new words when there is only a branch in the state transfer chart. For example, a text segment generated by Markov-Chain-Based as follows:

"... *I'll wait a year, according to the forest to tell each other than a brown thrush sang against a tree, held his mouth shut and shook it out, the elder Ammon suggested sending for Polly. ...* "

We can see that the algorithm adds white space between words "according" and "to", between words "sending" and "for" and so on in the text segment and these words are copied to generated text from sample text directly. This keeps more properties of normal text.

Fig. 4 shows testing results of all testing samples. Fig. 5 - Fig. 7 show testing results of testing samples generated by Markov-Chain-Based, NICETEXT and TEXTO respectively. As the discussion above, the accuracy of detecting Markov-Chain-Based method appears slightly lower. The results of detecting the other two algorithms appear ideal with the text segment size of 20kB. But when the segment sizes are smaller than 5kB, such as 2kB, the accuracies will decrease obviously. This is determined by characteristics of the statistical algorithm. So sample text segments with a size greater than 5kB are recommended.

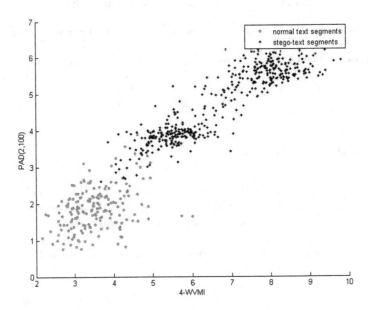

Fig. 4. Testing results of all testing samples

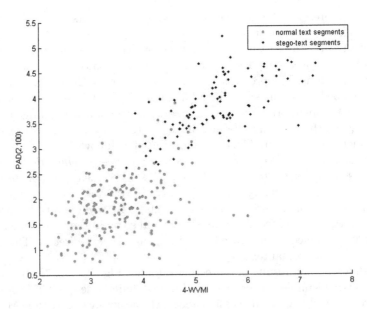

Fig. 5. Testing results of testing samples generated by Markov-Chain-Based

In addition, our algorithm is time efficient although we have not measured it strictly. It takes about 1 minute to complete our detection of more than 600 sample text segments.

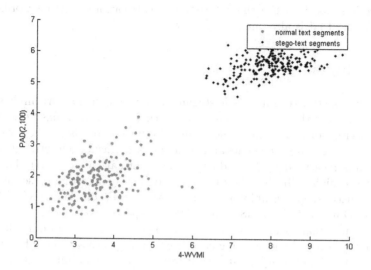

Fig. 6. Testing results of testing samples generated by NICETEXT

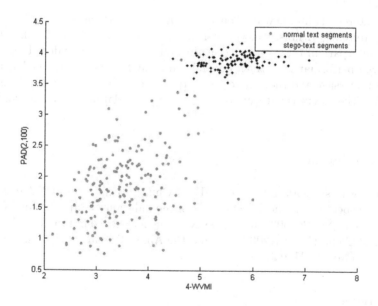

Fig. 7. Testing results of testing samples generated by TEXTO

After all, the results of our research appear pretty promising. We have detected the three forenamed linguistic steganography methods in a blind way accurately, and our method may suit to detect other or new linguistic steganography methods that generate nature-like cover text. For other linguistic steganography methods such as Synonym-Substitution-Based or translation-based steganography, the detection based on the characteristics of correlations between words may still work, and that is also our future work.

5   Conclusion

In this paper, a statistical linguistic steganography detection algorithm has been presented. We use the statistical characteristics of the correlations between the general service words that are gathered in a dictionary to classify the given text segments into stego-text segments and normal text segments. The strength of the correlation is measured by N-window mutual information (N-WMI). The total accuracy is as high as 97.19%. The accuracies of blindly detecting these three different linguistic steganography approaches: Markov-Chain-Based, NICETEXT and TEXTO are 94.01%, 98.48% and 97.96% respectively.

Our research mainly focuses on detecting linguistic steganography that embeds secret messages by generating cover text. But it is easy to modify our general service word dictionary to fit the detection of Synonym-Substitution-Based algorithm and other linguistic steganography methods modifying the content of the cover text. Therefore, our algorithm is widely applicable in linguistic steganalysis.

Many interesting and new challenges are involved in the analysis of linguistic steganography algorithms, which is called linguistic steganalysis that has little or no counterpart in other media domains, such as image or video. Linguistic steganalysis performance strongly depends on many factors such as the length of the hidden message and the way to generate a cover text. However, our research shows that the linguistic steganalysis based on correlations between words is promising.

Acknowledgement

This work was supported by the NSF of China (Grant Nos. 60773032 and 60703071 respectively), the Ph.D. Program Foundation of Ministry of Education of China (No. 20060358014), the Natural Science Foundation of Jiangsu Province of China (No. BK2007060), and the Anhui Provincial Natural Science Foundation (No. 070412043).

References

1. Winstein, K.: Lexical steganography through adaptive modulation of the word choice hash, http://alumni.imsa.edu/~keithw/tlex/lsteg.ps
2. Chapman, M.: Hiding the Hidden: A Software System for Concealing Ciphertext as Innocuous Text (1997), http://www.NICETEXT.com/NICETEXT/doc/thesis.pdf
3. Chapman, M., Davida, G., Rennhard, M.: A Practical and Effective Approach to Large-Scale Automated Linguistic Steganography. In: Davida, G.I., Frankel, Y. (eds.) ISC 2001. LNCS, vol. 2200, pp. 156–167. Springer, Heidelberg (2001)

4. Maher, K.: TEXTO,
   ftp://ftp.funet.fi/pub/crypt/steganography/texto.tar.gz
5. Shu-feng, W., Liu-sheng, H.: Research on Information Hiding. Degree of master,
   University of Science and Technology of China (2003)
6. Taskiran, C., Topkara, U., Topkara, M., et al.: Attacks on lexical natural language
   steganography systems. In: Proceedings of SPIE (2006)
7. Ji-jun, Z., Zhu, Y., Xin-xin, N., et al.: Research on the detecting algorithm of text
   document information hiding. Journal on Communications 25(12), 97–101 (2004)
8. Manning, C.D., Schutze, H.: Foundations of Statistical Natural Language Processing. Beijin Publishing House of Electronics Industry (January 2005)
9. Chang, C.-C., Lin, C.-J.: LIBSVM: a library for support vector machines (2001),
   http://www.csie.ntu.edu.tw/~cjlin/libsvm

A Data Mapping Method for Steganography and Its Application to Images

Hao-tian Wu[1], Jean-Luc Dugelay[1], and Yiu-ming Cheung[2]

[1] Department of Multimedia Communication, Eurecom Institute,
Sophia Antipolis, France
{Haotian.Wu,Jean-Luc.Dugelay}@eurecom.fr
[2] Department of Computer Science, Hong Kong Baptist University,
Hong Kong SAR, China
ymc@comp.hkbu.edu.hk

Abstract. In this paper, a new steganographic method that preserves the first-order statistics of the cover is proposed. Suitable for the passive warden scenario, the proposed method is not robust to any change of the stego object. Besides the relative simplicity of both encoding and decoding, high and adjustable information hiding rate can be achieved with our method. In addition, the perceptual distortion caused by data embedding can be easily minimized, such as in the mean squared error criterion. When applied to digital images, the generic method becomes a sort of LSB hiding, namely the LSB$^+$ algorithm. To prevent the sample pair analysis attack, the LSB$^+$ algorithm is implemented on the selected subsets of pixels to preserve some important high-order statistics as well. The experimental results of the implementation are promising.

Keywords: Steganography, LSB$^+$ algorithm, bijective mapping, first-order statistics, sample pair analysis.

1 Introduction

The art of steganography, i.e. covert communication by hiding the presence of a message from a third party, has been studied in the community (e.g. [1]-[3]). Although the early steganographic methods can imperceptibly embed data into a cover object, the technique of steganalysis [4] has been developed to detect the hidden data from the statistical characteristics of the stego object. It has been shown by the detection-theoretic analysis (e.g. [5,6]) that several data hiding methods are detectable. How to avoid being detected by the steganalysis technique is a central topic of the steganography research.

Since most of the steganalytic algorithms (e.g. [7]-[16]) exploit the statistics of the stego object for detection, quite a few steganographic algorithms (e.g. [17]-[23]) are designed to preserve the statistics of the cover object as much as possible. An early attempt is the F5 algorithm [17], in which some statistical characteristics in the histogram of DCT coefficients is preserved to prevent the χ^2 (chi-squared) attack [7]. In the detector designed by Fridrich et al. [8] to

K. Solanki, K. Sullivan, and U. Madhow (Eds.): IH 2008, LNCS 5284, pp. 236–250, 2008.

break the F5 steganography, the cover histogram is estimated from the suspected image for comparison. In Provos' Outguess [18], part of the JPEG coefficients are used to repair the histogram changed by data embedding. However, the changes at the JPEG block boundaries can be exploited because the embedding is performed in the block-wise transform domain [9]. A method attempting to preserve the histogram after LSB hiding is further presented by Franz [19], where a message that mimics the imbalance between the adjacent histogram bins is embedded in the pairs of values that are independent. Despite that a message with the unequal probabilities of 0 and 1 carries less information, the asymmetric embedding process determined by a co-occurrence matrix can be exploited for steganalytic attack, as shown in [10]. Similarly, Eggers et al. propose a histogram-preserving data-mapping (HPDM) method [20] by embedding a message with the same distribution as the cover object. Subsequently, the histograms of the cover object and the stego object can be matched so as to reduce the probability of being detected. However, it is shown by Tzschoppe et al. [21] that the HPDM can be detected by Lyu and Farid's steganalytic method [12] based on the high-order statistics. The reason given in [21] is that the higher frequency components have not been separately treated from the lower and direct current (DC) ones. In [22], a histogram restoration algorithm is proposed without embedding in the low-probability region. Within the embedding positions specified a secret key, a portion of eligible coefficients are used for embedding while the rest are used for compensation. In [23], the statistical restoration method is adopted to further preserve the second-order statistics of the cover image.

The model-based method [24] provides a new perspective for steganography by generating the stego object conforming to a given distribution model. For the lack of a perfect model, the steganographic algorithm using the Generalized Cauchy distribution [24] can be broken by only using the first-order statistics, i.e. the measures without considering the inter-dependencies between observations, such as mean and variance [25]. In this paper, a new steganographic method is proposed to preserve the first-order statistics inherently. By dividing the distribution range of the elements in a cover object into non-overlapped bins, two adjacent ones are utilized to form an individual embedding unit. Then the elements in the same embedding unit are bijectively mapped to each other for data embedding. Provided that the stego object is intact, the hidden message can be correctly extracted. Despite the relative simplicity of both encoding and decoding, high and adjustable information hiding rate can be achieved. Moreover, the distortion can be easily minimized in the minimum mean square error (MSE) criterion. When applied to digital images, the generic method becomes a sort of LSB hiding, namely the LSB$^+$ algorithm. To avoid being detected by the sample pair analysis (SPA) steganalysis [11], the LSB$^+$ algorithm is implemented on the subsets of pixels with the same neighbor values (up, down, left and right) to preserve some important high-order statistics as well.

The rest of this paper is organized as follows: In the next section, a novel data mapping method is presented for steganography. In Section 3, we apply it to digital images and further prevent the SPA attack by implementing it on the

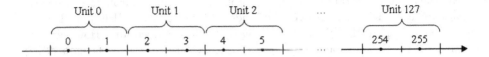

Fig. 1. Every two adjacent bins within the range from 0 to 255 are utilized to form an embedding unit for digital gray-scale images, respectively

selected subsets of pixels. The performance of the new approach is evaluated in Section 4. Finally, a conclusion is drawn in Section 5.

2   A Data Mapping Method for Steganography

In this section, a novel LSB hiding algorithm named LSB^+ is firstly introduced, which preserves the image histogram. Then the generic data mapping method is further proposed, applicable to the cover object represented by integers or floating point numbers. We further analyze the bounds of information hiding rate and perceptual distortion with the proposed method.

2.1 LSB^+ Algorithm

In [3], Cachin proposes an information-theoretic model for steganography with the relative entropy, also called the Kullback-Leibler (K-L) divergence, between the distribution P_C according to which the cover object is generated and the distribution P_S corresponding to the stego object:

$$D(P_C\|P_S) = \sum P_C \log \frac{P_C}{P_S}. \tag{1}$$

In general, $D(P_C\|P_S)$ is nonnegative and equal to zero if and only if $P_C = P_S$. As for digital images, the high-order statistics can still be exploited for steganalysis after the cover histogram is preserved. Nevertheless, we regard it as a necessary condition for a secure image steganography. In the following, a novel LSB hiding algorithm named LSB^+ is developed to preserve the image histogram, as well as the other first-order statistics:

Given a gray-scale image, we can easily calculate its histogram by counting the pixels having the same value, i.e. the amount of pixels within the same bin. As shown in Fig. 1, every two adjacent bins within the range from 0 to 255 are utilized to form an embedding unit, respectively. We restrict the change of a pixel value within each unit so that only the least significant bit is changeable. For example, a pixel with the value of 4 can only be modified to 5 or remain the same because only the two pixel values 4 and 5 are contained in the same unit. Since the operations in one embedding unit are independent from those in the other units, we only discuss the operations in an arbitrary unit.

In the normal LSB hiding, a string of bit values are used to replace the original LSBs of pixel values. The histogram of the cover image is probably changed

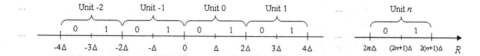

Fig. 2. Every two adjacent bins with the size Δ form an individual unit in the proposed data mapping method, respectively

due to the randomness of the embedded data. Obviously, the histogram can be preserved if the amount of pixels within each bin is unchanged. In the LSB$^+$ algorithm, the bit values are also embedded by replacement but the replacement operations are performed conditionally. The key idea is that the number of the embedded 0s and 1s should not exceed the original ones in the LSBs, respectively. Suppose that there are L and M pixels originally in the left and right bins, the time of embedding 0 should be no more than L and the time of embedding 1 should not exceed M. Once there are L 0s (or M 1s) having been embedded, all the unprocessed LSBs will be replaced with 1s (or 0s). In this way, the amounts of 0s and 1s in the LSBs are unchanged by data embedding. In the decoding process, the embedded bits are extracted one by one in the same order as in the embedding process. For each unit, the extraction process is finished once all the LSBs in either bin have been retrieved.

Since part of the LSBs are replaced to repair the cover histogram instead of embedding, the LSB$^+$ algorithm is a bit more complex than the normal LSB hiding. A portion of payload is also sacrificed to preserve the image histogram, as well as the other low-order statistics. In the following, a generic method that is applicable to any cover object represented by floating point numbers or integers will be further proposed.

2.2   The Generic Method

Suppose a cover object $\mathbf{C}$ consists of N data elements, i.e. $\mathbf{C} = \{e_1, e_2, \cdots, e_N\}$, where e_i is a data element with an index number $i \in \{1, 2, \cdots, N\}$. We use $\mathbf{R}$ to denote the distribution range of the data elements $\{e_1, e_2, \cdots, e_N\}$ and quantize $\mathbf{R}$ into the non-overlapping bins with the same size Δ. For the sake of simplicity, we only discuss the one-dimensional case because multiple dimensions can be addressed one by one. As shown in Fig. 2, every two adjacent bins in the range of $\mathbf{R}$ form an individual unit, within which the bit values 0 and 1 are assigned to the left and right bins, respectively. If the value of a data element e_i falls into the left bin, it represents a bit value of 0, or 1 if it is in the right bin. To embed a bit value of 0, the data element should be kept in the left bin if it was originally the case, or mapped to the left bin if it originally was in the right one. The process to embed a bit value of 1 is similar as long as we replace "left" by "right" and vice versa. The key idea of the proposed method is that the times of embedding 0 (1) should not exceed the amounts of elements originally in the left (right) bins, respectively. Therefore, we need to count the numbers of data elements in both bins before and during the embedding process. Once the time

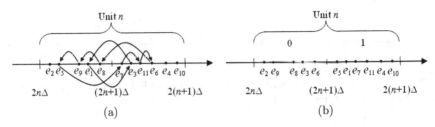

Fig. 3. The eleven data elements $\{e_1, e_2, \cdots, e_{11}\}$ in the embedding Unit n are used to embed a string of bit values "10011010010". Only the first nine bit values "100110100" can be embedded until the time of embedding a bit value 0 has reached the amount of those elements originally in the left bin. Then the bijective mapping between the eleven elements are performed with the minimum mean square error (MSE).

of embedding 0 (or 1) has reached the amount of elements originally in the left (or right) bin, no bit value can be further embedded to ensure that all elements in an embedding unit can be bijectively mapped to each other.

The detailed data mapping process can be illustrated in Fig. 3, where there are eleven data elements $\{e_1, e_2, \cdots, e_{11}\}$ with different values in the Unit n. To embed a string of bit values "10011010010", the data elements are processed in the order of their indices. Since e_1 is in the left bin, it corresponds to the bit value 0. Therefore, it should be mapped into the right bin to embed a bit value 1. As for e_2, it should remain in the left bin to embed a bit value 0. To embed the third bit value 0 in the string, e_3 needs to be mapped from the right to the left bin. The rest of the bit values are sequentially embedded until the ninth one, which leads e_9 to remain in the left bin. Since the number of the elements mapped to the left bin has reached 5, which is the amount of those originally in the left bin, no bit value can be embedded in the Unit n any more due to the randomness of data to be embedded. Therefore, only the first nine bit values "100110100" can be embedded by mapping the data elements with the indices 2, 3, 6, 8, 9 into the left bin and the rest elements into the right bin. To minimize the error caused by data mapping in the mean square error (MSE) criterion, the elements mapped to the same bin should be ordered according to their original values. In the optimal scheme, e_2, e_9, e_8, e_3, e_6 are mapped to the data elements e_2, e_5, e_9, e_1, e_8 while the elements with the indices 5, 1, 7, 11, 4, 10 are mapped to those with the indices 7, 3, 11, 6, 4, 10. It should be noted that the data mapping process can be performed no matter whether several elements have the same values (e.g. the pixels having the same value in a gray-scale image). If all elements originally in a destination bin have the identical values, there is no need to order the ones mapped to that bin.

The data mapping between the data elements in an embedding unit heavily depends on the order they are processed. In Fig. 4, the same data elements as shown in Fig. 3 are used to embed the bit values "100110100" except that the indices of the ninth and tenth elements are exchanged. To embed the ninth bit value 0, the data element e_9 in Fig. 4 should be mapped from the right bin to the left one. In contrast, the data element e_9 in Fig. 3 remains in the left bin.

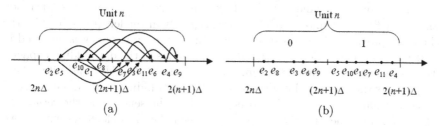

Fig. 4. The same data elements as shown in Fig. 3 are used to embed a string of bit values "100110100" except that the indices of the ninth and tenth elements are exchanged. As a result, the data mapping with the minimum MSE is greatly different from that in Fig. 3.

To minimize the error in the MSE criterion, the data elements e_2, e_8, e_3, e_6, e_9 are mapped to the elements $e_2, e_5, e_{10}, e_1, e_8$, while the data elements with the indices 5, 10, 1, 7, 11, 4 are mapped to those with the indices 7, 3, 11, 6, 4, 9.

The decoding process is much simpler: Given that the order of data elements in the stego object is the same as that in the cover object, the bit values can be extracted from the positions of data elements (i.e. in the left or right bin) one by one. The extracted bit value will be 0 if a data element is located in the left bin, or 1 if it is in the right one. For each embedding unit, once all elements in either bin (left or right) have been used up for data extraction, the extraction process is finished. For example, the bit values that can be extracted from the Unit n in Fig. 3 (b) and Fig. 4 (b) are not "10011010011", but "100110100". Since the embedding and extraction operations within each unit do not interfere with those performed in other units, the operations in every embedding unit can be carried out in parallel. So both of the encoding and decoding processes are performed in the order of all elements in a cover object. Furthermore, the order can be scrambled with a secret key shared by the sender and receiver.

2.3   Bounds of Hiding Rate and Perceptual Distortion

For each embedding unit, the amount of bit values that can be embedded depend on the amount of data elements in the two bins, respectively. Suppose there are L and M data elements in the two bins. Without loss of generality, we assume that M is always no more than L. Then the minimum and maximum amount of bit values that can be embedded in that embedding unit are M and $L + M - 1$. The upper bound of capacity is possible to be approached when M is close to L while the low bound is likely when M is close to 0. In particular, the capacity will be zero when $M = 0$. If we take digital images for instance, the proposed method tends to embed more when the histogram of the cover image changes slowly and the data hiding rate drops when the cover histogram fluctuates rapidly.

The data hiding rate is maximized by default because the embedding process will not stop until the bit values have been embedded to all elements in either bin (left or right). Alternatively, the hiding rate can be adjusted with a parameter

$\theta \in (0, 1]$, i.e. once the time of embedding a bit value 0 (or 1) reaches a fraction (denoted by θ) of the amount of elements originally in the left (or right) bin, the embedding process will be finished. Accordingly, the same policy is enforced in the extraction process. So the low and upper bounds of the data hiding capacity in the aforementioned embedding unit are $\lceil M\theta \rceil$ and $\lceil (L + M - 1)\theta \rceil$ bits, where $\lceil \cdot \rceil$ represents the ceil function. In this way, the data hiding rate can be adjusted with the parameter θ, which should be shared by the sender and the receiver.

By performing the bijective mapping between the data elements within two adjacent bins, the perceptual distortion caused by data embedding is bounded. Given a bin size Δ, the maximum change of a data element is always less than 2Δ. So the perceptual distortion of the stego object can be tuned by adjusting the bin size Δ. The proposed method can be applied to the cover object represented by integers or floating point numbers. As for the floating point numbers, there is no need to deal with the truncation error as no new value is generated in the stego object. In this paper, we concentrate on image steganography by applying the LSB$^+$ algorithm, which is a specific case of the proposed method applied to images with the bin size set to 1.

3   Image Steganography with the LSB$^+$ Algorithm

Since there is only one pixel value in each bin as shown in Fig. 1, there is no need to order the pixels mapped to the same bin. We perform the LSB$^+$ algorithm on all pixels within a cover image in the raster order, i.e. by rows from top to bottom and within each row from left to right. By setting the parameter θ to 1, the stego image is generated with the hiding rate at 0.9688 bit/pixel and $PSNR = 51.14dB$, as shown in Fig. 5 (a). Since the LSB$^+$ algorithm preserves the histogram, the steganalytic algorithms based on histogram are no longer efficient. Furthermore, it is performed in the spatial domain without differentiating the pixels at the block boundaries and those within the blocks. So the steganalytic algorithms designed to detect the message in a specific transform domain (e.g. JPEG) or a block structure are incapable of detection. Nevertheless, readers may argue that the hidden message may be detected by the steganalytic algorithms using high-order statistics (e.g. [6], [11]-[16]). In the following, we further take the SPA attack in [11] for instance and explore the inter-dependencies between pixels to prevent it.

Dumitrescu et at. develop the technique of SPA in [11] to detect the random LSB hiding in digital images. The key assumption for the SPA steganalysis can be summarized as follow: For the sampled pairs of pixels whose values differ by an odd number, the chances that the greater pixel value is odd or even are equal. The closed multi-set C_m under the LSB hiding is defined as the set of pixel pairs whose values differ by m in all the bits except the least significant one (i.e. by right shifting one bit to get rid of the LSB). But its submultisets D_{2m} (the set of pixel pairs whose value differ by $2m$), X_{2m-1} (the set of pixel pairs whose values differ by $2m - 1$ and the greater value is even), and Y_{2m+1} (the set of pixel pairs whose values differ by $2m + 1$ and the greater value is

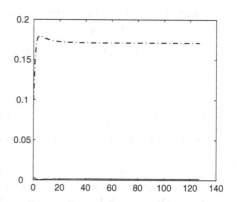

(a) The stego image of "lena" with the hiding rate at 0.9688 bit/pixel and $PSNR = 51.14dB$.

(b) The relative errors calculated from the original and stego images of "lena" as shown by the solid and dash-dot curves, respectively.

Fig. 5. The relative error $\frac{||\bigcup_{m=0}^{j} Y_{2m+1}| - |\bigcup_{m=0}^{j} X_{2m+1}||}{|\bigcup_{m=0}^{j} Y_{2m+1}| + |\bigcup_{m=0}^{j} X_{2m+1}|}$ is greatly increased for $0 \leq j \leq$ 127 after implementing the LSB$^+$ algorithm on all pixels in the cover image of "lena" with $\theta = 1$

odd), are not close under the LSB hiding. As shown in Fig. 5 (b), the relative error $\frac{||\bigcup_{m=0}^{j} Y_{2m+1}| - |\bigcup_{m=0}^{j} X_{2m+1}||}{|\bigcup_{m=0}^{j} Y_{2m+1}| + |\bigcup_{m=0}^{j} X_{2m+1}|}$ is greatly increased after implementing the LSB$^+$ algorithm on all pixels in the cover image of "lena" with $\theta = 1$, where $|X_{2m-1}|$ and $|Y_{2m+1}|$ denote the amount of pixel pairs in X_{2m-1} and Y_{2m+1}, respectively. The phenomenon is modeled by a finite-state machine in [11]. To further estimate the length of message embedded by the random LSB hiding, the fraction of the pixels modified in the embedding process is assumed to be equal to $\frac{p}{2}$ when the data hiding rate is p bit/pixel. However, the same conclusion cannot be drawn from the LSB$^+$ algorithm because part of the pixel values are modified not for data embedding purpose but to preserve the histogram of the cover. So we directly use α to denote the fraction of the pixels modified in the embedding process. Then the fraction of the pixels that are unchanged is $1 - \alpha$. For $m = 1, 2, \ldots, 127$, (2) and (3) in [11] become

$$|X_{2m-1}|(1 - 2\alpha)^2 = \alpha^2|C_m| - \alpha(|D'_{2m}| + 2|X'_{2m-1}|) + |X'_{2m-1}|, \qquad (2)$$

$$|Y_{2m+1}|(1 - 2\alpha)^2 = \alpha^2|C_m| - \alpha(|D'_{2m}| + 2|Y'_{2m+1}|) + |Y'_{2m+1}|, \qquad (3)$$

where $|C_m|$ denotes the amount of pixel pairs in C_m. $|X'_{2m-1}|$ and $|Y'_{2m+1}|$ denote the amount of pixel pairs whose values differ by $2m-1$ while the greater value is even and odd in the samples from the stego image, respectively. $|D'_{2m}|$ denotes the amount of pixel pairs whose values differ by $2m$ in the samples from the stego image. When $m = 0$, the (4) in [11] becomes

$$|Y_1|(1 - 2\alpha)^2 = 2\alpha^2|C_0| - 2\alpha(|D'_0| + |Y'_1|) + |Y'_1|. \qquad (4)$$

In [11], $|X_{2m+1}|$ is assumed to be equal to $|Y_{2m+1}|$ for $m = 0, 1, \ldots, 127$. With this assumption, we can obtain the following quadratic equation to estimate the length of the hidden message

$$(|C_m|-|C_{m+1}|)\alpha^2-(|D'_{2m}|-|D'_{2m+2}|+2|Y'_{2m+1}|-2|X'_{2m+1}|)\alpha+|Y'_{2m+1}|-|X'_{2m+1}|=0 \tag{5}$$

for $m \geq 1$ and for $m = 0$,

$$(2|C_0| - |C_1|)\alpha^2 - (2|D'_0| - |D'_2| + 2|Y'_1| - 2|X'_1|)\alpha + |Y'_1| - |X'_1| = 0. \tag{6}$$

It has been shown in [11] that the length of the hidden message is the smaller root of (5) provided that $|C_m| > |C_{m+1}|$ (or $2|C_0| > |C_1|$ for (6)). However, if $|X_{2m+1}| = |X'_{2m+1}|$ and $|Y_{2m+1}| = |Y'_{2m+1}|$, $|X'_{2m+1}| - |Y'_{2m+1}|$ in (5) is equal to 0 so that the estimated length will be zero. In the following, we will show how to prevent the SPA attack by implementing the LSB$^+$ algorithm on every special set of pixels.

For the better estimation, the SPA steganalysis is usually performed on the neighboring pixels to utilize the inter-dependencies between them. Since every sampled pixel pair are two neighboring pixels, we choose to implement the LSB$^+$ algorithm on the subset of pixels having the same neighbor values, i.e. the up, down, left, and right neighbor values (denoted by 4-N in short) of all pixels in the subset are the same. To generate a special subset, half of the pixel values, which are the neighbor values of the other pixels in a gray-scale image, are fixed during the embedding process. For each combination of the four neighbor values that appears, we count its occurrence in the first half pixel values and those pixels within them are grouped to a subset. Then the LSB$^+$ algorithm is implemented on every generated subset. By this means, the stego image of "lena" is generated with 5564 bits embedded and $PSNR = 65.17dB$, as shown in Fig. 6 (a). It should be noted that the subsets of pixels with the same neighbor values can exactly be generated from the stego image.

The effects of data embedding on the sampled pixel pairs are compensated by each other after implementing the LSB$^+$ algorithm on every subset of pixels having the same neighbor values. Consider a pixel P_i whose LSB has been changed from 0 to 1, its value is changed from $2n$ to $2n + 1$ with $n \in \{0, 1, \ldots, 127\}$. As the histogram is unchanged by the LSB$^+$ algorithm, there exists a corresponding pixel P_j whose neighbor values are the same as P_i's and its value has been changed from $2n + 1$ to $2n$. Given a neighbor value V_k of P_i and P_j, it is unchanged during the embedding process. So the difference between the value of P_i and V_k will increase by 1 after the value of P_i is changed from $2n$ to $2n + 1$ if $V_k \in [0, 2n]$, and the difference between the value of P_j and V_k will decrease by 1 after the value of P_j is changed from $2n + 1$ to $2n$. When $V_k \in [2n + 1, 255]$, the difference between the value of P_i and V_k will decrease by 1 after the value of P_i is changed from $2n$ to $2n + 1$, and the difference between the value of P_j and V_k will increase by 1 after the value of P_j is changed from $2n + 1$ to $2n$. As a result, $|X_{2m+1}|$ and $|Y_{2m+1}|$ will be unchanged by the embedding process for $m = 0, 1, \ldots, 127$. As shown in Fig. 6 (b), the values of $|X'_{2m+1}| - |X_{2m+1}|$ and $|Y'_{2m+1}| - |Y_{2m+1}|$ are zeros if we perform the SPA steganalysis on the stego

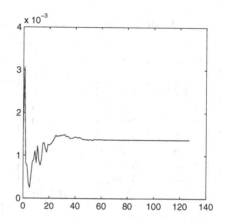

(a) By applying the LSB$^+$ algorithm on every subset of pixels having the same four neighbor values (up, down, left, and right), the stego image is generated with 5564 bits embedded and $PSNR = 65.17dB$.

(b) Solid curve: Relative error of the cover image "lena", which is the same as the solid curve in Fig. 5 (b); Lines at the bottom: $|X'_{2m+1}| - |X_{2m+1}|$ and $|Y'_{2m+1}| - |Y_{2m+1}|$, which are zeros for $0 \leq m \leq 127$ so that the relative error of stego image is the same as the cover one.

Fig. 6. By implementing the LSB$^+$ algorithm in the 4-N way, the relative error $\frac{\|\bigcup_{m=0}^{j} Y_{2m+1}| - |\bigcup_{m=0}^{j} X_{2m+1}\|}{|\bigcup_{m=0}^{j} Y_{2m+1}| + |\bigcup_{m=0}^{j} X_{2m+1}|}$ of the cover image is unchanged

image so that the relative error $\frac{\|\bigcup_{m=0}^{j} Y_{2m+1}| - |\bigcup_{m=0}^{j} X_{2m+1}\|}{|\bigcup_{m=0}^{j} Y_{2m+1}| + |\bigcup_{m=0}^{j} X_{2m+1}|}$ of cover image is unchanged. Under the assumption that $|X_{2m+1}| = |Y_{2m+1}|$, which can be taken for the most natural images, the length of the hidden message that can be estimated from (5) or (6) is zero because $|X_{2m+1}| = |X'_{2m+1}|$ and $|Y_{2m+1}| = |Y'_{2m+1}|$. As a matter of fact, we can directly generate the following equations from (2) and (3) if $|X_{2m+1}| = |X'_{2m+1}|$ and $|Y_{2m+1}| = |Y'_{2m+1}|$:

$$\alpha^2(|C_m| - 4|X'_{2m-1}|) = \alpha(|D'_{2m}| - 2|X'_{2m-1}|), \tag{7}$$

$$\alpha^2(|C_m| - 4|Y'_{2m+1}|) = \alpha(|D'_{2m}| - 2|Y'_{2m+1}|). \tag{8}$$

One root of (7) and (8) is zero, and the other root is

$$\alpha = \frac{|D'_{2m}| - 2|X'_{2m-1}|}{|C_m| - 4|X'_{2m-1}|} = \frac{|D'_{2m}| - 2|Y'_{2m+1}|}{|C_m| - 4|Y'_{2m+1}|}, \tag{9}$$

which implies that $(|C_m| - 2|D'_{2m}|)(|Y'_{2m+1}| - |X'_{2m-1}|) = 0$. Because $|X_{2m-1}|$ is unequal to $|Y_{2m+1}|$ for the cover image, we can conclude from (9) that $|C_m| = 2|D'_{2m}|$. Combined with $|C_m| = |X'_{2m-1}| + |D'_{2m}| + |Y'_{2m+1}|$, it can be seen that $|D'_{2m}| = |X'_{2m-1}| + |Y'_{2m+1}|$, which indicates that $\alpha = \frac{1}{2}$. Similarly, we can generate the following equation from (4) given that $|Y_1| = |Y'_1|$:

$$\alpha^2(|C_0| - 2|Y'_1|) = \alpha(|D'_0| - |Y'_1|). \tag{10}$$

Table 1. The experimental results on distortion and hiding rate

Images	Size	LSB$^+$: $\theta = 1$		LSB$^+$: 4-N, $\theta = 1$		
		PSNR (dB)	Rate (bpp)	PSNR	Bits	Rate
airfield	512×512	53.9397	0.5064	75.1562	574	0.0021
boats	720×576	51.1656	0.9628	60.1683	33264	0.0802
columbia	480×480	51.1480	0.9660	61.8852	12591	0.0546
crowd	512×512	51.9641	0.6430	62.4494	12474	0.0476
lena	512×512	51.1466	0.9688	65.1796	5564	0.0212
lighthouse	512×512	51.3676	0.8056	67.1048	3746	0.0143
peppers	512×512	51.1552	0.9641	67.9355	2857	0.0109
tank	512×512	57.7708	0.2045	74.1208	668	0.0025
truck	512×512	54.4157	0.4428	66.8681	4379	0.0167

Since $|C_0| = |D_0'| + |Y_1'|$ and $|D_0'| \neq |Y_1'|$, the two roots of (10) are 0 and 1. As the value of α (i.e. the fraction of the pixels modified in the embedding process) is zero, the length of the hidden message that is estimated by the SPA steganalysis is also zero. Whether $|X_{2m+1}| = |Y_{2m+1}|$ for $m = 0, 1, \ldots, 127$ or not, the image histogram as well as the values of $|X_{2m-1}|$, $|Y_{2m+1}|$ and $|C_m|$ can be preserved by implementing the LSB$^+$ algorithm on every subset of pixels having the same neighbor values. As a result, the SPA steganalysis is prevented.

4   Evaluation

In the experiments, the LSB$^+$ algorithm was implemented on the gray-scale images [1] listed in Table 1 with the parameter $\theta = 1$. In Table 1, we list the data hiding rates when the LSB$^+$ algorithm was implemented on all pixels in an image and on subsets of pixels having the same up, down, left, and right neighbor values (as denoted by 4-N), respectively.

4.1   Distortion

The peak signal-to-noise ratio (PSNR) of the stego image is used to represent the distortion caused by data hiding. As shown in Table 1, the PSNRs of the stego images are all above 51(dB) when the LSB$^+$ algorithm was implemented on all pixels in a gray-scale image with $\theta = 1$. When the LSB$^+$ algorithm was implemented only on every subset of pixels surrounded by the same neighbor values, the PSNRs of all the stego images were above 60(dB).

4.2   Hiding Rate

The information hiding rate using the generic method depends on both of the marginal distribution of the cover and the bin size Δ. In the LSB$^+$ algorithm

---

[1] The images are downloaded from http://www.hlevkin.com/TestImages/

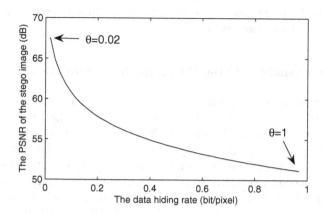

Fig. 7. The PSNR of the stego image "lena" at different hiding rate

where Δ is fixed at 1, the data hiding rate lies on the histogram of the cover image. As we can see in Table 1, less information can be hidden in the image "tank" (about 0.2045 bit/pixel if applied to all pixels) than in the image "lena" (about 0.9688 bit/pixel if applied to all pixels). This is due to that the histogram of "lena" changes slowly while the histogram of "tank" fluctuates rapidly.

Not surprisingly, the distortion of the stego image "tank" is less than that of the stego image "lena". Moreover, we can use the parameter θ to adjust the data hiding rate so as to tune the perceptual distortion caused by data embedding. As shown in Fig. 7, there is a trade-off between the distortion and the data hiding rate for the stego image of "lena". When implemented on subsets of pixels having the same neighbor values in the 4-N way, the amount of bits that can be embedded is affected by the histogram of the pixels in every subset. It can be seen from Table 1 that the hiding rate has been significantly reduced after restricting the embedding positions to prevent the SPA attack.

4.3   The Prevented Steganalytic Algorithms

The LSB$^+$ algorithm is consistent with the model-based steganography, in which two distinct parts are separated from the cover with one part unperturbed and the other replaced with the encoded message. Different from the algorithm of generating the encoded message following a given distribution as in [24], we directly use the cover histogram to generate the stego image so that the hidden message cannot be detected by using the first-order statistics (e.g. [7,25]). Since the LSB$^+$ algorithm is performed in the spatial domain without differentiating the pixels at the block boundaries and those within the blocks, the steganalysis designed for a block structure (e.g. [5], [9]) or a specific transform domain (e.g. [8], [10]) cannot detect the hidden message either. To further prevent the SPA attack [11], we implement it on the selected subsets of pixels having the same neighbor values. The experimental results show that some important high-order statistics have been well preserved.

4.4   Other Steganalysis Using the High-Order Statistics

How to prevent the other steganalytic algorithms using the high-order statistics (e.g. [6], [13]-[16]) from detecting the message hidden by the LSB$^+$ algorithm should be further investigated. In principle, it is possible to evade the two attacks against the LSB matching steganography as shown in [13]. The first algorithm calculates the histogram characteristic function (HCF) to calibrate the suspected image with the one down-sampled from it. In the second algorithm, the adjacency histogram is used for steganalysis instead of the usual one. By implementing the LSB$^+$ algorithm on every subset of pixels having the same neighbor values, both the usual and adjacency histograms of the cover image can be preserved. Therefore, the inequality relation between the center of mass (COM) of the stego HCF before and after down-sampling is probably broken. The experimental results on large image database are expected to justify our arguments.

5   Conclusion

In this paper, a new steganographic method has been presented for the passive warden scenario. By bijectively mapping the data elements within two adjacent bins to embed a secret message, the first-order statistics of the cover has been preserved inherently. Compared with the previous work in the domain, our method is relative simple and easy to implement. Furthermore, high and adjustable hiding rate can be achieved while the distortion (e.g. in the MSE criterion) can be easily minimized.

The generic method becomes a sort of LSB hiding when applied to digital gray-scale images, namely the LSB$^+$ algorithm. The SPA steganalysis [11] has been prevented by implementing the LSB$^+$ algorithm on the subsets of pixels having the same neighbor values. As a cost, the hiding rate has been significantly reduced by restricting the embedding operations to the selected positions. Our future work is to investigate how to preserve the high-order statistics so as to prevent the steganalytic attacks as shown in [6], [13]-[16]. We will also try to apply the generic method to some other covers such as 3D objects.

Acknowledgement

The authors would like to thank the anonymous reviewers for their valuable suggestions and comments. This work was partly supported by the Faculty Research Grant of Hong Kong Baptist University under Project FRG/06-07/II-07 and by a grant from the Research Grant Council of the Hong Kong SAR, China (Project No. HKBU 210306).

References

1. Anderson, R.J., Petitcolas, F.A.P.: On the limits of steganography. IEEE Journal on Selected Areas in Communications 16(4), 474–481 (1998)
2. Simmons, G.J.: The prisoner's problem and the subliminal channel. In: Advances in Cryptology: Proceedings of CRYPTO 1983, pp. 51–67. Plenum Press, New York (1984)
3. Cachin, C.: An information theoretic model for steganography. In: Aucsmith, D. (ed.) IH 1998. LNCS, vol. 1525, pp. 306–318. Springer, Heidelberg (1998)
4. Johnson, N.F., Jajodia, S.: Steganalysis of images created using current steganography software. In: Aucsmith, D. (ed.) IH 1998. LNCS, vol. 1525, pp. 273–289. Springer, Heidelberg (1998)
5. Wang, Y., Moulin, P.: Steganalysis of block-structured stegotext. In: Proceedings of the SPIE Electronic Imaging, San Jose, CA, vol. 5306, pp. 477–488 (January 2004)
6. Sullivan, K., Madhow, U., Manjunath, B.S., Chandrasekaran, S.: Steganalysis for Markov Cover Data with Applications to Images. IEEE Transactions on Information Forensics and Security 1(2), 275–287 (2006)
7. Westfeld, A., Pfitzmann, A.: Attacks on steganographic systems. In: Pfitzmann, A. (ed.) IH 1999. LNCS, vol. 1768, pp. 61–76. Springer, Heidelberg (2000)
8. Fridrich, J., Goljan, M., Hogea, D.: Steganalysis of JPEG images: Breaking the F5 algorithm. In: Petitcolas, F.A.P. (ed.) IH 2002. LNCS, vol. 2578, pp. 310–323. Springer, Heidelberg (2003)
9. Fridrich, J., Goljan, M., Hogea, D.: Attacking the OutGuess. In: Proceedings of the ACM Workshop on Multimedia and Security, Juan-Pins, France, December 2002, pp. 967–982 (2002)
10. Bohme, R., Westfeld, A.: Exploiting preserved statistics for steganalysis. In: Fridrich, J. (ed.) IH 2004. LNCS, vol. 3200, pp. 82–96. Springer, Heidelberg (2004)
11. Dumitrescu, S., Wu, X., Wang, Z.: Detection of LSB steganography via sample pair analysis. IEEE Transactions on Signal Processingy 51(7), 1995–2007 (2003)
12. Lyu, S., Farid, H.: Steganalysis using color wavelet statistics and one-class support vector machines. In: Proceedings of the SPIE Electronic Imaging, San Jose, CA, vol. 5306, pp. 35–45 (January 2004)
13. Ker, A.D.: Steganalysis of LSB matching in grayscale images. IEEE Signal Processing Letters 12(6), 441–444 (2005)
14. Avcibas, I., Memon, N., Sankur, B.: Steganalysis using image quality metrics. IEEE Transactions on Image Processing 12(2), 221–229 (2003)
15. Lyu, S., Farid, H.: Steganalysis using high-order image statistics. IEEE Transactions on Information Forensics and Security 1(1), 111–119 (2006)
16. Wang, Y., Moulin, P.: Optimized feature extraction for learning-based image steganalysis. IEEE Transactions on Information Forensics and Security 2(1), 31–45 (2007)
17. Westfeld, A.: High capacity despite better steganalysis (F5 - a steganographic algorithm). In: Moskowitz, I.S. (ed.) IH 2001. LNCS, vol. 2137, pp. 289–302. Springer, Heidelberg (2001)
18. Provos, N.: Defending against statistical steganalysis. In: Proceedings of the 10th USENIX Security Symposium, Washington, DC, pp. 323–335 (2001)
19. Franz, E.: Steganography preserving statistical properties. In: Petitcolas, F.A.P. (ed.) IH 2002. LNCS, vol. 2578, pp. 278–294. Springer, Heidelberg (2003)

20. Eggers, J.J., Bauml, R., Girod, B.: A communications approach to image steganography. In: Proceedings of the SPIE Electronic Imaging, San Jose, CA, vol. 4675, pp. 26–37 (2002)
21. Tzschoppe, R., Bauml, R., Huber, J.B., Kaup, A.: Steganographic system based on higher-order statistics. In: Proceedings of the SPIE Electronic Imaging, San Jose, CA, vol. 5020, pp. 156–166 (January 2003)
22. Solanki, K., Sullivan, K., Madhow, U., Manjunath, B.S., Chandrasekaran, S.: Provably secure steganography: Achieving zero K-L divergence using statistical restoration. In: IEEE International Conference on Image Processing 2006, Atlanta, USA, pp. 125–128 (Octobor 2006)
23. Sarkar, A., Solanki, K., Madhow, U., Chandrasekaran, S., Manjunath, B.S.: Secure steganography: Statistical restoration of the second order dependencies for improved security. In: Proceedings of the 32th IEEE International Conference on Acoustics, Speech, and Signal Processing (ICASSP), Honolulu, Hawaii (April 2007)
24. Sallee, P.: Model-based Steganography. In: Kalker, T., Cox, I., Ro, Y.M. (eds.) IWDW 2003. LNCS, vol. 2939, pp. 154–167. Springer, Heidelberg (2004)
25. Bohme, R., Westfeld, A.: Breaking Cauchy Model-based JPEG Steganography with First Order Statistics. In: Samarati, P., Ryan, P.Y.A., Gollmann, D., Molva, R. (eds.) ESORICS 2004. LNCS, vol. 3193, pp. 125–140. Springer, Heidelberg (2004)

Benchmarking for Steganography

Tomáš Pevný[1] and Jessica Fridrich[2]

[1] Department of CS, SUNY Binghamton
pevnak@gmail.com
[2] Department of ECE, SUNY Binghamton
fridrich@binghamton.edu

Abstract. With the increasing number of new steganographic algorithms as well as methods for detecting them, the issue of comparing security of steganographic schemes in a fair manner is of the most importance. A fair benchmark for steganography should only be dependent on the model chosen to represent cover and stego objects. In particular, it should be independent of any specific steganalytic technique. We first discuss the implications of this requirement and then investigate the use of two quantities for benchmarking—the KL divergence between the empirical probability distribution of cover and stego images and the recently proposed two-sample statistics called Maximum Mean Discrepancy (MMD). While the KL divergence is preferable for benchmarking because it is the more fundamental quantity, we point out some practical difficulties of computing it from data obtained from a test database of images. The MMD is well understood theoretically and numerically stable even in high-dimensional spaces, which makes it an excellent candidate for benchmarking in steganography. We demonstrate the benchmark based on MMD on specific steganographic algorithms for the JPEG format.

1 Introduction

Up until now, the security of steganographic systems was compared by reporting detection results for a specific blind steganalyzer [16,24,6]. This is clearly undesirable because the comparison is dependent on the steganalyzer feature set, the machine learning engine (SVM, neural network, etc.), and a functional assigning a single numerical value to the ROC curve (total minimal decision error [16,38], probability of detection for fixed false alarm rate [26], or false alarm for probability of detection 50% [20], accuracy [13], etc.). The goal of this paper is to provide a practical method for comparing security of steganographic systems that is free from such arbitrary choices and thus provides a more fundamental measure of security than previously proposed measures. We interpret the selection of the feature set as a low-dimensional *model* of covers and compute the steganographic security directly in the model space from empirical data obtained from a database of cover and stego images. We consider two different measures, each one of which has its own advantages and disadvantages—the Kullback-Leibler divergence and the Maximum Mean Discrepancy (MMD) two-sample statistics.

K. Solanki, K. Sullivan, and U. Madhow (Eds.): IH 2008, LNCS 5284, pp. 251–267, 2008.

In the next section, we introduce some basic concepts and explain the motivation for our approach. In Section 3, we describe a method for benchmarking steganographic systems using the KL divergence and discuss its limitations. The MMD is introduced in Section 4. We use MMD to compute benchmark values for selected known steganographic algorithms in Section 5. In the same section, we discuss the experiments and compare the benchmark to results obtained using SVMs. The paper is concluded in Section 6.

2   Steganographic Security and Cover Models

Denoting $\mathcal{C}$ the set of all covers c, Cachin's definition of steganographic security is based on the assumption that the selection of covers from $\mathcal{C}$ can be described by a random variable c on $\mathcal{C}$ with probability distribution function (pdf) P. A steganographic scheme, S, is a mapping $\mathcal{C} \times \mathcal{M} \times \mathcal{K} \to \mathcal{C}$ that assigns a new (stego) object, $s \in \mathcal{C}$, to each triple (c, M, K), where $M \in \mathcal{M}$ is a secret message selected from the set of communicable messages, $\mathcal{M}$, and $K \in \mathcal{K}$ is the steganographic secret key. Assuming the covers are selected with pdf P and embedded with a message and secret key both randomly (uniformly) chosen from their corresponding sets, the set of all stego images is again a random variable s on $\mathcal{C}$ with pdf Q. The measure of statistical detectability is the Kullback–Leibler divergence [5]

$$D(P||Q) = \sum_{c \in \mathcal{C}} P(c) \log \frac{P(c)}{Q(c)}. \tag{1}$$

When $D(P||Q) < \epsilon$, the stego system is called ϵ-secure.

The KL divergence is a very fundamental quantity because it provides bounds on the best possible detector one can build [8]. Thus, at least in theory, we could benchmark steganographic schemes by deriving Q from S and P and evaluating the KL divergence analytically. Of course, the real difficulty is that we have little information about the probability distributions involved due to the large dimensionality of the set $\mathcal{C}$. This problem is typically solved by working with simplified models of cover objects. There are basically two choices: 1) analytical models, in which c is modeled as a sequence of iid random variables [28] (or Markov chains [42]) and 2) high-dimensional models based on features extracted from the cover/stego objects [32,13,2,1,44,36,26,11]. The major advantage of analytical models is that we may be able to compute the distribution of stego images and derive the relationship between the KL divergence and the amount of embedded data [7]. The weakness of this approach lies in the fact that the analytical models are too simple to capture complex cover objects, such as digital images. Often, it is not difficult to detect the "provably secure" steganographic scheme by using a better model of cover objects and designing appropriate test statistics. As an example, we cite the successful attacks [32] on steganographic systems that preserve first order statistics of DCT coefficients in JPEG images [33,29,19,10,39]. Since at this point, there are no analytically tractable models that truthfully describe natural images, we turned our attention to models based on features.

Such models far better capture the complexity of cover objects but are no longer amenable to analytical study and thus we cannot derive the KL divergence (or some other statistic) analytically. Instead, we estimate it by calculating features from a large number of covers and stego objects. This approach, however, is not without problems. First, we have the uncomfortable dependence on the database of test images, and second, it is not clear how many bits we should be embedding in each image. We postpone discussion of the message length to subsequent sections. Presumably, the issue of the size and diversity of the database can be dealt with by including sufficiently many images. While the database choice is crucial for spatial domain steganography, it is less critical for steganography in JPEG images because JPEG compression removes high-frequency details from images and thus essentially narrows down the space of covers $\mathcal{C}$. Although in this paper our covers will be digital images in the JPEG format, the methods proposed here are by no means limited to such covers and can be extended to other objects, such as raw images or audio.

3   Benchmarking Steganographic Schemes

In this section, we explain the basic ingredients of our benchmark and study the feasibility of using the KL divergence for benchmarking.

3.1   Model Selection

As explained in Section 1, we model covers through a set of numerical features calculated from them. Formally, the model is a mapping

$$\psi : \mathcal{C} \to \mathbb{R}^d \qquad (2)$$

that assigns a d-dimensional feature vector $x = \psi(c)$ to every cover. This feature vector represents the cover in $\mathbb{R}^d$ and we interpret ψ as the cover model. Consequently, the benchmark that we propose will necessarily depend on the model. The mapping ψ induces two random variables on $\mathbb{R}^d$, $\psi(\mathsf{c})$ and $\psi(\mathsf{s})$, with their corresponding pdfs p and q, reserving from now on the letter x for features from covers and y for features from stego images.

By projecting $\mathcal{C}$ onto $\mathbb{R}^d$ for some "reasonably small" d, we obviously lose a lot of information. It is important that we preserve those properties of covers that typically get disturbed by steganographic embedding. Different authors proposed different feature sets for applications in blind as well as targeted steganalysis. In this paper, we selected the 274-dimensional feature vector described in [32]. The SVM steganalyzer based on this feature can reliably detect a large number of current steganographic techniques and provides state-of-the-art results based on comparative studies reported in [24,38,31].

3.2   Stego Images

Given two steganographic schemes, S_1 and S_2, we wish to know which method is more secure (less statistically detectable). This answer, however, will generally depend on how the steganography is used. It is well possible that S_1 may be more detectable than S_2 for one payload size and less detectable for a different payload size. For example, methods that use matrix embedding [14] exhibit sharp non-linear decrease in detectability with decreasing payload due to significantly lower number of embedding changes, while other methods do not allow matrix embedding (e.g., adaptive schemes). Moreover, some steganographic algorithms are inherently limited to binary codes, such as methods based on perturbed quantization [25,15], while methods that use ± 1 type of embedding can utilize more powerful ternary codes [14]. Thus, one steganographic method can be embedding significantly higher payload than some other method for the same distortion budget. Fixing the distortion budget instead of the payload would, however, benchmark the type of embedding operation rather than the whole scheme.

Perhaps, we first need to ask what it is that we want our benchmark to measure. If our goal was to evaluate the statistical detectability under conditions that somehow simulate real-life usage, we would need to know the statistical distribution of payloads that are typically embedded. It is, however, completely unclear if we can assume anything reasonable about this prior distribution. A tempting possibility is to choose an approach similar in spirit to the steganalysis benchmark proposed by Ker [22]. The reasoning is that over multiple uses of the stego channel, the relative change rate λ must converge to zero to avoid detection. Because for statistically detectable stego schemes the KL divergence is quadratic in λ, $D \approx Q\lambda^2$ as $\lambda \to 0$, it was proposed in [21] to take the constant Q for benchmarking steganalysis detectors. Adopting this approach for benchmarking steganography, we discover that the KL divergence may become non-quadratic in α due to matrix embedding. For example, for optimal codes $\lambda = H^{-1}(\alpha)$ and $D \sim \left(H^{-1}(\alpha)\right)^2$.[1] We acknowledge that this observation does not preclude the possibility to benchmark steganography in the limit $\alpha \to 0$, but do not pursue this approach further in this paper.

It seems that a reasonable option is to fix the message length with respect to the number of coefficients in the image usable for steganography. We fix the embedding rate or relative payload, α, as the ratio between the message length in bits and the number of non zero AC coefficients in the cover JPEG image (bpac). Thus, for each particular image every stego method will embed the same relative payload. By fixing $\epsilon > 0$, we could then state that a certain steganographic method becomes ϵ-secure at relative payload $\alpha(\epsilon)$. This way, the benchmark will stay compatible with the methodology accepted in previously published papers on steganalysis (see, e.g., [16]). Fixing the relative message length also makes intuitive sense because people might subconsciously use a bigger cover for large messages and a smaller cover for short messages. Also, there are some heuristic arguments that steganographic capacity might be linearly proportional to the number of pixels. Imagine that we take many pictures with a digital camera of exactly the same scene. Due to presence of random components, such as the shot noise (caused by quantum properties of light), each time we take a

---

[1] $H(x)$ is the binary entropy function.

picture, the pixel values will slightly vary. Subsequent in-camera processing will introduce local dependencies among the random components and thus the noise will correspond more to a Markov random field than a collection of iid variables. The entropy of this Markov field increases linearly[2] with the number of pixels [8]. Attempts to construct stego schemes around this idea include [12,30].

3.3 KL Divergence as Benchmark Statistics

Given a set of D database images, we generate two sets of samples

$$\mathbf{X} = (x_1, \ldots, x_D), \; \mathbf{Y}(\alpha) = (y_1, \ldots, y_D), \tag{3}$$

where we explicitly denoted the dependence of the samples of stego images $\mathbf{Y}$ on the relative message length α. We wish to emphasize that $x_i = \psi(c_i)$ and $y_i = \psi(s_i)$ are d-dimensional vectors (the features for cover and stego image i). Considering $\mathbf{X}$ and $\mathbf{Y}$ as vectors of D independent realizations of the random variables $\psi(\mathsf{c})$ and $\psi(\mathsf{s})$, we can estimate the KL divergence

$$D_{\mathrm{KL}}\left(\psi(\mathsf{c})\|\psi(\mathsf{s})\right) = \int_{\mathbb{R}^d} p(x) \log \frac{p(x)}{q(x)}$$

from the empirical data (3). The high dimensionality of the feature space makes the estimation quite challenging. A practically computable benchmark cannot rely on too large a database as that would incur impractical computing requirements and storage. Realistically, we need to obtain good estimates with $10^3 - 10^5$ images. The large dimensionality eliminates most estimators of KL divergence that we can potentially use. A good review of entropy estimators is in [3]. The only estimator that can provide accurate results in high dimensional spaces is the kNN estimator [4,37], which we now briefly describe.

3.4 The kNN Estimator of KL Divergence

The KL divergence can be written as

$$D_{\mathrm{KL}}(p\|q) = \int_{\mathbb{R}^d} p(x) \log p(x) - \int_{\mathbb{R}^d} p(x) \log q(x) = -H(p) + H_{\mathsf{x}}(p, q), \tag{4}$$

where H stands for the entropy of p and $H_{\mathsf{x}}(p, q)$ for the cross-entropy. Let $\rho_k(\mathbf{X}, z)$ and $\rho_k(\mathbf{Y}, z)$ denote the radius of the smallest ball centered at $z \in \mathbb{R}^d$ that contains exactly k samples from $\mathbf{X}$ and $\mathbf{Y}$, respectively. Then,

$$\hat{D}_{\mathrm{KL}}(p\|q) = \log \frac{D}{D-1} + \frac{d}{D} \left(\sum_{i=1}^{D} \log \rho_k(\mathbf{X}, x_i) - \sum_{i=1}^{D} \log \rho_k(\mathbf{Y}, x_i) \right) \tag{5}$$

---

[2] Note that this argument is not in contradiction with [21] because there exist no detectors for stego schemes that use this random field for embedding.

Table 1. Relative error of the KL-divergence estimate for two multi-variate Gaussian distributions for various combination of sample sizes, D, and data dimensionality d. The number of nearest neighbors was set to $k = \sqrt{D}$. Some combinations of d and k do not allow computing the KL divergence using the kNN method because it requires $k \geq d$.

d	2×500	2×1000	2×5000	2×10000	2×50000	2×100000	$D_{\mathrm{KL}}(p\|q)$
1	24.86%	23.62%	19.62%	16.05%	11.06%	9.41%	2
10	50.25%	41.15%	38.13%	38.14%	33.52%	32.58%	2
100	—	—	—	45.73%	44.10%	45.24%	2
200	—	—	—	—	45.45%	44.40%	2
300	—	—	—	—	—	50.66%	2

is a consistent and asymptotically unbiased estimator of the KL divergence as long as $k/D \to 0$, $k \geq d$, and $k \to \infty$ as $D \to \infty$. For large D, the first term is approximately zero. The second and third terms are estimates of the entropy $H(p)$ and the cross-entropy $H_{\times}(p, q)$.

We first tested this estimator on synthetic data generated from two d dimensional multivariate Gaussian distributions $p = N(-\mu, \mathbf{I})$ and $q = N(\mu, \mathbf{I})$, where $\mathbf{I}$ is the identity matrix and $\mu = \frac{1}{\sqrt{d}} \cdot \mathbf{1}$ with $\mathbf{1}$ being the vector of d ones. Note that $D_{\mathrm{KL}}(p\|q) = 2$. Table 1 shows the estimated values from $2 \times 500 - 2 \times 100000$ samples for $d = 1, 10, 100, 200, 300$. The estimates are clearly biased and this bias tends to zero very slowly with increasing number of data samples (it has to go to zero because the estimator (5) is asymptotically unbiased). The bias is due to the estimate of the cross-entropy. While entropy can be estimated accurately even in high-dimensional spaces with small number of data samples, the cross-entropy is harder to estimate. This is because we need to estimate $\log q(x)$ at x where $p(x)$ is still large but we may not have enough data points from $\mathbf{Y}$ in that region. This problem persists for other distributions, such as the Student's t-distribution, which seems to be a relevant model of output from some LSB detectors [23]. With μ approaching zero, the absolute error of the estimate stays approximately the same, producing a very large relative error of the estimated KL divergence. This is quite undesirable because our main interest is to use the benchmark for small payloads when the pdf of covers and stego images are close.

Without any doubts, the KL divergence in the model space is the preferable quantity for benchmarking steganographic schemes because it provides fundamental information about the limits of any steganalysis method. Also, it could be used for evaluating the suitability of models to distinguish between cover and stego objects for a fixed steganographic method (obtaining thus an interesting steganalysis benchmark). It appears, however, that we cannot simply apply existing estimators to data sets that are typically available for steganographic schemes ($d \sim 10 - 300$ and $D \lesssim 10^5$). The effort to remedy this situation could be directed towards deriving better behaved bias-free estimators and reducing the dimensionality of the model space [27].

The problems with the bias of the cross-entropy estimator prompted us to look for alternative statistics for benchmarking that exhibit more stable numerical behavior for sparse data in high-dimensional spaces. We turned our attention to the recently proposed two-sample statistics called Maximum Mean Discrepancy (MMD) [17,18], which has properties that make it a very good candidate for benchmarking in steganography.

4 Maximum Mean Discrepancy (MMD)

The problem of distinguishing between cover and stego features (3) is a two-sample problem [17]. Assuming the samples $\mathbf{X}$ and $\mathbf{Y}$ were generated from distributions p and q, we need to decide between two hypotheses

$$H_0 : p = q$$
$$H_1 : p \neq q \,.$$

From available methods for the two-sample problem (see the review in, e.g., [17]), we decided to use the Maximum Mean Discrepancy (MMD) [17,18], because of the following advantages relevant to our problem. MMD is numerically stable and scales well with data dimensionality. It has been shown that MMD converges almost independently on data dimension d with error $1/\sqrt{D}$, where D is the number of samples, which allows us to compute an accurate benchmark from $\sim 10^3$ images. Some experimental results on artificial data sets showing this phenomenon will be presented in Section 5 in Table 2. Second, MMD has been well established theoretically and can be linked to other methods, such as Parzen Windows estimates. Third, MMD's computational complexity is $O(D^2)$, which is fast in comparison to Support Vector Machines (SVM), which require expensive grid-search for hyper parameters. We now outline the principles on which MMD is constructed.

To this end, we assume that $\mathcal{X}$ is a separable metric space, and p,q are probability distributions defined on $\mathcal{X}$. The main idea behind MMD is based on Lemma 9.3.2 of [9] stating that $p = q$ if and only if $\forall f \in C(\mathcal{X})(\mathbf{E}_{x \sim p} f(x) = \mathbf{E}_{x \sim q} f(x))$, where $C(\mathcal{X})$ is the class of continuous bounded functions on $\mathcal{X}$. Because this function class is too rich, we cannot use the lemma in finite sample setting. The solution is to restrict the functions to a narrower class $\mathcal{F}$ and measure the disparity between p and q with respect to $\mathcal{F}$ as

$$\mathrm{MMD}[\mathcal{F}, p, q] = \sup_{f \in \mathcal{F}} \left(\mathbf{E}_{x \sim p} f(x) - \mathbf{E}_{y \sim q} f(y) \right), \tag{6}$$

or in finite sample setting,

$$\mathrm{MMD}[\mathcal{F}, \mathbf{X}, \mathbf{Y}] = \sup_{f \in \mathcal{F}} \left(\frac{1}{D} \sum_{i=1}^{D} f(x_i) - \frac{1}{D} \sum_{i=1}^{D} f(y_i) \right), \tag{7}$$

where $\mathbf{X} = \{x_1, \dots, x_D\}$, $\mathbf{Y} = \{y_1, \dots, y_D\}$ are samples (3) from p and q, respectively. To ensure that the measure (6) is useful, we have to choose $\mathcal{F}$ wisely. It has to be rich to distinguish $p \neq q$, yet restrictive enough to provide useful finite sample estimates. The next section shows how to construct such a function class.

4.1   Reproducing Kernel Hilbert Spaces

The class of functions $\mathcal{F}$ used in MMD is built from a symmetric, positive defi-nite[3] function $k : \mathcal{X} \times \mathcal{X} \mapsto \mathbb{R}$ called *kernel*. Using the kernel, we define $\forall x \in \mathcal{X}$ the function $K_x : \mathcal{X} \mapsto \mathbb{R}$ as $K_x = k(x, \cdot)$. It is easy to see that the set

$$\mathcal{H}_0 = \{\sum_{i=1}^{n} a_i K_{x_i} | n \in \mathcal{N},\ a_i \in \mathbb{R},\ x_i \in \mathcal{X}\}$$

of all finite linear combinations of K_x, $x \in \mathcal{X}$, forms a vector space of functions $\mathcal{X} \mapsto \mathbb{R}$. The vector space $\mathcal{H}_0$ can be endowed with a dot product defined as

$$\left\langle \sum_{i=1}^{n} a_i K_{x_i}, \sum_{j=1}^{m} b_j K_{y_j} \right\rangle_{\mathcal{H}_0} = \sum_{i=1}^{n} \sum_{j=1}^{m} a_i b_j k(x_i, y_j). \tag{8}$$

The symmetry and positive definiteness of the kernel function k guarantee that the dot product is well defined and indeed satisfies triangle inequality.

By completing the vector space $\mathcal{H}_0$, we construct Hilbert space $\mathcal{H}$ of real valued functions on $\mathcal{X}$ that can be approximated by finite linear combinations of $k(x, \cdot)$ centered at finite number of points x. This Hilbert space $\mathcal{H}$ has one key property. For each $x \in \mathcal{X}$, the point evaluation functional $\delta_x : \mathcal{H} \mapsto \mathbb{R}$, $\delta_x(f) = f(x)$, is a *continuous* linear functional[4]. This is because $\forall x \in \mathcal{X}$ and $\forall f = \sum a_i K_{x_i} \in \mathcal{H}$

$$\langle f, K_x \rangle_{\mathcal{H}} = \left\langle \sum a_i K_{x_i}, K_x \right\rangle_{\mathcal{H}} = \sum a_i k(x_i, x) = f(x) = \delta_x(f), \tag{9}$$

and the boundedness of δ_x (or continuity) follows from Cauchy-Schwartz inequal-ity $|\delta_x(f)| = |\langle f, K_x \rangle_{\mathcal{H}}| \leq \|f\|_{\mathcal{H}} \|K_x\|_{\mathcal{H}}$. Hilbert spaces $\mathcal{H}$ of functions $\mathcal{X} \mapsto \mathbb{R}$ where all point evaluation functionals δ_x are linear and continuous are called *Reproducing Kernel Hilbert Spaces* (RKHS) and (9) is called the reproducing property. Note that since $K_x \in \mathcal{H}$, it can be evaluated at $y \in \mathcal{X}$ by use of the functional δ_y, which yields

$$\delta_y(K_x) = \langle K_x, K_y \rangle_{\mathcal{H}} = k(x, y). \tag{10}$$

This property makes RKHSs very useful in the theory of SVMs [35].

We can see that an RKHS is tightly linked to its kernel. An important class of kernels are *universal* kernels [40]. We call kernel k universal if $\mathcal{X}$ is compact and its RKHS is dense in $C(\mathcal{X})$ in the maximum (infinity) norm $\|f - g\|_{\infty} = \sup_{x \in \mathcal{X}} |f(x) - g(x)|$. An example of a universal kernel, which we exclusively use in this paper, is the Gaussian kernel on $\mathcal{X} \subset \mathbb{R}^d$

$$k(x, y) = \exp(-\gamma \|x - y\|_2^2),\ \gamma > 0. \tag{11}$$

---

[3] $k(z_i, z_j)$ is a positive definite matrix for all $l \geq 2$ and all $(z_1, \ldots, z_l), z_i \in \mathcal{X}$.
[4] Convergence in norm in $\mathcal{H}$ implies point-wise convergence.

4.2 MMD

The role of a universal RKHS for MMD will become clear from the following theorem due to [17], which is a simple consequence of Lemma 9.3.2 of [9] and the fact that a universal RKHS is dense in $\mathcal{C}(\mathcal{X})$.

Let $\mathcal{F}$ be a unit ball in a universal RKHS. Then $\text{MMD}[\mathcal{F}, p, q] = 0$ if and only if $p = q$.

The MMD defined over a unit ball in an RKHS accepts a particularly simple form. In a separable Hilbert space, we can exchange expectation and dot product. Thus,

$$\mathbf{E}_{\mathsf{x} \sim p} f(\mathsf{x}) = \mathbf{E}_{\mathsf{x} \sim p} \langle f, K_{\mathsf{x}} \rangle_{\mathcal{H}} = \langle f, \mathbf{E}_{\mathsf{x} \sim p}[K_{\mathsf{x}}] \rangle_{\mathcal{H}} = \langle f, \mu_p \rangle_{\mathcal{H}}, \tag{12}$$

assuming the mean value exists $\|\mu_p\|_{\mathcal{F}}^2 < \infty$. Thus, the MMD (6) becomes

$$\text{MMD}[\mathcal{F}, p, q] = \sup_{f \in \mathcal{F}} \left(\mathbf{E}_{\mathsf{x} \sim p} f(\mathsf{x}) - \mathbf{E}_{\mathsf{y} \sim q} f(\mathsf{y}) \right) =$$

$$= \sup_{\|f\|_{\mathcal{F}} \leq 1} \langle f, \mu_p - \mu_q \rangle = \|\mu_p - \mu_q\|_{\mathcal{F}}, \tag{13}$$

because the supremum is reached for $f = (\mu_p - \mu_q)/\|\mu_p - \mu_q\|_{\mathcal{H}}$ from Cauchy-Schwartz inequality. Estimating $\text{MMD}[\mathcal{F}, p, q]$ by replacing μ_p and μ_q in (13) using finite sample estimates $\hat{\mu}_p(x) = \frac{1}{D} \sum_{i=1}^{D} k(x_i, x)$ and $\hat{\mu}_q(x) = \frac{1}{D} \sum_{i=1}^{D} k(y_i, x)$ in (7) leads to a biased estimate. An unbiased estimate based on U-statistics is

$$\text{MMD}_u[\mathcal{F}, \mathbf{X}, \mathbf{Y}] = \left[\frac{1}{D(D-1)} \sum_{i \neq j} k(x_i, x_j) + k(y_i, y_j) - k(x_i, y_j) - k(x_j, y_i) \right]^{\frac{1}{2}} \tag{14}$$

From the theory of U-statistics, under hypothesis H_1 $\text{MMD}_u^2[\mathcal{F}, \mathbf{X}, \mathbf{Y}]$ converges in distribution to a Gaussian according to $\sqrt{D} \left(\text{MMD}_u^2 - \text{MMD}^2[\mathcal{F}, p, q] \right) \xrightarrow{\mathcal{D}} N(0, 4 \cdot \sigma_u^2)$ [17], where σ_u^2 is the variance of $\mathbf{E}_{\mathsf{x}' \sim p, \mathsf{y}' \sim q}[k(\mathsf{x}, \mathsf{x}') + k(\mathsf{y}, \mathsf{y}') - k(\mathsf{x}, \mathsf{y}') - k(\mathsf{x}', \mathsf{y})]$. The convergence is uniform at rate $1/\sqrt{D}$. The distribution of $\text{MMD}_u[\mathcal{F}, \mathbf{X}, \mathbf{Y}]$ under H_0 can be obtained by bootstrapping (see the recommendations in [18]).

4.3 Analytical Calculation of MMD

We now give a specific example of an RKHS generated by the Gaussian kernel (11) $k : \mathbb{R} \times \mathbb{R} \mapsto \mathbb{R}$, $k(x, y) = \exp\left(-\gamma(x - y)^2 \right)$ by providing its orthonormal (ON) basis [41]

$$\left\{ e_n(y) = \sqrt{\frac{(2\gamma)^n}{n!}} y^n \exp(-\gamma y^2) \,\middle|\, n \geq 0 \right\}.$$

Having an ON basis enables us to evaluate the norm in (13) as

$$\text{MMD}^2[\mathcal{F}, p, q] = \|\mu_p - \mu_q\|_{\mathcal{F}}^2 = \sum_{n=0}^{\infty} (b_{p,n} - b_{q,n})^2,$$

where $b_{p,n} = \langle \mu_p, e_n \rangle_{\mathcal{H}}$ and similarly for q. From (12), (9), and (10)

$$\mu_p(y) = \langle \mu_p, K_y \rangle_{\mathcal{H}} = \mathbf{E}_{\mathsf{x} \sim p} \langle K_{\mathsf{x}}, K_y \rangle_{\mathcal{H}} = \mathbf{E}_{\mathsf{x} \sim p} k(\mathsf{x}, y) = \int_{\mathbb{R}} p(x) \cdot k(x, y) \mathrm{d}x$$

$$= \int_{\mathbb{R}} p(x) \cdot \exp(-\gamma(x-y)^2) \mathrm{d}x = \sum_{n=0}^{\infty} b_{p,n} \sqrt{\frac{(2\gamma)^n}{n!}} y^n \exp(-\gamma y^2).$$

Multiplying the whole equation by $\exp(-\gamma y^2)$, we obtain

$$\int_{\mathbb{R}} p(x) \cdot \exp(-\gamma(x^2 - 2xy)) \mathrm{d}x = \sum_{n=0}^{\infty} b_{p,n} \sqrt{\frac{(2\gamma)^n}{n!}} y^n.$$

From Taylor expansion of function $\int_{\mathbb{R}} p(x) \cdot \exp(-\gamma(x^2 - 2xy)) \mathrm{d}x$ at $y = 0$, we have

$$\sum_{n=0}^{\infty} b_{p,n} \sqrt{\frac{(2\gamma)^n}{n!}} y^n = \sum_{n=0}^{\infty} \frac{1}{n!} \frac{\partial^n}{\partial y^n} \left[\int_{\mathbb{R}} p(x) \cdot \exp(-\gamma(x^2 - 2xy)) \mathrm{d}x \right] \Bigg|_{y=0} y^n =$$

$$= \sum_{n=0}^{\infty} \frac{1}{n!} \left[\int_{\mathbb{R}} (2\gamma)^n x^n p(x) \cdot \exp(-\gamma x^2) \mathrm{d}x \right] y^n,$$

and thus

$$b_{p,n} = \int_{\mathbb{R}} p(x) \cdot \sqrt{\frac{(2\gamma)^n}{n!}} x^n \exp(-\gamma x^2) \mathrm{d}x = \int_{\mathbb{R}} p(x) \cdot e_n(x) \mathrm{d}x.$$

The coefficients $b_{p,n}$ are equal to the inner product of p and e_n in L_2.

Extension of this approach to more than one dimension is possible, but quickly becomes computationally intractable. The only exception is when the joint pdfs p and q is factorisable $p(x_1, \ldots, x_n) = p(x_1) \cdot \ldots \cdot p(x_d)$ and $q(y_1, \ldots, y_n) = q(x_1) \cdot \ldots \cdot q(x_d)$, in which case it can be easily shown that

$$\mathrm{MMD}^2[\mathcal{F}, p, q] = \left(\sum_{n=0}^{\infty} b_{p,n}^2 \right)^d - 2 \left(\sum_{n=0}^{\infty} b_{p,n} b_{q,n} \right)^d + \left(\sum_{n=0}^{\infty} b_{q,n}^2 \right)^d,$$

where $b_{p,n}$, $b_{q,n}$ are as above. This approach was used in Section 5.1 to calculate exact values of MMD for artificially generated data sets.

5   Experiments

In this section, we first discuss the choice of the Gaussian kernel parameter γ and then give comparison between the finite sample estimate of MMD (7) with the continuous value (6) on artificial data for various data sample sizes and dimensionality. Finally, we benchmark several popular steganographic techniques with MMD and discuss the results.

Even though universal kernels guarantee that $\text{MMD}[\mathcal{F}, p, q] = 0$ if and only if $p = q$, the choice of the kernel parameter γ has obviously a major influence on the finite sample estimate of MMD (14). If γ is large, the kernel is very narrow and thus $k(x_i, x_j) \approx 0$ (the discrete approximation to the RKHS "overfits" the data). On the other hand, a very small γ leads to a wide kernel and $k(x_i, x_j) \approx 1$ (the approximation is not "pliable" enough). We need the kernel to be aligned with our data[5]. Good results in practice are obtained using the "median" rule [35] (also used in one-class SVMs) according to which γ is set to $\gamma = \frac{1}{\eta^2}$, where η is the median of L_2 divergences between samples. This selection ensures the test statistics to be sensitive to data, because the Gaussian kernel will change its value rapidly.

We also point out that it is important to normalize the data using pre-whitening (setting the data samples to have zero mean and unit variance) before computing the MMD to obtain stable results. Here, we note that any pre-processing we might perform on the data before computing MMD, such as pre-whitening, changes the median and thus the kernel and finally the RKHS. Because for benchmarking of steganography we need one fixed RKHS for all stego methods, we determine the parameters of pre-whitening (and the kernel width γ) from the cover samples only.

5.1 Experiments on Artificial Data Sets

We calculated MMD for the same artificial data from two multinomial Gaussians $N(-\mu, \mathbf{I})$ and $N(\mu, \mathbf{I})$ as in Section 3.4. Table 2 shows that the relative

Table 2. Relative error of sample MMD for two d-dimensional multivariate Gaussian distributions computed from D data samples in d-dimensional space

d	2×500	2×1000	2×5000	2×10000	2×50000	2×100000	MMD
1	-1.29%	-4.17%	-0.57%	1.16%	-0.27%	0.24%	0.562
10	3.79%	2.05%	-0.89%	0.00%	-0.87%	-0.57%	0.123
100	-12.12%	1.71%	-2.41%	-3.50%	0.71%	0.83%	$1.44 \cdot 10^{-2}$
200	1.38%	-4.79%	-1.46%	-2.53%	-0.92%	-0.96%	$7.28 \cdot 10^{-3}$
300	-6.75%	-1.12%	-1.06%	0.48%	0.29%	0.39%	$4.87 \cdot 10^{-3}$

error of MMD calculated from sample data is remarkably stable across different dimensions d. The sample MMD quickly approaches its theoretical value with increased sample size. Tests with other probability distributions (Laplacian and Student's t-distributions) exhibited very similar convergence rates and errors but are not shown here due to lack of space.

5.2 Benchmarking Steganographic Methods

In this section, we use MMD to compare statistical detectability of 10 JPEG steganographic algorithms using the 274-dimensional Merged feature set [32].

---

[5] The role of the kernel in MMD is similar to the role of the kernel in Support Vector Machines.

We focus on low payloads to see if any of the tested steganographic techniques becomes undetectable (indistinguishable using finite sample MMD).

We used a database of 6000 images of a wide variety of scenes from 22 different digital cameras acquired in the raw uncompressed format. The images were embedded with pseudo-random payloads of 5%, 9%, 10%, 15%, and 20% bpac (bits per non-zero AC coefficient). The payloads 9% and 10% were chosen intentionally to see the effect of matrix embedding with Hamming codes (the 9% payload can be embedded with a more efficient code). The tested stego algorithms include F5 [43], –F5 [16], F5 without shrinkage [16] (nsF5), JP Hide&Seek[6], Model Based Steganography without deblocking [34] (MBS1), MMx [25], Steghide [19], Perturbed Quantization while double compressing [15](PQ) and its two modifications (PQt and PQe) as described in [16]). The cover images were prepared for every method as if zero message was embedded. The quality factor for the first seven methods was set to 70 and thus the cover images were single-compressed JPEGs with quality 70. Because the three versions of PQ produce double-compressed images, the covers were created by double-compressing the raw images with the same quality factors of 85 and 70.

The empirical estimates $MMD_u[\mathcal{F}, \mathbf{X}, \mathbf{Y}]$ were calculated from $D = 3000$ examples of $\mathbf{X}$ from the cover class and 3000 examples $\mathbf{Y}$ from the stego class embedded with a specific message length. In each test, the examples were always chosen so that each original raw image appeared either in $\mathbf{X}$ or in $\mathbf{Y}$ but never in both. We always repeated the calculation 100 times with a different split of the 6000 images and took the average as the value of MMD.

To make sure that the MMD was calculated in the same RKHS for every stego method and payload, we determined the whitening parameters and the Gaussian kernel width γ (by the "median" rule) only from the set of cover features $\mathbf{X}$.

In Figure 1 left, we show $-\log_{10} MMD[\mathcal{F}, \mathbf{X}, \mathbf{Y}]$ for 10 steganographic algorithms and 5 relative payloads. According to this benchmark, the PQ methods and the MMx are the least statistically detectable, while JP Hide&Seek, Steghide, and –F5 are the most detectable. F5 without shrinkage was the best algorithm that does not need side information (the raw image) at the embedder. The horizontal lines mark the value of MMD calculated from two disjoint samples of covers and thus indicate statistical undetectability with respect to the chosen feature set and database. One line is for 70% quality JPEGs for the algorithms producing single-compressed images, while the second line is for double-compressed covers for PQ, PQe, and PQt. We do not show the error bars from the bootstrap because the variances of MMD across different splits of the data set were too small to show in the graph.

To compare the MMD with previously used benchmarks, we show on the right the minimal decision error under equal priors $(P_{FA} + P_{MD})/2$, where P_{FA} is probability of false positives and P_{MD} the probability of missed detection, for a soft-margin SVM with a Gaussian kernel trained on the same data (one SVM was trained for each payload and method). This quantity was used for benchmarking in [16,38]. Despite the fact that both benchmarking methods estimate

---

[6] http://linux01.gwdg.de/~alatham/stego.html

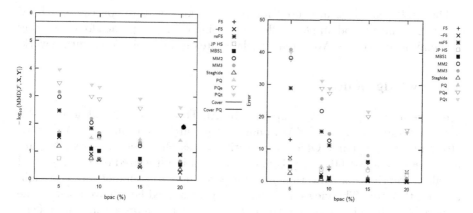

Fig. 1. MMD (left) and probability of error for an SVM (right) for 10 steganographic algorithms and 5 payloads. To obtain a better visual correspondence between the graphs, we show $-\log_{10} \text{MMD}[\mathcal{F}, \mathbf{X}, \mathbf{Y}]$. The horizontal lines indicate the threshold of undetectability determined as MMD from two samples of covers. Algorithms with MMD close to the line are recognized as secure with respect to the given set of features.

steganographic security in a different way, the graphs appear to be consistent in the sense that stego methods with small MMD tend to have higher classification error and vice versa. We stress that the computational complexity of calculating MMD is significantly smaller than that of training an SVM and calculating the probability of error.

The fast convergence rate and low estimation error even in high-dimensional spaces combined with low computational complexity make the MMD a potentially very useful steganographic benchmark.

6   Conclusions

We proposed a method for benchmarking steganographic schemes. The covers and stego images are first mapped to a feature space, which is viewed as a simplified model of natural images. The statistical detectability of a given method for a fixed payload is then evaluated as a measure of discrepancy between the sample pdf of cover and stego features. As a measure, we investigated the KL divergence and the two-sample statistics called Maximum Mean Discrepancy (MMD). Because the KL divergence is difficult to estimate accurately from sparse data in high-dimensional spaces, we proposed to use the MMD, which has properties useful for applications in steganography. The MMD has a fast convergence rate with respect to the number of data samples even in high-dimensional spaces. Moreover, its computational complexity is proportional to the square of the database size. The MMD thus replaces the need to train a classifier and enables evaluating statistical detectability from the features themselves. We demonstrate its use on 10 steganographic algorithms and compare the results with a previously used benchmarking method.

The MMD could be also used for benchmarking feature spaces for a fixed steganographic method and thus offers a very interesting approach for comparing steganalytic algorithms. We intend to elaborate on this topic in our future work.

Acknowledgments

The work on this paper was supported by Air Force Research Laboratory, Air Force Material Command, USAF, under the research grant number FA8750-04-1-0112 and by Air Force Office of Scientific Research under the research grant number FA9550-08-1-0084. The U.S. Government is authorized to reproduce and distribute reprints for Governmental purposes notwithstanding any copyright notation there on. The views and conclusions contained herein are those of the authors and should not be interpreted as necessarily representing the official policies, either expressed or implied, of AFRL, AFOSR, or the U.S. Government.

References

1. Avcibas, I., Kharrazi, M., Memon, N.D., Sankur, B.: Image steganalysis with binary similarity measures. EURASIP Journal on Applied Signal Processing 17, 2749–2757 (2005)
2. Avcibas, I., Memon, N.D., Sankur, B.: Steganalysis using image quality metrics. In: Delp, E.J., Wong, P.W. (eds.) Proceedings SPIE, Electronic Imaging, Security, Steganography, and Watermarking of Multimedia Contents III, San Jose, CA, January 22–25, vol. 4314, pp. 523–531 (2001)
3. Beirlant, J., Dudewicz, E., Gyorfi, L., van der Meulen, E.: Non-parametric entropy estimation: An overview. International Journal of Math. and Stat. Sci. 6, 17–39 (1997)
4. Boltz, S., Debreuve, E., Barlaud, M.: High-dimensional statistical distance for region-of-interest tracking: Application to combining a soft geometric constraint with radiometry. In: Proceedings IEEE, Computer Society Conference on Computer Vision and Pattern Recognition, CVPR 2007, Minneapolis, MN, June 18–23, pp. 1–8 (2007)
5. Cachin, C.: An information-theoretic model for steganography. In: Aucsmith, D. (ed.) IH 1998. LNCS, vol. 1525, pp. 306–318. Springer, Heidelberg (1998)
6. Chandramouli, R., Kharrazi, M., Memon, N.D.: Image steganography and steganalysis: Concepts and practice. In: Kalker, T., Cox, I., Ro, Y.M. (eds.) IWDW 2003. LNCS, vol. 2939, pp. 35–49. Springer, Heidelberg (2004)
7. Comesana, P., Pérez-Gonzáles, F.: On the capacity of stegosystems. In: Dittmann, J., Fridrich, J. (eds.) Proceedings of the 9th ACM Multimedia & Security Workshop, Dallas, TX, September 20–21, pp. 3–14 (2007)
8. Cover, T.M., Thomas, J.A.: Elements of Information Theory. John Wiley & Sons, Chichester (1991)
9. Dudley, R.M.: Real analysis and probability. Cambridge University Press, Cambridge (2002)
10. Eggers, J., Bäuml, R., Girod, B.: A communications approach to steganography. In: Delp, E.J., Wong, P.W. (eds.) Proceedings SPIE Photonic West, Electronic Imaging, Security, Steganography, and Watermarking of Multimedia Contents IV, San Jose, CA, January 21–24, vol. 4675, pp. 26–37 (2002)

11. Farid, H., Siwei, L.: Detecting hidden messages using higher-order statistics and support vector machines. In: Petitcolas, F.A.P. (ed.) IH 2002. LNCS, vol. 2578, pp. 340–354. Springer, Heidelberg (2003)
12. Franz, E., Schneidewind, A.: Pre-processing for adding noise steganography. In: Barni, M., Herrera-Joancomartí, J., Katzenbeisser, S., Pérez-González, F. (eds.) IH 2005. LNCS, vol. 3727, pp. 189–203. Springer, Heidelberg (2005)
13. Fridrich, J.: Feature-based steganalysis for JPEG images and its implications for future design of steganographic schemes. In: Fridrich, J. (ed.) IH 2004. LNCS, vol. 3200, pp. 67–81. Springer, Heidelberg (2004)
14. Fridrich, J., Lisoněk, P., Soukal, D.: On steganographic embedding efficiency. In: Camenisch, J.L., Collberg, C.S., Johnson, N.F., Sallee, P. (eds.) IH 2006. LNCS, vol. 4437, pp. 282–296. Springer, Heidelberg (2007)
15. Fridrich, J., Goljan, M., Soukal, D.: Perturbed quantization steganography. ACM Multimedia System Journal 11(2), 98–107 (2005)
16. Fridrich, J., Pevný, T., Kodovský, J.: Statistically undetectable JPEG steganography: Dead ends, challenges, and opportunities. In: Dittmann, J., Fridrich, J. (eds.) Proceedings of the 9th ACM Multimedia & Security Workshop, Dallas, TX, September 20–21, pp. 3–14 (2007)
17. Gretton, A., Borgwardt, K., Rasch, M., Schölkopf, B., Smola, A.: A kernel method for the two-sample-problem. Technical report, Max Planck Institute for Biological Cybernetics, Tübingen, Germany. MPI Technical Report 157 (2007)
18. Gretton, A., Borgwardt, K., Rasch, M., Schölkopf, B., Smola, A.: A kernel method for the two-sample-problem. In: Schölkopf, B., Platt, J., Hoffman, T. (eds.) Advances in Neural Information Processing Systems, vol. 19, pp. 513–520. MIT Press, Cambridge (2007)
19. Hetzl, S., Mutzel, P.: A graph–theoretic approach to steganography. In: Dittmann, J., Katzenbeisser, S., Uhl, A. (eds.) CMS 2005. LNCS, vol. 3677, pp. 119–128. Springer, Heidelberg (2005)
20. Ker, A.D.: Steganalysis of LSB matching in grayscale images. IEEE Signal Processing Letters 12(6), 441–444 (2005)
21. Ker, A.D.: A capacity result for batch steganography. IEEE Signal Processing Letters 14(8), 525–528 (2007)
22. Ker, A.D.: The ultimate steganalysis benchmark? In: Dittmann, J., Fridrich, J. (eds.) Proceedings of the 9th ACM Multimedia & Security Workshop, Dallas, TX, September 20–21, pp. 141–148 (2007)
23. Ker, A.D., Böhme, R.: A two-factor error model for quantitative steganalysis. In: Delp, E.J., Wong, P.W. (eds.) Proceedings SPIE, Electronic Imaging, Security, Steganography, and Watermarking of Multimedia Contents VIII, San Jose, CA, January 16–19, vol. 6072, pp. 59–74 (2006)
24. Kharrazi, M., Sencar, H.T., Memon, N.D.: Benchmarking steganographic and steganalytic techniques. In: Delp, E.J., Wong, P.W. (eds.) Proceedings SPIE, Electronic Imaging, Security, Steganography, and Watermarking of Multimedia Contents VII, San Jose, CA, January 16–20, vol. 5681, pp. 252–263 (2005)
25. Kim, Y., Duric, Z., Richards, D.: Modified matrix encoding technique for minimal distortion steganography. In: Camenisch, J.L., Collberg, C.S., Johnson, N.F., Sallee, P. (eds.) IH 2006. LNCS, vol. 4437, pp. 314–327. Springer, Heidelberg (2007)
26. Lyu, S., Farid, H.: Steganalysis using higher-order image statistics. IEEE Transactions on Information Forensics and Security 1(1), 111–119 (2006)
27. Miche, Y., Roue, B., Lendasse, A., Bas, P.: A feature selection methodology for steganalysis. In: Gunsel, B., Jain, A.K., Tekalp, A.M., Sankur, B. (eds.) MRCS 2006. LNCS, vol. 4105, pp. 49–56. Springer, Heidelberg (2006)

28. Moulin, P., Mihcak, M.K., Lin, G.I.: An information–theoretic model for image watermarking and data hiding. In: Proceedings IEEE, International Conference on Image Processing, ICIP 2000, Vancouver, Canada, September 10–13, vol. 3, pp. 667–670 (2000)

29. Noda, H., Niimi, M., Kawaguchi, E.: Application of QIM with dead zone for histogram preserving JPEG steganography. In: Proceedings IEEE, International Conference on Image Processing, ICIP 2005, Genova, Italy, September 11–14, pp. 1082–1085 (2005)

30. Petrowski, K., Kharrazi, M., Sencar, H.T., Memon, N.D.: Psteg: Steganographic embedding through patching. In: Proceedings IEEE, International Conference on Acoustics, Speech, and Signal Processing, Philadelphia, PA, March 18–23, 2005, pp. 537–540 (2005)

31. Pevný, T., Fridrich, J.: Towards multi-class blind steganalyzer for JPEG images. In: Barni, M., Cox, I., Kalker, T., Kim, H.-J. (eds.) IWDW 2005. LNCS, vol. 3710, pp. 39–53. Springer, Heidelberg (2005)

32. Pevný, T., Fridrich, J.: Merging Markov and DCT features for multi-class JPEG steganalysis. In: Delp, E.J., Wong, P.W. (eds.) Proceedings SPIE, Electronic Imaging, Security, Steganography, and Watermarking of Multimedia Contents IX, San Jose, CA, January 29 – February 1, vol. 6505, pp. 3-1-3-14 (2007)

33. Provos, N.: Defending against statistical steganalysis. In: 10th USENIX Security Symposium, Proceedings of the ACM Symposium on Applied Computing, August 13–17 (2001)

34. Sallee, P.: Model-based steganography. In: Kalker, T., Cox, I., Ro, Y.M. (eds.) IWDW 2003. LNCS, vol. 2939, pp. 154–167. Springer, Heidelberg (2004)

35. Schölkopf, B., Smola, A.: Learning with Kernels: Support Vector Machines, Regularization, Optimization, and Beyond (Adaptive Computation and Machine Learning). The MIT Press, Cambridge (2001)

36. Shi, Y.Q., Chen, C., Chen, W.: A Markov process based approach to effective attacking JPEG steganography. In: Camenisch, J.L., Collberg, C.S., Johnson, N.F., Sallee, P. (eds.) IH 2006. LNCS, vol. 4437, pp. 249–264. Springer, Heidelberg (2007)

37. Singh, H., Misra, N., Hnizdo, V., Fedorowicz, A., Demchuk, E.: Nearest neighbor estimates of entropy. American Journal of Math. and Management Sciences 23, 301–321 (2003)

38. Solanki, K., Sarkar, A., Manjunath, B.S.: YASS: Yet another steganographic scheme that resists blind steganalysis. In: Furon, T., Cayre, F., Doërr, G., Bas, P. (eds.) IH 2007. LNCS, vol. 4567, pp. 16–31. Springer, Heidelberg (2008)

39. Solanki, K., Sullivan, K., Madhow, U., Manjunath, B.S., Chandrasekaran, S.: Provably secure steganography: Achieving zero K-L divergence using statistical restoration. In: Proceedings IEEE, International Conference on Image Processing, ICIP 2006, Atlanta, GA, October 8–11, 2006, pp. 125–128 (2006)

40. Steinwart, I.: On the influence of the kernel on the consistency of support vector machines. Journal of Machine Learning Research 2, 67–93 (2001)

41. Steinwart, I., Hush, D., Scovel, C.: An explicit description of the Reproducing Kernel Hilbert Spaces of Gaussian RBF kernels. IEEE Transactions on Information Theory 52, 4635–4643 (2006); Los Alamos National Laboratory Technical Report LA-UR-04-8274

42. Sullivan, K., Madhow, U., Manjunath, B.S., Chandrasekaran, S.: Steganalysis for Markov cover data with applications to images. IEEE Transactions on Information Forensics and Security 1(2), 275–287 (2006)

43. Westfeld, A.: High capacity despite better steganalysis (F5 – a steganographic algorithm). In: Moskowitz, I.S. (ed.) IH 2001. LNCS, vol. 2137, pp. 289–302. Springer, Heidelberg (2001)
44. Xuan, G., Shi, Y.Q., Gao, J., Zou, D., Yang, C., Chai, Z.Z.P., Chen, C., Chen, W.: Steganalysis based on multiple features formed by statistical moments of wavelet characteristic functions. In: Barni, M., Herrera-Joancomartí, J., Katzenbcisser, S., Pérez-González, F. (eds.) IH 2005. LNCS, vol. 3727, pp. 262–277. Springer, Heidelberg (2005)

Information Hiding through Variance of the Parametric Orientation Underlying a B-rep Face

Csaba Salamon[1], Jonathan Corney[1], and James Ritchie[2]

[1] DMEM, University of Strathclyde, UK
[2] School of EPS, Heriot-Watt University, UK
Csaba.Salamon@strath.ac.uk, Jonathan.Corney@strath.ac.uk,
J.M.Ritchie@hw.ac.uk

Abstract. Watermarking technologies have been proposed for many different types of digital media. However, to this date, no viable watermarking techniques have yet emerged for the high value B-rep (i.e. Boundary Representation) models used in 3D mechanical CAD systems.

In this paper, the authors propose a new approach (PO-Watermarking) that subtly changes a model's geometric representation to incorporate a "transparent" signature. This scheme enables software applications to create fragile, or robust watermarks without changing the size of the file, or shape of the CAD model. Also discussed is the amount of information the proposed method could transparently embed into a B-rep model. The results presented demonstrate the embedding and retrieval of text strings and investigate the robustness of the approach after a variety of transformation and modifications have been carried out on the data.

Keywords: Digital Watermarking, Boundary representation (B-rep), Tweaking, Parametric orientation, Mechanical CAD.

1 Introduction

The increasing mobility of Computer Aided Design (CAD) data between design-centers, subcontractors and manufacturing facilities is creating a need to verify providence and protect the copyright of Boundary-representation (B-rep) CAD models.

Until recently, most intellectual property protection work has focused on audio, image and movie watermarking. But the spread of networks and digital multimedia materials, such as Web3D, MPEG4 and VRML has led to work on the development of watermarking techniques for 3D data represented as polygonal meshes. But despite the rapid evolution of dedicated hardware, software and methods to display and process 3D-CAD models effectively, no viable watermarking technique has yet emerged for the high value B-rep models used in mechanical CAD systems.

Our approach, called PO-Watermarking, described in this paper meets partly (and in some cases completely) many of the challenges associated with 3D CAD watermarking. The discussion at the end of the paper highlights the strengths and weaknesses of the proposed scheme in the context of mechanical CAD.

K. Solanki, K. Sullivan, and U. Madhow (Eds.): IH 2008, LNCS 5284, pp. 268–282, 2008.

The rest of this paper is structured as follows: the next section gives a brief summary of the requirements for watermarking three dimensional CAD models, while section three shows various established technologies for digital watermarking of 3D CAD models and methods of information encoding. Section four briefly reviews the nature of the B-rep data structure and describes the demands and processes B-rep data is exposed to. Section five describes the authors' proposed method with its possible applications. Section six presents testing procedures and results while sections seven and eight discuss the achievements of the work and lastly some conclusions are drawn.

2 Requirements for Digital Watermarking

One of the most important requirements of a watermark is its transparency. There are two kinds of transparency, namely functional and perceptual [1]. For most of the traditional data types such as image and audio data, transparency of a watermark is judged by human senses. If the original and watermarked data are indistinguishable to the human observer, then the watermark is perceptually transparent. For other data types, such as 3D geometric CAD data, transparency of the watermark is judged by considering if the functionality of the model is altered or not. For example, a perceptually transparent watermark incorporated in the CAD data of an engine cylinder may alter the shape of the cylinder enough (perhaps by only a few hundredths of a mm) to interfere with the simulated functionality of the engine.

According to the application purpose, watermarks can also be classified into robust and fragile schemes. Robust watermarking is usually designed for claiming ownership while fragile watermarking is used for digital content authentication and verification [2]. The design goal of robust watermarking is to make the embedded watermarks remain detectable after being attacked. In contrast, the requirements of fragile watermarking are to detect the slightest unauthorized modification. However, the requirements for watermarks to be both robust and transparent often contradict each other. In other words, making a watermark more robust tends to make it less transparent.

Other requirements for watermarking emerge when considering the representation of CAD models. It should be noted that many of these requirements are unique to B-rep CAD data and are not found in applications that use 3D mesh models. Specific features unique to the CAD applications are:

1. **No change in shape or dimension:** unlike mesh representations (e.g. VRML), B-rep models are required to support precision manufacturing. Consequently changes in shape are undesirable at any scale.
2. **Robust to translation:** it is common within CAD/CAM for an object to be translated between proprietary (e.g. .sat, .xt) and public (e.g. STEP, IGES) formats. Consequently it is desirable that any watermark should "survive" format translation.
3. **Robust to compression:** CAD data changes often between departments within a company or between sub-contractors and manufacturing facilities. Consequently very large sized files frequently need to be transmitted. Zip or Adobe 3D can be used to minimize the file size, however the embedded watermark should not be influenced or even erased while using these technologies.

4. **No incorporation of redundant entities:** internally commercial B-rep modeling systems use dramatically different precisions, and as a consequence translation is associated with so called "healing" operations that fill "virtual gaps" (between faces and their surrounding edges) and check data structures for redundancy or inaccuracies. Consequently a watermark based on the sub-division of faces or the splitting of edges is undesirable, as these might not be robust to the action of healing operations associated with common import/export functions.

5. **Robust to shape modification operations:** creation of models is labor intensive so designers will frequently "cut and paste" between old and new designs. However, despite this, it is rare for the origin of a new design to be explicitly documented and, as a consequence, impossible for an organization to track all the "parents" of a particular design. To facilitate this sort of traceability, once imported, a watermark should survive shape modification operations such as blending and Boolean operations (i.e. unite, subtract). In other words, if only a portion of a model is used the watermark should move with that volume.

3   Previous Work on 3D-Watermarking

In this section we provide a short overview of common algorithms for watermarking 3D models. In particular we consider the work of Ohbuchi et al. [3, 4] who proposed a large variety of techniques for embedding data into 3D polygonal mesh models. All watermarking algorithms developed by the authors are based on topological and geometrical modifications. For instance, the TSQ (Triangle Similarity Quadruple) embedding algorithm modifies vertices coordinates of four adjacent triangles to encode the watermark by setting the value of ratios between edge lengths of the triangle group. Another algorithm codes the hidden information by varying the ratio of tetrahedral volumes (TVR). Another algorithm proposed by Ohbuchi et al. is the TSPS (Triangle Strip Peeling Symbol) that uses topological modifications to embed a public watermark. Watermarks embedded by these algorithms are robust against some of the operations to which 3D models are routinely subjected such as affine transformation or arbitrary geometrical transformation [5]. However, at the same time they are not sufficiently robust enough for copyright protection, because they are vulnerable to common mesh operations e.g. remeshing, polygon simplification or noise addition [6].

The GEOMARK system developed by Benedens [7] implements three different algorithms: Vertex Flood Algorithm (VFA) for model authentication – a fragile watermark, the Affine Invariant Embedding algorithm (AIE) - robust against affine transformation of the model, and the Normal Bin Encoding (NBE) - robust against complex model modifications such as simplification and re-meshing. According to Corsini et al. [5] the novelty of this system is the combination of these three algorithms to obtain a watermarking scheme which is robust against randomization of vertices, mesh altering and polygon simplification operations.

Praun et al. [8] proposed a sophisticated robust mesh watermarking scheme that generalized a "spread spectrum" technique to 3D surfaces. First, they constructed a set of scalar basis functions over the mesh vertices using multi-resolution analysis and then perturbed vertices along the direction of the surface normal weighted by the basis functions. Their watermarking scheme is resistant to common mesh attacks such as translation, rotation, scaling, cropping, smoothing, simplification and re-sampling operations.

Another way to encode information into a 3D model is to fill the model with carrier objects that carry the watermark data as presented by Sonnet and Lange [9]. These carrier objects offer several possibilities to encode information in the form of binary codes. Amongst these possibilities are: object transformation such as rotation and scaling, the topology of the carrier object and the material's color can all be used for information encoding. Compared to other watermarking methods, the embedded data is imperceptible and robust to common geometric transformations. Besides this, the scheme enables to hide large amounts of data (several megabytes). On the negative side, by changing the model's triangle structure in file format conversion, it destroys the embedded data. Also, decreasing the accuracy of the model's geometry influences the embedded watermark.

Other digital watermarking methods proposed by Ohbuchi and Masuda [1] focus on providing authentication, tamper-detection, IP protection and other security related operations for 3D geometric CAD models consisting of parametric B-spline curves and surfaces (NURBS). Their two algorithms employ knot insertion and rational linear reparameterization to watermark NURBS curves and surfaces. The two approaches are called: Rational-Linear Reparameterization Based Algorithm and Knot Insertion Based Algorithm. Both methods preserve the exact geometric shape of NURBS curves and surfaces and the one based on reparameterization also preserves data size. However, the watermark embedded by this approach is not robust to some attacks. The second approach based on knot insertion, is robust against attempted removal. Obviously this approach is applicable only to shapes that contain NURBS geometry and the effects of format translation to IGES and STEP are unclear.

As presented above, nearly all 3D watermarking methods, schemes and algorithms are designed to work with shapes represented by meshes of polygons. Only Ohbuchi and Masuda [1] consider B-rep NURBS as a carrier of watermarks. But perhaps more importantly, no authors deal with the fact that those watermarked CAD data might be compressed for transmission or might be translated into neutral file formats such as IGES or STEP which could drastically influence the encoded information.

4 Boundary Representation

Before discussing the options for B-rep watermarking it is useful to briefly review the nature of the B-rep data structure. All commercial mechanical CAD systems use complex boundary representations to model shapes with great precision. Boundary representations, as the name suggests, define shapes in terms of their surface (i.e. the boundary between material and air; Figure 1). Early in the development of boundary representations it was realized that there were advantages in separating topology and geometry in the data structure. Hence the B-rep defines networks of boundary relationships between entities such as faces and edges that make no reference to their shape.

In this scheme the shapes of faces are defined by underlying surfaces characterized by analytical, parametric equations (e.g. plane, cone, sphere, torus). Similarly, edges are defined as the intersection curves of the surfaces of the adjacent faces. Likewise, vertices define the end point of curves and arise from the intersections of two or more edges.

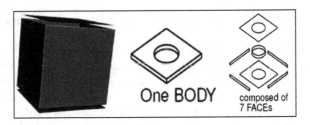

Fig. 1. Boundary representation of a 3D model

Consequently, the B-rep is a much richer and more complex data structure than the meshes of planar facets commonly used to define shape in digital animations. However the high degree of interconnections within the data structure means that even small changes have to be made with care. The interdependence inherent in the B-rep data structure is well described by Stroud [10] who says:

> "... the shape of an edge cannot be changed without changing the position of the surface, unless the new curve also lies in the surfaces of the faces adjacent to the edge. Similarly the position of vertices can not be changed unless they lie on the curves of all edges meeting at the vertex and hence the vertex position lies on the surfaces of all the faces meeting at the vertex."

Furthermore, the numerical values used to determine when geometry is coincident (i.e. "on") also vary greatly. In addition to this inherent sensitivity to change, watermarking also has to cope with the technologies (i.e. IGES, STEP and healing) developed to allow B-rep models to move between different vendor's CAD systems each with different precisions and formats.

Possible Mechanisms for watermarking B-rep faces

Given these constraints, what methods of watermarking might work for B-reps? The authors considered the following:

- **Explicit attribute addition:** it would be an easy task to associate additional data (i.e. attributes) with the entities of a model and with closed proprietary formats this information would be hard to see or remove. However such information would be lost during system translation, and consequently such a system would be limited in its scope.
- **Local operation to modify geometry:** there is a class of model editing operations known as "local ops" that facilitate small changes on geometry (e.g. offsetting, surface substitution etc.) that could be used to introduce a geometric watermark. However such an approach would not meet the "no change in shape" requirement.
- **Micro imprinting:** a Boolean operation could be used to "stamp" a pattern onto faces of the model (in other words create inner edge loops). Such a pattern could be so small as to be invisible to the naked eye and would not cause any change to the overall shape of the model. However, it could be easily removed by healing operations that detect its redundant nature.

- **Non-manifold entity addition** (flap faces, internal shells, and wire edges): visibly insignificant geometry could be created inside the model. Although this approach is potentially resistant to healing and would not change the external shape, such an approach could still create problems for CNC and RP systems that derive their movement directly from B-rep data. Furthermore, non-manifold geometry can be easily removed by standard modeling utilities.

Considering these constraints the authors hypothesize that a simple but effective watermark might be possible by altering the orientation of the parametric surfaces underlying B-rep geometry (see Figure 2).

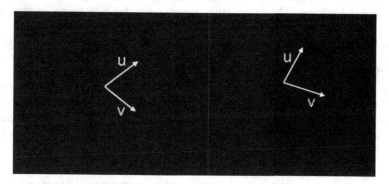

Fig. 2. ISO-parameter lines showing surface orientations

All faces (e.g. plane, cylinders, spheres etc.) have a parametric representation that allows them to be traversed in terms of (u, v) coordinates. The orientation of the u-v parameterization is largely determined by the operations used to create the model (i.e. the orientation of bodies united and subtracted to define the shape). The following section describes this approach in more detail and discusses the feasibility of using the orientation of a face's underlying geometry as a vehicle for watermarking.

5 Method Overview

Despite the complexity of the B-rep data structure many operators (e.g. Booleans, blending, warping) exist which modify a model's shape while automatically maintaining the integrity of the data structure. One well-known operator, termed a "tweak", modifies a face's surface (i.e. its geometry) and then automatically updates its topology (i.e. adjacency relationships) to accommodate the new surface. The key observation underlying the tweaking process is that if a face has been slightly changed (i.e. transformed) in some way, the edges which bound it can be recalculated by:

1. Intersecting the new (i.e. transformed) surface with the surface of each adjacent face: remember that the surface is the underlying, unbounded geometry on which the face sits - even if the existing face does not extend far enough to perform the intersection, the surface does. This process will define the curves, underlying the edges, which bound the "new" geometry of the face.

2. Intersecting each new curve with its neighbors will determine the bounding vertices of the updated edges.

So it is essential, when a new surface is inserted or modified by rotation of its parametric representation, that the tweaking process automatically intersects it with all the adjacent faces and so recalculates the geometry of the bounding edge's curves.

5.1 Proposed Scheme

Our watermarking scheme, called PO-Watermarking (Parameterization Orientation), is based on tweaking functions which are designed to enable operations such as offsetting or local editing. They also offer opportunities for inserting a watermark by varying the orientation of the underlying parametric surface. In other words, faces with different shapes can be tweaked (i.e. rotated) to *change the orientation of their defining surfaces without changing their shapes*. Figure 2 illustrates a component before (left) and after (right) all of its faces were rotated about their face normal vectors. To make this change visible the orientation of the u/v axis on one planar face are highlighted with white arrows. We have investigated the feasibility of encoding watermarks by tweaking the surface geometry of individual faces on the model. An overview of the proposed watermarking process is presented in the flowchart below (Figure 3).

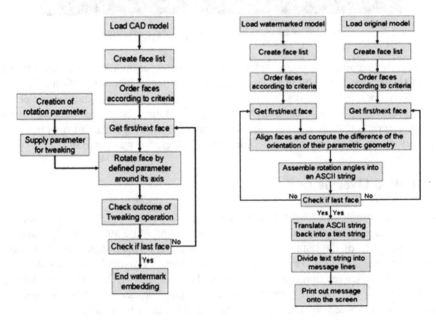

Fig. 3. Flowcharts of tweaking process (left) and retrieval process (right)

After loading a CAD model the program creates a list of planar, conical, spherical and toroidal faces and orders them on the basis of a criterion (e.g. surface area) from small to large. In the case of two or more faces with equal ranking another ordering is carried out which arranges them according to a series of criteria such as the lengths of their circumference and/or the number of edges and lastly the distance of a face centre from a plane defined by the principle axis of inertia. In the case of remaining identical (i.e. equal ranked) faces the first face will be chosen for watermark embedding.

5.2 Fragile Watermarking

Having established the number and order of faces to host the watermark, the next step is to determine the angle of each surface rotation, the magnitude of which is in fact the embedded information.

The angle for rotation of each face depends on the information to be encoded and its function. When the user enters product, or security, related information into the systems interface (Figure 4) the program arranges the text-information into a single line (text string) and converts it into ASCII code (ASCII string) (Figure 5).

Part number:	12-3456789-00-V01
Company name:	ALBATROSS
Contact details:	www.albatross.com

Fig. 4. Entry of information for embedding

Arranged information:

#12-3456789-00-V01#ALBATROSS#www.albatross.com#

ASCII code:

#049050045051052053054055056057045048048045...#...

Data embedding:

#049050045 051052053 054055056 057045048048...#...#

49.050045°	51.052053°	054.055056°	
for first face	for second face	for third face	....

Fig. 5. Information conversion and encoding

The ASCII standard defines numerical values, letters and specific characters using numbers between 32 and 127 (e.g. the number 101 is defined to be the letter "e"). In other words, a triple-digit is required to encode a single letter of the English alphabet. Investigations by the authors have suggested that rotation with up to six decimal places (no rounding influence) can be robustly applied to the model, so each face could potentially encode 3 letters in the following way:

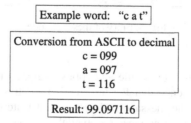

Example word: "c a t"

Conversion from ASCII to decimal
c = 099
a = 097
t = 116

Result: 99.097116

So a rotation of 99.097116° of a face encodes the word "cat". Large strings of text can be encoded across ordered sequences of faces in the following way.

Embedding procedure

Given a component with N distinctly different (i.e. differing area, shape or relative location) faces, it can hold up to 3N characters in the following way:

1. A list of faces is extracted from the model and ordered by geometric criteria as described above
2. Surface rotation watermark is applied to each face in the ordered list encoding three characters on each face (Figure 6).

This procedure is carried out until the whole information is encoded and embedded into the model. So, the more faces a model has, the more information can be embedded.

Retrieval procedure

The scheme described is a "Private Watermark" meaning that the original CAD model is required to decode the embedded information (Figure 4). This procedure can be summarized as follows:

1. A list of faces is extracted from both original and watermarked models and ordered using the same criteria as for embedding.
2. Faces of equal characteristics (e.g. area, circumferences, etc.) are aligned and the orientation of their parametric geometry computed.

The difference in angle between original and watermarked data (e.g. 28.097218) is broken into three triple-digit numbers (e.g. 028, 097 and 218) and converted back into readable text. This "re-gained" information is then made visible.

5.3 Robust Watermarking

The angle of rotation for robust watermarking is created in almost the same way as for fragile watermarking. However, in this case only a short data string such as a message digest (Figure 6) is converted into decimal value (Figure 7). When the code is converted the character's position (sequence number) is added (e.g. position 1 for K, position 2 for 5, position 3 for P, etc.). This enables the reassembly of the message digest characters when reading out. In this way the watermark on each face contains information analogous to a "packet" number in digital communication protocols.

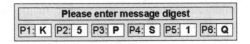

Fig. 6. Entry of message code

Embedding procedure

The embedding procedures for fragile and robust watermarking are the same, however with the slight difference that the information for fragile watermarking is embedded only once while the message code for robust watermarking is embedded as often as possible (i.e. as long as faces are available). The reason for this is that if a model with a fragile watermark is altered the single embedded fragile information would be destroyed (unreadable), and so the CAD model would lose its signature. On

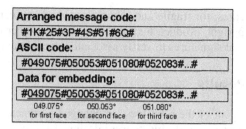

Fig. 7. Message code conversion

the other hand, for robust watermarking, the message code is embedded until the model is "full". This would increase the chances that despite modification to the model fractions of the code could be recovered to recreate the message digest.

Retrieval procedure

Here again the retrieval process for robust and fragile watermarking are very similar. The faces of the original and the watermarked models are ordered and aligned and the orientation of their parametric geometry is computed. While the fragile watermark is read out once, the robust watermark is retrieved several times (dependent on the size of the CAD file, or up to a user specified limit). In this way we can recover several duplicates of the embedded message code. Should there be any changes to the water-marked model, or if portions of the embedded data got lost (e.g. in translation), it is still possible to recreate the whole message within a few steps. These steps (illustrated in Figure 8) can be summarized as follows:

1. Read out orientation angle of 6 faces (Figure 8 illustrates only 6 faces but obviously this can be extended).
2. Convert orientation value back into readable text.
3. Sort message characters according to their position in the encoded data (recall that the sequence, or packet, number is encoded within the embedding process) and assign them to rows in the message recovery matrix (Figure 8).
4. By identifying common elements in each column of the message recovery matrix reconstruct the original watermark message digest code.

Now this "regained" message digest can be used to verify the correctness of any data or documents associated with the model.

| | Embedded message code | | | | | |
	P1	P2	P3	P4	P5	P6
Reading 1	K	5	P	S	1	
Reading 2		5	P		1	Q
Reading 3	K		P		1	Q
Reading 4		5		S	1	Q
Reading 5		5	P	S	1	
Reading 6	K		P	S		Q
Result:	K	5	P	S	1	Q

Fig. 8. Watermark recovery matrix

Both of these procedures, for fragile and robust watermarking, can be used to embed tracking devices, copyright, product, text, archiving, or any other type of confidential information (e.g. digital signatures to verify associated documents).

6 Testing and Results

To enable the assessment of the robustness of changed parameterization in mechanical CAD models, a series of test objects were designed in Solid Edge and translated into .sat file format. For these tests a watermark embedder and reader were written in C++ using the V16 of the ACIS kernel modeler.

This program was written to enable the rotation of the underlying parametric surfaces. For the purposes of the investigation the "easily" tweakable planar, closed conical, toroidal and spherical surfaces were modified, those with complex boundaries (i.e. geometry that could create chiralities in the solution) were stepped over at this stage, but will be considered in future embedding and testing procedures.

For further processing the models were imported into ACIS 3DT and healed to accommodate any differences between their originating CAD system's (i.e. the Parasolid kernel) representation and internal accuracy and ACIS. After embedding a watermark into a model the following series of transformations and modification where undertaken to test the robustness of the PO watermark:

- Export/import from SAT file to Solid Edge.
- Blending/chamfer of edges with constant radius blend/by 45 degree.
- IGES export/import: from SAT file into IGES and back into SAT format.
- STEP export/import: from SAT file into STEP and back into SAT format.
- Zip compression and decompression of CAD data.
- External Boolean subtract: remove the half of the model.
- Adding new component parts to the model.

After each of these operations the models were translated back into ACIS .sat format and the orientation of the tweakable faces recorded by the PO-watermark reader. The tests have been carried out using arbitrary values of rotation to test the robustness of the proposed PO watermarking scheme. The results are summarized in Table 1 where the second left column records how many faces of each type in the test object were watermarked, while the subsequent columns record how many of these orientations were still readable after each modification.

Although the number of detectable watermarks (recorded in the table) is lower after the Boolean subtraction, it represents a 100% success rate amongst the surfaces not removed or directly involved in the operation (the subtraction operation literally removed half the model). The orientation of the parametric surfaces is also unchanged by blending or chamfer their edges, adding new components to the model, or zip compression.

However, the tests have also shown some unexpected results for the effects of translation: for example, watermarks applied to planar (but not cylindrical) faces survive the IGES translation process, while STEP appears to preserve the orientation of cylinders (but not planes). The authors assume that this "phenomenon" is associated with, or generated by the way in which neutral formats represent the geometry of parametric surfaces. Future work will investigate this behavior.

Table 1. Test results of file conversion and model modification

Test object	After watermarking	Export/import into SolidEdge	After IGES export/import	After STEP Export/import	Zip compression	Blending of edges	Chamfer of edges	External Boolean	Adding components
	Planar 43 Cone 10 Torus 0 Sphere 0	Planar 43 Cone 10 Torus 0 Sphere 0	Planar 43 Cone 0 Torus 0 Sphere 0	Planar 0 Cone 10 Torus 0 Sphere 0	Planar 43 Cone 10 Torus 0 Sphere 0	Planar 45 Cone 10 Torus 0 Sphere 0	Planar 53 Cone 7 Torus 0 Sphere 0	Planar 18 Cone 3 Torus 0 Sphere 0	Planar 43 Cone 10 Torus 0 Sphere 0
	Planar 83 Cone 15 Torus 0 Sphere 34	Planar 83 Cone 15 Torus 0 Sphere 0	Planar 83 Cone 0 Torus 0 Sphere 0	Planar 0 Cone 15 Torus 0 Sphere 0	Planar 83 Cone 15 Torus 0 Sphere 0	Planar 87 Cone 13 Torus 0 Sphere 21	Planar 85 Cone 10 Torus 0 Sphere 18	Planar 40 Cone 5 Torus 0 Sphere 0	Planar 83 Cone 15 Torus 0 Sphere 34
	Planar 152 Cone 58 Torus 0 Sphere 0	Planar 152 Cone 58 Torus 0 Sphere 0	Planar 152 Cone 0 Torus 0 Sphere 0	Planar 0 Cone 45 Torus 0 Sphere 0	Planar 152 Cone 45 Torus 0 Sphere 0	Planar 150 Cone 45 Torus 0 Sphere 0	Planar 154 Cone 62 Torus 0 Sphere 0	Planar 74 Cone 22 Torus 0 Sphere 0	Planar 152 Cone 58 Torus 0 Sphere 0
	Planar 3 Cone 9 Torus 2 Sphere 0	Planar 3 Cone 9 Torus 1 Sphere 0	Planar 3 Cone 0 Torus 0 Sphere 0	Planar 0 Cone 9 Torus 1 Sphere 0	Planar 3 Cone 9 Torus 1 Sphere 0	Planar 1 Cone 9 Torus 1 Sphere 0	Planar 1 Cone 7 Torus 1 Sphere 0	Planar 1 Cone 3 Torus 1 Sphere 0	Planar 3 Cone 9 Torus 2 Sphere 0

Working with native .sat files both embedder and reader displayed a status output onto the screen and also wrote to a text file (Figure 9).

Before watermarking:	After watermarking:
planar watermark 0.000000,-1000.000000,0.000000	planar watermark 0.000000,-933.315112,359.058354
planar watermark -1000.000000,0.000000,0.000000	planar watermark -933.315112, 0.000000,359.058354
planar watermark 1000.000000,0.000000,0.000000	planar watermark 933.315112,359.058354, 0.000000
cone watermark 0.000000,0.000000,10.000000	cone watermark 0.000000, -3.590584, 9.333151
planar watermark 0.000000,0.000000,-1000.000000	planar watermark 0.000000,359.058354,-933.315112
planar watermark 1000.000000,0.000000,0.000000	planar watermark 933.315112, 0.000000,359.058354
torus watermark 0.000000, 0.000000, 1.000000	torus watermark 0.000000, 0.359058, 0.933315
sphere watermark 1.000000, 0.000000, 0.000000	sphere watermark = 0.933315, 0.359058, 0.000000
sphere watermark 1.000000, 0.000000, 0.000000	sphere watermark = 1.000000, 0.000000, 0.000000
sphere watermark 1.000000, 0.000000, 0.000000	sphere watermark = 0.933315, 0.359058, 0.000000
sphere watermark 1.000000, 0.000000, 0.000000	sphere watermark = 1.000000, 0.000000, 0.000000
cone watermark -20.000000,0.000000,0.000000	cone watermark -18.666302, -7.181167, 0.000000
planar watermark 1000.000000,0.000000,0.000000	planar watermark 933.315112,359.058354, 0.000000
planar watermark -1000.000000,-0.000000,0.000000	planar watermark -933.315112, -0.000000,359.058354
cone watermark 15.000000,0.000000,0.000000	cone watermark 13.999727, 0.000000, 5.385875

Fig. 9. Output of PO-watermark extractor

Figure 9 shows the parametric orientation of the different faces of a test object (Figure 10) before (left) and after (right) watermark embedding with six decimal places containing the embedded information. Faces with zero values for x, y and z coordinates, shown in the left column, contain no information at all. Faces in the right column are carrying the intended message. Here, faces with zero values for their co-ordinates show that the embedding process was not successful or this particular face was not considered for tweaking.

The results show that even using a very limited form of PO-watermarking it was possible to modify the geometry of a significant number of entities on a 3D model without significant increase in data structure size or changes to the model's shape. As Figure 10 shows the PO-watermark did not increase the size of the model data[1] and survived file conversion and model modification processes.

---

[1] The difference in file size in Table 1 is due to a side effect of the tweaking api (Application Procedural Interface) which created a bulletin board attribute for each of the changed faces. These can be easily removed and are not an inherent part of the model.

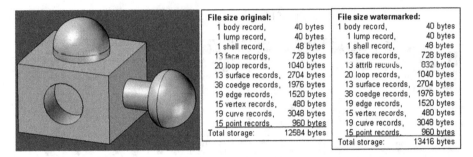

File size original:		File size watermarked:	
1 body record,	40 bytes	1 body record,	40 bytes
1 lump record,	40 bytes	1 lump record,	40 bytes
1 shell record,	48 bytes	1 shell record,	48 bytes
13 face records,	728 bytes	13 face records,	728 bytes
20 loop records,	1040 bytes	13 attrib records,	832 bytes
13 surface records,	2704 bytes	20 loop records,	1040 bytes
38 coedge records,	1976 bytes	13 surface records,	2704 bytes
19 edge records,	1520 bytes	38 coedge records,	1976 bytes
15 vertex records,	480 bytes	19 edge records,	1520 bytes
19 curve records,	3048 bytes	15 vertex records,	480 bytes
15 point records,	960 bytes	19 curve records,	3048 bytes
Total storage:	12584 bytes	15 point records,	960 bytes
		Total storage:	13416 bytes

Fig. 10. Test object with data structure before and after surface tweaking

7 Discussion

When considering the results, the approach described in this paper meets some of the requirements for 3D-watermarking presented in section two. Regarding file size and transparency, because the PO watermark does not exist in form of "added" data and does not increase the size of the CAD model data, it is difficult to estimate that additional information is hidden within the cover data, even when comparing it with the original unmarked data. Nor has the watermark any influences on the model's appearance when examined on a CAD system.

The Boolean, chamfer and blending results are understandable: any efficient algorithm will leave geometry not involved in the operation untouched and so it is reasonable to conclude, unless the watermarked surface is removed from the model, its orientation will not be changed. Even adding new components and faces has no influence on the watermark recognition. However, when reading out the watermark after blending and chamfering modification the reader shows sometimes more and sometimes less tweaked faces than actually exist (false positive identification). The authors believe this behavior reflects the process used to create chamfers where parametric orientation is inherited from the adjacent faces during the edge offset stage.

Finally, we can say that despite shape modification and native data export/import and data compression/decompression the watermark has survived and represents a robust characteristic.

However, the face ordering process has a number of negative effects (i.e. limitations). For instance, when ordering faces on a symmetric model it is difficult to identify a suitable or unique face for tweaking because all identical faces have the same characteristics. This leads to the fact that it cannot be guaranteed that exactly the same face is used for tweaking and watermark recovery, which might cause a false positive detection. Consequently, the face ordering process needs to be based on more sophisticated testing.

It is also surprising to see that IGES and STEP formats have effects on the CAD model. At first thought one might expect the behavior of the IGES and STEP translators to be predictable. The standards define the types of surface entities each can represent and so it should be clear if parametric orientation will be preserved. However there is choice in both which entities a cylinder is mapped to and how the geometry is represented internally within the translation system. Some systems translate all geometric surface entities to NURBS, others hold analytical representations. In many cases the preservation of parametric orientation will be down to a programmer's whim rather than the specific requirements of Part 42 of ISO 10303 and consequently the behavior can only be determined experimentally. Therefore, the behavior of PO-watermarks in translation to STEP/IGES is an area of further study for the authors.

Compared to other established watermarking algorithms for polygonal meshes or NURBS, our PO-watermarking scheme based on B-reps opens new ways/possibilities to hide information robustly into mechanical CAD data. For instance, Ohbuchi's method [1] could only be applied to B-spline surfaces and could not be used (unlike the PO-Watermark method) to watermark analytical surfaces like planes, cylinders and other face types, which are very common in mechanical CAD systems.

8 Conclusion

The PO-watermark appears to offer a simple and effective way of identifying and tracking B-rep models within a homogenous industrial CAD/CAM environment (i.e. one supplier, no translation). Additionally, this method can also be used for identifying the licensee or to prove ownership in dispute by showing a robust attribute to modification. The amount and uniformity of the surface rotation within a model can be varied to encode information in a manner analogous to the vertex moving watermarks applied to mesh models. However, the approach must be considered fragile at this stage as the combination of STEP and IGES translation is able to "wash" the watermark out of the model.

Future work will investigate translation issues and the magnitude limits of PO watermarking: what is the smallest and largest change in orientation that can be robustly recorded?

Compression/decompression of watermarked data with different systems (e.g. Adobe 3D) and the enlargement of this approach to achieve a public watermark are also areas of interest to the authors.

References

[1] Ohbuchi, R., Masuda, H.: Managing CAD data as a Multimedia Data Type Using Digital Watermarking. In: IFIP TC5 WG5.2 Workshop on Knowledge Intensive CAD to Knowledge Intensive Engineering, Deventer, The Netherlands, pp. 103–116 (2000)

[2] Chou, C., Tseng, D.: A public fragile watermarking scheme for 3D model authentication. Computer-Aided Design 2006 38, 1154–1165 (2006)

[3] Ohbuchi, R., Masuda, H., Aono, M.: Watermarking Three-Dimensional Polygonal Models. In: ACM International Multimedia Conference 1997, Seattle, Washington, USA, November 9-13, pp. 261–272 (1997)

[4] Ohbuchi, R., Mukaiyama, A., Takahashi, S.: A Frequency-Domain Approach to Watermarking 3D Shapes. Eurographics 2002 21(3), 373–382 (2002)

[5] Corsini, M., Barni, M., Bartolini, F., Caldelli, R., Cappellini, V., Piva, A.: Towards 3D watermarking technology. In: IEEE EUROCON 2003 Conference, Ljubljana, Slovenia, September 22-24, pp. 393–396 (2003)

[6] Rušinović, Z., Mihajlović, Ž.: Robust Watermarking for 3D Objects. In: MIPRO 2005: Hypermedia and GRID systems, Opatija, Croatia, 30 May-3 June, pp. 271–276 (2005)

[7] Benedens, O.: Geometry-Based Watermarking of 3D Models. IEEE Computer Graphics and Applications, 46–55 (January/February 1999)

[8] Praun, E., Hoppe, H., Finkelstein, A.: Robust Mesh Watermarking. In: International Conference on Computer Graphics and Interactive Techniques, pp. 49–56 (August 1999)

[9] Sonnet, H., Lange, S.: Carrier Objects as Illustration Watermarks for 3D Polygonal Models. In: Simulation und Visualisierung, pp. 305–316 (March 2005)

[10] Stroud, I.: Definition of solid modelling operations using uniform set of elementary procedures. In: GML 1992/3 Computer and Automation Institute, Hungarian Academy of Sciences, p. 89 (1992)

A Supraliminal Channel in a Videoconferencing Application

Scott Craver, Enping Li, Jun Yu, and Idris Atakli

Department of Electrical Engineering, Binghamton University

Abstract. Unlike subliminal or steganographic channels, a supraliminal channel encodes information in the semantic content of cover data, generating innocent communication in a manner similar to mimic functions. These low-bitrate channels are robust to active wardens, and can be used with subliminal channels to achieve steganographic public key exchange. Automated generation of innocent-looking content, however, remains a difficult problem.

Apple's iChat, a popular instant-messaging client and the default client on the Macintosh operating system, includes a video chat facility that allows the user to apply special effects such as replacing the user's background with a video file. We show how this can be used to implement a high-bitrate supraliminal channel, by embedding a computer animation engineered to communicate ciphertext by its pseudo-random behavior.

1 Introduction

The concept of supraliminal channels was introduced in 1998, as a steganographic primitive used to achieve public key exchange in the presence of an active warden.[1] Alice and Bob must communicate in the presence of Wendy, a warden; they have no shared keys in advance, and must enact a key exchange to use a steganographic algorithm. However, any overt key exchange is evidence of secret communication, and any steganographic bits embedded with a known key can be damaged by Wendy. Supraliminal channels allow robust and innocuous transmission of public key data in this environment.

In this paper, we describe how a new feature added to the video chat capabilities of iChat for the Apple Macintosh allows supraliminal content to be attached to a videoconferencing session. By implementing animation primitives that covertly accept ciphertext from an external application, and then fold this ciphertext into the evolution of a computer animation, ciphertext can be transmitted within the semantic content of the video.

This paper is organized as follows: in section 2, we review supraliminal channels and outline an efficient protocol to achieve a supraliminal channel from a steganographic channel and an image hash. In section 3 we explain our overall philosophy of data hiding and how it differs from the traditional approach of imperceptibly modifying cover data. In section 4 we describe our software architecture, and in section 5 the results of our supraliminal channel.

K. Solanki, K. Sullivan, and U. Madhow (Eds.): IH 2008, LNCS 5284, pp. 283–293, 2008.
© Springer-Verlag Berlin Heidelberg 2008

2   Supraliminal Channels

Unlike a steganographic channel, in which a multimedia object is indetectibly modified, a supraliminal channel chooses or controls the semantic content of the cover data itself. This can be achieved by a cover data generation program, or mimic function which transforms an input string reversably into a convincing piece of cover data. [2]. However, we will show that overt content generation is not strictly necessary to construct a supraliminal channel. Supraliminal channels are not keyed, and are readable by the warden. The main purpose of such a channel is ensuring total robustness of the message in the presence of an active warden, even if the embedding and detection algorithm is known. This follows from an assumption that the warden is allowed to add noise, but not make any modifications that effect the semantic meaning of the cover data being sent.

If Alice and Bob use such a channel to send a meaningful message, it will be readable to Wendy; however, they can send strings which resemble channel noise, so that Wendy cannot tell if an image is purposely generated. This is sufficient to transmit key data in order to accomplish key exchange, after which the shared key can be used in a traditional steganographic channel. The combination of a key exchange using subliminal and supraliminal channels achieves so-called *pure steganography*, that is, secure steganography without prior exchange of secret data. [1]

2.1   A Two-Image Protocol for Supraliminal Encoding

If one has a very low bitrate cover data hash function, it can be extended into a higher bitrate supraliminal channel by bootstrapping a keyed steganographic algorithm and extending the transmission over multiple steps. Suppose that Alice and Bob have access to a cover data hash algorithm $h : I \to \{0,1\}^n$. As a toy example, a recipient can choose a single word that best describes an image I, or other descriptive text suitably derived from I, and let $h(I)$ be the SHA-256 hash of that text.

This alone is not suitable for a supraliminal channel, firstly because the bit rate is extremely low, and secondly because the hash cannot be inverted into a generation function. However, Alice can perform the following:

1. Alice chooses two natural cover images I and J.
2. Alice embeds a message m in J, using a robust keyed steganographic algorithm with the hash of I as a key:

$$\hat{J} = \texttt{Embed}(m, J, \texttt{key} = h(I))$$

3. Alice sends $\hat{J}$ to Bob.
4. Bob confirms receipt of $\hat{J}$.
5. Alice sends I.
6. Bob (and Wendy) can extract the message $m = \texttt{Detect}(\hat{J}, h(I))$

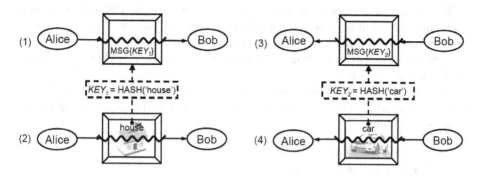

Fig. 1. The two-image protocol for establishing a supraliminal channel from an image hash. Alice and Bob's transmissions are each split across two images, with the semantic content of the second keying the steganographic content of the first.

This *two-image* protocol is illustrated in figure 1. Note that the message is public; the purpose of the channel is robust transmission without requiring a known key in advance, essentially robust publication. This approach to public-key steganography was introduced by Anderson, Petitcolas and Kuhn, requiring a keyed steganographic transmission followed by a broadcast of the key after the data is known to be securely received. [3] The authors point out that a broadcast of a key is suspicious, but can be plausibly explained in certain scenarios; this protocol exhibits such a scenario, by replacing the broadcast with the transmission of an arbitrary message.

This approach to creating a supraliminal channel has several desirable advantages. First, it can use any cover data hash algorithm, which need not be invertible. Second, it does not require any algorithm to *generate* content, which is difficult. Instead, Alice chooses a key by arbitrary choice of natural content.

2.2   Public Key Encoding

As mentioned above, the message m must be as statistically meaningless as channel noise—that is, it must resemble channel noise that would be found if Wendy attempted to decode an innocent message. In the sequel, we will show a channel where a computer animation, originally driven by a pseudo-random number generator, is instead driven by message bits. This means that if message bits are computationally indistinguishable from the PRNG output, it can be sent over the channel. This goal is trivially achievable if the PRNG is, say, a counter-mode AES keystream.

For this reason, we consider the problem of packaging key data to resemble n-bit strings of i.i.d. fair coin flips. Public keys are randomly generated, so it may seem that they can be convincingly disguised as random strings; however, keys have structure, as well as unlikely mathematical properties. An RSA key's modulus is not any random number, but one that just happens to be difficult to factor—a relative rarity among random strings.

To achieve random packaging of a public key, we use the Diffie-Hellman key exchange with a public prime p for which the discrete logarithm function is hard, and a generator for $\mathbb{Z}/p\mathbb{Z}$. Alice must transmit a single value $A = g^a \pmod{p}$ for a secret a, and Bob transmits the value $B = g^b \pmod{p}$. Thereafter their session key is $B^a = g^{ab} = A^b$.

The value of A is uniformly chosen over $p - 1$ values, and must be shaped so that it is uniform over all n-bit strings, where $n = 1 + \lfloor \log_2 p \rfloor$. The algorithm to do so is simple:

1. Set $n = 1 + \lfloor \log_2 p \rfloor$;
2. Generate a uniform n-bit number a;
3. `if`$(0 < a \le p - 1)\{$
     set $A = g^a \pmod{p}$;
   $\}$
4. else if $(n \ge p) : \{$
         repeat: $\{$
                 Choose b uniformly among $\{1, 2, \cdots p - 1\}$;
                 set $B = g^b \pmod{p}$;
                 set $A = p + B$;
         $\}$ while$(A \ge 2^n)$;
   $\}$
5. else set $A = 0$;[1]

This algorithm encodes a number of the form $g^a \pmod{p}$ such that any n-bit string is equally likely to be observed.

3   Manufacturing a Stego-Friendly Channel

The most common approach to steganography entails the subtle modification of a fixed but arbitrary piece of cover data. This must be performed so that no statistical test can distinguish between natural and doctored data. The challenge of this approach is that we have no complete statistical model for multimedia data, and cannot guarantee that any artificial modification of cover data can go undetected.

A second approach to steganography avoids "natural" data and instead places bits in simpler, artificial content, for example TCP packet timestamps or the ordering of note-on messages in MIDI data. [4,5]. While this data may be statistically simpler to characterize, the same modeling problem prevents an absolute guarantee of secrecy; another problem with this approach is that discrete data is often easy to overwrite without harming the content.

A third, extreme approach is to design a form of communication that makes an ideal cover for data embedding, and somehow convince the public to use it. Thus instead of using natural data, artificial data is *made natural* by placing it in common use. As a toy example, one could create a popular multi-player game

---

[1] Key exchange therefore fails with probability 2^{-n}, a virtual impossibility but necessary to make the distribution truly uniform.

or other multi-user application, and design a messaging protocol that makes considerable use of i.i.d. bit strings as random nonces. These could then be replaced by ciphertext to establish a covert channel.

The obvious flaw in this plan is convincing a large group of people to start using and sending the type of data we want. Users will not adopt a new media format *en masse* simply because it makes steganography harder to detect [2]. However, each emerging trend in social networking carries with it the possibility of an ideal stego channel.

3.1   Apple iChat

In late 2007, Apple announced version 10.5 of their operating system, Mac OS X. This included an extension to their bundled iChat instant messaging software that allows the user to apply special effects to a video chat session. Special effects include camera distortions, various image filters, and the ability to replace the user's background with a specific image or video file. The software allows users to drop in their own image and video backdrops. In January 2008, the operating system market share statistics for Mac OS X is a bit more than 7%. [7]

The authors suspected that if the software allowed image and video backdrops, then it would allow arbitrary multimedia files adhering to Apple's QuickTime standard. This includes *Quartz Compositions,* computer animations represented as programs rather than static multimedia data. Quartz Compositions are used within Mac OS X as animations for screen savers and within applications. They are composed of flow graphs of rendering and computation elements, called *patches,* that reside in user and system graphics libraries.

The ramifications of a computer-generated backdrop in a popular video chat application are significant: computer animations are often driven or guided by pseudo-random number generators, and if by some device we could replace the pseudo-random data with ciphertext, then we have a supraliminal channel within a video chat application. As long as an animation uses pseudo-random data transparently enough that the PRNG bits can be estimated from the video at the receiver, then *some of the semantic content of the video is generated from message bits.* The fact that this is possible within the default instant messaging client of a popular operating system creates the opportunity for a plausible, but stego-friendly form of communication.

3.2   Cultural Engineering

Social engineering is the act of beating a security system by manipulating or deceiving people, for example into revealing confidential information or granting

---

[2] This approach was taken to its logical extreme in 2001, when a software developer announced a simple LSB-embedding steganographic tool on Usenet cryptography fora. When people pointed out the well-known statistical attacks on brute LSB embedding, the author responded with the astonishing argument that if only the public would start randomizing the LSB planes of their images, his stego-images would be harder to detect. [6]

access to an adversary. [8] On a larger scale than the individual, we have the possibility for *cultural engineering*: achieving a security goal by swaying society in general towards a certain behavior. Popularizing a steganographically friendly form of communication is a form of cultural engineering.

A cultural shift that has greatly affected the status of cryptography is the public embrace of the Internet for electronic commerce, and other applications requiring secure HTTP connections. This made the public use of encryption far more common; not only did this phenomenon make encryption less conspicuous, but it fostered a general public expectation of privacy-enhancing technologies.

4   Software Overview

Our data-hiding channel is concealed in a computer animation, whose pseudo-random number generator occasionally outputs ciphertext. The overall transmitter architecture is shown in figure 2. The iChat application hosts a computer animated backdrop; the computer animation contains a doctored pseudo-random generator, that retrieves pseudo-random bits from an external server. The server can be fed data from an application, and outputs either pseudo-random bits or ciphertext bits.

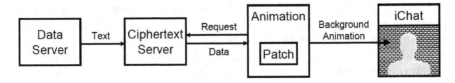

Fig. 2. The transmission pipeline. Data is fed to a ciphertext server, polled by a doctored PRNG patch in an animation.

The server is a rudimentary Tcl program with C extensions for generating pseudo-random data. It generates pseudo-random data using 128-bit AES in counter mode; when fed a request for data, of the form "$\{o\|b\|h\}$ [number]," the server returns a number of octal, binary, or hexadecimal digits from its store. The request "i $\{H\|C\}$ [data]" causes the server to input a data string specified either in hexadecimal or character format; upon future requests for random bits, this message data is exclusive-ored with the keystream.

4.1   Quartz Composer Animations

A Quartz Composition is a computer animation represented as a flow graph of fixed "patches." Patches are encapsulated procedures for rendering or computation with published inputs and outputs; they reside in system and user libraries, which can be extended with user-designed patches.

The animation we used for our experiments is a randomly changing grid of colored squares diagrammed in figure 4. The "ciphertext server" patch is a customized patch which connects to our server to retrieve pseudo-random data. The

```
#!/usr/bin/tclsh
set port 8080
proc answer {sock host2 port2} { fileevent $sock readable [list serve $sock] }
proc serve sock {
        fconfigure $sock -blocking 0 -translation binary
        gets $sock line
        if {[fblocked $sock]} return
        fileevent $sock readable ""
        set response [myServe $line]
        puts $sock $response; flush $sock
        fileevent $sock readable [list serve $sock]
}
puts "Bit server running on port $port, socket=[socket -server answer $port]."
vwait forever
```

Fig. 3. The 14-line ciphertext server, adapted from a 41-line web sever in [9]

data is requested as a string of octal digits, which are converted to the hue of each column. The remainder of the animation uses standard Quartz Composer patches.

4.2   Receiver Architecture and Implementation Issues

To establish a channel, the captured video at the receiver must be analyzed to estimate the pseudo-random bits used to drive the background animation. This requires that the animation uses its bits in a suitably transparent way, and that the background state can be estimated while partially occluded by a user. For our experiments, we capture the video on the receiving end as a video file for analysis; in the future we will implement a real-time receiver that polls the contents of the iChat video window.

Using our Ciphertext server and customized patch, a designer only needs to compose a computer animation, and write a corresponding C function to estimate the PRNG state given bitmap frames from the received video. The server, patch and receiver code is already written.

One implementation issue we have encountered is sandboxing of Quartz compositions by Apple. Because of the clear security risk of video files that can covertly access one's file system or connect to the Internet, Quicktime Player refuses to load any custom patches, and limits native patches that access the outside world, such as RSS readers. This prevented our customized patch from connecting to our server whenever it was installed as a backdrop for iChat.

Fortunately, the sandboxing was relatively simple to override. By examining the binary files of existing patches, we found that Quartz Composer patches simply implement the class method +(BOOL) isSafe, which by outputs NO. Subclassing the patch class circumvents this measure. This cannot be accomplished

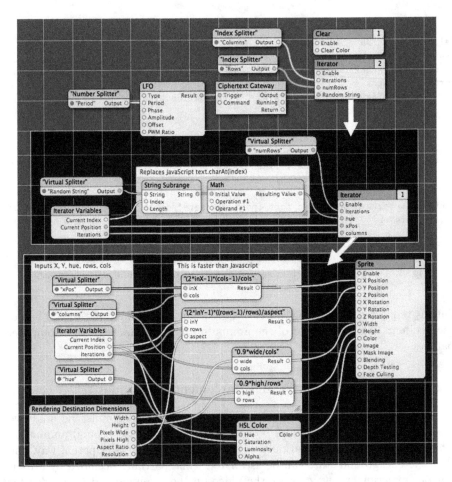

Fig. 4. Quartz composer flow-graph for our sample animation. At the top, the "Ciphertext Gateway" is polled by a clock to update the state of the display. The animation contains two nested iterators to draw columns and rows of sprites (blocks).

through Apple's public API, however; the public API does not allow a programmer to implement a patch directly, but only a "plug-in" object, a wrapper through which isSafe cannot be overridden. The ciphertext server patch had to be written directly as a patch, using undocumented calls [3].

Another implementation issue concerns random delays in rendering. When immersed in iChat, our animations do not render regularly, but experience random lag times between updates. This is a minor problem, because iChat does not *skip* frames of our animation; it merely delays animation frames over more frames. This only limits the speed of supraliminal transmission, and does not

---

[3] We are indebted to Christopher Wright of Kineme.net whose expertise on the undocumented API made our patch possible.

result in the dropping of message bits. To cope with the delays our decoder must be asynchronous, identifying from the received video when the animation has changed its pseudo-random state. This is easily accomplished with our animation, because block hues are dramatically altered across the entire frame during a state transition.

5   Results

For purposes of designing an optimal animation, we measured per-pixel occlusion of the iChat application. Pixels can be occluded either by the user in the foreground, or by misalignment of the camera or changes in lighting that confuse the background subtraction algorithm. We first replaced iChat's backdrop with a frame of bright green pixels, recorded the output as a video file, and computed the fraction of pixels in each pixel position position that were blocked. An occlusion graph for a 16-minute video chat is shown in figure 5.

Based on this data we determine that a pseudo-random state should be estimable given the upper left and right corners of video. We produced several animations that only utilized the top band of the frame, and could easily embed more data per frame by incorporating more of the sides of the frame. One animation featured a grid of colored blocks. We transmitted this backdrop with varying periods and grid sizes—each column transmits three bits of data. Decoding was accomplished by estimating the hue of the topmost row of blocks. The results of decoding are shown in figure 6.

These results show a limit of approximately 8 animation frames per second effectively transmitted, and to our surprise the BER decreased as we increased

Fig. 5. Average occlusion of background pixels over 31369 frames (16 minutes 28 seconds) of a video chat session

Blocks	Attempted period (s)					Blocks	Attempted period (s)			
	0.5	0.25	0.125	0.05			0.5	0.25	0.125	0.05
8	0.002	0.005	0.087	0.095		8	2.01	4.25	8.14	7.58
16	0.00	0.004	0.069	0.101		16	2.07	4.08	7.62	8.31
32	0.003	0.095	0.045	0.062		32	2.02	4.12	7.57	7.74
64	0.002	0.0015	0.003	0.006		64	2.05	4.01	7.36	8.21

Fig. 6. BER (left) and block rows transmitted per second (right) with our animation/decoder pair, for several block sizes and attempted periods

the block size. We believe this occurs because errors are largely due to intermittent errors, rather than general noise prohibiting hue estimation. This result indicates that backdrop computer animations can easily leak hundreds or thousands of bits per second. Hence this channel is suitable for public key exchange, and has a suitable bitrate for transmitting text messages as well.

Fig. 7. Supraliminal backdrops. On the left, colored blocks. On the right, the users's office superimposed with rain clouds. The animations are driven either by pseudo-random bits or ciphertext, estimable by the recipient.

6   Discussions and Conclusions

We have illustrated a means to smuggle ciphertext into a pseudo-random data source driving a computer animation, which can then be added as a novelty backdrop for a popular video chat application. The pseudo-random bits can be estimated at the other end of the channel, allowing the leakage of ciphertext.

Rather than hiding our information imperceptibly in the background noise of a multimedia file, we embed quite literally *in the background*, in an extremely perceptible fashion. Rather than achieving imperceptibility, we instead seek a different goal: plausible deniability. The background animation is obvious but plausibly deniable as innocent. Since it comprises the semantic content of the video, a warden cannot justifiably change it.

Our channel is designed so that new and creative animation/decoder pairs are easy to create. Once a designer has installed our ciphertext/PRNG patch and the corresponding server, designing a transmitter is a simple matter of using the patch in a Quartz Composition, a step that requires no coding. Decoding requires the implementation of a C function that inputs each video frame as a bitmap, and can estimate message bits. If the designer creates an animation whose bits are suitably estimable, for example our backdrop of colored squares, the decoder can be easily written. Data rates of thousands of bits per second are possible if the animation is properly designed. We hope that this framework will spur creative development of animation/decoder pairs, and encourage further search for possible supraliminal channels in emerging social networking applications.

Acknowledgments. This research was made possible by the generous support of AFOSR, under grant FA9550-05-1-0440.

References

1. Craver, S.: On public-key steganography in the presence of an active warden. In: Aucsmith, D. (ed.) IH 1998. LNCS, vol. 1525, pp. 355–368. Springer, Heidelberg (1998)
2. Wayner, P.: Disappearing Cryptography: Information Hiding: Steganography & Watermarking, 2nd edn. Morgan Kaufmann, San Francisco (2002)
3. Anderson, R.J., Petitcolas, F.A.P.: On the limits of steganography. IEEE Journal of Selected Areas in Communications 16(4), 474–481 (1998)
4. Giffin, J., Greenstadt, R., Litwack, P.: Covert messaging through TCP timestamps. In: Dingledine, R., Syverson, P.F. (eds.) PET 2002. LNCS, vol. 2482, pp. 194–208. Springer, Heidelberg (2003)
5. Inoue, D., Matsumoto, T.: Scheme of standard MIDI files steganography and its evaluation. In: SPIE Security and Watermarking of Multimedia Contents IV, vol. 4675, pp. 194–205 (2002)
6. Szopa, A.S.: New steganography innovation from ciphile software (August 2001) `talk.politics.crypto, 3B894FCE.FC4B729E@ciphile.com`
7. NetApplications.com: Operating system market share for January (2008), `http://marketshare.hitslink.com/report.aspx?qprid=8`
8. Mitnick, K., Simon, W.: The Art of Deception: Controlling the Human Element of Security. John Wiley & Sons, Chichester (2002)
9. Tcl programming, `http://en.wikibooks.org/wiki/Tcl_Programming/Print_version`

C-Mix: A Lightweight Anonymous Routing Approach

Vinayak Kandiah, Dijiang Huang, and Harsh Kapoor

Arizona State University

Abstract. Low latency mix networks such as onion routing (Tor), heavily utilize cryptographic operations for transmitting a message to the receiver resulting in substantial computational and communication overhead. To address the performance and security issues of low latency mix networks, we propose a novel anonymous routing scheme called C-Mix. Its design principles are inspired by network coding techniques and the properties of polynomial interpolation. Based on our security analysis and performance evaluations, C-Mix achieves same level of anonymity with comparable computation overhead in comparison to traditional low latency mix networks.

1 Introduction

Communication networks are used in various activities of our everyday life and have become commonplace. A significant portion of the communications taking place over a conventional wired network requires both cryptographic security and user anonymity. Cryptographic security ensures secrecy of the message while user anonymity deals with hiding the identities of the communicating users and the routing path in the network. Several techniques have been proposed to achieve anonymity over communication networks [1,2,3,4]. Extensive research has taken place in the last few decades in a great effort to keep data communications private and anonymous. One main class of solutions that achieves user and path anonymity is based on *Onion Routing*, such as [5,3] and I2P [6], which provide anonymity for low latency networks using cryptographic operations and overlay techniques. Under normal circumstances, mix networks which use several Chaumian nodes provide anonymity, i.e. attackers cannot gain end-to-end routing information from the network. However, they are vulnerable to various active and passive attacks [7,8,9,10,11]. Many implementations of anonymous services for low latency networks and the Internet such as Tor and I2P [5,6] are based on onion routing. For example, onion routing (Tor) performs multiple encryptions and decryptions for both path setup phase and data forwarding phase. The amount of computation performed by the sender of a message (i.e., the sender performs multiple encryption for both path set up and data transmissions) is not commensurate with the computation at the other nodes in the network. Hence, scalability suffers when implemented in networks with low computation capability. This situation is especially true when a user wants to voluntarily use his/her

K. Solanki, K. Sullivan, and U. Madhow (Eds.): IH 2008, LNCS 5284, pp. 294–308, 2008.

non-high-performance computer (no dedicated hardware for cryptography computation) as a relay node to improve the communication anonymity. Thus, it is highly desirable to improve the computation efficiency of mix networks.

To address above describe issues of Mix networks, we present a novel technique – C-Mix – a coding inspired anonymous routing scheme. This new technique is inspired by network coding [12] where the information is processed and coded by each forwarding node. However, instead of using XOR coding method, we utilize the properties of polynomial interpolations [13] to achieve our security goal. In particular, the proposed anonymous scheme requires the use of the onion structure (public key cryptography) only during the path setup phase. Once a packet forwarding path has been established, no encryption/decryption is required to forward messages. C-Mix reconstructs the message in a distributed hop-by-hop manner. In this way, the intermediate nodes are only required to perform a few multiplications and addition operations over a finite field $\mathbb{Z}_p$ instead of performing the decryption operation. As a result, less computation efforts required at mix nodes in the network, thus improving the efficiency of the system. When compared to AES encryption/decryption, C-Mix significantly reduces the computation involved at the sender nodes and some improvements are achieved at forwarding nodes as well. Specifically, in cases where the size of the message is significantly greater than the size of the finite field $\mathbb{Z}_p$, our scheme greatly reduces the computational overhead at the mix nodes. The primary goal of this new technique is to introduce a novel Mix technology to reduce the computational overhead for Mix nodes. At the same time, it provides same level of anonymity and security as onion routing based mix schemes under strong attack models. Compared to existing low-latency mix networks, C-Mix is built on a stronger attack model, i.e., the adversaries are global passive or active observers. We evaluate the security and anonymity performance of C-Mix under insider colluding attacks, blending attacks, and traffic analysis attacks. The message secrecy can be proven based on the polynomial interpolation properties. We will show that C-Mix has levels of security and anonymity akin to those of the onion routing–based mix networks. Performance testing of the underlying mathematical techniques used in the proposed scheme has been done using real experiments.

The rest of the paper is organized as follows. Section 2 contains the system and models that will be used in C-Mix. In section 3, the formal mathematical foundation of C-Mix is provided. The security, anonymity and performance of the proposed scheme is analyzed and compared with onion routing in section 4. Finally, the scope for future work and concluding remarks are provided in section 5.

2   System and Attack Model

In this section, we first present the fundamentals of polynomial interpolation and the attack models used to evaluate the proposed technique.

2.1   Polynomial Interpolation and Secret Sharing

Polynomial Interpolation based secret sharing scheme [13] has been proposed to share a secret among N_{usr} entities such that any $t \leq N_{usr}$ entities can recover the secret but any $t' < t$ entities know no more about the secret than any non-participating entity. This scheme is based on the interpolation property of polynomials computed over a finite field $\mathbb{Z}_p$ according to which, a polynomial equation $y(x)$ of degree $(t-1)$ can be reconstructed only if at least t points that lie on $y(x)$ are available. A degree $t-1$ polynomial of the form

$$y(x) = a_0 + a_1 x + a_2 x^2 + a_3 x^3 + \ldots + a_{t-1} x^{t-1} \tag{1}$$

is constructed, where a_0 equals the secret S (i.e., the y-intercept of the curve) and the other coefficients $a_1, a_2, \ldots, a_{k-1}$ are chosen randomly over the field $\mathbb{Z}_p$. Now, N_{usr} points $\{(x_j, y_j) | 1 \leq j \leq N_{usr}\}$ on the curve are obtained and distributed to the participating entities. Any t of these N_{usr} entities can combine their points to reveal the secret. The polynomial $y(x)$ can be reconstructed using the Lagrange Interpolation formula. If the points are represented as $\{(x_1, y_1), (x_2, y_2), \ldots, (x_t, y_t)\}$, the Lagrange Interpolation formula is given by:

$$y(x) = \sum_{i=1}^{t} b_i y_i \qquad \text{where, } b_i = \prod_{k=1, k \neq i}^{t} \frac{x - x_k}{x_i - x_k}. \tag{2}$$

The traditional secret sharing scheme is operated in a centralized system, i.e., all participants submit their points to a server which computes the secret. In C-Mix, we need to decentralize the secret sharing algorithm, and we require that without the destination's involvement, intermediate nodes cannot collude to derive the secret.

2.2   Attack Model

We now present the attack models, against which the new scheme is evaluated. The attacks chosen in this paper are the ones that are commonly used to evaluate an anonymous routing scheme. In addition, these attacks are representative of the various classes of attacks like passive/active, internal/external. A passive attack is one where the adversary does not modify or alter the functioning of the anonymous scheme. An active attack on the other hand involves some form of intentional modification to the working of the scheme by the attacker like dropping, modifying or delaying the messages. An external attack is a form of attack where the adversary only has access to the communication links and hence cannot affect the intermediate nodes and an internal attack is one where the adversary can observe and/or modify the internal operations performed by the forwarding intermediate nodes in the network. We do not make restrictive assumptions for the attack models enabling us to evaluate our new scheme against a powerful adversary. Proving the anonymity and security of our scheme against a powerful attacker will obviously show the scheme's security and anonymity in a practical attack which may be less powerful. Without losing generality, our discussion focuses on three attacks. The collusion attack is an internal attack, where two or more forwarding nodes share all their knowledge regarding the data transmissions. The blending [7] and traffic analysis attacks are external. However, the blending attack is active while the traffic analysis attack is passive. The C-Mix relies on hop-by-hop in-network data processing, and it does not use cryptographic method to protect the message integrity. We assume that the end-to-end message integrity checking is at the application layer. In section 4, we examine the security and anonymity provided by our scheme when these attacks are deployed.

3   C-Mix Anonymous Routing Scheme

In this section, we start with the principles of our approach and then iteratively refine it by adding new mechanisms to increase the security and anonymity of the scheme. A list of symbols that are frequently used in the description of the C-Mix is provided in Table 1.

C-Mix involves three phases: virtual circuit setup, data transmission, and virtual circuit termination, which are described as follows. However, unlike onion routing, we do not use any form of symmetric encryption or decryption during the data transmission phase. We do not provide much detail about the circuit termination phase as breaking down a virtual circuit is trivial and can be performed by transmitting some equivalent of a KILL message.

Virtual Circuit Setup. In the circuit initiation phase, the sender (or source) identifies the path to be followed to the intended receiver (or destination). Let

Table 1. List of Symbols

Symbol	Description
General	
L	Number of forwarding nodes on the path.
INIT	Integer value chosen by sender for circuit initiation.
$y_{init}(x)$	Polynomial used by sender for circuit initiation.
M_i	Forwarding node i.
sd	Sender.
dn	Destination.
NUM	Number of messages to be transmitted.
I_α	Indicates the current message being transmitted ($1 \leq \alpha \leq NUM$).
$y_\alpha(x)$	Curve chosen by sender for message α.
C-Mix Scheme	
$b_{init(i)}$	Secret b value for node i obtained during circuit initiation.
(x_i, y_i)	Secret point for node i obtained at circuit initiation.
$(x_{\alpha(L+2)}, y_{\alpha(L+2)})$	Point chosen by sender for transmission of message α.
$b_{\alpha(i)}$	b value to be used by node i for transmission of α message.

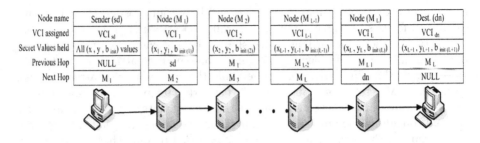

Fig. 1. Circuit Setup: Information distributed to the C-Mix nodes

there be L forwarding nodes in the path, which means $L + 2$ nodes (including sender and destination) are involved in the complete route. The sender now prepares an INIT value which is an integer over a finite field $\mathbb{Z}_p$. In rest of the paper, we assume all calculations are done over a finite field $\mathbb{Z}_p$ and we do not explicitly show it. The sender now chooses a polynomial $y_{init}(x)$ over the field $\mathbb{Z}_p$ which has INIT as the y–intercept:

$$y_{init}(x) = \text{INIT} + a_1 x + a_2 x^2 + a_3 x^3 + \ldots + a_L x^L.$$

The curve $y_{init}(x)$ has a degree L and the sender now determines $L + 1$ points that lie on it as $\{(x_1, y_1), (x_2, y_2) \ldots, (x_L, y_L), (x_{L+1}, y_{L+1})\}$. Now, in order to recompute the INIT value, we can substitute $x = 0$ and $t = L + 1$ in (2) to obtain these new equations:

$$y_{init}(0) = \text{INIT} = \sum_{i=1}^{L+1} b_{init(i)} \, y_i, \qquad \text{where} \quad b_{init(i)} = \prod_{k=1, k \neq i}^{L+1} \frac{x_k}{x_k - x_i}. \qquad (3)$$

Now, the sender calculates the values $(b_{init(i)} | 1 \leq i \leq L + 1)$ over the field $\mathbb{Z}_p$. In the circuit initiation phase, the INIT message need not be actually transmitted to the destination. The sender just uses this phase to distribute *triplets* of the form $(x_i, y_i, b_{init(i)}) \, | 1 \leq i \leq L)$ to the L forwarding nodes and the triplet $(x_{L+1}, y_{L+1}, b_{init(L+1)})$ to the destination. The x_i, y_i and $b_{init(i)}$ values will be used in the data transmission phase. Thus, the sender uses an onion to securely transmit the triplets to all forwarding nodes and the destination. The sender first prepares a header for the destination which contains the triplet $(x_{L+1}, y_{L+1}, b_{init(L+1)})$ and the public keys of the forwarding nodes in the path. This header is then encrypted using the destination's public key. To the resulting cipher text, the sender attaches a header containing $(x_L, y_L, b_{init(L)})$ along with the next hop and Time To Live (TTL) and encrypts the resulting content with the forwarding node M_L's public key. (Note that M_L is the last forwarding node on the path from sender to destination). In this way, the sender continues adding headers and encrypting iteratively in the reverse order of the path (i.e. last public key encryption will be using M_1's public key). The sender then transmits this onion message into the network. Each intermediate forwarding node i upon decryption of the onion message will perceive the message as:

$$\{nextHop, \{(x_i, y_i, b_{init(i)})\}, TTL, \{payload\}\},$$

where the $\{payload\}$ is an inner onion message. The first forwarding node M_1 on the path receives the onion message from the sender and decrypts it using its private key to read the header. M_1 realizes that this is a request to create a virtual circuit and hence generates a new VCI for this communication interface. The forwarding node then associates the previous hop, next hop and the triplet $(x_1, y_1, b_{init(1)})$ with the VCI and stores this information. This indicates to M_1 that for future data transmissions through the same interface it will have to use $(x_1, y_1, b_{init(1)})$ to operate on the message and forward it to the next hop (indicated by the VCI). In this way, as the onion message is transmitted through the network, a virtual circuit is created from the sender to the destination.

The triplets obtained by each node should not be disclosed as they are considered as secrets and will be used in the data transmission phase. The sender also retains all the triplets that it calculated and transmitted for this path. Note that each pair of neighboring nodes will choose their own VCI for the circuit being created. When the onion message reaches the destination the last layer of the onion message is decrypted and the destination obtains the triplet $(x_{L+1}, y_{L+1}, b_{init(L+1)})$. Figure 1 shows the values that each node on the path from sender to destination will store after the transmission of this onion message. Also in figure 1, though the previous hop of M_1 shows sd and the next hop of M_L shows dn these are not revealed as the sender and destination. This is because sd and dn are just identifiers of the nodes and are no different from the identifiers M_1 or M_L. We just use the sd and dn notations to clearly show the sender and destination to the reader. The destination will also receive the public keys of all the intermediate nodes in this path in the innermost layer of the setup message along with the triplet. Using these public keys, the destination now prepares a reply onion to the sender which will be sent through the reverse path (i.e. $M_L \rightarrow M_{L-1} \rightarrow \ldots M_1 \rightarrow Sender$). The sender on receiving this reply onion will know that the virtual circuit to the destination has been successfully setup and is ready for data transmission.

Data Transmission Phase. Let us assume that there are NUM messages to be sent by the sender. The sender then maps these NUM data packets to integers $I_1, I_2, \ldots, I_{NUM}$ over the field $\mathbb{Z}_p$ using a publicly known two–way function $Map()$. This function $Map()$ could be sent to the destination using the onion header during the circuit setup phase. To transmit an integer I_α, where, $1 \leq \alpha \leq NUM$, the sender uses the point $(0, I_\alpha)$ along with the points $\{(x_1, y_1), (x_2, y_2), \ldots, (x_L, y_L), (x_{L+1}, y_{L+1})\}$ to compute a polynomial $y_\alpha(x)$ of degree $L + 1$ using polynomial interpolation. The sender can now identify a new point $\{x_{\alpha(L+2)}, y_{\alpha(L+2)}\}$ that lies on the polynomial $y_\alpha(x)$. The construction of the curve $y_\alpha(x)$ and its relationship with the initial curve $y_{init}(x)$ are shown in figure 2. The nodes on the path already possess $L + 1$ points that lie on the

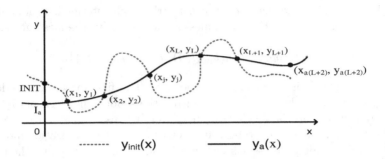

Fig. 2. Relationship between Circuit Initiation and Message Transmission Curves

polynomial $y_\alpha(x)$, i.e., the points $\{(x_1, y_1), (x_2, y_2), \ldots, (x_L, y_L), (x_{L+1}, y_{L+1})\}$ that were distributed during circuit setup. If we consider $\{x_{\alpha(L+2)}, y_{\alpha(L+2)}\}$ being the $L + 2^{th}$ point, then the sender along with the destination and the L forwarding nodes now have the potential to recalculate I_α using the following equations which are derived from (3):

$$y_\alpha(0) = I_\alpha = \sum_{i=1}^{L+2} b_{\alpha(i)} \, y_i \qquad \text{where,} \; b_{\alpha(i)} = \prod_{k=1, k\neq i}^{L+2} \frac{x_k}{x_k - x_i}. \tag{4}$$

For nodes $i = 1 \ldots L+1$ (i.e. the forwarding nodes and the destination), $b_{\alpha(i)}$ can be calculated as:

$$b_{\alpha(i)} = b_{init(i)} \, \frac{x_{\alpha(L+2)}}{x_{\alpha(L+2)} - x_i}. \tag{5}$$

From (5), each node i (where, $1 \leq i \leq L+1$) can calculate the $b_{\alpha(i)}$ values from $b_{init(i)}$, x_i and $x_{\alpha(L+2)}$. Each node i knows its $b_{init(i)}$ and x_i, and hence only needs the $x_{\alpha(L+2)}$ value. Also, the nodes are distributed over a network and hence the calculation specified in (4) should be done in a distributed manner while ensuring that the destination is able to determine I_α. The following procedure ensures that these requirements are satisfied.

1. The sender uses (4) to obtain $b_{\alpha(L+2)}$ from which $b_{\alpha(L+2)} \cdot y_{\alpha(L+2)}$ can be calculated.
2. The sender transmits this along with $x_{\alpha(L+2)}$ to the forwarding node M_1. (Note that the sender can calculate $b_{\alpha(L+2)}$ as it has stored all the points it distributed to the other nodes).
3. The intermediate node M_1 now computes $b_{\alpha(1)} \cdot y_1$ and adds this to the value $b_{\alpha(L+2)} \cdot y_{\alpha(L+2)}$ received from the previous hop to generate a new payload. (Note that the node can calculate $b_{\alpha(1)}$ using (5)). This new payload is then transmitted to M_2 along with $x_{\alpha(L+2)}$.
4. M_2 performs operations similar to node M_1 and forwards the payload to the next hop along the path.

This procedure is continued until the destination adds $b_{\alpha(L+1)} \cdot y_{L+1}$ to the payload it receives to reveal I_α. Remember that all the above calculations are performed over the finite field $\mathbb{Z}_p$.

An Example of Using C-Mix Basic Scheme. A simple example is provided to illustrate the operations of the C-Mix basic scheme. To simplify the presentation, the following example is demonstrated over the characteristic field zero. Assume the following 3-hop routing path for this example: $sd \to M1 \to M2 \to dn$, where sd is the sender and dn is the destination. Hence, for this case $L = 2$. Let the INIT value chosen by the sender be 20 and let the polynomial of degree 2 be: $y_{init}(x) = 20 + 4x + 3x^2$. The sender then locates the following 3 points on the curve: $\{(1, 27), (2, 40), (3, 59)\}$. The sender also calculates the $b_{init(i)}$ values as: $b_{init(1)} = 3$, $b_{init(2)} = -3$, $b_{init(dn)} = 1$. The sender distributes the triplets $\{(1, 27, 3), (2, 40, -3), (3, 59, 1)\}$ to the forwarding nodes and the destination. This completes the circuit setup phase. Now, let us assume that the sender needs to transmit $I_1 = 31$ to the destination. The sender first constructs a polynomial of degree 3 (as, $L + 1 = 3$) using the following points: $\{(0, 31), (1, 27), (2, 40), (3, 59)\}$. The resulting polynomial of degree $L + 1 = 3$ is $y_1(x) = -\frac{11}{6}x^3 + 14x^2 - \frac{97}{6}x + 31$.

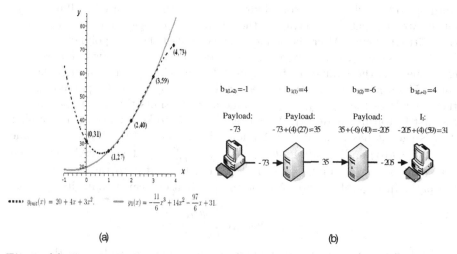

(a)   (b)

Fig. 3. (a) Shared points on the initialization and I_1 polynomials. (b) Calculations performed at each node during transmission of I_1.

Note that the two curves $y_1(x)$ and $y_{init}(x)$ share the points held by the intermediate nodes and the destination as shown in figure 3(a). The calculations performed at each node and the payload forwarded during transmission of I_1 is shown in figure 3(b). Next the sender finds the $L + 2^{th}$ point on this curve as $(4, 73)$. The $b_{1(L+2)}$ value is calculated by the sender as -1. The payload for initial transmission is prepared as $b_{1(L+2)} \, y_{1(L+2)} = -73$ which is transmitted along with $x_{1(L+2)} = 4$ to M_1. The forwarding node M_1 calculates $b_{1(1)}$ as: $b_{1(1)} = b_{init(1)} \frac{x_{1(L+2)}}{x_{1(L+2)} - x_1} = 3 \frac{4}{4-1} = 4$. Thus, the new payload is calculated as $-73 + (4)(27) = 35$ and it is forwarded to M_2. Similar to the previous step, M_2 can calculate $b_{1(2)} = -6$ and recompute the new payload as

$35 + (-6)(40) = -205$. The destination gets this new payload and calculates $b_{1(L+1)} = 4$ and $I_1 = -205 + (4)(59) = 31$. It can also be observed from this simple example that the intermediate nodes cannot collude to derive I_1.

Using Globally Determined $x_{\alpha(L+2)}$ Values. Previously presented C-Mix scheme is susceptible to colluding nodes or passive traffic analysis attack, which allow the adversary to obtain information about the path. The anonymous routing scheme based on polynomial interpolation needs to ensure that a forwarding node calculates different $b_{\alpha(i)}$ y_i values for each transmission along the virtual circuit. Also, colluding nodes on a virtual circuit should not be able to obtain path information by comparing $x_{\alpha(L+2)}$ values that are propagated by the sender.

To achieve the above desired property, we propose to use a globally known function $\Psi(\alpha)$ which determines an $x_{\alpha(L+2)}$ for every data transmission I_α where $(1 \leq \alpha \leq NUM)$. This function should be made accessible to all the users (senders and destinations) and forwarding nodes across the network. The forwarding nodes will use $\Psi(\alpha)$ for all virtual circuits that they are handling. Thus, all nodes on the path keep a track of the number of messages transmitted through each virtual circuit. After the sender has calculated the new polynomial $y_\alpha(x)$ for the message I_α, it uses $\Psi(\alpha)$ as its x–coordinate $x_{\alpha(L+2)}$ (where α is basically one plus the number of messages it has previously sent through the circuit). The sender obtains the corresponding $y_{\alpha(L+2)}$ from the polynomial. It then calculates the $b_{\alpha(L+2)}$ $y_{\alpha(L+2)}$ value and transmits this as the payload to the first forwarding node M_1. As it is easy for M_1 to keep track of the number of messages it has forwarded so far for this particular VCI, it can determine $x_{\alpha(L+2)} = \Psi(\alpha)$ and update its $b_{\alpha(1)}$ as $b_{init(1)} \frac{\Psi(\alpha)}{\Psi(\alpha)-x_1}$. The node M_1 can then determine $b_{init(1)} y_1$, update the payload and forward it to the next node on the path. In general, a node M_i (or the destination) can update its $b_{\alpha(i)}$ as:

$$b_{\alpha(i)} = b_{init(i)} \frac{\Psi(\alpha)}{\Psi(\alpha) - x_i}. \tag{6}$$

In this manner, all nodes in the network including the sender and the destination can calculate the appropriate value for each transmission α. This ensures that each node calculates different $b_{\alpha(i)}$ y_i for every transmission. This will prevent a passive attacker from correlating incoming and outgoing messages at a node because the difference in value between the incoming and outgoing messages is different for every transmission. This approach of using globally determined values also mitigates the collusion attack. Note that the forwarding node uses the same global function $\Psi(\alpha)$ for all the virtual circuits that it supports and the number of transmissions (α) for every virtual circuit begins at 1 and increments by 1 for every transmission. As a result, two or more colluding nodes cannot compare their $\Psi(\alpha)$ values to determine path information for a particular sender–destination pair because for a particular α the $\Psi(\alpha)$ value is the same for every virtual circuit in the system.

However, it is likely that different senders $(sd_1, sd_2, \ldots)$ have different number of messages to transmit $(NUM_{sd_1}, NUM_{sd_2}, \ldots)$. Consider a case where a sender has a lot of messages to transfer than the average in the network. After a period of time, only that sender will have very high α values. In this scenario, when forwarding nodes collude, they will notice the presence of a virtual circuit with a large α value. Although two or more non-contiguous forwarding nodes cannot determine with complete certainty that the virtual circuits with the high α are on the same path, the probability of these colluding forwarding nodes being on the same path is high. In order to offer better protection against collusion in such scenarios it is necessary to ensure that each virtual circuit can only transmit messages until a certain α_{max} and a corresponding $\Psi(\alpha_{max})$ are reached. After the sender has sent α_{max} messages through the path, the circuit must be broken down and a new virtual circuit (which may take a different path) must be created. Thus the sender needs to continually do this until all its NUM_{sd} messages are transmitted. The sender uses this new virtual circuit to transmit the remaining messages $(I_{\alpha_{max}+1} \ldots I_{NUM_{sd_X}})$ messages assuming $(NUM_{sd_X} < 2\alpha_{max})$. However, when the sender transmits the message $I_{\alpha_{max}+1}$, it is the first message transmitted through the new virtual circuit. As a result all nodes in the path consider $\alpha = 1$ and use $\Psi(1)$ to calculate $b_{\alpha(i)}$. Thus, the sender also uses $x_{\alpha(L+2)} = \Psi(1)$ to calculate $b_{\alpha(L+2)}$ and $y_{\alpha(L+2)}$. In effect, the virtual circuit uses $\alpha = 1 \ldots (NUM_{sd_X} - \alpha_{max})$ for the transmission of messages $(I_{\alpha_{max}+1} \ldots I_{NUM_{sd_X}})$. In this case, we assumed that the sender sd_X only needed 2 virtual circuits to transmit all messages to the intended destination. However, in general the number of virtual circuits that need to be constructed by a sender is given by the following equation:

$$\text{Number of VCs for } sd_X = RndUp(\frac{NUM_{sd_X}}{\alpha_{max}}),$$

where $RndUp()$ rounds the result to the ceiling function.

We must note that each forwarding node may support multiple virtual circuits. The forwarding node also keeps track of the α value for each of these virtual circuits. When the α_{max} value is reached for a particular VC, only that circuit is torn down while the functioning of all other VCs supported at the forwarding node is unaffected. Using this scheme of Globally determined $x_{\alpha(L+2)}$ values bounded by α_{max}, C-Mix scheme is resilient to collusion attacks by comparing α values.

4 Security, Anonymity, and Performance Analysis

In this section, we first discuss how the various attacks can be launched on the C-Mix scheme and what the attacker can learn from these attacks. The impact of the revealed information on the security and anonymity of the proposed scheme is also evaluated. In the second part of this section, we present the performance analysis of the C-Mix scheme which is based on experimental results.

4.1 Anonymity and Security Analysis of the C-Mix Scheme against Attacks

The attack model is described in section 2.2. The effect of the various attacks and the extent of information revealed from them are discussed here.

Resilience to Collusion Attack. This is a type of attack where several forwarding nodes in C-Mix collude and try to obtain the path information and the message being transmitted. In a scenario where the colluding nodes are contiguous, the path information will be revealed. This is obvious because a forwarding node can compare the messages it sent with the messages received by neighboring node. Now we consider a case where there is at least one uncompromised node FN_h in the network. This is sufficient to preserve the end–to–end path anonymity. The colluding nodes can track the path up to the node FN_h. However, the colluding nodes do not know the results of the calculations performed by FN_h. Hence, they cannot track the path by just observing the output messages of FN_h.

Thus, when a collusion attack is launched, the level of anonymity and security provided by the C-Mix scheme is similar to those provided by the onion routing–based schemes. Even in onion routing–based schemes, a single uncompromised node is sufficient to preserve end–to–end path anonymity and non-contiguous colluding nodes can compare the number of messages transmitted through a virtual circuit.

Blending Attack. A successful blending attack discloses the portion of the path which is enclosed by the compromised nodes. However, it is necessary to check if any other information is revealed by the attack. To increase the amount of information unknown to attacker at each node, we allow each node to have more than one triplet. We call the number of triplets held by a node for a virtual circuit as a "multiplicity". In the first case, assume that the attacker has also been able to obtain the secret multiplicities of each node. Consider a blending attack at a node on the transmission path. The adversary can observe the incoming and outgoing message at the compromised node and calculate their difference as a constant K over the field $\mathbb{Z}_p$. In this case, if the attacker can carry out adequate blending attacks he/she can construct sufficient equations which the forwarding node would have used to obtain K. If the number of equations is equal to or more than the number of unknowns, the system of equations can be solved over the field $\mathbb{Z}_p$. The solution will reveal the triplets held by the node i. However, this information in turn can only reveal the next hop (which is already known to the attacker) and does not compromise other forwarding nodes. In a more practical scenario where the adversary does not know the multiplicity, it is more difficult for the attacker to obtain equations and solve them. The attacker will have to guess the lowest and highest possible multiplicities and obtain systems of equations for each possible multiplicity value in the range. Also, the blending attack does not compromise the secrecy of the message I_α as the adversary cannot obtain the receivers triplets. When compared to onion routing–based schemes, the security of the C-Mix scheme is the same – the message cannot be revealed. However, in terms of anonymity C-Mix may reveal the triplets of forwarding nodes in addition to the next hop. But, this is not very useful as the compromised triplets cannot be used to track the path at other nodes.

Traffic Analysis Attacks. Finally, the impact of traffic analysis attacks on the proposed scheme is discussed. The simplest form of traffic analysis involves identifying transmission paths by examining the network for changes in the size of messages and similarities in the appearance of the messages. Both these techniques will be unsuccessful against our scheme because we use globally determined $x_{\alpha(L+2)}$ values and multiple $(x_i, y_i, b_{init(i)})$ triplets for each node. These two techniques make the same message I_α appear differently over different links. However, C-Mix is still vulnerable to long term traffic analysis attacks like the hitting set attack [14] as these attacks are based on the volume of traffic sent and received by the end users. The secrecy of the message I_α is not compromised by passive traffic analysis attacks. Even though the payloads are not encrypted, the attacker cannot deduce the final value of the message by observing the intermediate values. This is due to the fact that the values held by the destination can be obtained only if the exact polynomial used is known and there is no way for the passive attacker to determine the polynomial. Also, it is not possible for the adversary to deploy dictionary attacks on the observed data values to deduce the message (I_α). A dictionary attack is one where the adversary obtains various cipher–text messages which were encrypted using the same symmetric key. Then using frequencies of occurrence for the letters in the English Alphabet, the attacker decodes the cipher text to obtain the plain–text. In the proposed scheme, even though the same function $Map()$ is used for every transmission to convert text to integer messages, the value to be added by the destination to recover the integer I_α changes for every transmission. As a result, the frequency of occurrences of the numbers in the messages transmitted from the last forwarding node to the destination is distorted. As for anonymity of C-mix scheme the simplest form of traffic analysis involves identifying transmission paths by examining the network for changes in the size of messages and similarities in the appearance of the messages. Since all the calculations are performed in the finite field $\mathbb{Z}_p$, such attack will be unsuccessful. We note that the C-Mix scheme is potentially still susceptible to well-deployed traffic analysis attacks like the timing attack [15]. This is potentially because the existing low-latency mix networks are relatively static and only involve small number of mix nodes, for example, Tor only allows 3-hop path length route. Due to the computational and communication efficiency of C-Mix, we can allow a longer path and involve more mix relay servers. With more nodes involved the end-to-end latency may be deviated more and thus the consequence of timing attack can be also mitigated.

4.2 Computational Performance Assessment of C-Mix Based on Experimental Results

In this section, we present the performance assessment based on our experimental results. The time taken to perform the encryptions in AES and the field

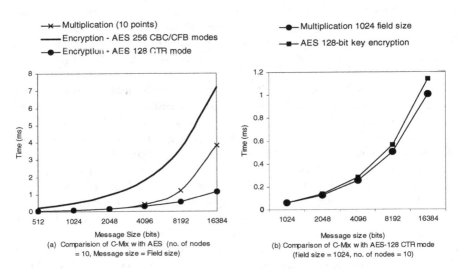

Fig. 4. Performance Evaluations

multiplications were measured using the C/C++ code [16] and Maple, respectively. The hardware configuration of the machine used for testing is: AMD 64 bit, 2 Ghz processor with 1G RAM. We assume an anonymous path that has 10 nodes. The encryption time was measured for AES 128-bit key and AES 256-bit key encryption in CTR, CBC and CFB modes for various message sizes (512 bits to 16,384 bits). The time taken to perform multiplications with various values of finite field and message sizes were recorded. The value of the finite field $\mathbb{Z}_p$ is determined by the bit representation size of this value i.e. a 512 bit field means that the value of the field is between $2^{511} + 1$ and 2^{512}. In the first case, we assumed the sizes (not values) of the message and the field to be the same. With this assumption, we compare the time taken to perform AES encryption with time taken to perform field multiplications on various message sizes in Figure 4(a). For message sizes up to 4096 bits, it can be seen that C-Mix scheme has computation cost between AES 128-bit key encryption and AES 256-bit key encryption.

However, the computation time for C-Mix can be further optimized by selecting a finite field size which is smaller than the message size. In this case, the C-Mix will process the message in fixed–size blocks (determined by field size). For example, a field size of 1024 bits can process a 2048 bit message by operating on the first 1024 bits and then on the second block. Note that choosing a field size smaller than message size does not compromise the security of the message. Each block of size k bits will have the same security offered by using a k bit field over a k bit message. The next comparison considers message whose sizes are multiples of 1024 and shows the time taken to perform AES encryption and C-Mix operations using a fixed 1024 bit size finite field. It can be seen from Figure 4(b) that the time taken for preparing messages of all sizes is least when C-Mix with a fixed size finite field. In onion–routing techniques, the intermediate node just needs to perform one decryption and forward the message. In C-Mix, the forwarding node needs to update its $b_{\alpha(i,j)}$ values for each point it holds. This involves one multiplication for each point possessed by the node. The time observed for decryption of various size messages using 128 bit keys is very close to the time taken to perform an encryption.

4.3 Communication Performance Analysis of C-Mix

After the path establishment phase, C-Mix sender does not need to create an onion structure for data transmission (see Figure 3). Instead, the sender just needs to specify the outgoing VCI number and attach the initial value I_0. Once the second C-Mix node received the message, it checks its routing table and swap a new outgoing VCI number and computer $I_1 = I_0 + b_1 y_1$ over the finite field $\mathbb{Z}_p$. Then the new computed value I_1 is the new payload. Due to the field operation, the payload size will never increase. Using C-Mix, the communication overhead is similar to the low latency mix network solutions such as Tor [17].

4.4 Storage Performance Analysis of C-Mix

In Tor, each intermediate node stores a shared key with the source. While in C-Mix, each intermediate node needs to store one or multiple coordinates distributed by the source. Thus, the storage complexity of C-Mix is at the same level of Tor.

5 Conclusion

Most of the existing anonymous routing schemes like Tor are based on the onion routing technique. Onion routing requires multiple encryptions to be performed by a sender for the transmission of each message. The forwarding nodes in the transmission path decrypt once and forward to the next hop. Due to the heavy use of encryption, these schemes have a considerable computational overhead (especially at the sender). As a result, scalability suffers in large networks.

In this paper, we have proposed a novel anonymous routing technique called C-Mix inspired by network coding and the properties of polynomial interpolation. C-Mix reduces the computation time required by the forwarding nodes for all message sizes. In general, our proposed C-Mix scheme is built on strong attack models and resilient to several global passive and active attacks, which are not addressed by existing low-latency mix networks.

However, there is still scope for improving C-Mix and for applying these techniques in other computing environments. Particularly, our research challenges are (a) Improving the computational efficiency further by reducing the number of multiplications performed by the sender. (b) Enabling the sender to dynamically change the path to the destination during the message transmission phase using predistributed secrets. (c) Anonymity and security performance under traffic analysis attacks is required for longer path length in large C-Mix networks. (d) Apply the principles of C-Mix in wireless network environments.

Acknowledgement

The authors would like to thank anonymous reviewers for their insightful comments to improve the quality of this paper.

References

1. Chaum, D.: Untraceable electronic mail, return addresses, and digital pseudonyms. Communications of the ACM 24(2), 84–88 (1981)
2. Chaum, D.: The dining cryptographers problem: Unconditional sender and recipient untraceability. Journal of Cryptology 1(1), 65–75 (1988)
3. Goldschlag, D.M., Reed, M.G., Syverson, P.F.: Hiding Routing Information. In: Anderson, R. (ed.) IH 1996. LNCS, vol. 1174, pp. 137–150. Springer, Heidelberg (1996)
4. Gulcu, C., Tsudik, G.: Mixing E-mail with Babel. In: Proceedings of the Symposium on Network and Distributed System Security, pp. 2–16 (1996)
5. Dingledine, R., Mathewson, N., Syverson, P.: Tor: The Second-Generation Onion Router. In: Proceedings of the 13th USENIX Security Symposium (August 2004)
6. I2P: Anonymizing Network, http://www.i2p.net/
7. Serjantov, A., Dingledine, R., Syverson, P.: From a Trickle to a Flood: Active Attacks on Several Mix Types. In: Petitcolas, F.A.P. (ed.) IH 2002. LNCS, vol. 2578, pp. 36–52. Springer, Heidelberg (2003)
8. Back, A., Moller, U., Stiglic, A.: Traffic analysis attacks and trade-offs in anonymity providing systems. In: Moskowitz, I.S. (ed.) IH 2001. LNCS, vol. 2137. Springer, Heidelberg (2001)
9. Danezis, G.: Statistical disclosure attacks: Traffic confirmation in open environments. In: Proceedings of Security and Privacy in the Age of Uncertainty (SEC 2003), pp. 421–426 (2003)
10. Levine, B., Reiter, M., Wang, C., Wright, M.: Timing Attacks in Low-Latency Mix Systems. In: Juels, A. (ed.) FC 2004. LNCS, vol. 3110, pp. 251–265. Springer, Heidelberg (2004)
11. Zhu, Y., Fu, X., Graham, B., Bettati, R., Zhao, W.: On flow correlation attacks and countermeasures in mix networks. In: Martin, D., Serjantov, A. (eds.) PET 2004. LNCS, vol. 3424, pp. 207–225. Springer, Heidelberg (2005)
12. Ahlswede, R., Cai, N., Li, S., Yeung, R.: Network information flow. IEEE Transactions on Information Theory 46(4), 1204–1216 (2000)
13. Shamir, A.: How to Share a Secret. Communications of the ACM 22(11), 612–613 (1979)
14. Kesdogan, D., Pimenidis, L.: The Hitting Set Attack on Anonymity Protocols. In: Fridrich, J. (ed.) IH 2004. LNCS, vol. 3200, pp. 326–339. Springer, Heidelberg (2004)
15. Murdoch, S., Danezis, G.: Low-cost Traffic Analysis of Tor. In: IEEE Symposium on Security and Privacy, pp. 183–195. IEEE CS, Los Alamitos (2005)
16. Gladman, B.: AES-CTR C Implementation,
http://fp.gladman.plus.com/cryptography_technology/fileencrypt/index.htm
17. Dingledine, R., Mathewson, N.: Tor Protocol Specification,
http://www.torproject.org/svn/trunk/doc/spec/tor-spec.txt

Strengthening QIM-Based Watermarking by Non-uniform Discrete Cosine Transform

Xianfeng Zhao, Bingbing Xia, and Yi Deng

State Key Laboratory of Information Security, Institute of Software,
Chinese Academy of Sciences, Beijing 100190, China
{xfzhao,xiabingbing,dengyi}@is.iscas.ac.cn

Abstract. Being extremely precise and at a low loss of perceptual quality, the attacks of value modification and optimized noise reduction still threaten the watermarking based on quantization index modulation (QIM). To resist them, the paper constructs a non-uniform discrete cosine transform (NDCT), and brings out an NDCT-QIM watermarking scheme, which embeds a watermark in a private NDCT domain with the parameters of NDCT as a secret key. The technique blinds the value modification by dispersing the attacking signal and changing its energy in the embedded domain. Because of the variable power spectrum of a watermark, the noise reduction becomes non-optimal. Some other advantages, including the ease of embedding, computational simplicity, etc., can also be acquired or maintained by the use of NDCT.

1 Introduction

B. Chen and G. W. Wornell [1], through quantization index modulation (QIM), proposed and, through dither modulation (DM) and distortion compensation (DC) [2], improved their QIM watermarking. We call their technique QIM-based watermarking. The QIM watermarking embeds a bit valued 1 or 0 by quantizing one or more signal samples with special quantizer(s). Since the quantized values for 1 or 0 do not overlap, the bit can be extracted accordingly. DM-QIM quantizes the samples with corresponding dither vectors to strengthen the security, and DC-QIM adds a portion of quantization error to the quantized data to improve the perceptual quality. Besides the above schemes, a scalar Costa scheme (SCS) [3] can also be regarded as QIM-based. All of the schemes can cancel the interference of an original signal without using the signal. Consequently the watermarking rate is high.

However, the following attacks can still accurately damage the watermarks by only introducing extremely slight perceptual distortion. That's to say, some security flaws remain.

- *Worst or Sub-worst Value Modification.* A worst case attack (WCA) [4-6] tries to find an additive noise that can minimize the channel capacity of QIM-based watermarking. When the attack is infeasible, an attacker can directly exploit the public knowledge that the quantization levels for the bits valued 0 and 1 are interleaved but non-overlapped. Having known or estimated the quantizers, the attacker can destroy a watermark by adjusting sample values onto or into their

K. Solanki, K. Sullivan, and U. Madhow (Eds.): IH 2008, LNCS 5284, pp. 309–324, 2008.

nearby borders [7, 8]. We call the latter sub-worst value modification. To our knowledge, the three existing methods can only partially resist the two attacks. The quantizers can be used as a secret key in QIM watermarking. Nevertheless, the method does not give an enough large key space, and the quantizers can be estimated [8-10]. In DM-QIM watermarking, the secret key can be a private dither sequence, the elements of which are evenly distributed [2]. However, it can also be estimated [11, 12]. Sect. 2 will show that the modification is still threatening because it is hard to keep the mean of the elements secret. The third method makes the choice of embedding positions key-dependent. But it wastes most of them, and the sparsely selected positions can be located [8].

- *Optimal Noise Reduction.* Another week property is the independence between the embedded signal and its host. An attack [13, 14] can optimally filter out the signal with the knowledge that the embedded signal in the spatial domain or transform domains has a power spectrum density (PSD) of a certain shape.

Notably, scaling samples is also a kind of value modification attack called value-metric attack. However, it is simpler because only a scale factor is needed to reverse it. The factor was estimated by J. J. Eggers et al. [3] who used an additive spread-spectrum pilot watermark and K. Lee et al. [9] who employed the expectation maximization algorithm. S. Kim and K. Bae [10] searched optimally for the scaled quantizer. Therefore the paper will no longer consider the attack.

Discrete cosine transform (DCT) is widely used in watermarking, and it is also suggested by B. Chen and G. W. Wornell in [2]. To resist the above attacks, the paper constructs a non-uniform DCT (NDCT), and proposes NDCT-QIM watermarking. With the parameters of NDCT as a secret key, the watermarking embeds and detects bits in a private NDCT domain, so that an attack can only modify the spatial domain or a guessed one. Since the attacking signal disperses in the embedded domain, and its energy also varies in an unpredictable way, the modification becomes puzzled. And since the watermarked signal is relevant to the NDCT depending on a secret key, its PSD becomes more variable, and the noise filtering not optimal.

Some *key-controlled transforms*, including the key-dependent orthogonal transform [15], parameterized wavelet transform [16], and non-uniform discrete Fourier transform (NDFT) [17], have been used to improve robustness other than security. The existence of their inverses is easy to prove. However, they have some limitations. Their original transforms are not so commonly embedded as DCT. An arbitrarily-generated orthogonal transform may not be fit for embedding. The adopted parameterized wavelet transform [18] just uses a part of wavelets, and it is not easy to change block by block. The experiments [16] show that the transform is not fit for protecting some early quantization-based watermarking schemes. Since the coefficients of NDFT are complex numbers, both the construction of NDFT and the embedding in its domain must keep conjugate symmetry of coefficients to guarantee the output of its inverse (INDFT) goes back to real numbers. The range of parameters and the capacity of embedding are restricted when the phases are not used. By giving NDCT, this paper will overcome some of the limitations. Besides, it will more fully explain the mechanism and advantages that a key-controlled transform can bring.

In Sect. 2, the related work will be further introduced. Sect. 3 gives the construction of NDCT and its inverse. And Sect. 4 proposes the NDCT-QIM watermarking, the properties of which are investigated in Sect. 5. The experimental results are given in Sect. 6. Finally, Sect. 7 arrives at the conclusions.

2 Related Work and Existing Problems

2.1 QIM Based Watermarking and Representative Low-Priced Attacks

QIM-based watermarking [1, 2] can be concisely interpreted by the concepts of lattice and coset [19]. A *lattice* is an additive group whose elements are some points in a set. If the set is an L-dimensional Euclid space, the elements constitute an L-dimensional lattice Λ by addition. Let Λ' be a sub-lattice of Λ. For $\forall a \in \Lambda$, $a + \Lambda'$ is a coset of Λ', and all the cosets come to be a partition of Λ. Let Δ be a quantizer, x a sample, and Z all integers. Then ΔZ is a sub-lattice of the lattice generated by $\pm\Delta/2$, and $\Lambda_0 = \Delta Z$ and $\Lambda_1 = \Delta/2 + \Delta Z$ are its cosets. In the QIM watermarking, the embedding of $m \in \{0,1\}$ can be represented by $y = Q_m(x) = \arg_\lambda \min(|\lambda - x|)$, $\lambda \in \Lambda_m$, where Λ_0 and Λ_1 are 2 cosets interleaved by $\Delta/2$. For vector quantization, the embedding can be generally expressed by

$$y = Q_m(x) = \arg_\lambda \min(\|\lambda - x\|), \ \lambda \in \Lambda_m, m \in \{0,1\}. \tag{1}$$

In (1), x, y, and λ are L-dimensional vectors, and $\|\cdot\|$ is the length of a vector. If Δ_i denotes the quantizer for quantizing the ith-dimensional component of a vector, $\Lambda_0 = [\Delta_1 Z, \cdots, \Delta_L Z]$ and $\Lambda_1 = [\Delta_1/2, \cdots, \Delta_L/2] + [\Delta_1 Z, \cdots, \Delta_L Z]$ are the cosets of the L-dimensional sub-lattice $[\Delta_1 Z, \cdots, \Delta_L Z]$. The Euclid distance between Λ_0 and Λ_1, i.e. $((\Delta_1/2)^2 + \cdots + (\Delta_L/2)^2)^{1/2}$, is called the *quantization distance*. Suppose that $\hat{y}$ is a vector from a watermarked copy, the extraction of a watermark bit can be expressed by

$$\hat{m} = \arg_{m \in \{0,1\}} \min(\|\hat{y} - \Lambda_m\|). \tag{2}$$

To improve the security, dithering is introduced in the DM-QIM watermarking [1,2]. With Δ as the scalar quantizer, the embedding can be expressed by

$$y = Q_m(x) = Q(x - d_m) + d_m, \ m \in \{0,1\}, \tag{3}$$

where for a sample s, $Q(s) = \Delta \cdot \lfloor s/\Delta \rfloor$, and d_0 and d_1 are two real numbers satisfying $|d_0 - d_1| = \Delta/2$. For example, if $d_0 = -\Delta/4$ and $d_1 = \Delta/4$, then $\Lambda_0 = -\Delta/4 + \Delta Z$ and $\Lambda_1 = \Delta/4 + \Delta Z$. When vector quantization is used, (3) should be expressed with vectors. Then $Q(s)$ becomes $Q(s) = [\Delta_1 \lfloor s_1/\Delta_1 \rfloor, \cdots, \Delta_L \lfloor s_L/\Delta_L \rfloor]$, and the two cosets become $\Lambda_0 = d_0 + [\Delta_1 Z, \cdots, \Delta_L Z]$ and $\Lambda_1 = d_1 + [\Delta_1 Z, \cdots, \Delta_L Z]$, where $d_0 = [-\Delta_1/4, \cdots, -\Delta_L/4]$ and $d_1 = [\Delta_1/4, \cdots, \Delta_L/4]$ are *dither vectors*, and Δ_i can vary each time. All dither vectors and quantization vectors constitute the *dither sequence* and *quantizer sequence* respectively. For either the case of scalar or vector quantization, (2) can still represent the watermark extraction. In the DC-QIM watermarking the quantization error is multiplied by a ratio, and the result is added to the quantized samples. The compensated signal improves the perceptual quality but disturbs the extraction.

In Sect.1 we have briefly surveyed the attacks which can still effectively damage QIM-based watermarks with a minor loss of perceptual quality. However, some of them, such as the 3-delta attack [5, 6], the dither estimation based on set-membership theory for KMA (known message attack) [11], the joint Baycsian and set-membership estimation for WOA (watermarked only attack) [12], the optimal filtering attack [14], etc., are conceptually complicated. We think the mechanism brought by NDCT can be more illustrative when the following simple but closely related attacks are analyzed.

- *Value Modification with Known Dither Sequence.* The QIM-based extraction is required to decide the coset nearest to a sample value. When an attack [7, 8] can know or estimate the quantizer(s), since Λ_0 and Λ_1 interleave with each other but do not overlap, it can change the value of a sample or sample vector by only about a half of the quantization distance to make it closer to the opposite coset. For scalar quantization, the amount of modification is about $\Delta/4$, and it is near to $\| d_0 - d_1 \| / 4$ for vector quantization. Moreover, the modification on half of the attacked samples even compensates the distortion resulting from watermarking. Therefore the attack is at a minor loss of perceptual quality (also see Sect. 6).

- *Value Modification with Unknown Dither Sequence.* Even suppose that d_0 and d_1 are private, where $d_0(i)$ and $d_1(i)$ are evenly distributed in $[-\Delta_i/2, \Delta_i/2]$, $| d_0(i) - d_1(i) | = \Delta_i/2$, and that the secret Δ_i, $1 \le i \le L$, vary in each quantization vector, since the ranges of Δ_i are limited, their mean $\overline{\Delta}$ is hard to keep secret. In an attack the quantized samples can be just modified by a quantity slightly larger than $\overline{\Delta}/4$ to destroy most watermark bits. Actually, on the positions where the bits are not damaged, $| d_0(i) - d_1(i) | > \overline{\Delta}/2$ holds. So the embedding has brought more distortion there.

- *Weiner Noise Reduction.* QIM-based watermarking results in embedding a signal w independent to the original x in the spatial domain or a transform one. The signals in a specific domain have similar flat PSDs. This can lead to the attacks of optimized noise reduction if the PSDs and those of the originals have different shapes. J. K. Su et al. [14] designed an attacking filter that exploits the PSDs $\Phi_{ww}(\omega)$ and $\Phi_{xx}(\omega)$ of w and x respectively. The frequency response can be expressed by

$$H(\omega) = A(\omega) \cdot \frac{\Phi_{xx}(\omega)}{\Phi_{xx}(\omega) + \Phi_{ww}(\omega)} . \qquad (4)$$

If $A(\omega) = 1$, (4) represents the frequency response of a Wiener filter [13] which is optimized under the criterion of mean square error (MSE). Otherwise, $A(\omega)$ is a much complicated function of $\Phi_{ww}(\omega)$ and $\Phi_{xx}(\omega)$, and we shall not make any further consideration of the cases.

2.2   Existing Key-Controlled Transforms and Their Limitations

Sect.1 briefly surveys the key-controlled transforms. Their inverses are easy to see but their original domains are not so commonly used as DCT domain. The inverse of a key-dependent orthogonal transform [15] is guaranteed by the orthogonality among the row vectors of the transform matrix. The parameterized wavelet transform [16] is constructed in compliance with the reconstruction condition. The transform matrix of NDFT is an invertible Vandermonde matrix [17]. However, DCT has not been made key-controllable. One of the reasons might be that it is not easy to show the stable existence of an inverse.

We shall supplement some details about the existing key-controlled transforms reviewed in Sect.1. A set of base vector dependent on a key will be orthogonalized to generate an orthogonal transform. The complexity of vector operations is $O(nm^2)$, where n and m are respectively the numbers of vectors and their dimensions. Since various transforms can all be generated likewise, different keys correspond to different kinds of transforms. Therefore it is difficult to design the embedding. In the generation of a parameterized wavelet transform [18], only three or four parameters in $[-\pi, \pi]$ are often used to solve the filter coefficients. However, the solved coefficients are interrelated, and more filters can not be generated in the parameterization. Therefore the features of the solved filters are not difficult to learn. And the experimental results [16] show that 2 quantization-based watermarks extracted from the different parameterized wavelet domains are mutually more correlative. As we know, since a wavelet multi-resolution decomposition can also be viewed as the partition of frequency components, a specific filter, low-pass or high-pass, gives the coefficients of the fixed time-frequency components. This means the difference between any two such transforms, which is often not enough to protect a QIM-based watermark, only results from the different ways of the computation. To keep the conjugate symmetry of frequency components, only one bit is embedded into every 8-sample piece of audio in the NDFT-based scheme. In addition, [15-17] rely mainly on experiments to show the improvement of robustness instead of the discussion of other properties and underlying principles.

3 NDCT and Its Inverse

To improve the security of QIM-based watermarking, we suggest using the domain of NDCT for embedding a watermark.

3.1 Construction of NDCT

Suppose that $X_{N \times N}$ is an image or an image block, the 2-demensional NDCT of it is

$$Y_{N \times N} = C_{N \times N} \cdot X_{N \times N} \cdot R_{N \times N}^{T}. \tag{5}$$

In (5), the *matrix of column transform* C is

$$\sqrt{\frac{2}{N}} \cdot \begin{bmatrix} 1/\sqrt{2} & 1/\sqrt{2} & \cdots & 1/\sqrt{2} \\ \cos\dfrac{\alpha_1 \pi}{2N} & \cos\dfrac{3\alpha_1 \pi}{2N} & \cdots \cos\dfrac{(2N-1)\alpha_1 \pi}{2N} \\ \vdots & \vdots & \ddots & \vdots \\ \cos\dfrac{\alpha_{N-1}\pi}{2N} & \cos\dfrac{3\alpha_{N-1}\pi}{2N} & \cdots \cos\dfrac{(2N-1)\alpha_{N-1}\pi}{2N} \end{bmatrix}, \tag{6}$$

where $\alpha_k \in (0, N)$, and $\alpha_{k-1} < \alpha_k$ for $k = 1, \cdots, N-1$, and R is the *matrix of row transform*. R has an expression similar to (6), where β_k are substituted for α_k. The parameters α_k and β_k, called *perturbation parameters*, control the non-uniformity of NDCT. Their values are around k and controlled by a secret key. If $\alpha_k = \beta_k = k$, NDCT becomes DCT.

3.2 INDCT and Its Stable Existence

Suppose that C and R are both invertible, i.e. nonsingular, the inverse of the NDCT is $X_{N \times N} = C_{N \times N}^{-1} \cdot Y_{N \times N} \cdot R_{N \times N}^{-T}$, where the superscript $-T$ means computing the inverse after the transpose. Next we shall demonstrate that C^{-1} and R^{-T} exist stably.

We do not directly use (6) to study its invertibility. Instead we use

$$
G(C) \triangleq CC^{T} =
\begin{bmatrix}
<c_1,c_1> & <c_1,c_2> & \cdots & <c_1,c_N> \\
<c_2,c_1> & <c_2,c_2> & \cdots & <c_2,c_N> \\
\cdots & \cdots & \cdots & \cdots \\
<c_N,c_1> & <c_N,c_2> & \cdots & <c_N,c_N>
\end{bmatrix},
\tag{7}
$$

where $<\cdot, \cdot>$ denotes the inner product, and c_i are the rows in C. We call $G(C)$ the *matrix of rows' inner products*. The appendix proves that C is nonsingular if and only if C is nonsingular. Let g_{ij} be the entries of $G(C)$. If

$$
|g_{ii}| > \sum_{j=1,\, j \neq i}^{N} |g_{ij}|, \quad i = 1, \cdots, N,
\tag{8}
$$

C^{-1} exists since $G(C)$ is strictly diagonally dominant. For R the case is similar. Let C also represent the matrix of column transform of DCT and $c_{ij}, 1 \leq i, j \leq N$, are the entries. Because of C's orthogonality, we have $CC^T = E$, where E is the identity matrix. Thus $<c_i, c_i> = 1$ if $i \neq j$, and $<c_i, c_j> = 0$ otherwise. Comparably, the NDCT defined by (6) only introduces some non-uniformity to the frequency samples, i.e. α_k is a value evenly distributed in $[k - \delta, k + \delta]$ rather than k. Since $\alpha_{k-1} < \alpha_k$, NDCT keeps most features of DCT. For example, $g_{ii} \approx 1$ if $i \neq j$, and $g_{ij} \approx 0$ otherwise. In practice, the coefficients of some lowest frequencies are not embedded such that we can let $\alpha_k = k$ and do not introduce non-uniform there. As a result, $G(C)$ has been found stably nonsingular.

Nevertheless, in our method the invertibility of C and R will still be tested before the use of them. First the multiplicative congruence algorithm [20] generates two pseudo-random sequences with N entries evenly distributed in $[0, \delta]$. Then α_k and β_k, $1 \leq k \leq N$, are acquired by subtracting each of their elements from k. If the determinant of either C or R is zero, these α_k and β_k are given up, and the next N-element segment of α_k and β_k will be generated and tested until the nonsingularity is guaranteed. When $N = 8$ and $\delta \leq 0.5$, however, we never find the case.

4 NDCT-QIM Watermarking Scheme

This section gives the NDCT-QIM watermarking scheme for images, which introduces NDCT to each of the 8×8-pixel blocks. The reasons for our choice of small blocks are: the non-uniformity of a frequency sample can be larger if N is smaller; it is reliable to ensure the nonsingularity of smaller C and R, and convenient to compute their inverses.

The input of the NDCT-QIM embedding consists of an original image, watermark bits encrypted by a stream cipher, and an initial state (seed) of the pseudo-random sequence generator (PRSG) which is the multiplicative congruence algorithm. The latter two as a whole can be viewed as a secret key. The steps of the embedding are:

a) Partition an image X into 8×8-pixel blocks. For each of them, do the b) ~ e).
b) Let B denote the current block. Use the PRSG to generate α_k and β_k, $1 \leq k \leq 7$, as in Sect. 3.2. Compute $F \leftarrow \text{NDCT}(B)$, and change the state of the PRSG.
c) Arrange $F(1,3)$, $F(1,4)$, $\cdots$, $F(1,8)$, $F(3,1)$, $F(4,1)$, $\cdots$, and $F(8,1)$ sequentially into a 1-dimemsional vector z containing 12 elements. Similarly use the PRSG to generate the current segment of quantization sequence Δ_j and segment of dither sequence $d_{0,j}$, $1 \leq j \leq 12$, where $-\Delta_j/2 \leq d_{0,j} \leq \Delta_j/2$, $0 < Q_1 \leq \Delta_j \leq Q_2$, and Q_1 and Q_2 are fixed. Compute the other dither sequence

$$d_{1,j} \leftarrow \begin{cases} d_{0,j} + \Delta_j/2, & d_{0,j} < 0, \\ d_{0,j} - \Delta_j/2, & d_{0,j} \geq 0. \end{cases} \tag{9}$$

d) Obtain the watermark bits b_i, $1 \leq i \leq M$, which is to be embedded into the current block. Let the length of a quantization vector be L. Partition the sequences of z, $\Delta_{1 \leq j \leq 12}$, $d_{0,1 \leq j \leq 12}$, and $d_{1,1 \leq j \leq 12}$ into M L-element vectors, denoted by z_i, Δ_i, $d_{0,i}$, and $d_{1,i}$ respectively. Embed b_i into z_i by

$$z_i \leftarrow Q_m(z_i) = Q(z_i - d_{m,i}) + d_{m,i}, \quad m = b_i \in \{0, 1\}, \tag{10}$$

where $Q(\cdot)$ quantizes a signal by Δ_i, and it becomes scalar quantization if $L = 1$.
e) Place the elements of z back in the accordant positions of F, and acquire $\tilde{F}$. Then output $\tilde{X} \leftarrow \text{INDCT}(\tilde{F})$ as the embedded copy.

In an NDCT domain, the above embedding is actually the DM-QIM watermarking using vector quantization. If $L = 1$, it becomes the DM-QIM watermarking using scalar quantization. And when Δ_j are all fixed, it is similar to the QIM watermarking.

In watermark extraction, the above a) ~ c) are first executed on the input consisting of $\tilde{X}$ and the initial state of the PRSG. Then the watermark bits are extracted by $\hat{m} \leftarrow \arg_{m \in \{0,1\}} \min\left(\|z_i - \Lambda_m\|\right)$ as in (2).

5 Analysis of the Properties

Three properties of the NDCT-QIM watermarking, including the dispersion of attacking signal, uncertainty of attacking energy, and variation of the watermark PSDs, help resist the value modification and optimal noise reduction. And the watermarking can have other good properties, such as the ample parameters, stable embedded domain, additive attack resistance, simplicity, and noninvertibility.

5.1 Dispersion of Attacking Signal and Watermark Signal

To damage the NDCT-QIM watermark, the value modification attack has to operate in a guessed domain instead of a fixed one. Then each sample of the attacking signal, when represented in the true embedded domain, disperses to other positions. The property is called the *dispersion of attacking signal*. We shall first study it by 1-dimensional signals. Let $\tilde{x}$ be a signal containing some watermark bits, $\tilde{y} = C_{N \times N} \cdot \tilde{x}$

the embedded domain, and $\tilde{y}' = C' \cdot \tilde{x}$ the guessed domain. We temporarily assume that an attack just modifies one sample $\tilde{y}'(k)$ in $\tilde{y}'$ and changes it to $\tilde{y}'(k) + a(k)$, i.e. $a(l) = 0$ when $l \neq k$. Then $\tilde{y}$ becomes

$$C \cdot (\tilde{x} + C'^{-1}[0, \cdots, a(k), \cdots, 0]^{\mathrm{T}}) = \tilde{y} + C \cdot C'^{-1}[0, \cdots, a(k), \cdots, 0]^{\mathrm{T}}. \tag{11}$$

By $C \cdot C'^{-1} \neq E$, the modification over $\tilde{y}'(k)$ spreads over all of $\tilde{y}$. We name $D \triangleq C \cdot C'^{-1}$ the *column dispersion matrix*. Then over $\tilde{y}$ the attacking signal resulting from the one-sample modification is

$$p \triangleq D \cdot [0, \cdots, a(k), \cdots, 0]^{\mathrm{T}} = a(k) \cdot [D(1,k), D(2,k), \cdots, D(N,k)]^{\mathrm{T}}. \tag{12}$$

The noise spreads onto $\tilde{y}(i)$ is $p(i) = D(i,k) \cdot a(k)$, $1 \leq i \leq N$. In the 2-dimentional cases, let $\tilde{Y} = C_{N \times N} \cdot \tilde{X} \cdot R_{N \times N}^{\mathrm{T}}$ be the embedded domain, and $\tilde{Y}' = C'_{N \times N} \cdot \tilde{X} \cdot R'^{\mathrm{T}}_{N \times N}$ the guessed domain. Besides D we also define $S \triangleq R'^{-\mathrm{T}} R^{\mathrm{T}}$ as the *row dispersion matrix*. Similarly, we begin with assuming only one sample $\tilde{Y}'(m,n)$ is modified by $a(m,n)$. Then the attacking signal introduced to the embedded domain $\tilde{Y}$ is

$$P = D \begin{bmatrix} & \mathbf{0} & \\ \mathbf{0} & a(m,n) & \mathbf{0} \\ & \mathbf{0} & \end{bmatrix} S = a(m,n) \begin{bmatrix} D(1,m)\,S(n,1) & \cdots & D(1,m)S(n,N) \\ D(2,m)\,S(n,1) & \cdots & D(2,m)S(n,N) \\ \cdots & & \\ D(N,m)S(n,1) & \cdots & D(N,m)S(n,N) \end{bmatrix}, \tag{13}$$

i.e. $P(k,l) = D(k,m) \cdot a(m,n) \cdot S(n,l)$, $1 \leq k, l \leq N$. When more samples of $\tilde{Y}'$ are modified, we have $P(k,l) = \sum_{m=1,n=1}^{N,N} D(k,m) \cdot a(m,n) \cdot S(n,l)$.

Correspondingly, an NDCT-QIM watermark disperses in the attacked domains likewise. The above results all imply that the value modification is hard to accurately control the effect of its attacking signal.

5.2 Uncertainty of Attacking Energy

Let T represent the DCT transform matrix. Then T and T^{-1} are all orthogonal, and

$$<x, \ x> = <Tx, Tx> = <T^{-1}x, T^{-1}x>. \tag{14}$$

It reveals that the signal energy is an invariant of the transforms, i.e. it complies with the Parseval's law.

Because NDCT and INDCT are all not orthogonal, they make the energy of an attacking signal not fixed. This further decreases the accuracy of a modification attack. As we know, such an attack is good at controlling the modification amplitude in attacking a common QIM-based watermark. However, it has to modify the spatial domain or a guessed one in attacking an NDCT-QIM watermarking scheme. The energy uncontrollably changes in the embedded domain. Sect. 6 will show that modifying a different domain can lead to a 10 dB PSNR difference.

5.3 Variation of Watermark PSDs

The optimal noise reduction faces the problem of correctly estimating a watermark's PSD. Under an NDCT-QIM watermarking scheme, however, the attack has to operate in the spatial or a guessed domain. The estimation becomes more difficult since the changes of NDCT parameters made the power spectrum more variable. Let W be a block of watermark, and let C and R define the NDCT used by the embedding. Then the watermark signal's spatial representation $\tilde{W}_{C,R} \triangleq C^{-1} \cdot W \cdot R^{-T}$ also depends on C and R, which are unknown to an attacker. In a guessed NDCT domain defined by C' and R', the watermark signal $W'_{C,C',R,R'} \triangleq C' \cdot C^{-1} \cdot W \cdot R^{-T} \cdot R'^{T} = D^{-1} \cdot W \cdot S^{-1}$ also depends on the guessed C' and R'. Since

$$\tilde{W}_{C,R}(k,l) = \sum_{m=1}^{N}\sum_{n=1}^{N} C^{-1}(k,m)W(m,n)R^{-T}(n,l) , \text{ and} \tag{15}$$

$$W'_{C,C',R,R'}(k,l) = \sum_{m=1}^{N}\sum_{n=1}^{N} D^{-1}(k,m)W(m,n)S^{-1}(n,l) , \tag{16}$$

one can use the direct method to estimate their PSDs by

$$\Phi_{\tilde{w}\tilde{w}}(u,v) = \frac{1}{N^2}\left| \sum_{m=0}^{N-1}\sum_{n=0}^{N-1} \tilde{W}_{C,R}(m+1,n+1)e^{-2\pi j\,(um+vn)/N} \right|^2 , \text{ and} \tag{17}$$

$$\Phi_{ww'}(u,v) = \frac{1}{N^2}\left| \sum_{m=0}^{N-1}\sum_{n=0}^{N-1} W'_{C,C',R,R'}(m+1,n+1)e^{-2\pi j\,(um+vn)/N} \right|^2 , \tag{18}$$

where $|\cdot|$ denotes the complex modulus. In practice, the noise reduction attack can estimate the PSDs and filter the watermarked signal block by block. Typically, a Wiener filter has the frequency response

$$H(u,v) = \frac{\Phi_{xx}(u,v)}{\Phi_{xx}(u,v) + \eta \cdot \Phi_{ww}(u,v)} , \tag{19}$$

where η is the parameter for adjusting the attacking energy, and $\Phi_{ww}(u,v)$ can be computed by (17) or (18). However, the NDCT settings have the influence on $\Phi_{ww}(u,v)$. The experimental results in Sect. 6 will show that the increased variation of $\Phi_{\tilde{w}\tilde{w}}$ and $\Phi_{ww'}$ makes the attack no longer be considered optimal.

5.4 Practical Security

We evaluate the covertness of an NDCT-QIM watermark by the error rate of the watermark bits extracted from a guessed NDCT domain. Let z and z' be the respective vectors of the embedded positions in an embedded domain and a guessed one. By Sect. 2.1 and Sect.4, we know if $\| z_i - z'_i \| \geq \| d_0 - d_1 \| / 4$, an extracted bit can deviate from the original bit. Let $\Pr(\cdot)$ represent probability. In practice if

$$\Pr\left(\arg_{m' \in \{0,1\}} \min\left(\| z'_i - \Lambda_{m'} \| \right) = 1 \,|\, m \right) \approx \frac{1}{2} , \tag{20}$$

i.e. the value of the extracted m' has an equal probability of being 1 and 0 no matter which value the embedded m has, z' can be regarded as being effectively hiding the watermark bit. For each block, the NDCT-QIM watermarking can apply a different NDCT, quantization sequence and dither sequence. They, just over one block, correspond to 14 perturbation parameters, 12 quantizers, and 12 dither values respectively. Let p denote the watermarking setting, i.e. all the parameters along all blocks. Let p' denote a guessed setting, and $e_{p,p'}$ the bit error rate (BER) of the watermark extraction in the domain defined by p' instead of p. Our experiments show that $e_{p,p'}$ can be around 0.54 when the quantization distance is 4. Thus $\Pr(\text{Extracted bit} = m \,|\, m) \approx 0.46$. Interestingly $e_{p,p'}$ can be larger than 0.5. The phenomenon implies that more quantized NDCT coefficient have been moved just into a nearby or opposite coset by another NDCT. In fact, we also find that the quantized values are less randomly distributed among the cosets in another NDCT domain when the coefficients are quantized by a longer quantization distance.

However, even if a watermark may have not been perfectly hidden by NDCT, it is still difficult for the attacks which we concern to exploit the situation. We define $e_{p',p}$ as the BER of watermark extraction after the signal containing a watermark has been attacked in a guessed NDCT domain. Let T be a threshold above which $e_{p',p}$ satisfies an attacker. In our experiments it is shown that $e_{p',p} \sim (m_e, \sigma_e^2)$, where m_e and σ_e are respectively the mean and variance of $e_{p',p}$. Therefore

$$\Pr(e_{p',p} > T) = \frac{1}{\sqrt{2\pi\sigma_e^2}} \int_T^{\infty} e^{-\frac{(x-m_e)^2}{2\sigma_e^2}} \, dx. \tag{21}$$

Sect.6 will demonstrate that when the scalar quantization is used, $e_{p',p}$ is around 0.368 under the modification attack, either with or without knowledge of the dither sequence, and when the vector quantization is used, $e_{p',p}$ is around 0.58. The reason why the second $e_{p',p}$ can be larger is not that apparent. Although in a guessed domain the attacks both introduce an amount of modification a little more than half of the corresponding quantization distances, the amount of the second modification is larger since the vector quantization distance is $\sqrt{3}$ times of the scalar quantization distance. Then in the embedded domain it is less likely that the quantized values can be pulled back from the nearby or opposite cosets by the effect of signal dispersion. In our experiments, a security level of $e_{p',p} \in (0.35, 0.39)$ and $\Pr(e_{p',p} > 0.39) \to 0$ can be achieved when the distance is 4, and $e_{p',p}$ increases when the distance becomes longer. Since the reciprocal of $\Pr(e_{p',p} > T = 0.39)$ can be regarded as the times of tries of a successful attack, it implies that the key space is large enough at such a security level. The case is similar for the attack filtering the spatial domain, and Sect. 6 will show that the attack filtering the NDCT coefficients is ineffective.

5.5 Other Properties

The NDCT-QIM watermarking can also have the following properties.

- Stable Domain Data. By $\alpha_{k-1} < \alpha_k$ and $\beta_{k-1} < \beta_k$, NDCT keeps most features of DCT. Since the embedded positions contain the low frequency components along row or column directions, the energy of the data is more stable than other part or some other transform domains such that it is fit for embedding.
- Attenuated Additive Noise. Because an additive noise can only attack the spatial domain or a guessed one. Since the noise disperses in the embedded domain, the attack signal over the embedded position is attenuated.
- Non-degraded Embedding Rate. NDCT provides the same number of embeddable positions as DCT. And in the NDCT-QIM watermarking no special treatment of the coefficients is required for making INDCT transform data back to real numbers. Thus a common embedding rate of QIM has been kept.
- Noninvertibility. The property indicates that an attacker is hard to claim the ownership of an intact distributed copy by the fabricated data [21]. Since the generation of the perturbation parameters of NDCT and that of the dither sequence

or quantization sequence can be one-way related, the attacker is infeasible to extract the wanted watermark in a claimed NDCT domain.

– *Simplicity*. The embedding on each image block is primarily composed of the computation of matrix multiplication at the complexity $O(N^2)$ of vector operation. If the parameters change on each block, the inverses of the matrices must be computed in the embedding at the complexity $O(N^3)$ of vector operation.

The NDCT-QIM watermarking only introduces NDCT to the common QIM-based watermarking in the DCT domain. Their other properties such as the robustness under lossy compression, signal processing, etc. are similar.

6 Experimental Results

We experimented on the watermarking schemes named NDCT-QIM, NDCT-QIM-O, DM-QIM, and DM-QIM-O respectively. The latter two embed watermark bits in DCT domain, and 'O' signifies that the dither and quantization sequences are public known. In experiments, the host signals are 256×256 grayscale images with 8-bit pixels. All quantizers vary in $[7.0, 9.0]$. The length of quantization vectors L are either 1 or 3. To compare the two cases, we embedded the same watermark bits but dealt with them by scalar ($L = 1$, quantization distance = 4) and vector operation ($L = 3$, quantization distance $= 4\sqrt{3}$) respectively. Although the quantization and dither sequences are different for each block, the mean of the quantizers is assumed known to an attacker. Fig. 1 gives some signals in the embedding, where the PSNR is computed in the spatial domain.

Fig. 1. The signals in a 41.5 dB PSNR NDCT-QIM embedding: the original (left), the NDCT domain of its blocks (middle), and the embedded (right)

The modification attacks on NDCT-QIM and NDCT-QIM-O operate in guessed NDCT domains. The results show that an attacking signal spreads over the embedded positions and even 15~18% of its energy disperses onto other locations (Fig. 2(a)). The BER of the watermark extraction is around 0.37 for $L = 1$ and 0.58 for $L = 3$ respectively (Fig. 2(b)), implying that the attack becomes blinded. The results also show the ineffectiveness of only using private quantization and dither sequences to resist the attack. Particularly, the BER in the case of $L = 3$ is higher by about 0.2 than that in the case of $L = 1$. The phenomenon has been explained at the end of Sect. 5.4.

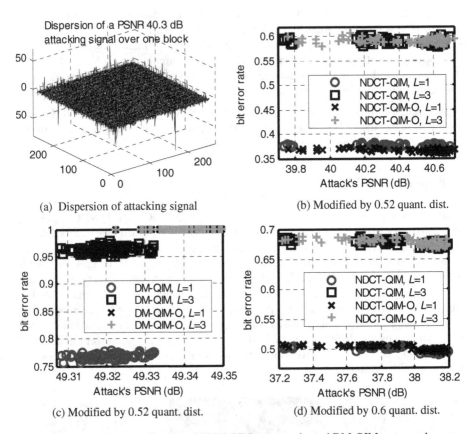

(a) Dispersion of attacking signal

(b) Modified by 0.52 quant. dist.

(c) Modified by 0.52 quant. dist.

(d) Modified by 0.6 quant. dist.

Fig. 2. Modification attacks on NDCT-QIM watermarks and DM-QIM watermarks

In the experiments DM-QIM-O and DM-QIM were attacked by the modification of DCT domain, i.e. the known embedded domain (Fig. 2(c)). After the attacks, the BERs of the former are 1.0 in both the cases of $L=3$ and $L=1$ whereas the BERs of the latter are about 0.765 and 0.963 in them respectively. It verifies the preciseness of the modification, and shows that using private quantization and dither sequences as a secret key has very limited effect in resisting the attack. And under the same amount of modification, the PSNRs computed in spatial domain, which is introduced by the modification attacks on NDCT-QIM and NDCT-QIM-O, can be 10 dB less than that introduced by attacking DM-QIM and DM-QIM-O (Figs. 2(b) and 2(c)).

The experimental results show that the modification attacks on NDCT-QIM and NDCT-QIM-O have to further increase the attacking energy to remove a watermark. When it is enlarged to 60 % of the quantization distance, the error rates for $L=1$ and $L=3$ respectively remains at about 0.5 and 0.68 (Fig. 2(d)). Notably, the former BER is more stably around 0.5 when the attacking energy is further increased.

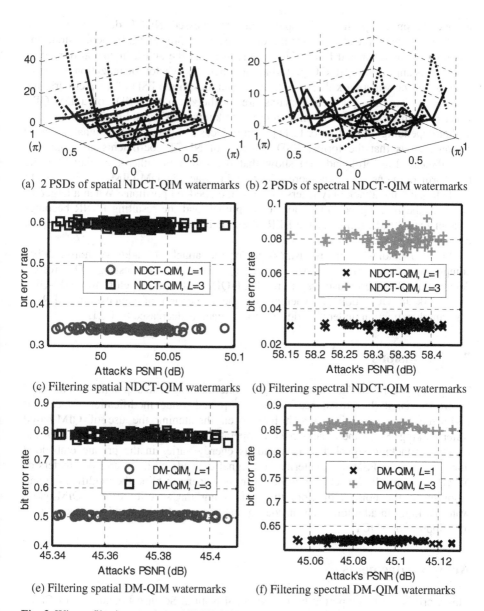

(a) 2 PSDs of spatial NDCT-QIM watermarks (b) 2 PSDs of spectral NDCT-QIM watermarks

(c) Filtering spatial NDCT-QIM watermarks (d) Filtering spectral NDCT-QIM watermarks

(e) Filtering spatial DM-QIM watermarks (f) Filtering spectral DM-QIM watermarks

Fig. 3. Wiener filtering attacks on NDCT-QIM watermarks and DM-QIM watermarks ($\eta = 3.3$)

In the experiments, the PSDs of NDCT-QIM watermarks were estimated in spatial domain and guessed NDCT ones, and the PSDs of DM-QIM watermarks estimated in spatial and DCT domain. The Wiener filters constructed by (19) where $1 \le \eta \le 4$ were used to attack watermarks in the accordant domains (Fig. 3). Since the attack on DM-QIM watermarking know the embedded positions in DCT domain, an attacking filter operates only on these positions. However, a filter attacking NDCT-QIM is assumed to operate on all positions in spatial or the guessed NDCT domain since the watermark signal spreads all over the domains. Figs. 3(a) and 3(b) demonstrate the variation of the estimated PSDs. Fig. 3(c) shows that the attack in spatial domain is more resistant to the NDCT perturbation when the vector quantization is used. Because of the watermark dispersion, the amplitudes in the PSD of a watermark that spreads all over the guessed domains are smaller than the PSDs of a DM-QIM watermark embedded on the limited number of known positions. Fig. 3(d) shows that a filter depending on the former PSD just introduces a slight attacking signal. Another reason here is that the former PSD and that of NDCT coefficients are both flat. Nonetheless, Fig. 3(e) and 3(f) show that the filters in either the spatial or the transform domains are both more effective in attacking DM-QIM watermarks. In DCT domain, the attack only filters the known embedded positions. When a larger η is taken, the filtering becomes more non-optimal, and the resulting PSNR becomes smaller than 39 dB. Similarly the BER of extracting a scalar NDCT-QIM watermark remains at about 0.5 in the case.

We also examined the robustness under the attacks of additive noise, JPEG compression, and various ways of filtering and signal processing. The results demonstrate that the robustness of an NDCT-QIM watermark is close to a DM-QIM watermark in DCT domain whereas, by the dispersion of signals, the BER of watermark extraction under the additive noise attack is decreased by 0.21.

7 Conclusions

This paper has shown that the NDCT-QIM watermarking with a quantization distance in proper length has resistance to the low-priced value modification attack and optimized noise reduction, which have been threatening the use of QIM-based watermarking. Since the attacks have to operate in spatial or a guessed domain, the resulting attacking signal disperses and its energy varies in the private embedded domain. And the PSD of a watermarked signal depends on the secret parameters of NDCT. As a result, the scheme proposed in the paper can blind the modification and de-optimize the noise reduction, thus improving the security of the QIM-based watermarking. In addition, other needed properties can also be acquired or kept after the adoption of NDCT.

Acknowledgements

This work is partly supported by the National Natural Science Foundation of China under the Grant No. 60573049 and 60633030. And the authors would like to thank the anonymous reviewers for their helpful remarks and suggestions.

References

1. Chen, B., Wornell, G.W.: An information-theoretic approach to the design of robust digital watermarking systems. In: Proc. IEEE Int. Conf. Acoustics, Speech, and Signal Processing (ICASSP 1999), Phoenix, AZ, March 15-19, pp. 2061–2064 (1999)

2. Chen, B., Wornell, G.W.: Quantization index modulation: a class of provably good methods for digital watermarking and information embedding. IEEE Trans. Information Theory 47(4), 1423–1443 (2001)
3. Eggers, J.J., Bauml, R., Tzschoppe, R., Girod, B.: Scalar Costa scheme for information embedding. IEEE Trans. Signal Processing 51(4), 1003–1019 (2003)
4. Pérez-González, F., Balado, F., Hernández, J.R.: Performance analysis of existing and new methods for data hiding with know-host information in additive channels. IEEE Trans. Signal Processing 51(4), 960–980 (2003)
5. Vila-Forcen, J.E., Voloshynovskiy, S., Koval, O., Pun, T., Perez-González, F.: Worst case additive attack against quantization-based watermarking techniques. In: Proc. IEEE 6th Workshop on Multimedia Signal Processing, September 29 - October 1, pp. 135–138 (2004)
6. Moulin, P., Goteti, A.K.: Block QIM watermarking games. IEEE Trans. on Information Forensics and Security 1(3), 293–310 (2006)
7. Eggers, J.J., Su, J.K., Girod, B.: Asymmetric watermarking schemes. In: Schumacher, M., Steinmetz, R. (eds.) Proc. Tagungsband des GI Workshop Sicherheit in Mediendaten, Berlin, Germany, September 19-22, pp. 107–123 (2000)
8. Bas, P., Hurri, J.: Security of DM quatization watermarking schemes: a practical study for digital images. In: Barni, M., Cox, I., Kalker, T., Kim, H.-J. (eds.) IWDW 2005. LNCS, vol. 3710, pp. 186–200. Springer, Heidelberg (2005)
9. Lee, K., Kim, D.S., Kim, T., Moon, K.A.: EM estimation of scale factor for quantization-based audio watermarking. In: Kalker, T., Cox, I., Ro, Y.M. (eds.) IWDW 2003. LNCS, vol. 2939, pp. 316–327. Springer, Heidelberg (2004)
10. Kim, S., Bae, K.: Robust estimation of amplitude modification for scalar Costa scheme based audio watermark detection. In: Cox, I., Kalker, T., Lee, H.-K. (eds.) IWDW 2004. LNCS, vol. 3304, pp. 101–114. Springer, Heidelberg (2005)
11. Pérez-Freire, L., Pérez-González, F., Furon, T., Comesña, P.: Security of lattice-based data hiding against the know message attack. IEEE Trans. on Information Forensics and Security 1(4), 421–439 (2006)
12. Pérez-Freire, L., Pérez-González, F.: Exploiting security holes in lattice data hiding. In: Furon, T., Cayre, F., Doërr, G., Bas, P. (eds.) IH 2007. LNCS, vol. 4567, pp. 159–173. Springer, Heidelberg (2008)
13. Su, J.K., Girod, B.: Power-spectrum condition for energy-efficient watermarking. In: Proc. ICIP 1999, Kobe, Japan, October 24-28, vol. 1, pp. 301–305 (1999)
14. Su, J.K., Eggers, J.J., Girod, B.: Analysis of digital watermarks subjected to optimum linear filtering and additive noise. Signal Processing 81, 1141–1175 (2001)
15. Fridrich, J., Baldoza, A.C., Simard, R.J.: Robust digital watermarking based on key-dependent basis functions. In: Aucsmith, D. (ed.) IH 1998. LNCS, vol. 1525, pp. 143–157. Springer, Heidelberg (1998)
16. Dietl, W., Meerwald, P., Uhl, A.: Protection of wavelet-based watermarking systems using filter parametrization. Signal Processing 83, 2095–2116 (2003)
17. Xie, L., Zhang, J., He, H.: Robust audio watermarking scheme based on nonuniform discrete Fourier transform. In: Proc. 2006 IEEE International Conference on Engineering of Intelligent Systems, April 22-23, pp. 1–5 (2006)
18. Schneid, J., Pittner, S.: On the parametrization of the coefficients of dolation equations for compactly supported wavelets. Computing 51, 165–173 (1993)
19. Moulin, P., Koetter, R.: Data-hiding codes. Proc. of the IEEE 93(12), 2083–2126 (2005)
20. Hammersley, J., Handscomb, D.: Monto Carlo Methods. Methuen, London (1964)
21. Craver, S., Memon, N., Yeo, B.L., Yeung, M.M.: Resolving rightful ownerships with invisible watermarking techniques: limitations, attacks, and implications. IEEE Journal on Selected areas in communications 16(4), 573–586 (1998)

Appendix

The claim that C is nonsingular if and only if $G(C) = CC^{\mathrm{T}}$ is nonsingular can be proved as follows.

If C is nonsingular, $c_1, c_2, \cdots, c_N$ are linearly independent. Assume that $G(C)$ is singular, then $G(C)x = 0$ has a non-zero solution. Let $x = [x_1, x_2, \cdots, x_N]^{\mathrm{T}}$ denote it. For $a = x_1 c_1 + x_2 c_2 + \cdots + x_N c_N$, there exist $a \neq 0$ and $<a, a> > 0$ because the c_i, $1 \leq i \leq N$, are linearly independent. However, since $G(C)x = 0$, there exists $<a, a> = x^{\mathrm{T}} G(C)x = 0$. The contradiction indicates the nonsingularity of C.

If $G(C)$ is nonsingular, then $G(C)$'s determinant $|G(C)| \neq 0$. Assume that C is singular, then $c_1, c_2, \cdots, c_N$ are linearly dependent. We have $c_N = \sum_{i=1}^{N-1} \gamma_i c_i$, where γ_i are the coefficients of the linear combination. Then, because

$$
|G(C)| = \begin{vmatrix}
<c_1, c_1> & <c_1, c_2> & \cdots & <c_1, c_{N-1}> & <c_1, \sum_{i=1}^{N-1} \gamma_i c_i> \\
<c_2, c_1> & <c_2, c_2> & \cdots & <c_2, c_{N-1}> & <c_2, \sum_{i=1}^{N-1} \gamma_i c_i> \\
\cdots & \cdots & \cdots & \cdots & \cdots \\
<c_N, c_1> & <c_N, c_2> & \cdots & <c_N, c_{N-1}> & <c_N, \sum_{i=1}^{N-1} \gamma_i c_i>
\end{vmatrix} \tag{A-1}
$$

$$
= \sum_{i=1}^{N-1} \gamma_i \begin{vmatrix}
<c_1, c_1> & <c_1, c_2> & \cdots & <c_1, c_{N-1}> & <c_1, c_i> \\
<c_2, c_1> & <c_2, c_2> & \cdots & <c_2, c_{N-1}> & <c_2, c_i> \\
\cdots & \cdots & \cdots & \cdots & \cdots \\
<c_N, c_1> & <c_N, c_2> & \cdots & <c_N, c_{N-1}> & <c_N, c_i>
\end{vmatrix} = 0
$$

contradicts to the known condition, C is nonsingular.

Distortion Optimization of Model-Based Secure Embedding Schemes for Data-Hiding

Benjamin Mathon[1], Patrick Bas[1], François Cayre[1],
and Fernando Pérez-González[2]

[1] Gipsa-Lab
Département Images et Signal
961 rue de la Houille Blanche
Domaine universitaire - BP 46
38402 Saint Martin d'Hères cedex, France
{benjamin.mathon,patrick.bas,francois.cayre}@gipsa-lab.inpg.fr
[2] Universidad de Vigo
Departamento de Teoría de la Señal y las Comunicaciones
Signal Processing in Communications Group
36200 Vigo, Spain
fperez@gts.tsc.uvigo.es

Abstract. This paper is the continuation of works about analysis of secure watermarking schemes in the case of WOA (Watermarked Only Attack) framework. In previous works, two new BPSK spread-spectrum watermarking modulations, Natural Watermarking (NW) and Circular Watermarking (CW), have been proposed and have been shown to be more secure than classical modulations. Because security is guaranted using specific distributions of watermarked contents, we propose to use optimal *model-based embedding* to ensure security while minimizing the overall distortion. Additionally, we propose a new secure watermarking scheme based on distribution of vector norms in the Gaussian case. We illustrate model-based embedding performance in the case of Gaussian signals and show that this approach not only allows to achieve excellent level of security in the WOA framework, but also allows to minimize distortion. Finally, a comparison of the robustness of the proposed embedding schemes is performed.

Keywords: Watermarking, Security, Hungarian method, Distortion Optimization.

1 Introduction

Watermarking is a mean to hide information into digital contents (images, sounds, videos). This hidden information can be used for copyright or copy protection applications, integrity checking, or fingerprinting in order to control each copy of a numerical document. Our works focus on copyright and copy protection. The embedding of the message must meet many constraints:

K. Solanki, K. Sullivan, and U. Madhow (Eds.): IH 2008, LNCS 5284, pp. 325–340, 2008.

- *imperceptibility*: the hidden information must not impair the original content for regular use,
- *capacity*: in multi-bit watermarking, one must ensure a sufficient number of bits can be reliably hidden into the host content,
- *robustness*: the hidden message should still be readable after common media processing,
- *security*: this last constraint can be viewed as *"the inability by unauthorized users to access, remove, read or write the hidden message"* [1]. Security in general is based on Kerckhoffs' principle [2]: the key is the only unknown parameter for the adversary.

This secret key is used to embed and detect (zero-bit watermarking) or decode (multi-bit watermarking) the watermark. Security is different from robustness. Robustness attacks relate to watermark survivability under common processing (in the case of still images, one may want to resist geometrical deformations, compression or noise addition). These attacks are generally not intentional.

On the contrary, security attacks are intentional and relate to the estimation of a part or all the secret key [3]. In multi-bit watermarking, the key is defined by the location of a set of codewords in a subspace. To embed a message in a host content, it must be placed in the decoding region of the right codeword. If an adversary learns the secret key, he can alter the message while minimizing the attack distortion with a 100% probability: his attack becomes deterministic. For example, he can design an attack in order to "push" the watermarked content into the nearest (wrong) decoding region, he can read the hidden message and copy the watermark in another content (copy attack [4]).

This paper deals with the case of WOA (Watermarked Only Attack) [5], the adversary has only access to several marked contents and to the source code of the watermarking algorithm (Kerckhoffs' principle). One should notice that the adversary can model the distribution of the host contents (Gaussian mixture or generalized Gaussian distribution for DCT or wavelet coefficients for example) since he knows the watermarking space. The adversary's goal is twofold. On one hand, he wants to model the conditional distribution of marked contents given the secret key, and on the other hand, he wants to estimate each codeword location.

Based on these ideas, we can find [6] the definition of four security classes to rank watermarking schemes security in the WOA framework (see Fig. 1 for relationships among them).

The first class is *insecurity*. In this class, the conditional distribution (given the key) of marked contents is not the same for all keys. By exhaustive search (or a more involved technique), he can estimate both the private subspace and the codewords.

A watermarking scheme belongs to the second class, *key-security*, if, for a subset of keys, the conditional distribution of the marked contents given each key is the same. The adversary can find this subset of keys and he can find the secret subspace but he cannot gain more information about the codewords.

The third class is called *subspace-security*. In this case, the conditional distribution of marked contents given the key will be the same for all keys. Therefore

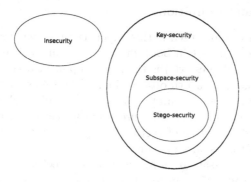

Fig. 1. Security classes in WOA framework

the pirate cannot gain any information about the key (he has not access to the secret subspace).

The last class *stego-security* relates to steganography: the distribution of marked contents is the same than that of the host contents. The adversary cannot decide whether the contents are marked or not.

Obviously, security in the WOA framework is strongly linked with the distribution of the contents after watermark embedding. In [7], authors have applied two secure modulations (namely Circular and Natural Watermarking, resp. CW and NW in the sequel) to still images. These modulations are used to modify the distribution of marked contents in order to be stego-secure or subspace-secure for NW and key-secure for CW. Note that such an approach is similar to the one proposed by Sallee in steganography [8], where perfect secrecy [9] is guaranteed by constraining the distributions of stego contents to be identical with the distributions of cover contents.

In this paper, we propose a new method to watermark signals in order to fit a chosen *target distribution* in an optimal way. This method uses the Hungarian algorithm, which minimizes distortion on average (in the sense of Euclidean distance) between points of host distribution and points of the target distribution. Section 2 recalls basics on BPSK-based SS watermarking schemes with an emphasis on unsecure and secure modulations and presents a watermarking scheme based on distribution of norm of signals. Section 3 presents our model-based embedding scheme by using Hungarian method. Section 4 compares our implementations of classical versus model-based embedding from security, distortion and robustness point of view over 2000 Gaussian signals.

2 Secure Watermarking Schemes

This section recalls definitions of unsecure and secure modulations, moreover we propose also a new secure embedding scheme based on the modification of the norm of the host vector.

2.1   Notations and Definitions

We first list the conventions used in this paper. Data are written in small letters. Vectors and matrices are set in bold fonts. Vectors are written in small letters and matrices in capital ones. $\mathbf{x}(i)$ is the i-th component of a vector $\mathbf{x}$ and $\mathbf{x}_j$ is the vector $\mathbf{x}$ associated to a j-th observation. We write $(\mathbf{x}(0), \mathbf{x}(1), \mathbf{x}(2), ...)$ the content of a vector $\mathbf{x}$. We note [a;b],]a;b[, [a;b[and]a;b] real-intervals. Sets are noted in capital letters and $vect\,(A)$ represents the vector space generated by A. $p\,(\mathbf{x}_j)$ denotes the distribution of vectors $\mathbf{x}_j$. $\sigma_{\mathbf{x}}^2$ denotes the variance of a signal $\mathbf{x}$ and $\langle.|.\rangle$ denotes the usual scalar product.

We want to hide a message $\mathbf{m}$ of N_c bits in a host vector $\mathbf{x} \in \mathbb{R}^{N_v}$. So we create a watermark signal $\mathbf{w} \in \mathbb{R}^{N_v}$ in order to obtain $\mathbf{y} = \mathbf{x} + \mathbf{w}$ the watermarked signal. The secret key K used to embed and decode the message $\mathbf{m}$ is the seed of a PRNG. With K, we generate N_c Gaussian carriers $\mathbf{u}_i \in \mathbb{R}^{N_v}$. Each carrier is able to hide one bit. In order to have a null ISI (Inter Symbol Interference), carriers must be orthogonal. Thanks to $s : \{0,1\} \to \mathbb{R}$, a modulation, we can create $\mathbf{w}$ by:

$$\mathbf{w} = \sum_{i=0}^{N_c-1} \mathbf{u}_i s(\mathbf{m}(i)). \tag{1}$$

Distortion is assessed by means of the WCR (Watermark-to-Content Ratio):

$$WCR_{[dB]} = 10 \log_{10}\left(\frac{\sigma_{\mathbf{w}}^2}{\sigma_{\mathbf{x}}^2}\right). \tag{2}$$

We model robustness attacks by adding Gaussian noise $\mathbf{n}$. So we consider the attacked vector $\mathbf{r} = \mathbf{y} + \mathbf{n}$. Attack strength is assessed by means of the $WCNR$ (Watermarked Content-to-Noise Ratio):

$$WCNR_{[dB]} = 10 \log_{10}\left(\frac{\sigma_{\mathbf{y}}^2}{\sigma_{\mathbf{n}}^2}\right). \tag{3}$$

Decoding is classically obtained by correlations z:

$$z_{\mathbf{r},\mathbf{u}_i} = \sum_{j=0}^{N_v-1} \mathbf{r}(j)\mathbf{u}_i(j). \tag{4}$$

We consider $\hat{\mathbf{m}}$ the estimated message, so we have for each bit:

$$\hat{\mathbf{m}}(i) = \begin{cases} 0 \text{ if } z_{\mathbf{r},\mathbf{u}_i} > 0, \\ 1 \text{ if } z_{\mathbf{r},\mathbf{u}_i} < 0. \end{cases} \tag{5}$$

We measure robustness of the watermarking scheme by BER (Bit Error Rate) between the estimated and the original message:

$$BER(\mathbf{m}, \hat{\mathbf{m}}) = \frac{1}{N_c} \sum_{i=0}^{N_c-1} \mathbf{m}(i) \oplus \hat{\mathbf{m}}(i). \tag{6}$$

For a pirate, there is no difference between estimating the carriers or getting K in the WOA context. According to [6], the security of a watermarking scheme relies on the properties of the conditional distribution $p(\mathbf{y}_j|K)$. In the case of spead-spectrum techniques, points of conditional distribution given the carriers are the N_c-tuples $(z_{\mathbf{y},\mathbf{u}_0}, ..., z_{\mathbf{y},\mathbf{u}_{N_c-1}})$ in the subspace spanned by the carriers.

2.2 Unsecure SS Modulations

Classical modulation SS (Spread Spectrum) is given by:

$$s_{SS}(\mathbf{m}(i)) = \gamma(-1)^{\mathbf{m}(i)}. \tag{7}$$

This modulation is analog to BPSK modulation. Parameter γ is used to set the power of watermark. It is a function of WCR. ISS (Improved Spread Spectrum) [10] uses side-information to improve robustness:

$$s_{ISS}(\mathbf{m}(i)) = \alpha(-1)^{\mathbf{m}(i)} - \lambda\frac{\langle\mathbf{x}|\mathbf{u}_i\rangle}{\|\mathbf{u}_i\|^2}, \tag{8}$$

where $\langle.|.\rangle$ denotes the usual scalar product, α and λ are computed to achieve host-interference rejection and error probability minimisation given Noise-to-Content power Ratio:

$$NCR_{[dB]} = 10\log_{10}\left(\frac{\sigma_{\mathbf{n}}^2}{\sigma_{\mathbf{x}}^2}\right), \tag{9}$$

where $\mathbf{n}$ denotes Gaussian noise. Previous works [5] have shown that SS and ISS are unsecure, and that carriers estimation is possible (see tests on [7]).

2.3 Secure Modulations

NW (Natural Watermarking) [6] modulation is defined by:

$$s_{NW}(\mathbf{m}(i)) = \left((-1)^{\mathbf{m}(i)}\frac{\langle\mathbf{x}|\mathbf{u}_i\rangle}{|\langle\mathbf{x}|\mathbf{u}_i\rangle|} - 1\right)\frac{\langle\mathbf{x}|\mathbf{u}_i\rangle}{\|\mathbf{u}_i\|^2}. \tag{10}$$

NW belongs to the so-called stego-secure class and is suitable for steganography applications.
CW (Circular Watermarking) [6] modulation is defined by:

$$s_{CW}(\mathbf{m}(i)) = \alpha(-1)^{\mathbf{m}(i)}\mathbf{d}(i) - \lambda\frac{\langle\mathbf{x}|\mathbf{u}_i\rangle}{\|\mathbf{u}_i\|^2}, \tag{11}$$

where α and λ are computed the same way than with ISS and $\mathbf{d}$ is generated at each embedding as follows from $\mathbf{g} \sim \mathcal{N}(0, 1)$, this parameter is used to randomly spread the correlations of the mixed signals on the whole decoding regions:

$$\mathbf{d}(i) = \frac{|\mathbf{g}(i)|}{\|\mathbf{g}\|}. \tag{12}$$

This parameter $\mathbf{d}$ enables the following property of circularity :

$$p\left(z_{\mathbf{y},\mathbf{u}_0}, ..., z_{\mathbf{y},\mathbf{u}_{N_c-1}}\right) = p\left(\sqrt{\sum_{i=0}^{N_c-1} z_{\mathbf{y},\mathbf{u}_i}^2}\right). \tag{13}$$

The circularity of the distribution allows us to say that for a subset of several keys (all bases of $vect(\{\mathbf{u}_i\})$), the distribution of marked signals will be the same. CW belongs to the so-called key-secure security class.

2.4   A New Secure Embedding Based on the χ^2 Distribution

Based on previous security assessment, we are able to propose a stego-secure watermarking scheme χ^2W (CHI2 Watermarking) by modifying norm of Gaussian host signals after embedding, while keeping the same distribution between original and watermarked contents. Distribution of these norms can be modeled by a χ^2 law. So we define codewords location by real-intervals in the set of norms of Gaussian vectors. Finally, in order to embed a secret message, we chose randomly a norm in the corresponding interval and we multiply the host vector in order to have the desired norm. Contrary to BPSK modulations, the watermarking subspace (space of norms) is not private, secret relies only on the partition of the real-positive axis representing the norms. There is no security flaw because we works on the WOA framework. Adversaries do not know the embedded message. However, this embedding is easy to implement, it enables to achieve stego-secure embedding since the distributions of original and watermarked contents are the same, and brings another scheme to compare with in term of robustness.

We use previous notations of Part. 2.1. We want to create a watermarked signal $\mathbf{y} = \alpha\mathbf{x}$, $\alpha \in \mathbb{R}^+$. This method is based on the distribution of the norms of host Gaussian vectors. In fact, if $\mathbf{x} \in \mathbb{R}^{N_v}$ with $\mathbf{x} \sim \mathcal{N}(0,1)$, $\|\mathbf{x}\|^2 \sim \chi^2(N_v)$ (Chi-2 law of degrees N_v), $\|.\|$ representing the euclidean norm. Codewords are sets in a partition of $[0,+\infty[$. To embed a secret message $\mathbf{m}$ in a host vector $\mathbf{x}$, we randomly choose a norm $\|\mathbf{y}\|^2$ in the corresponding real-interval and we compute:

$$\mathbf{y} = \sqrt{\frac{\|\mathbf{y}\|^2}{\|\mathbf{x}\|^2}}\mathbf{x}. \tag{14}$$

We obtain the watermark signal $\mathbf{w} = \mathbf{y} - \mathbf{x}$. This process can be considered as a variant of Moulin and Briassouli stochastic embedding [11] who work on different host distributions. Different consequences arise from this new embedding scheme:

- The means of choosing a norm in the right codeword is not optimal (from the distortion point of view): we generate real numbers until we have one of them in the desired interval.
- To define the secret partition on the real-positive axis, we use an estimator of the quantile function of χ^2 distribution.

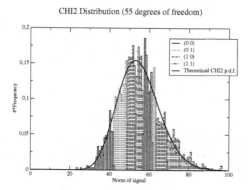

CHI2 Distribution (55 degrees of freedom)

Fig. 2. Secret partition of real-positive axis and associated distribution with parameters $N_c = 2, N_w = 8, N_v = 55$, each message is coded into 2 codewords. We have constructed the bins by generating 2000 Gaussian vectors for each message and calculating their respectives norms.

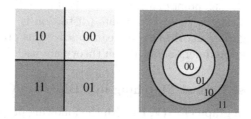

Fig. 3. 2D representations of coding regions for NW and CW (left part) and for χ^2W (right part) for 2 bits

- With the condition of message equiprobability, we must have more than one codeword for each message. Without this condition, a pirate can find the secret partition by using a quantile function (he separates the p.m.f. into 2^{N_c} parts of probability $\frac{1}{2^{N_c}}$). We denote N_w the number of codewords used.

Fig. 2 shows a secure partition of real positive axis and the associated distribution with parameters $N_c = 2, N_w = 8, N_v = 55$.

Note that the decoding regions are the same for NW and CW (they are delimited by hyperplanes) but different from the ones related to χ^2W (delimited by hyperspheres). Fig. 3 shows 2D representations of coding regions for spread-spctrum schemes and for χ^2W. We use $N_c = 2$.

3   Minimisation of the Embedding Distortion

We have seen that the level of security of the previously watermarking methods is given by the distribution of the signals after watermarking. Note that these

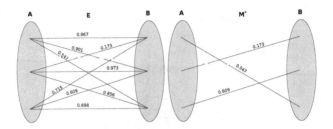

Fig. 4. Example of a weighted bipartite graph with two partitions of three vertices and minimal cost perfect matching found by Hungarian Method (weights between two vertices are noted on each corresponding edge)

distributions are defined by the distribution of correlations for BPSK modulations and the distribution of the norms for $\chi^2 W$. However, from the distortion point of view, these implementations are not optimal. We propose in the next section a new scheme which can ensure a given distribution of our marked signals while minimizing the embedding distortion. We want to associate each point of host distribution with each point of a chosen distribution with a minimal average Euclidean distance between these two points (distortion is proportional to the distance). The Hungarian algorithm is a mean to solve this problem. To explain this algorithm, some reminders about graph theory are useful.

3.1   Minimal Cost Perfect Matching in a Bipartite Graph

A bipartite graph is a graph $G = (V, E)$ with the following property: there exists a partition $V = A \sqcup B$, each edge of E is of the form $[a, b]$ with $a \in A$ and $b \in B$. Moreover G satisfy $|A| = |B| = N_m$. A weighted bipartite graph $G = (V, E, P)$ is a bipartite graph where each edge is weighted by a function $P : E \to \mathbb{R}$. A perfect matching M of G is defined as a subset of E with N_m elements where each vertex is incident with exactly one member of M. In this paper, we are interested in the Assignment Problem (AP), we search the minimal cost perfect matching M^*, i.e., a perfect matching whose the sum of weights of edges is minimal. More precisely we search:

$$M^* = \arg\min_{M} \sum_{t \in M} P(t). \tag{15}$$

Fig. 4 shows a weighted bipartite graph and its minimal cost perfect matching.

3.2   The Hungarian Method for the AP

The Hungarian method [12] is an efficient algorithm to solve the AP in a weighted bipartite graph in polynomial time $(O(N_m{}^3))$. We consider $G = (V, E, P)$ a weighted bipartite graph with:

- $V = A \sqcup B$,
- $A = \{a_0, ..., a_{N_m-1}\}$,
- $B = \{b_0, ..., b_{N_m-1}\}$.

We consider $\mathbf{D} \in \mathcal{M}_{N_m, N_m}(\mathbb{R})$, a matrix initialized with $\mathbf{D}(i, j) = P([a_i, b_j])$. The goal is to choose N_m elements of this matrix in order to have each row and each column containing one chosen element. In fact, the minimal cost perfect matching is the set of edges corresponding to these choosen elements. The Hungarian algorithm does the following:

1. Subtract the entries of each row by the row minimum: each row has at least one zero, all entries are positive or zero.
2. Subtract the entries of each column by the column minimum: each row and each column has at least one zero.
3. Select rows and columns across which to draw lines, in such a way that all the zeros are covered and that no more lines have been drawn than necessary.
4. A test for optimality:
   - If the number of the lines is n, choose a combination from the modified cost matrix in such a way that the sum is zero.
   - If the number of the lines is < n, go to 5.
5. Find the smallest element which is not covered by any of the lines. Then subtract it from each entry which is not covered by the lines and add it to each entry which is covered by a vertical and a horizontal line. Go back to 3.

So we have:

$$M^* = \{[a_i, b_j] : \mathbf{D}(i, j) = 0\}. \tag{16}$$

3.3 Application for NW and CW Embedding

Construction of bipartite graphs: We want to create 2^{N_c} bipartite graphs which contain, for the host partition, points of distribution of several host signals (correlations). We construct points of target distributions by selecting only points in codeword of the desired message. The goal is to find the minimal cost (euclidean distance) perfect matching between the two partitions. Formally, we use N_m host signals $\{\mathbf{x}_i\}_{i=0,\dots,N_m-1}$.

For each host signal $\mathbf{x}_i$ we construct the correlation host vector:

$$\mathbf{z}_{\mathbf{x}_i} = \left(z_{\mathbf{x}_i, \mathbf{u}_0}, \dots, z_{\mathbf{x}_i, \mathbf{u}_{N_c-1}} \right).$$

We want to construct 2^{N_c} target distributions. As we have seen before, NW and CW modulations can permit to construct distributions we want to obtain in order to match the security class we want (stego-secure, key-secure, ...).

We proceed by watermarking for each message $\mathbf{m}$, host signals $\mathbf{x}_i$ with the chosen modulation to obtain $\mathbf{y}_i$. Finally, we construct the correlation marked vector $\mathbf{z}_{\mathbf{y}_i} = \left(z_{\mathbf{y}_i, \mathbf{u}_0}, \dots, z_{\mathbf{y}_i, \mathbf{u}_{N_c-1}} \right)$. We obtain, for each message, the weighted bipartite graph $G = \{X \sqcup Y, A, P\}$ with:

- $X = \{\mathbf{z}_{\mathbf{x}_i}\}_{i=0,\dots,N_m-1}$,
- $Y = \{\mathbf{z}_{\mathbf{y}_j}\}_{j=0,\dots,N_m-1}$ (depends on $\mathbf{m}$),
- A defines the set of edges $[\mathbf{z}_{\mathbf{x}_i}, \mathbf{z}_{\mathbf{y}_j}]$ of the graph G,
- P is the weight function of the edges of G.

$$P([\mathbf{z}_{\mathbf{x}_i}, \mathbf{z}_{\mathbf{y}_j}]) = \|\mathbf{z}_{\mathbf{x}_i} - \mathbf{z}_{\mathbf{y}_j}\|_2.$$

We obtain 2^{N_c} minimal cost perfect matchings M_k^* between host correlations and marked correlations by using Hungarian method.

Mapping reduction: In previous section, we construct one bipartite graph for one message to embed. In order to reduce complexity of bijections calculus, we can use property of symmetry of our distributions (the axis of symmetry are the carriers); points of target distributions are computed in order to embed a constant message (for example the message $(1, 1, ..., 1)$). For the rest of this article, we notate N_m-map a triplet (X, Y, M^*) constructed with N_m host signals. Fig. 5 shows a correlation bipartite graph with $N_m = 3$, $N_c = 2$ and its minimal cost perfect matching found by Hungarian method.

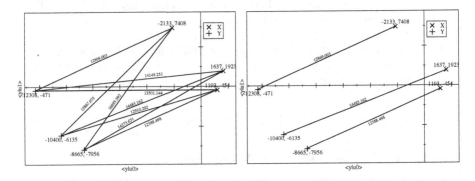

Fig. 5. Projection over two carriers ($N_c = 2$): correlation bipartite graph construction and minimal cost perfect matching found by Hungarian method with two partitions of three vertices, host correlations and marked correlations ($N_m = 3$). Euclidean distances (weights) between two vertices are noted on each corresponding edge. The minimal cost perfect matching associates elements of each vertex partition while minimizing the summation of the distances.

Model-based embedding: We consider (X, Y, M^*) the N_m-map constructed in the previous section. Now, we want to mark a signal $\mathbf{x}$ with any message $\mathbf{m}$ using the map. First, we compute the correlation host vector $\mathbf{z_x} = \left(z_{\mathbf{x},\mathbf{u}_0}, ..., z_{\mathbf{x},\mathbf{u}_{N_c-1}}\right)$ We want to associate $\mathbf{z_x}$ with a point of Y by using M^*.

We have seen that elements of Y have been constructed in order to embed the message $(1, ..., 1)$. We note indices of $\mathbf{m}$ where the bit is different from 1. Note that a matching from an original content to a given codeword enables to generate matchings to any codewords by symmetrising both points along appropriated axes. Consequently sign changes must be made on the coefficients of $\mathbf{z_x}$ in the indices that have undergone symmetries. Afterwards inverse symmetry must be performed after watermarking in order to embed the correct message $\mathbf{m}$. Formally, we construct $\mathbf{R z_x}$,

$$\mathbf{R} \in \mathcal{M}_{N_c, N_c}(\mathbb{R}), \mathbf{R}(i, j) = \begin{cases} 0 \text{ if } i \neq j, \\ (-1)^{\mathbf{m}(i)+1} \text{ if } i = j. \end{cases}$$

Next, we find the nearest neighboor (minimal euclidean distance) of $\mathbf{Rz_x}$ in X, for example $\mathbf{z_{x_{i_0}}}$. Thanks to the perfect matching M^* we find $\mathbf{z_{y_{j_0}}}$, the correspondance of $\mathbf{z_{x_{i_0}}}$. Next, we apply inverse symmetry to compute the correlation marked vector $\mathbf{z_y}$:

$$\mathbf{z_y} = \mathbf{R}^{-1}\mathbf{z_{y_{j_0}}} = \mathbf{Rz_{y_{j_0}}}.$$

So, we obtain the correlation vector of our marked signal. By a difference between $\mathbf{z_y}$ and $\mathbf{z_x}$, we have $\mathbf{z_w}$, the watermark correlation vector. Proper retro-projection of this signal in the $N_v\mathrm{D}$-space is assured by :

$$\mathbf{w} = \sum_{i=0}^{N_c-1} \frac{\mathbf{z_w}(i)}{\langle \mathbf{u}_i | \mathbf{u}_i \rangle} \mathbf{u}_i.$$

And finally, we compute the watermarked signal $\mathbf{y} = \mathbf{x} + \mathbf{w}$. Fig. 6 shows this process by using the 3-map constructed, see Fig. 5.

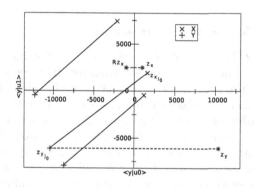

Fig. 6. Model-based watermarking scheme: illustration of Sec. 3.3. After calculating the correlation vector $\mathbf{z_x}$ of a host signal, we compute the watermarked correlations $\mathbf{z_y}$ by using the 3-map of Fig. 5 ($N_m = 3$) with the constant message $\mathbf{m} = (0,1)$ ($N_c = 2$).

3.4   Application for χ^2 Watermarking

Construction of bipartite graphs: We want to create 2^{N_c} bipartite graphs which contain, for the host distribution, norms of several host signals. We construct points of target distribution by selecting only real points in codewords of the desired message. We generate N_m Gaussian vectors $\mathbf{x}_i$ and, for each message, N_m Gaussian vectors $\mathbf{y}_j$ with $\|\mathbf{y}_j\|^2$ in the right codewords. We can construct, for each $k = 0, ..., 2^{N_c} - 1$ a bipartite graph $G = \{X \sqcup Y, A, P\}$ with:

- $X = \{\|\mathbf{x}_i\|^2\}_{i=0,...,N_m-1}$,
- $Y = \{\|\mathbf{y}_j\|^2\}_{j=0,...,N_m-1}$,
- A defines the set of edges $[\|\mathbf{x}_i\|^2, \|\mathbf{y}_j\|^2]$ of the graph G,
- P is the weight function of the edges of G. We use the absolute value of the differences of norms.

By using the Hungarian algorithm, we find 2^{N_c} minimal cost perfect matching M_k^* between host norms and marked norms (functions of embedded message). For the rest of this article, we denote N_m-smap the set $\{(X, Y_k, M_k^*)\}_{k=0,\dots,2^{N_c}-1}$ constructed with N_m signals.

Embedding: Process is similar to SS model-based embedding. To embed a vector $\mathbf{x}$ with message $\mathbf{m}$ and a N_m-smap; we calculate $\|\mathbf{x}\|^2$. Next we find the nearest neighboor of $\|\mathbf{x}\|^2$ in X. By M_k^* (k depends on $\mathbf{m}$), we find $\|\mathbf{y}\|^2$. Finally, we obtain $\mathbf{y} = \sqrt{\frac{\|\mathbf{y}\|^2}{\|\mathbf{x}\|^2}}\mathbf{x}$.

4   Experiments

The goal of this section is to assess the preservation of the distributions after the Hungarian method, the impact of this method on distortion and the general robustness of the three secure embedding schemes we presented.

4.1   Numerical Values and Assessments

In practice, $N_c = 2$. For NW and CW, we use $N_v = 256$ and for χ^2W, we use $N_v = 55$ (in order to have the same distortion for the three schemes, $WCR = -18dB$), $N_w = 8$. Tests are made with 2000 host Gaussian signals. For χ^2W, in order to have the equiprobable condition, we use an estimator of a fractile function of χ^2 distribution given in [13] which uses an estimator of the repartition function of a normal distribution in [14], we use the partition of the real-positive axis defined on Tab. 1. We have constructed a 10000-map and a 10000-smap with our signals database by using CW, NW and χ^2W and we have marked the initial 2000 signals by using on the one hand the secure modulation, and on the other hand the corresponding model-based found by Hungarian method (HCW, HNW and Hχ^2W).

Table 1. χ^2W: secret key used for $N_c = 2$, $N_w = 8$, $N_v = 55$. This table shows the real-interval functions of probability of messages. Each message appears with the same probability (0.25). This partition is the same than in Fig. 2.

message	probability	real-interval
(0 0)	0.1	[0;42.06]
(0 1)	0.2	[42.06;49.055]
(1 0)	0.15	[49.055;53.037]
(1 1)	0.15	[53.037;57.016]
(0 0)	0.15	[57.016;61.665]
(0 1)	0.05	[61.665;63.577]
(1 0)	0.1	[63.577;68.796]
(1 1)	0.1	[68.796;+∞[

4.2   Distribution Preservation after the Hungarian Method

Fig. 7 shows host, NW and HNW distributions on two carriers. As we can see, distribution of correlations after Natural Watermarking is the same than distribution of host correlations. It is consistent with the definition of stego-security. Moreover, correlations are the same after using Hungarian Method. Our model-based doesn't impair security. Distribution of CW and HCW on two carriers is shown on Fig. 8, we can see that the distribution is circular and we can conclude that for all bases $(\hat{\mathbf{u}}_0, \hat{\mathbf{u}}_1)$ of $vect(\mathbf{u}_0, \mathbf{u}_1)$ the distribution $p(\mathbf{y}_0, ..., \mathbf{y}_{1999}|\hat{\mathbf{u}}_0, \hat{\mathbf{u}}_1)$ will be the same (rotations of the secret subspace). It is consistent with the definition of key-security, the pirate can access the subspace of the codewords but has no information about the decoding regions. As HNW, HCW doesn't impair security. Fig. 9 shows projections of host, $\chi^2 W$ and $H\chi^2 W$ signals over the two first components. The distribution do not change with the two methods. As NW, $\chi^2 W$ is stego-secure.

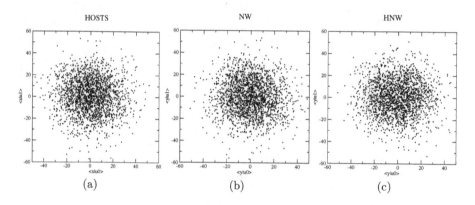

Fig. 7. (a): distribution of the projections of the host signals over two carriers. (b) and (c): distributions of the projection of the marked signals over two carriers for NW and HNW.

4.3   Distortion Minimisation

Tab. 2 shows the impact on distortion obtained on average on our 2000 signals for NW, CW, $\chi^2 W$, HNW, HCW and $H\chi^2 W$. We can see that we gain 2.7dB of distortion for NW, 1.1dB for CW and 3.6dB for $\chi^2 W$. This last result is due to the fact that there are two codewords for on message and these codewords are away in the real-positive axis.

4.4   Robustness

Beside distortion and security, the last constraint to assess is the general robustness of the presented schemes. We measure robustness of these secure modulations with and without distortion optimisation. Fig. 10 shows Bit Error Rate

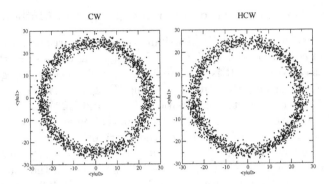

Fig. 8. Distribution of the projections of the marked signals over two carriers for CW and HCW

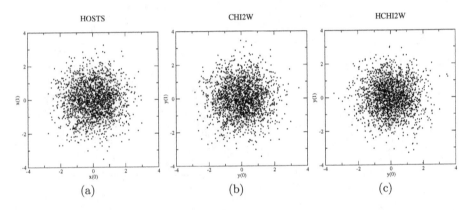

Fig. 9. (a): projection of host signals over the two first components. (b) and (c): projections of marked signals distributions over the two first components for χ^2W and Hχ^2W.

Table 2. Distortion for NW, CW and χ^2W on initial embedding schemes and after using the Hungarian optimisation scheme

	WCR (classical)	WCR (with the Hungarian method)
NW	-18.07	-20.76
CW	-17.97	-19.11
χ^2W	-18.02	-21.65

functions of chosen $WCNR$ over 2000 signals and we can verify that distortion optimisation does not modify robustness of our schemes. As we can see, CW is more robust than NW which is more robust than χ^2W. An insight of the poor robustness of χ^2W can be given by the fact that for this embedding, the decoding regions are always very close to each other (see Fig. 3). Consequently one

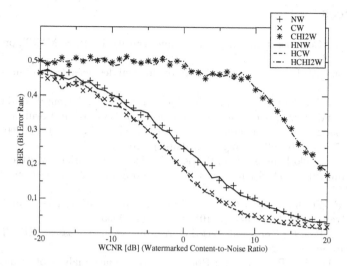

Fig. 10. BER vs WCNR for NW, CW and χ^2W. For NW, CW and χ^2W, we have $WCR = -18dB$. For HNW, HCW and $H\chi^2$W, we obtain respectively $WCR = -20.76\text{dB}$, -19.11dB and -21.65dB.

watermarked vector corrupted by noise will have a higher probability to change of coding regions for χ^2W than for NW or CW. Note that we cannot show robustness of the six schemes with the same distortion because NW modulation does not allow to set a target distortion.

5   Conclusion

The goals of this paper are twofold: to propose and compare secure embedding schemes for data-hiding and to propose a general method to minimise the global embedding distortion for each scheme. The first point is addressed by proposing the χ^2 embedding scheme which is more fragile than other scheme like NW or CW. The optimisation regarding robustness appears not to be straightforward and future works will be devoted to find more robust schemes and to find coding regions that will improve the robustness of χ^2W.

Moreover, we found that the Hungarian method is the ideal practical tool to minimize distortion while guaranteeing a given class of security.

Acknowledgments

Benjamin Mathon, François Cayre and Patrick Bas are supported (in part) by the European Commission through the IST Programme under Contract IST-2002-507932 ECRYPT and the National French projects Nebbiano ANR-06-SETIN-009, RIAM Estivale and ARA TSAR.

References

1. Kalker, T.: Considerations on watermarking security. In: Proc. MMSP, pp. 201–206 (October 2001)
2. Kerckhoffs, A.: La cryptographie militaire. Journal des Sciences militaires IX, 5–38 (1883)
3. Comesaña, P., Pérez-Freire, L., Pérez-González, F.: Fundamentals of data hiding security and their application to spread-spectrum analysis. In: Barni, M., Herrera-Joancomartí, J., Katzenbeisser, S., Pérez-González, F. (eds.) IH 2005. LNCS, vol. 3727, pp. 146–160. Springer, Heidelberg (2005)
4. Kutter, M., Voloshynovskiy, S., Herrigel, A.: The watermark copy attack. In: Electronic Imaging 2000, Security and Watermarking of Multimedia Content II, vol. 3971 (2000)
5. Cayre, F., Furon, T., Fontaine, C.: Watermarking security: Theory and practice. IEEE Trans. Signal Process. 53(10), 3976–3987 (2005)
6. Cayre, F., Bas, P.: Kerckhoffs based embedding security classes. IEEE Trans. Inf. Forensics Security (2007)
7. Mathon, B., Bas, P., Cayre, F.: Practical performance analysis of secure modulations for woa spread-spectrum based image watermarking. In: Proc. ACM MM&Sec 2007 (September 2007)
8. Sallee, P.: Model-based steganography. In: Kalker, T., Cox, I., Ro, Y.M. (eds.) IWDW 2003. LNCS, vol. 2939, pp. 154–167. Springer, Heidelberg (2004)
9. Shannon, C.E.: Communication theory of secrecy systems. Bell System Technical Journal 28, 656–715 (1949)
10. Malvar, H.S., Flôrencio, D.: Improved spread spectrum: a new modulation technique for robust watermarking. IEEE Trans. Signal Process. 53, 898–905 (2003)
11. Moulin, P., Briassouli, A.: A stochastic qim algorithm for robust, undetectable image watermarking. In: ICIP, pp. 1173–1176 (2004)
12. Kuhn, H.W.: The Hungarian method of solving the assignment problem. Naval Res. Logistics Quart. 2, 83–97 (1955)
13. Hill, I.D., Pike, M.C.: Algorithm 299. ACM TOMS, p. 185 (June 1985)
14. Ibbetson, D.: Algorithm 209. Collected Algorithms of the CACM, p. 616 (1963)

On the Design and Optimization of Tardos Probabilistic Fingerprinting Codes

Teddy Furon, Arnaud Guyader, and Frédéric Cérou

Centre de Recherche INRIA Rennes Bretagne Atlantique*

Abstract. G. Tardos [1] was the first to give a construction of a finger-printing code whose length meets the lowest known bound in $O(c^2 \log \frac{n}{\epsilon_1})$. This was a real breakthrough because the construction is very simple. Its efficiency comes from its probabilistic nature. However, although G. Tardos almost gave no argument of his rationale, many parameters of his code are precisely fine-tuned. This paper proposes this missing rationale supporting the code construction. The key idea is to render the statistics of the scores as independent as possible from the collusion process. Tardos optimal parameters are rediscovered. This interpretation allows small improvements when some assumptions hold on the collusion process.

1 In Gabor Tardos' Shoes

This article deals with active fingerprinting, also known as traitor tracing, or forensics, when applied on multimedia content. Fingerprinting is the application where a content server distributes personal copies of the same content to n different buyers. Some are dishonest users, called colluders, who mix their copies to yield a pirated content.

A binary fingerprinting code is a set of n different m bit sequences $\{\mathbf{X}_j\}_{j=1}^n$. Each sequence identifying a user has to be hidden in his/her personal copy with a watermarking technique. When a pirated copy is found, the server retrieves a m bit sequence $\mathbf{Y}$ and accuses some users or nobody. There are two kinds of errors: accusing an innocent (i.e. a false positive whose probability is denoted p_{fp}) and accusing none of the colluders (i.e. a false negative with probability p_{fn}). The designers of the fingerprinting code must assess the minimum length of the code so that the probabilities of error are below some significance levels: $p_{fa} < \epsilon_1$ and $p_{fn} < \epsilon_2$. One of the best fingerprinting codes is a probabilistic code proposed by G. Tardos, where $m = O(c^2 \log \frac{n}{\epsilon_1})$, where c is the number of colluders. Before Tardos' work, the existence of such a short code was proven. Tardos is the first to exhibit a construction which is surprisingly simple.

This breakthrough has appealed a numerous amount of research works. The goal of Tardos was to show a construction of an efficient fingerprinting code, where the length of the code was approximated. This yields a thread of works about refining the lower bound of the code length [2,3,4]. Improvements, such

---

* This work is supported by the French national programme "Securité ET INforma-tique" under project NEBBIANO, ANR-06-SETIN-009.

K. Solanki, K. Sullivan, and U. Madhow (Eds.): IH 2008, LNCS 5284, pp. 341–356, 2008.

as symmetric codes and q-ary codes have been proposed in [2]. Indeed, we study in this paper Skoric's symmetric version of the binary Tardos code. In the sequel, we abusively shorten this expression in 'Tardos code' in reference to the inventor of this family of codes. Implementation issues have also been addressed in [4,5].

1.1 A Pedagogical Approach

The nature of our article is very different. We are not providing better estimations of the code length. Our primary goal is to understand the key idea behind this code. Reading Tardos' seminal paper is very frustrating because Tardos proposes his construction hardly giving any clue on his rationale. His paper shows the code, gives a rough expression of its length, and chiefly proves that the probabilities of error match the constraints. Our aim is to rediscover how Tardos came up to invent this code. We have found different interpretations or explanations than those given in the previous works on Tardos codes, and we believe they help understanding how probabilistic codes work. Thanks to this better understanding, some small improvements are given at the end of the paper.

Another product of our analysis is that we create different classes of collusion. Usually, cryptographic papers dealing with traitor tracing use classes of collusion based on the nature of the symbols the collusion can forge: these are commonly denoted narrow or wide sense classes [6]. Nevertheless, these two classes are equivalent for binary codes studied in this article. Another variation is whether or not the collusion can produce erasures in detectable [7] or even undetectable positions [8]. We do not consider erasures here. We base the introduced four new classes of collusion not on the nature of the potentially forged symbols, but on side information the collusion has access to (see section 2 for details).

1.2 Probabilistic Codes

We keep the same structure of code than G. Tardos' one, what he defined as probabilistic codes. We denote random variables by capital letters and their occurences by their normal version. The sequence $\mathbf{X_j} = (X_{j1}, \cdots, X_{jm})$ identifying user j is composed of m independent binary symbols, with $P(X_{ji} = 1) = p_i$, $\forall i \in [m]$, with $[m]$ denoting $\{1, \ldots, m\}$. $\{P_i\}_{i=1}^m$ are independent and identically distributed random variables in the range $[0, 1]$: $P_i \sim f(p)$. They have been drawn, taking the values $\{p_i\}_{i=1}^m$, before the code construction. $\mathbf{Y} = (Y_1, \cdots, Y_m)$ is the sequence decoded from the pirated copy. The accusation process accuses user j if $S_j > T$, where $S_j = \sum_{i=1}^m U(Y_i, X_{ji}, p_i)$, and T is a threshold. Roughly speaking, $U(Y_i, X_{ji}, p_i)$ is positive when $X_{ji} = Y_i$, tending to accuse user j, $U(Y_i, X_{ji}, p_i)$ is negative when $X_{ji} \neq Y_i$, tending to plead user j as innocent.

The random variables $\{P_i\}_{i=1}^m$ are independent and identically distributed with a pdf f which is assumed to be symmetric around $1/2$: $f(p) = f(1 - p)$. It means that symbols '1' and '0' play a similar role with probability p or $1 - p$. This implies that the summands $U(Y_i, X_{ji}, p_i)$ in the accusation sum S_j follow the rules:

$$U(1,1,p) = g_1(p), \quad U(0,0,p) = g_1(1-p), \tag{1}$$
$$U(1,0,p) = g_0(p), \quad U(0,1,p) = g_0(1-p). \tag{2}$$

Functions g_0 and g_1 are notations from G. Tardos' paper, and common to Skoric's works [2,3]. The function g_1 is used when symbols X_{ji} and Y_i match, function g_0 when they are different. These weights depend on the probability to find symbol Y_i at this index, i.e. p_i if $Y_i = 1$, $1 - p_i$ if $Y_i = 0$.

Designing a binary probabilistic code means to find the optimal functions f, g_1 and g_0. But, the definition of optimality is not very clear. Skoric et al. took Chernoff's lower bound of the code length as the criterion, and they partially rediscovered Tardos functions [3]. We invoke a different rationale.

The main drawback of probabilistic codes is that, a priori, the score of the innocents is a random variable whose statistics depend on the collusion process, which is unknown at the decoding side. This also obviously holds for the scores of the colluders. On the other hand, Tardos announces two very astonishing facts:

1. The probabilities of error are guaranteed whatever the collusion process is. The threshold and the length are also fixed and independent of the collusion process (for a given collusion size c).
2. There is no need to calculate the scores of all the users. A user is deemed guilty if his accusation sum is greater than the threshold.

Although Tardos did not say anything on the key ideas supporting his code construction, we believe that his intuition was to render the scores as independent as possible from the collusion process. In other words, the first task is to render the statistics of the scores independent, before optimizing the code length.

The fingerprinting code being probabilistic, it is not surprising that our study is solely based on the statistics of the score of an innocent (section 3) and of the score of a colluder (section 4). The score being a sum of independent random variables, we consider it as Gaussian distributed. This assumption really helps interpretating what G. Tardos had in mind. Item number one in the list above implies that we need expectations and variances of the scores (innocents and colluders) to be independent of the collusion process. Item number two implies that the scores are also mutually independent. Tardos' choices of functions f, g_1 and g_0 do fulfill these two conditions. This paper studies the converse: we look for functions f, g_1 and g_0 achieving independence.

However, this use of the central limit theorem is absolutely not recommended when estimating the code length because it amounts to integrate the distribution function on its tail where the Gaussianity assumption does not hold. In other words, when the expectations and variances are set independent of the collusion process, the behaviour of the code is fixed up to the second order. Nevertheless, a precise evaluation of the threshold value and the code length would need further developments. The Berry-Esséen bound shows that the gap between the Gaussian law and the real distribution of the scores depends on their third moment, which a priori depends on the collusion process[1].

---

[1] Skoric et al. also stress the crucial role of the cutoff parameter in the convergence speed of the Berry-Esséen bound [2, Sec. 7.1].

2   The Marking Assumption and the Four Classes of Collusion

Fingerprinting code has been first studied by the cryptographic community. The marking assumption was a concept invented by Boneh and Shaw [7]. It states that, in its narrow-sense version, whatever the strategy of the collusion $\{j_1, \cdots, j_c\}$, we have $Y_i \in \{X_{j_1 i}, \cdots, X_{j_c i}\}$. In words, colluders forge the pirated copy by assembling chunks from their personal copies. It implies that if, at chunk i, the colluders symbols are identical, then this symbol value is decoded at the i-th chunk of the pirated copy.

This is what watermarkers have understood from the pioneering cryptographic work. However, this has led to misconceptions. Another important thing is the way cryptographers have modelized a host content: it is a binary string where some symbols can be changed without spoiling the regular use of the content. These locations are used to insert the sequence symbols. This implies that colluders disclose symbols from their identifying sequences comparing their personal copies symbol by symbol. Is this the case with multimedia fingerprinting?

In a multimedia application, the content is divided into chunks c_i. A chunk can be a few second clip of audio or video. Symbol X_{ji} is hidden in the i-th chunk of the content with a watermarking technique. This gives the i-th chunk sent to the j-th user: c_{ji}. In this paper, we only address the collusion process where the pirated copy is forged by picking chunks from the colluders personal copies. We do not address mixing of several chunks into one.

2.1   The Blind Colluders

We consider a first class of colluders. Before receiving the personal copies, these c dishonest users, denoted by their indices $\{j_1, \cdots, j_c\}$, have already agreed on how to forge the pirated copy. This strategy amounts to set an assignation sequence $(M_1, \cdots, M_m)$ with $M_i \in \{j_1, \cdots, j_c\}$, such that $Y_i = X_{M_i, i}$. We assume that the colluders share the risk, so that the cardinal $|\{i|M_i = j_u\}| \approx m/c$, for all $u \in [c]$. The assignation sequence is random and independent of the personal copies. We introduce the random variable Σ_i as the number of symbols '1' which the collusion gets at index i, the conditional probability concerning Y_i is given by: $P_{Y_i}(0|\Sigma_i = \sigma_i) = (c - \sigma_i)/c$. The important thing is that the blind colluders set their assignation sequence without observing their personal copies.

2.2   The Sighted Colluders

This second class of colluders differs in the fact that the assignation sequence is now a function of the personal copies. These colluders are able to split their copies in chunks and to compare them sample by sample. Hence, for any index i, they are able to notice that, for instance, chunks $c_{j_1 i}$ and $c_{j_2 i}$ are different or identical. For binary embedded symbols, they can constitute two stacks, each containing identical chunks. This allows new collusion processes such as a majority vote (the pirated chunk is taken for the stack whose size is bigger) or a minority vote... From a statistical point of view, the majority vote yields the following conditional probability: $P_{Y_i}(0|\Sigma_i = \sigma_i) = 1$ if $\sigma_i < c/2$, 0 else. For the minority vote: $P_{Y_i}(0|\Sigma_i = \sigma_i) = 1$ if $\sigma_i > c/2$, 0 else, with the noticeable exceptions due to the marking assumption: $P_{Y_i}(0|\Sigma_i = 0) = 1$ and $P_{Y_i}(0|\Sigma_i = c) = 0$.

The important thing is that colluders can notice differences between chunks, but they cannot tell which chunk contains symbol '0'. Hence, symbols '1' and '0' play a symmetric role, which strongly links the conditional probabilities:

$$P_{Y_i}(0|\Sigma_i = \sigma_i) = P_{Y_i}(1|\Sigma_i = c - \sigma_i) = 1 - P_{Y_i}(0|\Sigma_i = c - \sigma_i). \qquad (3)$$

2.3 The Cryptographic Colluders

In the third class, the colluders know parts of their code sequences. This is the case in the model used by cryptographers since Boneh and Shaw [7]. The bits are directly pasted in the host content string, and thus observable by the colluders. However, the marking assumption is still valid. New strategies are then possible like the 'All 0' (resp. 'All 1') consisting in putting a symbol '0' (resp. '1') in the pirated copy chunks whenever this is possible. This is the case when all the colluders do not have c embedded '1' (resp. '0') in their chunks: $P_{Y_i}(0|\Sigma_i = \sigma_i) = 1$ if $\sigma_i < c$, 0 else (resp. $P_{Y_i}(0|\Sigma_i = \sigma_i) = 0$ if $\sigma_i > 0$). Note that the relationship (3) does not hold anymore.

2.4 The Omniscient Colluders

In this last class, the colluders know the value of p_i for all index i. They can adapt their strategy for each index chunk according to its value p_i. From a statistical point of view, we just write that the conditional probabilities depend on σ_i and p_i: $P_{Y_i}(0|\Sigma_i = \sigma_i, P_i = p_i)$. Subsection 4.2 reveals the optimum values of the worst case collusion. This class of collusion breaks the code, in the sense that the omniscient colluders will not be accused almost surely. Therefore, it is mandatory that the value of p_i for all index i remains secret, so that, this class of colluders never exists. This threat considerably reduces the interest in making P_i discrete random variables as proposed in [4]. This option shortens the size of memory needed to store the value of p_i, but it introduces a security flaw as the set of possible values is public.

2.5 An Open Issue about Multimedia Fingerprint

Cryptographic fingerprinting codes and probabilistic codes target the third type of collusion. We do think that such powerful colluders are not realistic in multimedia fingerprinting. Colluders do not have the watermark decoder to disclose their embedded sequence. An open question is then: Provided the colluders are less powerful than foreseen, is there a hope to invent more suitable (i.e. shorter sequences) fingerprinting code?

3   User j Is an Innocent

In our quest of finding the optimal functions g_1, g_0 and f, we apply the idea of setting the statistics of S_j (knowing that user j is innocent) independent from the collusion process. We assume that symbols $\{Y_i\}_{i=1}^m$ are mutually independent and distributed such that $P(Y_i = 1) = q_i$ (denoted Q_i, when considered as a random variable). This distribution a priori depends on several parameters: the size of the collusion, the class of the collusion, the collusion process used at index i and the value of p_i.

3.1   Expectation of S_j

$\mathbb{E}(S_j) = \sum_{i=1}^m \mathbb{E}(U(Y_i, X_{ji}, P_i)) = m\mathbb{E}(U(Y_i, X_{ji}, P_i))$, where $\mathbb{E}$ denotes mathematical expectation. Dropping the subscripts and using (1) and (2):

$$\mathbb{E}(U(Y, X, P)) = \mathbb{E}_P \mathbb{E}_Y \mathbb{E}_X U(Y, X, P)$$
$$= \int_0^1 q(pg_1(p) + (1-p)g_0(p))f(p)dp$$
$$+ \int_0^1 (1-q)(pg_0(1-p) + (1-p)g_1(1-p))f(p)dp. \quad (4)$$

Now, the problem is that the detection side ignores many parameters of the distribution, so that q is unknown. We believe that Tardos had in mind to remove this dependence on q. The most general manner to achieve this, is the following:

$$\mathbb{E}(U(Y, X, P)) = \mathbb{E}(H(P)) + \mathbb{E}(QA(P)),$$

with

$$H(p) = pg_0(1-p) + (1-p)g_1(1-p), \quad (5)$$
$$A(p) = H(1-p) - H(p). \quad (6)$$

The expectation of the summand of the innocent's score is independent of the collusion process if and only if $A(p) = 0$, $\forall p \in [0,1]$. This implies that H is symmetric: $H(p) = H(1-p)$, $\forall p \in [0,1]$. In this case:

$$\mathbb{E}(U(Y, X, P)) = \int_0^1 H(p)f(p)dp.$$

Hence, we know in advance the expectation of the innocent's score, regardless of the collusion process. If it is not zero, we can always subtract this constant to the scores. Hence, without loss of generality, let us impose that $\mathbb{E}H(P) = 0$.

3.2   Variance of S_j

The variance of a random variable a is denoted by $\mathrm{Var}(a)$. The summands of the score are independent and their expectation is null. Hence: $\mathrm{Var}(S_j) = \mathbb{E}(S_j^2) = \sum_{i=1}^m \mathbb{E}(U(Y_i, X_{ji}, P_i)^2)$.;

$$\mathbb{E}(U(Y,X,P)^2) = \mathbb{E}_p\mathbb{E}_Y\mathbb{E}_X U(Y,X,P)^2$$

$$= \int_0^1 q(pg_1(p)^2 + (1-p)g_0(p)^2)f(p)dp$$

$$+ \int_0^1 (1-q)(pg_0(1-p)^2 + (1-p)g_1(1-p)^2)f(p)dp. \quad (7)$$

The most general manner to achieve independence is as follows:

$$\mathbb{E}(U(Y,X,P)^2) = \mathbb{E}(G(P)) + \mathbb{E}(QB(P)),$$

with

$$G(p) = pg_0(1-p)^2 + (1-p)g_1(1-p)^2, \quad (8)$$
$$B(p) = G(1-p) - G(p). \quad (9)$$

The variance of the summand of the innoncent's score is independent of the collusion process if and only if $B(p) = 0$, $\forall p \in [0,1]$. This implies that G is symmetric: $G(p) = G(1-p)$, $\forall p \in [0,1]$. In this case:

$$\mathbb{E}(U(Y,X,P)^2) = \int_0^1 G(p)f(p)dp.$$

Hence, we know in advance the variance of the innocent's score, regardless of the collusion process. If it is not one, we can always normalize the scores. Hence, without loss of generality, let us impose that $\mathbb{E}G(P) = 1$ so that $\text{Var}(S_j) = m$.

3.3 Cross-Correlation

Thanks to the CLT, when m is big enough, the score S_j for an innocent is approximately distributed as a Gaussian distribution $\mathcal{N}(0,m)$. We investigate here the dependence with the score S_k knowing that user k is also an innocent. This amounts to calculate their correlation since S_k and S_j are deemed Gaussian.

$$\text{Cov}(S_j, S_k) = \mathbb{E}(S_j S_k) = \sum_{i=1}^m \mathbb{E}(U(Y_i, X_{ji}, P_i)U(Y_i, X_{ki}, P_i)), \text{ with}$$

$$\mathbb{E}(U(Y,X_j,P)U(Y,X_k,P)) = \mathbb{E}(Q(Pg_1(P) + (1-P)g_0(P))^2)$$
$$+ \mathbb{E}((1-Q)(Pg_0(1-P) + (1-P)g_1(1-P))^2)$$
$$= \mathbb{E}(H^2(P) + Q(H^2(1-P) - H^2(P))). \quad (10)$$

A cross correlation independent of the collusion process is achieved for $H^2(p) = H^2(1-p)$. This condition was already fulfilled, *cf.* subsection 3.1. Thus we have $\mathbb{E}(U(Y,X_j,P)U(Y,X_k,P)) = \mathbb{E}(H^2(P))$, and scores S_j and S_k are independent if and only if $H(p) = 0$, $\forall p \in [0,1]$. Injecting this new result in the expression of $G(p)$ gives:

$$G(p) = p.\frac{(1-p)^2}{p^2}g_1^2(1-p) + (1-p)g_1^2(1-p) = \frac{1-p}{p}g_1^2(1-p). \quad (11)$$

Remembering the constraint on the variance of the innocent score, we have:

$$\int_0^1 g_1^2(1-p)\frac{1-p}{p}f(p)dp = \int_0^1 g_1^2(p)\frac{p}{1-p}f(p)dp = 1. \qquad (12)$$

We have also collected two other equations, $\forall p \in [0,1]$:

$$H(p) = 0 \;\rightarrow\; pg_0(1-p) = -(1-p)g_1(1-p) \qquad (13)$$
$$G(p) = G(1-p) \;\rightarrow\; (1-p)g_1(1-p) = pg_1(p) \qquad (14)$$

In this last equation, we assume that g_1 as a constant sign over $[0,1]$. We do not have enough equations to fully determine the three functions g_1, g_0, and f. However, any occurence of $g_0(p)$, $g_0(1-p)$, and $g_1(1-p)$ can be replaced by expressions involving only $g_1(p)$.

4   User j Is a Colluder

We seek more relations to find out the three functions. For the moment, we do not restrict our study to a particular collusion process.

4.1   Variance of S_j

The collusion process implies a distribution of the couple $\{Y_i, X_{ji}\}$, with user j being a colluder. Dropping the subscript but keeping in mind the dependence on p, this distribution equals $P_{YX}(y, x|p) = P_Y(y|x, p)P_X(x|p)$. Colluders do not receive sequences different in nature than the ones of the innocents: $P_X(x|p) = p^x(1-p)^{1-x}$. Finally, we can write:

$$P_{YX}(0, 0|p) = P_Y(0|0, p)(1-p) \qquad P_{YX}(1, 1|p) = P_Y(1|1, p)p$$
$$P_{YX}(1, 0|p) = (1 - P_Y(0|0, p))(1-p) \qquad P_{YX}(0, 1|p) = (1 - P_Y(1|1, p))p$$

Hence, the collusion process is only defined, from a statistical point of view, via two functions depending on p: $P_Y(0|0, p)$ and $P_Y(1|1, p)$. As done for the variance of the score of an innocent, we write:

$$\mathbb{E}(U(Y, X, P)^2) = \mathbb{E}(P_{YX}(0, 0|P)g_1^2(1-P) + P_{YX}(1, 1|P)g_1^2(P))$$
$$+ \mathbb{E}(P_{YX}(0, 1|P)g_0^2(1-P) + P_{YX}(1, 0|P)g_0^2(P)).$$

Knowing relations (13) and (14), we express the four summands with $g_1(p)$:

$$P_{YX}(0, 0|p)g_1^2(1-p) = P_Y(0|0, p)(1-p)g_1^2(1-p) = P_Y(0|0, p)\frac{p^2}{(1-p)}g_1^2(p),$$

$$P_{YX}(1, 1|p)g_1^2(p) = P_Y(1|1, p)pg_1^2(p),$$
$$P_{YX}(0, 1|p)g_0^2(1-p) = P_Y(0|1, p)pg_1^2(p) = (1 - P_Y(1|1, p))pg_1^2(p),$$
$$P_{YX}(1, 0|p)g_0^2(p) = (1 - P_Y(0|0, p))(1-p)g_0^2(p)$$
$$= (1 - P_Y(0|0, p))\frac{p^2}{1-p}g_1^2(p).$$

It appears that, whatever the collusion process, the expectation of the square of the summands in the colluders' score is constant:

$$\mathbb{E}(U(Y, X, P)^2) = \mathbb{E}\left(g_1(P)^2 \frac{P}{1-P}\right) = 1$$

Thus, given the results of Sect. 3, the variance of the score is already independent of the collusion process, equaling $\mathrm{Var}(S_j | j \in \mathcal{C}) = m(1 - \mathbb{E}(U(Y, X, P))^2)$. Hence, the impact of the collusion process is solely determined by $\mathbb{E}(U(Y, X, P))$: The lower this expectation is, the more difficult it will be to find back the colluders.

4.2   Expectation of S_j

The expectation of the score of one colluder is surprisingly much more involved. However, as G. Tardos did, it is simpler to calculate the expectation of the sum of the c scores of the colluders. If the colluders share the risk evenly, we can suppose that the expectation of one colluder's score is the average of this expectation: $\mathbb{E}(S_j | j \in \mathcal{C}) = c^{-1}\mathbb{E}(\sum_{k=1}^c U(Y, X_{j_k}, P))$. If this is not the case, we are sure that at least one colluder has an expected score bigger than this average. Hence, at the decoding side, it will be easier to distinguish the two hypothesis (j is an innocent, j is a colluder) when this expectation is bigger. We have:

$$\mathbb{E}\left(\sum_{k=1}^c U(Y, X_{j_k}, P)\right) = \mathbb{E}\left(\sum_{\sigma=0}^c P_{Y\Sigma}(0, \sigma|P)((c-\sigma)g_1(1-P) + \sigma g_0(1-P))\right.$$

$$\left. + \sum_{\sigma=0}^c P_{Y\Sigma}(1, \sigma|P)((c-\sigma)g_0(P) + \sigma g_1(P))\right). \quad (15)$$

As usual, we express the summands with function $g_1(P)$.

$$\mathbb{E}\left(\sum_{k=1}^c U(Y, X_{j_k}, P)\right) = \mathbb{E}\frac{g_1(P)}{1-P}\sum_{\sigma=0}^c (P_Y(0|\sigma, P) - P_Y(1|\sigma, P))P_\Sigma(\sigma)(cP - \sigma),$$

$$(16)$$

with $P_\Sigma(\sigma) = \binom{c}{\sigma}P^\sigma(1-P)^{c-\sigma}$.

The omniscient colluders. This last equation shows what the worst collusion process is. The goal of the colluders is to minimize this expectation, which happens if $P_Y(0|\sigma, p) = 1$ and $P_Y(1|\sigma, p) = 0$ when $cp < \sigma$, $P_Y(0|\sigma, p) = 0$ and $P_Y(1|\sigma, p) = 1$ else. This optimum strategy is only possible when the collusion knows exactly the values σ_i (number of symbols '1' it got) and $\{p_i\}_{i=1}^m$. This corresponds to the omniscient colluders class. The next subsection deals with the other classes of colluders.

4.3   Independence from the Collusion Strategy

The other classes of colluders have in common their ignorance of the values $\{p_i\}_{i=1}^m$. This translates in the fact that P can be forgotten in the conditional probabilities. Hence, we can exchange the expectation and sum in (16):

$$\mathbb{E}\left(\sum_{k=1}^{c} U(Y, X_{j_k}, P)\right) = \sum_{\sigma=0}^{c} (P_Y(0|\sigma) - P_Y(1|\sigma))\binom{c}{\sigma} I_c(\sigma) \qquad (17)$$

with

$$I_c(\sigma) = \mathbb{E}\left(g_1(P)P^\sigma(1-P)^{c-\sigma-1}(cP-\sigma)\right),$$

$$= \int_0^1 \frac{g_1(p)f(p)}{(1-p)} p^\sigma(1-p)^{c-\sigma}(cp-\sigma)dp \qquad (18)$$

This family of integrals has the following property:

Lemma 1. *c and σ being integers such that $0 \le \sigma \le c$, we have:*

$$I_c(\sigma) = -I_c(c-\sigma),$$

Therefore, $\sum_{\sigma=0}^{c}\binom{c}{\sigma}I_c(\sigma) = 0$ and $I_c(c/2) = 0$ when c is even.

The proof of this lemma is based on the change of variable $p' = 1 - p$ in the integral, knowing that this change lets $g_1(p)f(p)(1-p)^{-1}$ invariant according to (14) and the assumption that f is symmetric around $1/2$.

Inserting $P_Y(1|\sigma) = 1 - P_Y(0|\sigma)$ in (17), simplifies in:

$$\mathbb{E}\left(\sum_{k=1}^{c} U(Y, X_{j_k}, P)\right) = 2\sum_{\sigma=0}^{c} P_Y(0|\sigma)\binom{c}{\sigma}I_c(\sigma). \qquad (19)$$

The decoding side a priori ignores the values $\{P_Y(0|\sigma)\}_{\sigma=0}^{c}$, except for two cases: The marking assumption states that $P_Y(0|\sigma = 0) = 1$, and $P_Y(0|\sigma = c) = 0$. Hence, the only way to get rid of the remaining unknown conditional probabilities is to find function $g_1(p)f(p)$ such that $I_c(\sigma) = 0, \forall \sigma, 0 < \sigma < c$. (14) tells us that the block $g_1(p)f(p)/(1-p)$ is symmetric. For this reason, we define a symmetric function $T(p) = pg_1(p)f(p)$ which could cancel the $(c-1)$ integrals: $\forall \sigma, 0 < \sigma < c$

$$I_c(\sigma) = \int_0^1 T(p)P_{c,\sigma}(p)dp \quad \text{with} \quad P_{c,\sigma}(p) = p^{\sigma-1}(1-p)^{c-\sigma-1}(cp-\sigma).$$

Lemma 2. *The family of polynomials $\{P_{c,\sigma}\}_{\sigma=1}^{c-1}$ spans the subspace $\mathcal{P}$ of polynomials of degree equal or less than $(c-1)$ whose integral over $[0,1]$ is null.*

The proof is in Annex A.1. A corollary of this proposition is that such a function T exists: $T(p) = cst, \forall p \in [0, 1]$. The next subsection shows that Tardos actually made this choice while the last section of the paper considers other solutions.

4.4 Rediscovering Tardos' Solution

Suppose we have found a function S, such that its projection onto $\mathcal{P}$ is null (ie. $I_c(\sigma) = 0, \forall 0 < \sigma < c$), it is symmetric and positive (ie. $S(p) = S(1-p) \ge 0$). This means that S is a good candidate as a prototype for $pg_1(p)f(p)$. Note that

αS with $\alpha > 0$ also fulfills these requirements. What is the maximum α? Let us write $pf(p)g_1(p) = \alpha S(p)$. (12) and the fact that f is a pdf defines these two constraints for α:

$$\alpha^{-1} = \int_0^1 S(p)g_1(p)(1-p)^{-1}dp = \int_0^1 S(p)(pg_1(p))^{-1}dp$$

Thanks to the properties of S, the expectation of the sum of the colluders' score is now independent of their strategy and equal to:

$$\mathbb{E}\left(\sum_{k=1}^c U(Y, X_{j_k}, P)\right) = 2c\alpha \int_0^1 S(p)p^{c-1}dp, \tag{20}$$

$$= 2\frac{\int_0^1 S(p)dp}{\sqrt{\int_0^1 \frac{S(p)g_1(p)}{1-p}dp \cdot \int_0^1 \frac{S(p)}{pg_1(p)}dp}} \tag{21}$$

The simplification of the numerator happens thanks to lemma 2. The polynomial $p^{c-1} - c^{-1}$ has a degree equal to $c-1$ and a null integral. Hence, it belongs to the linear subspace $\mathcal{P}$. S being orthogonal to this subspace (with a scalar product defined as the integral over $[0, 1]$), we have $\int_0^1 S(p)p^{c-1}dp = c^{-1}\int_0^1 S(p)dp$.

At last, once we have rendered the statistics of the scores of the innocents and of the colluders independent from the collusion process, comes the criterion of optimality. We will define it as the choice of functions f and g_1 maximizing the expectation of the sum of the colluders. A Cauchy-Schwarz inequality on the product of the denominator shows the maximum:

$$\mathbb{E}\left(\sum_{k=1}^c U(Y, X_{j_k}, p)\right) \leq \frac{2\int_0^1 S(p)dp}{\int_0^1 S(p)(p(1-p))^{-1/2}dp} \tag{22}$$

with equality if $g_1(p) \propto \sqrt{(1-p)/p}$, and thus $f(p) \propto S(p)/\sqrt{p(1-p)}$. Note that this maximization holds for any choice of function S. For the simplest choice ($S(p) = 1$), we finally rediscover Tardos' functions:

$$f(p) = \frac{1}{\pi\sqrt{p(1-p)}}, \quad g_1(p) = \sqrt{\frac{1-p}{p}}.$$

This choice yields $\mathbb{E}(\sum_{k=1}^c U(Y, X_{j_k}, p)) = 2/\pi$.

5   How to Make a Better Choice?

We investigate whether there is still room for improvements compared to Tardos choice.

5.1   Fixed Size of Collusion

If the application scenario can assess that the colluders will always be no more than c, then the dimension of the space $\mathcal{P}$ is finite and equal to $(c-1)$. In order to use powerful mathematical objects such as Legendre polynomials, a change of variable $p = (1 + x)/2$ is advised. This transforms the rhs of (22) into:

$$\frac{\int_{-1}^{1} t(x)dx}{\int_{-1}^{1} t(x)(1 - x^2)^{-1/2}dx}, \quad \text{with } t(x) = S((1 + x)/2). \tag{23}$$

We are looking for the function t defined over $[-1, 1]$ which maximizes this ratio, while having the following properties:

- $t(x) = t(-x)$ because $S(p)$ must be symmetric wrt $1/2$,
- its projection onto $\mathcal{P}$ is null because $I_c(\sigma) = 0$, $\forall 0 < \sigma < c$.
- $t(x) \geq 0$, $\forall x \in [-1, 1]$,

Thanks to the change of variable, a basis of the linear space $\mathcal{P}$ is defined as polynomials of degree less or equal to $(c - 1)$ whose integral over $[-1, 1]$ are null, and orthonormal for the following scalar product: $< f, g > = \int_{-1}^{1} f(x)g(x)dx$. This exactly corresponds to the normalized Legendre polynomials[2]: $\{P_l^{\mathcal{L}}\}_{l=1}^{c-1}$. Odd order Legendre polynomials are anti-symmetric. Even order ones reach their maximum values at $x = \pm 1$, and $P_{2k}^{\mathcal{L}}(1) = 1$.

If t is smooth enough[3], it can be expressed as a series of Legendre polynomial: $t(x) = \sum_{k=0}^{\infty} \tau_k P_k^{\mathcal{L}}(x)$, $\forall x \in [-1, 1]$. The above listed properties imply that: $\tau_{2k+1} = 0$ $\forall k$, $\tau_k = 0$ for $0 < k < c$, and $\tau_0 + \sum_{k \geq \lceil (c-1)/2 \rceil} \tau_{2k} \geq 0$.

Lemma 3. $\beta_l = \int_{-1}^{1} P_{2l}^{\mathcal{L}}(x)(1 - x^2)^{-1/2}dx = \pi 2^{-4l} \binom{2l}{l}^2$.
Moreover: $0 < \beta_{l+1} < \beta_l$, $\forall l \in \mathbb{N}$.

Therefore:

$$\frac{\int_{-1}^{1} t(x)dx}{\int_{-1}^{1} t(x)(1 - x^2)^{-1/2}dx} = \frac{2}{\pi}\left(1 + \tau_0^{-1} \sum_{k > (c-1)/2}^{\infty} \tau_{2k} 2^{-4k} \binom{2k}{k}^2\right)^{-1}, \tag{24}$$

which is maximized under the constraint $\tau_0 + \sum_{k > (c-1)/2} \tau_{2k} \geq 0$, by setting $\tau_{2k} = 0$, except $\tau_{2\lceil(c-1)/2\rceil} = -\tau_0$. Table 1 gives the numerical values for the first sizes of collusion. Note that these expectations converges to Tardos' one as c increases. In fact, when we cannot make any assumption on the maximum size of the collusions, Tardos' alternative $T(p) = pf(p)g_1(p) = 1$ is the only choice.

Another important fact is that the function S has an impact on f, but not on g_1 (see (22) and the line after). Hence, the assumptions yielding function S must be known when generating the code, but not necessary on the decoding side.

---

[2] Without the change of variable, we would have resorted to the shifted Legendre polynomials which are less known.

[3] This assumption prevents us from looking for discrete random variable $\{p_i\}$, *i.e.* when f is a sum of Dirac distributions as in [4].

Table 1. Best expectations of the sum of the scores of the colluders for a code length $m = 100$, when the size of the collusion is known. Corresponding increase in percentage compared to Tardos solution for which $m\mathbb{E}(\sum_{k=1}^{c} U(Y, X_{j_k}, P)) = 2m/\pi = 63.7$.

c	2	4	6	8	10
$m\mathbb{E}(\sum_{k=1}^{c} U(Y, X_{j_k}, p))$	85	74	71	69	68
Increase in %	33.3	16.4	10.8	8.1	6.5

5.2   Unique Collusion Process

Suppose that we know what the collusion process is, *i.e.* we know all the probabilities $P_Y(1|\sigma, p)$ and $P_Y(0|\sigma, p)$ for any value of $p \in [0, 1]$ and $\sigma \in [c]$. We can simplify (16) in $\mathbb{E}(\sum_{k=1}^{c} U(Y, X_{j_k}, P)) = \mathbb{E}(g_1(P)(1 - P)^{-1} C(P))$, where C, defined accordingly, solely depends on the collusion process. We can always decompose $C(p)$ as the sum of a symmetric function $C_s(p)$ and an anti-symmetric function $C_a(p)$. As we have constrained $g_1(p)(1 - p)^{-1}$ to be symmetric, then $\mathbb{E}(\sum_{k=1}^{c} U(Y, X_{j_k}, P)) = \mathbb{E}(g_1(P)(1 - P)^{-1} C_s(P))$. A Cauchy-Schwarz inequality gives an upper bound of this expectation, which holds for any function g_1:

$$\mathbb{E}\left(\frac{g_1(P)}{1 - P} C_s(P)\right) \leq \sqrt{\mathbb{E}\left(\frac{P}{1 - P} g_1^2(P)\right)} \sqrt{\mathbb{E}\left(\frac{C_s^2(P)}{(1 - P)P}\right)} = \sqrt{\mathbb{E}\left(\frac{C_s^2(P)}{(1 - P)P}\right)}.$$

The first square root equals one thanks to (14). Equality holds when $g_1(p) = \lambda C_s(p)p^{-1}$. The value of λ is given by the constraint on the variance of the score of the innocent: $\lambda = 1/\sqrt{\mathbb{E}(C_s^2(P)/P(1 - P))}$, and the expectation is then equal to $\mathbb{E}(\sum_{k=1}^{c} U(Y, X_{j_k}, P)) = \lambda^{-1}$. In comparison, Tardos' choice yields a lower expectation:

$$\mathbb{E}\left(\sum_{k=1}^{c} U(Y, X_{j_k}, P)\right) = \mathbb{E}\left(\sqrt{\frac{C_s^2(P)}{P(1 - P)}}\right) \leq \sqrt{\mathbb{E}\left(\frac{C_s^2(P)}{P(1 - P)}\right)}. \tag{25}$$

Thanks to the concavity of the function $x \mapsto \sqrt{x}$, Jensen inequality ensures that our choice is better than Tardos' one with respect to the expectation of the sum of the scores of the colluders. Yet, this holds when the decoding side exactly knows what function C is (collusion process and size of the collusion). It is a kind of matched detection process, such as the matched filters receptors in digital communications. This condition is very restrictive. However, there are some interesting points:

- Lemma 1 tells us that $I_2(1) = 0$, hence the value of $P_Y(0|\sigma = 1)$ has no impact when $c = 2$. The marking assumption fixes the remaining term $P_Y(0|\sigma = 0) = 1 - P_Y(0|\sigma = c) = 1$. Therefore, for a given function g_1, any collusion process involving only 2 colluders yields the same expectation $\mathbb{E}(\sum_{k=1}^{2} U(Y, X_{j_k}, P))$.
- When the collusion belongs to the blind class, the size of the collusion doesn't matter: $C(p) = C_s(p) = 2p(1 - p), \forall c \in \mathbb{N}$.

Table 2. Expectations of the sum of the scores of the colluders for a given collusion process C, a given size c and a matched accusation function g_1. $m = 100$. Expectations are in boldface font when the accusation function matches the collusion process.

	class process size	blind $\forall c$	sighted Majority 3	4	5	Minority 3	4	5	crypto All-1 3	4	5	All-0 3	4	5	omniscient Worst 2	3	4	5
	blind	**71**	80	80	83	53	44	33	66	62	58	66	62	58	41	9	-19	-44
	Maj-3	67	**84**	84	92	34	17	-5	59	50	43	59	50	43	44	9	-23	-51
	Maj-4	67	84	**84**	92	34	17	-5	59	50	43	59	50	43	44	9	-23	-51
	Maj-5	63	83	83	**93**	24	4	-23	53	43	35	53	43	35	45	9	-25	-54
	Min-3	50	38	38	29	**75**	87	105	56	62	67	56	62	67	16	5	-2	-10
	Min-4	43	27	27	18	74	**89**	111	51	58	65	43	58	65	11	3	0	-3
	Min-5	40	24	24	15	73	89	**112**	48	57	63	48	57	63	9	2	0	-2
g_1	All1-3	69	73	73	73	62	59	55	**68**	66	64	68	66	64	36	8	-16	-37
	All1-4	65	63	63	60	70	72	76	66	**67**	68	66	67	68	30	7	-12	-28
	All1-5	59	53	53	47	73	80	90	63	66	**69**	63	66	69	25	6	-8	-21
	All0-3	69	73	73	73	62	59	55	68	66	64	**68**	66	64	36	8	-16	-37
	All0-4	65	63	63	60	70	72	76	66	67	68	66	**67**	68	30	7	-12	-28
	All0-5	59	53	53	47	73	80	90	63	66	69	63	66	**69**	25	6	-8	-21
	Tardos	64	64	64	64	64	64	64	64	64	64	64	64	64	32	7	-14	-32

For these two conditions, the above maximization shows that $g_1(p) = \lambda(1-p)$. Table 2 shows the values of the expectation times the length of the code $m = 100$, for some functions C (column) against some functions g_1 optimal for a given collusion process (line). The last line corresponds to Tardos' choice. The scores on this line are all equal reflecting the independence versus the collusion process. The first line corresponds to the choice $g_1(p) = \lambda(1-p)$. It is extremely important to notice that expectations have been measured with $f(p) = (\pi\sqrt{p(1-p)})^{-1}$. In other words, there is still a degree of freedom to improve these scores. Or, we can say that the assumptions yielding the function C have an impact on g_1 but not f, such that they are needed on the decoding side but not on the coding side while generating matrix $\mathbf{X}$.

The scores on the diagonal are always the best score of a column as they correspond to matched accusation function and collusion process. However these functions g_1 are very sensitive with respect to the collusion: for instance, function g_1 tuned to fight against minority vote has excellent expectations when matched, but very bad scores when the collusion process is indeed a majority vote. The worst case attack led by omniscient colluders always has a dramatic effect. This stresses the fact that $\{p_i\}_{i=1}^m$ must absolutely remain secret.

6   Conclusion

The key idea supporting the probabilistic fingerprinting code proposed by G. Tardos is to render the statistics of the scores of the innocents and of the colluders independent from the collusion process. Achieving the independence for the first (expectation) and the second (variance) moments freezes all the degrees of freedom, determining the functions involved in the code. Tardos' choice is the most general. There is no room for improvements, except if the maximum collusion size is known when generating the code or if the collusion process is known at the decoding side.

References

1. Tardos, G.: Optimal probabilistic fingerprint codes. In: Proc. of the 35th annual ACM symposium on theory of computing, San Diego, CA, USA, pp. 116–125. ACM, New York (2003)
2. Skoric, B., Katzenbeisser, S., Celik, M.: Symmetric Tardos fingerprinting codes for arbitrary alphabet sizes. Designs, Codes and Cryptography 46, 137–166 (2008)
3. Skoric, B., Vladimirova, T., Celik, M., Talstra, J.: Tardos fingerprinting is better than we thought (2006) arXiv:cs/0607131v1
4. Nuida, K., Hagiwara, M., Watanabe, H., Imai, H.: Optimal probabilistic fingerprinting codes using optimal finite random variables related to numerical quadrature (2006) arXiv:cs/0610036v2
5. Katzenbeisser, S., Skoric, B., Celik, M., Sadeghi, A.R.: Combining Tardos fingerprinting codes and fingercasting. In: Furon, T., Cayre, F., Doërr, G., Bas, P. (eds.) IH 2007. LNCS, vol. 4567, pp. 294–310. Springer, Heidelberg (2008)
6. Barg, A., Blakley, G.R., Kabatiansky, G.A.: Digital fingerprinting codes: problem statements, constructions, identification of traitors. IEEE Trans. Inform Theory 49, 852–865 (2003)
7. Boneh, D., Shaw, J.: Collusion-secure fingerprinting for digital data. IEEE Trans. Inform. Theory 44, 1897–1905 (1998)
8. Safavi-Naini, R., Wang, Y.: Collusion-secure q-ary fingerprinting for perceptual content. In: Sander, T. (ed.) DRM 2001. LNCS, vol. 2320, pp. 57–75. Springer, Heidelberg (2002)

A   Proof of Lemmas

A.1   Lemma 2

We show that the family of polynomials $\{P_{c,\sigma}\}_{\sigma=1}^{c-1}$ spans the subspace $\mathcal{P}$ of polynomials of degree equal or less than $(c-1)$ whose integral over $[0,1]$ is null.

$\deg(P_{c,\sigma}) = c - 1$ because $P_{c,\sigma}(p) = p^{\sigma-1}(1-p)^{c-\sigma-1}(cp-\sigma) = -\sigma p^{\sigma-1} + \ldots + (-1)^{c-\sigma-1}p^{c-1}$. Besides: $\int_0^1 P_{c,\sigma}(p)dp = c\frac{\sigma!(c-\sigma-1)!}{c!} - \sigma\frac{(\sigma-1)!(c-\sigma-1)!}{(c-1)!} = 0$.

Denote $N(p) = \sum_{\sigma=1}^{c-1} \alpha_\sigma P_{c,\sigma}(p) = \sum_{\ell=0}^{c-1} \beta_\ell p^\ell$ the null polynomial: $N(p) = 0$, $\forall 0 \le p \le 1$. The term in p^0 comes from the contribution of $\alpha_1 P_{c,1}(p)$. Hence $\beta_0 = 0$ implies $\alpha_1 = 0$. The term in p^1 comes from the contribution of $\alpha_1 P_{c,1}(p) + \alpha_2 P_{c,2}(p)$. Hence, $\beta_1 = 0$ implies $\alpha_2 = 0$ since $\alpha_1 = 0$, etc. Therefore, $\sum_{\sigma=1}^{c-1} \alpha_\sigma P_{c,\sigma} = 0$ implies $(\alpha_1, \ldots, \alpha_{c-1}) = \mathbf{0}$. This proves that the polynomials $\{P_{c,\sigma}\}_{\sigma=1}^{c-1}$ are linearly independent.

A.2   Lemma 3

We show that $\beta_l = \int_{-1}^1 P_{2l}^{\mathcal{L}}(x)(1-x^2)^{-1/2}dx = \pi 2^{-4l}\binom{2l}{l}^2$, and $0 < \beta_{l+1} < \beta_l$.

Even degree Legendre polynomials have the following generic expression:

$$P_{2l}^{\mathcal{L}}(x) = 2^{-2l}\sum_{k=0}^{l}(-1)^{l-k}\frac{(2l+2k)!}{(l-k)!(l+k)!(2k)!}x^{2k} \quad . \tag{26}$$

Besides:

$$\int_{-1}^1 \frac{x^{2k}}{\sqrt{1-x^2}}dx = \frac{\pi}{k!}\frac{1.3.5\ldots(2k-1)}{2^k} \quad . \tag{27}$$

Hence,

$$\beta_l = \frac{(-1)^l \pi}{2^{2l}}\sum_{k=0}^{l}c_{k,l} \quad \text{with } c_{k,l} = (-1)^k\frac{(2l+2k)!}{(l+k)!(l-k)!k!k!2^{2k}} \quad . \tag{28}$$

Note that $c_{0,l} = \binom{2l}{l}$, and $c_{k+1,l}/c_{k,l} = (k-l)(k+l+1/2)/(k+1)^2$. This means that β_l can be expressed thanks to an hypergeometric function of the second kind:

$$\beta_l = \frac{(-1)^l \pi}{2^{2l}}\binom{2l}{l} \, {}_2F_1(-l,l+1/2;1;1) \quad . \tag{29}$$

It turns out that ${}_2F_1(-l,l+1/2;1;1) = (1/2-l)_l/l!$, where $(k)_l$ is a Pochammer coefficient. Some more lines of calculus give $(1/2-l)_l = (-1)^l 2^{-2l}(2l)!/l!$. This produces the expected result. Secondly,

$$\frac{\beta_{l+1}}{\beta_l} = \left(\frac{l+1/2}{l+1}\right)^2 < 1 \quad . \tag{30}$$

Iterative Detection Method for CDMA-Based Fingerprinting Scheme

Minoru Kuribayashi and Masakatu Morii

Graduate School of Engineering, Kobe University
1-1 Rokkodai-cho, Nada-ku, Kobe, 657-8501 Japan
{kminoru,mmorii}@kobe-u.ac.jp

Abstract. Digital fingerprinting of multimedia data involves embedding information in the content signal and offers the traceability of illegal users who distribute unauthorized copies. One potential threat to fingerprinting system is collusion, whereby a group of users combines their individual copies in an attempt to remove the underlying fingerprints. Hayashi et. al have proposed hierarchical fingerprinting scheme using the CDMA technique which designed a fingerprint signal by a combination of quasi-orthogonal sequences to increase the allowable number of users. In this paper, we formalize the model of collusion from the viewpoint of a communication channel, and propose a removal operation considering the interference among fingerprints. We also explore the characteristic of the proposed detector and the effects of the removal operation on a detection sequence. By introducing two kinds of thresholds for the determination of the presence of fingerprints, the performance of the proposed detector is enhanced effectively.

1 Introduction

Digital fingerprinting is used to trace the illegal users, where a unique ID known as digital fingerprints [1] is embedded into a content before distribution. When a suspicious copy is found, the owner can identify illegal users by extracting the fingerprint. The research on fingerprinting techniques is classified into two studies; The designs of collusion-resistant fingerprint and secure cryptographic protocol. Since each user purchases a content involving his own fingerprint, each content is slightly different. A coalition of users will therefore combine their different marked copies of a same content for the purpose of removing/changing the original fingerprint. The other threats in the fingerprinting are dispute and repudiation of a purchase. The purpose of cryptographic protocols is to solve such threats by achieving the asymmetric property [2]. In spite of the property, the production of embedding information is based on the design of collusion resistant fingerprint.

One of the simple approaches for the collusion attack is to average multiple copies of a same content. By combining many copies sufficiently, the fingerprints will be weakened or removed by the attack. It is important to generate fingerprints that can be not only to identify the colluders, but also resilient against

K. Solanki, K. Sullivan, and U. Madhow (Eds.): IH 2008, LNCS 5284, pp. 357–371, 2008.

the collusion attack. A number of works on designing fingerprints that are resistant against the collusion attack have been proposed. Many of them can be categorized into two approaches. One is to exploit the Spread Spectrum (SS) technique [3,4,5,6], and the other approach is to devise an exclusive code, known as collusion-secure code [7,8,9,10], which has traceability of colluders.

The origin of the spread spectrum fingerprinting is Cox's method that embeds the sequence into the frequency components of a digital image and detects it using a correlator [3]. Since normally distributed values allow the theoretical and statistical analysis of the method, modeling of a variety of attacks have been studied. Studies in [4] have shown that a number of nonlinear collusions such as interleaving attack can be well approximated by averaging collusion plus additive noise. So far, many variants of the spread spectrum fingerprinting scheme are based on the Cox's method, especially for the usage of the sequence which elements are randomly selected from normally distributed values. Instead of such a random sequence, theoretically quasi-orthogonal sequences are designed in [11] using a PN sequence such as M-sequence and Gold-sequence [12], etc. combined with orthogonal transform like DCT, which basic idea is the exploitation of the CDMA technique. Using the orthogonality, it is possible to assign a unique combination of spectrum components to each user and provide a hierarchical structure using two kinds of SS sequences; one is for group ID, and the other for user ID. At a detection of the fingerprint information, we list the components which signal strengths exceed a threshold, and identify the corresponding colluders whose fingerprints are expressed by the combination of the listed components. After the detection of group ID, we detect each user ID which is corresponding to each group ID since the group ID is required for generating the detection sequence to examine the user ID within the group. Therefore, if we fail to detect the group ID at the first detection, the following procedure to detect user ID does not conducted, hence the probability of correct detection of user's fingerprint falls. In order to solve this problem, the threshold for a group ID is designed lower. Even if wrong group IDs are accidentally detected, user IDs associated with the wrong group IDs will be excluded with high probability.

Although the interference among inserted signals under averaging collusion is expected very small, the effects become considerably high with an increase of number of colluders. Here, it is remarkable that detected signals are assumed as the interference of other undetected signals. In this paper, we formalize the model of the CDMA-based fingerprinting scheme, and present a removal operation to minimize the interference. In [13], the analysis of collusion attacks for uniformly distributed watermarks employing one to two dozen independent copies of watermarked content. We further analyze the effects on the watermarks caused by the collusion attacks using the formalized model of the CDMA-based fingerprinting scheme, and it helps us to remove the noise signals involved in detection sequences from a pirated copy. Because the sequences contain some colluders' fingerprint signals, they work as an interference at the detection of each objective signal. Once a fingerprint signal is detected, the signal is removed from the detection sequence for the decrease of interference in our method. The effects of the removal operation on the detection sequence are explored, and the operation is adaptively customized. It is obvious that lower threshold for a group ID not only improves the true-positive detection rate, but also degrades the false-positive rate. Then, if wrong group IDs are accidentally detected, the signals which contain the undetected fingerprints' signals are removed regarding as the interference. In order to avoid such a removal as much as possible, two kinds of thresholds are introduced; one is for the detection of candidates for group ID, and the other is for the determination of removal operation. If detected signals for group IDs retain sufficiently large energy, clearly they are determined as the embedded fingerprints, otherwise they are listed as potential suspects. By separating the detected signals into such two cases using two thresholds, the removal operation is selectively performed in the proposed scheme. Final decision for the identification of colluders is based on a higher threshold for a user ID. Due to the successive removal of such signals, we can extract more objective signals of colluders and less that of innocent users.

2   CDMA-Based Fingerprinting

Hayashi et. al have proposed a CDMA-based fingerprinting scheme with high robustness against collusion attack [11]. In this section, we review the basic idea, and summarize the embedding/detection procedure with an hierarchical structure.

2.1   Basic Idea

Let a sequence $d = \{d_0, \ldots, d_{\ell-1}\}$ be constructed from DCT coefficients and be initialized to the zero vector. We assume that the i-th element d_i is assigned to the i-th user as a fingerprint and embedding strength β is added to it; Only i-th DCT coefficient retains strength β. Then, a spread spectrum sequence assigned to the i-th user is given by

$$w_i = pn(s) \otimes dct(i, \beta), \tag{1}$$

where $pn(s)$ is a PN sequence generated using an initial value s, $dct(i, \beta)$ is the i-th DCT basic vector of an ℓ-tuple of strength β, and $\otimes$ implies element-wise multiplication. The sequence w_i is embedded into the frequency components of a digital image.

At the detection, a sequence $\tilde{w}_i$ is extracted from the difference between an original image and a pirated one. Then, instead of the similarity measurement [3], we multiply a PN sequence and perform DCT to obtain the sequence $\tilde{d} = \{\tilde{d}_0, \ldots, \tilde{d}_{\ell-1}\}$;

$$\tilde{d} = \mathsf{FDCT}(pn(s) \otimes \tilde{w}_i), \tag{2}$$

where FDCT means fast discrete cosine transform algorithm. Illegal users can be determined if the corresponding coefficients exceed a threshold T.

The advantage of the detection method in a CDMA-based fingerprinting scheme [11] is the computational complexity because of the fast algorithm of DCT which requires $O(\ell \log \ell)$ operations [14].

2.2 Hierarchical Embedding Procedure

We suppose that each user's fingerprint information consists of two parts; "group ID," identifies the group to which a user belongs; and "user ID," represents an individual user within the group.

Exploiting the quasi-orthogonal property of a PN sequence, we introduce a dependency between the spread spectrum sequences generated from two sequences d_g and d_u. Before embedding a user ID, its corresponding DCT basic vector with strength β_g is multiplied by a specific PN sequence related to d_g. Thus, for fingerprint information (i_g, i_u), two spread spectrum sequences related to d_g and d_u with strength β_g and β_u are given by

$$w_{i_g} = pn(s) \otimes dct(i_g, \beta_g), \tag{3}$$
$$w_{i_u} = pn(i_g) \otimes dct(i_u, \beta_u), \tag{4}$$

respectively. Notice that w_{i_u} is bounded to the group ID i_g. The spectrum sequences are mutually independent if the applied PN sequences are different. Thus, an hierarchical structure is realized, which increases the number of users; ℓ^2 users with only 2ℓ spectrum components.

The procedure to embed a user's fingerprint into an $N \times N$ image is summarized as follows.

1. Perform full-domain DCT on the image.
2. Select ℓ DCT coefficients from low- and middle-frequency domains on the basis of a secret key key. We denote the selected coefficients by $v = \{v_0, \ldots, v_{\ell-1}\}$.
3. Generate two spectrum sequences w_{i_g} and w_{i_u} by using a secret key s, (i_g, i_u), β_g, and β_u.
4. Embed the spectrum sequences into v by addition.

$$v^* = v + w_{i_g} + w_{i_u} \tag{5}$$

5. Perform full-domain IDCT to obtain a fingerprinted image.

From the viewpoint of the CDMA technique, it is possible to detect w_{i_g} and w_{i_u} from v^* because of the quasi-orthogonal property.

2.3 Detection

At a detector side, an host image (host frequency components) and secret keys key and s are required. Since the group ID ig and the user ID i_u that comprise a user's fingerprint are embedded separately, the detection procedure consists of two stages. The first stage focuses on identifying groups involving colluders, and the second one is to identify colluders within each guilty group. The latter operation is performed on the sequence using the PN sequence generated from the identified group ID as a seed. At the detection of each ID, we compare the components in the detection sequence with a threshold.

The detection sequence is obtained by performing DCT after subtracting the host sequence from that of a pirated copy, which is denoted by $\tilde{d} = \{\tilde{d}_0, \ldots, \tilde{d}_{\ell-1}\}$.

To apply statistical decision theory, we assume that $\tilde{d}$ is composed of random variables and the sequence except for the fingerprinted component $\tilde{d}_k$, which is denoted by $\tilde{d}$, are distributed according to $N(0, \sigma^2)$, where σ is the variance of the sequence. If we insert a watermark to add β to d_k in order to satisfy the inequality

$$\tilde{d}_k > \max_{i \neq k}\{\tilde{d}_i\}, \tag{6}$$

then we can detect the embedded watermark by setting a threshold T to be imposed $\tilde{d}_k > T > \tilde{d}_i$. If $\tilde{d}_i > T$, then a detector decides that d_i is watermarked, and hence, it detects an innocent user by mistake. Therefore, $\Pr(\tilde{d}_i > T)$ is the probability of false-positive detection. Then, we can say that

$$\Pr(\tilde{d}_i > T) \leq \frac{1}{2} \operatorname{erfc}\left(\frac{T}{\sqrt{2\sigma^2}}\right), \tag{7}$$

from study in [15]. The knowledge of the variance σ^2 enables a fingerprint detector to obtain a proper threshold corresponding to a given probability of false-positive detection.

Under the above characteristic of the detection sequence, illegal users are detected as follows.

1. Perform full-domain DCT on the pirated copy.
2. Select ℓ DCT coefficients from low- and middle-frequency domains on the basis of a secret key key, which is denoted by $\tilde{v}$.
3. Detect a group ID by the following operations.
   3-1. Generate a PN sequence $pn(s)$ using a secret key s, and multiply $\tilde{v} - v$ by it.
   3-2. Perform one-dimensional(1D) DCT to obtain the detection sequence $\tilde{d}_g$;

$$\tilde{d}_g = \mathsf{FDCT}\big(pn(s) \otimes (\tilde{v} - v)\big) \tag{8}$$

   3-3. Calculate the variance of $\tilde{d}_g$ by considering the property of its distribution (See [11]) and determine a threshold T_g with a given false-positive probability Pe_g.
   3-4. If $\tilde{d}_{g,k} \geq T_g, (0 \leq k \leq \ell - 1)$, determine k as the group ID i_g.
4. Detect a user ID using the detected group ID by the following operations.
   4-1. Generate a PN sequence $pn(i_g)$, and multiply $\tilde{v} - v$ by it.
   4-2. Perform 1D DCT to obtain the detection sequence $\tilde{d}_u$;

$$\tilde{d}_u = \mathsf{FDCT}\big(pn(i_g) \otimes (\tilde{v} - v)\big) \tag{9}$$

   4-3. Calculate the variance of $\tilde{d}_u$ and determine a threshold T_u with a given false-positive probability Pe_u.
   4-4. If $\tilde{d}_{u,h} \geq T_u, (0 \leq h \leq \ell - 1)$, determine h as the user ID i_u.

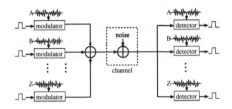 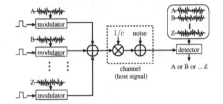

Fig. 1. The model of the CDMA technique

Fig. 2. The model of the CDMA-based fingerprinting scheme

Note that when some group IDs are detected, we examine each user ID corresponding to each group ID in order to identify all colluders. Therefore, this fingerprinting scheme is designed for *catch many*-type fingerprinting [1].

The detection of colluders are performed selectively depending on the detected group IDs, and FDCT is performed only once for the detection of a group ID and a few dozens of times for the corresponding user IDs. Suppose that the number of detected group IDs is much smaller than ℓ and it strongly depends on the number of colluders c. Then, the required number of operation for our detection method is approximately given by $O(c\ell \log \ell)$.

3   Proposed Detection Method

In this section, we formalize the averaging collusion as the CDMA channel and study the property of interference from noise elements. Based on the analysis, the interference can be removed efficiently from detection sequences in order to improve the true-positive detection rate.

3.1   Modeling

On the CDMA technique, signals of some users are multiplexed in one communication channel, and each detector checks the correlation with own PN sequence to decode an objective signal from the channel as shown in Fig.1. The CDMA-based fingerprinting scheme also follows the similar channel model except for the number of objective signals stored in a detector. Because the transmitting signals are assumed as the fingerprints of colluders and the objective signals should be correctly extracted from the channel which is an host signal. Since the host signal is known at the detector side, the received signal involves the objective signals and an additive noise. At the multiplexing process in a channel, the objective signals attenuate by a factor of the number of colluders, which is $1/c$, because of the effect of averaging. Such a channel model is illustrated in Fig.2. Our goal is to extract, not merely detect, the correct fingerprint signals as many as possible from the detection sequence with high probability.

The design of appropriate fingerprints must be complemented by the development of mechanisms that can capture those involved in the illegal user of content.

The detection of the signals, however, becomes difficult according to the increase of the number of colluders, and the difficulty is caused by the interference with each other. When a collusion occurs involving c colluders who form a pirated copy, the observed DCT coefficients after averaging collusion is

$$\tilde{v} = \frac{1}{c} \sum_{t=1}^{c} \tilde{v}_t + \epsilon, \tag{10}$$

where $\tilde{v}_t$ is the fingerprinted frequency components of the t-th colluder and ϵ is an additive noise that follows a Gaussian distribution with zero mean. Note that the additive noise is caused by the rounding-off effects when IDCT is performed to obtain a fingerprinted image. In this model, the number of colluders and the additive noise are unknown parameters. Since the host signal is available in our scenario, the detected signal sequence is represented by

$$\tilde{v} - v = \frac{1}{c} \sum_{t=1}^{c} (w_{i_g,t} + w_{i_u,t}) + \epsilon. \tag{11}$$

For the detection of a group ID, the PN sequence $pn(s)$ is multiplied and DCT is performed as explained in Eq.(8). It is remarkable that the detection sequence $\tilde{d}_g$ involves the noise signal $pn(s) \otimes (\sum_{t=1}^{c} w_{i_u,t}/c + \epsilon)$ as well as the signal corresponding to the colluders' group ID $pn(s) \otimes (\sum_{t=1}^{c} w_{i_g,t}/c)$. Although such a noise signal retains quasi-orthogonality, the effects are not negligible when the number of colluders is increased. The same effects are occurred at the detection of a user ID.

From the viewpoint of energy, the embedded signal strength β_g and β_u is attenuated into β_g/c and β_u/c, respectively. Notice that since the sequences $\tilde{d}_g$ and $\tilde{d}_u$ are transformed from the sequence $\tilde{v} - v$ by DCT, the energy of interference is also equal. Then, the energy of mutual interference at the sequence $\tilde{d}_g$ is given by $\beta_u + \beta_\epsilon$ because the spectrum sequence for the embedding is equal which is related to $pn(s)$, where β_ϵ is the energy of noise signal. If colluders are belonging to different groups, the energy at $\tilde{d}_u$ is $\beta_g + (c-1)\beta_u/c + \beta_\epsilon$ because each signal is embedded into quasi-orthogonal domain obtained by operating $pn(i_g)$ which is related to a group ID. Our objective is to remove the interference with energy β_u for the group ID and energy $\beta_g + (c-1)\beta_u/c$ for the user ID from $\tilde{v} - v$ as much as possible.

It is worth mentioning that the main source of interference, which is the original image, is removed at the detection because the access to it is allowed by the assumption of a fingerprinting scheme.

3.2   Removal Operation

The knowledge of fingerprinting sequences w_g and w_u enables a detector to remove the interference effectively from the detection sequences $\tilde{d}_g$ and $\tilde{d}_u$. Because once a certain group ID is detected, its signal is merely a noise for the detection of a user ID, hence it should be removed at the detection of the user

ID. Such a removal operation minimizes the effects of interference, and decreases the variance of $\tilde{d}_u$. As the results, the true-positive detection rate is increased with no sacrifice of false one.

The abstract of the detection procedure is illustrated in Fig.3. In this figure, some fingerprint signals are involved in the sequence $\tilde{v} - v$ with spread form, and at the first detection (detection of a group ID) two signals are found. Before the second detection, the detected signals are removed from $\tilde{v} - v$, which decrease the variance of noise elements. Since the detection of a user ID is performed using one of the detected group ID, the third detection is also performed with the similar procedure to the second one. In this stage, much interference from other fingerprint signals is removed, hence the number of detectable colluders is increased compared with the original method. If the detection operation is performed once again, some undetected signals at the first detection can be found because of the decrease of variances of noise elements.

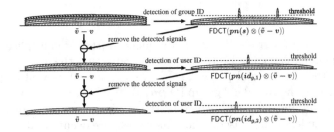

Fig. 3. Illustration of proposed detection procedure

To implement the procedure, the proposed removal operations described below are inserted in the original detection method.

3-5. The corresponding signals of detected group IDs are removed from $\tilde{v}$;

$$\tilde{v} \leftarrow \tilde{v} - \sum_k dct(k, \tilde{d}_{g,k}) \tag{12}$$

4-5. The corresponding signals of detected user IDs are removed from $\tilde{v}$;

$$\tilde{v} \leftarrow \tilde{v} - \sum_h dct(h, \tilde{d}_{u,h}) \tag{13}$$

5 If at least one user ID is detected by the Step 4, go to Step 3, otherwise quit the detection operation.

As described in Step 5, the detection of a group ID and a user ID with the above removal operations are repeatedly performed when at least one user ID is detected. As the consequence, the thresholds T_g and T_u related to the variance of $\tilde{v} - v$ is decreased without increasing the false-positive rate seriously.

3.3   Two Kinds of Thresholds

When embedded signals as fingerprint information are successively and correctly removed during the proposed detection process, the effects of mutual interference are minimized. Due to the increase of the number of colluders, wrong signals will be accidentally detected because the effects of interference are increased with respect to the number. In such a case, the undetected fingerprint signal is attenuated by the removal operation.

Since the characteristic of a CDMA channel at the detection sequence, an interference and noise signals follow normal distribution with zero mean. Considering the effects of such signals, fingerprinted signals are also represented by normal distribution which mean is β_g/c. Based on the Eq.(7), a false-positive probability Pe_g for the detection of a group ID is represented by,

$$Pe_g = \frac{1}{2} \operatorname{erfc}\left(\frac{T_g}{\sqrt{2\sigma^2}}\right), \tag{14}$$

where T_g is a threshold. The expected number of wrongly detected group ID from detection sequence $\tilde{d}_g$ is calculated from the false-positive probability Pe_g and the variance σ^2 of the sequence $\tilde{d}_g$. If the length of the sequence is ℓ, the number is given by $\ell \times Pe_g$. For example, when $\ell = 1024$ and $Pe_g = 10^{-3}$, which are used in the simulation of [11], are assigned, one of the detected group ID is wrong in average. Remember that some fingerprint signals will be covered by noise signals because of the attenuation of energy after averaging collusion. For the detection of a group ID, the false-negative detection of fingerprinted signals is much serious because the following detection of the user ID is not conducted. Even if the false-positive detection of a group ID is increased, the actual false-positive detection is bounded to the detection of the user ID. Hence, it is advisable to decrease Pe_g forgiving the false detection from this point of view.

When the threshold T_g for a group ID goes down, the number of detected group ID is increased. It provides the chance for mining the corresponding user ID from a detection sequence. If all detected signals are removed as an interference, wrongly detected signals at the detection of a group ID are also removed and the detection operation is performed again with the threshold which goes down after the removal under a constantly designed false-positive rate. Hence, the repeat of detection operation provides the chance, regretfully, to detect wrong ID by mistake, which causes the increase of the false detection. So our objective is to perform the removal operation selectively for the detection signals and to omit some repetition of detection. In order not to remove too much, two kinds of thresholds T_g^L and T_g^H, $(T_g^L < T_g^H)$ for group ID are introduced. If $\tilde{d}_{g,k}$, $(0 \le k \le \ell)$ are larger than the lower threshold T_g^L, they are regarded as the candidates of colluders' group ID. Then, some of them that exceed the higher threshold T_g^H are subtracted from the detection sequence as an interference, and the others are removed only when the corresponding signals of the user ID are detected, otherwise left the signals.

Similar to the above discussion, when the threshold T_u for a user ID decreases, the number of detected user ID is also increased. In this case, however, it directly raises the false-positive detection rate. By introducing two kinds of thresholds T_u^L and T_u^H, $(T_u^L < T_u^H)$, the objective signals are detected adaptively as follows. Our detector detects some candidates of the user ID using the lower threshold T_u^L and removes these detected signals as well as the corresponding signals of the group ID. Final decision are done by the threshold T_u^H to exclude the false detection.

Once user IDs are found at the detection sequence $\tilde{d}_u$, the repeat of detection operation will be needless. In order not to perform again the detection operation for such a case, when at least one user corresponding to a certain group ID has already been found, the repeat of detection operation for the user ID is omitted.

Based on the above two ideas, the proposed detection procedure is described as follows.

1. Perform full-domain DCT on a pirated copy.
2. Select ℓ DCT coefficients from low- and middle-frequency domains on the basis of a secret key key, which is denoted by $\tilde{v}$.
3. Detect group ID by the following operations.

   3-1 Generate a PN sequence $pn(s)$ generated by a secret key s, and multiply $\tilde{v} - v$ to it.

   3-2 Perform 1D-DCT to obtain the detection sequence $\tilde{d}_g$;

$$\tilde{d}_g = \mathsf{FDCT}\left(pn(s) \otimes (\tilde{v} - v)\right). \tag{15}$$

   3-3 Calculate the variance of $\tilde{d}_g$ considering the property of its distribution and determine two thresholds T_g^H and T_g^L with a given false-positive probability Pe_g^H and Pe_g^L, respectively.

   3-4 If $\tilde{d}_{g,k} \geq T_g^L, (0 \leq k \leq \ell - 1)$, determine k as the group ID, and store the signals,

$$\hat{d}_{g,k} = \begin{cases} \tilde{d}_{g,k} & (\tilde{d}_{g,k} < T_g^H) \\ 0 & \text{otherwise.} \end{cases}$$

   3-5 If $\tilde{d}_{g,k} \geq T_g^H, (0 \leq k \leq \ell - 1)$, the corresponding signals of detected group IDs are removed from $\tilde{v}$;

$$\tilde{v} \leftarrow \tilde{v} - \sum_{\tilde{d}_{g,k} \geq T_g^H} dct(k, \tilde{d}_{g,k}). \tag{16}$$

4. Perform the following operation for each group ID if no signal has detected from the corresponding detection sequence of the user ID.

   4-1 Generate a PN sequence $pn(i_g)$, and multiply $\tilde{v} - v$ to it.

   4-2 Perform 1D-DCT to obtain the detection sequence $\tilde{d}_u$;

$$\tilde{d}_u = \mathsf{FDCT}\left(pn(i_g) \otimes (\tilde{v} - v)\right). \tag{17}$$

4-3 Calculate the variance of $\tilde{d}_u$ and determine a lower threshold T_u^L with a given false-positive probability Pe_u^L.

4-4 If $\tilde{d}_{u,h} \geq T_u^L$, h is regarded as a candidate of the user ID i_u, and store

$$\hat{d}_{u,h} = \tilde{d}_{u,h} \tag{18}$$

as the detected signal strength for this candidate.

4-5 The corresponding signals of the candidates are removed from $\tilde{v}$;

$$\tilde{v} \leftarrow \tilde{v} - dct(k, \hat{d}_{g,k}) - \sum_h dct(h, \tilde{d}_{u,h}). \tag{19}$$

5. At least one candidate is detected by the Step 4, go to Step 3, otherwise, go to Step 6.
6. Perform the following operation for each candidate of the user ID.
   6-1 Perform the same operations as Step 4-1 and Step 4-2.
   6-2 Calculate the variance of $\tilde{d}_u$, and determine a threshold T_u^H with a given false-positive probability Pe_u^H.
   6-3 If $\hat{d}_{u,h} + \tilde{d}_{u,h} \geq T_u^H$, determine h as the user ID i_u.

It is noticed that the final decision of detected ID is determined at Step 6. Because the detected signals of the user ID at Step 4 may contain the noise and interference of undetected signals, the decision should be done after all removal operations. The noise and interference contained in the sequence $\tilde{d}_u$ when the user ID is detected at Step 4 are represented by $\tilde{d}_{u,h}$.

4   Computer Simulated Results

For the evaluation of the proposed detection method, we implement the algorithm and compare the number of detected colluders from a pirated copy with averaging collusion. As a host signal, we use a standard image "lena" that has 256-level gray scale with a size of 512×512 pixels. In our simulation, the embedding strengths are fixed by $\beta_g = 400$ and $\beta_u = 600$, respectively. Fingerprinted images are produced by embedding 10^4 patterns of randomly selected i_g and i_u, and a pirated copy is an averaged one of them and it is compressed by JPEG algorithm with a quality factor of 35%. Then, the value of PSNR is 45 [dB]. The detection of the fingerprint is performed with the knowledge of the host image. As a comparison, the proposed detection method with the removal operation introduced in subsection 3.2 applied for the original one is called method I, and the one with two kinds of thresholds for the detection of each ID is method II.

We explore the false-positive detection performance of our detection methods using the fingerprint sequences of length $\ell = 1024$. Thus, the allowable number of users is $1024^2(\approx 10^6)$. As discussed in Section 3, the actual probability P_{fp} of false-positive detection is dependent on the design of Pe_g and Pe_u for method I and Pe_g^L, Pe_g^H, Pe_u^L, and Pe_u^H for method II. The probability P_{fp} is defined as an average number of falsely detected innocent users at one detection. A threshold T

Table 1. The relations between $\overline{T}$ and a false-positive probability Pe

Pe	5×10^{-3}	1×10^{-3}	1×10^{-4}	1×10^{-5}	1×10^{-6}	1×10^{-7}	1×10^{-8}	2.5×10^{-9}
$\overline{T}$	1.82	2.19	2.63	3.02	3.36	3.68	3.97	4.13

Table 2. The actual probability of false-positive detection for different thresholds when method I with $\ell = 1024$ is applied

	original	method I	
$\overline{T_g}$	2.19	2.19	1.82
$\overline{T_u}$	3.97	3.97	3.97
P_{fp} [$\times 10^{-4}$]	2.00	2.63	17.46

Table 3. The actual probability of false-positive detection for different thresholds when method II with $\ell = 1024$ is applied

type	method II								
	i	$\ddot{\imath}$	$\dddot{\imath}$	$\dddot{v}$	v	$\ddot{v}$	$\dddot{v}$	$\dddot{v\ddot{\imath}}$	$\ddot{\imath}x$
T_g^L	1.82			1.82			1.82		
T_g^H	2.19			2.63			2.63		
T_u^L	3.97	3.68	3.36	3.97	3.68	3.36	3.36	3.02	2.63
T_u^H	3.97			3.97			4.13		
P_{fp} [$\times 10^{-4}$]	3.00	6.29	8.75	2.38	4.75	6.33	2.21	3.04	11.08

of a false-positive probability Pe is given by Eq.(7), and the relation is simplified by

$$T = \overline{T} \times \sqrt{2\sigma^2}, \tag{20}$$

where $\overline{T}$ is the relevant variable. Some values used in our simulation are listed at Table 1, and the false-positive probabilities using method I are at Table 2. It is confirmed that the probability P_{fp} is increased if $\overline{T_g}$ goes down. Table 3 shows the probabilities of method II for 9 types of thresholds considering the probability P_{fp}. Due to the precision of P_{fp} in our simulation, the probabilities in the table are the average number of falsely detected innocent users with the number of colluders from 7 to 40. Considering the size of P_{fp}, the number of detected colluders with original method, method I using $\overline{T_g} = 2.19$ and $\overline{T_u} = 3.97$, and method II of type i, $\dddot{v}$, $\dddot{v}$, and $\dddot{v\ddot{\imath}}$ are plotted in Fig. 4. The effectiveness of removal operations introduced in method I is confirmed, and using two kinds of thresholds at each level of detection the performance can be improved. Considering the trade-off between the number of detected colluders and the false-positive probability, the method II with type $\dddot{v\ddot{\imath}}$ holds a better performance. Hereafter, we simply denote the method with these specific parameters by proposed I and proposed II.

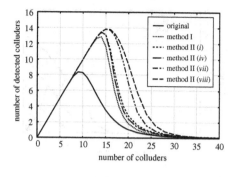

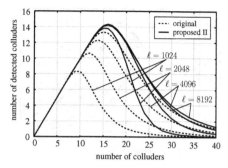

Fig. 4. The comparison of the number of detected colluders with $\ell = 1024$ for an image "lena"

Fig. 5. The number of detected colluders for an image "lena"

If ℓ is doubled, the false-positive probability also becomes double because the probability is proportionally increased by the number. For the evaluation of the true-positive detection of proposed II under an equal condition, the number of users is fixed to $2^{20}(= 1024 \times 1024)$ for different ℓ. The results for different length $\ell = 1024, 2048, 4096, 8192$ are plotted in Fig.5, and the actual probabilities of false detection are shown in Table 4. Since a short sequence is more volunerble to the interference of noise elements such as JPEG compression, P_{fp} of length $\ell = 1024$ is degraded. The false-negative rate, which is the error rate of catching no colluder, is also evaluated for proposed II, and the results are plotted in Fig.6. The results of other images with $\ell = 8192$ are shown in Fig.7, Fig.8, and Table 5. These results confirm that the proposed detection method can catch more colluders and less innocent users with high probability.

It is worth mentioning that the proposed removal operation is applicable to the conventional spread spectrum watermarking scheme [3]. However, considering the computational complexity required for the iterative detection procedure, the CDMA-based fingerprinting scheme is suitable to implement.

Table 4. The probability of false-positive detection for an image "lena"

ℓ	P_{fp} [$\times 10^{-4}$]		
	original	proposed I	proposed II
1024	2.00	2.63	3.04
2048	2.08	3.08	1.08
4096	1.54	3.17	1.08
8192	3.83	4.38	1.58

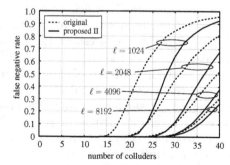

Fig. 6. The false-negative detection rate for an image "lena"

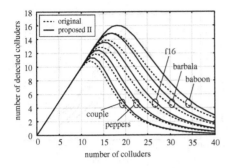
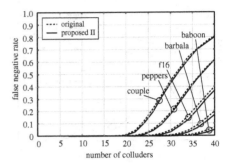

Fig. 7. The number of detected colluders for some images with $\ell = 8192$

Fig. 8. The false-negative detection rate for some images with $\ell = 8192$

Table 5. The probability of false-positive detection for some images with $\ell = 8192$

	$P_{fp}\ [\times 10^{-4}]$	
	original	proposed II
baboon	4.92	1.21
barbala	3.54	0.75
couple	3.13	1.21
f16	2.83	0.67
peppers	3.00	1.25

5   Concluding Remarks

In this paper, we proposed an effective detection method for the CDMA-based fingerprinting scheme. The model of the fingerprinting scheme gives us the way to attenuate the effects of a noise involved in detection sequences, which is a removal operation. The proposed removal operation implies that the detected signals are extracted from the detection sequence. We analyzed the effects of the removal operation on the detector, and introduced two kinds of thresholds. The detected signals of the group ID which exceed the higher threshold T_g^H are extracted from the detection sequence by a removal operation. The other detected signals which exceed the lower threshold T_g^L are removed when the corresponding user ID are detected using the lower threshold T_u^L, otherwise left the signals which are regarded as the interference of other undetected fingerprints. The final decision is done by the higher threshold T_u^H. From our simulation results, we found that the threshold T_g^H should be designed appropriately large in order not to remove undetected fingerprint signals. However, we have to remind that larger threshold T_g^H fails to remove the interference at the detection of the group ID, hence the detection of a user ID is missed because of the remained interference. By going down the threshold T_u^L, we collect more user ID as the candidates. Since the design of thresholds is dependent on the length of spread spectrum sequence, the determination of best parameters are left for our future work.

Acknowledgment

This research was partially supported by the Ministry of Education, Culture, Sports Science and Technology, Grant-in-Aid for Young Scientists (B).

References

1. Wu, M., Trappe, W., Wang, Z., Liu, K.J.R.: Collusion resistant fingerprinting for multimedia. IEEE Signal Processing Mag., 15–27 (2004)
2. Pfitzmann, B., Schunter, M.: Asymmetric fingerprinting. In: Maurer, U.M. (ed.) EUROCRYPT 1996. LNCS, vol. 1070, pp. 84–95. Springer, Heidelberg (1996)
3. Cox, I., Kilian, J., Leighton, F., Shamson, T.: Secure spread spectrum watermarking for multimedia. IEEE Trans. Image Process. 6(5), 1673–1687 (1997)
4. Zhao, H., Wu, M., Wang, Z., Liu, K.J.R.: Forensic analysis of nonlinear collusion attacks for multimedia fingerprinting. IEEE Trans. Image Process. 14(5), 646–661 (2005)
5. Wang, Z.J., Wu, M., Trappe, W., Liu, K.J.R.: Group-oriented fingerprinting for multimedia forensics. EURASIP J. Appl. Signal Process. (14), 2142–2162 (2004)
6. Wang, Z.J., Wu, M., Zhao, H., Trappe, W., Liu, K.J.R.: Anti-collusion forensics of multimedia fingerprinting using orthogonal modulatio. IEEE Trans. Image Process. 14(6), 804–821 (2005)
7. Boneh, D., Shaw, J.: Collusion-secure fingerprinting for digital data. IEEE Trans. Inform. Theory 44(5), 1897–1905 (1998)
8. Trappe, W., Wu, M., Wang, Z.J., Liu, K.J.R.: Anti-collusion fingerprinting for multimedia. IEEE Trans. Signal Process. 51(4), 1069–1087 (2003)
9. Zhu, Y., Feng, D., Zou, W.: Collusion secure convolutional spread spectrum fingerprinting. In: Barni, M., Cox, I., Kalker, T., Kim, H.-J. (eds.) IWDW 2005. LNCS, vol. 3710, pp. 67–83. Springer, Heidelberg (2005)
10. Tardos, G.: Optimal probabilistic fingerprint codes. In: Proc. 35th ACM Symp. Theory of Comp., pp. 116–125 (2003)
11. Hayashi, N., Kuribayashi, M., Morii, M.: Collusion-resistant fingerprinting scheme based on the CDMA-technique. In: Miyaji, A., Kikuchi, H., Rannenberg, K. (eds.) IWSEC 2007. LNCS, vol. 4752, pp. 28–43. Springer, Heidelberg (2007)
12. Gold, R.: Maximal recursive sequences with 3-valued recursive cross-correlation functions. IEEE Trans. Infom. Theory 14(1), 154–156 (1968)
13. Stone, H.: Analysis of attacks on image watermarks with randomized coefficients. NEC Res. Inst., Tech. Rep. 96–045 (1996)
14. Rao, K.R., Yip, P.: Discrete Cosine Transform: Algorithms, Advantages, Applications. Academic Press, Boston (1990)
15. Barni, M., Bartolini, F., Piva, A.: Improved wavelet-based watermarking through pixel-wise masking. IEEE Trans. on Image Process. 10(5), 783–791 (2001)

Author Index

Alkabani, Yousra   102
Alt, Stéphanie   195
Atakli, Idris   283

Barbier, Johann   195
Bas, Patrick   325
Böhme, Rainer   178

Cayre, François   325
Cérou, Frédéric   341
Chang, Ee-Chien   30, 87
Chen, Zhili   224
Cheung, Yiu-ming   236
Corney, Jonathan   268
Craver, Scott   283

Deng, Yi   309
Dugelay, Jean-Luc   236

Esponda, Fernando   15

Fang, Chen   132
Fang, Chengfang   30
Farid, Hany   72
Fridrich, Jessica   251
Furon, Teddy   341

Guyader, Arnaud   341

He, Hong-Jie   147
Ho, Nicholas Zhong-Yang   87
Huang, Dijiang   294
Huang, Jiwu   132
Huang, Liusheng   224

Kandiah, Vinayak   294
Kapoor, Harsh   294
Ker, Andrew D.   45
Kim, Hyoung-Joong   132
Kiyavash, Negar   102
Koushanfar, Farinaz   102
Kuribayashi, Minoru   357

Li, Enping   283
Li, Lingjun   224
Li, Ning   118

Mathon, Benjamin   325
Morii, Masakatu   357

Nagayoshi, Hiroto   1
Ni, Jiangqun   132

Pérez-González, Fernando   325
Pevný, Tomáš   251
Potkonjak, Miodrag   102

Ritchie, James   268

Sako, Hiroshi   1
Salamon, Csaba   268
Stinson, D.R.   209

Tai, Heng-Ming   147

Wang, Chuntao   132
Wang, Shuozhong   60
Wang, Weihong   72
Watanabe, Takashi   1
Westfeld, Andreas   161
Wu, Hao-tian   236
Wu, J.   209

Xia, Bingbing   309

Yang, Wei   224
Yu, Jun   283
Yu, Zhenshan   224

Zhang, Jia-Shu   147
Zhang, Rongyue   132
Zhang, Weiming   60
Zhang, Xinpeng   60
Zhao, Xianfeng   118, 309
Zhao, Xinxin   224
Zheng, Xueling   224